The Kifuliiru Language: Volume 1

Phonology, Tone, and Morphological Derivation

SIL International®
Publications in Linguistics

Publication 146

Publications in Linguistics are published by SIL International®. The series is a venue for works covering a broad range of topics in linguistics, especially the analytical treatment of minority languages from all parts of the world. While most volumes are authored by members of SIL, suitable works by others will also form part of the series.

Series Editor

Mike Cahill

Volume Editors

Rhonda Hartell Jones

Mary Huttar

Production Staff

Bonnie Brown, Managing Editor
Lois Gourley, Compositor
Barbara Alber, Cover design

Cover Photograph

Roger Van Otterloo

The Kifuliiru Language: Volume 1
Phonology, Tone, and Morphological Derivation

Karen Van Otterloo

SIL International®
Dallas, Texas

© 2011 by SIL International®
Library of Congress Catalog No: 2011929643
ISBN: 978-1-55671-261-6 (volume 1)
ISBN: 978-1-55671-279-1 (two-volume set)
ISSN: 1040-0850

Printed in the United States of America

All rights reserved

No part of this publication may be reproduced, stored in a retrieval system, or transmitted in any form or by any means—electronic, mechanical, photocopy, recording, or otherwise—without the express permission of SIL International®. However, short passages, generally understood to be within the limits of fair use, may be quoted without written permission.

Copies of this and other publications of SIL International® may be obtained from:

SIL International Publications
7500 W. Camp Wisdom Road
Dallas, TX 75236-5629

Voice: 972-708-7404
Fax: 972-708-7363
publications_intl@sil.org
www.ethnologue.com/bookstore.asp

Dedication

This book is dedicated to my sons, John, Nathan, Matthew, Daniel, and Isaac, whose lives were shaped by this language, its land, and its speakers.

Contents

Dedication. v
List of Tables. xiii
Preface xv
Acknowledgments xvii
Bafuliiru Foreword. xix
A Brief Background to Writing Grammars in Africa
    by Derek Nurse. xxi
Abbreviations xxvii
Maps xxxi
1 Conventions. 1
   1.1 Language name and classification 1
   1.2 Dialects. 2
   1.3 Previous language work; contributors to the present work 2
   1.4 Conventions. 3
2 Phonology 7
   2.1 Phoneme inventory 8
      2.1.1 Consonants 8
      2.1.2 Vowels 10
   2.2 Phonetic realization and distribution of phonemes 11
      2.2.1 Consonants 11
      2.2.2 Vowels 34
   2.3 Phonological rules and processes 37
      2.3.1 Phonologically governed rules and processes. 38
      2.3.2 Morphologically governed rules and processes 64
   2.4 Syllable structure, word structure, and syllable prominence 96
      2.4.1 Cliticization of monosyllabic words. 97
      2.4.2 Elimination of monosyllabic words by addition of morphemes 104
      2.4.3 Syllable structure inventory for noun stems 105

    2.4.4 Syllable structure inventory for verb bases 106
3 Tone **109**
  3.1 Assumptions from autosegmental theory 110
  3.2 The tone-bearing unit: mora or syllable? 113
  3.3 Tone inventory 117
    3.3.1 Underlying tones 117
    3.3.2 Surface realizations of tones 117
    3.3.3 Kifuliiru tone reversal vis-à-vis Proto-Bantu 123
  3.4 Functional load of tone 127
    3.4.1 Lexical tone contrasts 128
    3.4.2 Grammatical tone contrasts 128
  3.5 Tone on verbs 130
    3.5.1 Lexical tone in verbs 132
    3.5.2 Assignment of grammatical tone in verbs 141
    3.5.3 Stem-tone patterns in Kifuliiru verbs 143
    3.5.4 Tone assignment in verbs with adverbial auxiliaries 192
    3.5.5 Tone assignment in monosyllabic verb stems 194
    3.5.6 Tone in reduplicated verbs 198
    3.5.7 Overview of verb forms by stem-tone pattern 199
  3.6 Extratonality of the final syllable in nouns and verbs 203
  3.7 General characteristics of tone association in Kifuliiru 205
    3.7.1 Edge-in linking and double-linking of the penultimate 205
    3.7.2 Syllable, with modifications, as TBU 211
    3.7.3 Constraint against triple-linking to a single syllable 217
  3.8 General rules affecting tone at the word level 219
    3.8.1 Tone-spread rule 219
    3.8.2 Contour simplification rules 226
    3.8.3 Meeussen's rule 236
    3.8.4 T-drop 239
    3.8.5 Lexical level H float 242
  3.9 Lexical tone of verbal affixes 245
    3.9.1 Lexical tone of verbal prefixes 245
    3.9.2 Lexical tone of verbal suffixes 250
  3.10 Tone on nouns 252
    3.10.1 Lexical tone in noun affixes 252
    3.10.2 Lexical tone in noun roots 253
  3.11 Tone on other parts of speech 261
    3.11.1 Tone on adjectives 261
    3.11.2 Tone on demonstratives 262
    3.11.3 Tone on associative markers 265
    3.11.4 Tone on numerals 267

- 3.12 General rules affecting the tones of words on the phrase and clause level ... 269
  - 3.12.1 Postlexical H-spread ... 270
  - 3.12.2 Postlexical leftward H-shift ... 271
  - 3.12.3 Postlexical tonal changes due to coalescence of vowels ... 277
  - 3.12.4 Intonational raising indicating a non-final pause ... 278
  - 3.12.5 Final H contouring ... 279
- 3.13 Downdrift ... 280
- 3.14 Floating L tones and (non-automatic) downstep ... 282

4 Derivational processes ... 285
- 4.1 Noun derivations ... 285
  - 4.1.1 Nouns derived from verbs (deverbal nouns) ... 286
  - 4.1.2 Nouns derived from adjectives ... 296
  - 4.1.3 Nouns derived from other nouns by prefix change ... 297
  - 4.1.4 Nouns derived from another noun by the addition of a formative ... 305
  - 4.1.5 Compound nouns derived from two words ... 312
  - 4.1.6 Nouns derived from ideophones ... 314
- 4.2 Verb derivations ... 314
  - 4.2.1 Verbs derived from nouns ... 314
  - 4.2.2 Verbs derived from ideophones ... 315
  - 4.2.3 Verbs derived from adjectives ... 316
  - 4.2.4 Verbs derived from related verbs by way of extensions ... 317
  - 4.2.5 Verbal auxiliaries derived from verbs ... 317
- 4.3 Adjectives derived from verbs ... 319
  - 4.3.1 The closed set ... 319
  - 4.3.2 Productive derivations of stative verbal adjectives ... 320
- 4.4 Adverbs derived from verbs ... 321

5 Verb stems ... 323
- 5.1 Extensions: General considerations ... 325
- 5.2 Degrees of productivity in extensions ... 326
  - 5.2.1 Productive extensions ... 328
  - 5.2.2 Non-productive extensions ... 329
  - 5.2.3 Lexicalized extensions ... 330
- 5.3 Relative order of extensions ... 331
- 5.4 Extensions and their relationship to valence ... 334
- 5.5 Productive extensions ... 337
  - 5.5.1 Causative ... 339
  - 5.5.2 Passive ... 357
  - 5.5.3 Applicative ... 362
  - 5.5.4 Reciprocal ... 365

    5.5.5 Reversive (transitive) 372
    5.5.6 Reversive (intransitive) 375
    5.5.7 Intensive 378
    5.5.8 Emphatic. 380
5.6 Non-productive extensions and expansions 385
    5.6.1 Contactive. 386
    5.6.2 Extensive. 387
    5.6.3 Neuter 389
    5.6.4 Impositive. 391
    5.6.5 Positional 395
    5.6.6 Inchoative. 398
5.7 Other suffixes (expansions). 399
5.8 Various extension combinations 401
5.9 The resultative final: Structural considerations 412
    5.9.1 Interactions of the resultative with the verb stem. 413
    5.9.2 Irregular resultatives 416
    5.9.3 Resultatives of causatives. 419
    5.9.4 Resultatives of passives. 421

Appendix: Determining word boundaries and related orthography issues. 423

1 The relevant units: words, affixes, and clitics. 425
    1.1 Words 426
    1.2 Affixes. 427
    1.3 Clitics 429
2 Phonological indicators of word boundaries. 431
    2.1 Compensatory vowel lengthening 432
    2.2 Clitic-related vowel lengthening 433
    2.3 Mora-based vowel shortening 434
    2.4 Lexical and post lexical level vowel coalescence. 436
    2.5 Tonal contours 439
3 Grammatical indicators of word boundaries in verbs 441
    3.1 Multiple subject prefixes. 441
    3.2 Infinitive following auxiliary 442
    3.3 Subjunctive forms with no subjunctive FV. 444
    3.4 Placement of pre-final emphatic **-ag** extension. 446
    3.5 Grammatical tone of the verb stem 447
4 Other word break issues 448
    4.1 Clause-level clitics 448
        4.1.1 Clitics attached to the ends of verbs 451

    4.1.2 Single syllable verbs as enclitics 452
  4.2 Vowel coalescence, word breaks, and orthography 454
References. **457**
Person index **463**
Language index. **467**
Overall index **469**

List of Tables

Table 2.1. Consonant phonemes. 9
Table 2.2. Vowel phonemes 11
Table 2.3. Summary of consonant realizations and distribution 12
Table 2.4. Syllable structure inventory for noun stems 106
Table 2.5. Syllable structure inventory for verb bases 107
Table 3.1. Kifuliiru tone conventions 112
Table 3.2. Stem-tone patterns in Kifuliiru verbs 144
Table 3.3. Verb forms listed by stem-tone pattern 200
Table 3.4. Lexical tone of verbal prefixes 246
Table 5.1. Productive extensions 329
Table 5.2. Non-productive extensions 330
Table 5.3. General order of extensions within the verb 332
Table 5.4. Compound extensions 333
Table 5.5. Extensions and their relationship to valence 336
Table 5.6. Productive extensions in Kifuliiru, exemplified 338
Table 5.7. Non-productive extensions 385
Table 5.8. Extensions/expansions and combinations thereof. 401

Preface

This volume stems from our sixteen-year sojourn as a family (of two, then three, four, five, six and seven!) among the Bafuliiru people from 1980 to 1996. It describes the phonology, tonal system and derivational processes in Kifuliiru, a Bantu language of Zone J (J50). A chapter on orthographic word breaks is also included. Together with its companion volume on Kifuliiru grammar and discourse, written by my husband, Roger, this book forms a comprehensive documentation of the language. It is hoped that the information included in these two volumes will be helpful to those working in related languages, and perhaps suggest topics for further research.

The present time reflects a key point in the history of the language. With most of the children there now attending elementary school, and with a number of secondary schools in the area, the original richness of the language is being increasingly compromised by an overlay of Swahili, the Bantu trade language of the region, and to a lesser degree, of the national language, French. Because of this, much of the richness of the Kifuliiru grammar and vocabulary is in real danger of vanishing. These two volumes provide a record of the language as it is, and it is hoped that they will also help to renew in people's minds a sense of pride in their own beautiful and expressive language, the primary vehicle for the transmission of their own unique culture and heritage.

To maximize its viability over time, this description reflects a basic theory-neutral perspective wherever possible, but the reader will note influences from structuralism, early generative phonology, and autosegmental phonology, among others.

Karen Van Otterloo
August 2009

Acknowledgments

It was a privilege to live and work among the Bafuliiru people. We are grateful to them for their graciousness over the many years we resided among them, and for their patience in teaching us their language. We are honored that all of our sons had the privilege of speaking Kifuliiru as one of their two "first" languages. Special thanks goes to the family of the late Kashindi Ye'Mwana Adrien, on whose compound we lived. Their children were some of the many companions for our five boys growing up there.

This is the first of two volumes, the second of which is written by my husband, Roger. Though this work turned out to have two volumes, during much of our writing time we thought that we were working jointly to compile a single larger volume. We each read and made comments on the other's work, but each of us remains responsible for the content of the volume we wrote.

The Bafuliiru have a proverb: "No one shaves the back of his own neck": everyone needs help at some point. That proverb can be applied to this volume, to which so many people have made a significant contribution. Deep appreciation goes to SIL International Linguistic Coordinator Mike Cahill, who supervised this work and provided much wisdom, encouragement, and logistical help. In addition we're grateful to SIL- Eastern Congo Group, and especially our former directors, Jon Hampshire and Ed Lauber, for setting aside time for us to write. Without that, these books would never have been written.

We are grateful to the many Bafuliiru who provided the data used for this work. Our original texts and other data were collected before the days of computers and most of them were lost in the looting which took place at the beginning of the war in 1996. We are grateful to Kibambazi Zihindula for the collection of many new stories to analyze. Thanks goes to Juma Kinyamagoha for transcribing the texts, and to Sengoronge Katyera for dictating all the recordings which were used to put the tone markings on the data in both volumes. During the process of recording, Kamaro Busongoye assisted, and made many corrections and clarifications regarding the examples.

I should note that the turning point in my tonal analysis came in 1990, when I was able to access a copy of Pulleyblank's *Tone in Lexical Phonology*. Though much time and thought elapsed between that point and the present, it was that book which provided the keys that allowed me to see the Kifuliiru tone data as an amazing system, rather than as a confusing jumble.

Drafts of this volume have received extensive review and comments. Heartfelt thanks goes to all those who carefully read all or part of this document and provided helpful feedback. These include Cheryl Black, Leoma Gilley, Larry Hyman, Loren Koehler, Lana Martens, Derek Nurse, David Odden, Doris Payne, Kent Rasmussen, Thilo Schadeberg and Keith Snider. We also greatly appreciate the work of Bonnie Brown, Margaret González, Lois Gourley, George Huttar, Rhonda Hartell Jones, Mary Ruth Wise, and the rest of the staff at the editing and publishing department at Dallas SIL for their labor in bringing this work to publication. The reviewers and editors not only corrected many earlier errors, but also provided additional information and insights, and we are deeply grateful for the expertise they shared. We, of course, take full responsibility for any shortcomings.

Our ultimate thanks goes to God, our creator and sustainer, who not only led us to Africa in the first place, but also protected and provided for us all along the way, and by whose enabling we have been able to document what is in this work. To Him be all the glory!

Bafuliiru Foreword

Kifuliiru is a Bantu language spoken by more than 400,000 people, in the Uvira Territory of the Democratic Republic of Congo. In the beginning, Kifuliiru did not have the good fortune to be written. Nor was it taught in the schools. In fact when children spoke Kifuliiru on the school ground, they sometimes had a dead rat tied around their neck as punishment. There were many other types of punishment as well, such as writing lines over and over, saying "I will not speak Kifuliiru". As a result of such cultural arrogance on the part of teachers, some Bafuliiru no longer appreciate their mother-tongue. Many make mistakes when speaking it, mixing it indiscriminately with other languages.

Since Kifuliiru was not written down, people got used to speaking the trade language, Kiswahili. Kiswahili became the language of the primary school, and even the language for teaching God's Word in church. Everyone who could not speak Kiswahili well was viewed as an ignorant, backward person. Students were also taught in French, which further compromised the mother-tongue. Many children now speak Kifuliiru with French word order and mix words haphazardly from other languages. It's a very sad situation to find oneself in, losing one's language and cultural heritage!

All the same, most Bafuliiru living in their homes have continued to guard their language. And they now have the good fortune to have it written down, thanks to the work of SIL International. Many have begun to wake from sleep, and want to see their language given its proper place. In addition, many Bafuliiru are now happy to speak Kifuliiru even in church services. Kifuliiru has also begun to be resurrected in the area primary schools. The goal is that the children, from an early age, will be fluent in reading and writing their mother-tongue, as well as Kiswahili and French. This bodes well for generations to come.

In addition the Kifuliiru cultural association (Case Culturelle Fuliiru, or CACF) has published a variety of books to resurrect the language, including traditional stories, proverbs, and riddles, as well as books about traditional culture. The thirst to guard the language is now great!

This linguistic book is a like big sickle, to help the Bafuliiru harvest the riches of their language. Between its covers the essence of Kifuliiru is described at all levels, with all the original nuances. This will help all those writing the language to write with a pleasing style. Our desire is to adapt parts of this book into a form from which all the Bafuliiru people can benefit. This includes writing books for teaching the Kifuliiru language and culture in the primary schools. A Writer's Manual has also been produced, based on this grammar, for all who are interested in producing authentic literature that is sweet and clear.

The Bafuliiru, when they see this book, will laugh and dance, rejoicing in all the work that Roger and Karen Van Otterloo have done. Our language has been taken out of obscurity, and out of a slow death, and has been given a place among the languages of Africa. May God bless this work!

Elie Mushonio Banyimwire Rusati, President of Kifuliiru Cultural Association (CACF)
Phanuël Kibambazi Zihindula, Kifuliiru project director
December 2006, City of Uvira, Democratic Republic of Congo

A Brief Background to Writing Grammars in Africa

by Derek Nurse

When asked by the authors to contribute a short preface to this grammar, I thought it appropriate to set it in a historical context and sketch the evolution of the writing of grammars of sub-Saharan African languages, and of East African and Bantu languages in particular.

African languages and western writing systems came together in the mid nineteenth century, and over the following century they fused in several forms.

Churches were among the first developers of written material in the Roman script. They recognized the need to put the Scriptures, hymns, and later, other material into writing. Scriptures, containing as they do the same text across many languages, are not only a fine repository of classical language but also an invaluable source of comparative material, currently underused, for linguists. Equally important, and relevant here, churches saw that their representatives sent from Europe were eventually replaced by others, and that these successors needed instruction in the language, rather than reinventing the wheel every few years. So teaching materials, at first quite short and elementary, were developed, and some eventually developed into fuller grammars. These were often written by missionaries who had spent a long time in Africa and felt it would be a shame for their knowledge of the language to go to waste. From short teaching materials to a more complete grammar is a large step. Fine examples of more complete material by church representatives are the works of Barlow (1914, Great Britain), Hulstaert (1938, 1965, Belgium), Sacleux (1909, 1939, France) and Raum (1909, Germany). Raum's work on the Moshi dialect of Chaga resulted from many years' living on Kilimanjaro. Marred only by its lack of a list of contents, it is a real treasure trove, both of linguistic material and of stories. In the 1970s Gérard Philippson and I translated one of these stories for a student in Dar es Salaam, who was the grandson of the Chaga who had recorded them originally with Raum. The tradition of storytelling had meanwhile died out, and the grandson told us it was a fine story, that he had never heard, and that it even contained one or two names he recognized, and he asked where had it come from?!

Schools were initially run by the churches, later by the government. Schools had to have reading and instructional materials, which posed technical questions of how to reduce to writing languages which involved new difficulties not faced by those writing Western European languages. It also raised the issue of which variety or dialect to use, and what was to be the standard.

Professional administrators, established a little later, needed to communicate. With other senior administrators they used the colonial language but with junior, local employees they used a local language. Colonial administrators had limited tours of duty, and their replacements had to acquire that language. Both in Africa and Europe, pedagogical grammars were written and used, at first for major languages, later for the languages of some smaller communities.

The need on the part of the churches and of colonial governments for people who could speak African languages and thence for descriptive and instructional materials led gradually to the involvement of European universities. They sometimes absorbed clergy (Guthrie, for example) and administrators who had spent time in Africa, and they eventually set up institutes and departments of African languages, to produce pedagogical material, to write grammars, to broaden the general knowledge base. Invariably, most of the descriptions and grammars relied on the linguistic heritage and insights of the authors, most of whom had grown up in the Latin and Greek grammatical tradition and had only come to African languages later in life. Not surprisingly, many of these grammars use Latin models and theoretical terminology. Although some of their insights had to do with what we would now call linguistic universals, others look dated. It is appropriate here to mention the central role of the linguists at Tervuren and Brussels, under whose supervision a torrent of descriptions and theses on Bantu languages poured out in the second half of the twentieth century.

These strands continued and evolved until the dust of World War II settled and revealed a new world, where new factors came into play. The most obvious ones were the independence of African nations, coupled with the loss of a sense of colonial mission among western nations and a loss of Christian faith in Western Europe. These led to several immediate results: a drying up of the supply of the kinds of Western European individuals willing and able to write grammars, the establishment of African language departments in Africa, the emergence of African scholars, and the increased role of Americans in matters of faith and scholarship in Africa. A less salient factor was the emergence of linguistics, especially theoretical linguistics, as a discipline. Theoretical linguistics is primarily concerned with advancing the theoretical enterprise, and tends to produce short pieces—chapters, articles, squibs. It does not have the writing of grammars as a priority, and few of the theoretical grammars of African languages written during the heyday of transformational theory during the 1960s and 1970s have stood the test of time.

Have the changes just outlined led to an upsurge in the production of grammars? Put another way, are there enough grammars of sub-Saharan African, especially Bantu, languages? The answer is no. In preparing a forthcoming book, I wanted to do a survey of verbal phenomena in the languages of Guthrie's 85 Bantu groups, covering the whole Bantu area. Since no one can know so many languages, I had to rely on grammars and descriptions written by others. I made a list of all work I could find dealing with verbs in Bantu languages—books (especially), chapters in books, articles, theses, short discussions, unpublished work by others, my own work, and minor sources. Three rough general descriptive categories emerged: those groups of languages well described, those poorly described, and those in between, 'average'. These categories are relative. 'Well described' means that the verb system of at least one language in the group is reasonably described and that there exist descriptions for most of the other members of the group (some 20%); 'poorly described' means there is no good analysis of the verb system for any of the languages in the group and the whole group is poorly described (some 25%): 'average' is the remainder, the largest set of groups and languages (the rest, some 55%). Even the "well described' languages often suffer from a lack of examples, by which to test the descriptive or theoretical claims. I assume that what is true of the description or analysis of verb systems would in general be true of the rest of the grammatical system. So only 20% of the groups surveyed were reasonably described, and many languages were entirely undescribed or analysed. There is reason to think that non-Bantu languages or languages in other areas of Africa score even less well, using similar criteria. A few years ago Larry Hyman gave the keynote address at the Annual Conference for African Linguistics, and those who knew him expected a theoretical content. They were surprised to hear a speech strongly advocating the need for descriptive grammars (Hyman 2004).

If we compare who has written these grammars in the last fifty years, who are the authors? I examined a fairly comprehensive bibliography of Bantu languages for grammars of Bantu languages. With 'grammars' it is hard to know where exactly to draw the line. I included only published works which aimed at presenting all or most of the grammar, and excluded those which presented only partial analyses—sketches, descriptions or analyses of parts of the grammar, theoretical tracts, and most university theses. Most theses are excluded because writing grammars takes years, far longer than the time allowed for most theses, which concentrate on some aspect of the target language. The largest single producer of grammars over the last half century is still Europe, followed at some distance by Africa (especially South Africa) and then North America. The overwhelming impression is that of the small number of real grammars, and the number is not increasing. It is apparently so hard to write a grammar because certain conditions have to be met. The author needs to know the target language well, which means Africans, or non-Africans who have spent long years in Africa. The author needs courage, to venture into a language for which there is no grammatical tradition and little or no existing literature. Since writing a grammar takes years, the author needs a stable and adequate income over a long period. For many Africans and some non-Africans, that cannot be guaranteed, which is why most theses go no further. It also requires incentive, and neither African nor non-African universities encourage or reward the spending of long years on a grammar. Above all, it takes a certain kind of individual, an individual who is inspired, who loves language in general, the target language in particular, and is trained and happy to spend time doing this work. Small wonder that few grammars get written. No one forced the few authors, whether in the nineteenth or the twenty-first century, to do this work—they just want to do it.

And so it is with the two volumes of this grammar, too. The Van Otterloos spent thirteen years living with the Fuliiru, interspersed with three one-year periods of leave, plus several following years in Nairobi, a total of some twenty years each, forty in total, testimony to their amazing dedication, determination, and hard work, resulting in two extensive volumes, and 1,300 examples. This monumental reference work represents one of the most comprehensive grammars of any East African Bantu language. It combines masses of data and examples with linguistic argumentation and statements about all the basic topics to be expected in this kind of grammar: phonology, various word classes (noun, verb, pronoun/demonstrative, adjective, adverbials, and locatives), and sentence structure. It contains sections on topics not always adequately covered in conventional grammars: tone (a very long chapter), reduplication, ideophones, information theory (chapter 10), text analysis (chapter 12). To keep happy those who would say that grammars often make claims but do not show data to justify or falsify the claims, it provides many pages of examples and texts. It also deals with minor topics that do not often appear elsewhere: many 'adverbial auxiliaries' (fully grammaticalised auxiliaries expressing mainly aspect and mood), two verb forms expressing 'frustrated results', and the reduplication of nouns (the reduplication of 'mango' expresses multiple mangoes given out, one at a time, one to each worker, and successively acted on in the same way).

This grammar has been more than an academic exercise. Much of this material has already been adapted into a set of presentations in Swahili and French, for the benefit of the Bafuliiru themselves, as well as speakers of dozens of other Bantu languages East Africa. The idea is to stimulate local language awareness for mother-tongue speakers through a set of appropriately-graded seminars, so that this linguistic knowledge be brought back to the language communities themselves.

These two volumes would be a valuable addition to any Africanist's or linguist's bookshelf, appealing to several audiences. The general reader will find it very useful for reference and general interest. Theoretical linguists will find material and discussion for many current topics. Comparativists will find it a useful source for information on many topics.

References

Barlow, A. R. 1914 (reprinted 1951, 1960). *Studies in Kikuyu grammar and idiom*. Edinburgh: Blackwood.

Hulstaert, G. 1938. *Praktische grammatika van het Lonkundo (Lomongo)*. Antwerp: De Sikkel.

Hulstaert, G. 1965. *Grammaire du Lomongo, 2eme partie, morphologie*. Tervuren: MRAC.

Hyman, L. H. 2005. Why describe African languages? In A. Akinlabi and O. Adesola (eds), *Proceedings of the 4th World Congress of African Linguistics*. New Brunswick 2003, 21–42. Cologne: Ruediger Köppe Verlag.

Raum, J. 1909. *Versuch einer Grammatik der Dschaggasprache (Moschi-Dialekt)*. Berlin. G. Reimer. 1964 reprint. Farnborough: Gregg Press reprint.

Sacleux, C. 1909. *Grammaire des dialectes Swahilis*. Paris: Procure des R. P. du Saint Esprit.

Sacleux, C. 1939. *Dictionnaire Kiswahili-Francais*. Paris: Institut d'Ethnologie.

Abbreviations

1PL / 1.PL	first-person plural
1SG / 1.SG	first-person singular
2PL / 2.PL	second-person plural
2SG	second-person singular
A.M	associative marker
ADD.P	additive pronoun
ADD.V	additive verb
AG	agentive
APL	applicative
AU	augment
AUX	auxiliary
C	consonant, or predicate complement
C.F	contrary-to-fact
(cl.) 1, 2, etc.	noun class 1, class 2, etc.
CMP	complementizer
CND	conditional
CND.C.F	conditional, contrary-to-fact, pres.
CND.C.F.PST	conditional, contrary-to-fact, past
CND.RS	conditional, resultative
CND.TL	conditional, timeless
CNJ	conjunctive
CNT	contactive
COM	comitative
CON	continuative
COP	copula
CS	causative /cause
CTR.P	contrastive pronoun
D	distal

EMP / E	emphatic
F1	future, imminent
F2	future, default
F3	future, remote
Fa	final vowel -a
Fe	final vowel -e
Fi	final vowel -i
FOC	focus
Fr.	French
FRUS	frustrated
FV	final vowel
GNP	gender-number prefix
H	high tone
HL	falling contour on a single syllable
IMMED	immediately
IMP.P	imperative plural
IMPS	impositive
IMP.S	imperative singular
INTRANS	intransitive
INTL	intentional
INTS	intensive
INTV	intervening time
L	low tone
LH	L and H tone on a single syll. (mid tone)
MUT	mutual
N	nearby, or (unspecified) nasal
NEG	negative
NEG.FOC	negative focus
NEU	neuter
O1, O2, etc.	object marker cl. 1, cl. 2, etc.
O.P	object prefix
O.R	object relative marker
OBV	obvious
P	proximal
P.C	proximal contrast
P.R	previous reference
P1	past, recent
P2	past, unmarked
P3	past state
PERS	persistively
POS	positional

Abbreviations

POT	potential
PREV	previously
PRO	pronoun
PROG	progressive
PROG.INTL	progressive intentional
PS	passive
Q	question marker
R	remote
RCP	reciprocal
RDP	reduplication
REP	repeatedly
RFX	reflexive
RS	resultative
RV.I	reversive intransitive
RV.T	reversive transitive
S.P / sp.	subject prefix / specific variety
S.R	subject relative marker
SAME.SET	same set pronoun
SBSQ	subsequent
SBV	subjunctive
SF	surface form
SQ	sequential
Sw.	(Ki)Swahili
SYLL.	Syllable
TAM	tense/aspect/mood
TL	timeless
TRANS	transitive
UF	underlying form
UT	underlying (lexical) tone
V	vowel
~	alternate form
|	short pause
||	long pause

Maps

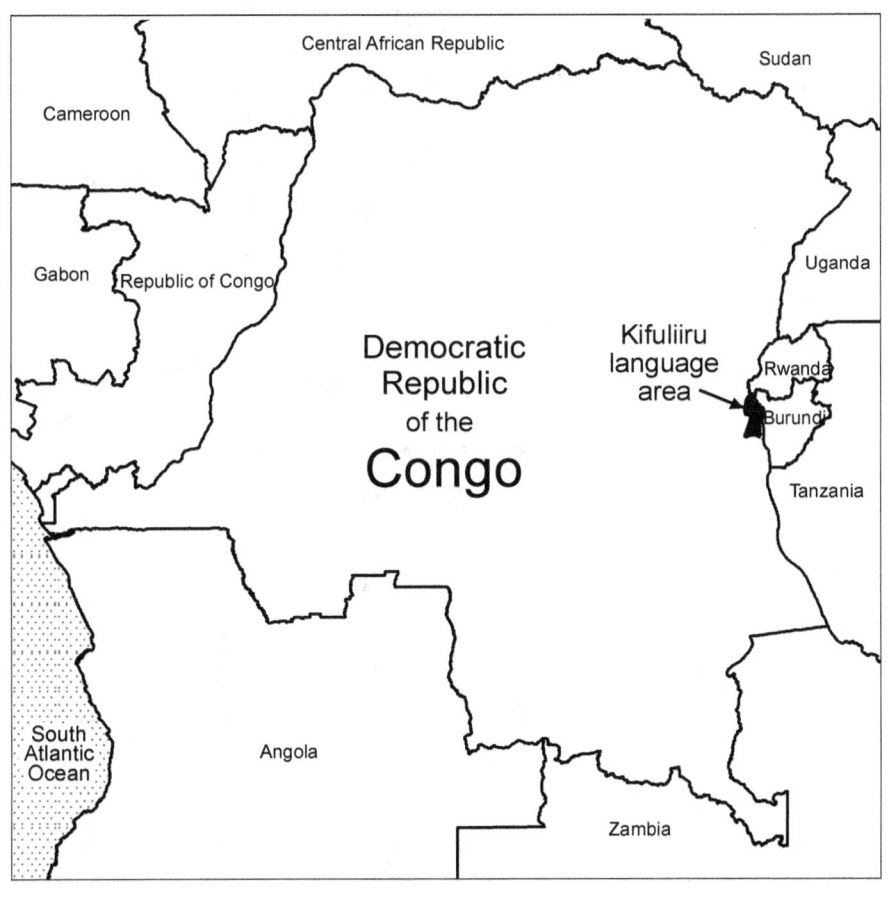

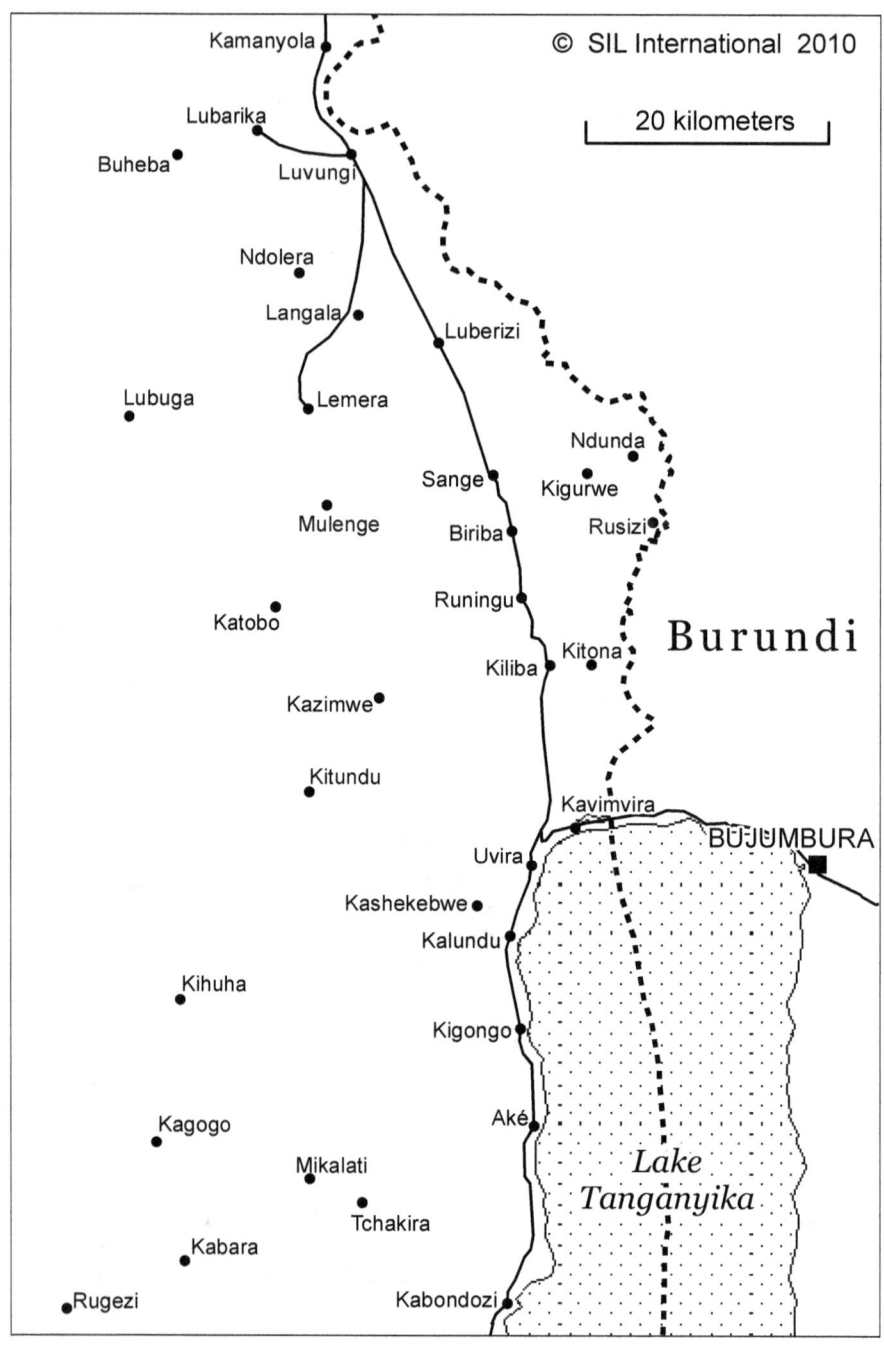

1
Conventions

1.1 Language name and classification

Kífùlìirû (complete with the cl. 7 prefix **kí-**) is the name the Bafuliiru people always use for their language. For reasons of convenience, linguists often reduce the name to **Fuliiru**. Non-speakers often pronounce the name with a short penultimate vowel, and often substitute **e** for **i** in that position, producing the variants of **Kifuliru, Fuliru, Kifulero**, or **Fulero**. The code letters in the *Ethnologue* are FLR (Gordon 2005).

Guthrie (1971) classified Kifuliiru in zone D as D.63 in the Ha group, which also includes Kinyarwanda, D.61 and Kirundi, D.62 among others.

Later this group was reorganized by Meeussen and is now commonly known as Zone J, also called "Great Lakes," or "Lacustrine." In the current classification, Kifuliiru is labeled as one of the J(D)50 languages (Bastin 2003) along with Kivira, Kinyindu, Mashi, Havu, Chitembo, and Kihunde, all situated along the eastern border of the Democratic Republic of Congo (DRC). Included in the larger J group, further north within the eastern DRC border, are Kinande, Talinga, and Hema. Other languages within the larger J group include Kirundi and Kinyarwanda, as well as all the languages of southern Uganda, the Luhya and Gusii groups of Kenya, and a number of languages in northern Tanzania. Geographically these languages are all in the area of the Great Lakes: Lake Albert, Lake Edward, Lake Kivu, Lake Tanganyika, and Lake Victoria.

Kifuliiru is most closely related to Kinyindu (80–90% cognate),[1] followed by the Mashi-Havu cluster.

1.2 Dialects

Kifuliiru enjoys a high degree of cohesiveness. Although the Bafuliiru people to the south are marginally influenced by Kivira, to the west by Kinyarwanda, and to the north by Mashi, still as a whole they are quite homogeneous; the language is easily understood across the area, with only minor phonological and vocabulary differences.

In this regard, there are a few words that vary relative to sounds which are otherwise contrastive in the language: **s/sh**, e.g. **músh̲ósì** 'man' and **mús̲ósi, sh̲ésh̲ēēzì** 'morning' and **s̲ésēēzì**. The sound **n** alternates in a few words with **ny**, such as **ny̲ínà** 'his/her mother' and **n̲ínà**, or **ny̲ândì** 'who' versus **n̲ândì**. Most say **bángérè** 'shepherds', but a few say **béngérè**. The word meaning 'a younger same-sex sibling' is pronounced either as **múlùmùn̲à** or **múlùmùl̲à**. Speakers from most areas delete a nasal before a fricative in verb forms such as **àgééz̲ìrì** 'he has gone', from -**génd**- 'go', while a few do not delete it, e.g. **àgéénz̲ìrì**. People influenced by Kivira use the -**ngwà** exclusive pronoun set, e.g. the cl. 2 **bóòngwâ** 'themselves' as well as the -**nyènè** set with the same meaning, e.g. **bóónyènè** 'themselves'. Such differences affect a few specific lexical items, or the presence/absence of a specific phonological rule, but there are no major differences that affect intelligibility.

1.3 Previous language work; contributors to the present work

In 2004, as a part of his master's degree program at the Nairobi Evangelical Graduate School of Theology, Kamaro Busongoye produced a thesis entitled "Complement Clauses in Kifuliiru".

Kifuliiru speakers whose input has contributed directly to this study of their language, listed alphabetically by second name, include Rev. Mushonio Banyimwire wa'Rusati, Pastor Kamaro Busongoye, Birunga Kaneneka, Asile Kashindi, Sengoronge Katyera, Pastor Juma Kinyamagoha, Kifuvyo Kwangiba, the late Pastor Kazera Kyula, the late Rev. Bahabwa Musobwa, Pastor Bugulube Mwemera, the late Pastor Nakalali Bukuru, Rev. Mulubi Ngalonga, Rev. Mulogoto Yunga, and Pastor Kibambazi Zihindula. Many others have contributed indirectly.

---

[1] This is based on personal research.

1.4 Conventions

VOWEL COALESCENCE is represented in the data only where it is mandatory in the pronunciation of the language. This means that it is indicated up to the level of the phonological word, which includes the cliticization of monosyllabic forms. In the example **á=bándú b̲é̲=kāāyà** 'people of the compound', **ba+i** (associative marker **ba+** cl. 23 locative clitic **i**) surfaces as **be**; coalescence is mandatory. Coalescence is not written at the level of the phrase, however, so that **ànágêndà í=kāāyà** 'he went home' is not written as usually pronounced at normal speed (i.e. **ànágêndé=kāāyà**), since it can also be pronounced in deliberate speech as two words without coalescence.

LONG VOWELS are marked as follows: All vowel length, whether underlying or produced by rules, is shown in examples in the chapters on Phonology and Tone, with the exception that on data within phonemic brackets, length produced by phonological rules is not indicated. In the remaining chapters, vowel length is written orthographically: only underlyingly (phonemically) long vowels are indicated. Any vowel length found preceding a nasal-plus-consonant, following a **w** or **y**, or resulting from word-initial morpheme concatenation, is not indicated. Note that no long vowel, whether underlying or the result of rules, ever occurs prior to the antepenultimate position, due to a shortening rule.

SURFACE TONE is marked in all data, as follows: The acute accent (**é**) is used to indicate high tone, e.g. **ú=múk̲é̲ngè** 'hollow grass used as straw'. The grave accent (**è**) indicates low tone, e.g. **ú=múk̲è̲ngè** 'monitor lizard'. The circumflex (**ê**) is used to indicate a phonetic falling contour on a word-final short vowel or on a phonologically conditioned long vowel (which is not written as a double vowel), e.g. **ú=múk̲ê̲ngè** 'wooden trough for making banana beer'. On a long vowel written as VV, a falling contour is marked with an acute accent on the first vowel and a grave accent on the second (**áà**). Such a contour reflects a lexical HL sequence e.g. **túgágáàjà** 'we will count'. Mid tone (the phonetic realization of an underlying low-high sequence, **ǐ**) is indicated by a macron (**ī**),[2] whether on a long vowel written as a single vowel, e.g. **ú=múvīndì** 'grasshopper dropping', or on a double vowel **á=mīījì** 'water'. In Kifuliiru there are no rising tones in the surface pronunciations; rather an underlying LH sequence is always pronounced as a mid tone.

A non-conjugated VERB BASE has tone indicated only on the first syllable (e.g. **-fùkam-** 'kneel') because this is where the underlying tone of a verb always surfaces. The tone of the following syllables within the verb stem will vary according to the tense/aspect/mood of a specific conjugated form. A verb

---

[2]Kifuliiru has no phonemic rising contours. Rather any underlying LH is pronounced on the surface as a level mid tone.

sequence on which there is no tone indicated is underlyingly toneless, e.g. -**laalik**- 'invite', since its tone depends completely on its TAM environment. Other toneless morphemes include certain prefixes, certain suffixes (including most verbal suffixes) and many single-syllable words.

IDEOPHONES AND INTERJECTIONS are also marked in examples by double chevrons, e.g. **Léézà náyè ngwà=vwómè, « shóóbè »**. 'Leeza, and she also, when she tried to get water, « frustration »'.

HYPHENS (-) are used to separate affixes from each other and from roots, when morphemes are separated for glossing purposes, e.g. **mú-kèngè** (3-monitor.lizard). They are also used to separate the parts of reduplicated items, e.g. **ká-síngé-síngè** (12-speedily-RDP), as well as to indicate morphemes or groups of morphemes which do not comprise whole words, e.g. the verb root -**génd**- 'go'.[3] Prefixes are followed by a hyphen, and suffixes are preceded by one. Verb bases are both preceded and followed by one.

EQUAL SIGNS (=) are used to join clitics to the word on which they depend, thus clearly distinguishing affixes and clitics. Clitics include monosyllabic words like **na** 'and' and **nga** 'like'. The initial augment **á** in **á=bándù** 'people' is a clitic also. In Kifuliiru, uninflected monosyllabic verb stems which follow an auxiliary are all clitics, and are also set off by an equal sign, e.g. the monosyllabic verb -**ly**- 'eat' in the phrase **ànákìzíí=ryà** 'he repeatedly ate'.

The term RESULTATIVE[4] (RS) is used to refer to Kifuliiru verb forms with the final -**ir-i**, which is the Kifuliiru reflex of the Proto-Bantu *-i̧d-e (or *- i̧de). In using the term resultative (related to, but not equal with "anterior") we follow Bybee, who uses this term for a verb where "an action in the past produces a state that persists into the present" (Bybee, Perkins, and Pagliuca 1994:318); for example the resultative **àtèzírì** 'he has set the trap, and the

---

[3]Verb roots and bases generally end in a consonant, e.g. the root -**gend**- 'go'. There are, however, a limited number of CV roots. Most of these end in a vowel which is changed by phonological rule to a glide preceding the obligatory FV, e.g. -**mo**- > -**mw**- 'shave'. Unless the underlying vowel is in focus in the discussion, we normally indicate these by a -Cw- or -Cy-. Two verbs with CV roots, the copula -**ba**- 'be, become' and the verb -**ha**- 'give', end in /a/, which does not undergo glide formation. Since long vowels are not used word finally, the addition of a FV to these does not result in a surface long vowel.

[4]The term "perfective", rather than resultative is often used in Bantu literature to refer to the final -**ir-i** suffix. It is also commonly used in reference to forms of the verb which include this morpheme. However, grammarians are quick to point out that this suffix is usually not associated with perfect aspect, as the name might imply, which "presents an event as an undifferentiated and time-bounded whole" (Nurse 2003:96) but rather with anterior, which "refers to an earlier action which produced a state which either lives on or whose consequences or relevance live on" (ibid.). Thus both in reference to tense/aspect forms created by the use of this suffix, and in reference to the suffix itself, we have used the term "resultative" (which is a subset of anterior) when referring to any inflected verb form which includes the use of this suffix. We also use RS as the gloss for this suffix in morpheme-by-morpheme glosses.

resulting state still obtains: the trap remains set'. Thus **à-tèz-ír-ì** is glossed morpheme-by-morpheme as (1-trap-RS-Fi).

The **e/o** morpheme of PREVIOUS REFERENCE (P.R) is a pronominal word-building component that is found in several classes of words in Kifuliiru, including many pronouns and qualifiers, as well as the focus copulas. In the morpheme glosses, these P.R morphemes are sometimes not specified, as the previous reference is already clear, and to add an additional "P.R" tends to clutter the gloss, making it more difficult to follow.

The glosses of most free-standing (whole word) PERSONAL PRONOUNS are written in caps, e.g. "THEY", to demonstrate the emphatic nature of the self-standing pronoun.

Third-person singular is morpheme-glossed as (cl.) 1 (not 3SG), and the third plural is glossed as (cl.) 2 (not 3PL). Note that third-person singular pronouns are free-glossed 'he' or 'she', depending on the context from which the example is taken.

PAUSES in Kifuliiru are important in isolating various components of information structure at the clause and sentence level. Thus all clause and sentence examples in this book have been carefully marked for pause. Long pauses of one-half second or longer are marked with two vertical lines (‖). Pauses shorter than one-half second are marked with one vertical line (|).

SQUARE BRACKETS ([ ]), besides indicating phonetic transcription, are also used to separate morphemes within word formulas. In formulas, every prefix is marked only by a left bracket ([ ) and every suffix is marked only by a right bracket ( ]). The root has a bracket both preceding and following ([ ]). The parentheses in formulas represent optional morphemes. Thus the formula for the direct imperative singular is: [verb base] -a]. The formula for the simple subjunctive is: [S.P [(NEG) [Ø [(O.P) [(RFX) [base] -e], which means obligatory subject prefix, optional negative prefix, null TAM prefix, optional object prefix, optional reflexive prefix (or 1SG object), base, and -**e** final vowel.

2

Phonology

This chapter[1] begins with an overview of the contrastive segments with their realizations and distribution. Rules and processes are then divided into two sections, the first of which presents the phonologically-governed rules and processes and the next which describes those which are morphologically governed. The final section includes a brief discussion of syllable and word structure. The following offers a short overview of typologically significant features of the language.

Kifuliiru is a five-vowel language, with contrastive long vowels at each of the five points of articulation. It has twenty-two consonants.

There is widespread presence of **p**-lenition, by which Proto-Bantu *p > h in most cases, e.g. Proto-Bantu *-**pik**- 'arrive' > -**hík**- in Kifuliiru.

There is extensive spirantization in the lexicon—Proto-Bantu obstruents realized as fricatives when followed by what were in Proto-Bantu "first degree"[2] vowels (2.3.2.5). Spirantization of the final consonant of a verb base is observed in the environments of agentive -**i** (2.3.2.5.3), causative -**i** (2.3.2.5.2),

---

[1] In regard to transcription in this chapter, data may be bracketed as phonemic, with slashes (//), or as phonetic, with square brackets. (See table 2.1. for consonant symbols used in phonemic transcription.) Slashes are also used to set off forms in which individual morphemes given in their underlying form differ from the surface form. Data in this chapter which have no brackets are written phonemically with the exception that all vowel length, both phonemic and non-phonemic, is indicated for clarity. For further transcription conventions, see chapter 1.

[2] "First degree" vowels are those with the greatest degree of closure. These vowels in Proto-Bantu have sometimes been called "heavy" or "superclose" because of their tendency to spirantize preceding consonants, but the preferred term, according to Schadeberg, is "first degree" (Schadeberg 2003b).

resultative -**ir**-**i** (2.3.2.5.1), and in at least two cases in a lexicalized adjective with the suffix which is the reflex of *-ų: -**novu** 'soft', from **kúnōgà** 'to be soft, limp', and -**jáávù** 'tasteless, plain' (possibly from an earlier meaning of **kújāāmbà** 'to become thin').

Kifuliiru exhibits only diachronic traces of Dahl's law (2.2.1.3) by which there is voicing of C1 when the consonant in C2 position within the word is voiceless. There are also some traces of Meinhof's law, with the simplification of NC V N(C) to N V N(C) (2.2.1.4).

Voiceless consonants become voiced following a nasal (2.3.1.1.3). For example, the **p** of **kúpúúmúkà** 'to dash off' becomes **b** after the nasal object marker in **ámbúmúkírà** 'he dashed away from me'.

There is no juxtaposition of unlike vowels in surface realizations. High vowels (**i, u**) undergo glide formation (i.e. become **y** or **w**) when followed by any unlike vowel, and the following vowel is compensatorily lengthened, e.g. the underlying **kí-úsí** (7-smoke) is realized as **kyúúsì**, underlying **mú-ázì** (3-news) becomes **mwáàzì**. Compensatory lengthening also takes place preceding a **NC** cluster, cf. **í=kííndù** 'a thing'.

There is a rule of mora-based vowel shortening,[3] so that any long vowel, e.g. the long **oo** of **àyòònérà** 'he poured on (recent past, P1)' is shortened when followed within the word by three (or more) morae, e.g. **àyòníírì** 'he poured on (resultative, RS)' (2.3.1.2.6).

Of special interest are the two different vowel coalescence rules, one which works at the lexical (word-building) level, and one which works at the postlexical (syntactic) level. At the lexical level, there is total elision (with the exception of high vowels, which undergo glide formation) of the first vowel: e.g. **bá-īīrù** (2-black) is realized as **bíírù**. In postlexical coalescence, when two underlying vowels are juxtaposed, they are realized by a vowel which has the height of the first and front/back quality of the second, e.g. **a + i → e**. For example, **yé-úgáyáàngà** 'she whom you will marry' is realized as **yó=gáyáàngà**, and **bà=í=nyúùmbà** '(cl. 2) of the house', as **bé=nyúùmbà** (2.3.1.2.2).

2.1 Phoneme inventory

2.1.1 Consonants

Kifuliiru has a total of twenty-two consonant phonemes, which occur at the labial, labiodental, alveolar, pre-palatal, velar, and laryngeal places of articulation.[4] A chart showing only the unmodified consonant phonemes of

---

[3]Any syllable with a short vowel comprises one mora, while a syllable with a long vowel counts as two morae.

[4]This number includes three consonants with contrastive prenasalization, but does not in-

2.1 Phoneme inventory

Kifuliiru is provided in table 2.1. (See 2.2.1.2 for labialized and palatalized versions of the consonants.)

Table 2.1. Consonant phonemes

	Labial	Labio-dental	Alveolar	Pre-palatal	Velar	Laryn-geal
Plosives, voiceless	p		t		k	
Plosives, voiced			d		g	
Fricatives, voiceless		f	s	sh		h
Fricatives, voiced		v	z	j		
Plosives, pre-nasalized	mb		nd		ng	
Nasals	m		n	ny		
Liquids			l/r			
Approximants	b					
Glides				y		

There is a phoneme /l/ which alternates non-contrastively with /r/ following front vowels. There is also a phoneme /r/ which contrasts with /l/ in all environments. The contrastive /r/ seems to be the result of borrowings from Kinyarwanda.

The sound **w**, although present in Kifuliiru, is very rare, occurring as **w** only in pronominal/prefixal forms. When it occurs without a preceding consonant, it is always synchronically traceable to a high back vowel, **u**, which has undergone glide formation, and so **w** is not included in the phoneme inventory.

Only the prenasalized consonants which occur within a single morpheme are listed in the consonant inventory above in table 2.1. These are the prenasalized plosives **mb, nd**, and **ng** ([ŋg]). Within a single morpheme, these occur only in C2 position or later. A prenasalized plosive found in syllable-initial position is always bi-morphemic, with the nasal comprising one morpheme and the plosive being the initial segment of another.

The nasal-fricative[5] combinations [ɱv], [nʒ], and [nz] do occur in Kifuliiru, but they occur only at morpheme junctions, where the nasal component

---

clude labialized and palatalized consonants, many of which, if considered as single segments, would contrast with their unmodified counterparts.

[5]These are continuant sequences realized generally as nasal plus fricative, and not as nasal plus affricate. Some people do pronounce the fricative as an affricate following a nasal, but the nasal plus fricative pronunciation is more common, especially in older speakers. Affricates are used in loan words which have not been adapted, but are not generally used in original Kifuliiru words. Even the borrowed words which are sometimes pronounced with affricates,

comprises a separate morpheme. These combinations may result from the juxtaposition of a fricative-initial noun root with the cl. 9/10 nominal prefix N-, cf. (2.1a). Alternatively, they may also result from the prefixation of a verbal first-person object prefix, n-, to a fricative-initial verb stem, cf. (2.1b, c). (All nasal prefixes assimilate to the place of articulation of a following consonant.) Since the nasal/fricative combinations are exclusively bi-morphemic, they are not included in the phonemic inventory.

(2.1) a. /í=N-jánga/ [ínʒááŋgà] AU=10-dried fish 'dried fish'
b. /a-à-ń-vwom-er-a/ [áɱvwóómérà] 1-P1-O1.SG-get.water-APL-Fa 'he drew water for me'
c. /a-à-ń-zìmb-a/ [ánzìimbà] 1-P1-O1.SG-steal-Fa 'he stole from me'

There are a few words in which the N + fricative ([ɱv], [nʒ], and [nz]) appears to occur morpheme internally, but it seems that these cases are probably the result of reinterpretation of combinations of what was historically a nasal morpheme preceding a fricative-initial morpheme. This has occurred where a cl. 9/10 prefix, N- is re-lexicalized as a part of the stem, either when another prefix is added or as a result of reduplication. E.g. **í=kì-njògòlò** (AU=7-unripe.peanut.seed) is derived probably from the non-attested form **N-jogolo**, where the N- is the cl. 9 prefix. Likewise, **í=n-záá(n)zàgè** (AU=9-men's.woven.bag) is from **i=N-za-(n)zage**, where the stem is formed by a reduplication of the first syllable of the noun, **n-zage** which includes the nasal cl. 9 prefix (though this form is not synchronically attested separately, either). The medial **nz** in this word is retained by some speakers, while in the speech of others, the medial **nz** is reduced to **z**. There are also some borrowings from Kiswahili in which the Kiswahili **nz** is replaced by [nʒ], e.g. [í-káànʒù] (5-robe) from Kiswahili **kanzu** 'robe'.

2.1.2 Vowels

The vowel phonemes are shown in table 2.2.

---

e.g. Kiswahili words pronounced with **ndj** (nasal plus affricate), also have an adapted version in Kifuliiru, as Kiswahili **kuvunja** 'to break' (often used of changing money), **kúvùújà** 'to change money' (with effacement of the nasal segment). In cases with no prenasalization, Kiswahili affricates are always adapted to fricatives, e.g. **tch** > **sh**: Kiswahili **chaaki** 'chalk' > **í=sháàkì**.

2.2 Phonetic realization and distribution of phonemes

Table 2.2. Vowel phonemes

	Front	Central	Back
High	i ii		u uu
Mid	e ee		o oo
Low		a aa	

Because there are no unambiguous VV sequences, the long vowels are interpreted as long segments rather than as two vowels together.[6] Orthographically, however, and for the purposes of this book, they are written as VV rather than as V:.

2.2 Phonetic realization and distribution of phonemes

2.2.1 Consonants

2.2.1.1 *Realizations/distribution*

The various realizations of each consonant phoneme are given in this section, with examples. Most of the variants comprise what some might term "morphophonemic" variation, in that they involve the change from one contrastive segment to another contrastive segment at morpheme boundaries. Nevertheless, as long as the motivation is phonetic, the variations are included in this section. The generalizations that can be drawn from the allophonic realizations of the individual phonemes, such as rules of voicing and of strengthening, are found in 2.3.1.

In table 2.3, note that "suffix-final consonants" include those found in what are known as verbal expansions – suffixes which are not identifiable extensions having inherent morphological significance. A suffix-final C is always followed either by a -VC expansion or by a FV, and thus is never found word finally.

---

[6]However, a VV sequences at the syntactic level can be created by the concatenation of vocalic morphemes or vowel-initial morphemes with vowel-final morphemes.

Table 2.3. Summary of consonant realizations and distribution

Phonemic	Phonetic realizations	Prefix initial	Suffix final	Stem initial	Stem medial
p	[p] [b]			x	x[a]
t	[t] [d]	x	x	x	x
k	[k] [g]	x	x	x	x
b	[b] [β]	x	x	x	x
d	[d]		x[b]	x	x
g	[g]	x	x	x	x
mb	[mb]				x
nd	[nd]				x
ng	[ŋ]	x[c]			x
f	[f] [v]			x	
v	[v]			x	x
s	[s] [z]		x[d]	x	x[e]
z	[z]		x	x	x
sh	[ʃ] [ʒ]			x	x
h	[b] [h]	x	x	x	x
j	[ʒ]			x	x
m	[m]	x	x	x	x
n	[m] [ŋ] [ɲ] [m̩] [n]	x	x	x	x
ny	[ɲ]	x		x	x
r	[ɾ] [d]	x	x	x	x
l	[ɾ] [l] [d]	x	x	x	x
y	[y][f]	x		x[g]	x

[a] **p** occurs medially only as the result of reduplication.

[b] **d** occurs suffixally only in one combination of verbal expansions: -**ad-ik**, e.g. -**fùmb-adik-** 'hand to'. This is the result of diachronic voicing of the final **t** of -**at** 'contactive' by Dahl's law i.e. **at-ik > ad-ik** by the diachronic application of Dahl's law.

2.2 Phonetic realization and distribution of phonemes

^cThis comes only in the verbal conditional prefix **nga-** which always follows the P1 **à-**. The two could be interpreted as a single prefix **ànga-** and thus the /ng/ could be seen as prefix internal rather than prefix initial.

^d**s** and **z** occur in suffixes only as a part of the causative suffix or as a result of the spirantization of another consonant, conditioned by a following morpheme (causative, resultative, etc.).

^e**s** and **z** occur stem medially only as the result of spirantization conditioned by a following morpheme. Proto-Bantu ***c** seems to be quite regularly realized as **sh** in Kifuliiru, e.g. the PB verb root ***dác-** 'throw' is realized in the verb **kú-làsh-à** 'throw'. (Note that **kúlásâ** 'to make something sound (play instrument, etc.)' is the causative form of **kúlàkà** 'to resound, make a noise'.)

^fThe IPA symbol for **y** (alveolar glide) is actually **j**. However, we are not using **j** here (due to reviewer feedback) as it is too easily confused with the phonemic /j/ in Kifuliiru which is a pre-palatal voiced fricative.

^g**y** is found stem-initially only in verbs. Kifuliiru has a constraint against V-initial verb roots.

Prefixes are of the form N(C)(V)-, or (C)V-. Suffixes are of the form -(VC)V(C). In prefixes and prefixal formatives, consonant inventory is restricted to **h, b, t, l/r, k, g, m, n, ng, ny**. In (verbal) suffixes, only **h, b, t, d, l/r, k, g, m,** and **n** occur, of which **l/r** may be spirantized to **z**, and **t** or **k** may be spirantized to **s**. Any special notes on distribution of an individual phoneme follow the examples for that segment.

/h/ → [b] / nasal __
    → [h] elsewhere

(2.2) a. /í=hí-hènè/   [íhíhènè]   AU=19-goat 'small goat'
      b. /í=N-hènè/   [íímbènè]   AU=9/10-goat
      c. /ú=lú-hāndè/   [úlúhāāndè]   AU=11-groundnut
      d. /í=N-hândè/   [ímbáàndè]   AU=10-side
      e. /ú=mú-hyâhyá/   [úmúhyáàhyâ]   AU=1-new
      f. /í=N-hyâhyá/   [ímbyáàhyâ]   AU=9/10-new
      g. /ú=kú-heek-a/   [úkúhéékà]   AU=15-carry-Fa[†]
      h. /a-à-ń-heek-a/   [ámbéèkà]   1-P1-O1.SG-carry-Fa
                                           'he carried me'
      i. /í=kí-hálo/   [íkíhálò]   AU=7-one.edged.knife
      j. /í=kí-hé/   [ííkíhê]   AU=7-time
      k. /í=kí-hínda/   [íkíhííndà]   AU=7-granary
      l. /í=kí-hóma/   [íkíhómà]   AU=7-puff.adder
      m. /í=kí-húlu/   [íkíhúlu]   AU=7-darkness
      n. /í=í-vùha/   [íívùhà]   AU=5-bone
      o. /ú=kú-róh-a/   [úkúróhà]   AU=15-throw.in.fire.
                                           or.river-Fa

[†]Cl. 15 is the class used for infinitives. Wherever there is a morpheme-by-morpheme gloss which contains 15- followed by a verb (in this case 'carry') it should be interpreted as an infinitive, i.e. 'to carry'.

The phoneme **h** is the Kifuliiru reflex of Proto-Bantu *p. Whereas other voiceless consonants, when preceded by a nasal consonant, gain voicing but stay at the same or nearly the same point of articulation, **h** is pronounced as [b] when it is preceded by a nasal. One could assume that the weakening that took place for the *p to become **h** did not occur in the environments where the *p was protected by prenasalization. However, this has resulted in synchronic alternation between **h** and **b**. Cases in which such prenasalization and concurrent strengthening and voicing occurs always involve the juxtaposition of an **h**-initial root with a nasal prefix. Such juxtaposition is in nouns (2.2b, d) cf. (2.2a, c); in adjectives (2.2f), cf. (2.2e); and in verbs (2.2h), cf. (2.2g). In some words, there is free variation between forms with and without a root-initial **h**, e.g. **múhóbò** ~ **mwóóbò** 'hole'.

2.2 Phonetic realization and distribution of phonemes

/p/ → [b] / nasal __
    → [p] elsewhere

(2.3) /ú=kú-puumuk-a/ [úkúpúúmúkà] AU=15-dash.off-Fa
/a-à-ń-puumuk-ir-a/ [ámbúmúkíɾà] 1-P1-O1.SG-dash.off-APL-Fa
'he dashed away from me'
/ú=kú-pwepuz-a/ [ukúpwéépúzâ] AU=15-squint.and.blink-Fa
/í=kí-pànga/ [íkípààŋgà] AU=7-male.sheep
/nàpéèyá/ [nàpéèyâ] 1a+woman.w.no.propriety
/í=kí-pòòngòsho/ [íkípòòŋgòʃò] AU=7-elongated.back.of.skull
/ú=kú-píís-á/ [úkúpíísâ] AU=15-cs.many.to.be.killed-Fa

The phoneme **p** is somewhat rare in Kifuliiru, following the historical process of p-lenition, by which Proto-Bantu *p became **h**. The phoneme **p** occurs in a limited number of words (in roughly forty words out of 5,475, as compared to **h** with 794 occurrences in the same corpus). These words with **p** include words derived from ideophones,[7] as well as words reintroduced through borrowing or by analogy. For the most part, **p** occurs only morpheme initially except in reduplicatives and loan words.

In (2.4) we see **p** and **h** in analogous environments, preceding vowels of all points of articulation. In (2.4e) **p** and **h** are in free variation. There are other examples in the corpus of free variation between **p** and **h**.

(2.4)   Words with **h** and **p**
        Words   Gloss

    a. /í=kí-pààngà/   [íkípààŋgà]   AU=7-ram
        /í=kí-hāāngò/   [íkíhāāŋgò]   AU=7-covenant

    b. /ú=kú-puumuk-a/   [úkúpúúmúkà]   AU=15-dash.off-Fa
        /ú=kú-huumur-a/   [úkúhúúmúɾà]   AU=15-be.strong.
                                                    smelling-Fa

    c. /í= í-páàmbà/   [ípáàmbà]   AU=5-cotton (Sw.)
        /í-hèèmbà/   [íhèèmbà]   5-sorghum

    d. /pépéépé/   [pépéépé]   very.white (ideophone)
        /íí=n-gùhé/   [ííŋgùhé]   AU=9-type.of.fish

---

[7]Such as **-puumuka, -pwepuuza,** and **-piisa** in 2.3.

	Words with **h** and **p** Words		Gloss
e.	/ú=kú-yìpàlalik-a/	[úkúyìpàlálíkà]	AU=15-attempt. impossible-Fa
	/ú=kú-yìhàlalik-a/	[úkúyìhàlálíkà]	AU=15-attempt. impossible-Fa

/t/ → [d] / nasal __
   → [t] elsewhere

(2.5)	/u-tábaal-e/	[ùtáβáàlè]	2SG-help-Fe 'you (SG) help!'
	/u-ń-tábaal-e/	[úndáβààlè]	2SG-O1.SG-help-Fe 'you (SG) help me!'
	/í=N-tàngiro/	[índààŋgírò]	AU=9-beginning
	/í=N-tāmbo/	[índāāmbò]	AU=9-step
	/í=kí-tóle/	[íkítólè]	AU=7-eggplant(sp.)
	/í=kí-tùgo/	[íkítùgò]	AU=7-shoulder
	/í=kí-tèér-o/	[íkítēērò]	AU=7-attack
	/ú=kú-tíbit-a/	[úkútíβítà]	AU=15-run-Fa

/k/ → [g] / nasal __
   → [k] elsewhere

(2.6)	/u-kéngeer-e/	[ùkéŋgéèrè]	2SG-remember-Fe '(that) you remember'
	/u-ń-kéngeer-e/	[úŋgéŋgèèrè]	2SG-O1.SG-remember-Fe '(that) you remember me'
	/ú=kú-keek-a/	[úkúkéékà]	AU=15-guess-Fa
	/nkèèkà/	[ŋgèèkà]	maybe
	/í= í-kééta/	[íkéétà]	AU=5-knife
	/í=kí-kàmo/	[íkíkàmò]	AU=7-dry.season
	/ú=mú-káka/	[úmúkákà]	AU=3-small.fish
	/bìkòra/	[βìkòrà]	1a+type.of.fish
	/í=kí-kúmba/	[íkíkúúmbà]	AU=7-porridge

2.2 Phonetic realization and distribution of phonemes

/d/ → [d] in all instances

(2.7)
/ú=lú-dáha/	[úlúdáhà]	AU=11-bag/pocket
/ú=kú-deek-a/	[úkúdéékà]	AU=15-cook-Fa
/ú=kú-dèdemb-a/	[úkúdèdéémbà]	AU=15-quarrel.endlessly-Fa
/ú=mú-dóódo/	[úmúdóódò]	AU=3-ride
/ú=bú-dìku/	[úβúdìkù]	AU=14-liver
/í=í-dúùdu/	[ídúùdù]	AU=5-processed.cassava.piece

The phoneme **d** rarely occurs as the second consonant in a stem, whether noun or verb. In C1 position, it is often followed by an unvoiced C in C2 position. This may be a result of the application of Dahl's law, which causes voicing of a consonant in C1 postion if C2 is voiceless. In the few cases where **d** does occur in C2 position, it is a product of reduplication or of assimilation to the first C, which would also be **d**, as in **kú-dóód-à** (15-go.for.a.ride.on.bike-Fa), **kú-dèdéémb-à** (15-quarrel.incessantly-Fa).

/g/ → [g] in all instances

(2.8)
/ú=mú-gàzi/	[úmúgàzì]	AU=3-mountain
/í=kí-gábi/	[íkígáβì]	AU=7-gift
/ú=kú-génd-a/	[úkúgééndà]	AU=15-go-Fa
/ú=kú-gír-a/	[úkúgírà]	AU=15-do/make-Fa
/ú=kú-góh-a/	[úkúgóhà]	AU=15-coax-Fa
/ú=kú-gúg-a/	[úkúgúgà]	AU=15-gather.into.pile-Fa

/b/ → [b] / nasal __
→ [β][8] elsewhere

The bilabial approximant **b** ([β]) patterns phonologically with the liquids **l** and **r**, and the voiceless fricative **h** in undergoing a fortition (strengthening) process following nasal consonants. Thus the approximant becomes a plosive in post-nasal position, cf. final example in (2.9).

---

[8]Note that the symbol [β] (which usually denotes a voiced fricative) is used (in keeping with what appears to be the most common transcriptions for these sounds in Bantu languages) for the labial approximant, in place of the IPA symbol [ʋ]. It should be noted, however, that this sound is most often produced as an approximant in Kifuliiru, and usually has little, if any, friction.

(2.9) /ba-à-génd-a/ [βàgéénda̋] 2-P1-go-Fa 'they went'
/í=bí-hándo/ [íβíháándò] AU=8-sores
/í=N-kúlube/ [íŋgúlúβè] AU=9-pig
/ú=kú-lòb-a/ [úkúlōβà] AU=15-get.wet-Fa
/ú=mú-bùsi/ [úmúβùsì] AU=1-parent
/a-à-ń-biik-ir-a/ [ámbííkírà] 1-O1.SG-put-APL-Fa
  'he put something away for me'

/f/ → [v] / nasal __
  → [f] elsewhere

(2.10) /í=fùlà/ [íífùlà] AU=9+eldest.son
/í=kí-fúnè/ [íkífúnè] AU=7-fist
/ú=kú-fu-a/ [úúkúfwâ] AU=15-die-Fa
/ú=kú-fuuh-a/ [úkúfúúhà] AU=15-blow-Fa
/a-à-ń-fuuh-ir-a/ [ánvúúhìrà] 1-P1-O1.SG-blow-APL-Fa
  'he blew on me'
/ú=kú-fín-a/ [úkúfínà] AU=15-tread.on-Fa

The alternation between **f** and **v** is seen only in verbs, when the first-person object marker **n-** precedes an **f**-initial verb stem. In nouns, the voicing of **f** is not attested because in cl. 9 nouns, the nominal prefix **n-** is deleted preceding a voiceless fricative, as seen in the first example in (2.10), where the cl. 9 augment is present, but there is no overt nominal prefix (2.3.2.3.3).

The phonemes **f** (2.10) and **v** (2.12) in the majority of cases are followed by **u** (see all examples but the last one in (2.10) above), and in some cases are followed by **i**, see final example in (2.10) and final example in (2.12). Besides occurring in a **vi** or **vu** sequence, **v** can also occur morpheme finally following **u** or **i**, such as in **kú-hīīv-a**, in (2.12), where it is followed by the final vowel. However, in morpheme-initial position, neither **f** nor **v** ever occurs preceding **a, e**, or **o**. This distribution results from the fact that historically **f** and **v** were the result of spirantization (mainly of *k > f and *g > v) when they followed the first degree vowels *i̜ and *u̜, which later merged with /i/ and /u/. However, the distribution of these segments seems to have been interpreted as a synchronic constraint against sequences other than **fu/fw** and **fi, vu/vw** and **vi** except in cases where the **f** or **v** is morpheme final. The phonological changes made in the French loan word, **fwárááŋgà** 'franc/money' in (2.11) shows the strategy of epenthesizing **u**, which subsequently undergoes glide formation, following the **f** to avoid having the **fa*** sequence morpheme initially.

(2.11) /ú=lú-fuáranga/   [úlúfwáráángà]   AU=11-money

/v/ → [v] in all instances

The distribution of **v** is as described above. Note that **v** is more likely than **f** to occur in C2 position.

(2.12) /í=í-vùha/   [íívùhà]   AU=5-bone
        /á=má-àvu/   [ámààvù]   AU=6-beer
        /í=fùúvi/   [ífūūvì]   AU=(9)+orphan
        /ú=kú-vúnd-ik-a/ [úkúvúúndíkà]   AU=15-ferment-IMPS-Fa
        /ú=kú-jàvuur-a/   [úkúʒàvúúɾà]   AU=15-despise-Fa
        /ú=kú-hòov-a/   [úkúhōōvà]   AU=15-hunt.birds-Fa
        /ú=kú-hìiv-a/   [úkúhīīvà]   AU=15-hunt.animals-Fa
        /ú=kú-víg-a/   [úkúvígà]   AU=15-fish.get.mealy-Fa

/s/ → [z] / nasal __
    → [s] elsewhere

(2.13) /í=í-sù/   [íìsù]   AU=5-eye
        /í=kí-úsì/   [íkyúúsì]   AU=7-smoke
        /ú=kú-sìg-a/   [úkúsīgà]   AU=15-leave.behind-Fa
        /a-à-ń-zìg-a/   [áánzìgà]   1-P1-O1.SG-leave.behind-Fa
                                            'he left me behind'

        /ú=kú-sook-a/   [úkúsóókà]   AU=15-pass.behind.sthg-Fa
        /ú=kú-seeh-a/   [úkúséého]   AU=15-transport.in.groups-Fa
        /ú=kú-súm-a/   [úkúsúmà]   AU=15-go.to.buy.food-Fa
        /ú=kú-sánganir-a/ [úkúsáŋgáníɾà]   AU=15-go.meet-Fa

Neither **s** nor **z** ever occurs in a non-initial position in a verb stem unless as the result of preceding a morpheme which triggers spirantization/frication. These spirantizing morphemes include the resultative, agentive, and causative (2.3.2.5).

/z/ → [z] in all instances

(2.14)
/í=í-zìína/	[ízīīnà]	AU=5-name
/í=í-zùúba/	[ízūūβà]	AU=5-sun
/ú=kú-zìmb-a/	[úkúzīīmbà]	AU=15-steal-Fa
/ú=kú-zaat-a/	[úkúzáátà]	AU=15-walk-Fa
/ú=kú-zòbek-a/	[úkúzòβékà]	AU=15-hobble.with.rope-Fa
/ú=kú-zègemb-a/	[úkúzègéémbà]	AU=15-carry.heavy.load-Fa

/sh/ → [ʒ] / nasal __
→ [ʃ] elsewhere

(2.15)
/í=í-shámba/	[íʃáámbà]	AU=5-barren.flatland
/í=shèény-o/	[íʃēēɲò]	AU=9+axe
/í=shòni/	[íʃònì]	AU=9+shame
/í=shúúli/	[íʃúúlì]	AU=9+bull
/ú=kú-shiig-a/	[úkúʃíígà]	AU=15-smear-Fa
/a-à-ń-shiig-a/	[áánʒíìgà]	1-P1-O1.SG-smear-Fa
		'he smeared me w/something'
/ú=lú-shènga/	[úlúʃèèŋgà]	AU=11-fishing.net
/í=N-shènga/	[ínʒèèŋgà]	AU=10-fishing.nets

There are a few words with root-initial **sh** which have colloquial variants with **s**. E.g. **ú=múshósì ~ ú=músósì** 'man', **Sháàngê ~ Sáàngê** 'Sange' (place name), **kúshéézì ~ kúséézì** 'tomorrow', **shéshéézì ~ séséézì**[9] 'morning'. The **sh ~ s** alternation is observed only in a certain few of the words which contain **sh**. It is not observed in cases where the **sh** is not root initial, and is rarely noted in verbs, with the exception that -**saaz**- ~ -**shaaz** 'remove' is commonly heard.

---

[9]This is a compound word derived from **shé** 'father of' **kú-shéézì** 'tomorrow'. Thus both instances of the **sh/s** alternation are root initial.

2.2 Phonetic realization and distribution of phonemes

/j/ → [ʒ] in all instances

(2.16) /í=bí-góòjè/ [íβígóòʒè] AU=8-maize
/í=kí-júmbu/ [íkíʒúúmbù] AU=7-potato
/ú=kú-jánd-a/ [úkúʒáándà] AU=15-forsake-Fa
/ú=kú-jìgimb-a/ [úkúʒìgíímbà] AU=15-be.burned.up-Fa
/ú=kú-jòm-a-joma/ [úkúʒòmá-ʒómà] AU=15-urinate-Fa-RDP
(as male dog)

/m/ → [m] in all instances

(2.17) /máàwé/ [máàwê] 1a+my/our.mother
/á=mí-īno/ [ámīīnò] AU=6-teeth
/ú=kú-mók-a/ [úkúmókà] AU=15-bark-Fa
/ú=kú-kàm-a/ [úkúkāmà] AU=15-squeeze.out-Fa
/ú=mú-mírò/ [úmúmírò] AU=3-throat

/n/ → [m] / __ labial
→ [ŋ] / __ velar
→ [ɲ] / __ y
→ [ɱ] / __ f, v
→ [n] elsewhere

Note that the above is assuming that the first-person singular verbal subject and object prefixes are underlyingly **n-**, and not **N-** with assimilation to the place of the following consonant.[10] In the dialect spoken around Mugule and by people whose families came from there, **ny** is used in place of **n** in many morpheme(s) of the form **na-**. For example, such speakers would say **à-nyá-géènd-à** (1-SQ-go-Fa) 'and he went' in place of the standard **à-ná-géènd-à**.

---

[10]The subject prefix occurs as **n-** before a vocalic or vowel initial prefix, e.g. **n-à-géénda** 'I went'. The object prefix never occurs prevocalically, as it always directly precedes the verb stem and there are no vowel-initial verb stems.

(2.18) /ú=bú-núnu/ [úβúnúnù] AU=14-sweetness
/ú=kú-nán-a/ [úkúnánà] AU=15-refuse-Fa
/a-à-ń-téb-a/ [áándéβà] 1-P1-O1.SG-trick-Fa
'he tricked me'

/a-à-ń-bon-a/ [áámbònà] 1-P1-O1.SG-see-Fa 'he saw me'

/a-à-ń-vuom-er-a/ [áŋvwóómérà] 1-P1-O1.SG-draw.water-APL-Fa
'he drew water for me'

/a-à-ń-kéngeer-a/ [áŋgéŋgèèrà] 1-P1-O1.SG-remember-Fa
'he remembered me'

/a-à-n-yíbagir-a/ [áɲíbàgìrà] 1-P1-O1.SG-forget-Fa
'he forgot me'

/ny/ → [ɲ] in all instances

The first two of the following examples show **ny** as a realization of the 9/10 nominal prefix, while the rest show it as part of a root.[11] Note that **ny** is the form that the cl. 9/10 nominal prefix, N-, takes before vowel initial roots. In consonant-initial roots the cl. 9/10 nominal prefix assimilates to the place of articulation of the initial consonant.

(2.19) /í=ny-áma/ [íɲámà] AU=9-meat
/í=ny-úùmba/ [íɲúùmbà] AU=9-house
/ú=kú-mény-a/ [úkúméɲà] AU=15-know-Fa
/ú=kú-nyaafu-l-a/ [úkúɲááfúlà] AU=15-whip-Fa
/ú=mú-nyófu/ [úmúɲófù] AU=3-flesh
/ú=mú-unyu/ [úmúùɲù] AU=3-salt
/ú=mú-nyére/ [úmúɲérè] AU=1-girl
/nyóko/ [ɲókò] 1a+your.mother
/nyína/ [ɲínà] 1a+his/her/their.mother
/í=kí-ànya/ [íkyààɲà] AU=7-time

---

[11]In the first two examples, there is never an alternation which changes the form, so it would also be possible to interpret the **ny** as part of the root, with deletion of the nasal prefix preceding the nasal root. There are, however, other words in which there is alternation, such as **lwáàlà/nyáàlà** 'boulder, cave/boulders, caves' and **lwímbó/nyímbò** 'song/songs'. Because of this, we assume that **ny** is the prevocalic form of the prefix, and do not attempt to distinguish in cl. 9/10 between **ny**- initial noun roots and V-initial noun roots with the **ny**- prefix.

2.2 Phonetic realization and distribution of phonemes

There are some words in which **n** may be substituted for **ny** in some dialects. For instance, some speakers say **nyákásàrè** as **nákásàrè**, and **nyínà** 'his/her/their mother' as **nínà**. It is clear that **ny** and **n** do constitute contrastive phonemes, however, as witnessed by pairs such as **kúnágà** 'to coagulate, thicken' and **kúnyágà** 'to take by force'. The palatal nasal **ny** ([ɲ]) also contrasts with palatalized **n** ([ny] alveolar nasal plus **y**[12]) in words such as **kúkáányà** 'to make a cracking sound when breaking' and **kúkàníá** ~ **kúkànyâ** 'to grasp tightly, make firm'.

/l/   → [d] / n __
      → [ɾ] / e, i __
      → [l] elsewhere

(2.20) /ú=kú-leet-a/   [úkúléétà]   AU=15-bring-Fa
        /ú=kú-ń-leet-er-a/   [úkúndéétéɾà]   AU=15-O.1SG-bring-APL-Fa
        /ú=kú-gì-leet-a/   [úkúgìɾéétà]   AU=15-O4/O9-bring-Fa
        /ú=kú-té†=leet-a/   [úkútéɾéétà]   AU=15-first=bring-Fa
        /ú=lú-lèhe-lehe/   [úlúlèhè-ɾèhè]   AU=11-longing-RDP
        /í=N-lèhe-ndehe/   [índèhè-ndèhè]   AU=10-longings-RDP
        /ú=mú-lòndo/   [úmúlòòndò]   AU=3-garment
        /í=mí-lòndo/   [ímíɾòòndò]   AU=4-garments
        /ú=bú-lúlù/   [úβúlúlù]   AU=14-bitterness
        /ú=mu-hùli/   [úmúhùlì]   AU=3-cluster.of.grain/fruit
        /ú=bú-híli/   [úβúhíɾi]   AU=14-heavy.knobbed.stick
        /í=kí-tólo/   [íkítólò]   AU=7-piece
        /ú=kú-kùl-à/   [úkúkūlà]   AU=15-grow-Fa
        /ú=kú-kòl-a/   [úkúkōlà]   AU=15-work-Fa
        /ú=kú-mál-a/   [úkúmálà]   AU=15-finish-Fa

†**te** is not a prefix, but an procliticized auxiliary which has apparently evolved from the verb **kútáángà** 'to come first'. There is a word break following the auxiliary. Because it is procliticized, the **e** in **te** still conditions the change of **l** to **r** in the main verb.

The liquid **l** has an allophone [ɾ] that occurs following front vowels as seen in (2.20). Besides the [ɾ] which is an allophone of **l**, many words have a phoneme /r/ which does not alternate with [l] (2.21). Words containing this sound

---
[12]This latter is indicated orthographically as **ni**, e.g. **kúkàniâ** 'to grasp tightly, make firm'.

can almost always be traced to borrowings from Kinyarwanda or Kirundi. The non-alternating phoneme /r/ is also found in words which are obvious borrowings from Kiswahili (2.21g) and French (2.21h). This non-alternating **r** acts phonologically just like **l**. It undergoes strengthening to [d] after nasals, just as **l** does (2.21f). The following is a pair of words which illustrates well the contrast between /r/ and /l/: **ú=kúl̠ààmbà** 'to lick' and **ú=kúr̠áámbà** 'to live'. Normally, the difference between **l** and **r** is neutralized following a high front vowel, e.g. **ú=múl̠òòndò** 'garment' > **í=mír̠òòndò** 'garments'. However, the contrast between the two sounds is maintained in subjunctive forms of **ú=kúl̠àmbà** 'to lick' and **ú=kúr̠ámbà** 'to live' which have an **i**-final subject prefix: **zì-l̠áámb-è** (10-lick-Fe) 'that they lick' still contrasts with **zì-r̠áámb-è** (10-live-Fe) 'that they live'.

/r/ → [d] / n __
    → [ɾ] elsewhere

(2.21) a. /í=í-tàrà/   [íítàɾà]   AU=5-lamp
       b. /rúréma/   [ɾúɾémà]   1a+God (the creator)
       c. /ú=ru-kūndo/   [úɾúkūūndò]   AU=15-love
       d. /ú=bú-râmbe/   [úβúɾáàmbè]   AU=14-long.life
       e. /ú=kú-raakar-a/   [úkúɾáákáɾà]   AU=15-become.angry-Fa
       f. /a-ń-raaka-í-a/   [ándáákázá]   1-O1.SG-be.angry-CS-Fa
                                              'he made me angry'
       g. /á=ká-rátààsi/   [ákáɾátààsì]   AU=12-paper (Sw. **karatasi**)
       h. /lú-fuáranga/   [lúfwáɾááŋgà]   11-piece.of.money
                                              (Fr. **franc**)

The non-alternating **r** occurs in verbal suffixes as well as in roots. There are verbal extensions containing **r**, which correspond to each of the **a**-, **u**-/**o**-initial extensions which end with **l**, e.g. **-uur/-oor**, corresponding to the reversive transitive extension, **-uul/-ool**, etc. Other extensions with **r** include **-ur/-or**, **-urur/-oror**, **-ar**, **-arar**, **-aar**. However, these **r**-final suffixes always seem to be lexicalized as part of specific words and are no longer productive in any cases we have found. Examples are found in (2.22).

(2.22) /ú=kú-bwàndarar-a/ [úkúβwàndáɾáɾà] AU=15-be.all.broken-Fa
/ú=kú-yáárar-a/ [úkúyááɾáɾà] AU=15-be.red-Fa
(as hair from kwashiorkor)

/ú=kú-hángaar-a/ [úkúháŋgááɾà] AU=15-challenge.
stronger.one-Fa

/ú=kú-gémur-a/ [úkúgémúɾà] AU=15-food.to.herdsmen-Fa

/ú=kú-yògoror-a/ [úkúyògóɾóɾà] AU=15-come.from.water-Fa

/ú=kú-fyòngoor-a/ [úkúfyòŋgóóɾà] AU=15-kill.by.choking-Fa

Some cl. 11 nouns, which are probably of Kinyarwanda/Kirundi origin, have the prefix **ru-** instead of the usual **lu-**. However, the concord used with other parts of speech to mark agreement with such nouns is the normal cl. 11 concord, **lu-**. E.g. **ú=rúsóòzò** 'drinking gourd', but **ú=rúsóòzò lúhámù** (*not* **u=rusoozo *ruhamu**) 'big drinking gourd'. The fact that the nominal prefix is **ru-** but the adjective prefix is **lu-** is also an indication that the prefix is lexicalized with the root in the case of the noun, while there is no productive prefix **ru-** to be affixed to the adjective base.

/y/ → [y] in all instances

(2.23) /ú=kú-kúy-a-kuya/ [úkúkúyá-kúyà] AU=15-attend.someone-Fa-RDP
/ú=kú-yòboh-a/ [úkúyòòβóhà] AU=15-be.afraid-Fa
/ú=kú-yák-a/ [úkúyáákà] AU=15-burn.brightly-Fa
/ú=kú-yìg-a/ [úkúyīīgà] AU=15-learn-Fa
/á=ká-āya/ [ákāāyà] AU=12-compound/village/town
/ú=bú-òya/ [úβwòòyà] AU=14-fur
/í=í-yúnga/ [íyúúŋgà] AU=5-ankle.bell (for dancing)
/yùguó/ [yùùgwó] that.N+3

It is interesting to note that **y** is the consonant which is epenthesized in the formation of certain demonstratives whose roots are V-only (7.7.1), and is also the consonant which is the unspecified "copy" of a specified prefix C in the formation of demonstratives whose roots are of the CV shape. The consonant **y** is also dropped in derived nominal forms of verbs whose roots begin with **y**, for example **mw-áámbáló** (3-garment) from **-yáámbal-** 'put on clothing'. It can optionally be dropped from at least some conjugated verb forms. For instance, **námúyììtè** 'and if I kill him' can also be pronounced as **námwììtè**.

Some instances of **y** are obviously derived from a high front vowel (**i**) as the result of glide formation. Others, such as that in **á=kāāyà** 'compound, village', or that in the verb -**káy**- 'be fierce, harsh' would seem to be underlyingly consonantal. It is a matter of interpretation whether one posits an underlying /y/ phoneme or derives all instances of **y** from **i** by glide formation. There is evidence for both views. We have posited a /y/ phoneme because it sometimes occurs within a single morpheme, where it would appear to be underived. Also, in demonstrative forms which would otherwise consist of VV, the **y** is inserted to modify the form so that its form is VCV. That its function is to add a consonant to what would otherwise be a VV sequence points to its underlying status as a consonant.

It could of course be possible that even such **y**s derive from a high vowel. Compensatory lengthening of a V which follows a glide points to a vocalic origin for that glide. In Kifuliiru there is lengthening of (all but word final) vowels following *all* instances of **y**. This would seem to indicate that all **y**s are derived from a high vowel. However, this lengthening in the case of an underlying **y** could also be due to analogy with **y**s which are derived from a high vowel.

/mb/ → [mb] in all instances

(2.24) /í=ny-ûmba/ [ínyúùmbà] AU=9-house
/ú=kú-bámb-a/ [úkúβáámbà] AU=15-stretch.out.and.nail -Fa
/ú=kú-bómb-a/ [úkúβóómbà] AU=15-die-Fa (of a twin only)
/ú=kú-hémb-a/ [úkúhéémbà] AU=15-reward-Fa
/í=N-hēmb-o/ [ímbēēmbò] AU=9/10-reward
/ń-heez-a/ [mbéézâ] O1.SG-give-Fa
'give me something!'

/mb/ never occurs morpheme initially in underlying forms. It can occur in a word-initial syllable as the result of morpheme juxtaposition as in the final example of (2.24), or in forms such as **mbéémbò** 'reward', when used without the augment.

2.2 Phonetic realization and distribution of phonemes

/nd/ → [nd] in all instances

(2.25) /ú=kú-hónd-a/ [úkúhóóndà] AU=15-pound-Fa
/ú=kú-hùnd-a/ [úkúhūūndà] AU=15-compact-Fa
/ú=kú-hánd-a/ [úkúháándà] AU=15-rent-Fa
/ú=kú-hènd-a/ [úkúhēēndà] AU=15-deceive-Fa
/ú=kú-hínd-a/ [úkúhííndà] AU=15-circle-Fa
/í=N-dà/ [ìindà] AU=9-louse
/n-ta-looz-iiz-i/ [ndàlózíìzì] 1SG-NEG-want-RS+CS-Fi
'I don't want (sthg.)'

/nd/ never occurs morpheme initially in underlying forms. It can occur in a word-initial syllable as the result of morpheme juxtaposition as in the final example of (2.25).

/ng/ → [ŋg] in all instances

(2.26) /í=kí-ìbùngu/ [íkìβùùŋgù] AU=7-cloud
/ú=kú-hìng-a/ [úkúhīīŋgà] AU=15-cultivate-Fa
/ú=bú-ēnge/ [úβwēēŋgè] AU=14-cleverness
/á=má-lánga/ [ámáláángà] AU=6-face
/ú=kú-lóng-a/ [úkúlóóŋgà] AU=15-get-Fa

/í-N-gwí/ [ííŋgwî] AU=9-leopard
/ngèèka/ [ŋgèèkà] 'perhaps'
/ngábà/ [ŋgáβà] 'perhaps'
/ngú/ [ŋgú] 'that'

/ng/ never occurs morpheme initially in underlying forms of nouns, verbs, etc. It does occur word initially in several grammatical functors which are probably historically multimorphemic forms, as in the last three examples of (2.26).

2.2.1.2 Labialization and palatalization of consonants

Like many other Bantu languages, Kifuliiru also has a series of phonetic labialized and palatalized consonants (Cw or Cy) which are in surface contrast with their plain counterparts, but which are all either historically or synchronically the product of desyllabification of high vowels. These are interpreted as labialized and palatalized consonants (CG) rather than as CC sequences, since there are no unambiguous CC sequences in the language. In stems and roots, the modified segments tend to occur only in the initial- or final-consonant position, and not in stem-medial slots.

All consonants except **ny, y, s, j**, and **z** occur with palatalization. All consonants occur with labialization.[13] In general, in roots and stems, these modified segments tend to occur only in the initial-consonant position, with any apparent exceptions caused primarily by reduplication. Both can occur in final syllables of verbs and words of verbal derivation when the final C of the verb stem is followed by the passive or causative extension, since both of these extensions may consist only of a high vowel which is then turned into a glide when followed by the final vowel, e.g. **kú-hùm-ú-a** > **kúhùmwâ** 'to be touched', **kúhùm-í-a** > **kúhùmyâ** 'to cause to touch'.

Though traceable to a sequence of high vowel plus non-high vowel, the glide segments found in labialized and palatalized consonants are not usually noticeably vocalic in nature in speech of normal speed. That having been said, the pronunciation by some speakers of some words would call for a phonetic transcription of CiV or CuV, especially where the palatalization or labialization occurs in the penultimate or ultimate syllable, and where the point of articulation of the preceding consonant is near the same general area as the point of articulation of the high vowel, e.g. **ty, my**, or **fy; kw** or **hw**. The high vowel in a CiV sequence more often sounds vocalic than does the vowel in a CuV sequence. The vocalic passive and causative suffixes (**u** and **i**, respectively) often retain some vocalic nature, especially when they follow a nasal (**m** or **n**) such as in **kúhùmyâ** ~ **kúhùmíà** 'to cause to touch'. For consistency, these glides are represented here always with **w** or **y** rather than a vowel, with the exception of the cases where the alveolar nasal **n** is palatalized. In this case, **ni**V is used rather than **ny**V, in order to distinguish a palatalized alveolar **n** from the alveopalatal nasal which is symbolized by the digraph **ny**. It is especially obvious that **ni**V contrasts with **ny**V in the final syllable of verbs, such as **kúményà** 'to know', versus **kú-màníà** 'to cause to patch a leak', where the **i** of the second example is the causative morpheme.

Example (2.27) lists all of the palatalized and labialized segments. The number of occurrences found in a database of 5,475 words is shown in the "Freq." column. This is a list of words, not of stems. Thus, synchronic morphologically derived palatalization and labialization are included in the count.

An asterisk (*) following the number indicates that the total number includes words containing nominal prefixes which have undergone

---

[13] Some, such as **z** occur with labialization only in the context of ideophones, e.g. **zwí** ~ **yúwí** 'sound of something whizzing by', and in verbs derived from ideophones, e.g. the toneless verb root -**zwiririk**- 'spurt'.

2.2 Phonetic realization and distribution of phonemes

desyllabification before a vowel initial root (e.g. **mu- > mw-, ki- > ky-**, etc.) A double asterisk (**) following the number indicates that none of the examples given in the count is unambiguously monomorphemic synchronically. A triple asterisk (***) following the number means that though these appear on the surface to contain **ry**, they are traceable back to an **ly** which has been altered at a morpheme boundary.

(2.27)

	Palatalized: Cy	Gloss	Freq.
p	lú-pépyâ	11-wanton.adulterer	1
t	kú-tyáá-z-â	15-be.sharp-CS-Fa	13
k	kú-kyóókól-à	15-provoke-Fa	47*
b	kú-byóól-à	15-burp-Fa	39*
d	mú-dyóòtyò	3-finger.banana	2
g	Ø-m-búú-z-àgy-â	IMP.S-O1.SG-ask-CS-EMP-Fa 'ask me!'	0**
l	kú-ly-â	15-eat-Fa	46
r	kí-ryáàmù	7-lightning	11***
y	----------------		0
f	kú-fyáátúr-à	15-make.bricks-Fa	12
s†	----------------		0
sh	kú-shy-â	15-grind-Fa	8
h	kú-hy-â	15-ripen-Fa	28
v	kú-vyúúk-à	15-awaken-Fa	42
j	----------------		0
z	----------------		0
mb	kú-dúgúúmb-y-â	15-make.noise-CS-Fa	1**
nd	n-dyáàlyà	9-deceiver	1**
ng	kí-shóóngyà	7-banana.shoot	2**
m	kú-myógóól-à	15-steal.maize-Fa	41*
n	kú-kàn-í-à	15-be.firm-CS-Fa	
ny	----------------		0
	Labialized Cw	Gloss	Freq.
p	kú-pwáág-à	15-suffer.loss-Fa	4
t	kú-twáán-à	15-light.fire-Fa	37*
k	kú-kwéég-à	15-drag-Fa	52*

	Labialized Cw	Gloss	Freq.
b	kú-bwáátál-à	15-sit-Fa	89*
d	í=ì-dwì	AU=5-knee	23
g	kú-gwíím-à	15-blaze-Fa	33
l	kú-lwáál-à	15-get.sick-Fa	45*
r	í=n-dèngèèrwà	AU=9-pity	53
y	bà-yày-w-íír-ì	2-yawn-PS-RS-Fi 'they are yawning'	0**
f	kú-fwīīj-à	15-snore-Fa	29
s	kú-swár-úúk-à	15-disperse-RV.T-Fa	3
sh	kú-shwéék-à	15-tie-Fa	16
h	kú-hwīīj-à	15-skirt.issue-Fa	25
v	kú-vwóóm-à	15-draw.water-Fa	28
j	kú-jwéég-à	15-talk.at.once-Fa	9
z‡	kú-zwíírík-a	15-spurt.out-Fa	1
mb	kú-túmbwííj-à	15-speak.incorrectly-Fa	17
nd	kí-róóndwê	7-tick	9**
ng	nángwììkê	1a+lazy.woman	24
m	kú-mwéémúz-â	15-chuckle-Fa	70*
n	ká-nwâ	12-mouth	
ny	kú-nyw-â	15-drink-Fa	

†For **s** and **z**, a rule causes absorption of the palatalization in any such sequences.

‡No labialized **z** is underived except in ideophones and words derived from them, such as this example from **zwi** 'spurt!'. Morphological constraints prevent any such sequences being formed by passivization. The **z** occurs in base-final position of verbs only as a result of a following a resultative -**ir-i** or causative -**i**. If passive follows the causative -**i**, it takes its post-vocalic form, -**ibu**, rather than the simple -**u**.

A palatalized consonant may not be further modified by labialization (i.e. *****byw**, etc. do not occur). A labialized consonant may not be further modified by palatalization (i.e. *****bwy**, etc. do not occur).

Some of these palatalized and labialized segments occur within morphemes, where they are in phonemic contrast with their counterparts without the glide, e.g. **kúkùlà** 'to grow' versus **kúkyúúlà** 'to order', and

kúmyógóólà 'to steal maize from field' versus **kúmógólà** 'to rip apart with the fingers (as the stalk of a banana plant)'.

However, other modified (i.e. labialized or palatalized) segments occur only as a result of what can easily be posited as desyllabification of a high vowel at synchronic morpheme boundaries. In that case they will occur as a non-modified consonant followed by a high vowel, if a consonant rather than a vowel follows that high vowel. For example, the sequence **gy** does exist, but there is no word in which **g** contrasts with **gy**, e.g. *__kú-gyuul-a__ to contrast with **kú-gúl-à** 'to buy'. In order to find palatalized **g**, one must put morphemes together, e.g. **Ø-bùù-z-àgy-â!** 'ask! (EMP)' where the **y** is a form of the causative morpheme, -**i**, changed to a glide because it precedes a vowel.

Thus the modified consonants occurring in what are synchronically non-alternating, monomorphemic forms such as the **ky-** above, might be more easily explained as units, i.e. palatalized or labialized consonants, while most others, such as the **gy-** discussed above, might be better explained as a sequence of a consonant plus a following non-syllabic segment. However, there are also many cases in which **ky-** alternates with **kí-**, notably in the cl. 7 concord prefix, e.g. **kí-kúúmbà** (7-porridge) versus **ky-úúsì** (7-smoke). Historically, it seems likely that all consonant modifications (with the possible exception of many or all of those in ideophones) are the result of the desyllabification of a vocalic segment, **i** or **u**. However, synchronically, the origins of some are more readily apparent than the origins of others.

In cases where the non-alternating modified consonant belongs to a single synchronic morpheme, palatalized and labialized consonants seem to occur mostly, but not exclusively, in verbs and lexicalized words of verbal derivation. In the case of verb roots which contain Cy or Cw, one can easily posit that such modification has its origin either in an **i**- or **e**- final, or **u**- or **o**- final, monosyllabic verb root, e.g. **kú-ly-â** (15-eat-Fa) is from **kú-li-a**; while **kú-ky-â** (15-dawn-Fa) is underlyingly **kú-ke-a**; **kú-mw-â** (15-shave-Fa) is from **kú-mo-a**; **kú-lw-â** (15-fight-Fa), from **kú-lu-a**, etc. In longer verbs and deverbal nouns, adjectives, etc., we can posit that final-syllable palatalization is due to the addition of the causative morpheme -**i**, or passive morpheme, -**u**, to a CVC verb root, e.g. **mu-kòlwà** (3-work) from the passive form of **kú-kōl-à** (15-work-Fa). These are processes which have occurred historically, and the forms in many cases are now 'frozen' (i.e. lexicalized) especially in the case of nouns of verbal derivation.

The suffixation of the causative morpheme, and especially of the passive morpheme, to verb stems is also still a productive source of palatalized consonants and labialized consonants. See example (2.28).

(2.28)

Inf (CS or PS)	Gloss	Cf. Non-PS/CS	Gloss
ú=kúhúmyâ	'to cause to be blind'	ú=kúhúmà	'to be blind'
ú=kúhíságyâ	'to cause to arrive EMP'	ú=kúhíkágà	'to arrive EMP'
ú=kúyáángúhyâ	'to cause to become light'	ú=kúyáángúhâ	'to become light'
ú=kúhèèmbwâ	'to be rewarded'	ú=kúhēēmbà	'to reward'
ú=kútéérwâ	'to be attacked'	ú=kútéérà	'to attack'

Another synchronically productive source of labialized and palatalized consonants is the desyllabification of the vowel of a concord prefix which ends with **i** or **u** (1PL, 2SG, 2PL, and classes 1, 3, 4, 5, 7, 8, 11, 13, 14, 15, 16, 17, 18, 19) when it is juxtaposed to a V-initial lexical item. Examples of the desyllabification of the final **i** or **u** of a nominal prefix are given in (2.29).

(2.29)

/ú=mú-ēzi/	ú=mwēēzì	AU=3-moon
/í=mí-àzi/	í=myààzì	AU=4-news
/lì-a-wè/	lyààwè	5-A.M-2SG 'your (sg.)'
/í=kí-úsi/	í=kyúúsì	AU=7-smoke
/ú=lú-íguzo/	ú=lwíígúzô	AU=11-key
/tu-a-génd-a/	twàgééndà	1PL-P1-go-Fa 'we went'

2.2.1.3 Dahl's law

Dahl's law is not active in Kifuliiru. Dahl's law states that "when two successive syllables in a stem each begin with a voiceless plosive, then the first of these becomes voiced".[14] There are some lexical items in Kifuliiru in which the historical effects of Dahl's law are clearly evident. Comparing Kifuliiru data with Proto-Bantu reflexes, we see that there are traces of Dahl's law not only in some monomorphemic lexical roots, but also in at least one lexicalized combination of verbal extensions.

Some of the single morpheme roots which seem to exhibit the effects of this process are shown in (2.30). Note that the first consonant of the stem has become voiced (by Dahl's law) in Kifuliiru, while the Proto-Bantu forms have unvoiced consonants in both C_1 and C_2 position.[15]

---

[14] Schadeberg (1999:391), translation of a quote from Meinhof (1904).

[15] Other changes, such as **k** (>**g**) being spirantized to **v** in **má-vùtà** 'oil', from PB **mà-kútà**, are caused by other rules.

(2.30) PB   Kifuliiru   Gloss
       *kù-yí-kùt-a   kú-yìgút-à   15-become.satisfied-Fa
       *mà-kútà   má-vùtà   6-fat/oil

Example (2.31a) shows what seem to be the effects of Dahl's law in a combination of verbal extensions. This combination of extensions has been lexicalized in Kifuliiru[16] and is no longer productive. However, it shows that when the contactive extension -**at** (which has a voiceless consonant) was followed by the impositive extension -**ik** (which also has a voiceless consonant) the consonant of the first extension became voiced, i.e. **atik** > **adik**. The effects of this voicing are seen in (2.31a), while the two following examples show the contactive extension in normal -**at** form, when it appears as the final extension, as in (2.31b), or is followed by the applicative extension -**ir** with a voiced, rather than voiceless consonant, as in (2.31c).

(2.31)   Infinitive   Gloss
       a.   kú-fùmb-ád-ík-à   15-place.in.hand-CNT-IMPS-Fa
    cf. b.   kú-fùùmb-át-à   15-hold.in.fist-CNT-Fa
    cf. c.   kú-fùmb-át-ír-à   15-hold.in.fist-CNT-APL-Fa

Because Dahl's law is no longer productive in Kifuliiru, we do *not* find voicing of the C of a CV- prefix when the stem begins with a voiceless C. Nor are the effects of this voicing rule evident in *all* lexical stems, as witnessed by such verbs as **kúkééka** 'to guess', which is not modified to **kugeeka* nor to **gukeeka*. The same is true of **kútákà** 'to play jacks', which though it has two voiceless Cs in its stem, has not become **kudaka*, nor **gutaka*, and of nouns such as **í-kéétà** (5-knife), which has not become **igeeta*, and **kí-tālà** (7-drying. platform) which has not become **gi-tala*, etc. However, such words as those just mentioned, which have two successive syllables beginning with voiceless consonants, are noticeably less common in the lexicon than words where C_1 and C_2 are both voiced or of opposite voicedness. This is probably an indication that Dahl's law was active in the past, and has fallen out of use.

---

[16]With respect to voicing in combinations of verbal extensions, in a corpus of roughly 3,000 verbs, there are six which are of the form **kú**-CVC-**adika**, and none of the shape **kú**-CVC-**atika**. This -**adika** extension seems to be a combination of the -**at** 'contactive/tentive' and the -**ik**/-**ek** 'stative/impositive' extensions. -**at** contactive, which is no longer a productive extension in Kifuliiru, is the only extension besides -**ik**/-**ek** which has a voiceless consonant, so there are not many contexts in which to explore the theory that Dahl's law was active in combinations of suffixes.

2.2.1.4 *Meinhof's law*

Meinhof's law, though not synchronically active in Kifuliiru, seems to have been active in the past. In its basic form, this law states that when there are subsequent nasal-plus-consonant combinations in one word, i.e. NC V NC, or a nasal-plus-consonant followed by a syllable with a simple nasal, i.e. NC V N, the initial NC is simplified by the deletion of the consonant, leaving only the nasal, thus giving the output N V NC or N V N. Thus the rule can be summarized simply as:

NC V N(C) → N V N(C)

No such law is synchronically active in Kifuliiru, as there are many multimorphemic NC V NC sequences, e.g. **í=m-bāāndè** (AU=10-groundnuts) which result from the addition of a cl. 9/10 N- prefix to a C V NC noun root, and many NC V N sequences in verb stems (e.g. -**gììngam**- 'be in position of responsibility, be haughty', where the sequence **ng-am** is found). These result historically from extensions/expansions of verb roots (e.g. -**am** in -**gììngam**) that are now lexicalized in stems. It is interesting, however, that all such cases involve morpheme juxtaposition, and any sequences which seem to violate Meinhof's law are not originally root internal.

There are no known root-internal sequences of NC V NC in Kifuliiru. There are no root-initial NC sequences in historically monomorphemic roots. This seems to be an indication that Meinhof's law was active in the past history of the language and has since been dropped. For other nasal-related alternations possibly attributable to Meinhof's law, see the section on nasal deletion preceding another nasal (2.3.1.1.5).

2.2.2 Vowels

2.2.2.1 *Phonetic realization of vowel phonemes*

	Front	Central	Back
High	i		u
	ii		uu
Mid	e		o
	ee		oo
Low		a	
		aa	

2.2 Phonetic realization and distribution of phonemes

The front and central vowels are unrounded, while the back vowels are rounded, but not as much as their English counterparts. The high vowels may be either close or lax, while the non-high vowels all seem relatively lax. Contrastive long vowels are found at all five points of articulation in Kifuliiru. In addition, underlyingly short vowels can surface as long due to compensatory lengthening.

While the lengthened vowels are longer than the short ones, the actual duration of voicing is relative to the rate of speech production. The phonetic length of a long vowel does not seem to be influenced by whether the vowel is underlyingly long or compensatorily lengthened at some point in the derivation. Word finally, long vowels are only found in cases where there is an underlying H tone on the final vowel. This word final length is only phonetic and is not contrastive.

2.2.2.2 Distribution of vowels

The vowels **i**, **u**, and **a** are the only vowels that occur in prefixes, whether nominal or verbal. The vowels **i**, **u**, and **a** can all occur word initially, as a V-only syllable.[17] These V-only syllables always constitute an entire morpheme of the shape V, such as the nominal augment, verbal subject agreement marker, etc.

Other vowels occur only within stems, or as suffixes, and never in prefixes. As nominal derivational suffixes, all vowels are attested. In verbal suffixes, the following occur: **a**, **i** (not subject to harmony, as in the resultative -**ir-i**), **u** (not subject to harmony, as passive -**u**), and the high vowels which are subject to harmony: **i** ~ **e** and **u** ~ **o**.

The vowel **e** occurs word initially only as a monosyllabic clitic, **è!** 'vocative (O/hey)' or, **é!** (followed by a glottal stop) 'an exclamation of unpleasant surprise or displeasure', or in interjections, such as the affirming interjection **éégò!** 'Oh, is that so!'. The phoneme /o/ does not ever occur in the word initial position. This lack of word initial **o** seems morphologically determined at this point in time, rather than phonologically motivated. There is no rule to eliminate **o** word initially. Examples of word initial vowels are given in (2.32). These are all interpreted as monosyllabic clitics, and not as prefixes. All vowels also are attested in the initial position of noun or adjective roots.

---

[17]According to letter counts done on natural discourse, **a** is the most frequently occurring vowel (regardless of word position), followed by **u**, **i**, **e**, and **o**.

(2.32) /í=bí-ndù/ í=bííndù AU=8-things
/ú=bú-ndù/ ú=búúndù AU=14-ugali (stiff porridge)
/á=bá-ndù/ á=báándù AU=2-people
/e=bá-ndù/ é=báándù Oh=2-people (vocative)

A vowel of any quality may occur medially or finally, as shown in (2.33).

(2.33) Word medially   Word finally
  í=kí-<u>híí</u>ndà   AU=7-storehouse   ú=mú-só<u>sì</u>   AU=1-man
  í=kí-<u>hè</u>bè   AU=7-male.goat   í=í-hū<u>tè</u>   AU=5-boil (infection)
  í=kí-<u>háá</u>ndò   AU=7-sore   í=í-gù<u>shà</u>   AU=5-bee.larva
  í=<u>kòò</u>ndò   AU=+5-navel   í=n-gíín<u>gò</u>   AU=9-bed
  í=í-<u>fù</u>nù   AU=5-edible.root(sp.)   ú=búú-<u>ndù</u>   AU=14-ugali

Phonemically contrastive long vowels may occur on the surface only in the antepenultimate or penultimate position in a word. The mora-based vowel shortening rule shortens any long vowel occurring before the antepenultimate position in a word, and a long vowel is not found word finally (2.3.1.2.6). Non-contrastive vowel length, including all length shown in (2.33), may be phonologically or morphologically derived, and can be realized in initial or medial position, but not word finally.[18]

An example of each phonemic vowel is given in (2.34), showing contrast between the short and long vowel of each quality in both a verb and noun. Though phonemically long vowels in the list below appear only in the penultimate syllable, they may also occur in the antepenultimate syllable position, e.g. **kúbííkirà** 'to put away for'.

(2.34)   Infinitive cl. 15   Gloss
  i   ú=kú-bìk-à   AU=15-crow-Fa
  ii   ú=kú-bíík-à   AU=15-put-Fa

  e   ú=kú-hék-à   AU=15-come.to.end-Fa
  ee   ú=kú-héék-à   AU=15-carry-Fa

---

[18]The exception to this is in interjections, e.g. **èè** 'yes', in which the vowel is sometimes very long (with low or rising tone, **èèè** or **èèèéé**), for intonational effect.

2.3 Phonological rules and processes

(2.34)   Infinitive cl. 15   Gloss
a   ú=kú-sháb-à   AU=15-ask-Fa
aa   ú=kú-shááb-à   AU=15-knock.down-Fa

o   ú=kú-gók-à   AU=15-bend.down-Fa
oo   ú=kú-góók-à   AU=15-be.in.trouble-Fa

u   ú=kú-hún-à   AU=15-be.a.rebel-Fa
uu   ú=kú-húún-à   AU=15-ask.for-Fa

i   íí=kí-kô   AU=7-hard.end.of.cassava.root
ii   í=kīīkò   AU=7-three.stone.fireplace

e   ú=mú-shègò   AU=3-pillow
ee   ú=mú-shéégò   AU=3-supper

a   í=í-shálì   AU=5-hunger
aa   í=shààlì   AU=9+firewood

o   íí=n-gòkò   AU=9/10-chicken
oo   í=n-góókô   AU=9/10-woven.bowl.for.ugali

u   úú=mú-shì   AU=1-person.of.Shi.ethnicity
uu   ú=mú-úshì   AU=3-pestle

2.3 Phonological rules and processes

This section presents phonological rules and processes, grouped here not by what phonemes they affect, but by what process is taking place: rules like voicing, vowel lengthening, etc.[19] These rules are divided into two major sections:

- rules and processes which are phonologically motivated and phonologically governed, applying wherever the structural description of the rule is met, whether that occurs within a morpheme, or at a morpheme or word boundary.
- rules and processes which apply only to certain morphemes, or which are conditioned only by certain morphemes, i.e. which are morphologically governed, though still having some phonological motivation. For such rules, there are other phonologically identical environments in the language where

---

[19]These rules express the generalizations that can be observed in the alternate phonetic realizations of phonemes which are presented in 2.2, phonetic realization and distribution of phonemes. For example, all the voiceless obstruents become voiced when they follow a nasal.

the rule does not apply, just because the environment is not found within an affected morpheme or juxtaposed to a conditioning morpheme. All these morphologically conditioned changes are found only at morpheme boundaries, and never within a single morpheme.

2.3.1 Phonologically governed rules and processes

2.3.1.1 Phonological rules affecting consonants

Segments affected by the rule are shown in parentheses following the name of the rule. The domain of the rule, whether it is active at the lexical (word-building) or postlexical (syntax) level, or both, is also indicated. Any rule which plays a part in the word building process, whether in derivation or in primary morphology, is considered here to be a lexical rule, whether or not it is morphologically conditioned or motivated. Postlexical rules are those that act at or across word boundaries.

2.3.1.1.1 l/r rule (l) (lexical, postlexical)

/l/ is realized as [ɾ] following front vowels (**e** or **i**)

(2.35)

/ú=mú-lòndò/	ú=múlòòndò	AU=3-garment
/í=mí-lòndò/	í=míròòndò	AU=4-clothes
/a-à-gù-leet-a/	àgùléétà	1-P1-O3-bring-Fa 'he brought it'
/a-à-gì-leet-a/	àgìréétà	1-P1-O4-bring-Fa 'he brought them'
/leet-a/	léétà	bring.something-Fa (Imp.SG)
/tē=leet-e/	té=rēētè	FIRST=bring.something-Fe (Imp.SG)

2.3.1.1.2 Strengthening rule (h, l, r) (lexical)

An **h**, **l**, or **r** becomes a plosive when preceded by a nasal. As seen in (2.36), this voicing rule applies when a nasal prefix, either the cl. 9/10 nominal prefix, or the first-person singular subject or object prefix, is juxtaposed to a root or stem beginning with one of these non-plosive segments. Note in example (2.36a), that when **h** undergoes strengthening, it also undergoes voicing. Theoretically the strengthening rule only changes the **h** to a plosive, **p**, and it is the voicing rule that causes it to become voiced. The **l** and **r** are already voiced, so only the strengthening rule applies in examples (2.36b–e).

(2.36) a. /lú-hù/ lúhù 11-skin
/í=N-hù/ íì=mbù AU=10-skins

b. /mu-langi/ múlaangi 1-fierce
/N-langi/ ndaangi 9/10-fierce

c. /a-à-mú-lím-ir-a/ àmúlímìrà 1-P1-O1-farm-APL-Fa
'he farmed for him'
/a-à-ń-lím-ir-a/ ándímìrà 1-P1-O1.SG-farm-APL-Fa
'he farmed for me'

d. /a-à-mú-raakar-ir-a/ àmúrákárírà 1-P1-O1-get.angry-APL-Fa
'he got angry with him'
/a-à-ń-raakar-ir-a/ ándákárírà 1-P1-O1.SG-get.angry-APL-Fa
'he got angry with me'

e. /n-à-mú-leet-er-a/ nàmúléétérà 1SG-P1-O1-bring-APL-Fa
'I brought something for him'
/a-à-ń-leet-er-a/ ándéétérà 1-P1-O1.SG-bring-APL-Fa
'he brought something for me'

2.3.1.1.3 Voicing rule (h, t, k, f, s, sh) (lexical)

An unvoiced segment becomes voiced when it is preceded by a nasal. As seen in (2.37) this voicing rule applies when a nasal prefix, either the cl. 9/10 nominal prefix, or the verbal first-person singular subject or object prefix, is juxtaposed to a root or stem beginning with one of these unvoiced segments.

(2.37) /a-à-ń-<u>h</u>eek-a/ ám<u>b</u>éèkà 1-P1-O1.SG-carry-Fa
'he carried me'

/a-à-ń-<u>t</u>ábaal-a/ án<u>d</u>ábààlà 1-P1-O1.SG-help-Fa
'he helped me'

/n-<u>f</u>ùmb-iit-i/ n<u>v</u>ùmbíítì 1.SG-hold-RS-Fi
'I am holding in my hand'

/a-à-ń-<u>k</u>éngeer-a/ án<u>g</u>éngèèrà 1-P1-O1.SG-remember-Fa
'he remembered me'

/a-à-ń-<u>sh</u>iig-a/ án<u>j</u>íìgà 1-P1-O1.SG-smear-Fa
'he smeared me'

/n-<u>s</u>ìg-e/ n<u>z</u>ígè 1.SG-leave-Fe
'that I leave something'

/í=N-<u>k</u>óma/ íí=<u>ng</u>ómà AU=9/10-drum

/í=N-<u>h</u>ène/ íí=<u>mb</u>ènè AU=9/10-goat

2.3.1.1.4 Nasal assimilation rule (n or N) (lexical)

As shown in (2.38) a non-syllabic nasal (this is always either the first-person singular subject or object marker, **n-**, or the cl. 9/10 concord prefix **N-**, which is an unspecified nasal consonant) assimilates to the place of articulation of a consonant which directly follows it.

(2.38) /a-à-<u>ń</u>-heek-a/ á<u>m</u>béèkà 1-P1-O1.SG-carry-Fa 'he carried me'

/a-à-<u>ń</u>-téb-a/ áá<u>n</u>débà 1-P1-O1.SG-trick-Fa 'he tricked me'

/a-à-<u>ń</u>-bèg-a/ áá<u>m</u>bègà 1-P1-O1.SG-cut.hair-Fa 'he cut my hair'

/í=<u>N</u>-bìsh-o/ íí=<u>m</u>bìshò AU=9-hiding.place

/í=<u>N</u>-límu/ íí=<u>n</u>dímù AU=9-orange/lemon

/í=<u>N</u>-gòko/ íí=<u>ng</u>òkò AU=9-chicken

2.3.1.1.5 Nasal deletion preceding another nasal (n, m, or N) (lexical)

Because of morphological constraints, there are only two environments where the rule of nasal deletion before another nasal is observed. Both involve the addition of a nasal-only prefix to a stem that is nasal initial. One such environment is in verbal constructions containing the first-person singular object marker, and the other is in nouns of cl. 9 or 10.

In verbal constructions, nasal deletion takes place when a first-person singular object concord, which consists only of a nasal (**n-**), is juxtaposed to a

2.3 Phonological rules and processes

morpheme which begins with a nasal consonant, either **m** or **n**. In the case of the first-person singular object concord, as in examples (2.39a, c) below, the high tone of the object prefix is transferred to the preceding vowel, which in these cases is the subject prefix + tense marker.[20]

(2.39) a. /a-à-ń-mólek-er-a/ ámólèkèrà 1-P1-O1.SG-shine-APL-Fa
'he shined on for me'

cf. b. /a-à-mòlek-er-a/ àmólékérà 1-P1-shine-APL-Fa
'he shined on (for someone)'

c. /a-à-ń-níg-à/ áánígà 1-P1-O1.SG-choke-Fa
'he choked me'

cf. d. /a-à-níg-à/ àànígà 1-P1-choke-Fa
'he choked (someone)'

Besides the verbal cases of nasal juxtaposition, there is also a small subset of cl. 9/10 nouns such as **í=maana** 'luck', where the cl. 9/10 prefix, **N-** is deleted because the noun stem begins with a nasal. Examples are found in (2.40).

Such nouns may begin with any of the nasal phonemes: **n**, **m**, or **ny**.[21] The group of cl. 9/10 nouns, which is nasal initial and does not merely have the normal prevocalic form of the cl. 9/10 prefix **n-**, followed by a vowel initial stem, but begins with another nasal, can be interpreted synchronically as consisting of words with a nasal-initial root and no prefix. Since the usual cl. 9/10 prefix consists of a nasal, **N-**, the lack of prefix in this group of nasal-initial nouns can be seen as the result of a synchronic rule which

---

[20]Orthographically, the first-person singular object, when it precedes a nasal-initial verb stem, is indicated by a doubling of the nasal consonant, even though the only phonetic indication of its presence is in the tone of the preceding subject prefix/tense marker. This orthographic choice was made because a high tone on this prefix could indicate a certain subjunctive form rather than the presence of the object marker, and speakers of Kifuliiru are not generally consciously aware that tone is the signal for the presence of the object marker in these cases. They are aware only that one can hear the difference between the form with the first-person singular object and the corresponding form without it. Thus the orthographic presence of the segmental representation of the object marker itself, indicated by the extra nasal, is more intuitive for readers of the language than a tone marking would be in this case.

[21]There are both words with **ny-** initial stems, and also vowel-initial roots in which the usual form of the cl. 9/10 prefix is **ny-**, so that they *appear* to be nasal initial, **ny-úùnù** (SG **ú=lúùnù**) 'claws, fingernails', etc. In non-alternating forms, it is difficult to tell whether the **ny-** is a prefix or part of the stem. In other nouns, alternate forms such as diminutives, related derivations etc. show that the **ny** is actually root initial, such as **nyáàbù** 'cat/s', (cf. **nyááù** the ideophone describing sound made by a cat), **nyóótà** 'thirst' (cf. **kúnyóótérwâ** 'to be thirsty'), **nyúùmbà** 'house/s' (cf. diminutive **hí-nyúùmbà**.) However, because of the debatable status of the initial **ny** in many such words, we do not include them in the count of cl. 9/10 nouns with nasal initial stems.

deletes the nasal prefix that would otherwise directly precede the stem-initial nasal in this context.

We have observed seventeen of these nasal-initial noun roots of cl. 9/10 (**i-N-**) or cl. 11 (**u-lu-**), listed in (2.40). Ten of the seventeen, found in (2.40a–j) have a nasal or a prenasalized stop as the onset of the second syllable of the root, i.e. in the C_2 position of the root.

(2.40)		SG	PL (if different)	Gloss
	a.	í=<u>m</u>ànè-mánè		AU=9/10+myrrh (Sw.)
	b.	í=<u>m</u>āānà		AU=9/10+luck
	c.	ú=lú-<u>m</u>ínà	íí=<u>m</u>ina (cl.10)	AU=11-centipede
	d.	í=<u>m</u>éémbò		AU=9/10+erosion.on.slope
	e.	í=<u>m</u>óòndò		AU=9/10+mat.making.string
	f.	í=<u>n</u>āāmà		AU=9/10+council
	g.	í=<u>n</u>áàndá		AU=9/10+sewing.needle
	h.	í=<u>n</u>ííngù		AU=9/10+fish(sp.)
	i.	í=<u>n</u>úúngò		AU=9/10+seasoning
	j.	í=<u>n</u>ùùngù		AU=9/10+seal/stamp
	k.	í=<u>m</u>áájò[†]		AU=9/10+adze
	l.	ú=lú-bààjà	í=<u>m</u>ààjà[†](cl.10)	AU=11-law/judgement
	m.	íí=<u>m</u>òtò		AU=9/10+type.of.fish
	n.	í=<u>n</u>ágíîrâ		AU=9/10+fertilizer
	o.	í=<u>n</u>óòrô		AU=9/10+gold (from Fr. **or**)
	p.	í=<u>n</u>óózì		AU=9/10+fish(sp.)
	q.	í=<u>n</u>íízô		AU=9/10+bird.landing.place

[†]One of the (non-loan) words which does not have a nasal in the second syllable is **í-máájò** 'adze', which is defined as a tool with which to 'carve out' (**ú=kúbāājà**) wood. The correspondence in form between the verb **kú-bāāj-a** and the tool **í-mááj-ò**, coupled with the fact that the verb has L tone rather than being toneless (see "Toneless verbs" in 3.3.3.1), makes it look like the original form of the noun might have been *imbaanjo, though this, to my knowledge, is nowhere attested. A seemingly related word, with the same irregularity, and which does have a singular form occurring synchronically with a **b**, is **ú=lú-bààjà/í=mààjà** 'judgment(s)/law(s)'. Synchronically, it is not clear what caused the loss of the voiced stop following the nasal, however, since there is no nasal

2.3 Phonological rules and processes

in the C_2 position of the root, which would have allowed Meinhof's law to take effect. The common Proto-Bantu root for **kúbāājà** has been reconstructed as PB *baaj- or *baij. It is interesting, however, that in neighboring Kinyarwanda/Kirundi, the word corresponding to Kifuliiru **ú=lúbààjà/í=màajà** is listed by Bastin (2003:511) as **ùrùbàánzà, ìmàánzà**.

The fact that in many of these examples in (2.40) a long vowel precedes the second syllable of the stem e.g. **í=nāāmà** 'council', **ú=lúbààjà** 'law, judgment', etc. may suggest that in some cases the N or the C of the NC in the second syllable dropped out, leaving only the lengthened vowel. In other cases the full NC remains, e.g. **í=móòndò** 'local mat string', **í=náàndà** 'needle', etc.

Another word which, in its two possible pronunciations, shows the alternation of a nasal with a non-nasal, but not in the C_1 position of the stem, is **múlùmùṉà ~ múlùmùḻà** 'younger same-sex sibling'. This may reflect a historical alternation between **l** and **n** in some positions.

2.3.1.1.6 Compensatory nasal syllabification (m only) (postlexical)

Compensatory nasal syllabification is a postlexical rule which is only observed to take place after optional **u** deletion has taken place. In this case, **m** becomes syllabic when it immediately precedes a consonant which is at another point of articulation, as in (2.41). When the syllabified nasal is word initial as in examples (2.41b, c), the extra syllable can usually be heard, but when it is word medial, the syllable it forms is often so short that it sounds more like a syllable-final consonant. The nasal, when syllabified, is tone bearing, and this is especially audible in word-initial position when it takes on the H tone of the deleted vowel, as in (2.41b, c). The fact that this is a postlexical rule can be seen by the fact that it occurs subsequent to the process of optional **u**-deletion. It is generally agreed that any optional processes are postlexical.

(2.41)		Phonemic	Phonetic	Gloss
	a.	/n-à-lámu̱s-a/	[nàlám̥sà]	1SG-P1-greet-Fa 'I greet (you PL)'
	b.	/mú̱zíbò/	[m̥zíbò]	1a+lastborn
	c.	/mú̱tààmà/	[m̥tààmà]	1a+title.of.moderate.respect (used for men)

2.3.1.1.7 y absorption (y) (lexical)

A **y** is always absorbed[22] following an **s** or **z**. The (pre)palatal glide (**y**) is absorbed into an alveolar fricative, losing its phonetic realization. This rule explains the fact that **sy** and **zy** are never observed in Kifuliiru. The palatal glide is absorbed by the palatal fricative in all cases.

Examples of this rule affecting **sy** can be found in the context of the short form of the causative morpheme. The short form of the causative morpheme is -**i** in underlying form. It is a morpheme which causes spirantization (5.23.1) of the final consonant of the stem, as seen in (2.42a), where the final consonant of the verb stem -**hík**- 'arrive' is spirantized to **s**. In (2.42b) the final consonant of -**nòg**- 'be soft' is spirantized to **z**. After causing the spirantization, the -**i** undergoes high vowel glide formation (2.3.1.2.1.1), and becomes **y** since it precedes the final vowel. This **y**- is subsequently deleted by **y**-absorption. Note that in (2.42c, d), provided for contrast, neither the **m** of the verb stem -**hím**- 'surpass', nor the **h** of the verb stem -**yòfih**- 'be short' is affected by the spirantization rule. In such cases the causative -**i**, though it still becomes -**y**, does not follow **s** or **z**, and is, therefore, not absorbed.

(2.42)	Cl.	Stem	CS	Fa			Infinitive	Gloss
a.	/kú-	hík-	-í	-a/ →	kú-hís-y-á spiran. + glide formation	→	kúhísâ by y- absorption	'to marry wife'
	15-	arrive	CS	Fa				
b.	/kú-	nòg-	-í	-a/ →	kú-nòz-y-á spiran. + glide formation	→	kúnòzâ by y- absorption	'to soften'
	15-	be.soft	CS	Fa				
cf. c.	/kú-	hím-	-í	-a/ →	kú-hím-y-á glide formation	→	kúhímyâ	'to CS to surpass'
	15-	surpass	CS	Fa				
cf. d.	/kú-	yòofi-h-	-í	-a/ →	kú-yòòfíh-y-á glide formation	→	kúyòòfíhyâ	'to shorten'
	15-	short- INC	CS	Fa				

Examples of the **y**-absorption rule affecting **zy** can also be seen in the context of the cl. 10 verbal subject prefix, as seen in (2.43a). The underlying form

---

[22]The term absorb is used rather than "delete" as an indication that the loss of the glide is phonetically motivated by the fact that the preceding segment is a fricative at the same point of articulation, and it is not merely a random deletion.

2.3 Phonological rules and processes

of this morpheme is **zi-**. When it is followed by a vowel, such as the tense marker **à-** of the recent past (P1) the **i** of **zi-** undergoes glide formation, yielding **zy-**. At that point, the **y** is deleted by the above rule. Compare (2.43b), where the **zi-** prefix is followed by a consonant, and is therefore not deleted.

(2.43) a. /zi- à- génd -a/ → zy-à-géénd-a → zàgééndà 'they went'
         10 P1 go Fa   by glide formation by y-absorption

cf. b. /zi- ká- génd -a/ → zí-ká-géénd-à → zíkágééndà 'they went'
         10 P2 go Fa

This rule can also be seen to affect the long form of the causative: e.g. **kúhìng-iisi-a > kúhìing-íísy-a > kúhìngíísâ** 'to have a field farmed'.

Note that the **y**-absorption rule is a lexical rule, applying only within the word level, and does not affect postlexical (phrasal) combinations containing **si#V** or **zi#V**, e.g. **Sì àgééndà ~ syàgééndà** 'But (it's obvious that) he went.'

2.3.1.2 Phonological rules affecting vowels

2.3.1.2.1 Glide formation rules

2.3.1.2.1.1 High vowel glide formation (**i, u**) (lexical, postlexical)

A high vowel (**i** or **u**) becomes a (non-syllabic) glide (**y** or **w**) when it is followed by an unlike vowel. The following vowel is then lengthened by the compensatory lengthening rule. Thus in (2.44a) the vowel **i** found in the cl. 7 concord prefix **ki-** is followed by the unlike vowel **u**, causing **ki-** to be changed to **ky-**, etc.

(2.44) a. /kí-úsi/ → kyúúsì 7-smoke
     b. /bí-âsi/ → byáàsì 8-leaf/grass
     c. /mí-âzi/ → myáàzì 4-news (PL)
     d. /mú-âzi/ → mwáàzì 3-news (SG)
     e. /mú-ērù/ → mwéérù 1/3-white
     f. /bú-ólo/ → bwóólò 14-weakness

When a high vowel is followed by an identical vowel, (i.e. **i + i**, or **u + u**) glide formation does not take place.

(2.45) /mí-îmbu/ → míìmbù   4-harvests
      /mú-ùka/ → mùùkà   3-air/breath

2.3.1.2.1.2 Back vowel glide formation (u, o) (lexical)[23]

A back vowel (**u** or **o**) becomes a (non-syllabic) glide (**w**) when it is followed by an unlike vowel. The following vowel is then lengthened by the compensatory lengthening rule.

In effect, the back vowel desyllabification rule is the same as high vowel glide formation. The only difference is that it also affects a surface **o**, which is not a high vowel. The effect of this rule on **o** (as well as on **u**) is exemplified within the word in cases where the final **l** of a verb stem is deleted by the process of deletion of stem-final consonants in resultative verb forms (2.3.2.3.2). The vowel affected in each example in (2.46) is the vowel of the reversive transitive extension -**ul** ~ -**ol**. The vowel in both examples is underlyingly the same, while on the surface, the vowel in (22.46b) shows the effects of vowel height harmony, being lowered to a mid vowel following a stem which has the back mid vowel. The fact that both the **o** and the **u** are merely different forms of the same morpheme here, affected by vowel harmony, is likely the reason why glide formation applies to **o** in this case, whereas glide formation usually does not apply to the mid vowels. There are no other morphological environments where this rule of back vowel glide formation ever applies as far as we have observed.

(2.46) a. a- bètul -ir -i → à-bètu -ir-i → àbètwíírì 'he is carrying'
          1 carry RS Fi

      b. a- shóbol-ir -i → à-shóbo-ir-i → àshóbwììrì 'he is able'
          1 be.able RS Fi

Back vowel glide formation does not apply at the postlexical level. Rather, postlexical vowel coalescence applies to **o**, as it is a non-high vowel (2.3.1.2.2.3), whereas high vowel desyllabification applies to **u**, a high vowel, at the postlexical level. The lack of effect of back vowel glide formation on **o** is shown in (2.47), where the relative marker **bó** plus the following **a** becomes **bá**, and not *****bwá**.

---

[23] This rule is not necessary if one assumes that the underlying form of the reversive extension (-**uul** ~ -**ool**) has a high vowel, i.e. is -**uul**, and that the rule which desyllabifies the vowel is ordered before the action of the rule which lowers it to -**ool** when the stem has a mid vowel. If one assumes that the -**ool** is either the underlying form of the extension or selected lexically rather than formed by rule, this back vowel desyllabification rule is necessary.

(2.47) á=báándú   →   á=báándú   'the people whom he ruled'
        bó=ákátwáálà   bá=kátwáálà

2.3.1.2.2 Vowel coalescence

Vowel coalescence in Kifuliiru is of three different types. Vowel coalescence of two like vowels always results in a long vowel identical in nature to the original vowels. Vowel coalescence involving unlike non-high vowels[24] works differently at the lexical level (i.e. at morpheme boundaries within the word) than at the postlexical level (i.e. at a boundary between words, which includes boundaries between phonological clitics and words.) At the lexical level, a non-high vowel assimilates completely to the following vowel, while at the postlexical level, there is coalescence in which the resultant vowel may be different from either of the original juxtaposed vowels. Thus these vowel processes will be described by three separate rules below.

2.3.1.2.2.1 Identical vowel assimilation (lexical and postlexical)

Two identical vowels may be juxtaposed at the lexical level, as when a CV-prefix is added to a V-initial noun stem. This produces combinations like those found in (2.48), with a long vowel identical in articulation to the original vowels. Note that prefixes exhibit a limited subset of the possible vowels, so that the combinations shown in (2.48) are the only ones attested.

(2.48) a+a → aa   bá-ānà   →   báánà   2-children
        i+i → ii   mí-îmbu   →   míîmbù   4-harvests
        u+u → uu   mú-ùkà   →   mùùkà   3-breath

At the postlexical level as well, morphology is a limiting factor in the variety of combinations of identical vowels attested within a phrase, since with the exception of interjections, every word-initial vowel represents either a prefix or an augment. Thus **a, u,** and **i** are the again only combinations of identical vowels involved at this level. Combinations of unlike vowels within word-formation processes are discussed in the next section (2.3.1.2.2.2).

Postlexical vowel coalescence, i.e. vowel coalescence at boundaries within a phrase, is dependent on the rate of speech. In slow speech, the vowels may be pronounced separately, with no coalescence. Thus the pronunciation may remain as indicated below in the "Underlying" column, or, in more normal speech, pronounced as shown in the "With coalescence" column. In

---

[24]The high vowel glide formation rule, which works the same at all phonological levels, takes care of instances where a high vowel is followed by any non-like vowel.

(2.49) are the combinations of identical vowels possible. Note that the long vowels produced by coalescence are usually shortened by the shortening rule, due to the number of following morae (2.3.1.2.6). Combinations of non-like vowels at word boundaries are dealt with in the postlexical vowel coalescence section (2.3.1.2.2.3).

(2.49) Vowels   Underlying   With coalescence   Gloss
  a. a+a → a(a)†   àshúlìkà ábátábánà   [àshúlìká̠bátàbánà]   'he hit the boys'
  b. i+i → i(i)   ti: «Ikòlà ígáàhyà» [ti̠ìkòlégáàhyà]   '<quote>: "It's about ready."'
  c. u+u → u(u)   úmúndú úkáyíjà   [úmúúndú̠káyííjà]   'the person who came'

†The length of the vowel produced by the postlexical coalescence of a word-final vowel and a word-initial vowel depends on the number of morae following it within the word, not within the phrase. For example, in (2.49c), the length on the initial **u** of **úkáyííjà** 'who came', produced by the coalescence of the final **u** of **ú=múúndù** 'person' and the initial **u** of **úkáyííjà** is neutralized by the mora-based shortening rule, due to the number of following morae within the word. The fact that the compensatory vowel length in **úmúúndù** is still present shows that this still patterns as a separate prosodic word from the following relative verb, and that the postlexical coalescence does not eradicate the prosodic word boundary between the two words. In the example in (2.49b), by contrast, the long **i** of **tii** is not shortened, being followed within the word by only two morae: **tììkòlà**, even though the final vowel of **ìkòlà** also undergoes postlexical coalescence with the initial vowel of **ígáàhyà**.

2.3.1.2.2.2 Lexical unlike vowel assimilation (lexical)[25]

At the lexical (word-building) level (i.e. at boundaries between a prefix or suffix and a root or stem) the following rule of vowel coalescence always applies: A non-high, non-back vowel (**e** or **a**) assimilates totally to a following vowel at morpheme boundaries within the word.

Theoretically, this rule operates when any non-high, non-back vowel (**e** or **a**) is followed directly within the word by any vowel. However, not all combinations are attested at the lexical level in the data, because prefixes, whether verbal or non-verbal, have a limited subset of vowels (**a, i, u**) of which only **a** is

---

[25]The long vowel produced by this rule may subsequently be shortened by the mora-based shortening rule, so this assimilation does not necessarily result in a long vowel on the surface.

2.3 Phonological rules and processes

a non-high vowel, and suffixes, though more diverse in their range of vowels, tend to be of the shape V(C), and suffixed onto C final roots, so there is not a lot of VV juxtaposition in suffixes.

This rule of total assimilation of vowels on the lexical level is most often observed in two contexts.[26] One of these is the formation of words such as nouns, adjectives, and pronouns[27] in which an **a**-final prefix is juxtaposed to a V-initial stem. In such an instance, **a** assimilates totally to the following vowel, and the result is a lengthened vowel.[28] There are also cases of VV juxtaposition within verbal prefixes, but these are always a high vowel (**i** or **u**) plus **a**, or **a** plus **a**.

(2.50)

			Word type	Cl.	Prefix	Stem		Surface	Gloss
a+i	→	ii	adjective	2	bá-	īru		bíírù	'black'
a+i	→	ii	noun	2	bá-	ìra	→	bììrà	'friends'
a+e	→	ee	adjective	2	bá-	ēru		béérù	'white'
a+e	→	ee	noun	6	má-	ēnge	→	mééngè	'cunning'
a+a	→	aa	noun	2	bá-	āna	→	báánà	'children'
a+o	→	oo	pronoun	2	bá-	ôhe	→	bóòhê	'they'
a+o	→	oo	adverb	16	há-	òofi	→	hòòfì	'near'
a+u	→	uu	noun	2	bá-	ùbási	→	bùùbásì	'builders'

The second context where lexical vowel assimilation is often observed is in verbs which have the resultative suffix. A morpheme-specific rule deletes[29] the final consonant of a verbal extension ending in **l** or **r** when it is followed by the resultative suffix (2.3.2.3.2). After this deletion of **l** or **r**, the remaining **a** or **e** at the end of the verb stem assimilates totally to the **i** of the resultative morpheme, resulting in a long **ii**, as shown in (2.51a, b).

---

[26] A third context where apparent complete assimilation of unlike vowels is often observed is in the interaction between the associative marker and nouns of cl. 5. A phrase like **áá=mágí gí'báátà** 'the eggs of the duck' (from **á=mágì gà í=íbáátà**) is an example.

[27] In verbs stems, the only time that two vowels are juxtaposed is in the imbrication of the resultative morpheme following certain extension-final consonants. Kifuliiru has no vowel-initial verb stems, and the reflexive marker is **yì-**.

[28] The long vowel produced by this rule may subsequently be shortened by the mora-based shortening rule, so this assimilation does not necessarily result in a long vowel on the surface.

[29] Or perhaps circumscribes. (See footnote 57, and the final paragraph under 2.3.2.3.2.)

(2.51) a. /a-bwatal- iri/ → abwaata- iri → àbwátíìrì 'he is sitting'
       1-sit   RS   → C-deletion   Tot. V assim.

       b. /a-yòn-er- iri/ → ayòone- iri → àyòníírì 'he has
          1-pour-APL RS   → C-deletion   Tot. V assim. poured on'

   cf. c. /a-yòn- iri/ → ayòon- iri → àyòònírì 'he has
          1-pour   RS   ----------   ---------- poured out'

2.3.1.2.2.3 Postlexical vowel coalescence[30]

Coalescence of a non-high vowel plus any other vowel at the postlexical (syntactic) level, that is, at the boundaries of lexical words, results in what can be termed partial or reciprocal assimilation, following this rule:

When a non-high vowel (**e**, **o**, or **a**) is juxtaposed to another vowel at a word boundary, the result is a long vowel which exhibits the height of the first vowel (i.e. non-high) and the "backness" (or lack of it) of the second vowel. (Here it is helpful to remember that **e** is a front vowel, **o** is a back vowel, and **a** is neither front nor back.) For example, the coalescence of **e** (a non-high front vowel) with **u** (a high back vowel) results in **o** (a non-high back vowel).[31]

In (2.52) are examples of each vowel combination that has been observed between words. Note that some of these combinations are different from the ones listed in the section on lexical coalescence, because of the difference in the shapes of the morphemes involved at the two levels. The vowel combinations do overlap, however, in the combinations **e + i**, **o + i**, **a + i**, and **a + u**. In these, the results of back vowel desyllabification (in the case of **o + i**) and of lexical coalescence (assimilation) (in the cases of **a + i** and **a + u**) are different from the results of the postlexical coalescence, as can be seen by comparing the postlexical coalescence in (2.52d, e), with the lexical coalescence in (2.52f); the postlexical coalescence in (2.52h, i) with the lexical coalescence in (2.52j); that in (2.52k) with that in (2.52l); and that in (2.52m) with that in (2.52n).

Note in cases such as (2.52b, d, e, g), etc., that because there are three or more morae following, the vowel shortening rule neutralizes the vowel length produced by coalescence. The shortening rule works only at the word level, however, so when there are two words joined by coalescence in a phrase, each

---

[30] Affects **e + u**, **o + a**, **o + i**, **a + i**, **a + u**, **o + e**, i.e. any non-high vowel plus any unlike vowel.

[31] As noted above, when two vowels coalesce, they form a long vowel. However, whether or not the surface result is a long vowel depends on prosodic factors: when there are three or more morae following within the word, the long vowel is shortened.

2.3 Phonological rules and processes

may still have a long vowel. The symbol = below indicates cliticization (which results in a single phonological word to which the vowel shortening rule applies), while # is used below to indicate a (non-audible) word break within a phrase.

	(2.52)	Vowels	Morphemes/phrase	Coalescence effect	Gloss
	a.	e+u → oo	yé=ùlyà	yóò=lyà	'he is that.R one'
	b.	e+u → oo	yé=úgáyáángà	yó=gáyáàngà	'whom you will marry'
	c.	e+u → oo	ùhámágálè ùmwānà	ùhámágál(y)ò#mwāānà	'(that) you (SG) call the child!'
	d.	e+i → ee	yé=ígávwejagira	yé=gávwèjàgìrà	'whom it will devour'
	e.	e+i → ee	àgééndé íkāāyà	àgééndé#kāāyà	'may he go home'
cf.	f.	e+i → ii	a-yòn-e-ir-i†	àyòníírì	'he has spilled on'
	g.	o+a → aa	bó ákábùngánà	bá=kábùùngánà	'those he moved with'
	h.	o+i → ee	mwó=iísìkù zìbìrì	mwéé=sìkù#zìbìrì	'in there two days'
	i.	o+i → ee	yó=ìlyòsírì	yé=lyòsírì	'that (4) come from...'
cf.	j.	o+i → wii	a-shób-o-ir-i	àshóbwììrì	'he is able'
	k.	a+i → ee	yà=ííngòkò	yéé=ngòkò	'of the chicken'
cf.	l.	a+i → ii	bá-ìra	bììrà	'friends'
	m.	a+u → oo	yà=úmúúndù	yó=múúndù	'of the person'
cf.	n.	a+u → uu	bá-ùbásì	bùùbásì	'builders'

†This form is an intermediate stage in the derivation of the resultative form of the applicative verb whose infinitive form is **kúyòònérà** 'to pour/spill (sthg) out for/at'. The original morphemes are **a-yòn-er-ir-i** (1-pour-APL-RS-Fi).

Between two separate phonological words, each of which is more than monosyllabic, such as examples (2.52c, e) above, postlexical vowel coalescence is optional, depending on the rate of speech flow. Very slow speech would involve no coalescence at such junctures. The normal rate of speech involves coalescence between words of a phrase. This is the same principle that was illustrated above under (2.3.1.2.2.1).

However, vowel coalescence is not optional when monosyllabic forms are involved, since monosyllabic words are not allowed to stand alone within a phrase. All monosyllables are joined to a following or preceding word through the rule of monosyllable cliticization (2.4.1). In these cases vowel coalescence is mandatory, and follows this rule of postlexical coalescence. Thus all of the examples of postlexical vowel coalescence in (2.52) above except (2.52c, e) are mandatory, since the first element of each phrase is monosyllabic, e.g. **ye** in examples (2.52a, b). In (2.52c, e) the coalescence could be reversed at an unnaturally slow rate of speech.

2.3.1.2.3 Vowel weakening

There are two rules of vowel weakening, both of which are optional.

2.3.1.2.3.1 Final vowel devoicing (any vowel) (postlexical, optional)

A word-final vowel may be devoiced or even elided at the end of a phrase or utterance. This optional rule is most often applied to high vowels, and especially when the preceding consonant is an unvoiced fricative or plosive. However final vowel devoicing can also occur with other vowels and in the environment of other consonants. The examples in (2.53) illustrate this very common phenomenon. (A ring under the vowel indicates voicelessness.)

(2.53) a. /ú=mú-jà-kàzi/ → ú=mújààkàzị̀ AU=1-slave-woman
b. /ú=mú-gìsi/ → ú=múgìsị̀ AU=3-idol
c. /nárùfu/ → nárùfụ̀ 1a+spirit.of.death
d. /í=n-gòkò/ → íí=ngòkọ̀ AU=9/10-chicken
e. /í=n-gòòtì/ → í=ngòòtị̀ AU=9/10-dagger
f. /í=n-gùngùlà/ → í=ngùùngùlḁ̀ AU=9/10-type.of.fish
g. /í=n-gùndàshì/ → í=ngùùndàshị̀ AU=9/10-reddish.soil

It is possible that the process of final vowel devoicing has contributed to the realization of the final vowel of the resultative suffix as **i** (-**ir**-**i**) in Kifuliiru

2.3 Phonological rules and processes

(rather than **e** (-**ir**-**e**) as is the usual realization in related languages). The final vowel is very often devoiced or mostly devoiced in these verb forms, especially when they are phrase final, as they often are. The process of devoicing weakens the features of the vowel and makes it more susceptible to harmonization with the preceding vowel, which is always the **i** of the resultative morpheme, -**ir**-**i**. Thus it has likely gone from -**ire** > -**ir e̥** > -**iri**. Some speakers, especially those who have more Mashi or Kinyindu influence, still use the -**ire** form, but it is not considered standard by Kifuliiru speakers.

2.3.1.2.3.2 Optional u deletion (u) (post lexical)

A **u** following an **m** and preceding one of the following alveolar or nasal consonants: **s, z, t, l**, or **m** may be weakened or deleted, as shown in (2.54), before **s** (2.54a, b), before **z** (2.54c), before **t** (2.54d), before **l** (2.54e), or before **m** (2.54f). As seen in the phonetic forms of the examples, this rule feeds the rule of compensatory nasal syllabification.

(2.54) a. /m**ú**-sìngo/ → m̩sììngò   3-greeting
      b. /n-à-lá**mu**s-a/ → nàlám̩sà   1SG-P1-greet-Fa 'I greet'
      c. /m**ú**-zíbò/ → m̩zíbò   1-last.born.child
      d. /m**ú**-tààma/ → m̩tààmà   1-title.of.respect
      e. /tw-à-m**ú**-laalik-a/ → twàm̩láálíkà   2PL-P1-O1-invite-Fa 'we invited him'
      f. /m**ú**=mw-āka/ → m̩mwāākà   18=3-year 'in the year'

2.3.1.2.4 Compensatory vowel lengthening

A mora is a unit of prosodic length or syllable weight. In general terms, we can say that all vocalic segments are moraic. Each short vowel counts as one mora, while a long vowel counts as two morae. Nasals are also underlyingly moraic in Kifuliiru when they precede a consonant in an NC cluster, though they are never moraic (or syllabic) on the surface.[32] It is very common in Bantu languages that when a moraic segment loses its moricity, there is compensatory lengthening of a juxtaposed moraic segment. There are two compensatory vowel lengthening rules in Kifuliiru which are occasioned by

---

[32]Except following optional /**u**/-deletion.

2.3.1.2.4.1 Post-glide lengthening (all vowels) (lexical)

A vowel is always lengthened when it follows a high vowel **i** or **u** which has undergone glide formation, i.e. following the glide **y**[33] or **w**, in non-word final position.[34] Thus the vocalic segment, **i** or **u**, shifts its moricity to the vowel immediately following it within the word. This occurs whether **w** or **y** is alone, as in (2.55a–d), or whether it occurs as palatalization or labialization following a consonant, as in (2.55e–g). This is compensatory lengthening, making up for the loss of moricity of the underlying **i** or **u** which has become a glide.

If the vowel following the glide is word final (2.55h) the extra mora is deleted rather than being transferred to the word-final vowel. No length appears in that vowel if the phonological word break is subsequently shifted rightward by the addition of an enclitic. Notice in (2.55i) that neither the **a** following **bw**, nor the **o** following **kw** is lengthened, as compensatory lengthening is a lexical rule, and both of the aforementioned vowels were word final in the lexical stage. Thus the extra morae were deleted, and cliticizing the pronominal form **kw-o** (17-P.R) to the verb at the postlexical stage does not invoke the action of this rule.

(2.55)
    a. /ú-à-ní/   wààní   1-A.M-1SG 'my'
    b. /í-à-gè/   yààgè   4/9-A.M-1 'his, her'
    c. /ú=kú-yòboh-a/   ú=kúyòòbóhà   AU=15-fear-Fa
    d. /ú=kú-yák-a/   ú=kúyááká   AU=15-burn-Fa
    e. /ú=kú-vyuk-a/   ú=kúvyúúkà   AU=15-wake.up-Fa
    f. /ú=kú-vwom-a/   ú=kúvwóómà   AU=15-draw.water-Fa
    g. /ú=mú-âzì/   ú=mwáàzì   AU=3-news

    cf. h. /í-n-vwì/   íì=nvwì   AU=9/10-white.hair
    cf. i. /a-à-haab-ú-à=kw-o/   àháábwà=kwò   1-P1-give-PS-Fa=17-P.R
                                                                                           'he was given part of'

---

[33]In some related languages, there are **y**s which condition following vowel lengthening and others which do not condition length in the following vowel. To our ear, Kifuliiru does not have these two types of **y**.

[34]However, any word-final vowel with underlying H tone is phonetically lengthened in utterance-final position when it has an intonational falling contour, whether or not there is a preceding glide.

2.3.1.2.4.2 Pre-N+C lengthening (all vowels) (lexical)

A vowel is lengthened when it precedes a prenasalized consonant. Lengthening in this position is generally recognized to be compensatory lengthening, i.e. the vowel length compensates for the loss of moricity of the nasal.

(2.56)
mb	/ú=mú-mbáti/	ú=múúmbátì	AU=3-cassava
nd	/ú=mú-ndù/	ú=múúndù	AU=1-person
ng	/í=kí-pànga/	í=kípààngà	AU=7-ram
nd	/ú=mú-lòndo/	ú=múlòòndò	AU=3-garment
nd	/ú=kú-génd-a/	ú=kúgééndà	AU=15-go-Fa

2.3.1.2.5 Clitic-related vowel lengthening (all vowels, postlexical)

There is lengthening of the vowel in any phrase-level monosyllabic proclitic when fewer than three morae follow. There is also lengthening in the final vowel of a host word to which a monosyllabic verbal, nominal, or adjectival enclitic is attached.[35]

All monosyllabic words are cliticized, either to a preceding or following word (2.4.1). The lengthening which takes place in connection with this process seems to affect any phrase-level procliticized element, and encliticized stems which are nouns, verbs, or adjectives. The lengthening is seen clearly with the augment **á, í,** or **ú**, where the augment proclitic is lengthened in (2.57a, c, e), where it is attached to a word of fewer than three morae. The lengthening does not take place when the word following the augment is three or more morae, as in (2.57b, d, f).

---

[35] It is tempting to posit a long vowel form of all the clitics, in which case the vowels would be shortened when appropriate by the mora-based shortening rule, which has massive application elsewhere in the language. However, there were four reasons we could not justify positing long vowel UFs for these morphemes. First, they all seem to have short vowels both in PB and in other Bantu languages. Secondly, all of these have in common the fact that they are not prefixes but clitics. It seems strange that all clitics and (nearly) no prefixes would have long vowels if the vowel length itself were not predicated on the fact that they are clitics. Thirdly, there are prefixal forms of some of these same morphemes (e.g. the locative markers.) These prefixal forms occur in adjectives, as verbal subject markers etc. In all cases where these markers have become bound prefixes, they are not lengthened, e.g. the **ha-** in **hánò** is a locative prefix, not a clitic, and it does not have a lengthened vowel. Lastly, there is very similar lengthening of the final vowel of a host word when the following enclitic is a monosyllabic noun, verb, or adjective. For all these reasons, we have posited this mora-based lengthening rule to lengthen the underlyingly short vowel of such forms in the appropriate contexts.

(2.57) a. /á̱=ká-sà/   á̱á=kásà   AU=12-antelope
      b. /á̱=ká-fùlò/   á̱=káfùlò   AU=12-turtle
      c. /í̱=kí-hé/   í̱í=kíhê   AU=7-time
      d. /í̱=kí-nògosho/   í̱=kínògòshò   AU=7-hoof
      e. /ú̱=mú-kó/   ú̱ú=múkô   AU=3-blood
      f. /ú̱=mú-ùkà/   ú̱=mùùkà   AU=3-air

The lengthening rule is also observed with the proclitic locative markers. These markers include the cl. 16 **há**, cl. 17 **kú**, cl. 18 **mú**, and cl. 23 **í**, and are exemplified by **há** in (2.58). In (2.58a) the vowel of the cl. 16 locative marker is lengthened before the noun **kítì** 'tree', which contains only two morae. However that locative marker retains its short vowel when occurring before the noun **lwīījì** 'river', which contains three morae.

(2.58) a. /ha̱=kí-tì/   ha̱á=kítì   16=7-tree   'at the tree'
      b. /ha̱=lú-ījì/   há̱=lwīījì   16=11-river 'at the river'

In (2.59a), the progressive aspect marker **mu**,[36] is lengthened when cliticized to a verb stem which contains only two morae, giving the phonological word **múú=gúlà**. In (2.59b) that same marker **mú** retains its short vowel, when it is followed by three morae in **mú=byáálà**.

(2.59) a. /a-a-shuba mú= gul-a/ > ààshùbà **mú̱ú**=gúlà   'he was buying'
          1-P1-PREV PROG=**buy-Fa**

      b. /a-a-shuba mú= byal-a/ > ààshùbà **mú̱**=byáálà 'he was planting'
          1-P1-PREV PROG=**plant-Fa**

When the associative marker (A.M) or the conjunctive **na** (CNJ) precede a noun of fewer than three morae, the vowel of these clitics also always undergoes lengthening. In most cases where these markers are used, there is coalescence with the augment of the following noun. Any lengthened vowel found in such an environment could thus simply be attributed to coalescence. However, when we look at cl. 1a nouns, which never take an augment, we see that the proclitic A.M or CNJ demonstrates vowel length which is obviously attributable to clitic lengthening. Examples in which the vowel of the clitic is lengthened when preceding a noun of fewer than three morae are found in (2.60a, c, e).

---

[36]The progressive aspect marker **mú**, is a grammaticized use of the cl. 18 locative marker **mú** 'within'.

(2.60) a. /á=má-kàlà gà nyínà/ ámákàlà gàà=nyínà 'the charcoal of
   AU=6-charcoal 6-A.M-his.   his mother'
   mother

cf. b. /á=má-kàlà gà dáàtà/ ámákàlà gà=dáàtà 'the charcoal of
   AU=6-charcoal 6-A.M-my.   my father'
   father

 c. /á=ká-bwá kà nyókò/ ákábwá kàà=nyókò 'the dog of
   AU=12-dog 12-A.M-your.   your mother'
   mother

cf. d. /á=ká-bwá kà yîshò/ ákábwá kà=yîshò 'the dog of
   AU=12-dog 12-A.M-your.   your father'
   father

 e. /nà=nyókò/   nàà=nyókò   'and your mother'
cf. f. /na=dáàtà/   nà=dáàtà   'and my father'

Vowel lengthening is not seen, however, in clause-level proclitics, e.g. the quote marker, **ti**, pronominal focus markers and relative markers which are procliticized to a conjugated verb, e.g. **kíshókómà kyó=kìrì**... 'the leopard is the one which is...', and monosyllabic interjections, such as the vocative **e** 'Oh', etc.[37]

Lengthening also affects the final vowel of nouns and verbs to which an *enclitic* of certain word classes is added. This lengthening seems to be a function of minimality constraints, an effort to add to the number of morae in the enclitic in order to allow the monosyllabic word to meet the minimality requirements of its word class. We have observed examples of this in verbal, nominal, and adjectival enclitics: auxiliary plus monosyllabic verb stem, verb plus monosyllabic noun, and noun plus monosyllabic adjective. The same lengthening occurs in a reduplicated monosyllabic stem, whether verbal, nominal, or adjectival.

---

[37]This lack of lengthening may be simply due to the number of morae following. More research could be done on this: most such clause-level clitics are encliticized to words of three or more morae, so environments in which the vowel of such proclitics would be lengthened are infrequently observed.

(2.61) Auxiliary plus monosyllabic verb stem

  a. /á-gá-kìzì mo-a/   ágáákìzíí=mwâ   'he will repeatedly
    1-F2-REP shave-Fa   shave'

cf. b. /á-gá-kìzì gúl-a/   ágákìzì gúlà   'he will repeatedly
    1-F2-REP buy-Fa   buy'

  c. /tu-áyè mo-e/   twáyéé=mwè   'we will shave
    1-F3.shave-Fe   someday(F3)'

cf. d. /tu-áyè gúl-e/   twááyè gúlè   'we will buy
    1-F3.buy-Fe   someday (F3)'

Verb plus monosyllabic noun

  e. /i-li n-dá/   ìríí=ndâ   'it is a pregnancy'
    9-is 9-pregnancy

cf. f. /i-li n-dàre/   ìrí ndàrè   'it is a lion'
    9-is 9-lion

cf. g. /lù-lì lúfú/   lùlì lúfú   'it is death'
    11-is 11-death

Noun plus monosyllabic adjective

  h. /í=ny-úùmbà N-bí/   ínyúùmbáà=mbì   'the bad house'
    AU=9-house 9-bad

cf. i. /í=ny-úùmbà N-hámù/   ínyúùmbà mbámù   'the big house'
    AU=9-house 9-big

Reduplicated monosyllabic stems

  j. /kú-hy-á=hyá/   kúhyáá=hyâ   'to get ripe/
    15-get.ripe=RDP   cooked (RDP)'

cf. k. /kú-kìt-á-kítà/   kúkítá-kítà   'to rush around
    15-rush.around-Fa-RDP   (RDP)'

  l. /kí-hy-á=hyá/   kíhyáàhyâ   'new'
    7-new

cf. m. /kí-lúlù/   kílúlù   'bitter'
    7-bitter

In (2.61j) there is lengthening of the final vowel of the verb stem because the reduplicated portion is a monosyllable, and because it is a monosyllable, it is encliticized to the original verb. In (2.61k), by contrast, the reduplicated portion is bisyllabic, so there is no lengthening of the final vowel of the original verb. Note in (2.61k) that there are only two morae in the reduplicated

2.3 Phonological rules and processes

section following the final vowel of the original verb, so that the mora-based vowel shortening rule would not apply here to shorten any lengthened vowel in this position (2.3.1.2.6).

In (2.61l) there is also lengthening of the vowel when the adjective is derived using the -CV- verb root -**hy**- 'get ripe, ready to eat', but no lengthening when a -CVC- root is used with a derivational final vowel, as in (2.61m) where the verb root is -**lul**- 'be bitter'. Note that the lengthening in (2.61l) is not due to the preceding glide, as word-final vowels are not compensatorily lengthened, even when followed by a clitic. This is shown below in (2.62).

Though the lengthening is seen when the enclitic is a noun or verb, as above, there is no lengthening when the enclitic is a pronominal element, such as in (2.62). Lengthening of the final vowel preceding such an enclitic is not seen even when a glide plus vowel precedes the enclitic, as in (2.62b, c).

(2.62) a. /a-à-bà-gwat-ir-a=by-o/ àbàgwáátírà=<u>by</u>ô 'he held them (cl. 8)
       1-P1-O2-hold-APL-Fa=8-P.R   for them'

    b. /a-à-haab-w-a=ky-o/ àháábwà=<u>ky</u>ô 'he was given it (cl. 7)'
       1-P1-give-PS-Fa=7-P.R

    c. /a-à-shúlik-w-a=y-o/ àshúlìkwà=<u>y</u>ô 'he was hit there'
       1-P1-hit-PS-Fa=23.P.R

    d. /a-à-hááb-w-à=kw-o/ àháábwà=<u>kw</u>ò 'he was given part'
       1-P1-give-PS-Fa=17-P.R

2.3.1.2.6 Mora-based vowel shortening (all vowels, lexical, post lexical)

The mora-based vowel shortening rule (vowel shortening) states that "any long vowel is shortened if it is followed by three or more morae within the domain of the phonological word". This rule applies to all long vowels, whether underlyingly long or lengthened by phonological rule. This rule applies after any phonological lengthening rules have applied.

By definition, a mora constitutes one unit of prosodic length. In Kifuliiru, a syllable with a short vowel contains one mora, while a syllable having a long vowel consists of two morae. Thus the "three or more morae" which trigger application of the rule may consist of a long-vowel syllable plus one (or more) short-vowel syllables, or it may consist of three (or more) short-vowel syllables.

In (2.63a), the first vowel of the verb root is lengthened to **oo**, since it follows a **y**. Given the fact that the last two syllables of the word contain short vowels, adding up to only two morae, the vowel shortening rule does not apply. In (2.63b), however, the final two syllables of the stem contain three morae (the long penultimate **ii** counting as two morae, plus the final short **i** counting as one) and thus the vowel shortening rule applies. As seen in these two examples, the effect of this rule sometimes gives the impression that long vowels are playing leapfrog across a word as its form changes, since vowel length often seems to "jump" from a more leftward syllable towards the right as suffixes are added.

Likewise in (2.63c) the first vowel of the verb root is lengthened to **uu**, as it precedes an **mb**. Since there are two or fewer morae in the following syllables in (2.63c, d), vowel shortening does not apply. In (2.63e), by contrast, there are three morae following the **u**. The presence of three following morae triggers the vowel shortening rule, producing a phonetically short **u** in the verb stem.

(2.63) UF   SF   Gloss
 a. /a-à-yòn-er-a/   àyòònérà   1-P1-pour-APL-Fa 'he poured on'
 b. /a-yòn-er-ir-i/   àyònííri̇̀   1-pour-APL-RS-Fi 'he has poured on'

 c. /kú-húmb-a/   kúhúúmbà   15-dig-Fa 'to dig up something'
 d. /kú-húmb-ir-a/   kúhúúmbírà   15-dig-APL-Fa 'to dig up for someone'
 e. /kú-húmb-irir-a/   kúhúmbírírà   15-dig-INTS-Fa 'to dig up intensively'

This rule is, in effect, a constraint against having more than one long vowel per word. Since the rule shortens all vowels to the left of the final three morae, the only vowel that remains phonetically long is the one that is rightmost in the word. Furthermore, since word final vowels are not lengthened, this rule has the effect that only the penultimate or antepenultimate syllable is allowed to have a long vowel.

The fact that this rule does not apply across word boundaries in phrases shows that this rule operates over the domain of the word, at the word-building (lexical) stage.[38]

---

[38]Note that the rule does *not* count the enclitic (clitic which attaches to the end of a word) as a mora in the host word when deciding which vowels to shorten within the host word, e.g. in combinations of verb plus pronominalized object. This rule also applies *before*, or is overruled by, the rule which lengthens the final vowel of host word whose enclitic is a monosyllabic noun, verb, or adjective.

2.3.1.2.6.1 Origins of long vowels affected

The following observations concerning the vowel shortening rule will be documented in the sections below:
- The rule applies to any long vowel, whether the length was the result of a phonemic long vowel in a certain morpheme, or the result of a phonological process such as being compensatorily lengthened by any of the lengthening rules noted above, or resulting from the juxtaposition of the vowels of two separate morphemes.
- The rule applies to all phonological words. Two of the environments in which it is most evident are verb prefixes and verb stems to which suffixes have been added.

Example (2.64) illustrates this, listing examples of long vowels from all possible sources. In (2.64a), the long **ii** in the first syllable of the verb base -**biik-ir** 'put something away APL' is underlyingly long (cf. **kúbííkà** 'to put, place' and **kúbìkà** 'to crow of a rooster'). In (2.64b) that long **ii** is shortened to **i**, since the resultative morpheme -**ir** has been suffixed, so that the long vowel is now followed by three morae within the word, thus meeting the conditions of the vowel shortening rule.

In (2.64c), the long **ii** in the first syllable of the verb root -**línd**- 'wait' is the result of a phonological process, Pre-N+C lengthening, whereby a vowel is compensatorily lengthened when it precedes a prenasalized consonant. In the extended form **àlííndìrà** 'he waited for', the **ii** is not affected by vowel shortening rule, as only two morae follow. However in (2.64d) the long **ii** of the stem is shortened, again because the addition of the resultative morpheme, with its final vowel, to the extended base, making a total of three morae to the right.

Example (2.64e) shows another long vowel which is the result of a phonological process; the long **oo** in the verb **àyòònérà** 'he poured APL' is the result of post-glide lengthening. This long **oo** also is affected by the vowel shortening rule when the verb is in the resultative form, as in (2.64f), since it is followed by three morae.

In (2.64b, d, f), the long vowel **ii** in the suffix -**iiri** is itself the result of a juxtaposition of two separate morphemes. In this case the resultative suffix -**ir** is added to the applicative (APL) extension -**ir**/-**er**. The **r** of -**ir**/-**er** (APL) is deleted by a morpheme-specific rule, and the remaining -**e** or -**i** assimilates completely to the vowel of the resultative suffix, by the lexical coalescence rule, thus giving -**iir**.

(2.64)   UF (P1 + APL)   SF   Gloss
   a. /a-à-<u>biik</u>-ir-a/   àb<u>íí</u>kírà   1-P1-put-APL-Fa
                                'he put something away for someone'
   b. /a-<u>biik</u>-ir-ir-i/   àb<u>í</u>kîìrì   1-P1-put-APL-RS-Fa
                                'he has put something away for s/o'

   c. /a-à-<u>lín</u>d-ir-a/   àl<u>íí</u>ndìrà   1-P1-wait-APL-Fa 'he waited for s/o'
   d. /a-<u>lín</u>d-ir-ir-i/   àl<u>í</u>ndîìrì   1-wait-APL-RS-Fi 'he is waiting for s/o'

   e. /a-à-<u>yon</u>-ir-a/   ày<u>òò</u>nérà   1-P1-pour-APL-Fa 'he poured on/for...'
   f. /a-<u>yon</u>-ir-ir-i/   ày<u>ò</u>níírì   1-pour-APL-RS-Fi 'he has poured on/for...'

The mora-based vowel shortening rule applies wherever a long vowel is followed within the word by more than two morae. Because verbs are the word class with the most affixes, both prefixes and suffixes, verbs are the arena in which the shortening rule is most often seen to work. The long vowels in verbs stems are shortened when suffixes totaling three or more morae are added. In addition, the long vowels resulting from the juxtaposition of morphemes in verb prefixes are shortened when the total morae following within the verb are three or more.

The examples in (2.65) show the results of the vowel shortening rule as it applies to *long vowels in the verb stem*. In (2.65a) the long **oo** in the radical of the infinitive **kúhóóhà** 'to become calm' is lexically long. Example (2.65b) shows the same radical with the addition of an extension which has a long vowel, in this case -**eesi** 'causative' (CS). The long vowel **ee** of the extension, plus the final vowel **a**, add up to three morae, causing the long vowel of the verb root -**hooh**- to be shortened, so that the root is now -**hoh**-.

In (2.65c), the long **aa** in the stem of the verb **bákátāāngà** 'they offered' is the result of the phonological process of Pre-N+C lengthening. In (2.65d), however, that long **aa** is shortened, since the following causative extension -**iisi**, together with the final vowel **a**, add up to three morae.

(2.65)   UF infinitive   SF   Gloss
   a. /kú-<u>hooh</u>-a/   kúh<u>óó</u>hà   15=be.calm-Fa
   b. /kú-<u>hooh</u>-eesi-a/† kúh<u>ó</u>héésâ   15=be.calm-CS-Fa

   c. /ba-ka-<u>tàng</u>-a/   bákát<u>āā</u>ngà   2-P2-offer-Fa
   d. /ba-ka-<u>tàng</u>-iisí-a/ bákát<u>à</u>ngíísâ 2-P2-offer-CS-Fa

2.3 Phonological rules and processes

†The final **i** of the causative morpheme is changed to a glide (**y**) because it precedes a vowel (the final vowel). Following glide formation, the **y** undergoes **y**-absorption.

The effects of the vowel shortening rule are also often commonly observed in *verb prefixes*. For example, the vowel shortening rule often has the effect of neutralizing the marking of the recent past (P1) tense which is indicated segmentally by the morpheme **à-**. When this tense marker follows the cl. 1 subject marking, which is indicated by the morpheme **a-**, the result is a word initial long vowel, **aa**. However, when followed within the word by three or more morae, this initial long vowel, formed by the merging of the two **a-** morphemes, is shortened, leaving only a single **à-**.

In (2.66a) the two above-mentioned morphemes are both reflected in the surface form by the phonetically long **aa** of **ààhíkà** 'he arrived'. However in (2.66b) the same two combined morphemes surface phonetically as a short **a**, as seen in the form **àbúgùmùlà** 'he shook out something', having been affected by the shortening rule since the remainder of the word contains four morae.

Likewise in (2.66c), both the cl. 1 morpheme **a-**, and the **à-** marking the P1 tense are reflected in the first syllable of the verb **ààsìgà** 'he left'. However, in (2.66d) the addition of the cl. 1 object prefix **mú-** means that there are now three morae following **a-à**, and so it is shortened: **àmúsìgà** 'he left him'.

(2.66e, f) shows the same shortening happening in the case where the vowel of the negative marker **ta-** is the morpheme which is juxtaposed to the **a-** of recent past (P1). Negative **ta-** plus P1 **à-** surfaces as **taa-** when fewer than three morae follow as in (2.66e), but as **ta-** when followed by three or more morae as in (2.66f).

(2.66)	UF recent past (P1)	SF	Gloss
a.	/a-à-hík-a/	ààhíkà	1-P1-arrive-Fa 'he arrived'
b.	/a-à-búgumu-l-a/	àbúgùmùlà	1-P1-shake.out-Fa 'he shook out...'
c.	/a-à-sìgà/	ààsìgà	1-P1-leave-Fa 'he left'
d.	/a-à-mú-sìgà/	àmúsìgà	1-P1-1.O-leave-Fa 'he left him'
e.	/a-tà-à-sìgà/	àtààsìgà	1-NEG-P1-leave-Fa 'he did not leave'
f.	/a-ta-à-mú-sìgà/	àtàmúsìgà	1-NEG-P1-1.O-leave-Fa 'he did not leave him'

In (2.67a) the future tense marker **gáá-** has a long vowel in the word **ágááhíkà** 'he will arrive', while in the form in (2.67b) **ágábàlàmà** 'he will travel', the vowel in the future tense marker is shortened, since there are three following morae. Though the future tense marker appears more often with a short vowel than with a long one, the long-vowel form must be taken as the current underlying form, since none of the lengthening rules would account for its length in the cases where it appears as long on the surface.[39] Additional examples with long and short vowels in the future marker are found in (2.67c–f). In each case, the short vowel form, **gá-** is followed by three or more morae in the verb.

(2.67)   UF future (F2)   SF   Gloss
     a. /a-gáá-hík-a/   ágááhíkà   1-F2-arrive-Fa 'he will arrive'
     b. /a-gáá-bàlam-a/   ágábàlàmà   1-F2-travel-Fa 'he will travel'
     c. /a-gáá-ly-a/   ágáàlyà   1-F2-eat-Fa 'he will eat'
     d. /a-gáá-téb-a/   ágáátébà   1-F2-trick-Fa 'he will trick'
     e. /a-gáá-tíbit-a/   ágátíbìtà   1-F2-run-Fa 'he will run'
     f. /a-gáá-génd-a/   ágágéèndà   1-F2-go-Fa 'he will go'

2.3.2 Morphologically governed rules and processes

There are several phonological rules and processes which affect only selected morphemes, rather than applying in a general way wherever the phonological requirements of the rule are met. There are also certain processes which affect or are conditioned by the presence of certain morphemes, rather than by purely phonological criteria. All these "morphologically governed" rules will be discussed below, grouped according to the type of process going on: assimilation, epenthesis, deletion, transposition, spirantization.

2.3.2.1 Vowel harmony rules

In Kifuliiru there are two rules of vowel harmony that apply to various derivational verbal suffixes; back vowel height harmony applies to the extensions with back vowels: the transitive reversive -(**u**)**ul**/(**u**)**ur** and the intransitive reversive -(**u**)**uk**. Front vowel height harmony applies to the extensions with front vowels: the applicative (-**ir**), intensive (-**iirir**/-**iiriz**), impositive/neuter (-**ik**), and the first (long) vowel of the long causative (-**iisi**).

---

[39]The long-short alternation of the **gáá-** future marker could be an indication that it was formerly a clitic, and as such was affected by the rule of mora-based lengthening in cliticized monosyllabic words. This is the only monosyllabic prefix which has a long vowel.

2.3 Phonological rules and processes

Vowel height harmony (VHH) means that high vowels in the extension suffixes are lowered to mid when there is a mid vowel in the immediately preceding syllable.[40] For example, in the verb **kúyònóólà** 'to retrieve cows which are eating someone's crops' (cf. **kúyōnà** 'to spill something' or 'cows to go into someone's field of crops'), the reversive suffix **-uul** is realized as **-ool**, harmonizing with the mid vowel **o** in the stem **-yòn-**. Likewise, in the verb **kúyònékà** 'to be spilled' the stative suffix **-ik** is realized as **-ek**, again harmonizing in vowel height with the mid vowel **o** in the stem.

There is some evidence that the initial vowel of the long passive extension is or was subject to vowel height harmony in Kifuliiru.[41]

In Kifuliiru, as is typical of five-vowel languages in zone J, the vowel height harmony rules follow a pattern which Hyman (1999:238) terms canonical VHH.[42] Inclusion in the canonical group includes the fact that the VHH is asymmetrical. The term "asymmetrical" means that there is different conditioning for the front harmony than for the back. For back vowel height harmony, the lowering of the suffixal high vowel **u** to the mid vowel **o** is triggered by only the mid back-vowel **o** in the stem (and is not triggered when the stem contains a mid front vowel **e**) while for front vowel height harmony the vowel lowering in the suffix is triggered *either* by **e** *or* by **o** in the stem.[43]

---

[40] "The immediately preceding syllable" is the last vowel of the verb stem, which may be part of the original verb root, or may be a non-productive extension.

[41] It "was" subject because the **o** or **e** in the roots of the only verbs which exhibit this form of the passive is no longer discernable synchronically except by the fact that these verbs take the o/e VHH extensions. The **o** of **mwa** 'shave' (presumably from **mo-a**) and **nyw-a** 'drink' (from **nyo-a**) never shows up in any surface form. The evidence that the vowel of the passive undergoes VHH comes from such forms as **kú-mw-éébwâ** 'to be shaved' from **kú-mw-â** 'to shave', the root of which underlyingly is **mo-**. **Kú-nywâ**, (though it has a lexicalized related word **kú-ny-wíísâ** 'to water a field', using the high vowel **i**), also takes the mid-vowel form of the extensions, including the causative form, **kú-nywéésâ** 'to give someone a drink', and the long (post-vocalic) form of the passive, **kú-nyw-éébwâ**. The use of this form is also reinforced by the noun **kí-ny-wèèbwà** (7-beverage). The mid vowel form of the long passive is also heard in the form **kúhéébwâ** 'to be given'. More often heard these days is the alternative **kúháábwâ** 'to be given'. Both are from the verb **kúhâ**. The verb **kúhâ** 'to give' is very rarely used in its base form, never occurring without at least an incorporated object, and with the usual citation form given instead with the reciprocal extension as **kúháánà** 'to give'. In conjugated form it most often appears in pseudo-causative form as **kúhéézâ** ~ **kúhéérézâ** 'to give'.

[42] As described by Hyman, a "canonical" VHH system is characterized by the following: it is asymmetrical, as defined above; it does not affect extensions with the vowel a, nor does an a in the stem condition any lowering in any extensions; it does not affect the final vowel of the verb; it does not apply to prefix vowels, i.e. they are not lowered or otherwise affected by vowels in the verb stem.

[43] In symmetric vowel height harmony, by contrast, a single set of conditioning vowels in the stem would trigger lowering both for back vowel suffixes and for front vowel suffixes.

It should be noted that though the Kifuliiru vowel system contains three non-high vowels (**e, a, o**) only a stem containing **e** or **o** can trigger vowel height harmony; the non-front, non-back **a** never triggers VHH. Furthermore, as is typical, suffixes in which the vowel is **a** are never affected by VHH. The exclusion of **a** from the system of height harmony is the usual case in Bantu languages.

2.3.2.1.1 Back vowel height harmony

In Eastern Bantu, when the back mid vowel **o** occurs in the syllable immediately preceding the reversive extensions, -(**u**)**ul/r** or -(**u**)**uk**, then the vowel in those extensions is realized as the mid vowel **o**, producing -(**o**)**ol/r** and -(**o**)**ok**, respectively.

The data in (2.68) demonstrate that in Kifuliiru only the back mid vowel **o** triggers back vowel height harmony. As can be seen in (2.68a), the **o** in the verb stem -**shòn**- 'climb' causes the reversive suffix -**uuk** to be realized as -**ook**. By contrast, the verbs containing the stem vowels **i**, **u**, **a**, and **e** (2.68b–e) do not trigger BVHH.

(2.68)	Stem	Gloss	RV ext.	Reversive infinitive	Gloss
a.	-**shòn**-	'climb up'	-**ook**	kú-shòn-óók-à	15-climb-RV-Fa
b.	-**shwek**-	'tie'	-**uuk**	kú-shwék-úúk-à	15-tie-RV-Fa
c.	-**bìsh**-	'hide'	-**uuk**	kú-bìsh-úúk-à	15-hide-RV-Fa
d.	-**dúb**-	'fish'	-**uuk**	kú-dúb-úúk-à	15-fish-RV-Fa
e.	-**bàlam**-	'travel'	-**uk**	kú-bàlám-úk-à	15-travel-RV-Fa

It should be noted that back vowel height harmony operates consistently on all forms that have the -(**u**)**uk** and -(**u**)**ul** shape of the reversive extensions. This is true whether those extensions occur with a productive reversive meaning, as in (2.68), or in frozen forms where a reversive meaning is not transparent, as in (2.69) below. In (2.69a) the verb **kúlóngóólà** 'to quarrel sharply' cannot be said to be a productive reversive form of the verb **kulóóngà** 'to get'. Nevertheless, the form -**ool** does still harmonize in vowel height with the **o** in the previous syllable. The verbs in (2.69b–e) below all retain the **u** in the "non-productive reversive extension", since the vowels in the stem (**i, uu, a,** and **e**) do not trigger BVHH.

2.3 Phonological rules and processes

(2.69)   Infinitive   Frozen ext.   Gloss
- a. kú-lóngóól-à   -ool   15-quarrel.sharply-Fa
- b. kú-yììmúl-à   -ul   15-chase.away-Fa
- c. kú-púúmúk-à   -uk   15-dash.off-Fa
- d. kú-zàmúúk-à   -uuk   15-go.up-Fa
- e. kú-géndúúk-à   -uuk   15-make.profit-Fa

As stated in the definition at the beginning of this section, only the vowel in the syllable which immediately precedes the extension is able to trigger back vowel height harmony. Thus, if after a mid vowel **o** in the stem there is an intervening non-**o** vowel before the reversive extension, then the **o** in the stem will not trigger vowel lowering in the reversive extension. Such cases, though quite rare, do exist, as in the infinitive **kúkòmágúlà** 'to beat with a stick'. In this case, the high **u** in the lexicalized extension -**ul** is not lowered by the **o** in the stem, because there is an intervening **a**, which does not trigger BVHH.

Finally, it should be noted that while verbs stems with the mid vowel **o** in the last syllable always condition back vowel height harmony in the extension, it is not true that *only* verbs with **o** in the last syllable of the stem have extensions containing **o**. In a few cases, a mid vowel **o** occurs in the extension without being triggered by a mid vowel in the verb stem. These exceptions, interestingly, all have **si** or **zi** initial roots, and include: **kúsíngóólà** 'to burn up' and **kúsíngóókà** 'to be burnt up', both of which seem to be derived from **búsííngò** 'materials for starting fire without matches' (which also ends in an **o**), as well as **kúyìsìndóólà** 'to make slow headway' and **kúzìhóólà** 'to wound by striking', both of which possibly may be derived from ideophones. No other such examples have been observed.

2.3.2.1.2 Front vowel height harmony

When either of the mid vowels **e** or **o** occurs in the vowel immediately preceding verbal extensions containing the high front vowel **i**, then the **i** of those extensions is realized as the mid vowel **e**. The verbal extensions affected are the following: applicative (-**ir**), intensive (-**iirir/-iiriz**), stative intransitive/neuter (-**ik**), and the first vowel only of the long causative (-**iisi**).

High front vowel extensions/suffixes not affected by this rule are the resultative final -**ir-i** and the short causative -**i**, which are distinguished from the other high vowel verbal extensions in that they both are descended historically from forms which in Proto-Bantu had the high close vowel.[44]

---

[44]Hyman (1999) posits that the mid vowel forms of the extensions may have been historically

In (2.70a) the mid front vowel **e** in the verb stem -**shék**- 'laugh' causes the applicative suffix -**ir** to be realized as -**er**.[45] Likewise in (2.70b) the mid back vowel **o** in the verb stem -**yon**- 'spill out' causes the neuter suffix -**ik** to be realized as -**ek**. By contrast, the verbs containing the stem vowels **i**, **u**, and **a** (2.70c–e) do not trigger front VHH.

(2.70)	Stem	Gloss	Extended form	Gloss
a.	-shék-	'laugh'	kú-shék-ér-à	15-laugh-APL-Fa 'to laugh at'
b.	-yòn-	'spill'	kú-yòòn-ék-à	15-spill-NEU-Fa 'to be spilled'
c.	-gír-	'do'	kú-gír-íírír-à	15-do-INTS-Fa 'to do intensively'
d.	-bùl-	'lack'	kú-bùl-ík-à	15-lack-NEU-Fa 'to be lacking'
e.	-twal-	'take away'	kú-twáál-ír-à	15-take-APL-Fa 'to take to/for'

Just as with back vowel height harmony, front vowel height harmony affects productive extensions (2.70a–e), as well as their lexicalized equivalents, seen in (2.71). For example, the intensive suffix -**erer** on the verb **kúgéndérérà** 'to continue' (2.71a) is not a productive extension. Nevertheless -**erer** still harmonizes in vowel height with the mid vowel **e** in the previous syllable. Likewise the frozen suffix -**er** in the verb **kújòjóbérà** 'to be weak and pitiful' harmonizes in vowel height with the **o** vowels in the stem. By contrast, the verbs in (2.71c–e) all retain the **i** in their non-productive extensions, as the vowels to the left (**i**, **u**, and **a**) do not trigger front VHH.

(2.71)	Verb with frozen ext.	Frozen ext.	Gloss
a.	kú-géndérér-à	-erer	15-continue-Fa
b.	kú-jòjóbér-à	-er	15-be.weak/pitiful-Fa
c.	kú-yííník-à	-ik	15-give.name-Fa
d.	kú-shúlík-à	-ik	15-hit-Fa
e.	kú-sángánír-à	-ir	15-go.meet.someone-Fa

---

prior. I will not comment on that except to note that Kifuliiru contains one interesting case, the verb **kúhâ** 'to give' in which the mid vowel form of the extensions is used even though the root has the vowel **a**. The mid vowel form of the long passive is also heard in the form **kúhéébwâ** 'to be given'. More often heard these days is the alternative **kúháábwâ** 'to be given'. The verb **kúhâ** 'to give' is very rarely used in its base form in Kifuliiru, almost never occurring without at least an incorporated object, and with the usual citation form given instead with the reciprocal extension as **kúháánà** 'to give (to someone)'. In conjugated form it most often appears in pseudo-causative form as **kúhéézâ** ~ **kúhéérézâ** 'to give', also with the mid vowel extensions.

[45]These suffixes which come from the former Proto-Bantu first degree front vowel still condition spirantization in preceding consonants as well.

2.3 Phonological rules and processes

As previously stated in relation to back vowel harmony and the reversive extensions, the vowel of the syllable which immediately precedes the extension is the one that triggers front vowel height harmony. This is illustrated by the applicative extension in the verb **kújéjágízâ** 'to help weak person walk', as well as in its non-causative form, **kújéjágírà** 'to lack strength'. Since the non-productive expansion -**ag** follows the root and is closest to the extensions -**iz** and -**ir** in these forms, it is the vowel **a** with which the extensions harmonize. Thus *kujejageza and *kujejagera are not allowable forms.

Finally, it should be noted that while verb stems with the mid vowels **e** and **o** always trigger front vowel height harmony in the extension, is not true that *only* verbs with **e** or **o** in the last syllable of the stem have extensions containing **o**. Especially in the intensive extension and in frozen extensions which look like the intensive extension (-**iirir**/-**iiriz**), a mid vowel **e** can occur in the extension without being triggered by a mid vowel in the verb stem. Examples include **kúdúméérézâ** 'to agree by humming' and **kúfùndéérézâ** 'to put something in a well-hidden place'.

2.3.2.1.3 Historical vowel harmony/harmonizing suffixes

There is significant evidence in the lexicon of further types of vowel harmony in verb stems. Historically, there has been widespread partial reduplication, which involved identical vowels in the two or more syllables thus produced. Some examples are shown in (2.72).

(2.72) Infinitive	Gloss	Compare to	Gloss
kútùtúúmbà	'to pound with fists'	**kútìtíímbà**	'to hit much'
kúdíídíkà	'to throw down'	**kúdéédékà**	'to throw down heavy thing'
kúdóódókà	'to snap off and fall'	**kudúúdúkà**	'to snap under tension'

There is also evidence in the lexicon of historical suffixes (expansions) with the forms -V**t**, -V**m**, -V**b**, -V**g**, etc. which underwent complete vowel assimilation. For example, -**at** 'contactive' is a recognizable, though no longer productive, extension. Examples (2.73d-f) show words with -**at**, and compare them across the column to similar words in which the extension is -**et** or -**ut**. Examples (2.73a, c) also use -**ut**, which seems to be a vowel harmonized form of -**at**, while (2.73b) shows the same extension with the mid back vowel, -**ot**.

Though most of the words in (2.73) can no longer be broken down into synchronically identifiable extensions, words such as the following exemplify the effects of historical vowel harmonization in lexicalized verb stems. There is no consistent relationship between the forms in the left column and the forms in the right column. These forms are included here just as an indication of historical vowel harmonization in suffixes.

(2.73)   Infinitive   Gloss   Infinitive   Gloss
   a. **kú-nyúgútúl-à** 15-snatch-Fa   **kú-nyág-à**   15-steal-Fa
   b. **kú-yòngótól-à** 15-suck.lots-Fa   **kú-yōōng-à**   15-suckle-Fa
   c. **kú-yùbútúl-à**   15-shell-Fa   **kú-yúúbúl-à** 15-shell-Fa
   d. **kú-hùmbát-à**   15-get.thin-Fa   **kú-bègét-à**   15-embrace-Fa
   e. **kú-fùmbát-à**   15-grasp-Fa   **kú-kègét-à**   15-chew.on-Fa
   f. **kú-bàlágát-à**   15-wither-Fa   **kú-bùlúgút-à** 15-dawdle-Fa
   g. **kú-tòndóból-à** 15-explain-Fa   **kú-tìndíbúz-â** 15-belittle-Fa
   h. **kú-jójóból-à**   15-talk.slowly-Fa **kú-jájábír-à** 15-roar-Fa
   i. **kú-tìndímál-à** 15-stay.small-Fa   **kú-gìshímál-à** 15-get.rusty-Fa
   j. **kú-jójómól-à**   15-peck-Fa   **kú-vwógómól-à** 15-take.lots-Fa
   k. **kú-shòlógót-à** 15-nauseated-Fa   **kú-shùlúgút-à** 15-cast.far-Fa
   l. **kú-mérégéz-â**   15-thrive-Fa   **kú-mér-à**   15-grow-Fa
   m. **kú-gérégéz-â**   15-try.hard-Fa   **kú-gér-à**   15-try-Fa

2.3.2.2 *Epenthesis rules*

Epenthesis rules are needed to account for the shape of:
- Certain forms of demonstratives.
- Certain first-person singular verb forms.[46]
- Stand-alone forms of certain monosyllabic words.

Though we have listed the first of these as **y**-epenthesis, in theory, all of these could be seen as **i**-epenthesis. In the first case, the epenthetic segment is intervocalic, so that the high vowel glide formation rule (2.3.1.2.1.1) would change it from an **i**- to a **y**-. A possible motivation for these epenthetic segments, clearest in the epenthesis in NC initial verbs, is to protect the tonal configuration of the words involved.

2.3.2.2.1 y-epenthesis in demonstratives

A **y** is epenthesized to make a two-syllable word of the proximal demonstrative of cl. 1, 4, and 9.

---

[46]Though the historical form of the first-person subject and object markers in Proto-Bantu is said to be **ni**-, the usual form in Kifuliiru synchronically is **n**-, so that what might historically be merely the exemption of a form from the loss of the final **i**- is now reinterpreted as epenthesis.

2.3 Phonological rules and processes

The proximal demonstrative with the meaning of "this one" is formed by a copy rule. This copy rule alone is sufficient to explain the formation of the demonstrative for classes which have a CV demonstrative prefix. However, for a class which has a demonstrative prefix of a V- only form, another rule is needed to complete its formation. This "y-epenthesis in demonstratives" is that rule.

The copy rule referred to above will produce a demonstrative of the form VV for cl. 1, 4, and 9, while the actual form has a **y** separating the two vowels. Notice that for a class which has a CV demonstrative prefix, the copy rule gives yVCV.

(2.74)

	Cl.	DemPfx	Copy rule	y-epenthesis	Gloss
	1	u	uu	úúyù	'this.P'
	4	i	ii	ííyì	'this.P'
	9	i	ii	ííyì	'this.P'
cf.	7	ki	yiki	yííkì	'this.P'

Thus the **y**-epenthesis (demonstrative) rule will generate a **y** to stand between the two vowels, making the word two syllables rather than one. The avoidance of a monosyllabic form is probably at least part of the phonological motivation for this rule. As such it would complement the other rules which eliminate monosyllabic words. The epenthesis of a **y** between the vowels of these forms also complements the copy rule mentioned above, which "copies" the C of a CV form as a **y** (an unspecified C) giving **yúgù** 'this.P' (not ***gúgù**, as it would be if the C were copied as a specified C) from the cl. 3 demonstrative prefix **gu**, **yíkì** 'this.P' from the cl. 7 demonstrative prefix **ki**, etc.

Another possible motivation for the epenthetic **y** in the cl. 1, 4, and 9 forms is tonal. The tone of this particular demonstrative, in all classes, is always HL (when used as a copula) or LH (when used attributively). If the demonstrative were monosyllabic, both these tones would have to occur on the single syllable. However, since a HL or LH tone may only occur on a penultimate syllable of a word, the demonstrative, if only consisting of VV, would not be able to bear either of these tonal configurations. It would rather, as a monosyllable, be cliticized to another word. With the epenthetic **y**- serving as the onset of a second syllable, however, it becomes bisyllabic, and is thus able to stand alone and to bear the two hallmark tones of this form on its two separate syllables.

2.3.2.2.2 *i-epenthesis in NC-initial verb words with H-tone initial prefix*

A word-initial **i** is epenthesized in a verb form when there is a high tone assigned to the subject morpheme, and that subject morpheme is first-person singular and therefore consists of only a non-syllabic nasal.[47] Usually a tone assigned to a non-syllabic nasal is shifted to the next leftward tone-bearing unit in the word. However, when the non-syllabic nasal is word initial, as subject morphemes always are in Kifuliiru,[48] the only way to get a tone-bearing unit to the left of it within the word is to add an epenthetic vowel word initially.

This motivation for epenthesis is found in the first-person singular of certain dependent verb forms, one of which is the conditional form of the verb form which expresses unrealized expectation. This conditional unrealized expectation form is marked segmentally by the usual "not yet" aspect morpheme **ta-zi**, and marked tonally as conditional by a certain tonal configuration which includes high tone on the subject marker. This dependent form, when combined with a negative form in the main verb of the clause, means 'if/when I have not x'ed', e.g. **ndágályòkà hánó, ííndàzì múbōnà** 'I will not leave here *when* I have not yet seen him', (epenthetic **i** underlined) or **ndágálúhùùkà átàzí bònèkà** 'I will not rest *when* he is not yet found'.[49]

The other form with an initial **i** epenthesized to accommodate a high tone on the subject marker is the conditional contrary-to-fact persistive, which includes, besides the H tone on the subject prefix of all its forms, a L-toned **kì**- morpheme, and means 'if only I had x'ed (but I did not...)', e.g. **ííngìbè nié=ngáàfwà** 'If (only) I had been the one who died (but I was not)'.

Following are some examples of the two forms that take epenthesis, along with comparative forms of other persons which do not require the epenthetic vowel. These are given to show the contexts of the verb forms in which

---

[47]In verbs with other than first-person singular subject, the subject prefix is of the form (C)V, and is thus able to bear the characteristic H tone of such verb forms. The "true Kifuliiru" way to solve such problems as the lack of a necessary tone bearing segment is to epenthesize a word-initial **i**-, as seen in the forms given. However, another method, which is becoming popular among many young people for all first-person singular subject markers, not just those needing to bear a H tone, is to use a **ni**- form rather than a nasal-only **n**- form for first-person singular. This is probably being adopted from Kiswahili, the relevant language of wider communication, which always uses **ni**- for the first-person singular subject marker.

[48]The only morpheme which might possibly precede the verbal subject morpheme is the relative marker, which is a clitic rather than a prefix. In any case, the relative marker is never used with a first-person subject, so is irrelevant in regard to the initial position of the **n**- subject marker.

[49]With a positive form in the main verb of the dependent clause, this same form can be given the gloss 'before I x', e.g. **ngályòòkà hánó ííndàzì múbònà** 'I will leave here before I see him'. Either way, 'without having x'ed' expresses the intent of the form.

2.3 Phonological rules and processes

such epenthesis takes place. For explanatory purposes, the epenthetic vowel is labeled EP in the morpheme-by-morpheme gloss, though it is not actually a morpheme.

(2.75) ...ná-n-gú-gáshààn**ì**r-é | **í**-n-dà-zíì   =fw-à.
       CON-1SG-O2.SG-bless-Fe   EP-1SG-NEG-YET   =die-Fa.

'...(that) I bless you | before I die.'

Compare this in (2.76) with third-person singular subject instead of first-person:

(2.76)...à-ná-kú-gáshààn**ì**r-é | á-tà-zíí   =fw-à.
       1-CON-O2.SG-bless-Fe   1-NEG-YET   =die-Fa

'...(that) he bless you | before he dies.'

Compare it also with the indicative form of the verb form meaning in (2.77a) 'I have not yet died' and in (2.77b) 'he has not yet died'. In these indicative forms, no H tone is required on the subject morpheme, so no epenthesis is necessary in the first-person singular.

(2.77) a. /n-dà-zí =fw-à/   >   ndàzíìfwà   'I have not yet died'

       b. /à-tà-zí =fw-à/   >   àtàzíìfwà   'he has not yet died'

Another example is given in (2.78).

(2.78) **Kéèrà**   **n-à-shííkíz-á** | **kwó=**   **n-dá-gá-lyòòk-à**   **há-nó** |
       ALREADY   1SG-P1-swear-Fa   that   1SG-NEG-F2-leave-Fa   16-here.P.C

       íí-n-dà-zí   **yìhóól-à.**
       EP-1SG-NEG-YET   take.revenge-Fa

'Already I have sworn | that I will not leave here | before I have taken revenge.'

Compare the epenthesized form in (2.78) **ííndàzí** with (2.79) where the verb in first-person singular is not subjunctive, but indicative, and thus where there is no high tone on the subject prefix, and therefore no epenthetic **i**.

(2.79) **N-dà-zí**　　yìhóól-à.
　　　　1SG-NEG-YET　take.revenge-Fa

'I have not yet taken revenge.'

The other verb form that takes the epenthetic **i** is the conditional contrary-to-fact persistive. These forms also have H tone on the subject prefix.[50] The epenthesis works in exactly the same way as it did in the forms above. In (2.80) the epenthesis is seen.

(2.80) **Í-n-gì-dèt-è**　　‖　ngà=　kwó=　b-áàlì　kìzí　dēt-à...
　　　　EP-1SG-PERS-speak-Fe　like　CMP=　2-P1　REP　speak-Fa

'If I had spoken ‖ as they always spoke...' (Psa 73:5)

Compare this to a third-person form in (2.81), where the high tone is carried on the subject marker, **a**-, and there is no epenthesis needed.

(2.81) **Á-kì-dèt-è**　　|　ngà=　kwó=　bá-àlì　kìzí　dēt-à...
　　　　1-PERS-speak-Fe　like　CMP=　2-P3　REP　speak-Fa

'If he had spoken | as they always spoke...' (Psa 73:5)

2.3.2.2.3 i-epenthesis to avoid n plus nasal

In certain verb forms, **i**-epenthesis is used as a way of avoiding an **n** plus nasal sequence.[51] Speakers may epenthesize an -**i** in the first-person subject marker, making it **ni**- instead of the usual **n**-. Ordinarily this is not considered "good Kifuliiru", but it seems that it is more acceptable in verbs that follow **ìrí** 'while/when (at the same time)' as in the examples below. The epenthesis avoids having forms like **n-ná-dètà** 'and I am speaking'.

---

[50]The epenthesis seems limited to verbal subject prefixes. There are other forms where a H tone on an initial prefix does not trigger epenthesis. CV initial cl. 9/10 nouns without the augment do not undergo epenthesis, e.g. **ndàrè** 'lion', though the unaugmented form usually appears only within a copula phrase, where the noun is preceded by a vowel final word, e.g. **ìrí ndàrè** 'it is a lion', and the H tone of the prefix is shifted left onto the final mora of the preceding word. In another context, the imperative with a first-person singular object prefix also appears without epenthesis. A frequently heard phrase from children is **mbéèzâ!** 'Give me (sthg)!'

[51]There are no surface juxtaposed nasals in the language.

2.3 Phonological rules and processes

(2.82) ...írí   nì̱-ná-dèt-à   'while I am speaking'
       ...írí   nì̱-ná-lír-à   'while I am crying'

In cases of the first-person singular **n-** followed by the consecutive **na-**, and the subjunctive final vowel, **-e**, either the epenthesis option or the morpheme transposition option may be used (see 2.3.2.4). Thus some speakers would use **nì-ná-mú-bwììr-è** (1SG-CON-O1-tell-Fe) 'and I tell him' in place of **ná-mú-bwììr-è**, from UF **ná-n-mú-bwìr-è** (CON-1SG-O1-tell-Fe) 'and I tell him'. It should be noted, however, that while such forms as **nì-ná-mú-bwììr-è** are heard, especially from younger speakers, the epenthesis forms for this type of case are considered to have Kiswahili influence, and are not considered "proper Kifuliiru" by older speakers.

An epenthetic **i** may also be added in cases where **n**-plus-nasal sequence is avoided between the first-person subject marker and a nasal-initial verb stem. In (2.83a, b) the first-person singular subject prefix on the subjunctive form of a verb would, without the epenthesis, be assimilated to the following nasal segment, and deleted by the rule of nasal deletion preceding another nasal, leaving a verb with no observable subject prefix. Rather than allowing this to happen, an **i** is epenthesized, yielding a bisyllabic form with a **ni-**, rather than **n-**, prefix. Compare this to (2.83c), where the verb stem is not nasal initial, and the first-person singular subject retains the usual **n-** form.[52]

(2.83) a. ní̱-nyw-è   1SG-drink-Fe '(that) I drink'
        b. nì̱-nyót-fîr-w-ì 1SG-thirst-RS-PS-Fi 'I am thirsty'

   cf. c. n-géndérér-è   1SG-continue-Fe '(that) I continue'

2.3.2.2.4 i-epenthesis in monosyllabic words

There are several strategies in Kifuliiru for eliminating monosyllabic words.

With monosyllabic adjective roots, **i**-epenthesis is mandatory in the case of cl. 9/10 concord marking on an adjective root which does not have an initial plosive, such as is the case with **-là** 'long/tall' in example (2.84a).[53] Because the usual cl. 9/10 concord prefix on adjectives is just an unspecified non-syllabic

---

[52]Though some younger speakers have regularized the first-person singular subjunctive prefix to **ni-**, by analogy to Kiswahili.

[53]However, in the case of plosive-initial monosyllabic adjective roots, such as **-bí** 'bad', it will be seen that **i**-epenthesis is an optional alternative to the strategy of cliticization of the monosyllabic word. Cl. 9 is the only case in which these CV adjectives are monosyllabic in prefixed form. **-bí** 'bad' and **-lá** 'long' are the only two CV adjectives, as the others are used adjectivally only in reduplicated form, **-hyâhyâ** 'new', **-lúlù** 'bitter', **-núnù** 'sweet', **-nììní** 'little', etc.

nasal consonant, it does not add an extra syllable to the adjective, as do all the other concord prefixes (e.g. the cl. 1 prefix, **mú-** illustrated in (2.84b)). The cl. 9/10 prefix is normally realized as **ny** before a vowel, and in the case of a following consonant, it is realized as a nasal which assimilates to the place of articulation of the consonant. However, in the case of a monosyllabic root, the cl. 9/10 prefix may be realized with an epenthetic **i** as **nyi-**, thus adding an extra syllable to a form which would otherwise be monosyllabic.

The monosyllabic adjective stem **-là** 'long/tall' does not begin with an plosive. Thus the only permissible form of this adjective in cl. 9/10 is **nyírà** 'tall', which includes the epenthetic **i**.[54] Such forms with epenthetic **i** are only observed with monosyllabic adjective roots in cl. 9/10 (cf. (2.84b) with a cl. 1 prefix), and are never seen with adjective stems consisting of two or more syllables, as examples (2.84e–h).

(2.84)

	UF of Adj		SF	Gloss	In phrase	Gloss
a.	/N-là/	→	nyí-rà	9/10-long	í=njírá nyírà	'long road/s'
cf. b.	/mú-là/	→	mú-là	1-long	ú=múúndú múlà	'tall person'
c.	/N-bí/	→	nyí-bì	9/10-bad	í=njírá nyíbì	'bad road/s'
cf. d.	/N-bí/	→	m-bî	9/10-bad	í=njíráà=mbî	'bad road/s'
e.	/N-langi/	→	n-dààngì	9/10-fierce	í=ngáàvú ndààngì	'fierce cow/s'
f.	/N-òòfì/	→	ny-òòfì	9/10-short	í=njírá nyòòfì	'short road/s'
g.	/N-lulu/	→	n-dúlù	9/10-bitter	í=nyámá ndúlù	'bitter meat/s'

Note that in (2.84b), the same monosyllabic adjective root as found in (2.84a), when used with cl. 1 concord, does not need an epenthetic vowel because the prefix already consists of a complete syllable, **mu-**. Examples (2.84c, d) show that with a monosyllabic adjective which is plosive initial, there are two options for realization, either with an epenthesized **i** as in **nyíbì** 'bad' (2.84c) or cliticized to the noun, as =**mbî**[55] (2.84d). In (2.84e–g) by contrast, the roots are not monosyllabic, so they do not trigger the rule of **i**-epenthesis when used with the cl. 9/10 prefix. Rather, the prefix is realized in its usual

---

[54]It is **nyírà** rather than *__nyílà__ because **l** changes to **r** following front vowels, **i** and **e**.

[55]Though linguistically I posit epenthesis because the usual surface form of the cl. 9 prefix has no vowel, the NCV form **mbî** is considered by speakers to be a short or contracted form of **nyíbì**, rather than **nyíbì** being considered a lengthened form of **mbî**.

2.3 Phonological rules and processes

form, as a non-syllabic nasal, which then triggers strengthening of the following consonant **l** to a plosive **d**, in (2.84e, g).

The strategy of avoiding monosyllabic words by the epenthesis of an **i-** is also noticeable in some Kifuliiru speakers' pronunciation of monosyllabic words in Kiswahili which begin with NC. In this case the initial syllabic nasal of Kiswahili is typically pronounced by speakers of Kifuliiru with an initial **i-**. For example, the Kiswahili word **mbwa** 'dog' is often pronounced as **íímbwà**, by Kifuliiru speakers, cf. Kifuliiru **ká-bwá** (12-dog); Kiswahili **mbu** 'mosquito' is often pronounced **íímbù**, cf. Kifuliiru **mú-bù** (3-mosquito), etc.

2.3.2.3 Deletion rules

Morphologically triggered deletion rules are needed in order to account for the variations in the shape of:
1) **y**-initial verb stems, when used in derivative nouns or adjectives
2) The loss of the final consonant of certain verb stems in the resultative form
3) The deletion of nasal consonants preceding fricatives in resultative verbal stems, noun roots, agentive nouns, and causative verb forms.

2.3.2.3.1 y-deletion in non-verbal derivations from verb stems

A **y** is deleted at the beginning of a **y**-initial verb stem[56] when that verb stem is used derivationally in a non-infinitive noun or an adjective. In (2.85) each stem is shown first with an infinitival and then with a non-verbal prefix. It can be observed that the **y** present in the first of each pair is absent in the second.

---

[56]There are no V-initial verb stems in Kifuliiru. Those that are V-initial in some related languages all have initial **y** in Kifuliiru. Some speakers optionally delete the **y** in conjugated forms of **kúyììtà** 'to kill' in which it follows the third-person singular object marker **mú-**, e.g. ...**ànámwììtà** 'and he killed him' (**ànámwììtà** is an alternate form of **ànámúyììtà**.) However, it has not been observed with other verbs, nor with this verb except when it has the **mú-** object. A likely source for this initial **y-** in verbs where other languages have V-initial roots is the historical use in Kifuliiru of the cl. 5 infinitive (with initial **í-**) of which synchronic signs remain. It is possible that the initial **í-** (whose surface realization in V initial roots would have been **y-**) was reinterpreted as part of the verb root during the time when the transition was made to cl. 15 (**kú-** initial) infinitives. The resulting absence of V-initial roots could have, in turn, been reinterpreted as a constraint against V-initial verb roots. In any case, it seems that synchronically, the verbs are interpreted as underlyingly **y**-initial.

(2.85)

UF	SF	Gloss
/ú=kú-yòboh-a/	úkúyòòbóhà	AU=15-fear-Fa
cf. /ú=mú-ōba/	úmwōōbà	AU=1-fearful.person
/ú=kú-yámbal-a/	úkúyáámbálà	AU=15-wear-Fa
cf. /ú=mú-ámbalo/	úmwáámbálò	AU=3-garment
/ú=kú-yèruus-a/	úkúyèrúúsâ	AU=15-whiten/clean-Fa
/mú-ēru/	mwéérù	1-white
/ú=kú-yìr-a/	úkúyīīrà	AU=15-get.dark-Fa
/mú-īru/	mwíírù	1-black

Having the **y-** present in the verb protects the tonal integrity of the initial syllable of the stem. Verbal tone is quite complex, with the tonal identity of the verb carried by the initial syllable of the stem, and grammatical tones indicated on the preceding and following syllables. If the verb stem were vowel initial, the vowel of the prefix would coalesce with the initial vowel of the stem, causing the tones to coalesce as well, and thus "muddying the waters" tonally and sacrificing the clear identity of the underlying tone of the verb. By contrast, nominal and adjectival stems do not have to carry any grammatical tone to indicate tense, mood, etc., and their prefixes have a non-alternating H tone, so the protection of the first syllable of the stem is not so important.

The alternation between the presence and absence of **y** in the verbal base could theoretically be either a result of **y**-epenthesis in the verbal forms or of **y**-deletion in the non-verbal forms. There are two reasons for positing a case of **y**-deletion in the nominal forms rather than **y**-epenthesis in the verbal forms.[57] 1) One reason is that the reflexive is historically reconstructed as **yi-**. When one nominalizes a verb in which this **yi-** has become lexicalized as part of the stem, the **y** of the reflexive is no longer present in the nominal form; e.g. **kúyìtègéérézâ** 'to be careful' yields the nominal derivative **úbwìtègèèrèzè** 'wisdom'. Such nominal forms are the only cases in which the reflexive morpheme lacks the initial **y**. 2) The other argument for

---

[57]There is also one argument for saying that the **y-** is epenthesized in verbs. If one assumes that the adjective, rather than the verb, is primary in verbs with the inchoative extension, and that the adjective does not have an underlying initial **y**, then there is a need for **y-** epenthesis in the verb form. E.g. -òòfi 'short', yields the verb **kúyòòfíhà** 'to be/become short'. So we can either take this to mean that the verb is actually primary, or that there is a constraint against V-initial verb stems which does indeed necessitate the epenthesis of a **y-** in such cases.

deletion rather than epenthesis is that many of the **y**-initial verb stems in Kifuliiru are reconstructed in Proto-Bantu with an initial ***j**- (i.e. the glide **y**), e.g. *-**jóg-a** 'swim, bathe' (FLR **kú-yōōg-à**), *-**jél-a** 'be white' (FLR **ku-yēēr-à**); while the related adjectives and nouns which have no initial **y** in Kifuliiru are also reconstructed with an initial glide, e.g. *-**jél-ʋ** 'white', cf. FLR -**ēru**, e.g. **mw-ēērù** (1/3-white).[58]

2.3.2.3.2 Deletion of final consonants in resultative verb forms (lexical)

A verb base which ends with an extension which ends with **l, r, n,** or **t** undergoes deletion of the final consonant of the verbal extension when followed by the resultative final -**ir-i** ending.

First, let us look at C-deletion in extensions ending in **l** or **r**: the -**er**/-**ir** applicative, -**ol**/-**ul** reversive transitive, and -**al** extensive extensions. The final C of each of these is deleted when followed by the resultative final suffix -**ir-i**.[59] This suffix has a tense/aspect related function, and is associated across Bantu with a wide range of modifications to the verb base to which it is affixed, including spirantization (also called frication) of the final consonant of a root, and fusion with an extended verbal base. Part of this fusion involves the loss of a consonant.

Following the deletion of the consonant, there is vowel coalescence between the last V of the verb stem and the **i** of the resultative suffix. Since this is coalescence at the lexical level, the rules of lexical vowel coalescence take effect, with a back vowel undergoing glide formation to **w**, as in (2.86c, d), and any other vowel plus the resultative **i** yielding **ii**. This can be seen in (2.86).

---

[58]Lexical reconstructions here from Bastin, Coupez, and Mann (1999).

[59]The analysis given here, the deletion of the final consonant of the extension, is a simplified explanation of the process. An alternative, more involved explanation is that rather than the deletion of the final consonant of the extension, it is the **r** of the resultative -**ir-i** which is deleted. This might involve circumscription of the final consonant of the extension, and the insertion of the resultative immediately following the vowel of the extension, e.g. **bwatal-ir-ir-i** > **bwatali-ir-r** -**i**> **bwatali-i-r** -**i**> **bwataliiri**. This would be in keeping with the processes which historically resulted in resultative forms like -**fùmbiitì** from -**fùmb-at-a** > -**fùmba-ir-t-i** > -**fùmbiiti**. For a more thorough discussion of this topic, see 5.9.1. For a presentation of several options of analysis which have been used in a very similar situation in Cibemba, see Hyman (1995).

(2.86) Sbj. Stem   RS+Fi   By C-deletion   By V coalescence
   a. /a- bwatal-ir̲-ir-i/ → abwatali-ir-i → àbwátálíìrì
                                                    'he is sitting (on sthg)'

   b. /a- bwatal̲   -ir-i/   → a-bwata-ir-i   → àbwátíìrì
                                                    'he is sitting'

   c. /a- gálul̲   -ir-i/   → a-galu-ir-i   → àgálwììrì
                                                    'he has returned (sthg)'

   d. /a- shóbol̲   -ir-i/   → a-shobo-ir-i   → àshóbwììrì
                                                    'he is able'

   e. /a- bèr-er̲   ir-i/   → a-ber-e-ir-i   → àbèríírì
                                                    'he has cut for...'

This process, by which the resultative suffix seems to fuse with the stem, is often referred to as "imbrication" (Bastin 1983). Verb stems affected by imbrication (here referring only to the deletion of the final consonant and the subsequent vowel coalescence) in Kifuliiru are generally those which have an extension, whether frozen or productive.[60] This is to say that they have more than just a CV(V)C stem.[61] In this analysis, we have attributed the application of imbrication to the presence of a certain verbal extension at the end of the stem. In (2.87) it can be seen that the final **l** or **r** of a CV(V)C root with no extension (2.87a, c) is not deleted, while the final **l** or **r** of a longer CV(V)CVC(VC) stem, which ends with an extension as in (2.87b, d, f), does undergo deletion.

While in (2.87a, c) the final consonant of the stem does undergo spirantization, there is no deletion of the final consonant, so no vowel coalescence takes place. In (2.87e), there is neither imbrication nor spirantization, because the final consonant of the stem, **m**, is not affected by either rule. In (2.87b, d, f) there is imbrication, i.e. the final **l** or **r** is deleted and vowel coalescence takes place.

---

[60]There are several irregular forms which undergo deletion of the final C even though not longer than CV(V)C, namely **-bwini** (from **bòn-a** 'see', probably originally *bo-an-a), **-gweti** 'have' (a lexicalized form originally probably from **-gwata** (**gw-at-a**) 'grasp', **-hiiti** 'have' (which speakers say has no synchronic root, but linguistically, most likely comes at some point from **-ha-at-a** (give-contactive-Fa). These are all forms which are often irregular (usually in the same or similar ways) in many Bantu languages.

[61]It seems to be generally accepted among Bantuists that the original Bantu verb roots consisted of -CV(V)C- or less commonly -CV-, and that longer roots are always indicative of the addition of extensions/expansions, processes of full or partial reduplication, etc.

2.3 Phonological rules and processes

(2.87) Sbj.   Stem   RS +Fi   Surface
  a. /a- gàl   -ir-i/   → a-gàz-ir-i   → àgàzírì
                                                'he is rich'

  b. /a- bwatal-ir-i/   → a-bwata-ir-i → àbwátíìrì
                                                'he is sitting'

  c. /a- bèr   -ir-i/   → a-bèr-ir-i   → àbèzírì
                                                'he has cut'

  d. /a- bèr-er -ir-i/   → a-bèr-e-ir-i → àbèríírì
                                                'he has cut for...'

cf. e. /a- hím   -ir-i/   → a-hím-ir-i   → àhímìrì
                                                'he has conquered'

  f. /a- hím-ir -ir-i/   → a-him-i-ir-i → àhímììrì
                                                'he has conquered for...'

Imbrication affects the resultative forms of all verb stems ending in extensions which have a final **r** or **l**, whether or not the extension is still productive or whether it is lexicalized in the word in question. Many of the extensions affected have become "frozen" as a part of a verb form which can no longer be reduced into a non-extended form. For example, the root of (2.87b), **kúbwátálá** 'to sit', does not alternate with a non-extended form *kubwata. The extensive -**al** is no longer a productive extension in Kifuliiru; **kúshóbólà** 'to be able' does not have a synchronic related unextended form *kushoba. The lexicalization of these extensions does not alter the fact that these verbs, as well as all others containing frozen extensions, undergo imbrication. (For more on the resultative suffix see 5.23.)

The continued use of the imbricated form for verbs with lexicalized extensions could point to phonological rather than truly morphological conditioning in the verbs that undergo this rule. One possibility for a phonological motivation for imbrication only in longer stems is to posit that the shorter stems are exempt from the process by reason of minimality conditions. Hyman (1995), in his treatment of imbrication in Chibemba, analyzes the fact that the process of imbrication works differently in verb stems of different lengths as a function of a language-specific minimality condition.[62] It would certainly be possible to posit such an analysis for Kifuliiru, as well.

We look now at C-deletion in final extensions ending in **n** and **t**. This affects the final consonant of the -**an** 'reciprocal/comitative' extension, and of the -**at** 'contactive' extensions, when followed by the resultative suffix.

As can be seen in (2.88a, b), in verbs with the -**an** reciprocal/comitative extension, the resultative suffix appears as -**in**,[63] as seen in (2.88a), and in verbs having the -**at** contactive extension the resultative appears as -**it**, seen here in (2.88b). Both of these forms of the resultative behave identically to the -**ir** form in conditioning the deletion of the final consonant of the extension they follow.

(2.88) Sbj.   Stem   RS + Fi   By C-deletion   Surface
   a. /ba-   shúsha̠n-in-i/ → ba-shúsha-in-i → bàshúshììnì
                                                    'they look alike'

   b. /a-   fùmba̠t -it-i/ → a-fùmba-it-i → àfùmbíítì
                                                    'he has (sthg) in hand'

It seems that the use of the variant forms of the resultative (-**in** and -**it**) is in flux in Kifuliiru, and has been/is being lexicalized, at least in certain cases. Examples (2.89e, f) below show that there are often two possibilities for the resultative form of a single verb, one in which the variant form is used and imbrication is seen (2.89e) and the other (2.89f) in which the final **n** is treated as a consonant unaffected by either deletion or spirantization. The form in (2.89f) is considered sub-standard by many speakers, but is attested.

The form with the variant form of the resultative sometimes also has a specialized meaning, as in (2.89b). Examples (2.89c, d) show that some verbs with the -**at** ending, such as **kúfùmbátà** 'to have something in hand' (2.89c), follow the deletion rule and use the specialized allomorph, while others, such as **kúhàgátà** 'to carry on shoulder' (2.89d), seem to regularly follow only the rule of final consonant spirantization, and use the basic -**ir-i** allomorph of the resultative.

Other verbs, such as (2.89g, h) show the use of the -**it-i** form of the resultative in verbs whose current non-resultative forms do not even contain the -**at** extension. In these forms, the use of the special allomorph is clearly lexicalized.

---

[62]This minimality condition states, in part, that a consonant may not be morphologically circumscribed, i.e. made temporarily invisible to the morphology rules, if to circumscribe it would leave less than the minimal requirement of the language for a root.

[63]The -**in-i** form of the resultative also appears in the lexicalized resultative form of the verb -**bòn**- 'see', -**bwini**.

2.3 Phonological rules and processes 83

(2.89) Infinitive Gloss Resultative Gloss
a. **kúgwáátà** 'to hold' **à-gwáás-ír-ì** 'he is holding'
cf. b. **kúgwáátà** 'to hold' **à-gwéét-ì** 'he has/owns'

c. **kúfùùmbátà** 'to grasp' **à-fùmb-íít-ì** 'he is grasping'
cf. d. **kúhàgátà** 'to carry on shoulder' **à-hàgás-ír-ì** 'he is carrying on shoulder'

e. **kútùngáánà** 'to be perfect' **bì-tùng-íín-ì** 'it is perfect'
cf. f. **kútùngáánà** 'to be perfect' **bì-tùngáán-ír-ì** 'it is perfect'

g. **kúyáámbálá** 'to get dressed' **à-yámb-ìít-ì** 'he is dressed'
h. **kúyùùvwâ** 'to hear' **à-yùvw-íít-ì** 'he hears'

2.3.2.3.3 Nasal effacement preceding fricatives

Hyman (2003b) states that there are three different strategies in Bantu languages for dealing with the combination nasal plus voiceless fricative. Two of these strategies, post-nasal voicing (of **h, f, s,** and **sh**) and nasal effacement, are seen in Kifuliiru.

This section deals with nasal effacement in Kifuliiru, which is used in the contexts of nominal morphology and suffixal (but not prefixal) verbal morphology.[64]

In four separate morphological contexts,[65] outlined below, an alveolar nasal (**n**) is effaced (deleted) when it directly precedes a fricative. The deletion of the nasal in such an environment is referred to as "nasal effacement" before fricatives. In Kifuliiru effacement is in most cases conditioned only by the voiceless fricatives, **h, f, s, sh,** though the examples of lexicalized agentive nouns and causative verbs show that in the past it was in some cases conditioned also by the voiced fricatives **v** and **z**. It is still productively conditioned by these voiced (as well as voiceless) segments in the case of spirantization due to the resultative morpheme. Nasal effacement is not synchronically attested before the voiced prepalatal fricative, **j**, though this also seems to have conditioned effacement at some point historically.[66] Conditioning environments are listed for each morphological context.

---

[64] By contrast, post-nasal voicing is seen in the prefixal morphology of verbs.

[65] I list the various morphological environments for nasal effacement separately because there seem to be various parameters operating in the different situations as far as exceptions to the rule are concerned.

[66] The H-tone verb **kúgáájà** 'to count' provides evidence that nasal effacement was once also

a) In cl. 9/10 nominal prefixes, N- is deleted before stems with an initial voiceless fricative, including those in loan words. In this environment the deletion of the nasal seems to occur with any of the voiceless fricatives (**f** (2.90a, b, c), **h** (2.90d), **s** (2.90e, f), **sh** (2.90g)).

(2.90)
	Singular	UF (PL)	Plural	Gloss
a.	íí=fùkà	/í=N-fùkà/	íí=fùkà	AU=9/10-hoe
b.	úú=lú-fwì	/í=N-fwì/	íì=fwì	AU=11/10-fish
c.	ú=lú-fwàabé	/í=N-fwàbé/	í=fwààbé	AU=11/10-letter (Fr.)
d.	í=hóóngò	/í=N-hóngò/	í=hóóngò	AU=9/10-commotion
e.	ú=lú-sìkù	/í=N-sìkù/	íí=sìkù	AU=11/10-day
f.	í=sààbúnì	/í=N-sààbúnì/	í=sààbúnì	AU=9/10-soap (Sw.)
g.	ú=lú-shààlì	/í=N-shààlì/	í=shààlì	AU=11/10-firewood

But in other similar words, the nasal is retained, and the fricative becomes voiced (2.91a, b, f), or remains voiced (2.91c–e). There are no examples in the data of nasal effacement occurring in nouns which have a stem-initial voiced fricative in the underlying form.

(2.91)
	SG	UF (PL)	PL	Eff?	Gloss
a.	ú=lú-sháándò	/í=N-shándò/	í=n-jáándò	no	AU=11/10-foot
b.	ú=rú-sààtì	/í=N-sààtì/	í=n-zààtì	no	AU=11/10-walking.stick
c.	ú=lú-zígè	/í=N-zígè/	íí=n-zígè	no	AU=11/10-locust
d.	ú=lú-jáángà	/í=N-jángà/	í=n-jáángà	no	AU=11/10-small.dried.fish
e.	íí=n-vùlà	/í=N-vùlà/	----	no	AU=9-rain
f.	í=fììzì	/í=N-fììzì/	í=n-vììzì	SG	AU=9/10-large.bull

Note that in (2.91f) the singular and plural of the same word are differentiated by the presence or absence of the nasal effacement rule. This seems to be a good indication that the status of this rule is in flux in the language. The alternation seen in (2.91f) may be influenced by analogy with the words in

---

conditioned by **j**. This verb is not among the toneless class of verbs, as all historically CVVC stems are (but CVVNC stems are not). This indicates that it was historically **kúgáánjà**, and that the **N** underwent effacement at some point in the past.

2.3 Phonological rules and processes

(2.91a–d) which have the N+fricative combination in the cl. 10 plural but not in the cl. 11 **lu-**.

There are also indications that the some of the cl. 9 nouns subject to nasal effacement may be gradually being reinterpreted by some speakers as cl. 5 nouns, but only in that the plural is sometimes found in cl. 6, e.g. the plural of Ø-**shúúlì** (9-bull) is found in our texts both as cl. 10 **shúúlì** and as cl. 6 **máshúúlì**. Likewise, the plural of **íí=fùkà** (9-hoe) is generally found as cl. 10 **íí=fùkà**, but is also attested as cl. 6 **máfùkà**. No regular cl. 9 nouns take their plurals in cl. 6, but cl. 5 always has its plural in cl. 6.

b) Nasal deletion preceding fricatives is seen in nouns derived from verbs by the addition of the -**i** suffix which is usually called *agentive*, but which in Kifuliiru has a wider usage than just "agent", and is often used with non-animate subjects, as is seen in (2.92f).

In all examples in (2.92), the NC found in the infinitive form of the source verb has been changed in the derived noun to a simple fricative by the rule of spirantization and the subsequent nasal effacement.

In the context of this "agentive" suffix, we have found no exceptions to these rules, but are of the opinion that these are all lexicalized forms rather than active synchronic derivations. It should also be noted in all these forms that the vowel length conditioned by the NC is retained in the derived nouns even though the conditioning environment (the following NC cluster) has been lost.

(2.92)

	Infinitive	Gloss	Derived noun	Gloss
a.	ú=kúgéénda̖	'to go'	ú=mú-géez̲-ì	AU=1-traveller-AG
b.	ú=kúláángà	'to guard'	ú=mú-lááz̲-ì	AU=1-guard-AG
c.	ú=kúhīīngà	'to cultivate'	ú=mú-hīīz̲-ì	AU=1-farmer-AG
d.	ú=kúbūūmbà	'to mould clay'	ú=mú-būūv̲-ì	AU=1-potter-AG
e.	ú=kúshūūngà	'to dance'	ú=mú-shūūz̲-ì	AU=1-witch-AG
f.	ú=kúgòlóómbà	'to flow'	á=má-gòlóóv̲-ì†	AU=6-water-AG

†Alternate word for **ámìíjì** 'water'. A Mufuliiru friend told me that the use of these "alternate" terms for the same thing or idea is often the result of cultural taboos. For example, if your father-in-law is named **Miiji** 'water' you are prohibited from pronouncing that word. So you have to come up with another term you can use for the same concept.

c) Nasal deletion is also observed in verbs whose final C has been spirantized by the addition of the resultative final morpheme -**ir-i**.

Many final consonants in the verb root, including **nd** and **ng**, are spirantized when followed by the resultative morpheme. In the case of **nd** or **ng**, which are spirantized to **nz**, the nasal is subsequently deleted by the nasal deletion rule, leaving only **z**. The phoneme **b** is not affected by resultative spirantization, and **mb** is not affected in this context either, as seen in (2.93f). This makes it seem that the spirantization of **mb** seen in agentive examples like (2.92d, f) has probably been lexicalized.

It should be noted that Kifuliiru as spoken by those from the area of Mangwa[67] is characterized by the lack of nasal deletion following spirantization in the resultative. This is shown in the "Mangwa form" column in (2.93), where the nasal is retained preceding the spirantized consonant. Note that in (2.93f), where the final C of the base is **mb**, there is no difference between standard Kifuliiru and the Mangwa form, since **mb** does not undergo spirantization.

(2.93)	Infinitive	Gloss	w/resultative	Mangwa form	Gloss
a.	**kúbííngà**	'to chase'	**àbíízìrì**	**àbíínzìrì**	'he has chased'
b.	**kúlēēngà**	'to pass'	**àlèèzírì**	**àlèènzírì**	'he has passed'
c.	**kúláángà**	'to guard'	**àláázìrì**	**àláánzìrì**	'he is guarding'
d.	**kúlóóngà**	'to get'	**àlóózìrì**	**àlóónzìrì**	'he now has'
e.	**kúkūūndà**	'to love'	**àkùùzírì**	**àkùùnzírì**	'he loves'
cf. f.	**kúhāāmbà** 'to carry in bag'		**àhààmbírì**	**àhààmbírì**	'he is carrying'

d) There are definitely some words in the lexicon which still exhibit the effects of nasal effacement before spirantization caused by causative **-i**, but they seem to be "frozen" relics of a process that is no longer productive.

The words in (2.94) show the effects of nasal effacement with the historical use of the short causative following NC. If there is an alternate (productive) causative form related to the same infinitive, without spirantization, and therefore, without nasal effacement, that also is listed. We did not find any examples of the short causative following **-nd**, either with or without nasal effacement.

---

[67]Mangwa is a small mountain village west of Kiliba. The speech of this area is not really a separate "dialect" but more of an "accent", since the most noticeable difference is that people from the area of the mountain village of Mangwa lack the rule of nasal deletion in the resultative forms of verbs.

2.3 Phonological rules and processes

(2.94)

	Final C	Non-CS Inf.	Gloss (non-CS)	-i causative form	Productive form
a.	mb	kúdàláámbà	'to walk far'	kú-dàláá<u>v</u>-y-â	---------
b.	mb	kúkùlúúmbà	'to roll'	kú-kùlúú<u>v</u>-y-â	---------
c.	mb	kújāāmbà	'to get thin'	kú-jàà<u>v</u>-y-â	kú-jàmb-íís-â
d.	mb	kújùgúúmbà	'to shake'	kú-jùgúú<u>v</u>-y-â	kú-jùgúúmby-â[†]
e.	ng	kúkāāngà	'to be startled'	kú-kàà<u>z</u>-â	kú-kàngíísâ
f.	ng	kúyōōngà	'to suck breast'	kú-yòò<u>z</u>-â	kú-yòngéésâ

[†]In the causative form **úkújúgúúvyâ** (2.94d) there is a somewhat specialized meaning of shaking a container to see what sound it makes (in order to deduce from that sound what kind of thing/how much is in it) or to rinse out a container (put water in, shake it around, and then pour water out again). It is not clear whether there is a difference in meaning between this and the **úkújúgúmbyâ** form. Note that in the alternate form of **úkújúgúmbyâ**, though the short causative is used, spirantization does not take place, and thus the environment for nasal effacement is not met. Thus the spirantization rule itself has fallen out of use at some point in this context with this consonant. The fact that there are other verbs ending in **mb** and **ng** for which one hears not only the short causative form, but also the long causative, e.g. **kujààvyâ/kújàmbíísâ** (2.94c) shows that even the use of the short causative form with NC final verbs is becoming/has become a lexical phenomenon rather than a productive process.

The lexicalization of the forms in (2.94) which exhibit spirantization is further evidenced by the fact that several of these forms have developed somewhat specialized meanings. For example, **kúdàláávyâ** (2.94a), rather than being an innocent instance of causing someone to walk a long ways, has the meaning of 'deliberately causing someone trouble by making it necessary for them go a long ways when they do something'.

In conclusion, it seems clear from many of the examples above that this rule of nasal effacement is in flux in the language. It is still well attested in many frequently used nominal forms and is widely active in the resultative verb forms used by most speakers.

However, even for the speakers whose spirantized resultative verb forms always show nasal effacement, there are other environments in their speech in which nasal effacement before fricatives does not ever take place. In verbs with an initial alveolar fricative, the addition of a first-person singular object marker, which is of the form **n-**, does not trigger nasal effacement in any verbs. The fact that the **n-** here is a separate morpheme with significant semantic content may play a role in its stability in this context.

(2.95) a. a- a- ń- sìg- -a > áánzìgà 'he left me'
 1 P1 O1.SG leave Fa

b. ba- a- ń- fùkam–ir -a > bánvùkámírà 'they knelt before me'
 2 P1 O1.SG kneel APL Fa

As was shown in (2.91) above, the same type of exception is noted in nouns of cl. 11 which take a plural in cl. 10, with its **N-** prefix. Even when such a noun stem begins with a fricative, the nasal prefix still appears on it.

Thus the frequent exceptions to the nasal effacement rule, in verbal as well as nominal contexts, along with the existence of a subdialect that never observes the rule of nasal effacement in resultative verb forms, all seem to be indications that this rule in general is in the process of being lost from the language.

2.3.2.4 Nasal commutation rule (avoidance of N + N sequences)

A nasal-plus-nasal (N + N) sequence is not allowed in the language and is avoided in one of two ways. In section 2.3.1.1.5, we saw the strategy of nasal deletion before nasals. The other strategy for the avoidance of nasal plus nasal sequences, used only in verbs, is the transposition of certain morphemes containing nasal segments.

The morpheme transposition strategy is found in the first-person singular form of continuative verbs, as in (2.96a), and resultative forms as in (2.96b) which contain the additive **ná-** marker. The verb forms in question have an empty tense slot, and so according to the normal order of morphemes in verbs, the subject marker is directly followed not by the usual tense marker, but by the conjunctive **ná-** marker.

In the case where the subject is first-person singular, as in (2.96a, b), the subject marker is **n-**, which when juxtaposed to **ná-** would produce **n-ná-** (were they to be aligned in the normal order).[68] In order to avoid that sequence, the normal order of these morphemes is reversed, yielding **ná-n-**instead, as in

---

[68] In the case where the verb stem or macrostem also begins with a nasal, transposing the morphemes does not evade the problem, e.g. **írí nàngàmúhímà, námwìitè** 'if I defeat him and I kill him'. In the word **námwìitè (n-ná-mú-yìit-e)** (1SG-SBSC-O.1-kill- Fe) no matter where the first-person subject marker is placed, it precedes a nasal, because of the initial position of the cl. 1 object marker in the verb macrostem.

(2.96a, b). Note that in both (2.96a, b)⁶⁹ the **ná-** morpheme precedes the subject marker. Compare those with the continuative form in (2.96c), and the resultative form in (2.96d), where the subject is third-person singular rather than first-person singular, so that the normal order of the prefixes is observed: the subject comes first and the **ná-** marker afterwards.

(2.96)   a.   <u>ná-n</u>-gánùùl-è   =nà   wéèhê   'and I converse with you'
               CON-1SG-converse-Fe   CNJ   you (SG)

          b.   <u>ná-n</u>-gì-góóz-ír-w-ì   'and I still have a problem'
               ADD.V-1SG-PERS-have.problem-RS-PS-Fi

cf.   c.   <u>à-ná</u>-gánùùl-è   =nà   wéèhê   'and he converse with you'
               1-CON-converse-Fe   CNJ   you (SG)

cf.   d.   <u>à-ná</u>-kì-góóz-ír-w-ì   'and he still has a problem'
               1-ADD.V-PERS-have.problem-RS-PS-Fi

2.3.2.5 Spirantization rules

Spirantization (sometimes also called frication) is the phonological process by which a plosive or other non-fricative phoneme becomes a fricative. Historically this process happened following the Proto-Bantu "first degree" high tense vowels of the original seven vowel system, *i̧ and *u̧ (which were distinct from the more lax second degree vowels *ɪ and *ʊ). Kifuliiru has only five vowels, as the result of a merger of the first degree and second degree vowels.

Historically, spirantization took place preceding any first degree vowel, so that Proto-Bantu *-kádi̧ 'woman' became -kàzì (**múkàzì**) in Kifuliiru (with the plosive *d becoming the fricative z preceding *i̧). Likewise, PB*-jògu̧ 'elephant' became -jóvù (**njóvù**) (with plosive *g becoming fricative v preceding *u̧). In the same way, PB*-ku̧du̧ 'tortoise' became -fùlò (**káfùlò**) (with *k being spirantized to **f**), etc.

Though the effects of this historical spirantization remain in the Kifuliiru lexicon, there is no longer any phonologically motivated spirantization in the language. However, morphologically motivated spirantization is a productive

---

⁶⁹Note that in (2.96b), **ki-** 'persistive, durative' (which surfaces **gi-** because of the voicing conditioned by the preceding nasal subject marker) is an aspect marker, and so is in aspect position, which follows the consecutive. It is not in the tense position; if it were, it would precede the consecutive marker.

process today in Kifuliiru. It is conditioned by two specific morphemes which historically had a first degree vowel, the resultative final -**ir**-**i**, and causative -**i**. In the synchronically active resultative and causative spirantization, one can roughly say that **t, k, g, l/r, nd**, and **ng** become either **s** or **z**, depending on the voicedness of the original segment, cf. (2.97).

Besides the synchronically active spirantization conditioned by these two morphemes, and the lexicalized spirantization observable within lexical roots, there are also agentive, adjective, and some causative forms in which the effects of derivational spirantization have been lexicalized. In certain lexicalized forms of the agentive and causative, and in adjectives, it can be seen that **mb**, which is not affected by the currently active process of spirantization, was at one time affected, becoming **mv** by the spirantization rule.[70]

The two verbal morphemes which condition spirantization in Kifuliiru today, resultative -**ir**-**i** and causative -**i**, work a bit differently from each other, and so are discussed separately below. Neither affects **mb**. Their effect on other prenasalized segments also seems to be in flux in the language, as is further detailed below.

2.3.2.5.1 *In verbs with resultative suffix*

The final consonant of a CV(V)C verb root ending in **k, t, l, r, g, ng**, or **nd** (plosives and laterals, with the exception of **b/mb**), or a longer stem with an extension ending in **k**, is spirantized when followed by the resultative suffix. Voicedness remains the same as that of the original stem-final segment.

The effects of the spirantization rule are shown in (2.97). Notice in (2.97g and h) that it affects both the reversive intransitive extension, -**uk**/-**ok** and the stative/neuter/impositive extensions -**ek**/-**ik**. Note in (2.97c, d) that the treatment of the **t** of the -**at** extension is in flux in the language. It is sometimes spirantized as in (2.97c) and sometimes used with an imbricated form as in (2.97d).

In general, voiceless segments **t** and **k** are spirantized to **s**, and the voiced segments **r, l, nd, ng**, and **g** are spirantized to **z**.[71] Other consonants are unaffected by the spirantization rule. Free glosses in the right hand column below are 'he has ..... (and the effects remain)'.

---

[70]It then was changed to **v** by the rule of nasal effacement preceding fricatives.

[71]Recall, however, that **l** and **r** in particular and sometimes **t** and **n** are sometimes deleted (instead of being spirantized) when they are the final consonant of a verbal extension. This is discussed above in section 2.3.2.3.2, deletion of stem-final consonants in resultative verb forms. When they are the final consonant of a CV(V)C verb stem, they are spirantized.

2.3 Phonological rules and processes

(2.97)

	C	Infinitive	Gloss	w/resultative	Gloss
a.	t	ú=kúgwáátà	'to grasp'	à-gwáá<u>s</u>-ír-ì	1-hold-RS-Fi
b.		ú=kúdètà	'to speak'	à-dè<u>s</u>-ír-ì	1-speak-RS-Fi
c.		ú=kúhàgátà	'to hang on shoulder'	à-hàgá<u>s</u>-ír-ì	1-hang.on. shoulder-RS-Fi
cf. d.		ú=kúfùùmbátà	'to have in hand'	à-fùmb-íít-ì	1-have. in.hand-RS-Fi
e.	k	ú=kúbííkà	'to put'	à-bíí<u>s</u>-ír-ì	1-put-RS-Fi
f.		ú=kúfúkà	'to pour water'	à-fú<u>s</u>-ìr-ì	1-pour.water-RS-Fi
g.		ú=kúshònóókà	'to climb down'	à-shònóó<u>s</u>-ír-ì	1-climb.down-RS-Fi
h.		ú=kúfùmbádíkà	'to hand to s/o'	à-fùmbádí<u>s</u>-ír-ì	1-hand.to.s/o-RS-Fi
i.	r	ú=kúgírà	'to do'	à-gí<u>z</u>-ìr-ì	1-do-RS-Fi
j.		ú=kúbwíírà	'to tell'	à-bwíí<u>z</u>-ír-ì	1-tell-RS-Fi
k.	l	ú=kúgúlà	'to buy'	à-gú<u>z</u>-ìr-ì	1-buy-RS-Fi
l.		ú=kúhúúlà	'to grind'	à-húú<u>z</u>-ír-ì	1-grind-RS-Fi
m.	g	ú=kúsháágà	'to go away'	à-sháá<u>z</u>-ír-ì	1-go.away-RS-Fi
n.		ú=kútègà	'to trap'	à-tè<u>z</u>-ír-ì	1-trap-RS-Fi
o.	nd	ú=kúgééndà	'to go'	à-géé<u>z</u>-ìr-ì	1-go-RS-Fi
p.		ú=kúkūūndà	'to love'	à-kùù<u>z</u>-ír-ì	1-love-RS-Fi
q.	ng	ú=kúlēēngà	'to pass'	à-lèè<u>z</u>-ír-ì	1-pass-RS-Fi
r.		ú=kúlóóngà	'to get'	à-lóó<u>z</u>-ìr-ì	1-get-RS-Fi

If the verb stem ends with a labial consonant, a nasal, a glide, or a fricative, there is no change to the consonant when it is juxtaposed to the resultative suffix. That is to say that **b, m, mb, n, ny, j, h, sh, y, v** (and **s** and **z**, which in verb stem-final position are always themselves the product of spirantization from the causative extension) remain unchanged when followed by the resultative ending, as shown in (2.98).

(2.98)

Final C	Infinitive	Gloss	w/resultative	Gloss
b	ú=kúyìtábà	'to respond'	à-yìtáb-ír-ì	1-respond-RS-Fi
mb	ú=kúráámbà	'to live long'	à-ráámb-ìr-ì	1-live.long-RS-Fi
m	ú=kúhéémà	'to swell'	à-héém-ír-ì	1-swell-RS-Fi
n	ú=kútònà	'to think.sthg'	à-tòn-ír-ì	1-think.sthg-RS-Fi
ny	ú=kúshéényà	'to get firewood'	à-shéény-ír-ì	1-get.firewood-RS-Fi
j	ú=kúyáájà	'to spread out'	à-yááj-ìr-ì	1-get-RS-Fi
y	ú=kúkáyà	'to be fierce'	à-kááy-ìr-ì	1-be.fierce-RS-Fi
vw	ú=kúyùùvwâ	'to hear'	à-yùùvw-ít-ì	1-hear-RS-Fi
h	ú=kúyòòbóhà	'to fear'	à-yòbòh-ír-ì	1-fear-RS-Fi
sh	ú=kúbìshà	'to hide'	à-bìsh-ír-ì	1-hide-RS-Fi
s	ú=kúhísâ	'to bring home bride'	à-hís-īīz-ì	1-bring.home.bride-RS-Fi
z	ú=kúbúúzâ	'to ask'	à-búz-fìz-ì	1-ask-RS-Fi

2.3.2.5.2 In the causative form of verbs

The short form of the causative morpheme, -i, (historically *-į) conditions spirantization of the voiced segments **r**, **l**, and **g** to **z**, and the voiceless segments **t** and **k** to **s**. In addition, (historically at least) **ng** is spirantized to **z** and **mb/b** to **v**. Other consonants which occur stem finally preceding the short causative, notably **h**, **m**, and **n**, remain stable and do not spirantize.

This short form of the causative may occur as the only form of the causative within a given verb, or it may be a "copy" of the causative, used in a verb which also contains either the long or short causative further to the left. Such a "copy" is added following a subsequent extension, in order to keep the causative in the position immediately preceding the final vowel.

The long form of the causative morpheme, -iisi/-eesi, does not condition spirantization of the final consonant of the verb stem, as only the final -i of this morpheme (and not the initial ii of the long form) causes spirantization, e.g. **kúgúlíísâ** 'to sell' (from **kú-gúl-iisí-a**) versus **kúgúzâ** (from **kú-gúl-í-a**) 'to put something up for sale'.

Words in which **mb/b** spirantizes to **v**, or **ng** to **z**, may well be "frozen" relics of a process that is no longer productive. The process of spirantization and even the use of the short causative with NC-final verb stems seems to have fallen (or be falling) out of use. Example (2.99) shows forms which exemplify spirantization, as well as the alternate forms which are used. Such alternate forms are either used interchangeably with the

2.3 Phonological rules and processes

spirantized form, or in cases where the spirantized form has taken on a specialized meaning, as a productive causative of the original base word. The words in (2.99) which have prenasalized final consonants also show the effects of nasal effacement. The last three examples show the non-spirantizing consonants, for contrast. Each causative example is formed as follows: (AU=15-stem-CS-Fa), and has the gloss of causing the action of the verb to be done.

(2.99)	Final C	Non-CS infinitive	Gloss (non-CS)	-i CS form	Alternate form (if any)
	mb	ú=kú-kùlúúmb-à	AU=15-roll-Fa (INTRANS)	ú=kú-kùlúú<u>v</u>-y-â	
		ú=kú-jāāmb-à	AU=15-become.thin-Fa	ú=kú-jàà<u>v</u>-y-â	ú=kú-jàmb-íís-â
		ú=kú-jùgúúmb-à	AU=15-shake-Fa (INTRANS)	ú=kú-jùgúú<u>v</u>-y-â	ú=kú-jùgúúmb-y-â
	ng	ú=kú-kāāng-à	AU=15-startled-Fa	ú=kú-kàà<u>z</u>-â	ú=kú-kàng-íís-â
		ú=kú-yōōng-à	AU=15-suck.the.breast-Fa	ú=kú-yòò<u>z</u>-â	ú=kú-yòng-éés-â
	b	ú=kú-lób-à	AU=15-get.wet-Fa	ú=kú-ló<u>v</u>-y-â	
		ú=kú-shób-à	AU=15-be.messed.up-Fa	ú=kú-shó<u>v</u>-y-a	
	g	ú=kú-nòg-à	AU=15-be.soft-Fa	ú=kú-nò<u>z</u>-â	
	r	ú=kú-gér-à	AU=15-measure-Fa	ú=kú-gé<u>z</u>-â	
		ú=kú-kìr-à	AU=15-get.well-Fa	ú=kú-kì<u>z</u>-â	
	l	ú=kú-ból-à	AU=15-rot-Fa	ú=kú-bó<u>z</u>-â	
	t	ú=kú-dèt-à	AU=15-speak-Fa	ú=kú-dè<u>s</u>-â	
		ú=kú-fùùmbát-à	AU=15-grasp.in.hand-Fa	ú=kú-fùùmb-á<u>s</u>-â	

Final C	Non-CS infinitive	Gloss (non-CS)	-i CS form	Alternate form (if any)
k	ú=kú-làk-à	AU=15-resound-Fa	ú=kú-là s̱ â	
	ú=kú-lálúk-à	AU=15-be.drunk-Fa	ú=kú-lálú s̱ -â	
cf. m	ú=kú-hám-à	AU=15-get.big-Fa	ú=kú-hám-y-â	
cf. h	ú=kú-lááh-à	AU=15-get.long-Fa	ú=kú-lááh-y-â	
cf. n	ú=kú-kàn-à	AU=15-be.firm-Fa	ú=kú-kàn-í-à	

2.3.2.5.3 In the agentive form of nouns

The "agentive"[72] suffix -**i**, for deriving agentive nouns from verbs, always triggers spirantization in the final consonant of a verb stem which ends with **t**, **k**, **g**, **r**, **l**, **mb**, **nd**, **ng**, but does not condition spirantization in stems ending with **m** or **n**. In stems that already end with a fricative or approximant, e.g. **b**, **s**, **z**, **v**, **f**, **j**, there is no change. In (2.100) are provided some examples of the agentive suffix. We consider at least some of these nominal forms to be lexicalized (not productively derived.)

(2.100) <u>The following C's undergo spirantization preceding the agentive</u>

C	Infinitive	Gloss	UF agentive	SF agentive	Gloss
t	ú=kúdètà	'to speak'	/ú=mú-dèt-i/ /í=n-dèt-i/	ú=múdè s̱ ì/ íí=ndè s̱ ì	'speaker'
k	ú=kúyáándíkà	'to write'	/ú=mú-ándik-i/	ú=mwáándí s̱ ì	'writer'
g	ú=kúnyágà	'to rob'	/ú=mú-nyág-i/	ú=múnyá ẕ ì	'bandit'
r	ú=kúgálúkírà	'to return to (place)'	/í=N-galukir-i/	í=ngálúkí ẕ ì	'sthg. returning'
l	ú=kúkòlà	'to work'	/ú=mú-kòl-i/	ú=múkò ẕ ì	'servant'
mb	ú=kúbūūmbà	'to work clay'	/ú=mú-bumb-i/	ú=múbūū v̱ ì	'potter'
nd	ú=kúgééndà	'to go'	/ú=lu-génd-i/	ú=lúgéé ẕ ì	'journey'
ng	ú=kúhīīngà	'to farm'	/ú=mú-hīng-i/	ú=múhīī ẕ ì	'farmer'

---

[72]The same suffix is used on abstract nouns, with the same resultant spirantization, e.g. **kútábáálà** 'to help' > **ú=bútábáázì** 'help', **ú=kúyìgéndérérà** 'be patient' > **ú=bwìgéndérézì** 'patience', etc.

2.3 Phonological rules and processes

The following do not undergo spirantization preceding the agentive

C	Infinitive	Gloss	UF agentive	SF agentive	Gloss
m	ú=kúlímà	'work soil'	/ú=mú-lím-ì/	ú=múlímì	'farmer'
n	ú=kúyìtánà	'kill each other'	/ú=mú-ìt-an-i/	ú=mwììtánì	'murderer'
b	ú=kúdúbà	'to fish (w/net)'	/ú=mú-dúb-i/	ú=múdúbì	'fisherman'
j	ú=kúshōōjà	'to row boat'	/ú=mú-shòój-i/	ú=múshōōjì	'boatman'
v	ú=kúhīīvà	'to hunt'	/ú=mú-hìív-i/	ú=múhīīvì	'hunter'
z	ú=kútwéézâ	'to dip food'	/ú=mú-twéz-i/	ú=mútwéézì	'food dipper'

2.3.2.6 Copy rule: demonstrative

As is typical for Bantu languages, there are several different demonstratives in Kifuliiru. It can be posited that two of these demonstrative forms are produced (at least partially) by a morpheme-specific rule of phonological copying, a sort of modified reduplication.

The base of these two demonstratives is the demonstrative prefix of the appropriate class. The CV pattern of these two demonstrative forms differs according to whether the base of the form consists of V (as in cl. 1, 4, 9) or CV (as in the other classes.) These demonstratives have yV^1CV^1 forms in classes where there is a CV base, and V^1yV^1 forms for classes which have a V base (the V^1s here indicate identical vowels). For example cl. 3 (with a **gu-** demonstrative prefix) has the 'proximal' demonstrative **yúúgù** 'this.P+3'. Cl. 1, with a **u-** demonstrative prefix, has the proximal demonstrative **úúyù** 'this.P+1'.[73] The 'nearby' form, e.g. **yùùgwó** 'that.N+3', **ùùyó** 'that.N+1' is produced by adding the "**o** of (previous) reference" to the proximal form.

The rule which produces the proximal form (e.g. **yúúgù**) "reduplicates" the demonstrative prefix, except that the C of a CV prefix is copied not as the specific consonant found in the prefix (which would instead yield the non-existent form *****gugu**), but as the unspecified consonant, **y-** (see also 2.101a–d).

Demonstrative prefixes of V-only form (as found in cl. 1, 4, and 9) are copied or reduplicated only as a V, and then a **y** is epenthesized by a subsequent rule, between the two vowels, to separate the two identical vowels which

---

[73]There is lengthening of the initial vowel in the case of these V initial forms, apparently due to the same sort of minimality constraints which cause lengthening of vowels in clitics. The lengthening in the **y**VCV forms is due to post-glide compensatory lengthening.

result from the copy rule. A few examples are given in (2.101e–g). The gloss in each case is 'this/these.P' (**yáábà, yúúgù**, etc.) or 'that/those.N' (**yààbô, yùùgwô**, etc.)

Note that (2.101a–d) (cl. 2, 3, 7, and 10), as well as any other class with a demonstrative prefix (DP) of the shape CV, have an initial **y**- produced by the copy rule. Those classes with a V-only DP, shown in (2.101e–g), i.e. cl. 1, 4, 9, lack the initial **y**-. Tone on these examples reflects use with no following substantive, and a copulative meaning, e.g. **yáábà** 'they are these (people)'.

(2.101)

	Class	Copy C	Copy V	DP	this proximal	Gloss	that nearby	Gloss
a.	2	y	a	ba	**yáábà**	'these'	**yààbô**	'those'
b.	3	y	u	gu	**yúúgù**	'this'	**yùùgwô**	'those'
c.	7	y	i	ki	**yííkì**	'this'	**yììkyô**	'that'
d.	10	y	i	zi	**yíízì**	'these'	**yììzô**	'those'
e.	1	--	u	u	**úúyù**	'this'	**ùùyô**	'that'
f.	4	--	i	i	**ííyì**	'these'	**ììyô**	'those'
g.	9	--	i	i	**ííyì**	'this'	**ììyô**	'that'

2.4 Syllable structure, word structure, and syllable prominence

Kifuliiru has two basic syllable types: V and CV.

The C in a CV syllable may be realized as a simple C, or as N, NC, (N)(C)w, or (N)(C)y. Thus, a labialized or palatalized consonant is interpreted systemically as a modified C, and not as a CC sequence. There are no unambiguous CC sequences in Kifuliiru.

The V in either the V or CV syllable may be short or long (i.e. the possibilities for syllables are: V or VV, CV or CVV). Thus, long vowels are interpreted as V:,[74] rather than as two separate vowels. There are no disparate VV sequences in surface forms, except in borrowed words, where they are pronounced as glides.

A V-only syllable is always word initial and followed by a CV syllable, never by another V syllable. That is, a VV sequence anywhere in the language is always monosyllabic, and never constitutes two separate syllables (though it may be bimorphemic). Thus, words are of the type (V)CV(CVCV...).

A long vowel (V:) is not normally allowed in word final position.[75] There are no word final long vowels at the lexical level. However, a final vowel may be

---

[74]Long vowels in this book are transcribed as VV, instead of V: .

[75]However, a word which has underlying H tone on the final syllable displays phonetic length-

2.4 Syllable structure, word structure, and syllable prominence

lengthened at the discourse level, if a person is stressing the great extent of something indicated by a word, e.g. **à-ná-gèènd-ááá** (1+P1-SQ-go-Fa) 'and he went...(on and on and on)'. Note from the retention of vowel length in the verb stem that at this level, the rule of mora-based vowel shortening is not triggered. A vowel may also be lengthened like this while thinking up what to say next, much as in English one might say, "Welllllll...." or "Hmmm...". Exceptions to this constraint against word final long vowels are also found in interjections, e.g. **yééé!** 'interjection of surprise or disbelief', **yóóó!** 'interjection of surprise', **yòòò!** 'exclamation of sympathy, disappointment', **tííí** 'ideophone showing continuation, rapid progression', etc.

As mentioned above, the mora-based vowel shortening rule precludes the possibility of more than one long V in any phonological word. This is because a long V may not precede more than two morae within the word. Each short vowel counts as one mora, while each long vowel counts as two. The effect of the shortening rule plus the constraint against long vowels in the final syllable is that the antepenult and penultimate syllables are the only ones that may have long vowels.

The surface penultimate syllable in Kifuliiru seems to be the one with the most prominence. This is evidenced by the fact that phonemic HL (realized on the surface as a mid tone) and LH tones occur only on the penultimate syllable.[76]

There is a strong tendency in Kifuliiru to avoid monosyllabic phonological words. The optimal phonological word consists of at least two syllables, and at least three morae. Monosyllabic lexical words do exist, as will be shown below. However, a monosyllabic lexical word is never allowed to stand alone within a phrase as a surface phonological word. There are three strategies in Kifuliiru which seem to be aimed specifically at the elimination of monosyllabic words. These strategies are:

- cliticizing the monosyllabic word to a preceding or following word within the phrase;
- adding an extra morpheme or clitic to the word; or
- epenthesizing a vowel in order to add an extra syllable (2.3.2.2.4).

2.4.1 Cliticization of monosyllabic words

If a monosyllabic word is used in Kifuliiru without any epenthesis or morpheme addition to make it at least bisyllabic, it must be joined to any

---

ening of the final vowel in utterance-final position.

[76]There is a phonetic rule that can produce HL also on a final syllable. But in this case, the underlying tone is H, and only the surface realization is HL.

preceding or following word by the rule of monosyllable cliticization. Thus a word like **fwì** 'fish (PL)', though it can be pronounced in isolation, if used in a phrase, and without the augment, must be encliticized to the preceding word, e.g. **yììzó=fwì** 'those.N=fish'.

Cliticization of a monosyllabic lexical word to a preceding or following word within the phrase is the most common strategy in Kifuliiru for eliminating monosyllables.[77] This strategy is illustrated below with monosyllables of various grammatical categories, with evidence from various phonological phenomena.

2.4.1.1 Evidence from tone and vowel length phenomena

The fact that the cliticization takes two lexical words and makes them into a single phonological word is indicated by what happens both in the vowel length phenomena and in the tones. This will be illustrated first by the comparison of examples taken from monosyllabic adjectives.

As was stated in the section on **i**-epenthesis in monosyllabic words, if a monosyllabic adjective stem begins with a plosive, **i**-epenthesis is only one of the strategies available for making its cl. 9/10 forms polysyllabic. There is also the option of forming a monosyllabic adjective and cliticizing it to the preceding noun. The two strategies available for such an adjective are illustrated in (2.102) with the plosive-initial monosyllabic adjective stem -**bi** 'bad'. As is seen in (2.102a, b), in cl. 9/10 there are two alternative forms. The meanings of these two forms are identical, and either may be used in any context.[78]

(2.102)	Class	Pref + stem		Adjective	SF	Gloss
a.	9/10	N+bí	→	nyíbì	ínyúùmbà <u>ny</u>íbì	'bad house'
b.	9/10	N+bí	→	mbî	ínyúùmbáa̲m̲bî	'bad house'
cf. c.	1	mu+bí	→	múbì	úmúúndú múbì	'bad person'
cf. d.	9/10	N+hámu	→	mbámù	ínyúùmbà mbámù	'big house'

As seen in the orthographic and phonetic forms of (2.102b), if the choice is made to not use **i**-epenthesis to avoid having a monosyllabic adjective, the monosyllabic adjective must then be cliticized to the preceding noun,[79] since

---

[77] For further discussion of word boundary issues, see appendix.

[78] The form in (2.102b) is, however, considered by some to be more "authentic." It is not used as a citation form, though. Either the **nyíbì** form, or one of a different noun class (with a CV prefix) would be chosen for a citation form of the adjective.

[79] It is actually much more common to cliticize a monosyllable to a following word. This is

2.4 Syllable structure, word structure, and syllable prominence

there is no following word within the phrase. Note that the monosyllabic adjective, **mbí** 'bad' is cliticized to the preceding noun, **ínyúùmbà** 'house'. This cliticization is attested by the vowel length and tonal phenomena.

First let us look at the vowel length phenomena. In (2.102a) **ínyúùmbà nyíbì** 'bad house', the noun **ínyúùmbà** 'house' displays compensatory vowel lengthening before the NC cluster, shown by the **uu** preceding **mb**, while the final vowel, as is always the case for word final vowels, is short. When we look at the phonetic form of (2.102b), we see that the **u** of **í=nyúùmbà** has not been shortened to **í=nyúmbá**, as it would be if the adjective were actually a part of the lexical word. However, compensatory vowel length is now found also in the following syllable, which now has **áà** preceding the initial NC cluster of the adjective, **m-bì** 'bad': **í=nyúùmbáà=mbî**.

Observation of the vowel length in (2.102b) shows two things: First, we note that the long vowel in **í=nyúùmbà** 'house' has not been shortened by the mora-based shortening rule. This shows that there are still no more than two morae following it within the lexical word.[80] Secondly, we see the lengthening of the final **a** of **í=nyúùmbà** preceding **mbì**. The presence of a long vowel here shows that the **a** is no longer (only) a word-final vowel, since word-final long vowels are disallowed. The formerly-final **a** is lengthened because it now precedes the cliticized adjective. The lengthening of the vowel here is obligatory for word-final vowel which is followed by an encliticized monosyllabic noun (including verbal infinitive) or adjective (2.3.1.2.5).

This is not merely compensatory lengthening triggered by the following NC sequence, since the same lengthening is seen in environments where there is no following NC, such as the compound word **námúlóbáà=fwì** 'type of water bird' or **ànákìzíì=ryâ** 'and he repeatedly ate' (cf. **ànákìzì gééndà** 'and he repeatedly went', where the final word is not monosyllabic, and therefore not cliticized, and where there is no lengthening of the final **i** of **kizi**). Instead, this lengthening of a vowel which precedes a nominal or adjectival clitic seems to be a strategy to increase the syllable count of the cliticized monosyllabic word. It does not happen when the following word has two or more syllables: compare (2.102d), **í=nyúùmbà mbámù** 'big house', where the final syllable of the noun **í=nyúùmbà** is not lengthened, but has a short vowel even though it precedes (within the phrase) a word which begins with a NC cluster. The difference between (2.102b, d) is the fact that the monosyllabic adjective

---

done whenever there is a following word within the phrase. The cliticization of the associative marker, e.g. **wa** in **ú=múúndú wá=kàbìrì** 'the second person', is a common example of cliticization to a following word.

[80]If pronounced quickly, however, this phrase becomes **í=nyúmbáà=mbì** with a short H-toned vowel in **nyúmbá** rather than a long vowel with a HL tone.

m-bí (9/10-bad) has been cliticized, and the bisyllabic adjective, m-bámù (9/10-big) has not.

The minimality requirement that a noun, verb, or adjective should have at least two syllables and three morae seems to take precedence here over the vowel shortening rule which works towards no more than one long vowel per phonological word. Thus the second long vowel in í=nyúùmbáà=mbî functions on two levels. Its first mora serves as a final vowel for the host word, while at the same time one or both morae serve as part of the structure of the following cliticized monosyllabic adjective.

Tonal phenomena observable in (2.102b) also give evidence that the monosyllabic adjective has been cliticized. In the cliticized form, í=nyúùmbáà=mbì the HL contour originally seen on the **uu** of í=nyúùmbà is still there. The presence of this HL contour on the **uu** is significant because a HL contour in Kifuliiru may only be realized on a *long* vowel in a *penultimate* syllable. This means that the syllable **nyúù** is still penultimate at some level. Observe, however, that the **aa** now also bears a HL contour in í=nyúùmbáà=mbî. Because there has been cliticization, there has been reinterpretation of the compound unit from [í=nyúù-mbà]_w [mbí]_w to [í=nyúùmb[á]à=mbî]_w.[81] Since a HL contour will surface only in the penultimate syllable position, the fact that there is now a HL contour in both long vowels of this word show that both are counted as penultimate syllables, one the penultimate of the original bisyllabic word, **nyúùmbà**, and the other on the penultimate syllable of the product of encliticization. Thus there is a mismatch between the lexical level and the phrase level.

2.4.1.2 *Evidence from vowel coalescence*

Besides the tonal and vowel length phenomena noted above as evidence for cliticization of monosyllables at the phrase level, in instances where a monosyllabic word is cliticized to a following vowel-initial word (such as is the case with associative markers) vowel coalescence is also a strong indicator of the nature of this process.

As was noted earlier, Kifuliiru has one vowel coalescence rule that works at lexical (word building) level (see 2.3.1.2.2.2) and another, with different outputs, that works at the postlexical (phrase-building) level (see 2.3.1.2.2.3). When non-like vowels are coalesced, the two rules result in different output vowels. For example, **a** + **i** > **ii** at lexical level (prefix plus stem **bá-** **īru** > **bíírù** 'black ones'), or suffix plus suffix in verbs (-**bwata-ir-i** > -**bwatiiri** 'sitting'), but

---

[81] The brackets are intended to show that the final long **a** functions as a part of two underlying words.

2.4 Syllable structure, word structure, and syllable prominence 101

a + i > ee at postlexical level as seen in (2.103a).[82] That it is postlexical vowel coalescence which takes place between a cliticized monosyllable and the word to which it is attached is a clear indicator that there were two lexical words[83] to begin with, and not just a prefix and a stem. Coalescence between a prefix and a stem follows the lexical coalescence rules and not the postlexical rules.

Associative markers are always monosyllabic words, and thus are always cliticized onto the following noun. This is shown by the mandatory vowel coalescence that takes place between them and the augment of the following noun, illustrated in the example phrases in (2.103). These phrases cannot be pronounced as phrases without the vowel coalescence having taken place.

(2.103)	Cl. A.M	AU	A.M + AÚ=noun	SF	Gloss
a.	3 gu-a	í →	gw<u>a+í</u>=mbènè	gwéémbènè	'of the goat'
b.	6 ga-a	ú →	g<u>aa+ú</u>=kúnywâ	góókúnywâ	'of drinking'
c.	6 ga-a	ú →	g<u>aa+ú</u>=kúyìkàrábà	g<u>ó</u>kúyìkàrábà	'of washing oneself'
d.	7 ki-a	à →	ky<u>a+á</u>=bákàzì	ky<u>á</u>bákàzì	'of the women'

The augment (AU) in Kifuliiru is a phrase level clitic which, if present, is positioned on the initial word of its phrase (see Vol. 2, 7.2). Thus that the augment is present on the noun in the "A.M+AU=noun" column above indicates that this noun is functioning as the initial word of a noun phrase. The associative marker (A.M) is not a prefix on this augment-plus-noun unit, but a proclitic in the associative phrase. Though syntactically a phrase, it comprises a single (postlexical) phonological word consisting of the associative marker plus the augment plus the noun. The quality of the vowel produced by the coalescence of the A.M and the AU shows that postlexical rather than lexical vowel coalescence takes place between the associative clitic and the following augment-plus-noun.

That postlexical coalescence is happening here shows that the associative marker is a separate (monosyllabic) lexical word and not a "formative" nor a prefix. If the associative markers were prefixes rather than separate words, lexical vowel coalescence would take place in this environment, resulting in the faulty output ***uu=muko gwii=mbene** and ***a=miiji guu=kunywa**, for the

---

[82] The same sort of coalescence that takes place between the associative marker and noun also takes place between any two vowels juxtaposed and coalesced within a phrase. Recall the earlier example, **àgééndà íkâāyà > àgééndé#kâāyà** 'he went home'.

[83] Some might be more comfortable calling the monosyllabic words "clitics" rather than "words". However, it is clear that they are functioning as separate entities at the beginning of the postlexical level, rather than functioning at the sublexical level as prefixes do. See appendix on word boundaries for more discussion of "What is a word?".

first two examples above rather than **úú=múkó gwéé=mbènè** 'the blood of the goats' and **á=mììjí góó=kúnywà** 'water for drinking'.[84]

While it is the quality of the vowel produced by coalescence that proves that there were two words to begin with, it is the vowel length phenomena in the resultant vowel that shows that the result of that coalescence is a single phonological word. When two vowels coalesce, theoretically the resultant vowel consists at some level of two morae. However, the surface length of the vowel which results from coalescence of a clitic plus the initial vowel of a host word is dependent on the number of morae in the word to which the clitic is attached. If there are three or more morae following the clitic within the word, the vowel is short. If there are two or fewer, the vowel is long.

Comparing the length of the vowels of the A.Ms in (2.103b, c), i.e. **á=mììjí góó=kúnywà** 'water for drinking' and **á=mììjí gó=kúyìkàrábà** 'water for washing oneself', we see that the vowel shortening rule which shortens the vowel of a clitic which is followed by fewer than three morae operates on the vowel of the A.M. There is a long **o** in **góó=kúnywâ**.[85] This vowel length results from the coalescence of the vowel of the associative marker and the vowel of the augment on the following noun. Compare this to the short **o** in (2.103c), **gó=kúyìkàrábà**. This **o**, like the one in (2.103b), results from the coalescence of two vowels, and should therefore be long. However, in the case of **gó=kúyìkàrábà**, the **o** is followed *within the word* by more than three morae, and thus is shortened by the rule of mora-based vowel shortening (**ga=ú=kúyìkàrábà** > **góó=kúyìkàrábà** > **gó=kúyìkàrábà**.) This shortening applies over the domain of the phonological word, and the fact that it applies to the combination of the associative marker plus noun is clear evidence that such a clitic group is treated as a single phonological word.

2.4.1.3 Proclitics versus enclitics

A proclitic is a word cliticized to "lean on" a following word, while an enclitic is cliticized to the end of a preceding word. In Kifuliiru, cliticizing a monosyllable to a following word, producing a proclitic, is the strategy preferred over cliticizing it to the preceding word, producing an enclitic.

The monosyllabic forms which best illustrate both proclitics and enclitics are the pronominal forms which are formed using what Ashton (1959:19) called the "**o** of reference". They include relative pronouns like (2.104a, b);

---

[84]Orthographically, the fact that the associative markers are separate words which have undergone coalescence, rather than prefixes, is marked by the presence of an apostrophe, e.g. **úúmúkó gwéé'mbènè; ámììjì góó'kúnywà**.

[85]Orthographically, both **á=mììjì góó=kúnywà** and **á=mììjì gó=kúyìkàrábà** are written with a short **o**, as **amiiji go'kunywa** and **amiiji go'kuyikaraba** since speakers of Kifuliiru will automatically lengthen the **o** in the proper place.

2.4 Syllable structure, word structure, and syllable prominence

non-incorporated pronominal object markers, as in (2.104c); and locative pronominal forms, as in (2.104d, e). Comparable pronominal forms in related languages are often referred to as "suffixes" in the literature, but the fact that they cliticize to a following word when possible, rather than attaching to the preceding word, shows that they are clitics rather than suffixes, at least in Kifuliiru. Only when the monosyllabic word is the final word in the utterance does it become an enclitic, leaning on the preceding word, as seen in (2.104c, d). If there is a following word within the phrase, the monosyllable is cliticized to this following word, as in (2.104a, b, f, g).

(2.104)	Type of functor	SF	Gloss
a.	Focus pronoun	**tw-é=tú-gá-gèènd-à** 2PL-FOC=2PL-F2-go-Fa	'we are the ones who will go'
b.	Relative pronoun	**tw-é=bá-kòzì bà-à-wè** 2PL-FOC=2-servants 2-A.M-2SG	'we who are your servants'
c.	Extra obj. mkr.	**à-bà-gwát-ír-à=byô** S.R-2-hold-APL-Fa=8	'he held them (8) for them (2)'
d.	Loc. obj. mkr.	**bà-ná-béèr-à=mwô** 2-SQ-remain-Fa=18	'and they remained in there'
cf. e.	Explicit obj., no extra obj. mkr	**à-bà-gwáát-ír-à í-bí-kòlànwà** S.R-2-hold-APL-Fa AU= 8-equipment	'he held the equipment for them (2)'
f.	Loc. obj. mkr.	**bà-ná-mál-á mw-éé=sìkù zì-shàtù** 2-SQ-finish-Fa 18+AU=days 10-three	'and they finished in there 3 days'
g.	Loc. obj. mkr.	**bà-ná-mál-á mw-é=my-èèzí í-shátù** 2-SQ-finish-Fa 18+AU=4-month 4-three	'and they finished in there 3 months'

Looking at (2.104c, e) we see that there is a difference in vowel length in the applicativized verb -**gwaat-ir**- 'hold for'. In (2.104e) the compensatory vowel lengthening following the glide in **à-bà-gwáát-ír-à** (1+P1-O2-hold-APL-Fa) 'he held for them' is present in the surface form. However in (2.104c), where the pronoun **byô** 'them (8)' is cliticized to the verb, adding another mora to the phonological word, the rule of mora-based vowel shortening has neutralized the compensatory lengthening and we find **àbàgwátírà=byô**. The fact that the pronoun and verb are combined in a single phonological word might lead us to think that the pronoun is perhaps a suffix. However, suffixes on Bantu verbs always precede the final vowel. If this were a suffix, it would be exceptional, in that it *follows* the final vowel of the verb.

Besides that, this alleged "suffix", if followed by another word within the utterance, becomes instead a proclitic, attaching itself to the beginning of the following word, as seen by comparing (2.104d, f). In (2.104d) where there is no word following, the pronoun is cliticized to the preceding word. As soon as there is another word within the utterance, however, as seen in (2.104f) with the addition of the oblique phrase **sìkù zì-shàtù** 'three days', the monosyllable is no longer cliticized to the verb as an enclitic, as it was in (2.104d), but rather is joined as a proclitic to the first element of the oblique phrase. The fact that the **mwó** is joined to the first word of the oblique phrase in (2.104e) is indicated by the (mandatory) vowel coalescence between **mwó** 'in there' and **ísìkù**, resulting in **mwéé=sìkù**. The vowel length seen in **mwéé** in (2.104f), compared with the lack of length in the same spot in (2.104g), where the long vowel has been shortened by the lexical level rule of mora-based vowel shortening, shows that the proclitic and its "host" are joined into a single phonological word.

2.4.2 Elimination of monosyllabic words by addition of morphemes

Besides cliticization, another strategy used in Kifuliiru to avoid the pronunciation of a monosyllabic word is the addition of an extra morpheme to the word. This strategy is often used when the monosyllabic word is alone in its phrase. This is illustrated by the imperative singular form of monosyllabic verb stems.

The imperative form of the verb consists of the verb root with final vowel and a null prefix, e.g. **sháágà!** 'you (SG) go away!' or **shàágî!** 'you (PL) go away!' As in most languages, imperatives are often "stand-alone" forms, used as an utterance in and of themselves, with no preceding or following words. The imperative form of a verb such as **kúlyâ** 'to eat', **lyâ**, gives the example of a situation in which there is a monosyllable with no preceding or following word to which the monosyllable could be cliticized.[86] In such a case, the monosyllabic imperative may be pronounced alone, but more often it is augmented,

---

[86]In Kiswahili, the problem is solved for such verbs by retaining the infinitive prefix in forms such as the imperative, which would otherwise be monosyllabic. Cf. Kiswahili **ku-la** 'eat!' versus **piga** 'hit!'.

2.4 Syllable structure, word structure, and syllable prominence

either by a following object, e.g. **lyá=byó=kúlyâ** 'eat the food'; by an interjection such as **ngànà** or **nyènê**, which give a sense like 'just ..!', e.g. **lyá=ngànà** 'just eat!'; or by the addition of a subject prefix or an object prefix. If an object or subject prefix is added, the final vowel is changed to the subjunctive final vowel -**e**, e.g. **úúbìlyè!** 'you (SG) eat them!'.

(2.105)

	Infinitive	Imperative		Imperative with added morpheme or word	Gloss
a.	**kú-gw-â**	**Ø-gw-â**	→	**gwáá=ngànà**	'just fall!'
b.	**kú-tw-â**	**Ø-tw-â**	→	**kí-twê**	'cut it (7)!'
c.	**kú-mw-â**	**Ø-mw-â**	→	**mwáá=ngànà**	'just shave!'

The strategy of adding another morpheme is also used with monosyllabic nouns, as, for example, **n-dá** (9-pregnancy). Such a word, though a complete word with prefix and stem, because of its brevity is not comfortably pronounceable unless one adds an augment, a locative marker, etc. With the extra morpheme it is pronounceable as **íí=ndá** 'the pregnancy', or **múú=ndá** 'in the abdomen', etc. If there is no added morpheme, the word is encliticized to another word (2.4.1), e.g. **ìrìì=ndá** 'it is a pregnancy'. A monosyllabic noun is very rarely used in isolation without an additional morpheme.

2.4.3 Syllable structure inventory for noun stems

The vast majority of noun stems[87] in Kifuliiru are at least bisyllabic, with a significant percentage having three syllables or more. Table 2.4. presents a count of all the simple noun stems found in a random database of Kifuliiru words. Based on this table, the following observations can be made:

A strong majority of Kifuliiru noun stems (64.3%) are comprised of two syllables. A smaller, but still relatively large, number have stems of more than two syllables (21.5% composed of three syllables stems and 9.2% with four syllable stems.) The smallest number of stems (4.9%) is composed of one syllable. Of these one-syllable stems, only those with cl. 9/10 prefixes and no augment will yield a monosyllabic noun word.

---

[87]Note: This section is focused on noun stems (not roots), the majority of which are derived from verbs. It is meant to give a "feel" for the way the language is put together. "Stems" here refers to the part of the noun which does not include the prefixes, though all nouns except cl. 1a require a concord prefix, and the use of the augment (pre-prefix) is usual in most cases in Kifuliiru. Complete nouns, including both prefix and augment, can be seen in the next to last column of table 2.4.

Any stem-initial vowel will interact with any vowel of a noun prefix, thus appearing in context as a noun with one of the following in the prefix syllable (first syllable following the augment): a long vowel, e.g. **íkíìtâ** 'share of meat', labialization, e.g. **úbwìtègèèrèzè** 'wisdom', or palatalization, e.g. **íkyùùbàtì** 'knife sheath', depending on the qualities of the vowels interacting.

Table 2.4. Syllable structure inventory for noun stems

# Syll	CV pattern of stem w/out pfx.	Total	% of Total	% Sub-total	Noun w/AU	Gloss
1	CV	58	4.9%	4.9%	íí=**kí-tá**	AU-7-largeness
2	V CV	92	7.7%	64.3%	í=**kí-ìtà**	AU-7-share of meat
	CV CV	520	43.7%		í=**kí-tùgò**	AU-7-shoulder
	CVV CV	154	12.9%		í=**kí-góòjè**	AU-7-maize
3	V CV CV	11	0.9%	21.5%	í=**ky-ùùbàtì**	AU-7-knife sheath
	V CVV CV	4	0.3%		í=**ky-ànyàànyà**	AU-7-sky
	CV CV CV	163	13.7%		í=**kí-shókómà**	AU-7-leopard
	CVV CV CV	26	2.2%		í=**kí-húúhúlù**	AU-7-dead thing
	CV CVV CV	52	4.4%		í=**kí-húhúùtà**	AU-7-strong wind
4	V CV CV CV	5	0.4%	9.2%	í=**ky-énènèkè**	AU-7-in public
	CV CV CV CV	95	8.0%		í=**kí-hòmógólò**	AU-7-small erosion
	CV CVV CV CV	4	0.3%		í=**kí-shókóólólò**	AU-7-thick brush
	CV CV CVV CV	6	0.5%		í=**kí-hùngùlèèrè**	AU-7-poor eyesight
Total		1190	100%			

2.4.4 Syllable structure inventory for verb bases

Table 2.5 presents a count of all the simple verb bases found in a random database of Kifuliiru words. Note that although the following count is approximate and includes a small number of reduplicated forms, productively derived forms, etc., nevertheless it gives a good idea of relative percentages. Note also that the final vowel is not included here in the CV pattern of the base, since it is always a separate morpheme, though it is a mandatory part of any verb word.

A '+' preceding the CV pattern in table 2.5 indicates that the reflexive object prefix forms the first syllable in at least some of the forms with this syllable pattern. Such verbs are included either because the reflexive form has been lexicalized as a part of the verb, i.e. the stem is not used without the reflexive,

2.4 Syllable structure, word structure, and syllable prominence

or the stem when used with the reflexive has a slightly different meaning (in addition to the connotation of reflexive action) from the same stem used without the reflexive.

Table 2.5. Syllable structure inventory for verb bases

# Syll	CV pattern of base	Total	% of Total	% Sub-total	Example, verb base	Gloss
1	CV	15	0.57	0.57%	-li-	'eat'
2	CV C	496	18.94	25.81%	-dèt-	'speak'
	CVV C	180	6.87		-beer-	'remain'
3	CV CV C	761	29.07	49.2%	-láhir-	'refuse'
	CVV CV C	106	4.05		-kuuman-	'gather'
	CV CVV C	421	16.08		-kúbeet-	'take by force'
4	CV CV CV C	433	16.54	22.38%	-dìbagul-	'cs.get fat'
	+CV CVV CV C	110	4.20		-híduukir-	'work hard'
	+CV CV CVV C	43	1.64		-yì-jèjeet-	'waddle'
5	+CV CV CV CV C	45	1.72	1.99%	-jàjagulik-	'be ripped up'
	+CV CV CVV CV C	7	0.27		-yì-yogookol-	'separate self'
6	CV CV CV CV CV C	1	0.04	.04%	-kòngobedekan-	'get thin'
Total		2,618	100%			

3

Tone

This chapter presents a detailed autosegmental analysis of Kifuliiru tone, with special emphasis on tone in verbal forms and constructions. We posit that the syllable is the basic tone-bearing unit (TBU), and that the penultimate syllable of a stem has the special ability to bear two tones regardless of whether it has one mora or two. Also, whereas in many Bantu languages a high tone seems to contrast synchronically only with its absence,[1] the analysis of Kifuliiru indicates a three-way distinction between high (H), low (L), and toneless (Ø). Kifuliiru has undergone a nearly total tone reversal relative to Proto-Bantu.

Following the presentation of the basics of Kifuliiru tone, details of verbal tone are described and discussed at length. The passive and causative extensions in Kifuliiru add a H tone to the right end of the verb, so forms with these extensions are included in the discussion of each grammatical stem-tone pattern.

Next we discuss general characteristics of tone association in Kifuliiru, followed by a presentation of the rules affecting tone at the word level, e.g. tone spread, various contour simplification rules, etc. There is also a description of lexical tone of various affixes and parts of speech, followed by a description of rules which affect tone at the phrase level, as well as of downdrift (very pervasive in the language) and downstep (quite rare).

---

[1]Including Mashi, according to the analysis by Louise Polak-Bynon (1975). Mashi is a language quite closely related to Kifuliiru and is spoken just to the north of the traditional Bafuliiru homeland.

3.1 Assumptions from autosegmental theory

The analysis of Kifuliiru tone presented here is based primarily on the theory of autosegmental phonology,[2] which posits that tones are not, at the most abstract level, connected to the individual sound segments of the word. Instead they are independent units (autonomous segments) on a separate level or "tonal tier". These independent tonal units are then "linked" or "associated" to the tone-bearing units (TBUs) by a process of derivational rules.[3] In the original formulation of the theory, it was posited that these rules, in the unmarked case, link the tones from left to right, with a one-to-one correspondence between tones and TBUs.[4] Any tone or tones related to a given lexical item (morpheme) at the underlying level are known as that morpheme's "lexical" tone(s).

There are three possible types of morphemes in any given language:
- morphemes consisting of both segment(s) and tone(s);
- morphemes consisting only of tone(s);
- morphemes consisting only of segment(s).

In a tonal Bantu language, all three of these morpheme types are typically present. The morphemes which consist of both segment(s) and tone(s) are usually the most common. Morphemes of the type consisting solely of a tone or combination (pattern) of tones usually have some sort of grammatical function, such as the indication of a verb tense or a syntactic role, and are used in conjunction with other morphemes, e.g. a verb stem and affixes, which would provide segments in the context of which the tone-only morphemes can be realized. The third type, the morphemes not underlyingly specified for tone, are said to be underlyingly "toneless". They are assigned tones by the tone rules of the language.

Though there are some general principles which are assumed to govern the way tones are assigned to segmental TBUs,[5] each language has its own language-specific tone assignment rules as well. If there are not enough lexical tones present to give each TBU in the word a tone, the tones that are present

---

[2] The references to domains and constraints are taken roughly from Optimality theory. For more information, see Prince and Smolensky (1993).

[3] For a helpful overview of autosegmental theory, see the early chapters of Snider (1999), *The Geometry and Features of Tone*.

[4] This left-to-right, one-to-one linking was first proposed by Goldsmith (1976) as a potential "universal principle", but it has been shown that linking often does not follow this pattern. Individual languages have their own rules and conventions for linking. Hyman and Ngunga (1994) proposed in their treatment of Ciyao that underlying tones may be associated only by language-specific rules, which may or may not reflect left-to-right linking. The only remaining "universal" of tone association seems to be that association lines never cross each other.

[5] Snider (1999:6–12) also gives a brief overview of these principles.

3.1 Assumptions from autosegmental theory

link according to such language specific rules, and tones must be assigned to the remaining TBUs by another language-specific rule such as a spreading rule, which "spreads" (usually) a high (H) tone onto successive unassigned (usually referred to as "empty") TBU(s) and a "default Tone Insertion" rule which assigns a tone (for most two-tone languages the default tone is L) to any TBU which, after all rules have applied, still lacks a tone. Such rules assure that there are no phonetically toneless TBUs on the surface level. If, on the other hand, there are more lexical tones than there are TBUs, each language has its own strategies to merge tones, delete tones, shift tones, or otherwise get the available tones and segments to match up.

For Kifuliiru, the linking of underlying tones can generally be explained by the Edge-in Association Convention, as proposed by Yip (1988) and reformulated by Hewitt and Prince (1989) (3.7.1). During word formation, this principle applies within morphological domains, such as that of a word stem, distributing the tones relevant to that domain to the TBUs available within the domain. Such domains may also serve as the units within which certain rules apply. For example, the verb stem serves as the domain for the application of Meeussen's rule in certain verb forms (3.8.3).

We shall propose for Kifuliiru that a TBU in stem-penultimate position initially receives two tones if there are enough underlying tones to supply them (this is similar to Goldsmith's (1976) automatic contouring proposal). The double-linking of the penultimate syllable is aided in many forms by the edge-in tone association (3.7.1) which associates the final tones of a tonal melody to the rightmost available TBU. Thus the final tone of stem-tone patterns and the right-linking H tones of the passive and causative extensions, as well as the second tone of any nominal tone melody, all link to the right end of the stem, rather than linking from left to right (see 3.7 for details on linking constraints).

All basic tone of Kifuliiru words is explained using only the following:
- lexically and grammatically determined underlying tones, with Meeussen's rule active in certain grammatically determined contexts (3.8.3);
- initial tone association using edge-in linking;
- double-linking of the penultimate;
- extratonality of FV in all but exceptional nouns and in non-passive/non-causative verbs;
- constraint against three tonal association lines to any one syllable;
- simple left to right H and L spread rules;
- four basic rules which provide a phonetic interpretation of tonal contours.

The presentation of Kifuliiru tone will include derivations and rules formulated according to the autosegmental model. Conventions used in derivations, rules, and data tables are found in table 3.1.

Table 3.1. Kifuliiru tone conventions

Symbol/term	Designates
H	High tone
L	Low tone
T	any tone, either H or L
Ø	toneless; or in derivations, shows that a tone has been deleted
acute accent, e.g. á, í, etc.	H tone
grave accent, e.g. à, ì, etc.	L tone
circumflex accent, e.g. â, î, etc.	short falling contour at the phonetic level, resulting from an utterance-final H tone
acute followed by grave, e.g áà, íì	HL contour on a double mora
macron, e.g. ā, ī, āā, īī, etc.	Mid tone (underlying LH)
polar tone	a "polar" tone is realized as the tone opposite from a preceding tone (i.e. L when the preceding tone is H, or H when the preceding tone is L).
H^l or L^l	H or L linked to the left node of a monomoraic penult[a]
H^r or L^r	H or L linked to the right node of a monomoraic penult
μ	mora
σ	syllable
TRN	tonal root node (underlying linkage site for tones)
[ ]$_w$	word boundary (used in rule)
H̵ or L̵	a deleted H or L tone
solid line (e.g. |, /, or \\)	association between tone and TBU
cross hatched line (e.g ǂ)	delinking of a tone

Symbol/term	Designates
dashed line (¦)	new linking (labeled to its right as to which rule is applying)
down arrow	in derivations: change of a tone to null (deletion) or to a different tone, indicated below arrow
<a>, <e>, or <i>	extratonal FV (non-interaction of FV with tone association rules)
UF	underlying form, i.e. form at the point of initial tone association
SF	surface form, i.e. form given with surface tones on segments
visibility	point at which the FV is eligible to be assigned tone
kúbēgá ~ kúbègà	alternate pronunciations, depending on dialect
> (as in HL > H)	"is realized as" (read: HL is realized as H)
/(as in /L _ H)	"in the environment of" (read: where it follows a L tone and precedes a H tone)
MR	Meeussen's rule (3.8.3)

Note: In order to focus on tone linking on the verb stem, the association lines linking verbal prefixes with tones are not shown in the derivations. These tonal association lines can, for the most part, be assumed from the surface tone marks on the prefixes themselves, as prefixal tones are straightforward and except in monosyllablic stems, stem tones are never realized on prefixes. In no case is a prefix tone ever realized on the verb stem (underlying prefix tones can be found in 3.9.1).

^aFor further detail, see (3.7).

3.2 The tone-bearing unit: mora or syllable?

In a tonal language, there is always the question of whether the syllable or the mora is the basic unit to which tone is assigned, i.e. the basic tone-bearing unit (TBU). We will posit for Kifuliiru that the syllable is the basic TBU, and that the penultimate syllable of a stem has the special ability to bear two tones regardless of whether it has one mora or two. But first, a quick review of the situation concerning morae and syllables in Kifuliiru.

A syllable in Kifuliiru may consist of V(V) (word initially, only) C(G)V(V) or NC(G)V(V). A syllable which includes VV occurs only in the antepenultimate or penultimate positions in a word.[6]

---

[6]This is due to the rule of mora-based vowel shortening, which shortens any long vowel that is followed by three or more morae within the word.

A mora is a measure of syllable "weight" or prosodic length. One mora is equivalent to a "light" (V or CV) syllable, and two morae, to a "heavy", VV or (N)C(G)VV, syllable.[7] Each syllable with a short vowel comprises one mora (is monomoraic) and a syllable with a long vowel constitutes two morae (bimoraic). In Bantu languages, the norm seems to be that there is an upper limit of two morae per syllable, and this is true for Kifuliiru.[8] The mora is a relevant unit in Kifuliiru for the rule of mora-based vowel shortening (2.3.1.2.6).

In Kifuliiru, all vowels are moraic. Long vowels always comprise two morae. A nasal adds a mora to a word only if that nasal occurs in the sequence VNC. A nasal which does not precede a consonant, i.e. which occurs as NV or VNV, does not add a mora, nor does a nasal add a mora when it occurs in a word-initial NC sequence. The mora carried by the nasal in a VNC sequence is transferred to the vowel which precedes the nasal, yielding VVNC. Nasals themselves are rarely tone bearing on the surface[9] and only underlyingly tone bearing when used as a word-initial prefix on a monosyllabic form.[10]

The segments which appear on the surface as glides (**y** and **w**) are derived from high vowels, so they are also underlyingly moraic. The moricity for these underlyingly moraic, but non-vocalic surface units is transferred by rule to the following vocalic segment, thus adding a mora to that vocalic segment. The vowel is thus compensatorily lengthened and becomes bimoraic (yielding **y**VV or **w**VV). (See the discussion in (2.3.1.2.4) on compensatory vowel lengthening preceding a NC cluster and following a glide.)[11] All compensatory lengthening of vowels is done prior to initial tone association.

---

[7]In Kifuliiru, morae are the relevant units for a lexical rule of vowel shortening. The rule of mora-based vowel shortening states that a long (bimoraic) vowel is shortened whenever there are three or more morae following it within the word. For this rule, the number of syllables following is irrelevant; the three morae may comprise either two or three syllables. See "Mora-based Vowel Shortening" in chapter 2.

[8]Hubbard (1995:152) notes this in her discussion of nine Bantu languages including Runyambo, Luganda, KiLega, KiNdendeule, CiYao, Kikerewe, CiTonga, Bukusu, and Chichewa, languages from Tanzania, Kenya, Malawi, Uganda, Mozambique, and the Democratic Republic of Congo.

[9]Nasals may take on a tone when they become syllabic following the optional deletion of a following /u/. (See 2.3.1.1.6).

[10]However, the lexical representation of a morpheme which consists only of a nasal, such as the first-person singular object marker, or a cl. 9 noun prefix, may also include a tone. This tone is part of the morpheme/lexeme, but is never linked to the nasal by a tonal association line in the process of tone association. Thus though the morpheme consists of a nasal and a tone, the nasal does not "bear" the tone. The only instances in which a nasal does bear a tone is when it becomes syllabic and moraic in response to the deletion of a following vowel in the process of optional **u** deletion, e.g. **ṁsííngò** 'Greetings!', or when it comprises the initial prefix of a single syllable noun in isolation, e.g. **ṁbú** 'skins' (but not in a longer noun such as **mbúhù** 'cape gooseberry/ies'.)

[11]However, a long vowel in any syllable preceding the antepenultimate will be shortened by

3.2 The tone-bearing unit: mora or syllable?

Hyman (1992:255) notes that it is widely assumed in Bantu languages that the mora is the basic TBU. Very simply put, this means that a syllable with a short vowel is assigned one tone and that a syllable with a long vowel, being bimoraic, is automatically assigned two tones.

However, as Kisseberth and Odden (2003:60) note, the surface evidence indicating whether the syllable or the mora is the TBU is often contradictory, since the distribution of contour tones in Bantu languages is usually limited. This is very true in Kifuliiru. In Kifuliiru a HL contour may surface *only* on a bimoraic syllable. In a noun with underlying HL tone such as **bí-góòjè** (8-maize), both of the underlying tones appear on the bimoraic syllable of the stem. This contour on a bimoraic syllable seems to be one indication of tone assignment to the mora.

On the other hand, surface tonal contours are determined by syllable position. Contours appear *only* in a penultimate syllable. On the surface, any bimoraic syllables in non-penultimate positions bear only a single tone. To assume that the mora is always the basic TBU at the underlying level would necessitate an extra rule, antepenultimate contour simplification. This rule would then account for the fact that there are no surface contours in non-penultimate positions. It would delink the second of the two tones which are associated to any non-penultimate bimoraic syllable.

To avoid the need for this contour simplification rule by positing the syllable as the TBU would somewhat simplify derivations,[12] but at least in the penultimate syllable, data from verbs, especially, show us that linking is clearly to a subsyllabic unit. For instance, rightward tone-spread rules may not target a bimoraic penultimate syllable if its left-hand mora is already linked to a tone.[13] Instead, the tone linked to the left-hand mora of the penultimate will spread onto its right-hand mora. However, a bimoraic penultimate of which only the *right-hand* mora is already linked to a tone *may* be targeted by these same rightward spread rules, since there is a free TBU at its left[14] (3.7 and 3.8.1 for details). This discrepancy in the application of tone-spread rules to bimoraic

---

the mora-based shortening rule, and will not appear in surface forms. Long vowels may appear either in the antepenultimate or the penultimate syllable, but not in both, since the shortening rule affects any long vowel followed by three or more morae.

[12]There are still other cases of contour simplification in which a tone must be delinked following its association, but one can avoid having initial tone association necessitate such a process by positing association to the syllable rather than the mora.

[13]Such linking only of a left-hand mora or only of a right-hand mora is done by edge-in linking (see next footnote.)

[14]Linking is done from the edge of a domain inwards toward the center of the word, so the initial tone in any melody is linked to the leftmost free TBU while the final tone of the melody is linked to the rightmost TBU. Thus, with a subsyllabic unit as the TBU, the assignment of the tone can be pinpointed as to which mora it targets.

penultimates indicates that at least in the penultimate, the underlying TBU is some subsyllabic unit. The natural assumption would be that this unit is the mora.

However, even more significant in determining the identity of the underlying TBU is that exactly the same parameters also apply to a monomoraic stem-penultimate syllable. A monomoraic penultimate may also be targeted by tone-spread rules, with the very same delimiting factors explained in the preceding paragraph for bimoraic penults. Thus, even a monomoraic penult has the underlying ability to bear two tones. This indicates that the assignment of two tones to a bimoraic penultimate is due not to the presence of two morae but to some other quality of the penultimate syllable.

The presence of a such an underlying contour in a monomoraic penult is seen as a surface LH contour in words such as **gàfúsīrwì** 'it has been poured', where the macron represents an underlying LH contour which surfaces on a single mora.[15] Some might claim that this LH contour represents not a doubly linked penult, but a penult linked to a H tone and preceded by a floating L tone. However, this is not the case in Kifuliiru. The double-linking of tone to the penultimate syllable is documented specifically in 3.7.

To explain the lack of contour in non-penultimate syllables and the ability of even a monomoraic penult to bear two tones, we posit that for Kifuliiru the basic TBU is the syllable, and that a penultimate syllable has two tonal root nodes (TRN),[16] each of which can bear one tone (for details 3.7).

Further evidence of the significance of the syllable in tone association is seen in the constraint against linking more than two tones to any one syllable (3.7.3). We will continue to mention morae in the discussions of the forms however, because though the mora is not the underlying TBU, it is still a significant factor in the phonetic pronunciation of a vowel (long versus short) as well in the phonetic realization of an underlying contour. In a bimoraic syllable, we will use the term mora interchangeably with "node" in referring to the two tone-bearing units.

---

[15]The acceptability of a doubly-linked monomoraic penultimate is clearly the case in verbs, but is less clearly the case in nouns. Though speakers will comply with a request to separate what appear to be H-L-L nouns of the configuration PFX-CV-CV nouns (where H is the prefix tone) into two separate tonal groups, it is not clear to my ears that one group is actually H-LH-L while the other is H-LL-L. This may, however, be the case. Two facts are clear: first that there is no semantically significant contrast between LH and LL on a monomoraic nominal penult; and second, that nouns of CVV-CV structure definitely have underlying contours on the bimoraic syllable. If in CVCV nouns there is only a L melody, while LL and LH are found in CVVCV nouns, this would argue that the penultimate syllable in a noun may not take two tones unless it has two morae. Further research is needed to clarify the situation.

[16]A term taken from Snider (1999). He uses the tonal root node as a rendevouz point for the tonal feature and the register feature in his Register Tier Theory.

3.3 Tone inventory

3.3.1 Underlying tones

Kifuliiru has two underlying tones, high (H) and low (L). Morphemes can also be underlyingly toneless (∅). Thus there is a three-way distinction on the underlying level between high (H), low (L), and toneless (∅). This three-way distinction is directly reflected in the three tonal classes of verb stems (3.5.1).

3.3.2 Surface realizations of tones

Since tone in verbal forms is complicated not only by segmental prefixation and suffixation but also by grammatically dictated tonal affixation, let us begin by looking instead at the surface realization of tones in nominal forms,[17] which are morphologically and tonally much less complex while still including the full range of surface tones. The possible combinations of tones in non-derived Kifuliiru noun stems are H(H), L(L), LH, or HL. As will be seen below, LH when realized on any single syllable surfaces phonetically as a level mid tone, while HL on a single bimoraic syllable is realized as a falling contour.[18]

In regard to phonetic realization, we should mention the presence of downdrift, discussed in 3.13. One should also note that in an utterance-initial sequence of two or more H tones, or such a sequence following a L tone, the highest absolute pitch is sometimes not reached until the second H tone. This may give the impression that the initial H is not actually H. However, such variations in pitch are merely phonetic. Speakers asked to whistle the melody of such words whistle the initial H tone at the same pitch as the following ones.

To see the various surface realizations of the four possible underlying tone patterns of noun stems, let us look first at single syllable stems. Though theoretically a noun may have any one of the four given tone patterns, no single-syllable stem can bear more than one surface tone. Thus a single-syllable noun stem can have either a H tone or a L tone,[19] but never the HL or LH tone pattern. In (3.1) the underlined stem is one mora and bears one tone. The final syllable of a single-syllable noun stem is not extratonal.

---

[17]This overview is a condensation of the more complete discussion of tone in nouns found in (3.10).

[18]HL on a single monomoraic syllable is phonetically interpreted as H.

[19]Note that VV is not allowed word finally in Kifuliiru, so that a stem/root consisting of a single syllable is always monomoraic at the time of tone association. Data indicate that in such cases, the prefix is reanalyzed as part of the stem before tone association takes place, in order to meet prosodic minimality constraints: the stem must have at least two syllables.

(3.1) Tone patterns in single-mora noun stems
    H   **úú=bú-lá**   AU=14-intestine
    L   **úú=bú-là**   AU=14-length

One would expect that in bisyllabic noun stems (CVCV) since there are two TBUs in the stem, that all of the four possible tone combinations, H, L, HL, and LH, would be found. However, in these CVCV noun stems, the possible number of tone patterns is still only three, that is, either H, LH, or L, as seen in (3.2). This is because the final syllable of a regular non-monosyllabic noun stem is extratonal in Kifuliiru, and thus does not bear lexical tone[20] (see discussion of extratonality in 3.6). The tone on the final syllable of regular, non-monosyllabic nouns in isolation is provided by a default rule/boundary tone, and is always low.

(3.2) Tone patterns in bimoraic bisyllabic noun stems
    H   **í=kí-rígò**   AU=7-spring.of.water
    LH   **í=kí-rīmì**   AU=7-sore.throat
    L   **ú=lú-sìkù**   AU=11-day

However, the penultimate syllable can bear two tones. In the case that the two tones are HL, they are realized only as H on a monomoraic syllable, so that in CVCV noun stems, there is neutralization of any difference between underlying H and HL. The same neutralization of contrast seems to be the case with L and LH in such nouns. However, at least with some speakers, LH still seems to be phonetically distinguishable from L in a monomoraic penultimate syllable of CVCV nouns, as heard in the final two examples in (3.2). It is possible, however, that the H tone which optionally co-occurs with L on the penultimate of CVCV nouns is only intonational, as it does not seem to be contrastive. Thus, though there may still be some phonetic difference between LH tone and L(L) tone on the monomoraic penult of a CVCV noun stem, speakers are not able to consistently distinguish any difference in phonetic tone between the two.[21] In (3.2), the first (underlined) syllable of the bisyllabic stem bears the lexical tone(s) while the final syllable bears a default L tone.

---

[20] By "regular" noun root, we mean those with an extratonal final mora. As noted in (3.10.2), there are exceptional cases in which the final syllable bears a lexical H tone in isolation.

[21] It will be shown that there is still an underlying difference between LH and LL on a single penultimate mora, at least in verbs, where more flexible morphology enables us to show that a monomoraic penult with LH will be realized phonetically as H when preceded by a L tone, while a monomoraic penult with LL will be realized as L in the same environment.

3.3 Tone inventory

In a noun with two or more available TBUs (i.e. non-word final TBUs)²² in the stem (i.e. a noun stem of CVVCV or CVCVCV or longer) all four possible patterns, HH..., LL..., HL..., or LH... are attested. Even when a noun has three, four, five, or more available TBUs in its stem, these four patterns are the only basic tone patterns found in noun stems.²³ Thus we speak of the underlying tonal pattern of a lexical item being realized over the domain of the lexical stem. The examples in (3.3) show noun stems of three syllables, illustrating the four different tonal patterns.

(3.3)   Tonal patterns on trimoraic trisyllabic noun stems

	H	í=kí-<u>míníkà</u>	AU=7-epidemic
	L	í=kí-<u>nògòshò</u>	AU=7-hoof
	LH	í=kí-<u>shàkúlò</u>	AU=7-mortar.for.grinding
	HL	í=kí-<u>kómèrè</u>	AU=7-wound

In a two-syllable noun stem with a bimoraic penultimate syllable (CVVCV) as shown in (3.4), all four patterns are also present. The lexical tone(s) of the noun are realized on the bimoraic syllable, underlined in (3.4). This means that both of the tones of a HL or LH pattern are realized on the bimoraic syllable.

(3.4)   Tonal patterns on bisyllabic trimoraic noun stems

	H	ú=mú-<u>kééngè</u>	AU=3-hollow.grass.used.as.straw
	L	ú=mú-<u>kèèngè</u>	AU=3-monitor.lizard
	LH	ú=mú-<u>vīīndì</u>†	AU=3-grasshopper.secretion
	HL	ú=mú-<u>kéèngè</u>	AU=3-wooden.beer-making.trough

†**Múvìíndè** is that small bit of dark liquid which a grasshopper secretes if you try to hold it in your closed fist. It is not just coincidental that the word which here illustrates the LH tone pattern differs segmentally as well as in tone from the others. No minimal pairs of nouns have been found in the language in which the only difference is the LL vs. LH pattern. The contrast between the two in nouns of this CV pattern is in the process of being lost.

---

²²I say non-extratonal rather than non-final here because in some exceptional nouns, as well as in monosyllabic noun roots, the final syllable is not extratonal.

²³There are some exceptional patterns, including a small percentage of compound nouns which demonstrate combinations of the tonal patterns plus prefixes (**mú-tó-kì-íkò** H H LH L 'ashes', perhaps from **mú-tò** 'lesser one', and **kì-íkò** 'fireplace') and partially reduplicated nouns with partial reduplication of the tonal pattern (**kí-húhúùtà** H H HL L 'strong wind').

As seen in (3.4), the two underlying tones, H and L, combine to form four contrastive[24] surface tones in the penultimate syllable position. These four tones include three level tones, H, L, and LH (phonetically a level mid tone) and HL, a falling contour. The two "combination" tones, LH and HL, are contrastive only on a bimoraic penultimate syllable.[25] In non-penultimate syllables, whether monomoraic or bimoraic, there is only a two-way phonemic contrast possible, between H and L.

Thus in two-syllable nouns which have long vowels in the penultimate syllable (these are bisyllabic trimoraic noun stems) such as those in (3.4), all speakers still seem to differentiate in pronunciation between nouns with LH tone on the penultimate and those with LL tone.

A final syllable in Kifuliiru is always monomoraic, and just as other non-penultimate monomoraic syllables, may bear only one tone underlyingly. The most common case for a final syllable is a default L tone on the final mora of a surface form. Monosyllabic stems, e.g. **íí=kí-hê** (AU=7-time), and forms with a special H tone suffix, e.g. **kí-bèèmbê** (7-Bembe.language), or some with an underlying final GV, e.g. **ká-húùmbwê** (12-solitude) may, however, exhibit a H tone on the final syllable of the surface form (see 3.10). An utterance-final H underlying tone is realized phonetically as a short falling contour, always marked in this position in the examples by a circumflex accent. Such an utterance-final falling contour never reflects a lexical level HL sequence.[26]

3.3.2.1 *Restrictions on tautosyllabic contours*

As just mentioned, the distribution of combinations of two unlike tones (LH or HL) linked to a single syllable is restricted to the penultimate syllable. The HL contour is further restricted in that it may not be realized on a single mora, and it may not be realized following a preceding L tone within the same word. It remains unsimplified only on bimoraic (CVV) penultimate

---

[24]Just as is true with the CVCV roots, even with the CVVCV noun roots, speakers have a hard time dividing into separate groups those nouns in which the CVV syllable has LL tone and those in which that same syllable has LH tone. Thus the contrast, though phonetically very discernable, retains no lexically significant contrast in the ears of native speakers.

[25]The LH is phonetically discernable also on a monomoraic penultimate syllable, especially of verbs, in the speech of some speakers, including the one from whom I elicited most of my verb paradigms.

[26]Though it possibly reflects a phonetic level L boundary tone in addition to the H lexical tone. There is no double-linking of the ultima at lexical level, but at the phonetic level it is possible that a boundary tone can link together with the lexical tone.

3.3 Tone inventory

syllables, e.g. **í=ny-úùmbà** (AU=9-house), and only in the environment of a preceding H within the word, or in word-initial position.[27]

Though tautosyllabic[28] HL is realized as a falling contour tone, in which the tone starts high and becomes lower, tautosyllabic LH, as mentioned above, is never realized as a rising contour tone, but rather as a level, phonetically mid tone. As is true in many Bantu languages, there are no rising contours in Kifuliiru.[29] In the realization of LH, the initial L tone is expressed phonetically only by the lowering of the H tone, which is pronounced as a level "mid" tone, phonetically somewhere about midway between H and L on the register.[30]

The tautosyllabic LH is restricted in that it may remain unsimplified only on a penultimate syllable, just as was true for the HL contour. LH (mid) is further restricted in its surface realization by the constraint that it must follow a H tone, and precede a L tone, e.g. **ú=lú-hāāndè** (AU=11-groundnut). LH is lowered to L whenever it precedes a H tone, and raised to H between two L tones or word initially preceding a L tone. Thus it is realized phonetically on the surface only on a penultimate syllable where it follows a H tone and precedes a L tone.

In some people's speech, any phonetic realization of LH seems perhaps to have largely disappeared, being replaced by a simple L or H, depending on the conditioning environment.[31] For other speakers, LH is restricted to bimoraic (CVV) penultimate syllables. Still other speakers pronounce LH

---

[27]There are seeming exceptions in (arguably lexicalized) cases where cliticization are involved. Words such as **nàmúlòbáà=fwì** 'a type of bird which catches fish' (from the verb **lòb-** 'to fish without a net' and the noun **fwì** 'fish') seem to have undergone reinterpretation so that the long vowel with HL contour is considered word initial, since word-initial position is the the only case in which HL is realized as a phonetic contour without a preceding H tone within the word. Other cases involve the elision of a H tone syllable in compound words such as **mùkáàgè** 'his wife' (from **mùká (ú)a=gè**) or **mùkíìbà** 'the wife of her husband' (from **mùká yíìbà**).

[28]"Tautosyllabic" means "same-syllable".

[29]Kisseberth and Odden (2003:66) say, "There is a particularly strong tendency to avoid rising tones in Bantu." Hyman (p.c.) notes that if a language does have rising tones, they will occur only following a L tone.

[30]Tautosyllabic LH could be described as a "downstepped H" tone, as it has the same phonetic realization as a H tone which is lowered automatically by downdrift following a L tone in the preceding syllable. However, "downstepped H" is a term that usually infers a preceding unassociated or "floating" L tone, whereas in Kifuliiru the L tone (as well as the H tone) of a tautosyllabic LH is always linked to the TBU on which it is realized. For this reason, I prefer not to use the term "downstepped H" to describe it.

[31]For these speakers, LH is realized as L in the environment/H _ L. The fact that the surface realization of LH depends on surrounding tonal context seems to indicate that the contour is still present underlyingly. It may just be difficult to hear in the pronunciation of some speakers. We have no statistics or dialectical information on which speakers have retained a contrastive phonetic realization of LH and which have not. More research could be done on this subject.

as a phonetically mid tone even on a monomoraic (CV) penultimate syllable, especially in verbal forms (e.g. some speakers pronounce **tùgúúzīrwì** 'we have been cheated', while others say **tùgúúzìrwì**).[32] LH never contrasts phonemically with L on a monomoraic syllable, and there is almost never significant contrast even on a bimoraic syllable.

There are however, certain environments in verbs where LH and LL are contrastive. In L-toned verb stems, e.g. -**hììng**- 'farm', the first-person singular past form **n-gá-hīīng-à** (1SG-P2-farm-Fa) 'I farmed (P2)' and the first-person singular future form, e.g. **n-gá-hììng-à** (1SG-F2-farm-Fa) 'I will farm (F2)' differ only in the fact that the P2 past has LH tone on the stem, while the F2 future has LL. In this case, the identity of the tense prefix (**ká-** in P2 and **gá-** in F2) is neutralized when the nasal-only first-person subject marker precedes it, triggering voicing of the stop in the P2 marker, so that both are **gá**. Thus the difference between LH and LL on the stem is the only distinguishing factor which shows the tense. Speakers do recognize the difference in forms here by the tone (LL versus LH) in this case. In all other cases, the shape of the prefixes, in addition to the tone on the verb stem, serve to provide redundancy in distinguishing the two tenses.

3.3.2.2 *Phonetic realizations*

The initial tone of an utterance, whether H or L, is often realized on a lower pitch than an underlyingly identical tone which directly follows it. Thus when an utterance begins with two or three successive H tones, the pitch often begins fairly low and increases with each successive H tone. A sequence of #H H L# may be phonetically realized by the pitch sequence ⁻ ⁻ _, while a sequence of #H H H L# may be phonetically realized with a pitch sequence like ⁻ ⁻ ⁻ _. Such sequences can be distinguished from a #L H H... sequence by the fact that in a sequence of #L H H..., the second H will not be realized on a higher pitch than the H which immediately follows the L. Instead, downdrift (lowering) affects any H tones which follow an L. The H tone of a HL contour is always higher in pitch than the pitch of a preceding H tone. This may be partially due to the penultimate position of all HL contours, and partially a mere rise in pitch to allow contrast between the H and the following L without lowering the pitch to a level below the comfort range of the speaker.

The same sort of pitch increase may be observed between the first and second Ls in a sequence of #L L H.... However, if a word in isolation consists only of L tones or only of H tones, e.g. #L L L# or #H H H# the pitch tends to be much more even. Another general principle of phonetic pitch realization

---

[32]There is audible contrast in the penultimate vowel in the future form **túgáábègà** 'we will cut someone's hair', and that in the P2 past **túkábēgà** 'we cut someone's hair (before yesterday)'.

3.3 Tone inventory

is that the shorter the word, the less pitch variation will be seen in an initial sequence of identical tones.

Utterance-final L tones are also usually realized on a lower pitch than previous L tones. Utterance-final H tones are given a falling contour. This lower tone may be the result of the addition of a L boundary tone utterance finally. Often, a L-tone utterance-final vowel is totally devoiced.

Other phonetic phenomena include the addition of an intonational H tone to a noun in isolation which would otherwise have no H tones. For example, the noun **bììra** 'friends' has LL tone. When pronounced with an augment, it is realized as **ábììrà**, because the augment provides a H tone. When pronounced in isolation without an augment, however, it is realized as **bíírà**.[33] It is possible that when there is no preceding word on which to realize the floating H tone which occurs at the left edge of such a L-initial noun or adjective, it is shifted rightward onto the noun itself. A conjugated verb with no underlying H tones does not evidence any added H tones when pronounced in isolation, e.g. **ààdètà** 'he spoke'.[34]

A L tone between two H tones may be realized at a pitch barely lower than the preceding H tone, but will still trigger downdrift in the following H tone.

3.3.3 Kifuliiru tone reversal vis-à-vis Proto-Bantu

When compared with the tones proposed by Guthrie and others for Proto-Bantu, it is clear that Kifuliiru has undergone an almost total tone reversal. One major exception to this is the nominal augment, which is H both in the PB tone reconstructions and in Kifuliiru. If the passive and causative "extensions" also had H tone in PB, as Meeussen (1967) suggested, then these too have been preserved unchanged in Kifuliiru.[35]

Noun stems and adjectives exhibit clear tone reversal. Because the final syllable in Kifuliiru is extratonal at the time of initial tone association, some tone patterns have been collapsed in words of CVCV pattern. In nouns of two single-mora syllables, the Proto-Bantu LL and LH patterns have merged as H in Kifuliiru, e.g. (3.5a, b), while the PB HH and HL have merged as L (3.5c, d).

In cases where there are at least two non-final morae in the Kifuliiru noun stem, as in examples (3.5e–i) the tones appear with complete reversal of the

---

[33] In isolation this sounds like H L. When pronounced in a list where it follows an augmentless noun of the same CV pattern but which has an underlying H tone, there is however, a difference. The initial tone of the H noun is higher and the intial tone of the L noun is more of a mid tone.

[34] Though passing observation indicates that in verbal relative forms in isolation or in utterance final position, there is sometimes an added H tone in penultimate position. Minimal research has been done on negative forms and relative forms of verbs.

[35] There may be other exceptions; no real comparative study on Kifuliiru has been done.

tones of the PB starred forms (though in stems with bimoraic penultimate syllables, both the tones appear together on the penultimate syllable, rather than occurring on separate syllables).

(3.5)	PB Tone	Cl.	PB† form	FLR tone	Cl.	FLR form	Gloss
a.	LL	9	*-jìdà	H	9	n-jírà	9-path
b.	LH	9	*-jùnį́	H	12	ká-nyúnì	12-bird
c.	HH	1	*-kádį́	L	1	mú-kàzì	1-woman
d.	HL	9	*-júkì	L	9	n-jùkì	9-bee
e.	LL	9	*-gòįnà	HH	9	n-góónà	9-crocodile
f.	LH		*-pàndé	HL	11	lú-háàndè	11-piece
g.	HL		*-kų́ndò	LH	7	kí-fūūndò	7-knot
i.	HH		*-jį́ngí	LL		-ìingì	-many

†Most forms here are Guthrie's starred forms, but (3.5f) and (3.5g) follow C. Ehret (1999).

The verbal object prefixes are reconstructed for PB as having L tone in first-, second-, and third-person (cl. 1) singular, and H tone for the rest of the object prefixes.[36] For Kifuliiru, exactly the opposite is true, as is seen in (3.6).

(3.6)	Object prefixes	Proto-Bantu	Kifuliiru
	1SG	*NÌ-	Ń-
	2SG	*KÒ-	kú-
	1 (3SG)	*MÒ-	mú-
	1PL	*TÓ-	tù-
	2PL	*MÓ-	mù-
	2 (3PL)	*BÁ-	bà-
	cl. 3–23	all H	all L

Casual observation of verb roots also supports the occurrence of tone reversal in Kifuliiru lexical forms. A few examples are provided in (3.7).

---

[36] Guthrie (1971), Vol. 2, p. 10.

3.3 Tone inventory   125

(3.7)
Tone of PB verb root	Guthrie's P-B form	Gloss	Tone of FLR verb root	FLR form	Gloss
L	*-gùd-	'buy'	H	-gúl-	'buy'
L	*-dìd-	'cry'	H	-lír-	'cry'
L	*-dìm-	'cultivate'	H	-lím-	'cultivate'
L	*-pònd-	'pound'	H	-hóónd-	'strike'
L	*-mɩ̀d-	'swallow'	H	-mír-	'swallow'
H	*-dʊ́g-	'cook, boil'	L	-dùg-	'cook ugali'
H	*-tég-	'set (trap)'	L	-tèg-	'trap'
H	*-kín-	'dance; sing'	L	-kìn-	'dance'
H	*-kúd-	'grow'	L	-kùl-	'grow'
H	*-bón-	'see'	L	-bòn-	'see'

Even the tones of the suffixal stem-tone patterns of verbal tenses exhibit tone reversal. Goldsmith (1987) lists several typical stem-tone patterns for Lacustrine Bantu languages. In his "Simple Stem-tone" pattern, which he has found in the infinitive and sometimes a few other tenses, the verb stem bears the tone of the radical on the first syllable, followed by L tones on all the other syllables. In Kifuliiru infinitives, this same pattern is found, except that the verb stem bears the tone of the radical followed by H tones, rather than L, on all the other syllables.[37]

Another pattern Goldsmith mentions, the "Complex Stem-tone pattern" involves a H tone on the second vowel of the stem (which is changed to L by Meeussen's rule if it follows a H radical tone) plus a H tone linked to the final vowel (FV) of the verb. In Kifuliiru, the tone of the second TBU of the stem is exactly as Goldsmith described, having a H tone which is changed to L following a H-toned radical. Because this H tone, by virtue of the effects of Meeussen's rule, is a type of "polar tone" (a tone whose surface form is the opposite of some conditioning tone in its environment) it has not been reversed, and remains H.[38] However, the tone on the FV in this pattern in Kifuliiru is L, rather than the H which Goldsmith found in related zone J languages which have not undergone tone reversal.[39]

---

[37] With the exception of the final syllable of active, non-causative forms, which is extratonal at the point of initial tone association, and bears a default L tone.

[38] However, because in the reflex of any given verb, the lexical tone of the verb has been reversed, this polar tone will be H in Kifuliiru reflexes of verbs in which it is found as L in languages which have not undergone tone reversal.

[39] There is another pattern in Kifuliiru which has a L tone on the second vowel of the stem

3.3.3.1 Toneless verbs

Verbs which have an underlyingly bimoraic syllable in the root-initial position exhibit toneless behavior in Kifuliiru. Most Kifuliiru verb roots have either a lexical H tone or a lexical L tone, to which suffixal tones are added according to the tense, aspect, etc. of the verb. However, there is a third tonal grouping of verb roots, with underlying CVV... pattern, which does not exhibit any lexical tone, but only the suffixal (grammatically determined) tone(s). These we refer to as toneless verb roots. These toneless verbs are reflexes both of verbs reconstructed as H in Proto-Bantu, e.g. **kúbííkà** from *-**bíik**- 'to put', and of those reconstructed as L, e.g. **kúhéékà** from *-**pèek**- 'to carry'.

This toneless class includes most[40] verb stems with underlying C(G) VV in the root-initial position, e.g. -**biik**- 'put', -**bwaatal**- 'sit', and -**byaal**- 'plant', as well as the monosyllabic CV-only verbs (which are underlyingly CV, but become CG-FV) e.g. -**fu**- 'die', -**li**- 'eat', -**gu**- 'fall'. However, the toneless class does *not* include verbs in which the VV in the initial syllable is conditioned by a following NC, e.g. -**géend**- 'go', -**bùumb**- 'work clay', -**hèend**- 'deceive'. This is true even when the initial syllable begins with a CG, such as in -**fyèèng**- 'pinch together'. (For further discussion of toneless verbs, see 3.5.1.1.)

A three-way distinction between H, L, and toneless verbs is similarly noted by Kaji (1996) in regard to Chitembo (J57).[41] He states that "-CV- and -CVVC- [verb radicals]...had a proper lexical tone in Proto-Bantu, but in Chitembo [the reflexes of *-CV- and most of the reflexes of *-CVVC- verbs] cannot be given a proper tone as they turn out to be H or L in different conjugational forms..." (Kaji 1996:8). The existence of just such a three-way distinction is also attested in various Bantu A languages in Cameroon. In Kóózime (A80) Beavon (1991) lists six toneless verbs, whose tonal behavior contrasts with that of both H and L-toned verbs, and Beavon (2005) has a very similar list from a related language, Njyem: -**de** 'eat'; -**jwe** 'die'; -**je** 'give'; -**be** 'be', -**nsye** 'come'; -**cwe** 'stumble'. Teresa Heath (p.c.) states that a comparable list of toneless verbs also exists in Makaa (A83). In these verbs the tone varies between H and L, depending on the grammatical tone which is added to the verb, just as is the case with toneless verbs in Kifuliiru.

---

and a right-linking H tone.

[40]No complete listing has been made of the toneless verbs.

[41]Blanchon (1998) also notes a three-way distinction in verbal infinitives for Yoombi (H.12b) with classes "A, B and C"; the example given for "class B" is of CVVC configuration. He attributes the three-way distinction in verbs to what he calls "the Great *HL Split" (Blanchon 1990).

3.3.3.2 Default tone

In view of the tone reversal found in this language, the question may be raised as to whether tone reversal has affected the default tone in Kifuliiru.⁴² Has this also undergone reversal from the usual L default found in most two-tone languages, and become instead a H tone? Our answer is no. The default tone in Kifuliiru, as in most Bantu languages, is L. Besides appearing in the word final position,⁴³ default L tone can be seen in the subject prefixes of verbs.⁴⁴ Subject prefixes are toneless, and in any case in which there is not a H tone assigned to them by a specific morpheme (such as a directly-following future (F2) prefix, **gáá**- or past (P2) prefix, **ká**-, or the subjunctive H tone linked to the subject marker in certain forms) they exhibit L tone. That they are toneless, and not underlyingly L-toned, is shown by the tonal behavior of subjunctive forms. Any subjunctive form which has no prefix with an underlying tone exhibits the Complex HH stem-tone pattern, while a subjunctive verb which does have a prefix with an underlying tone exhibits the V_2 stem-tone pattern. The subjunctive forms with only a toneless (surface L tone) subject marker are the only forms which exhibit the Complex HH pattern (3.5.3.3.6). This shows that the subject prefixes, which have surface L tone, are underlyingly toneless. The negative prefix is also lexically toneless, and it also has a surface L tone, with the same exceptions as noted above in regard to the subject prefixes.

3.4 Functional load of tone

Tone is contrastive both grammatically and lexically in Kifuliiru. Lexical roots which differ only in tone can be found in both nouns (roughly 1%) and in verbs (between 1 and 2%).⁴⁵ For nouns, there are a few sets of three words which differ only in tone. For verbs, there have never been observed to be

---

⁴²The default tone is the tone associated by rule to any TBU which is still toneless following the application of all specific tone assignment rules.

⁴³The default L tone at the ends of words whose final mora is underlyingly extratonal could also be seen as a boundary tone, but even if considered so, the default boundary tone is L. High boundary tone only occurs to signal a pause or raise the register in an incomplete utterance, while L occurs in all other "boundary" positions, including utterance medial and utterance final.

⁴⁴Because of the H- and L-spread rules which apply within stems, there is little need for default tones in post-prefix positions, with the exception of the word-final position, to which H-spread, and probably L-spread rules do not apply. The L tone found at the right boundary of most words in isolation could be seen as a default tone, as well, since it can be replaced by a H tone in marked pause positions within a discourse context.

⁴⁵Lexical minimal pairs are rare enough, and different enough semantically, that the correct meaning of the word is always clear from context. Thus the Kifuliiru orthography does not indicate lexical tone.

more than two words, a H verb and a L verb, in such a set differentiated only by tone (since the toneless verbs all have a distinctive syllable pattern which further distinguishes them from the others). There are however, verbal "triplets" in which the consonantal segments are identical. See the **-hum-/-huum-** examples in (3.9) where the first two forms are H and L, respectively, while the third is a toneless verb.

3.4.1 Lexical tone contrasts

In (3.8) are some examples of minimal pairs/triplets for nouns. The contrastive syllable in each example below is underlined. Numbers indicate noun class.

(3.8)	UT	SF	Gloss	UT	SF	Gloss
	HL	ítáàngà	'sail (5)'	HH	ú=múkééngè	'grass stem sp. (3)'
	LH	ítāāngà	'offering (5)'	HL	ú=múkéèngè	'beer trough (3)'
				LL	ú=múkèèngè	'monitor lizard (3)'
	HH	í=kyóóbà	'mushroom (7 aug)'	H	íí=ndá	'pregnancy (9)'
	LL	í=kyòòbà	'fear (7)'	L	îì=ndà	'louse (9)'
	LL	í=nyùùngù	'squash seed (9)'	H	úú=búlá	'intestine (14)'
	HL	í=nyúùngù	'cooking pot (9)'	L	úú=búlà	'length (14)'

There are also minimal pairs among verbs, as seen in (3.9).

(3.9)	UT	SF	Gloss	UT	SF	Gloss
	H	ú=kúshébà	'to sift'	H	ú=kúyálíkà	'to cloister'
	L	ú=kúshēbà	'to have trouble'	L	ú=kúyàlíkà	'to heat water for ugali'
	H	ú=kúhúúmbà	'to dig'	H	ú=kúhúmà	'to be blind'
	L	ú=kúhūūmbà	'to end off'	L	ú=kúhùmà	'to touch'
				Ø	ú=kúhúúmà	'to become much'

3.4.2 Grammatical tone contrasts

Tone is contrastive grammatically in verbal forms, though considering the number of verb forms in the language, there are relatively few minimal pairs,

3.4 Functional load of tone

since segmental differences in the prefixes, suffixes, and sometimes in the final vowel of the verbs also signal the form of the verb. All the same, there are still various forms which are distinguished only by tone.[46] For example, the recent past (P1) and unmarked past (P2) forms of the conditional contrary-to-fact (CND.C.F) are distinguished by tone on the prefixes, as well as by differences in the suffixal tone on the verb stem in L and Ø verb forms, though the suffixal tone pattern in a H-tone verb stays the same in most forms. This tonal contrast and segmental similarity is shown in (3.10), where the underlining shows the syllables in each pair that are different in the two forms.

(3.10) H **twàngàbàgúúzìrì**   'we could have cheated them (P1) (but haven't)'
       H **twángábàgúúzìrì**   'we could have cheated them (P2) (but didn't)'

       L **twàngàbàfyèèzírì**   'we could have pinched their noses shut (P1) (but haven't)'
       L **twángábàfyèèzìrì**   'we could have pinched their noses shut (P2) (but didn't)'

       Ø **twàngàbàdííhírì**   'we could have beaten them (P1) (but haven't)'
       Ø **twángábàdìȉhìrì**   'we could have beaten them (P2) (but didn't)'

Several other grammatical forms are distinguished only by tone as well, as exemplified briefly in (3.11) by the difference between a frustrated resultative form (RS.FRUS) (3.11a) and the negative of a resultative form (RS) (3.11b); between the first-person singular of before-yesterday past (P2) (3.11c, e), and unmarked future (F2) (3.11d, f); and between conditional resultative (CND.RS) (3.11g) and resultative forms (RS) (3.11h). Note that in (3.11a, b), as well as (3.11g, h), there are tonal differences both in the prefixes and in the suffixal tones on the verb stem, while in the pairs in (3.11c, d), and (3.11e, f), the only difference is found in the suffixal tone on the verb stem. The suffixal tone is H in the past forms (3.11c, e) and L in the future forms (3.11d, f). In both cases the suffixal tone is realized on the second mora of the bimoraic penultimate syllable. In (3.11e, f) the two forms are only distinguished by the LH versus LL on the verb stem.

---

[46]Because grammatical tone indicates semantic differences which are generally less discernable by context than the lexical differences are, the Kifuliiru orthography includes conventions for marking various tonally indicated tense or mood differences by means of an accent mark or other diacritc.

(3.11) a. átámúgúúzīrì   'he cheated him, (but then...)' RS.FRUS
       b. àtàmúgúúzírì   'he is not in the state of having cheated him'
                          Neg of RS

       c. ngámúgúúngà   'I cheated him (before yesterday)' P2
       d. ngámúgúùngà   'I will cheat him' F2

       e. ngáh<u>īī</u>ngà   'I farmed (before yesterday)' P2
       f. ngáh<u>ìì</u>ngà   'I will farm' F2

       g. túgúúz<u>ī</u>rì   'if/whether we have cheated someone' CND.RS
       h. tùgúúz<u>ì</u>rì   'we are in the state of having cheated someone' RS

3.5 Tone on verbs

The context in which the tone rules and processes of a Bantu language are most clearly seen is that of verbs. Though complex, Bantu verbs are ideal for tone observation due to their great morphological flexibility. By making use of the agglutinative nature of verbs, it is fairly simple to get the environment needed to test a hypothesis. The affixes make it simple to maintain the basic verb and the tense/aspect/mood as constants, while varying other factors. By adding a H or L-toned object prefix, one can modify the tonal environment preceding the verb radical without changing anything else about the verb. To "stretch" the verb, and see what the language does when there are more TBUs than tones, simply add one or more toneless extensions. To see how the language deals with less TBUs than available tones, one only has to use a verb stem consisting only of CVC. The various grammatical stem-tone patterns and the basic tone rules of Kifuliiru have been formulated by extensive comparison of verbs having different underlying lexical tones and various syllable patterns.

This section on verbal tone is divided into six parts:
- lexical tone on Kifuliiru verb roots and selected affixes
- background on the tone patterns of verb stems
- the realization of stem-tone patterns on various basic verb forms
- tone assignment in some of the multiword verb forms
- characteristics unique to monosyllabic verb stems
- tone in reduplicated verbal forms

All of these sections assume two basic principles of tone assignment in Kifuliiru: 1) underlying extratonality of the final vowel, except in passive and causative forms (3.6) and 2) the double linking of the penultimate syllable (3.7). Also assumed are edge-in initial tone association (3.7.1) (unless otherwise noted) and commonly invoked processes such as default L-insertion, merger of adjacent identical tones, and stray erasure. Argumentation for and formulation of language specific rules necessary for the derivation of surface patterns are found in (3.8). A cross-reference to the description of each rule will be given when the rules are first mentioned.

It should also be noted that the Bantu verb is commonly regarded as having several subparts. These can be listed as inflectional prefixes (including subject, tense, aspect), object prefixes (including the reflexive prefix), root (also called radical), extensions, and final vowel (FV). The root and extensions together make up what is called the verb base, and the base together with the FV make up the stem. It is to these that the inflectional prefixes are added. If there is any incorporated object marker(s) these are included with the stem in a unit referred to as the macrostem. For example, the sections of the verb **tú-ká-mú-shòn-óól-à** (1PL-P2-O1-climb-RV.T-Fa) 'we lowered him down', are as shown in (3.12).

(3.12)

	tú	**ká**	**mú**	**shòn**	**óól**	**à**
	1PL	P2	O1	climb	RV.T	FV
[subject, negative, TAM prefixes]		[object prefix(es)†]		[root]	[extension(s)]	FV
				[base]		
				[stem]		
		[macrostem]				

†Kifuliiru verbs may have two object prefixes only if one of the two is either reflexive **yì-** or first-person singular **ń-**. These prefixes are an incorporated pronominal reference to an object of the verb.

The domains which are relevant to tone association in Kifuliiru are the prefixes and the stem, the latter of which is initially separated into the base and the FV. There is a distinct domain boundary between the prefixes (including the object prefixes) and the stem. Though there are tone spread rules which spread tone rightward, tone from the prefixes never spreads rightward across this domain boundary onto the stem.

Most of the prefixes and the object markers each have their own tone, which is assigned to the prefix itself except in the case of the first-person singular object prefix, which consists of a nasal and a H tone. Since the nasal-only prefix is not syllabic and cannot bear a tone, the H tone of this prefix is not able to link to the prefix, and is instead realized on whatever prefix occurs directly to the left of the object marker. Thus the object prefixes group together with the rest of the prefixes in regard to tonal domains. The macrostem, though relevant in other contexts in Kifuliiru, does not function as a domain for Kifuliiru tone assignment.

3.5.1 Lexical tone in verbs

In Kifuliiru verbs, the majority of prefixes and roots, along with two suffixes, bear lexical tones. The verb stem as a unit bears any lexical tone of the root and suffixes, plus obligatory grammatical tones. The lexical tones of the root and suffixes interact with the grammatical tones of the stem as a whole, so that all of these must be discussed together.

Because the tones of verbal prefixes do not interact with the tone of the stem in most cases,[47] they do not need to be presented here in order to understand the more general points of verbal tone. Thus, for the sake of simplicity of presentation, the discussion of tone in verbal affixes in general is presented much later (3.9). In this section, we include only the discussion of the lexical tone of verb roots, immediately below, and of the two suffixes which have tone, the causative and passive, which are discussed in (3.5.1.2).

3.5.1.1 *Lexical tone of verb roots*

Verb roots have at maximum one underlying lexical tone. The lexical tone, if any, of the verb always links to the first syllable of the root, to the left of any other tones which link to the stem. It never spreads to the second mora of a bimoraic/penultimate stem-initial syllable in a -CVV(N)C- base such as **-gúung-** 'cheat',[48] nor to any other syllables of the stem, because initial tone association invariably associates the obligatory grammatical tone of the verb directly to the right of the lexical tone, thus blocking any rightward spreading which might otherwise take place. As mentioned above, the tones of prefixes never spread onto TBUs of the verb stem, even in the case of a toneless verb stem.

Verb roots in Kifuliiru fall into three tonal classes, H, L, and toneless (Ø). The H verbs have a fixed H tone, which is realized on the first TBU of the root, the L verbs have a L tone in that same position, but the toneless verbs have

---

[47]The exception to this is in the subjunctive forms, where there is a single, predictable interaction between prefix tones and stem-tone pattern.

[48]But the lexical tone is phonetically realized on both morae of a non-penultimate bimoraic syllable (e.g. in a CVV(N)CVC- base, such as **-yòòfih-** 'be short'). This is not due to spreading, but to the fact that a non-penultimate bimoraic syllable bears only a single tone, which is phonetically realized over the whole of the syllable.

3.5 Tone on verbs

no fixed tone. The tone of the first TBU of the root of a toneless verb varies, reflecting the suffixal tone (determined by the grammatical form of the verb).

Every surface form of any verb, whether imperative, infinitive, past, future, etc., in addition to any lexical tone, also bears a "stem-tone pattern", i.e. a pattern of grammatical tones, characteristic of the individual tense/aspect/mood of the verb form. This stem-tone pattern or grammatical melody is overlaid on the verb stem, and interacts with any lexical tones of the stem. There are seven distinct stem-tone patterns in Kifuliiru, all of which are discussed below in (3.5.3). They are mentioned here only to provide explanation for the fact that the various verb forms in (3.13) have tones other than their lexical tones on the syllables which follow the first syllable of the stem.

The forms in (3.13) show the distinctions among the three lexical tonal classes of verbs: H, L, and Ø. The presentation uses two different verb forms, infinitive (INF) and unmarked future (F2) in order to illustrate the fluctuation in the tone of the initial TBU of a toneless (Ø) root, and to contrast that fluctuation with the stable tone seen on the first syllable of the H and L verbs.

(3.13)   H 'return'   L 'kneel'   Ø 'invite'
  INF   ú=kú-gálúkà   ú=kú-fùkámà   ú=kú-láálíkà
  F2   tú-gá-gálùkà   tú-gá-fùkàmà   tú-gá-lààlìkà

Note in (3.13) that in the H-tone verb, **-gáluk-** 'return', the tone of the first syllable of the stem (underlined) in both the infinitive and future forms is H, while in the L-tone verb, **-fùkam-** 'kneel' the tone of the first syllable of the stem in both forms is L. These are the lexical tones of the respective verb roots. Now compare just the infinitive forms of these same two verbs. The second syllable of the stem in the infinitive form has a H tone in both the H verb **kúgálúkà** and the L verb **kúfùkámà**. This H tone is the suffixal stem tone of the infinitive form.

In the future tense, the suffixal stem tone is L. Thus, the tone on the second syllable of the stem is L in the future forms, whether in the H verb **túgágálùkà** 'we will return', or the L verb **túgáfùkàmà** 'we will kneel'.

Looking next at the two forms of the toneless (Ø) verb, **-laalik-** 'invite', we see that the tone of the first syllable of the stem varies. In the infinitive, the first syllable of the verb stem, **kúláálíkà** 'to invite' exhibits H tone,[49] which

---

[49]Though the first syllable of a verb like **-láálíkà** has two morae, we assume that since linking is to the syllable there is only one underlying H tone on this bimoraic syllable. We will indicate this by association lines in derivations, but will continue to mark each mora with an accent mark (**láálíkà** and not **láalíkà**) just to avoid creating the impression that there is a contour in such a syllable.

is the suffixal stem tone of the infinitive form. In the future form of -**laalik**-, that same first syllable exhibits the L tone which is the suffixal stem tone of future forms: **túgáláàlìkà** 'we will invite'.

The suffixal tone in any verb always links to the leftmost free TBU. In a verb which has a lexical H or L tone, the lexical tone always links to the first syllable of the stem, so that the leftmost free TBU is the second TBU of the stem. Thus in verbs of the H or L class, the suffixal tones must link to the right of the lexical tone, on the second TBU of the root. However, in a toneless verb, there is no lexical tone to link to the initial TBU of the stem, so that this initial position of the stem is a free TBU. Thus the suffixal tone is able to link to the leftmost position in the stem of toneless verbs, producing the fluctuation of tones such as is seen on -**laalik**- in (3.13).

Derivations from underlying form (UF) to surface form (SF)[50] are shown in (3.14) for the infinitive form of a H, a L, and a toneless (Ø) verb, using the examples found in (3.13). Infinitives display what is known as the simple stem-tone pattern, whose grammatical tone is a H tone which links to the leftmost free TBU (3.5.3.1 for more on the simple stem-tone pattern). For each form, the surface tones and its lexical tone class (in parentheses) are shown in the first line of the respective derivations. Then the morphemes, separated by hyphens and shown with any underlying tones, are presented in the UF of the derivation. Morphemes of the verbs in (3.14) are the augment, the cl. 15 (infinitive) prefix, verb base, and final vowel (FV). The chevrons around the FV indicate that it is extratonal at the outset of the derivation. At the stage where the FV becomes visible, the chevrons are removed.

---

[50]Stages (i.e. the restatement of the form, labeled UF, Next, SF etc.) used in the derivations in this chapter are not intended to accurately reflect cycles or other specified underlying stages of derivation, except insofar as labeled as UF, or with terms such as (by visibility). A new "stage" of the derivation is begun when it would otherwise become confusing to follow the application of the rules and processes listed. UF represents the form as found immediately preceding tone association. Prefixes are included for the identification of the form, but it is assumed that they comprise a separate domain, and the association of the tones of the prefixes is not shown in any of these derivations (except in cases of monosyllabic stems, where stem tones may associate to the rightmost mora of the prefixes).

3.5 Tone on verbs

(3.14) Derivation of H, L, and Ø infinitives[51]

ú=kú-gálúk-à (AU=15-return-Fa) 'to return' (H)

UF **ú=kúgáluk\<a\>** initial tone association
     | |
     H H lexical H tone, simple pattern H [52]

SF **ú=kúgálúkà** by visibility
    | | |
    H H L by default L-insertion on FV

Note that H-spread will not spread a tone onto a word-final TBU (3.8.1), so a default L tone is associated to the FV.

ú=kú-fùkám-à (AU=15-kneel-Fa) 'to kneel' (L)

UF **ú=kúfùkam\<a\>** initial tone association
     | |
     L H lexical L tone, simple pattern H

SF **ú=kúfùkámà** by visibility
    | | |
    L H L by default L insertion

---

[51] All penultimate syllables have two tonal root nodes, (see 3.7) but for simplicity and space saving in the case of a monomoraic penult, these nodes are not shown individually unless each has a contrastive lexical or grammatical tone. Note that in derivations of forms with a monomoraic penult, the tones linked to the penult are marked with a superscript **r** or **l** to show whether they are linked to the right or left node of the penult. If a left node is linked, and the right node is not shown, it may be assumed that the right node is linked identically, by tone spread from the left node. Tone spread to an unlinked penultimate can be assumed to target both nodes.

[52] Every penult underlyingly has both a left and a right node and can bear two tones. The grammatical tone of the stem-tone pattern links to the left node of the penult.

ú=kú-láálík-à (AU=15-invite-Fa) 'to invite' (Ø)

UF ú=kúláalik<a>   initial tone association
        |
        H   simple pattern H (links to leftmost TBU)

Next ú=kúlaalik<a>
        |⟋
        H   H-spread to all non-final TBUs

SF ú=kúláálíkà   by visibility
    |⟋ |
    H   L   by default L insertion

Note that in verbs of all tone types, as mentioned above, the grammatical tone of the stem-tone pattern associates to the leftmost free TBU in the stem. In a H or L verb, this leftmost free TBU is in the V_2 position. In a Ø verb, it is in the V_1 position, since there is no lexical root tone present.

The toneless class of roots is especially interesting, because the only verbs in this class[53] are the verbs with a single CV root, or verbs in which the first syllable of the stem has a phonemically long vowel, as in (3.15d) or those which have a long vowel in the first syllable due to a preceding glide (**Cw** or **Cy**)[54] as (3.15e, f).

(3.15) Configurations of stem-initial syllable in toneless verbs

a.	CV	kú-<u>bà</u>	'to be'
b.	CV	kú-<u>lyâ</u>	'to eat'
c.	CV	kú-<u>mwâ</u>	'to shave'
d.	CVV	kú-<u>bííkà</u>	'to put'
e.	CwVV	kú-<u>bwíírà</u>	'to tell'
f.	CyVV	kú-<u>kyúúlà</u>	'to command'

---

[53]One can say that if a verb is toneless, it must have one of these three CV configurations, but the converse is only true as long as there is not a fricative in the C_2 position, as will be seen below.

[54]Verbs with a CGV initial syllable may be considered to be derived from a CVV in which the first V is a high vowel, and the second is an unlike vowel. Thus even preceding compensatory lengthening of the vowel, there are two moraic segments in the first syllable of the radical.

3.5 Tone on verbs

A verb which begins with **yVV** is never in the toneless class as far as we have determined. This would seem to suggest that the initial **y-** in such verb stems is not historically a part of the verb radical.[55] If it is the case that the **y-** is inserted by rule, then preceding the **y-** epenthesis the underlying radical would have only one moraic segment in its initial syllable, and would not have the bimoraic initial syllable which is the underlying configuration of the toneless class.

A verb which begins with a CVVNC pattern, e.g. **kú-hēēnd-à** (L) 'to trick' or **kú-géénd-à** (H) 'to go', in which a nasal-consonant (NC) sequence is the conditioning factor for the long vowel, never falls in the toneless class. This may be related to the fact that prior to compensatory lengthening of the vowel preceding the NC, there is only one mora in the initial syllable of the verb. However, even when there is a CG (Cy or Cw) stem initially in a verb containing NC in the second syllable such as in **kú-fyēēng-à** (L) 'to pinch something together' the verb is not in the toneless class, even though there are two morae in the first syllable.

There are some apparent exceptions to the statement that verbs with a CVV or CGVV initial syllable are always toneless. Note that these are only apparent exceptions, rather than true exceptions. There is a reason that these verbs, though having a C(G)VV initial syllable, are not toneless. This is because historically, they had an NC cluster following the VV: the H verb **kúgáájà** 'to count' and the L verbs **kúhīīvà/kúhōōvà** 'to hunt', **kúfwīījà** 'to snore', **kúbāājà** 'to carve', **kúshōōjà** 'to paddle or pole a boat', and **kúsùùzâ** 'to bother', and **kúgwèjérà** 'to lie down'. All of these apparent exceptions have a voiced fricative in the C_2 position.[56] There is a phonological rule which operated historically in Kifuliiru to delete a nasal preceding a fricative. Thus we posit that each of these "exceptional" verbs originally had not a C(G)VVC stem, but a C(G)VVNC base, giving a historical, phonological reason to explain why these "exceptions" are not found in the toneless class of verbs.[57] The H-tone

---

[55] There are no V-initial verb stems in Kifuliiru. Any verb stem which would otherwise be V-initial begins with **y**. This **y-** may have its source in the cl. 5 infinitive prefix **i-** of which traces remain in Kifuliiru. This **i-** would have undergone glide formation and could have been reinterpreted as a part of the verb stem at the time when the switch to cl. 15 infinitives was in process. Nouns and adjectives derived from such verbs do not contain the **y**.

[56] Recall that **j** in Kifuliiru is a voiced alveolar fricative (IPA ʒ).

[57] There are also some verbs which are toneless which do *not* have a long vowel in the first syllable of the stem, but which are derived from a verb with an underlying long vowel in the first syllable, e.g -**komeer**- 'get used to'; -**yitubaanul**- 'make oneself sweat, work very hard' from -**tuuban**- 'sweat'. This long vowel in the initial syllable is shortened by phonological rule when three or more morae follow, as happens when an extension with a long vowel is added. These verbs have may have no synchronic form with a long vowel in the first syllable of the stem, as -**komeer**- does not.

causative verb **kúlóózâ** 'to want, look for', derived from **kúlóóngà** 'to get' is an example of a verb which still has a synchronic form with the NC cluster.

The data in (3.16) compare a CVVC verb of the toneless class, in several conjugated forms, to the "exceptional" (non-toneless) CVVC verbs, one with lexical H tone and one with lexical L tone. This data is presented merely to exemplify the differences in the tone realization of three different stem-tone patterns on H, L, and Ø verbs, all of CVVC configuration.[58] (For explanation of stem-tone patterns, see 3.5.2. For information on the specific patterns see 3.5.3.)

(3.16) Ø, H and L verbs of CVVC configuration in infinitive, RS, and F2

Lex. T	Gloss	Infinitive	Resultative (RS)	Future (F2)
Ø	'put'	**kú-bíík-à**	**tù-bíís-ír-ì**	**tú-gá-bììk-à**
H	'count'	**kú-gááj-à**	**tù-gááj-ìr-ì**	**tú-gá-gááj-à**
L	'hunt'	**kú-hīīv-à**	**tù-hììv-ír-ì**	**tú-gá-hììv-à**

Note in (3.16) that in the infinitive column the Ø and H verbs pattern identically, with a H tone on the first stem syllable, while the L verb **kúhīīvà** has underlying LH tone (level mid tone, phonetically) on the corresponding syllable.

In the following column, the resultative forms (all in first-person plural, **tù-bíís-ír-ì** (1PL-put-RS-Fi) 'we have put', etc.) each verb patterns separately: the Ø verb has only H tones on both non-final syllables of the stem, while the H verb shows a HH tone followed by a L tone on its non-final stem syllables, and the L verb shows a LL followed by a H tone on the corresponding syllables.

In the third column, showing unmarked future (F2) forms, the Ø and L verbs pattern identically, with a L tone on the non-final stem syllable, while the H verb displays a HL contour on the corresponding syllable.

The fact that these three segmentally comparable CVVC verbs all pattern differently is clear evidence that toneless verbs are indeed identifiable as a class separate both from H and from L in Kifuliiru. The toneless class is not just the result of predictable changes happening to a H or L stem due to the CVVC configuration of the verb stem.

---

[58]Reading an earlier version of this chapter, which lacked this comparison of CVVC stems of different tone classes, some reviewers were led to conclude that the "toneless" nature of the Ø verbs was merely due to the interaction of synchronic tone rules with the CVVC configuration of the stem. The data in (3.16) merely show that this is not the case. Example (3.16) is not intended to be a presentation or explanation of the different stem-tone patterns.

3.5.1.2 Lexical H tone of causative and passive suffixes

It is recognized that though Bantu verbal extensions in general are toneless, the causative and passive morphemes often seem to be an exception. Meeussen (1967:92) states in regard to his historical reconstructions that "The high tone of [the Proto-Bantu causative and passive] suffixes is set up tentatively, and in any case its manifestations seem to have been very much limited". Kifuliiru is one of the languages in which the H tone of these suffixes is quite apparent. Despite the tone shift in Kifuliiru relative to Proto-Bantu (3.3.3) these suffixes clearly exhibit a H tone.[59]

The causative and passive extensions each consist of a segmental morpheme as well as a lexical H tone, as shown in (3.17).

(3.17) Causative and passive morphemes[†]

    a. **-i/-iisi**   causative (CS)   H

    b. **-ú** (following C)/**-bú** (following V)   passive (PS)   H

    [†]Both the final -i of the causative and the final -u of the passive morpheme undergo glide formation when juxtaposed to the FV of the verb. The final vowel of the causative morpheme is then deleted/absorbed by phonological process if it follows an **s** or **z**, as it most often does, due to its spirantizing effect on a preceding consonant. Thus the final -i of the causative does not appear on the surface as **y** except when it immediately follows a consonant not affected by spirantization, such as **h** or a nasal.

When both passive and causative are present in the same verb form, we never see evidence of more than one H tone. We must assume that when the passive and causative appear together, they are treated as a single unit: a passive-causative morpheme **-ibw-/-iisibw-/-eesibw-** with a single lexical H tone.

These two suffixes are unique among verbal suffixes in that they bear a tone at all, since all other verbal suffixes are toneless. The H tones of these two morphemes are considered the second (and final) tone of the lexical tonal melody of the verb stem (3.5.2), and as such will link only to the rightmost available position in the word.[60] That position is the FV in a verb form whose

---

[59]Hyman and Katamba (1990) presents much more information on H tones in these extensions with focus on Luganda. They note that in general the H tone is evident only in stem-tone patterns with a suffixal H tone, or in languages having undergone tone reversal, such as Kifuliiru, only in stem-tone patterns with a suffixal L tone. We show that in Kifuliiru the H is present underlyingly in all instances, though its presence is neutralized in various contexts by the normal processes of tone spread and contour simplifications.

[60]Because the H of passive will only link to the rightmost available TBU, we assume that the

suffixal grammatical melody has only a single tone, and the right-hand node of the penultimate syllable in a verb form whose grammatical melody has both an initial and a final tone. Any final tone of a grammatical melody links to the FV in all passive and causative forms.

This right-linking behavior of the extension tones is partially due to the application of the edge-in linking convention (3.7.1). In that convention, for any melody /$T_1...T_n$/, T_1 is associated to the leftmost TBU and T_n to the rightmost, with any intervening tones associated to the next most peripheral TBUs according to their left or right placement within their original melody. The H tone of an extension is always the rightmost tone of the lexical melody. If it is also the last tone in the combined melody of a verb stem as in (3.18c), it is linked to the rightmost free TBU. However, if there is a final grammatical tone present, that grammatical tone is the last tone of the combined melody. In such a case, the extension tone still links rightward, associating to the TBU directly to the left of the final grammatical tone. The right-linking quality of these tones, just as that seen in the final-linking tones of the complex stem-tone patterns, is thus synchronically partially attributable to edge-in linking of the combined melody (3.5.2) and partially attributable to the rightward placement of the extension tone within the lexical melody.

The rightward placement of the tones of causative (CS) and passive (PS) within the lexical melody has its roots in the rightward placement of the segmental portion of these morphemes. Both causative and passive are unique among the extensions in the requirement that they be placed as close as possible to the right end of the verb. PS never appears in any position other than that directly preceding the FV, e.g. **kú-gúl-w-â** (15-buy-PS-Fa) 'to be bought' and the CS's final **i**- takes that same position in a non-passive verb, e.g. **kú-gúl-iisi-a** > **kúgúlíísâ** (15-buy-CS-Fa) 'to sell (cause to buy)'. CS directly precedes PS in the passive of a causative verb, e.g. **kú-gúl-íísí-bw-â** (15-buy-CS-PS-Fa) 'to be sold'.

It is also essential to make special note of another unique characteristic of verbs which include the causative or passive morpheme. The final vowel of these verbs is not extratonal. In all non-passive, non-causative forms, the final vowel is extratonal at the time of initial tone association, and is only assigned a tone at a later point in the derivation. In passive or causative forms only, the final vowel of the verb may be linked to a tone at the point of initial association.[61] Causative and passive forms are presented under the discussion

---

original lexical melody of a toneless verb includes a "placeholder" null marker which occupies the left-hand position in the melody. A passive or causative verb whose root has lexical H tone would have a lexical melody of H H, a verb with a L-toned root would have a lexical melody of L H, and a toneless verb would have a lexical melody of Ø H.

[61]The lack of extratonality in the FV of passive and causative forms, as well as the rightward position of the segmental suffix, is likely affiliated with the fact that each of these morphemes is V-final. All other non-final verbal suffixes are C-final. Being V-final, causative and passive

3.5.2 Assignment of grammatical tone in verbs

Verbal tone assignment in Kifuliiru reflects the basic divisions of the verb word into prefixes, base, and final vowel (FV) as laid out in (3.12). In Kifuliiru, the tones, if any, of the prefixes link to the prefixes. The lexical tone, if any, of a verb root links to the first TBU of the verb base. The H tones of passive and causative link to the FV if it is not linked to a grammatical tone, or to the TBU which immediately precedes the FV, if the FV is linked to a grammatical tone.

As mentioned in (3.5.1.2), the FV of the verb is always extratonal in all underlying forms except for passive and causative verbs. When the FV is extratonal, it does not receive a tone in the initial association of lexical and grammatical tones. Before the end of the derivation, the FV loses its extratonality. The point at which the FV becomes interactive with the tonological processes is termed "visibility" following the term used by Bickmore and Doyle (1995) in their discussion of Chilungu (M14) tone.

In addition to the lexical tones (if any) of the prefix(es) and of the stem, a tense or mood puts its own tonal grammatical "suffix" on the verb. It is termed a "suffix" because it is placed on the stem of the verb, following any underlying root tone of the verb, and ignoring the prefixes to the left, though they may be toneless. In Kifuliiru, the tonal grammatical suffix usually appears as an overlay on the free TBUs of the verb base. (The base is the root plus all suffixes, but does not include the FV.) This can be illustrated by any CVCVC-FV infinitive, such as **kú-tèm-ér-à** (15-cut-APL-Fa) 'to cut for/at' where the infinitive prefix **kú-** has its own H tone, the first syllable of the radical **-tèm-** bears the underlying lexical L tone of the verb, and the underlyingly toneless applicative extension **-er** displays the H suffixal tone of the infinitive, which has associated to the only free syllable of the verb stem.

---

each add a mora to the final syllable without adding a corresponding extra syllable to the verb. Another tack of analysis, which I initally took, would be to assume that the final vowel is initially extratonal even in the passive and causative forms and that it is non-interactive to the extent that it does not trigger glide formation in the vowel of the preceding V-final extension. Then, since the vowel at the end of these suffixes remains vocalic, it allows the final syllable, despite the invisibility of the FV, to meet the moricity requirements of a syllable. Because of this, initial tone association would link the rightmost tone of the tonal melody to this final syllable. The tone(s) thus linked would be delinked when the vowel of the suffix underwent glide formation at the point of visibility of the final vowel and would then relink rightward, onto the FV. This relink and delink analysis adds a good deal of complexity to the explanation of verbal tone, but is more explanatory (than assuming ad-hoc non-extratonality of the FV) as to *why* the final vowel of causative and passive displays the final linking tones found in the penultimate syllable of non-passive, non-causative forms.

All verb stems, when used in any surface form are given such a suffixal overlay of grammatical tones by one of the various stem-tone patterns. Some stem-tone patterns have only one tone, while others have two. The tones of the verb stem associate to the syllables according to the normal linking process of tones in Kifuliiru, i.e. edge-in linking (3.7.1). If the grammatical melody has only one suffixal tone, this single tone links to the first free TBU to the right of any lexical tone of the verb stem. If there are two suffixal overlay tones, the first links to the leftmost free TBU in the verb stem (still to the right of any lexical tone) and the second to the rightmost available TBU.[62]

The stem-tone pattern is referred to here as a "suffixal overlay" because its left-hand tone links to the right of any lexical tone of the verb root, while its right-hand tone links to the right of any extension tone. Thus the possible underlying tones of the lexical and grammatical melodies (3.18 a, b) are laid out on the verb stem in what we call the combined tonal melody as shown in (3.18c). Tones (T) shown in parentheses may or may not be present, depending on the verb form.

(3.18) a. Lexical melody :   (root T), (extension T)

      b. Grammatical melody :   left-linking gr.T, (right-linking gr. T)

      c. Combined melody :   (root T), left gr.T, (ext. T), (right gr. T)

Thus underlyingly there are two separate but overlapping melodies: the lexical melody and the grammatical melody, each of which may have both a left-edge tone and a right-edge tone. The grammatical melody is overlaid on the lexical melody to form a single combined melody as shown in (3.18c). As noted, the tones indicated in parentheses are lacking in some verb forms. Some verb roots are lexically toneless, lacking the initial lexical root tone in the layout. Because most extensions are toneless, the lexical extension tone is present only in a passive or causative form. The grammatical stem-tone pattern also may consist of only one tone, as is true in the case of the simple and V_2 stem-tone patterns. In such cases, the right-linking grammatical stem tone would be lacking. Thus the only tone obligatory in every verb form is the left-linking grammatical stem tone.

The combination melody created by the overlay of the grammatical melody on the lexical melody is associated by edge-in linking (3.7.1). The lexical tone of a H or L verb always links to the first TBU of the verb stem, while the

---

[62]This is to say the rightmost TBU, with the exception of any which is extratonal.

3.5 Tone on verbs

grammatical tones, those of the stem-tone pattern and any extension link to TBUs to the right of this lexical tone.

3.5.3 Stem-tone patterns in Kifuliiru verbs

In the following discussion we make repeated reference to terms used by Goldsmith (1987) in describing tone patterns of verbs in Lacustrine Bantu. In his article he notes that throughout the Lacustrine Bantu (Bantu J) group, of which Kifuliiru is a member, stem-tone patterns of verb tenses usually fall into three certain types. He terms these three "Simple", "V_2", and "Complex" stem-tone patterns. His "Simple" pattern consists of the lexical stem tone on the first vowel of the stem, and L tones on all other syllables. His "V_2" pattern has the lexical tone of the root on the first vowel of the stem, followed by a polar[63] H tone on the second vowel of the stem, while his "Complex" pattern is the "V_2" pattern *plus* a H tone which links to the final vowel.

In Kifuliiru, these three patterns are all evident. However, Kifuliiru, unlike the Lacustrine languages discussed by Goldsmith, has undergone a total tone reversal compared to Proto-Bantu, and because of this, there are some differences between Goldsmith's "typical" patterns and the Kifuliiru ones. Except for the polar H tone of the complex stem-tone pattern, all the other tones are reversed from what Goldsmith describes:

The Kifuliiru "simple" pattern consists of the lexical stem tone followed by H tones on all the following syllables (except for the syllable of the FV, which bears a default L).[64]

The Kifuliiru "V_2" pattern is characterized by a (non-polar) L tone which associates to the first free TBU of the stem. All remaining TBUs bear L surface tones with the exception of the FV in causative and passive forms, which have H tone. Of the three patterns in Kifuliiru, this one is the farthest from the description Goldsmith posits as "typical" in Lacustrine Bantu, since the V_2 tone in Kifuliiru is not only L instead of H, but is also non-polar. This lack of polarity of the L tone is not surprising, however, if one interprets the "polarity" of

---

[63] Saying it is a "polar" H tone here simply means that it is a H tone which is in a form subject to Meeussen's rule, a rule which lowers a H tone following another H tone. That the underlying form of this "polar" tone is H rather than L is discernable from observing the Ø verbs.

[64] As noted, Goldsmith (1987) in describing and naming the tone patterns in Lacustrine Bantu, was focusing on languages which have not undergone tone reversal. He named the "simple" pattern "simple" because it had no grammatical H tones, only L tones, which he considered "default". However, since Kifuliiru has undergone tone reversal, the pattern which corresponds to Goldsmith's "simple" pattern is characterized by H tones. In order to keep the correspondences straightforward, I keep the names as Goldsmith had them. In Kifuliiru they are no longer quite as appropriate, but this way anyone comparing Lacustrine languages will find it easier to compare what tenses are found in each of these patterns across the language family.

the H tone in the complex HL pattern as a result of the action of Meeussen's rule, which affects only H tones.

Besides the "simple" pattern and the V_2 pattern, Kifuliiru has five different "complex" (two-tone) stem-tone patterns.[65] The Kifuliiru "complex" pattern which most probably corresponds to Goldsmith's "Complex" pattern is the complex HL pattern, which has a "polar" H tone that links to the leftmost free TBU of the stem, plus a right-linking L tone which surfaces on the penultimate TBU in a non-passive non-causative form, or on the FV in a passive or causative verb.

An overview of all the basic stem-tone patterns in Kifuliiru is presented in table 3.2. For examples of the various verb forms, see (3.5.7).

Table 3.2. Stem-tone patterns in Kifuliiru verbs

Pattern	Stem tone(s)	Characteristics	Verb forms in which the pattern is found
Simple	H	links to leftmost free TBU	Infinitive Unmarked past (P2)
V_2	L	links to leftmost free TBU	Future (F2) Any structurally subjunctive form[a] in which an underlying tone is realized on a prefix Unrealized expectation (present)
Complex HL	H L	H links to leftmost free TBU, L links to rightmost free TBU (Meeussen's rule[b] affects all HH sequences)	Recent past (P1) Sequential Potential/conditional Potential/conditional, contrary-to-fact Present resultative state Timeless

---

[65]The fact that Kifuliiru has five "complex" patterns does not necessarily imply that Kifuliiru is not typical of Lacustrine Bantu. Goldsmith mentions that he did not deal in his article with imperatives and subjunctives, which account for two of these extra "complex" patterns in Kifuliiru, and there are very possibly other forms, as well, which he did not treat.

3.5 Tone on verbs

Pattern	Stem tone(s)	Characteristics	Verb forms in which the pattern is found
Complex LH	L H	L links to leftmost free TBU, H links to rightmost free TBU	Resultative, frustrated Remote past state (P3) Imperative Singular
Complex LH-IP	L H	L links to leftmost free TBU, H links to FV	Imperative plural
Complex LL	L L	L links to leftmost free TBU, L links to rightmost free TBU	Potential/conditional, contrary-to-fact (past)
Complex HH	H H	H links to first TBU of stem, replacing any lexical tone; H links to the rightmost free TBU (Meeussen's rule affects all HH sequences)	All subjunctive forms in which there are no underlying tones which link to any prefixes

[a]There are five forms in Kifuliiru which are structurally subjunctive, having the characteristic FV -**e**, as well as various dependent (if/when conditional) forms of other tenses/aspects which also take stem-tone patterns characteristic of the subjunctive.

[b]Meeussen's rule lowers the second of a sequence of two H tones to L. (See 3.8.3 for details.)

The sections under 3.5.3 examine in some depth the various stem-tone patterns in Kifuliiru, showing their realization on passive and causative verbs, as well on as passivized causatives and on verbs of various syllable patterns.[66] The stem-tone patterns are presented in the order given in table 3.2.

---

[66]In the sections describing the stem-tone patterns, we have used a limited number of verbs mainly for convenience and so that the reader may become somewhat familiar with them. Every verb of a given lexical tone class and a given syllable pattern reacts to the tonal overlays of the stem-tone patterns in exactly the same way as every other verb of that same class and configuration. For this reason, it is more helpful to see a verb of each of three or four different syllable configurations in the various stem-tone patterns than it is to see many different verbs of the same syllable configuration.

3.5.3.1 *Simple stem-tone pattern*

The "simple" stem-tone pattern is the name given to forms in which the lexical tone of the verb stem appears on the first TBU of the stem, and all other non-final TBUs bear H tone. The grammatical tone of this pattern is a single H tone which links to the leftmost free TBU in the stem. This H tone is then spread onto other non-final TBUs by the rule of H-spread. In the passive or causative of these forms, the H tone of the PS or CS extension surfaces on the FV. Meeussen's rule does not operate in verbs of the simple stem-tone pattern.

In the simple stem-tone pattern, we find the infinitives (INF) and the unmarked past (P2) which has the **ká-** prefix, e.g. **túkálágáánà** 'we agreed together'. The infinitives include the regular cl. 15 infinitive, e.g. **kúlágáánà** 'to agree together', as well as the cl. 5 infinitive forms[67] used as the main verb of a multiword verb form, e.g. the second word of **kúkìzí lágáánà** 'to repeatedly agree together', or the final word of the progressive form **tùlì mú=géèndà** 'we are going'.

Let us look at the infinitive as an example of the simple stem-tone pattern in Kifuliiru. The infinitive, besides having the typical cl. 15 (**ú=**)**kú-** prefix, is always characterized by the suffixal H tone of the simple pattern, which is linked to the leftmost free TBU of the stem and spreads rightward onto any free non-final TBUs. In the case of a H or L-tone verb, the first free TBU is the second TBU of the stem (Goldsmith's V_2 position) since the first TBU of the stem (the V_1 position) always displays the lexical tone of the verb. In the case of a toneless verb, the first free TBU of the stem is the first TBU (the V_1 position) of the stem, since there is no lexical tone which must link there. Thus, in **kúláálíkà** 'to invite', the toneless verb shown in (3.19), the infinitive form's suffixal H tone associates initially to the first syllable of the stem, i.e., **laa**.[68] The rule of H-spread applies in all cases (3.8.1).

The syllables on which the H tone of the simple pattern is realized on each stem are underlined in (3.19).

---

[67]Kifuliiru no longer uses infinitives with the cl. 5 prefix, using instead cl. 15 infinitives, but these aspectual auxiliaries with "prefixless" infinitives seem to reflect the historical use of cl. 5 infinitives in the language. Some related languages, such as Kinande (JD40) and Kihunde (JD50) use cl. 5 infinitives exclusively (Bastin 2003:523).

[68]In the case of any verb with a C(G)VV(N)C-FV configuration, (i.e. where the VV is both stem initial and in penultimate position) the first mora of the penultimate constitutes the V_1 position, and the second mora, the V_2 position, e.g. **kúdííhà** 'to beat someone'.

3.5 Tone on verbs

(3.19) Stem tone patterns on infinitives

UT	Infinitive	Gloss
H	kúlágáánà	'to agree together'
L	kúbètúlírà	'to carry on head or shoulders for someone'
Ø	kúláálíkà	'to invite'

Note that the first syllable of the stem in the H verb **kúlágáánà** displays the H lexical tone of the stem, the first syllable of the stem of the L verb **kúbètúlírà** displays the L lexical tone of that stem, but the first syllable of the stem of the toneless verb **kúláálíkà** displays the H tone of the simple stem-tone pattern.

In (3.20) are examples of the simple stem-tone pattern on infinitives of all three tone classes (labeled in the left-hand column as H, L, or Ø) and of various syllable patterns.

(3.20) Simple stem-tone pattern with assorted verb types

UT	Syll. pattern	Base	Gloss	Infinitive
H	CVC	-fúk-	'pour on'	kúfúkà
H	CVVNC	-gúung-	'cheat'	kúgúúngà
H	CVCVVC	-báraat-	'make wattle frame'	kúbáráátà
H	CVCVVNCVC	-gógoombek-	'barge in'	kúgógóómbékà
L	CVC	-bèg-	'cut hair'	kúbēga/kúbègà
L	CVVNC	-fyèeng-	'shut off breath'	kúfyēēngà
L	CVNCVVC	-shàmbaal-	'rejoice'	kúshàmbáálà
L	CVCVVNCVC	-bèraangir-	'call from afar'	kúbèráángírà
L	CVCVCVVNC	-gòloloomb-	'flow'	kúgòlólóómbà
Ø	CVVC	-diih-	'beat'	kúdííhà
Ø	CVVCVC	-laalik-	'invite'	kúláálíkà

In (3.20) the following observations can be made regarding the forms with the simple stem-tone pattern:

(a) In H and in Ø verbs, the first syllable of the stem always has H tone in the simple stem-tone pattern. In H verbs, this is the result of a H lexical tone. The lexical H of a H verb always appears on the surface as H in the simple stem tone forms, in verbs of all syllable pattern types. In Ø verbs, the stem-initial

H tone is the direct realization of the H tone of the simple pattern, since the H tone of the simple pattern associates to the V_1 position in a Ø verb.

(b) In H and Ø verbs, not only the first syllable of the stem, but all other non-final syllables as well have H tone. In H verbs, the H in the V_2 position is the H of the simple stem-tone pattern. Any Hs in post-V_2 position are due to H-spread, as are all the post-stem-initial Hs in Ø verbs.

(c) In L verbs, all syllables which are non-stem initial and non-word final have H tone. Note in (3.20) that the first syllable of the stem of L verbs longer than CV(VN)C, e.g. -**shàmbaal**-, -**bèraangir**-, etc., always has a L tone. This is because the lexical tone of any verb always links only to the first (leftmost) TBU of the stem, and the lexical tone here is L. The H tone of the simple stem-tone pattern links to the TBU directly to the right of the lexical tone.

In the shorter (CV(VN)C-FV) L-toned verbs, e.g. -**bèg**-, **fyèeng**-, the stem-initial syllable displays LH (mid) tone (indicated by a macron.) (Some speakers have a rule which reduces a LH on a single mora to L. This is why there is an alternate pronunciation given for **kúbēgà/kúbègà** 'cut hair'.) It is possible for this stem-initial syllable to bear LH contour because it is penultimate, and a penultimate syllable receives two association lines. For details on the double linking of the penultimate syllable, see (3.7). Thus the L lexical tone of the verb and the H tone of the simple stem-tone pattern are both associated to the stem initial syllable of these CV(VN)C verbs. Keep in mind that the FV in these forms never has a tone associated to it in the initial association (3.6).

In a CVC L-tone verb like -**bèg**-, the double linking of the penultimate syllable means that the single mora of the stem is double linked to the lexical L and the grammatical H of the simple pattern. In the CVVNC-FV verb such as -**fyèeng**-, the same double linking of the initial/penultimate syllable is seen. The only difference is that here it is on a bimoraic syllable, so that it is easier to see that the first TBU is associated to the lexical L and the second TBU to the H tone of the simple pattern, as shown in (3.21).

(3.21) **kú-fyèéng-à** (15-shut.off.breath-Fa) 'to shut off breath' (L)

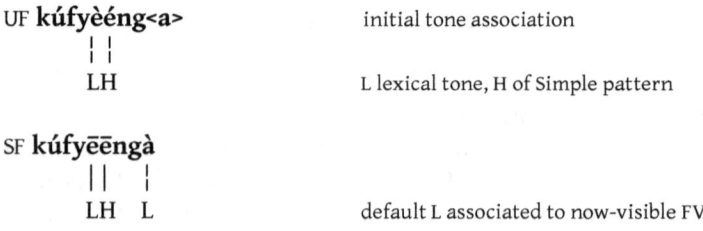

3.5 Tone on verbs

Because the L tone of a lexically L CV(VN)C verb and the H tone of the simple stem-tone pattern are both realized on the same syllable, there is an underlying tautosyllabic LH contour. There are several phonetic rules which affect the surface realization of a tautosyllabic LH contour (3.8.2.1). Thus the manner in which the tautosyllabic LH contour is pronounced in a L CV(VN)C verb depends upon the preceding and following tones. The data in (3.22), all of which exemplify different forms of L verbs in the simple stem-tone pattern, compare the basic infinitive to infinitive forms which have an added affix to alter the tonal environment. This demonstrates the surface tones which can result from the underlying LH contour which results from the interaction of the H of the simple stem-tone pattern and the lexical L of the verb stem in CVC and CVVNC forms. Observations and explanations follow.

(3.22)
	UT	Base	Gloss	Added affix	Infinitive
a.	L	-bèg-	'cut hair'	---	**kú-bēgà/kú-bègà**
b.				H tone (cl. 1 obj.)	**kú-múbēgà/kú-múbègà**
c.				L tone (cl. 2 obj.)	**kú-bàbégà**
d.	L	-fyèeng-	'pinch shut'	---	**kú-fyēēngà**
e.				H tone (cl. 1 obj.)	**kú-múfyēēngà**
f.				L tone (cl. 2 obj.)	**kú-bàfyééngà**

Note that in (3.22a) the simple base -**bèg**-, when occurring with an infinitive, has a surface LH (mid) or L tone (depending on dialect). This is the realization of the underlying LH contour when it follows a H tone and precedes a L tone. In (3.22d) the infinitive form of -**fyèeng**- has LH (mid) tone.

In (3.22b, e) there is a H-toned cl. 1 object prefix (**mú**- 's/he') preceding the stem. Thus the tonal environment preceding the stem in rows (3.22b, e) is identical to that in the simple infinitive seen in (3.22a, d). Accordingly, the realization of the underlying LH contour on the first syllable of the verb stem in all these cases is identical.

In (3.22c, f) there is instead a L-toned cl. 2 object prefix (**bà**- 'them') preceding the stem. We see in (3.22c, f) that when preceded by a L tone and also followed by a L tone, LH is realized as H due to the application of the rule of LH raising (LH > H/L_ L, (see 3.8.2.1.1 LH raising). The tone rules have exactly the same effect whether the tautosyllabic LH is on a single mora or a single bimoraic syllable. Thus each of the verb stems in these rows begins with an initial surface H tone: -**bégà**, -**fyééngà**, though the underlying initial tone is LH.

3.5.3.1.1 Simple stem tone pattern with causative and passive

Let us look next at the effect of adding causative and passive morphemes to forms of the simple stem-tone pattern.

Causative and passive morphemes add an additional H tone to the verb (3.5.1.2). This H tone links as far to the right as possible. In passive and causative forms, unlike other verb forms, the FV is not extratonal. Since the simple stem-tone pattern has no right-linking grammatical tones, the H tone of the passive or causative can link directly to the FV. Included in (3.23) are simple infinitives of the three tone classes, for comparison with the passive, causative, and passive-of-causative forms.

(3.23) Simple stem-tone pattern with causative and passive

	UT	Syll. pattern	Base	Gloss	Infinitive
a.	H	CVC	**-fúk-**	'pour on'	**kúfúkà**
b.	H	CVC w/PS	**-fúk-u-**	'pour on (PS)'	**kúfúkwâ**
c.	H	CVC w/CS	**-fúk-iisi-**	'pour on (CS)'	**kúfúkíísâ**
d.	H	CVC w/CS+PS	**-fúk-iisi-bu-**	'pour on (PS of CS)'	**kúfúkíísíbwâ**
e.	L	CVC	**-bèg-**	'cut hair'	**kúbēga/kúbègà**
f.	L	CVC w/PS	**-bèg-u-**	'cut hair (PS)'	**kúbègwâ**
g.	L	CVC w/CS	**-bèg-eesi-**	'cut hair (CS)'	**kúbègéésâ**
h.	L	CVC w/CS+PS	**-bèg-eesi-bu-**	'cut hair (PS of CS)'	**kúbègéésíbwâ**
i.	Ø	CVVC	**-diih-**	'beat'	**kúdííhà**
j.	Ø	CVVC w/PS	**-diih-u-**	'beat (PS)'	**kúdííhwâ**
k.	Ø	CVVC w/CS	**-diih-iisi-**	'beat (CS)'	**kúdíhíísâ**
l.	Ø	CVVC w/CS+PS	**-diih-iisi-bu-**	'beat (PS of CS)'	**kúdíhíísíbwâ**

In looking at (3.23), note that in all (H, L, and Ø) the verbs with passive and/or causative morphemes, the final syllable of all passive and causative (and passive-of-causative) forms has a H tone. This is the realization of the H tone of the passive or causative morpheme. In final position in isolation, H is always realized phonetically as a short falling contour (marked by the circumflex) due to the presence of a phonetic L boundary tone in phrase-final and utterance-final positions.

The stem-initial tone of each form is identical to the initial tone of the unextended infinitive with the exception of the L-tone verbs. In these, the stem initial tone of the causative or passive verb is L rather than LH, as it is in the

3.5 *Tone on verbs* 151

unextended form. In (3.23g, h) this is because the addition of the causative adds another syllable to the verb, causing the shortening of any long vowel in this position, and causing the H tone of the simple stem-tone pattern to link to a syllable farther to the right than the initial syllable.[69]

In (3.23f) the passive form **kú-bègwâ** also exhibits a L tone in the stem-initial position. In passive forms the total number of syllables is the same as it was in the unextended form, so the H tone of the simple pattern still links to the stem-initial syllable of the verb, causing an underlying LH contour there. However, the realization of the resultant LH contour is simplified to L now because the H tone of the passive directly follows it. This environment triggers the application of LH lowering (LH > L/_ H see 3.8.2.1). Observe the derivation in (3.24).

(3.24) **ú=kú-bèg-w-â** (AU=15-cut.hair-PS-Fa) 'to have hair cut' (L)

    UF **ú=kúbegwa**   initial tone association
           |\ |
           LH H   lexical L, H of Simple pattern, PS H

    SF **ú=kúbègwâ**
          |≯ |
          LH H   H of LH deleted by LH lowering

In the passive form of a CVC verb, as shown in (3.24), the first syllable of the stem, being in surface penultimate position, takes two association lines by initial tone association. Both the lexical L tone and the grammatical H tone of the simple stem-tone pattern link to this stem-initial/penultimate syllable. The H of PS links to the rightmost available position in the verb, in this case, the FV. (The surface falling contour is the phonetic realization of a H tone in utterance-final position.)

Since the grammatical tone of the simple stem-tone pattern is a H tone, we might be tempted to attribute the final H tones in the forms in (3.23) to the process of H-spread onto the non-extratonal FV. However, lexical level H-spread will not spread a tone onto a final syllable, and the final H tones in the passive and causative forms here are caused by the linking of the H of passive or causative to the FV as shown in (3.24). The fact that the causative and passive actually do have a lexical H tone will become more evident as we look at other stem-tone patterns.

---

[69] The mora-based vowel shortening rule shortens any long vowel when three or more morae follow within the word. A single mora may be assigned two tones only when it is in the penultimate position of the word.

3.5.3.2 V_2 stem-tone pattern

In Kifuliiru, the V_2 pattern displays a L tone on the first free TBU of the stem, which in a verb with lexical H or L tone is the second vowel (V_2) of the stem,[70] hence the name from Goldsmith (1987)[71] "V_2". All following TBUs within the verb word also have L tone, unless there is a causative or passive morpheme, either of which adds a final H tone. A final H tone will surface on the FV itself in all passive and causative forms in the V_2 pattern. Meeussen's rule does not operate in V_2 forms.

In the group of tenses/moods which exhibits the V_2 stem-tone pattern, we find the unmarked future (F2) tense, as well as all subjunctive forms which have any prefix which bears a lexical or grammatical tone.[72] Besides basic subjunctive (SBV) forms with such prefixes, there are also four other subjunctive patterns which always fall in this pattern, as listed in table 3.4: Continuative (CON), intervening time (INTV), future remote (F3), conditional contrary-to-fact persistive (CND.CF.PERS). In addition, the V_2 pattern applies to the timeless and resultative forms which have been rendered subjunctive by the addition of a H-toned subject prefix, mentioned briefly in the discussion of (3.94).

In (3.25) we will use the F2 tense as an example of the V_2 pattern. As background, note that the future prefix, **gá(a)-** bears a H tone which spreads one syllable leftward onto the preceding prefix syllable. This preceding prefix is the subject prefix unless the form includes a negative prefix, in which case it is the negative **ta-** onto which the H of **gá-** spreads. It will also be noted that the vowel of the future prefix is lengthened (**gáá-**) when it precedes fewer than three morae within the word. Prefix tones do not spread onto the verb stem in any circumstances.

As stated, the V_2 stem-tone pattern is defined by a suffixal L tone which links to the leftmost free TBU. Any following TBUs are given L tones by the rule of L-spread. Thus in the unmarked future tense (F2), the H-tone verb **gógoombek-** 'to barge in, intrude', in first-person plural takes the form **tú-gá-yì-gógòòmbèk-à**[73] (1PL-F2-RFX-intrude-Fa) 'we will intrude'. Notice that the H lexical tone of the verb links to the V_1 position of the stem, while the

---

[70]In a toneless verb, this L tone is placed on the first vowel of the stem.

[71]Because of the lack of tone reversal in the languages he worked with, Goldsmith's V_2 pattern had a H tone on the second vowel, rather than a L.

[72]Subjunctive forms with only toneless subject marker (which displays default L tone) have the complex HH pattern, which includes a H tone which replaces the lexical tone of the verb and spreads onto all free non-final morae of the verb.

[73]This verb is most often used with the L-toned reflexive **yì-** prefix. Literal meaning is something like 'push oneself in where one doesn't belong'. In table forms, and in reference to the forms shown in the tables, we omit the reflexive prefix for brevity and so as not to obscure the fact that this is a H-tone verb.

3.5 Tone on verbs

grammatical L tone links to the following syllable. Because of L spread, all following syllables also have L tone.

Note especially in (3.25) that the L tone of the stem-tone pattern is apparent in nearly all forms. Only in a H tone CVC verb is there no direct evidence of the L grammatical tone of the V_2, e.g. **túgááfúkà** 'we will pour'.[74] The L of the V_2 pattern has no distinctive surface realization in such a form because it links, along with the H lexical tone of the verb, to the only non-final syllable, giving two association lines to this penultimate TBU.[75] This double linking results in a HL contour on the monomoraic first syllable of the stem. This contour is reduced to a single H tone by the phonetic rule of single-mora HL simplification (3.8.2.2). A derivation is given in (3.26).

---

[74] The final L is best interpreted as a default or intonational tone, and not as a realization of the L tone of the stem tone. The final vowel is extratonal and does not accept a grammatical tone at the time of initial linking. The penultimate, on the other hand, always accepts two tones by initial linking. The second of the two tones in many cases is deleted by a contour simplification rule. That at least in some cases the tone is not simply delinked and then relinked to the FV is shown by comparable examples in which the tone which is delinked/deleted is H. This H does not appear on the FV in these cases. We posit that a tone which is subject to contour simplification is initially delinked, and then is deleted if there is no non-final syllable to which it can link.

[75] One could also assume here that the grammatical L remains floating until it can link to the FV, but since we have seen in L verbs of the simple pattern that both the lexical and grammatical tones link to a single mora in simple forms (e.g. **kúbēgà** 'to cut hair') there is no reason to assume that the L tone does not link similarly in the case of the V_2 pattern verbs. Though we show the L tone being delinked again here, this is merely to clarify the phonetic interpretation of the surface form. The contour simplification rules are phonetic interpretation rules and likely do not actually delink or delete any tones, but merely give them a phonetic interpretation. The interpretation of a monomoraic HL is H.

In verbs with the complex LH stem-tone pattern, it becomes patently obvious that all grammatical tones are either linked by initial association, or deleted by T-drop in cases where linking would violate constraints against linking three tones to a single syllable. It is possible to account for all Kifuliiru verb forms with one basic set of assumptions regarding linking procedures and a single set of rules.

(3.25) V₂ stem-tone pattern with assorted verb types

UT	Syll. pattern	Base	Gloss	Future (F2)
H	CVC	-fúk-	'pour on'	**túgááfúkà**
H	CVVNC	**-gúung-**	'cheat'	**túgágúùngà**
H	CVCVVC	**-báraat-**	'make wattle frame'	**túgábáràatà**
H	CVCVVNCVC	**-gógoombek-**	'barge in'	**túgágógòòmbèkà**
L	CVC	**-bèg-**	'cut hair'	**túgáábègà**
L	CVVNC	**-fyèeng-**	'shut off breath'	**túgáfyèèngà**
L	CVNCVVC	**-shàmbaal-**	'rejoice'	**túgáshàmbààlà**
L	CVCVVNCVC	**-bèraangir-**	'call from afar'	**túgábèrààngìrà**
L	CVCVCVVNC	**-gòloloomb-**	'flow'	**gágágòlòlòòmbà**[†]
UT	Syll. pattern	Base	Gloss	Future (F2)
Ø	CVVC	**-diih-**	'beat'	**túgádììhà**
Ø	CVVCVC	**-laalik-**	'invite'	**túgálààlìkà**

[†]Note that in the case of this verb, a first-person plural prefix is less semantically compatible, so the cl. 6 subject prefix, referring to **á=mí-íjì** (AU=6-water) 'water' is substituted in this case. A plural personal subject would be taken figuratively as masses of people "flowing" by like a river (more likely to be used in the third-person plural by an observer rather than in first-person plural by a participant in the flow of people.)

(3.26) **tú-gáá-fúk-à** (1PL-F2-pour-Fa) 'we will pour' (H)

UF **túgááfúk<a>**
    |⋰
    H L   lexical H, L of V₂ pattern

Next **túgááfúka**
    |╤
    H L   delink by single-mora HL simplification

SF **túgááfúkà**
    | |
    H L   by default L insertion

3.5 Tone on verbs

In a H verb of CVVNC shape, the grammatical L is evident on the second mora of the bimoraic initial/penultimate syllable of the verb stem, underlined in **túgágúùngà** 'we will cheat someone'. Notice in this form that the H-toned future prefix immediately precedes the verb stem. This allows the HL contour to surface phonetically on a bimoraic syllable as a falling contour. However, if instead a L-tone prefix immediately precedes the verb stem, the underlying HL contour is simplified to H by the rule of post-L HL simplification (HL >H/L_ see 3.8.2.2). Thus if one adds a L-toned cl. 2 object prefix immediately to the left of the verb stem, as in **tú-gá-bà-gúúng-à** (1PL-F2-O2-cheat-Fa) 'we will cheat them', the HL contour surfaces as a simple H tone.

In longer H verbs in (3.25), all the post-prefix TBUs have L tone except for the V_1 position of the stem, which bears the lexical H tone, e.g. **tú-gá-gógòòmbèk-à** 'we will barge in'.

In the L verbs, the grammatical L never effects a change in the first syllable of the verb stem, since like-tone simplification will simplify any tautosyllabic LL combination which might occur due to double linking of tones on a CVC base. In L verbs of the V_2 pattern, the first syllable of the stem always has L tone, and all post-prefix morae also have L tone.

In the Ø verbs of the V_2 stem-tone pattern, the first syllable of the verb stem always displays L tone, since the grammatical L tone of the stem-tone pattern links to that syllable. All following morae of Ø verbs also have L tone, spread onto them by the L-spread rule.

In (3.27) is provided a derivation of the first-person plural future form of the lexically H-tone verb, -**báràat**- 'make a wattle frame (for a mud and wattle house)'.

(3.27) **tú-gá-báràat-à** (1PL-F2-make.wattle.frame-Fa) 'we will make a wattle frame' (H)

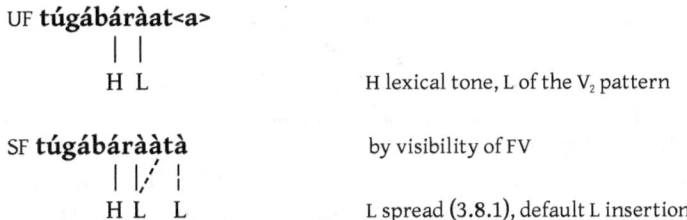

Note in this form that because the only tone of the stem-tone pattern is a L tone, there are no H tones to the right of the lexical H tone of the verb stem. The grammatical L tone of the V_2 stem-tone pattern links to the second syllable of the stem, on the left-hand mora of the bimoraic penultimate, directly following the lexical tone of the verb.

3.5.3.2.1 V_2 stem-tone pattern with causative and passive

Because there are no grammatical H tones in the V_2 stem-tone pattern, evidence of the rightward linking of causative and passive's H tone can be seen most clearly in these forms. The chart in (3.28) gives examples of passive and causative verbs in the unmarked future (F2) tense.

(3.28) V_2 stem-tone pattern with assorted causatives and passives

	UT	Syll.pattern	Base	Gloss	Future (F2)
a.	H	CVC	**-fúk-**	'pour on'	**túgááfúkà**
b.	H	CVC w/PS	**-fúk-u-**	'pour on (PS)'	**túgááfúkwâ**
c.	H	CVC w/CS	**-fúk-iisi-**	'pour on (CS)'	**túgáfúkììsâ**
d.	H	CVC w/CS+PS	**-fúk-iisi-bu-**	'pour on (PS of CS)'	**túgáfúkììsìbwâ**
e.	L	CVC	**-bèg-a**	'cut hair'	**túgáábègà**
f.	L	CVC w/PS	**-bèg-u-**	'cut hair (PS)'	**túgáábègwâ**
g.	L	CVC w/CS	**-bèg-eesi-**	'cut hair (CS)'	**túgábègèèsâ**
h.	L	CVC w/CS+PS	**-bèg-eesi-bu-**	'cut hair (PS of CS)'	**túgábègèèsìbwâ**
i.	Ø	CVVC	**-diih-**	'beat'	**túgádììhà**
j.	Ø	CVVC w/PS	**-diih-u-**	'beat (PS)'	**túgádììhwâ**
k.	Ø	CVVC w/CS	**-diih-iisi-**	'beat (CS)'	**túgádìhììsâ**
l.	Ø	CVVC w/CS+PS	**-diih-iisi-bu-**	'beat (PS of CS)'	**túgádìhììsìbwâ**

Looking at (3.28) we see that in all the passive and causative forms in the V_2 pattern, there is a final H tone (phonetically, a short falling contour, and marked with a circumflex.) This contrasts with the non-passive and non-causative forms, seen in (3.28a, e, i) which always end with a L tone. The final H tone in the passive and causative forms is the realization of the H tone of the passive or causative extension. This tone links directly to the FV in these forms, since the FV is not extratonal in passive and causative verbs.

The fact that the H tone of passive and causative links to the FV rather than to the right-hand node of the penultimate syllable is evidence that there is no final-linking tone in this stem-tone pattern. (This will become evident as we look at the "Complex" stem-tone patterns, which do have a final-linking tone, and in which the H of passive and causative is not able to link to the FV.)

3.5 Tone on verbs

The derivation in (3.29) shows the causative form **túgábáràtììsâ**[76] 'we will cause someone to build a wattle frame'. Note that the H tone of the causative associates to the right end of the verb (FV), ignoring the free TBUs to its left.

(3.29) **tú-gá-báràt-ììs-â** (1PL-F2-make.wattle.frame-CS-Fa) 'we will cause someone to make a wattle frame' (H)

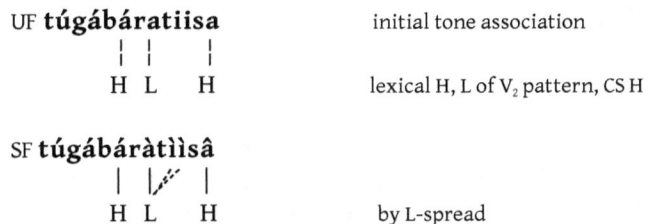

UF **túgábáratiisa**	initial tone association
| | |	
H L H	lexical H, L of V_2 pattern, CS H

SF **túgábáràtììsâ**

   | |⁄ |

H L   H   by L-spread

In (3.29) if the H tone of the causative had linked initially in a left-to-right manner, i.e., immediately following the grammatical L tone of the V_2 stem-tone pattern, the surface form, following H-spread, would be *__túgábáràtíísâ__ rather than the correct form, with low tones on the penult: **túgábáràtììsâ**.

The passive forms in the V_2 stem-tone pattern exhibit exactly the same behavior as the causative forms, having a final H tone, the source of which is the passive extension, e.g. **ígábáràátwâ** 'it will be built (with a wattle frame)', **ágáhàmàgàlwâ** 'he will be called', **túgágúùngwâ** 'we will be cheated'. The H of the PS links to the rightmost available TBU in its underlying form, i.e. the FV, which is not extratonal in passive or causative forms.

The derivation in (3.30) shows the passive of a causative default future tense (F2) verb: **tú-gá-gúng-ììsì-bw-â** 'we will be caused to cheat'. The only surface H tone in the verb stem besides the H lexical tone of the root is the H tone on the FV. Note that we assume here that there is only one H tone provided by the combination of causative plus passive.[77]

---

[76]Note that the long vowel in the antepenult has been shortened by the phonological rule of mora-based vowel shortening because the addition of the causative extension has increased the number of following morae to three.

[77]In this case, where the stem-tone pattern includes no final-linking tone, the derivation would produce the correct output even if we assumed that passive and causative each provided a H tone, because the combination of L-spread and LH lowering would neutralize the H which would link to the penultimate. However, there are cases in which positing two H tones for passive-of-causative would produce the wrong output, so we assume only one H for the passive-of-causative in all cases.

(3.30) **tú-gá-gúng-ììsì-bw-â** (1PL-F2-cheat-CS-PS-Fa) 'we will be caused to cheat' (H)

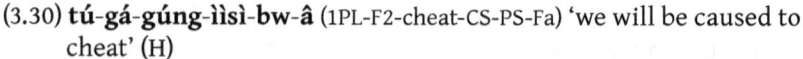

UF **túgágúngììsibwá**   lexical H, L of F2, H of CS/PS

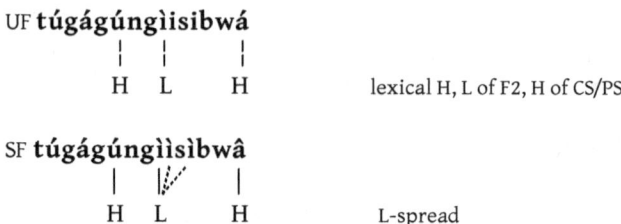

SF **túgágúngììsìbwâ**   L-spread

As seen in (3.30), in the initial tone association, the final H tone links to the final vowel, while the L of the V_2 stem-tone pattern links to the leftmost free TBU, the V_2 position. L-spread spreads this L tone onto the following free TBUs, giving the correct surface result.

3.5.3.3 *"Complex" stem-tone patterns*

There are five stem-tone patterns in Kifuliiru which have two grammatical tones. In all these patterns, the first tone links to the leftmost free TBU in the stem, while the second associates to the rightmost free TBU. It was such a pattern that Goldsmith (1987) termed "Complex". In the "complex" pattern as found in many Lacustrine languages, and described by Goldsmith for Kihunde, there is a polar H tone which links immediately to the right of the lexical tone of the verb stem, in the V_2 position, as well as a H tone which links to the final vowel (FV) of the verb.

The most common of the five distinct stem-tone patterns in Kifuliiru which fall in the double-toned "complex" category is found in at least five different Kifuliiru verb forms, including the recent past (P1). It is probably this pattern which corresponds historically to the pattern which Goldsmith originally described. This pattern in Kifuliiru has a "polar" H tone in the V_2 (in Kifuliiru, leftmost free TBU) position, and a L tone which links rightward to the final free TBU. This pattern in Kifuliiru we will call the complex HL stem-tone pattern.

The four remaining "complex" patterns are each found in different verb forms (ranging from one to four "tenses" represented). Complex LH stem-tone pattern has a L tone in V_2 position, and a final, right-linking H tone. The complex LL stem-tone pattern also has a L tone in V_2 position, but its final, right-linking tone is a L rather than a H. The imperative plural's complex LH-IP forms constitute a special case, with an invariable LH overlay on all forms, including passive and causative forms. The L of this imperative plural

3.5 Tone on verbs 159

pattern links to the leftmost free TBU position, while the H links to the final vowel. Any TBUs between these two positions bear L tone. The subjunctive's complex HH pattern has one special feature which distinguishes it from the other complex patterns: it has a H tone that replaces any lexical tone of the verb rather than linking to the V₂ position of the stem. Its final H tone is lowered by MR in all but passive and causative forms, in which the passive and causative H tones are lowered instead, protecting the final H from lowering. All the complex patterns will be illustrated in separate sections below. The subjunctive forms receive special consideration, because of the many peculiarities of this pattern.

3.5.3.3.1 Right-linking of the final tones of the complex stem-tone patterns

As mentioned above, the complex patterns are characterized by having two suffixal tones, the first of which links immediately to the right of the verb's lexical tone, and the other of which links as far to the right end of the verb stem as possible. Because of the extratonality of the FV in non-passive/non-causative forms in Kifuliiru, the "final" tone of each complex pattern has its primary linking to the rightmost available TBU, i.e. the right-hand node of the penultimate syllable. This is where we find its surface realization in these forms, and not on the FV.

In passive and causative forms, however, the final-linking tones of a complex stem-tone pattern link directly to the FV by initial tone association. The final-linking tone of the stem-tone pattern always links farther to the right than the right-linking H tones of causative and passive. This is evidenced by the fact that in a complex pattern with a final-linking L, there is never a H tone on the FV of a passive or causative form. Instead, in the complex forms, the H tones of the passive and causative link to the left of the final tone of the complex pattern, on the right-hand node of the penultimate syllable. Thus, if not neutralized by a combination of spread rules and contour simplification rules, the H tone of passive or causative is realized in the surface form on the penultimate mora of a verb with a complex stem-tone pattern. This is in contrast to what we saw in the simple and V₂ patterns, which have no final-linking tones, so that a PS or CS H tone always links to and is realized on the FV.

3.5.3.3.2 Complex HL stem tone pattern

The complex HL pattern is characterized by a H tone which links to the leftmost free TBU of the stem, and a L tone which links rightward to the final free TBU. Meeussen's rule (3.8.3) which lowers the right-hand H tone of a HH sequence (i.e. HH > HL) applies to any juxtaposed HH sequences *within the verb stem* in all complex HL forms.[78] It applies not only to the H grammatical tone of the stem-tone pattern when it is juxtaposed to the lexical H tone of a verb stem, but also to the H tone of a passive or causative extension when juxtaposed to the H tone of the complex HL stem-tone pattern. The grammatical H of the complex HL pattern is the target of MR in a verb with lexical H tone, being lowered itself. In a lexically L verb, the grammatical H is not lowered, but serves as the trigger for MR to apply to a following passive or causative H.

The final-linking L of this pattern links to the right-hand node of the penultimate in non-passive, non-causative forms, and to the FV in a passive or causative verb. Because the final-linking L of this pattern links to the right of any passive or causative H tone, the FV of a verb with the complex HL stem-tone pattern never has a H tone, even in passive or causative forms.

The complex HL pattern is found in six different verb forms. These forms include the recent past (P1), e.g. **twàgéénda** 'we went'; "not yet", e.g. **tùtàzí géèndà** 'we haven't gone yet'; potential-conditional (POT-CND), e.g. **twàngàgéénda** 'we could/would go'; conditional contrary-to-fact (CND.C.F), e.g. **twàngàgéézìrì** 'we could have gone'; resultative (RS), e.g. **tùgéézìrì** 'we have gone (and are still gone)', and the timeless form that follows **máángò** 'when' or is used in proverbs (always true/habitual) (TL), e.g. **máángò tùgéénda** 'when(ever) we go' or **í=rúbàkò ìtàgéénda múkàzì** 'a woman doesn't (ever) go to the forest' (literally 'to the forest there does not ever go a woman').

The data in (3.31) includes examples of two of complex HL verb forms: the recent past (P1) and resultative (RS). We include two forms in this chart, rather than just one, in order to exemplify both the forms which take the basic form of the verb base, and the forms which make use of the resultative form of the verb.[79] The stem-tone patterns on these forms exemplify all the other verb forms which exhibit the complex HL stem-tone pattern.

---

[78]Goldsmith (1987) described the H of his complex pattern as "polar" which also means that it was changed to L following a H. Since in Kifuliiru such lowering applies not only to the grammatical H, but to any HH sequences in these forms, it is more accurate to describe this form in terms of the activity of Meeussen's rule. Besides this complex HL stem-tone pattern, there are only one or two other environments in which MR has been observed in Kifuliiru.

[79]The term "resultative" here refers to the inclusion in these forms of the suffix normally referred to in Bantu literature as the "perfective". The perfective or "resultative" suffix in Kifuliiru is -**ir-i**; thus it adds an extra syllable to the verb stem, as well as causing the spirantization (also called frication) or elimination of many preceding consonants. The combination of these qualities results in a verb stem of different syllable pattern than the non-resultative stem.

3.5 Tone on verbs

(3.31) Complex HL stem-tone pattern with assorted verb types

UT	Syll. pattern	Base	Gloss	Recent past (P1)	Resultative
H	CVC	-fúk-	'pour on'	twààfúkà	tùfúsìrì
H	CVVNC	-gúung-	'cheat'	twàgúúngà	tùgúúzìrì
H	CVCVVC	-báraat-	'build wattle'	twàbáràatà	tùbáràasìrì
H	CVCVVNCVC	gógoombek-	'barge in'	twàgógòòmbèkà	tùgógòmbèsìrì
L	CVC	-bèg-	'cut hair'	twààbègà	tùbèzírì
L	CVVNC	-fyèeng-	'shut off breath'	twàfyèèngà	tùfyèèzírì
L	CVNCVVC	-shàmbaal-	'rejoice'	twàshàmbáálà	tùshàmbíírì
L	CVCVVNCVC	-bèraangir-	'call from afar'	twàbèráángírà	tùbèrángîirì
L	CVCVCVVNC	-gòloloomb-	'flow'	gàgòlólóòmbà†	gàgòlólóómbírì
Ø	CVVC	-diih-	'beat'	twàdííhà	tùdííhírì
Ø	CVVCVC	-laalik-	'invite'	twàláálíkà	tùlálísírì

†The cl. 6 subject marker ga- (here referring to water) is used here for semantic reasons.

We can make many observations about the forms in (3.31). First, let us look at the realizations of the H suffixal tone of this pattern. Since it is a "polar" tone, the H tone of the HL pattern is most easily discerned in the forms of the L and Ø verbs, since in these forms it appears as H rather than being lowered to L. In the lexically L forms with a base of at least CVCVC, such as twàbèrángírà, gàgòlólóòmbà, tùbèrángíìrì, tùbèzírì, tùfyèèzír-ì, and in all the Ø forms such as tùdííhírì, twàdííhà, twàláálíkà, and tùlálísírì, the H tone of the complex HL pattern is evident in the underlined syllables. Since in Ø verbs, the first tone of a stem-tone pattern always appears on the first TBU of the verb stem, the H tone in underlined syllables of the Ø verbs is a definitive indicator of the identity of the H tone of this pattern. This H tone associates to the first free TBU of the stem, and spreads onto any free TBUs.

However, there is no evidence of the stem-tone pattern's H tone in the recent past (P1) forms of the CVC and CVVNC L verbs: twààbègà, twàfyèèngà, etc. If there were an underlying LH contour on the penult, it would be realized as a H tone in these forms, because the application of the rule of LH raising (tautosyllabic LH > H/ L _ L see 3.8.2.1.1) would be triggered by the presence of a preceding L tone (on the prefix) and a following L tone. Instead, the tone in this position is L. The absence of the grammatical H in these surface forms is completely explainable in terms of triple-linking constraints, which trigger the application of the rule of T-drop (3.7.3) as shown by the following derivation of **tw-à-fyèèng-à** 'we shut off someone's breath'.

(3.32) **tw-à-fyèèng-à** (1PL-P1-choke-Fa) 'we shut off someone's breath' (L)

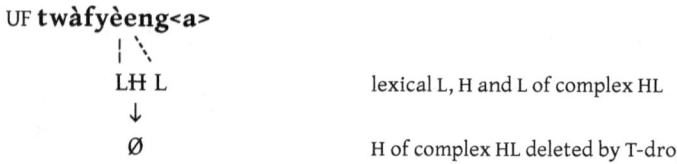

As shown in (3.32) the lexical L tone of the verb root links to the first TBU of the first (and also penultimate) syllable of the verb stem, while the two tones of the complex HL stem-tone pattern also both attempt to link to the following TBU of that same syllable. Even though this syllable is penultimate, and may have two association lines (3.7) there is a constraint against three association lines to any single syllable, whether that syllable is monomoraic or bimoraic (3.7.3 for details on triple-linking constraints). Because of this, the rule of T-drop applies (3.8.4). This rule gives preference to the tones which link first, and deletes the tone which is the last to link. In this case, the third-linked tone is the grammatical H tone of the complex HL pattern. The fact that T-drop applies in cases where there is a only single syllable of the verb stem available for initial tone association is one clear indication that there is a final-linking L tone in this stem-tone pattern.[80]

Further evidence that it is T-drop which causes the failure of the H tone to link in the CV(VN)C verbs is found by looking at the toneless verbs. In these forms, there is no lexical tone, so that there are only two tones (the H and L of complex HL) vying for position on the stem of a CVVC toneless verb. In these forms, we see that both of these tones *are* permitted to associate to the first syllable of the stem. The contour thus produced is clearly seen when a H-toned prefix precedes the verb stem, as in **tw-à-mú-díìh-à** (1PL-P1-O1-beat-Fa) 'we beat him', where the H-toned cl. 1 object prefix **mú-** precedes the stem, and in **tw-à-ná-díìh-à** (1PL-P1-SQ-beat-Fa) 'and we beat (someone)', where the conjunctive **ná-** precedes. In these forms, the contour is heard on the surface, so that both the H and the L tone of the stem-tone pattern are evident. When there is no preceding H-toned prefix, e.g. **tw-à-dííh-à** (1PL-P1-beat-Fa) 'we beat

---

[80]See (3.7.3) for evidence that the failure of the H tone to link here is due only to triple-linking constraints and not to a general constraint against linking a H tone to the first syllable of a CV(VN)C stem. In the P2 tense, where there is no final-linking tone, H tones regularly link in that same second mora position, e.g. **túkáfyèéngà** 'we pinched shut'.

(someone)', or **tw-à-bà-dííh-à** 'we beat them', with the L-toned cl. 2 object prefix **bà-**, the underlying HL contour does not surface, since a HL contour is simplified to H when it follows a L tone.

Toneless verbs, as those in the last two rows of (3.31) are also a clear indicator of the true identity of the initial tone of the complex HL pattern: a H tone. Since this H tone surfaces as a H in L verbs, and as a L in H verbs, it is very helpful to have toneless verbs, which clearly evidence the basic tone as H.

Having discerned that the initial grammatical tone of this stem-tone pattern is indeed H, we look now at the longer of the lexical H-tone verbs, **tw-à-gógòòmbèk-à** (1PL-P1-force.in-Fa) 'we forced in' and **tù-gógòmbès-ìr-ì** (1PL-force.in-RS-Fi) 'we are in the state of having forced in'. In these forms, it can be seen that the initial tone of the HL pattern is realized as L when it follows a H tone. We posit that this is due to the activity of Meeussen's rule (3.8.3) in this stem-tone pattern.

In Kifuliiru, MR lowers the second H of any sequence of two H tones which are both found within the domain which is subject to MR (see 3.8.3 for details). In the various verb forms in which MR is active, the domain of MR is the entire stem of the verb (but MR does *not* apply among the prefixes or across the boundary between prefixes and stem: observe the successive lexical H tones in **tw-à-ná-mú-báràatìr-à** (1PL-P1-SQ-O1-make.wattle.frame-Fa) 'and we made a wattle frame for him'). It is evident in the forms of the lexical H verbs, e.g. **twàbáràatà** 'we built a wattle frame', **tw-à-shúlik-à** 'we hit (someone)', **tw-à-shálik-à** (1PL-P1-be.hungry.Fa) 'we were hungry', **tw-à-kónòòlèr-à** (1PL-P1-stare-Fa) 'we stared wide eyed at something', etc., that MR lowers the H tone which links immediately to the right of the lexical H in these complex HL forms. Thus there are no H tones other than the lexical H in the surface forms of non-passive, non-causative forms of H verbs. Instead, there are L tones in these forms, in the same syllable positions where the longer L-tone verbs (**twàbèrángírà**, etc.) had H tones.

Just as the grammatical H tone of this pattern was not permitted to link in L-toned CV(VN)C verbs such as **tw-àà-bèg-à** (1PL-P1-shave-Fa) 'we shaved' and **tw-à-fyèèng-à** (1PL-P1-choke-Fa) 'we choked', in the same way, the L which, because of MR, is the realization of this tone in H verbs, is not permitted to link in H-toned CV(VN)C verbs. Just as was seen in the L verbs, the absence of this tone is due to the constraint against the triple-linking of any syllable. In complex HL forms of H-toned CV(VN)C verbs, e.g. **tw-àà-fúk-à** (1PL-P1-pour-Fa) 'we poured', **tw-à-gúúng-à**, (1PL-P1-cheat-Fa) 'we cheated 'etc., the lexical H, the grammatical H and the final L all compete for association to the single non-final TBU, i.e. the penultimate syllable. The constraint against triple linking to a single syllable causes the deletion of the grammatical H tone (for details and argumentation see 3.7.3). The lexical H and the final-linking

L both associate to the penultimate syllable. This creates a HL contour on the penultimate syllable of the stem. Though the contour does not appear in surface forms like **twàgúúngà**, where there is a preceding L tone, we can be sure that there is an underlying HL contour there. This contour only surfaces when it is on a bimoraic syllable and preceded by another H tone, such as the H-toned cl. 1 object marker **mú-** in **twàmúgúùngà** 'we cheated him', or the H-toned consecutive/subsequent prefix **ná-** **twànágúùngà** 'and we cheated (someone)'. When these two conditions are not met, the underlying HL contour is simplified phonetically to H, either by the rule of post-L HL simplification, e.g. **twàgúúngà**, **twàbàgúúngà** 'we cheated them', **twànábàgúúngà** 'and we cheated them', etc. or by the rule of single-mora HL simplification, e.g. **twàfúkà** (3.8.2.2).

In the resultative forms of H verbs, **tù-gúúz-ìrì** (1PL-cheat-RS+Fi) 'we have cheated him', etc., there is no HL contour on the first syllable of the verb stem because a bimoraic syllable in non-penultimate position receives only one tone. Because no tautosyllabic HL contour is permitted in this syllable position, adding a H-tone prefix to these forms does not have the effect of causing an underlying contour to be realized: **tù-mú-gúúz-ìrì** (1PL-O1-cheat-RS+Fi) 'we have cheated him'. The lexical tone of the radical is linked to that stem-initial syllable, while the H and L of the stem-tone pattern both link to the penultimate. The H of the stem-tone pattern is then lowered to L by MR, resulting in LL on the penult. This L tone is evident in the surface form.

Returning now to the issue of the final-linking L of the complex HL pattern, it should be noted that this tone links to the rightmost available TBU, which because of the extratonality of the FV, is the surface penultimate syllable. It links to this position because the FV is extratonal in a non-passive, non-causative verb form, making the right-hand node of the penultimate syllable the rightmost available TBU. This final-linking L is evidenced in several ways in the surface forms. As noted above, the fact that the triple-linking constraint takes effect in CV(VN)C verbs is one major indicator that there are two grammatical tones, rather than just one, involved in this stem-tone pattern (3.8.4).

There are also cases in which the final-linking L is clearly seen in surface forms. One such case is found in lexically L verbs with a CVCVCVVC base, such as the recent past form **gàgòlólóòmbà** 'it (water) flowed' or the resultative form **tùbèrángíìrì** 'we had called out'. In these forms the final-linking L tone is seen clearly on the second mora of the bimoraic penultimate. Similarly, the two grammatical tones of the complex HL produce an underlying HL contour in CVVC toneless forms. When such verbs have a H-tone prefix preceding the stem, such as **twàmúdíìhà** 'we beat him', **twànádíìhà** 'and we beat (someone)' this contour is heard on the surface, so that both the H and the L tone of the pattern are evident. When there is no preceding H-toned prefix, e.g.

twàdííhà 'we beat (someone)' or twàbàdííhà 'we beat them', the underlying HL contour does not surface, since a HL contour is simplified to H when it follows a L tone.

There are many reasons why the final-linking L tone is not particularly evident in many verbs of the complex HL pattern. The penult in verb forms which have any complex stem-tone pattern always has two association lines. The leftmost of these two association lines, in a CV(VN)C verb, e.g. twàgúúngà or twàfyèèngà is linked to the lexical tone of the verb, while in CVCVC (or longer) stem, the leftmost of the two penultimate association lines is either the grammatical polar H tone of the stem-tone pattern, as in twàbáràatà, or results from H or L spread from the preceding grammatical tone, as in twàbèráángírà. The rightward of the two association lines on the penultimate of all these forms is from the final-linking tone which is linked there.

Thus, in a H-tone verb of the complex HL pattern, e.g. twàgógòòmbèkà, the tone preceding this penultimate syllable will be the H of the complex HL, lowered to L, since it follows the lexical H tone. Because of this, it is a L tone which spreads, providing the leftmost of the two tones on the penult in all the longer lexically H verbs. (The penultimate of twàgógòòmbèkà is thus underlyingly linked to LL, the left-hand L resulting from L spread and right-hand one being the final-linking L of the complex HL pattern.) The resultant LL combination on the penultimate syllable is simplified to L, and since this L tone on the penultimate follows another L tone, (the lowered polar H) as well as preceding the L that has spread onto the FV, it is not immediately apparent that it is actually the realization of the final-linking L.

In a lexical L-tone verb with a CVCV(V)C base, e.g. twàbètúlà 'we carried on our heads', the H tone of the complex HL and the final-linking L will both link to the V₂ position of the verb, since it is penultimate. Many forms, however, including twàbètúlà, have only a monomoraic penult, and on a single mora, such a HL contour will always be simplified to H. Thus the presence of the final-linking L is neutralized in lexically L-tone verbs with a monomoraic penult. Even in an L verb which does have a bimoraic penult, any HL contour which is a result of initial linking, as in twàshàmbáálà, will not show up as a surface HL contour because there is a lexical L tone, rather than a H tone preceding the contour. A HL contour which follows a L tone is pronounced as H, due to the phonetic rule of post-L HL simplification. In lexically L-toned verbs then, the HL contour on the penultimate syllable will only be realized when the verb has a bimoraic penult, *and* is long enough to have at least one syllable where the grammatical H tone can link between the L-toned initial syllable of the stem and the bimoraic penult. This is indeed the case in tùbèrángîìrì, and gàgòlólóòmbà, where the H grammatical tone of the complex HL is realized on the syllable preceding the bimoraic penult, thus allowing the HL contour (produced by spread of the grammatical H onto the left mora of the penult, plus the linking of the final-linking L to the right mora) to surface on the penult.

3.5.3.3.2.1 Complex HL stem tone pattern with causative and passive

The final-linking L of the complex HL pattern is actually most clearly evidenced by the fact that a passive or causative form in this stem-tone pattern always ends in a L tone, rather than the H which would result there (at least in H verbs) if the H of these extensions were linked to the FV. Note in (3.33) that there are no forms which end with a H tone. This is because the H tone of CS and PS links not to the FV in these forms, as it did in the simple and V_2 patterns, but to the penultimate syllable. Instead, the final-linking tone of a complex stem-tone pattern is always realized on the FV of a passive or causative form as in (3.33) and (3.34).

Thus in these complex HL forms, the final vowel always bears the final-linking L tone. The H tones of causative and passive link to the penultimate in these forms, but it will be shown that these H tones are subject to lowering by Meeussen's rule, just as was seen with the grammatical H tone of the complex HL pattern. Observe the causative and passive forms of the complex HL pattern in (3.33).

(3.33) Complex HL stem-tone pattern with causative and passive

	UT Syll. pattern	Base	Gloss	Recent past (P1)	Resultative (RS)
H	CVC	-fúk-	'pour on'	twààfúkà	tùfúsìrì
H	CVC w/PS	-fúk-u-	'pour on (PS)'	twààfúkwà	tùfúsīrwì/ tùfúsìrwì
H	CVC w/CS	-fúk-iisi-	'pour on (CS)'	twàfúkīīsà	tùfúkìsíízì
H	CVC w/CS+PS	-fúk-iisi-bu-	'pour on (CS+PS)'	twàfúkììsíbwà	tùfúkìsííbwì
L	CVC	-bèg-	'cut hair'	twààbègà	tùbèzírì
L	CVC w/PS	-bèg-u-	'cut hair (PS)'	twààbégwà	tùbèzírwì
L	CVC w/CS	-bèg-eesi-	'cut hair (CS)'	twàbègéésà	tùbègésîìzì

3.5 Tone on verbs

UT	Syll. pattern	Base	Gloss	Recent past (P1)	Resultative (RS)
L	CVC w/CS+PS	-bèg-eesi-bu-	'cut hair (CS+PS)'	twàbègéésíbwà	tùbègésíîbwì
Ø	CVVC	-diih-	'beat'	twàdííhà	tùdííhírì
Ø	CVVC w/PS	-diih-u-	'beat (PS)'	twàdííhwà	tùdííhírwì
Ø	CVVC w/CS	-diih-iisi-	'beat (CS)'	twàdíhîîsà	tùdíhísîîzì
Ø	CVVC w/CS+PS	-diih-iisi-bu-	'beat (CS+PS)'	twàdíhíísíbwà	tùdíhísíîbwì

Note that in the L verb, **twààbègà** there is a L tone on the first syllable of the stem in the non-passive form, but a H tone in that same spot in the corresponding passive verb, **twààbégwà**. This is due to two factors. First, in passive and causative forms, the final vowel is not extratonal. The final-linking L of the complex HL pattern can link to the FV. The second factor is that the passive contributes a H tone to the equation. Thus there are still three tones vying for position on the first syllable of the stem. The lexical L of the verb root, the H of the complex HL, and the H of passive all compete for linking to that position. Just as we saw in the non-passive form, when three tones are competing for position on a single syllable, the one that would link last is deleted by T-drop. Thus the H of the passive drops out, leaving the H of the complex HL pattern. The lexical L and the complex HL's H link to the first syllable of the stem, creating a LH contour. This contour surfaces as a H tone because of the preceding and following L tones. By adding a H-tone prefix, we can cause this LH contour to surface as a LH (mid) tone: **twànábēgwà** 'and we had our hair cut'.[81] Note that the final-linking L is always realized on the FV in passive and causative forms.

In a longer L verb, such as **twàbèráángírwà** 'we were called from afar', there are enough TBUs for all the tones to link. In such a case, the H tone of passive follows the H grammatical tone of the complex HL, and is therefore lowered to L by MR. However, it links to the right node of the penultimate, which is always double linked by spread rules if not by initial linking. Since the preceding tone is H, spread from that H gives a HL contour on the penultimate syllable in a form like **twàbèráángírwà**. However, because this syllable is monomoraic here, the contour is simplified to H, masking the presence of the lowered passive tone.

Though the underlying tones in passive forms are identical to those in causative forms, causative verbs provide a better view of what happens to the

---

[81]This is pronounced as **twànábègwà** by those who do not pronounce a mid tone on a single mora.

H extension-tone. This is because the long causative -**iisi**/-**eesi** morpheme gives causative verbs a bimoraic penultimate syllable. This bimoraic syllable provides a better setting for seeing the tonal contours which result from tone spread onto the syllable linked to the H tone of the passive or causative extension.

In such verbs, the HL contour which is formed by the H tone of the complex HL pattern plus the lowered (by MR) H of the causative extension is easy to see because it falls on the bimoraic penultimate syllable of the extension itself, e.g. the Ø verb **twàdíh̭îsà** 'we caused someone to beat someone', or the L verb **twàhàmágáḽîsà** 'we caused someone to call someone'.

In H verbs longer than CV(V)NC the H of passive or causative is never lowered by MR, since the H of the complex HL, lowered by MR to L, is associated to the TBU which follows the lexical tone H of the radical. The lowering of the grammatical H to L removes the trigger which would otherwise allow MR's application to the H of the extension. Also, since the tone which precedes the H of passive or causative in these verbs is the lowered grammatical H, now a L tone, it is this L which spreads onto the left-hand node of the penultimate syllable, where the H of passive or causative is linked to the right-hand node. This creates a LH contour on the penultimate syllable. This LH on the penultimate is always followed by the final-linking L of the complex HL, creating an environment where the LH contour is found between two L tones. This environment triggers the application of LH raising, causing the LH contour to be realized phonetically as a H tone.

Such a case is seen in **twàbárààṱírwà** 'we had a house frame made for us' or **twàgúngìḽs̭íbwà** 'we were caused to cheat someone'. Thus the H of passive or causative is discernable in these forms as a H tone, which follows the lowered H of complex HL. In shorter H verbs, this H extension tone is discernable as the H of the LH contour. Such a contour is most discernable in a causative verb, where the long **ii** of the causative morpheme provides a bimoraic syllable where the LH is easily heard, e.g. **twàfúk̭īsà** 'we caused someone to pour'.

Recall that when both passive and causative are present in the same verb form, we never see evidence that they contribute more than one H tone. We must assume that when the passive and causative appear together, they are treated as a single unit: a passive-causative morpheme -**ibw**-/**iisibw**-/-**eesibw**- with a single lexical H tone. The derivations in (3.34) show the places of association of right-linking tones in a passive form with the complex HL. We use the present resultative forms here, e.g. **tùgúngìsííbwì** 'we have been caused to cheat' because with the passive of causative, these forms have a bimoraic penult, and the addition of the resultative suffix makes the verbs long enough to allow the H grammatical tone of the complex HL to link to a separate syllable from the extension tone. This creates a tonal environment

3.5 Tone on verbs

which allows contours to surface, as well as demonstrating that the H of the extension links to the right-hand mora of a bimoraic penult.

Note in (3.34) how Meeussen's rule (MR), active in all complex HL forms, lowers the H tone of the complex HL pattern in H verbs, but lowers the H of passive/causative in L and toneless verbs.

(3.34) H, Ø, and L verbs in present resultative, with passive of causative
tù-gúng-ìsíí-bw-ì (1PL-cheat-CS-PS-RS+Fi) 'we have been caused to cheat' (H)

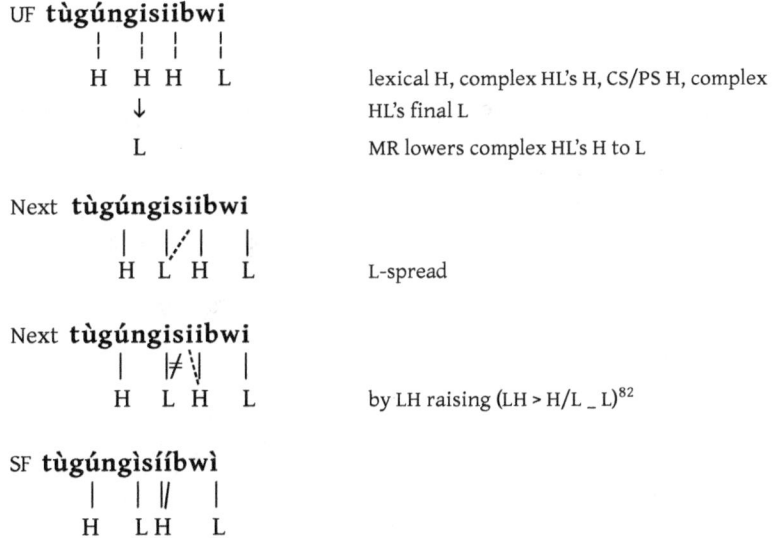

---

[82] Some might ask: Why spread the L rightward only to delink it again in the next step? It is likely that the rules of contour simplification: LH raising and LH lowering, post-L HL lowering, single-mora HL simplification, etc. are all phonetic rules, and that they merely interpret the lexical level tones, rather than actually manipulating them. Thus in a case like that seen here, the L of the LH contour on the penultimate would not actually be deleted, and there would not be an empty mora here. For the sake of easy phonetic interpretation, we show the L as being deleted, and the H as spreading leftward to "cover for" the "missing" tone. If instead an intonational H tone had been placed on the FV, the underlying LH contour would have surfaced as L by the rule of LH lowering (LH > L/_ H). The fact that the behavior of the tone on this penultimate syllable thus reflects a LH contour shows that the L-spread is indeed active in these forms.

tù-díh-ísíì-bw-ì (1PL-beat-CS-PS+RS-Fi) 'we have been caused to beat (someone)' (∅)

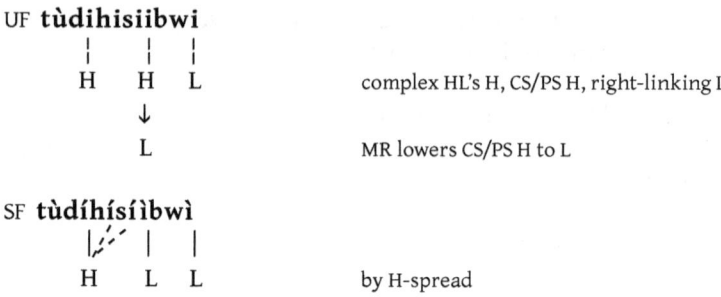

UF **tùdihisiibwi**

H H L   complex HL's H, CS/PS H, right-linking L
↓
L   MR lowers CS/PS H to L

SF **tùdíhísíìbwì**

H L L   by H-spread

tù-bèg-és-íìbw-ì 'we have been caused to get our hair cut' (L)

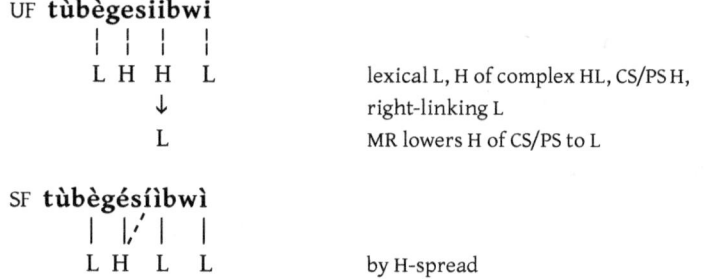

UF **tùbègesiibwi**

L H H L   lexical L, H of complex HL, CS/PS H,
      ↓   right-linking L
      L   MR lowers H of CS/PS to L

SF **tùbègésíìbwì**

L H L L   by H-spread

3.5.3.3.3 Complex LH stem-tone pattern

The complex LH stem-tone pattern has a L tone which links to the leftmost free TBU in the stem, and a final, right-linking H tone. This pattern is found in the frustrated resultative (e.g. **tútágúúzīrì** 'we had just cheated, but...') and the past resultative forms (e.g. **twáàlí gúúzīrì** 'we had cheated') as well as in the dependent form of the present resultative (e.g. **túgúngīīrì** 'if/when we are in the state of having cheated APL') and in the imperative singular (e.g. **gúùngâ** 'cheat!').

In these forms, MR does not operate. If it did, the final-linking grammatical H would always be lowered by the presence of a passive or causative H, and would never appear as a H tone on the FV in passive and causative forms. It would instead appear as a L on the FV of such forms. However, the right-linking H tone does appear as H on the FV in passive and causative forms, so we can assume that MR is not operative in any verb forms of the complex LH pattern.

3.5 Tone on verbs 171

The forms in (3.35) exemplify various verbs in the frustrated resultative. Glosses for the frustrated resultative forms are 'we had just...ed, but...'. A subsequent chart gives the imperative singular forms.

(3.35) Complex LH stem-tone pattern with assorted verb types

UT/Syll. pattern		RS stem	Gloss	Frustrated resultative†
H	CVC	-fúk-ir-i	'pour on'	tútáfúsīrì/ tútáfúsìrì‡
H	CVVNC	-gúung-ir-i	'cheat'	tútágúúzīrì/ tútágúúzìrì
H	CVCVVC	-báraat-ir-i	'make wattle frame'	tútábárààsírì
H	CVCVVNCVC	-gógoombek-ir-i	'barge in'	tútágógòmbèsírì
L	CVC	-bèg-ir-i	'cut hair'	tútábèzírì
L	CVVNC	-fyèeng-ir-i	'shut off breath'	tútáfyèèzírì
L	CVNCVVC	-shàmbaal-ir-i	'rejoice'	tútáshàmbíírì
L	CVCVVNCVC	-bèraangir-ir-i	'call from afar'	tútábèràngíírì
L	CVCVCVVNC	-gòloloomb-ir-i	'flow'	gátágòlòlòòmbírì
Ø	CVVC	-diih-ir-i	'beat'	tútádììhírì
Ø	CVVCVC	-laalik-ir-i	'invite'	tútálàlìsírì

†The use of the resultative suffix in these forms triggers spirantization or absorption of the final consonant of the base, so that these forms display what is sometimes called the "modified base". The long vowel seen in the penultimate of some forms results when the final consonant of the base is absorbed.

‡Note that though on a single-mora syllable, the mid tone on the penultimate syllable is pronounced only by some speakers, a universally pronounced phonetic mid tone on this syllable can be easily elicited by using an applicative form of the verb, e.g. **kúfúkírà** 'to pour on (APL)', which gives the form **tútáfúkīīrì**, pronounced by all speakers with a mid (LH) tone on the bimoraic penultimate syllable.

The stem-tone pattern in these forms, as stated above, is a L tone which links to the first free TBU of the verb stem, plus a final-linking H tone. This pattern is quite transparent in much of the data in (3.35). Look, for example, at the Ø verbs **tútádììhírì** 'we had just beat (someone), but...' and **tútálàlìsírì** 'we had just invited (someone), but...'. The L tone links to the first syllable of the stem, while the H tone links to the rightmost available TBU of the underlying form, which is the right-hand node of the penultimate syllable of the surface form. The pattern is also clearly discernable in H and L verbs. Observe especially the longer forms such as **tútágógòmbèsírì** and **tútábèràngíírì**.

The LH contour seen in the penultimate syllable of verbs with H-toned CV(VN)C roots, e.g. **tútáfúsīrì** and **tútágúúzīrì** reflects both the L and the H of the stem-tone pattern. The same LH contour exists underlyingly in the L and Ø verbs, as well, but in these cases it surfaces as a H tone due to the application of LH raising which causes a LH contour to surface as H when preceded and followed by a L tone (3.8.2.1.1).

3.5.3.3.3.1 Complex LH stem tone pattern with causative and passive

It might be assumed from the majority of the forms in (3.35) that the H tone of this pattern is "attracted to the penultimate syllable". However, by looking at the passive and causative forms in (3.36), we can see that it is not the *penultimate* which is the target of this H tone, but as usual with right-linking tones, the rightmost available TBU. Since the rightmost available TBU *is* the penultimate syllable in a non-passive, non-causative form, that is where the H is linked in those forms. But because the FV is not extratonal in passive and causative forms, the FV is the rightmost available TBU here. Thus we find the final grammatical H not in the penultimate position, but associated to the FV in these forms.

Assuming, then, that the H of the FV in these causative and passive forms is that of the complex LH pattern, one might wonder what happens to the H tones of the causative and passive extensions in these forms. A look at a derivation would reveal that the H tones of PS and CS are still there on the underlying levels, but their presence is not noticeable on the surface due to the application first of L spread and then of LH lowering. Because the final H of the stem-tone pattern links to the FV in these forms, the H of the causative or passive links to the right-hand node of the penultimate syllable. Then, because L spread from the preceding L tone of the stem-tone pattern links an L to the left-hand node of that same syllable, there is always a LH contour on the penultimate of passive and causative forms. When LH is followed by a H tone, as it always is here because of the final-linking grammatical H, it is lowered by the phonetic rule of LH lowering, and appears on the surface as L. Thus all forms below have a L surface tone on the penultimate syllable.

3.5 Tone on verbs

(3.36) Complex LH stem-tone pattern with causative and passive

UT	Syll. pattern	RS stem	Gloss	Frustrated resultative
H	CVC-ir	-fúk-ir-i	'pour on'	tútáfúsīrì/ tútáfúsìrì
H	CVC-ir/PS	-fúk-ir-u-i	'pour on (PS)'	tútáfúsìrwî
H	CVC -ir w/CS	-fúk-iisi-ir-i-i	'pour on (CS)'	tútáfúkìsìizî
H	CVC -ir w/CS+PS	-fúk-iisi-ir-i-bu-i	'pour on (PS of CS)'	tútáfúkìsìibwî
L	CVC-ir	-bèg-ir-i	'cut hair'	tútábèzírì
L	CVC -ir w/PS	-bèg-ir-u-i	'cut hair (PS)'	tútábèzìrwî
L	CVC -ir w/CS	-bèg-eesi-ir-i-i	'cut hair (CS)'	tútábègèsìizî
L	CVC -ir w/CS+PS	-bèg-eesi-ir-i-bu-i	'cut hair (PS of CS)'	tútábègèsìibwî
Ø	CVVC-ir	-diih-ir-i	'beat'	tútádììhírì
Ø	CVVC -ir w/PS	-diih-ir-u-i	'beat (PS)'	tútádììhìrwî
Ø	CVVC -ir w/CS	-diih-iisi-ir-i-i	'beat (CS)'	tútádìhìsìizî
Ø	CVVC -ir w/CS+PS	-diih-iisi-ir-i-bu-i	'beat (PS of CS)'	tútádìhìsìibwî

Derivations follow for the passive forms **tútábèzìrwî** 'we just had our hair cut, but...' and **tútáfúsìrwî** 'we just had something poured on us, but...'

(3.37) Derivations of passive L and H verbs in frustrated resultative
tú-tá-bèz-ìr-w-î (1PL-FRUS-cut.hair-RS-PS-Fi) 'we just had our hair cut, but...' (L)

tú-tá-fús-ìr-w-î (1PL-FRUS-pour.on-RS-PS-Fi) 'we just had something poured on us, but...' (H)

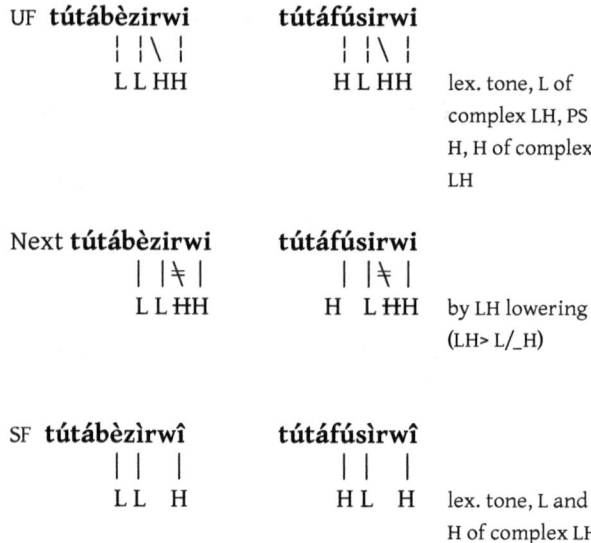

Since there is a right-linking H tone from the stem-tone pattern, that tone is associated by initial tone association to the FV. The H of passive links to the penultimate, together with the L of the complex LH. The resulting LH contour is then simplified to L by LH lowering (LH > L/_ H) due to the following H tone. In the case of a longer verb, such as **tútábègèsììbwî** 'we were just caused to cut hair, but...' the H tone of passive/causative would link to the right-hand mora of the penultimate, with a free TBU to its left. L spread from the L of the complex LH pattern to the left-hand mora of the penultimate would then produce a LH contour on this syllable. This H would then undergo LH lowering, just as it does in the derivations in (3.37).

3.5.3.3.4 Imperative singular: another complex LH form

Another form which takes the complex LH stem-tone pattern is the imperative singular. Because of the difference in the morphemic composition between these forms and the frustrated resultative forms discussed above, the

3.5 Tone on verbs

surface tonal patterns seen in these forms are also different from those shown above, and deserve some discussion here. The differences are mainly attributable to the fact that the forms in (3.35) and (3.36) involve the resultative form of the verb stem, while the imperatives involve the unextended stem. This means that in the imperative forms, the tones have fewer syllables on which to be realized. However, especially in imperatives with longer stems, the complex LH pattern is still easily discernable. In (3.38) are examples of the imperative singular forms.

(3.38) Imperative singular (another Complex LH form) with assorted verb types

UT	Syll. pattern	Base	Gloss	Imperative SG
H	CVC	**-fúk-**	'pour on'	**fúkà/fúkâ**
H	CVVNC	**-gúung-**	'cheat'	**gúùngà/gúùngâ**
H	CVCVVC	**-báraat-**	'make wattle frame'	**báráātà**
H	CVCVVNCVC	**-gógoombek-**	'barge in'	**gógòòmbékà**
L	CVC	**-bèg-**	'cut hair'	**bégà**
L	CVVNC	**-fyèeng-**	'shut off breath'	**fyééngà**
L	CVNCVVC	**-shàmbaal-**	'rejoice'	**shàmbáálà**
L	CVCVVNCVC	**-bèraangir-**	'call from afar'	**bèrààngírà**
L	CVCVCVVNC	**-gòloloomb-**	'flow'	**gòlòlóómbà**
Ø	CVVC	**-diih-**	'beat'	**dííhà**
Ø	CVVCVC	**-laalik-**	'invite'	**lààlíkà**

Note that in the imperative forms in (3.38) which have three or more syllables, the LH complex pattern is quite transparent. For example, **gógòòmbékà** (H), **bèrààngírà** (L), and **lààlíkà** (Ø) all have L tones in the first free TBU position, followed by a penultimate H tone. In the shorter forms it is much more difficult to see how the tones have interacted to produce the surface forms. Forms with a base of CVC and CVVNC are problematic.

There are two variations elicited (from the same speaker) for the CVC and CVVNC forms of H verb stems. One form has a final H tone, and the other seems to have a final L rather than the final H, e.g. **fúkà**, **gúùngà**. This could theoretically be attributed to the use of different intonational boundary tones (see Hyman (1990) for more discussion). A L tone is the default for lexical items in isolation or final position. A H boundary tone is used in discourse to indicate non-finality where finality might otherwise be assumed, and is often observed in subjunctives and imperatives, especially when there is some degree of impatience being expressed. However, if the final H tones in these imperatives are purely boundary tones, there is some further explanation needed for the fact that the infinitives of toneless or L-toned verbs rarely, if ever, exhibit the final H tone in our elicitation, and why it only occurs with the CV(VN)C verbs, and not with longer ones.

Assuming that the FV of such forms is extratonal, and the LH grammatical pattern competes for linking, along with the lexical H tone of the radical, on the (initial) penultimate syllable, normally the middle tone (in this case the grammatical L) would be dropped out by T-drop, leaving the final H linked to the second mora of the penultimate. However, because there is a surface HL contour audible in lexically H verbs with a bimoraic first syllable, such as **gúùngà**, it seems that instead it must be the grammatical L which links to the second node of the penultimate, while the final H does one of two things. In the cases where a final H tone surfaces in the form, we posit that it is this grammatical H which remains floating until it is allowed to link to the final vowel.

In the cases where the final tone on these lexically H CV(VN)C verbs is L rather than H, we posit that rather than remaining floating, the final H of the grammatical pattern has been trimmed out by some process similar to T-drop (3.8.4). Because there is always a HL contour in a bimoraic first syllable in imperatives of lexically H verbs, it is not possible to posit that it is the grammatical L tone which is dropped. It is not clear why the final H would drop rather than the L. Usually the tone dropped is that which is the third linking of the three tones, which in this case, would be the L. One possible reason for the difference here might be that an invariable "imperative" tone pattern has been established for imperatives of bisyllabic verbs. Since the lexically L and toneless verbs have a surface pattern which is H-L, perhaps the lexically H verbs are fit into the same pattern. This is not an unreasonable hypothesis, since the imperative plural forms have a single invariable pattern for all verbs of any syllable type.

Whatever the reasons, the CV(VN)C forms can be described as follows: A lexically H verb with a CVC base has a H initial tone and either a H or L final tone. A lexically H verb with a CVVNC base has a HL contour on the bimoraic penult and either a H or L final tone.

A lexically L verb with a CVC or C(G)VV(N)C base, e.g. **bégà** 'cut hair!' and **fyééngà** 'pinch something shut!', has a H tone on the initial TBU and a L final tone. We assume that the initial surface H tone of both the L verbs is the phonetic realization of an initial LH, since a word-initial LH which precedes an L tone is always realized as H. This would leave the final L to be provided by the default rule. So in the case of a lexically L-toned verb, the underlying LH on

3.5 Tone on verbs

the initial syllable would be composed of the lexical L tone plus the final H of the complex LH pattern, with the grammatical L, the last linking of the three tones, being dropped by T-drop.[83] The LH contour on the initial syllable is phonetically interpreted by the rule of LH raising (LH > H/#_ L) being heard as a surface H tone. This would correctly yield forms such as **bégà** and **fyééngà**.

The imperative of Ø CVVC verbs patterns identically to a L verb as regards surface tones. It is formed in the same manner as the imperative of L verbs, except that in toneless forms there is no T-drop. In the case of the toneless CVVC verb, the underlying LH on the initial syllable would be the two grammatical tones of the complex LH pattern, which both are linked by initial tone association to the two free nodes of that syllable. Just as in the L verbs, phonetic interpretation of the LH contour by LH raising (LH > H/#_ L) occurs here, yielding forms like **dííhà** 'beat!'.

3.5.3.3.4.1 Imperative singular stem tone pattern with causative and passive

Causative and passive forms of the imperative singular are found in (3.39).

(3.39) Imperative singular stem-tone pattern with causative and passive

UT	Syll. pattern	Base	Gloss	Imperative SG
H	CVC	-fúk-	'pour on'	fúkà/fúkâ
H	CVC w/PS	-fúk-u-	'pour on (PS)'	fúkwâ
H	CVC w/CS	-fúk-iisi-	'pour on (CS)'	fúkììsâ
H	CVC w/CS+PS	-fúk-iisi-bu-	'pour on (PS CS)'	fúkììsìbwâ
L	CVC	-bèg-	'cut hair'	bégà
L	CVC w/PS	-bèg-u-	'cut hair (PS)'	bègwâ
L	CVC w/CS	-bèg-eesi-	'cut hair (CS)'	bègèèsâ
L	CVC w/CS+PS	-bèg-eesi-bu-	'cut hair (CS+PS)'	bègèèsìbwâ
Ø	CVVC	-diih-	'beat'	dííhà
Ø	CVVC w/PS	-diih-u-	'beat (PS)'	dììhwâ
Ø	CVVC w/CS	-diih-iisi-	'beat (CS)'	dìhììsâ
Ø	CVVC w/CS+PS	-diih-iisi-bu-	'beat (CS+PS)'	dìhììsìbwâ

Looking at the forms which have three or more syllables, we can see that the complex LH pattern is realized as expected, with the final H tone linking

---

[83] It is not totally clear why T-drop would work normally in imperatives of lexically L verbs when it does not do so in lexically H verbs. The pattern in these short verbs may instead reflect an invariable pattern.

to the FV in these causative and passive forms. The H tone of the passive or causative extension is not noticeable in any of these forms. This is just as we saw in the non-imperative causative/passive complex LH forms such as **tútábègèsìibwî** 'we were just caused to cut hair, but...' described above under (3.36). The H of the extension links to the penultimate syllable, which is also linked by L spread from the preceding syllable. This produces an underlying LH contour which undergoes LH lowering because of the following H tone. Thus in all the causative forms of the imperative singular, there is a L tone in the penultimate of surface forms, e.g. **bègèèsìbwâ** 'be caused to get your hair cut!', **fúkììsìbwâ** 'be caused to pour water on something!', **dìhììsìbwâ** 'be caused to beat!'

In the CVC and CV(VN)C verbs of lexically H and L verbs, the tonal pattern of the passive or causative of the imperative is identical to their non-passive counterparts, with the exception that the final syllable in all cases bears H tone and the initial syllable of L and Ø verbs is now L rather than H. This alternation in the initial syllable of L and Ø verbs is another indication that the underlying tone is LH on these syllables, here predictably undergoing LH lowering preceding the final H.

In H verbs of CV(VN)C configuration, we find that there is still a HL contour in an initial bimoraic syllable, e.g. **gúùngwâ** 'be cheated', maintaining the LH pattern. A bisyllabic H verb in which the initial syllable is monomoraic has a H tone on both syllables, e.g. **fúkwâ** 'be poured out'.

3.5.3.3.5 Imperative plural stem-tone pattern (complex LH-IP)

The imperative plural forms, like the imperative singular, have a LH stem-tone pattern. However, the plural imperatives are exceptional in that they have a set pattern consisting of L tones on all non-final free TBUs, with an invariable H tone on the final vowel -**i**, whether or not there is a passive or causative in the form. This leads us to posit that the final vowel of the imperative plural is not extratonal in any instances. As always, a word-final H tone is phonetically realized as a short falling contour, and is shown below as a circumflex accent. The stem-tone pattern for imperative plural will be called the complex LH-IP (IP for imperative plural).

The imperative plural forms are exemplified in (3.40). The only forms in which the two tones of the pattern are not both evident are the lexically H-toned CVC-FV forms. These can easily be derived using the basic contour simplification rules, however, since a HL on a single syllable is simplified to H. Forms here are self explanatory.

(3.40) Imperative plural (Complex LH-IP stem-tone pattern) with assorted types

UT	Syll. pattern	Base	Gloss	Imperative PL
H	CVC	-fúk-	'pour on'	fúkî
H	CVVNC	-gúung-	'cheat'	gúùngî
H	CVCVVC	-báraat-	'make wattle frame'	báràatî
H	CVCVVNCVC	-gógoombek-	'barge in'	gógòòmbèkî
L	CVC	-bèg-	'cut hair'	bègî
L	CVVNC	-fyèeng-	'shut off breath'	fyèèngî
L	CVNCVVC	-shàmbaal-	'rejoice'	shàmbààlî
L	CVCVNCVC	-bèraangir-	'call from afar'	bèrààngìrî
L	CVCVCVVNC	-gòloloomb-	'flow'	gòlòlòòmbî
Ø	CVVC	-diih-	'beat'	dììhî
Ø	CVVCVC	-laalik-	'invite'	làalìkî

3.5.3.3.5.1 Imperative plural forms with causative and passive

As can be seen by comparing (3.40) with (3.41), there is no difference between the tonal pattern of the usual imperatives and that of the causatives and passives, since the active forms all have final H tones as well. It would appear here, just as in the causatives of other complex LH forms, that there is no sign in these causative and passive forms of the characteristic H extension tones. This is because the H of the extension always links to the right-hand node of the penultimate syllable (as long as there is no shortage of TBUs) in cases where there is a final-linking stem tone. Then, because of L spread from the preceding L tone of the stem-tone pattern, there is a LH contour on the penultimate of most passive and causative forms. When LH is followed by a H tone, it is lowered by the rule of LH lowering, and appears on the surface as L.

(3.41) Imperative plural with causative and passive

UT	Syll. pattern	Base	Gloss	Imperative PL
H	CVC	-fúk-	'pour on'	fúkî
H	CVC w/PS	-fúk-u-	'pour on (PS)'	fúkwî
H	CVC w/CS	-fúk-iisi-	'pour on (CS)'	fúkììsî
H	CVC w/CS+PS	-fúk-iisi-bu-	'pour on (PS CS)'	fúkììsìbwî

UT	Syll. pattern	Base	Gloss	Imperative PL
L	CVC	-bèg-	'cut hair'	**bègî**
L	CVC w/PS	-bèg-u-	'cut hair(PS)'	**bègwî**
L	CVC w/CS	-bèg-eesi-	'cut hair(CS)'	**bègèèsî**
L	CVC w/CS+PS	-bèg-eesi-bu-	'cut hair (CS+PS)'	**bègèèsìbwî**
Ø	CVVC	-diih-	'beat'	**dììhî**
Ø	CVVC w/PS	-diih-u-	'beat (PS)'	**dììhwî**
Ø	CVVC w/CS	-diih-iisi-	'beat (CS)'	**dìhììsî**
Ø	CVVC w/CS+PS	-diih-iisi-bu-	'beat (CS+PS)'	**dìhììsìbwî**

The imperative plural of lexically H CVVNC verbs, just as in the imperative singular, has a HL contour in the first syllable, for example, **gúùngwî** 'you (PL) be cheated!'. Though the final grammatical H links in these forms to the final syllable, there are still two tones, the grammatical L and the H of passive, vying for position on the right-hand node of the penultimate. The grammatical L is given precedence, probably to maintain the surface LH pattern.

3.5.3.3.6 *Complex LL stem tone pattern*

The complex LL stem-tone pattern has a L tone in V₂ position, and a final, right-linking L tone. This pattern is found only in the conditional contrary-to-fact past (CND.C.F.PST) form of the verb. This form has H tones on the tense prefixes and uses the resultative form of the verb stem. In these forms it is impossible to tell if MR operates or not, because there are no sequences of H tones in a position that gives a clear indication of the underlying tonal configuration. Thus MR is irrelevant in such forms. In (3.42) we see examples of this form. The gloss for each would be: 'If we had.... (but we didn't)'.

(3.42) Complex LL stem-tone pattern with assorted verb types

UT	Syll. pattern	RS stem	Gloss	CND.C.F.PST
H	CVC-ir	-**fúk-ir-i**	'pour on'	**twángáfúsìrì**
H	CVVNC-ir	-**gúung-ir-i**	'cheat'	**twángágúúzìrì**
H	CVCVVC-ir	-**báraat-ir-i**	'make wattle frame'	**twángábáràasìrì**
H	CVCVVNCVC-ir	-**gógoombek-ir-i**	'barge in'	**twángágógòmbèsìrì**

3.5 Tone on verbs

UT	Syll. pattern	RS stem	Gloss	CND.C.F.PST
L	CVC-ir	-bèg-ir-i	'cut hair'	twángábèzìrì
L	CVVNC-ir	-fyèeng-ir-i	'shut off breath'	twángáfyèèzìrì
L	CVNCVVC-ir	-shàmbaal-ir-i	'rejoice'	twángáshàmbììrì
L	CVCVVNCVC-ir	-bèraangir-ir-i	'call from afar'	twángábèràngììrì
L	CVCVCVVNC-ir	-gòloloomb-ir-i	'flow'	twángágòlòlòòmbìrì
∅	CVVC-ir	-diih-ir-i	'beat'	twángádììhìrì
∅	CVVCVC-ir	-laalik-ir-i	'invite'	twángálàlìsìrì

The fact that there is a L grammatical tone in these forms is not hard to see by looking at the data in (3.42). In the non-passive, non-causative forms, there are no H tones to the right of the prefixes other than the lexical H tones of the H verbs.

That there are *two* grammatical L tones in this pattern, one of which is final linking, is best seen by observation of the passive and causative forms in (3.43). These forms all have a L tone on the FV. This shows that the passive/causative H tone is not the rightmost-linking tone in these forms. If it were, the extension's H tone would link to the FV. Instead, the H tone of the passive and causative links to the penultimate (note the LH and H tones on the penultimate syllables of all the passive and causative forms in (3.43)), while the final-linking L of the complex LL pattern links to the FV, resulting in a surface L tone on the FV in each case.

3.5.3.3.6.1 Complex LL stem-tone pattern with causative and passive

(3.43) Complex LL stem-tone pattern with assorted causatives and passives

UT	Syll. pattern	RS stem	Gloss	CND.C.F.PST
H	CVC	-fúk-ir-i	'pour on'	twángáfúsìrì
H	CVC w/PS	-fúk-ir-u-i	'pour on (PS)'	twángáfúsīrwì/ twángáfúsìrwì
H	CVC w/CS	-fúk-iisi-ir-i-i	'pour on (CS)'	twángáfúkìsíízì
H	CVC w/CS+PS	-fúk-iisi-ir-i-bu-i	'pour on (CS+PS)'	twángáfúkìsííbwì

UT	Syll. pattern	RS stem	Gloss	CND.C.F.PST
L	CVC	-bèg-ir-i	'cut hair'	twángábèzìrì
L	CVC w/PS	-bèg-ir-u-i	'cut hair (PS)'	twángábèzírwì
L	CVC w/CS	-bèg-eesi-ir-i-i	'cut hair (CS)'	twángábègèsíízì
L	CVC w/CS+PS	-bèg-eesi-ir-i-bu-i	'cut hair (CS+PS)'	twángábègèsííbwì
Ø	CVVC	-diih-ir-i	'beat'	twángádììhìrì
Ø	CVVC w/PS	-diih-ir-u-i	'beat (PS)'	twángádììhírwì
Ø	CVVC w/CS	-diih-iisi-ir-i-i	'beat (CS)'	twángádìhìsíízì
Ø	CVVC w/CS+PS	-diih-iisi-ir-i-bu-i	'beat (CS+PS)'	twángádìhìsííbwì

The fact that the complex LL stem-tone pattern includes only L tones makes the presence of the H tones of causative and passive all the more clear in these forms. In this stem-tone pattern, the H of passive or causative surfaces on the penultimate syllable, either as part of a mid (LH) tone (in verbs such as **twángáfúsīrwì**) or as a H tone. As is always the case when there is a final-linking tone in the stem-tone pattern, the H of passive and causative links to the right-hand node of the penultimate syllable.

The underlying tone on the penultimate syllable is LH in all the passive and/or causative forms, because in a CVC -**ir** verb base the left L grammatical tone of the stem-tone pattern is also linked to the penultimate, and in longer stems, there is L spread from the L grammatical tone onto the penultimate. It is only in the CVC H-tone verb, **twángáfúsīrwì**, where this LH is preceded by a H tone and followed by L, that the tonal environment allows this LH contour to be realized as a phonetic mid tone. In all other cases, there are both a preceding and a following L tone, which causes the LH to be simplified to H by the rule of LH raising (LH > H > L _ L). The underlying presence of the penultimate LH in all the forms above can be shown by a derivation, but it can also be proven by elicitation in a context in which the form has an intonational final H tone. When verbs of this form are pronounced with the marked[84] *pre-pause intonation* (3.12.4) with a final H tone, the surface H tone of the penultimate syllable seen in the forms in (3.43) changes to L. For example, **twángágúngìsíízì** 'we could have cheated' is pronounced pre-pausally as **twángágúngìsììzí**. The switch of the H penultimate syllable to L here is a clear indication that the underlying tone on that syllable is actually LH.

---

[84]In these forms, the prepause intonation is frequently heard since this verb form (we could have...) is often in a clause followed by another clause detailing the consequences of not having done whatever it was.

3.5 Tone on verbs

(LH always undergoes lowering to L preceding a H tone, while surfacing as H between two L tones.)

3.5.3.3.7 Subjunctive: Complex HH with replacive H stem-tone pattern

The subjunctive has a unique type of complex pattern which includes two H tones. We call this the complex HH stem-tone pattern. The initial H tone of this pattern replaces the lexical tone of the verb and then spreads rightward. Because it replaces the lexical tone of the verb root, rather than linking to its right, we term it "replacive" H tone. The final-linking H tone of this pattern links to the rightmost available TBU, but is lowered to L by Meeussen's rule, which is active in these forms. In passive and causative forms, however, it is the H of the PS or CS extension that is juxtaposed to the replacive H of the complex HH, with the result that the H extension tone is the one that is lowered, becoming L. In these cases the final-linking H tone of the stem-tone pattern is protected from lowering, and surfaces as H on the final vowel of the verb.

The first H tone of complex-HH is a replacive tone, which "preempts" or neutralizes the lexical tone of the verb stem.[85] This replacive H tone alone is associated to the first syllable of the verb stem. The replacive H tone remains H whether it links to a lexically H-toned verb root, a lexically L-toned one, or a lexically toneless one. This is shown by the following examples: **àhámágàlè** 'that he call' from **hàmagal** (L), **àgálúkè** 'that he return' from **gáluk** (H) or **àláálíkè** 'that he invite' from **laalik** (Ø). The complex HH pattern is found only in the simple subjunctive (SBV) illustrated by the examples just given, and on the verb stem in the remote future (F3), e.g. **twááyè hámágálè** '(someday) we will call'.

Because there are no differences of tonal pattern due to the underlying lexical tones of the radical (since the tone of the radical is dropped) all of the "basic" subjunctive forms (toneless subject marker+verb stem+Fe)[86] pattern identically, whether formed from lexically H, L, or toneless verbs. Example (3.44) provides some subjunctive (SBV) forms.

---

[85] A tone with this characteristic is sometimes described as "feature changing" rather than "feature filling." Feature filling tones can only link to empty nodes, while feature changing tones will link to a node which is already filled. Schadeberg (2003b: 151) states that such a neutralization of underlying lexical tone can be reconstructed in PB for the "optative" (which corresponds to our subjunctive forms here). In PB, the tones are neutralized to L, whereas here, because of tone reversal, the tones are neutralized to H.

[86] As will be seen below, the lexical tone of the radical is replaced by the subjunctive H tone only in the "basic" subjunctive forms. Any subjunctive form which has an added prefix of any kind (aspectual, negative, incorporated object, etc.) whether segmental or tonal, reverts to the V_2 stem-tone pattern, in which the lexical tone associates as usual to the first mora of the stem.

(3.44) Complex HH stem-tone pattern with assorted verb types

UT	Syll. pattern	Base	Gloss	Subjunctive
H	CVC	-fúk-	'pour on'	tùfúkè
H	CVVNC	-gúung-	'cheat'	tùgúúngè
H	CVCVVC	-báraat-	'build wattle frame'	tùbáráàtè
H	CVCVVNCVC	-gógoombek-	'barge in'	tùgógóómbékè
L	CVC	-bèg-	'cut hair'	tùbégè
L	CVVNC	-fyèeng-	'shut off breath'	tùfyééngè
L	CVNCVVC	-shàmbaal-	'rejoice, celebrate'	tùshámbáàlè
L	CVCVVNCVC	-bèraangir-	'call from afar'	tùbéráángírè
L	CVCVCVVNC	-gòloloomb-	'flow'	tùgólólóòmbè
Ø	CVVC	-diih-	'beat'	tùdííhè
Ø	CVVCVC	-laalik-	'invite'	tùláálíkè

Looking at the data in (3.44), the replacive H tone of this pattern is easy to spot, but the right-linking H tone is not evident as a H in any forms. However, the usual quick method of determining if there is a final H tone in complex patterns, that is, looking for a H tone on the FV of passive and causative forms (3.45), immediately shows that this stem-tone pattern involves a final H. This leads us to posit that in non-causative, non-passive forms, the final-linking H is lowered by the activity of Meeussen's rule. If we look at the two examples in (3.44) which have a bimoraic penultimate syllable, e.g. **tùbáráàtè** 'let's build a wattle frame' and **tùshámbáàlè** 'let's celebrate', the presence of the right-linking L is obvious. It is this right-linking L (underlyingly a H) which gives the falling contour in the penultimate syllable of such forms.

In a verb stem longer than just CV(V)C, we see that the replacive H tone of complex HH spreads to all free non-final TBUs up to and including the underlying rightmost available TBU. H-spread also spreads the H tone onto the penultimate syllable, which is linked to the lowered right-linking H tone of the complex HH pattern. Because the rule of single-mora HL simplification (HL> H on a single mora) the L is not evident in any monomoraic penult. For example, in **tùgálúkè** 'let's return' the underlying HL contour on the penultimate syllable is simplified by single-mora HL simplification. This contour only shows up in a CVCVVC-stem verb, where the surface penultimate is bimoraic. In such a case, as noted above, the right linking L shows up as the L in the HL contour on that penultimate syllable, e.g. **tùbáráàtè** 'let's build a wattle frame'. In a bimoraic penultimate which directly follows the L-toned

3.5 Tone on verbs

prefix however, e.g. **tùbííkè** 'let's put something', the underlying HL contour on **bii** is simplified to H by the rule of post-L HL simplification.

The remote future (F3) tense is a two-word verb form. The presence of a word break in this form can be discerned from the fact that there is still a long vowel in the prefix/tense marker combination,[87] even when more than three morae follow in the verb stem, e.g. **twááyè báráàtè** 'someday we will build a wattle frame'. If the whole verb form were a single phonological word, the mora-based shortening rule would shorten the vowel in the initial syllable when three or more morae follow. The fact that this is a two-word form is very significant in tone assignment, since, as will be seen in the section below on subjunctive forms of the V_2 pattern below, a subjunctive form which has prefixes preceding the verb stem does not take the complex HH stem-tone pattern. These remote future forms do, however, take the complex HH pattern. The tones on the self-standing stem are just as seen above in the stems of the SBV subjunctive forms (3.44).

3.5.3.3.7.1 Complex HH stem tone pattern with causative and passive

We now look at the causatives/passives with the complex HH stem-tone pattern, exemplified in (3.45). Note that there is a H tone on the FV of every passive or causative subjunctive. This is the final H tone of the complex HH. In these forms, the H tone of the passive or causative extension, which directly precedes the final-linking tone of the stem-tone pattern, is the H tone which is juxtaposed to the replacive H. Therefore the extension tone is the one which is lowered by the application of Meeussen's rule, leaving the H tone of the stem-tone pattern to surface on the FV as a H tone. It is this lowered H of the extension which produces an underlying HL contour in the penultimate syllable of all causative and passive subjunctive forms. Just as was seen in the non-extended forms, this contour is simplified to H on any monomoraic syllable. It is heard as a surface contour only on a bimoraic syllable which is preceded by a H tone, e.g. **tùfúkîsê** 'let's have something poured on/into someone/something'. The effect is the same as was seen in non-causative forms which have a bimoraic penult, e.g. **tùbáráàtè** 'let's build a wattle frame' and **tùshámbáàlè** 'let's rejoice', but in those forms the L of the penultimate contour resulted from the lowering of the final H of the stem-tone pattern, while in these forms, the L in that same position results from the lowering of the H of the extension.

---

[87]By contrast, in the case of a monosyllabic verb stem, e.g. **mw-** 'shave', the **aa** in the prefixes is shortened following the lengthening of the final vowel of the auxiliary, preceding the encliticized monosyllabic verb stem: **twáyéémwè**. (See 3.5.5 for more on the treatment of monosyllabic stems.)

(3.45) Complex HH stem tone pattern with causative and passive

UT	Syll. pattern	Base	Gloss	Subjunctive
H	CVC	**-fúk-**	'pour on'	**tùfúkè**
H	CVC w/PS	**-fúk-u-**	'pour on (PS)'	**tùfúkwê**
H	CVC w/CS	**-fúk-iisi-**	'pour on (CS)'	**tùfúkîisê**
H	CVC w/CS+PS	**-fúk-iisi-bu-**	'pour on (PS of CS)'	**tùfúkíísíbwê**
L	CVC	**-bèg-**	'cut hair'	**tùbégè**
L	CVC w/PS	**-bèg-u-**	'cut hair (PS)'	**tùbégwê**
L	CVC w/CS	**-bèg-eesi-**	'cut hair (CS)'	**tùbégéèsê**
L	CVC w/CS+PS	**-bèg-eesi-bu-**	'cut hair (PS of CS)'	**tùbégéésíbwê**
Ø	CVVC	**-diih-**	'beat'	**tùdííhè**
Ø	CVVC w/PS	**-diih-u-**	'beat (PS)'	**tùdííhwê**
Ø	CVVC w/CS	**-diih-iisi-**	'beat (CS)'	**tùdíhîisê**
Ø	CVVC w/CS+PS	**-diih-iisi-bu-**	'beat (PS of CS)'	**tùdíhíísíbwê**

3.5.3.3.8 *Subjunctive forms of the V₂ pattern*

The subjunctive forms are unique in that if there is *any* prefix (segmental or tonal) on the verb stem, besides the surface L-toned (toneless in UF) subject prefix, the complex HH stem-tone pattern otherwise found in subjunctive forms is "cancelled".[88] If even so much as a H tone is added to the usual subject prefix of a subjunctive form, the verb stem does not have the replacive H tone and lowered right-linking H tone of the complex HH tone pattern. Instead the verb stem displays a V₂ stem-tone pattern. It is interesting to note that all forms which have the V₂ stem-tone pattern are irrealis forms with a prefix; the V₂ pattern is characteristic of future (F2) forms, prefixed subjunctive forms, and in forms denoting not yet realized events (such as the NEG.YET forms, e.g. **àtàzí lààlìkà** 'he has not yet invited' or **àtáàlì záàzí lààlìkà** 'he had not yet invited').

The V₂ stem-tone pattern is characterized by the appearance of the lexical tone of the radical on the first syllable of the verb stem, followed by a L tone on the first free TBU. This L tone thereafter spreads to all free TBUs to the right.

---

[88]However, in a CV verb stem, e.g. **túmwè** 'let's shave', because of minimality constraints, the normal replacive tone of the subjunctive actually appears on the subject prefix rather than on the verb stem. For this reason, this H tone on the subject in this case is not considered as an "extra" prefix, and the H replacive tone remains (though on the prefix, not on the stem).

3.5 Tone on verbs

Take, for example, the basic subjunctive form of a L-tone verb stem such as -hàmagal- 'call': ùhámágálè '(that) you call'. This typical subjunctive form has a surface L-tone on the subject prefix, followed by the stem, which displays replacive H tone. The H tone spreads up to but does not include the FV. With the addition of an object prefix (in this case a L-toned object, but a H-toned object or any other extra prefixation invokes the same reaction) this form trades the complex HH pattern seen above for the V_2 stem-tone pattern, becoming ùb̠àhàmàgàlè '(that) you call them', displaying nothing but L tones from beginning to end.

Any prefix in any position preceding the verb stem (whether H- or L-tone) triggers the switch to the V_2 pattern. Even a non-segmental H-tone "conditional" prefix realized on the subject marker is followed by the V_2 pattern, e.g. the Ø verb: túlààlìkà 'if/when we invite'. Examples of other prefixes which trigger the V_2 pattern include the toneless negative marker (which in the subjunctive forms takes a H tone) e.g. tùt̠álààlìkè 'that we *not* invite'; any object marker e.g. tùm̠úlààlìkè 'that we invite *him*'; the consecutive/additive ná- e.g. tùn̠álààlìkè 'that we *also* invite';[89] and several mood markers, such as kì- 'if it were that', túk̠ìlààlìkè 'if we had invited', or ká- 'distal', e.g. tùk̠álààlìkè '(and following something else) you invite'. As seen in all these examples, the tones on the verb stem are the L of the V_2 pattern as shown in (3.25).

As just noted, there are several subjunctive forms, if one terms a "subjunctive" as a form with the subjunctive stem-tone pattern and the final vowel -e.[90] The "basic" subjunctive (SBV) is the archetypical subjunctive form, e.g. the H verb àgééndè 'that he go'. The SBV and the remote future (F3) are the only forms which exhibit the complex HH stem-tone pattern, and they exhibit this pattern only in their minimally prefixed forms. All the other subjunctive forms, by virtue of the fact that it is their prefixes which define them as distinct forms of the subjunctive, exhibit only the V_2 stem-tone pattern, and are never found with the complex HH stem-tone pattern. These forms are the conditional contrary-to-fact ki-...-e form (CND.C.F), e.g. àkìgééndè 'if he had gone', the intervening time (INTV) ka-...-e future form, e.g. àkágéèndè 'he will go (following some other action)' and the narrative continuative (CON) na- -e forms, e.g. àn̠ágéèndè 'and he went'. In all these forms, the prefixes kì-, ká-, and ná- themselves function to keep the complex HH stem-tone pattern from ever appearing on the verb stem.

---

[89]This form is used in the continuative (SBSC) where it indicates an action in a series of consecutive past events in which the progression is fairly predictable, but can also function with a subjunctive meaning: 'that we also invite (someone)'.

[90]In the case of verbs with an adverbial auxiliary, the subjunctive final vowel -e is not present, as the main predicate appears as a "dead" verb, in the form of a prefixless infinitive, and the auxiliary, which should carry the subjunctive FV, if any form were to do so, has an invariable FV.

As already noted, the addition of a negative marker (as of any other prefix) changes the stem-tone pattern of a subjunctive form from the complex HH to V_2.[91] A further characteristic of negation in the subjunctive is that the negative marker, which is underlyingly toneless, always exhibits H tone in a subjunctive form. This H on the negative marker does not spread rightward, since it is a prefix; because of domain constraints, tones linked to prefixes never spread to the stem, e.g. **ùtáhàmàgàlè** 'don't call (someone)', **ùtábàhàmàgàlè** 'don't call them', or **ùtámúhàmàgàlè** 'don't call him'.

The fact that the toneless negative marker **ta-** has a H tone in the subjunctive presents an interesting option for the analysis of why subjunctive forms switch stem-tone patterns when prefixes are added. One option is to posit that the replacive H tone of the subjunctive is a prefixal tone (i.e. a tone that links from the left edge, not of the verb stem, but of the verb word, i.e. prefixes plus stem) rather than being a suffixal tone like all the other stem-tone patterns which form an overlay on the verb stem only, and link to the right of a verb's lexical tone. It must also be posited that the replacive H of the subjunctive stem-tone pattern is marked for linking only either to a negative marker, in which case it spreads no further, or to the first TBU of a verb stem where it is a replacive tone, and spreads rightward onto all available free TBUs.

According to such an analysis, if there is no lexical tone in any of the prefixes to the left of the negative marker or, lacking a negative marker, to the left of the verb stem, the H subjunctive tone is able to move rightward and link to the negative marker, if there is one, or if there is no negative marker, to replace the lexical tone of the verb stem. If however, there is any prefix with its own lexical or grammatical tone, whether H or L, this tone blocks the rightward movement of the H subjunctive tone, so that it cannot reach its target. If the initial H links to the negative marker, it stops there, and is followed by the verb stem with V_2 stem-tone pattern. If there is a tonal prefix to the left of the negative marker, the H tone is blocked and instead, the complex HH stem-tone pattern is replaced by the V_2 pattern.

The data in (3.46) illustrate the subjunctive form, both with the basic complex HH tone pattern and with examples of how prefixes change the stem-tone pattern to V_2 with its L suffixal tone. The final column shows how the negative marker takes on the H tone of the subjunctive mood. Subject markers are first-person plural, and forms indicate a polite imperative. Note that in order to include only verbs which semantically allow both H and L tone objects, our usual CVC H verb -**fúk**- 'pour' has been

---

[91]In negative subjunctive forms such as these, as well as in other non-simple subjunctive forms of the V_2 pattern, there is sometimes a final H tone. More study could be done on the nature and occurrence of these final H tones.

3.5 Tone on verbs

replaced in (3.46) by -níg- 'choke someone' and the toneless applicative extension -ir- has been included in the forms **tùbáráátírè, tùmúbáràatìrè**, and **tùbàbáràatìrè** 'let's build (him/them) a wattle frame'.

(3.46) Complex HH subjunctives and V₂ subjunctives

Base, UT	Gloss	Complex HH Subjunctive	V₂ pattern w/H tone Obj.	w/L tone Obj.	w/negative
-níg- H	'choke'	tùnígè	tùmúnígè	tùbànígè	tùtánígè
-gúung- H	'cheat'	tùgúúngè	tùmúgúùngè	tùbàgúúngè	tùtágúùngê
-báraat- H	'build frame'	tùbáráátírè	tùmúbáràatìrè	tùbàbáràatìrè	tùtábáràatìrè
-bèg- L	'cut hair'	tùbégè	tùmúbègè	tùbàbègè	tùtábègè
-fyèeng- L	'pinch shut'	tùfyééngè	tùmúfyèèngè	tùbàfyèèngè	tùtáfyèèngè
-hàmagal- L	'call'	tùhámágálè	tùmúhàmàgàlè	tùbàhàmàgàlè	tùtáhàmàgàlè
-diih- ∅	'beat'	tùdííhè	tùmúdìihè	tùbàdìihè	tùtádìihê
-laalik- ∅	'invite'	tùláálíkè	tùmúlààlìkè	tùbàlààlìkè	tùtálààlìkè

The remote future (F3) tense, another complex HH form, shown in the final column of (3.47), presents some interesting data, by virtue of the fact that it is a two-word verb form. The presence of a H tone in the first word of this complex form, because it is in a separate word, does not affect the ability of the main verb stem to display the complex HH stem-tone pattern. (In contrast, as will be shown in the last three columns of (3.48), when there is a prefix *directly attached to the verb stem itself*, these forms, just like every other more-than-minimally-prefixed subjunctive form, do exhibit the V₂ stem-tone pattern.)

(3.47) Complex HH stem-tone pattern in two-word verb form (F3)

UT	Syll. pattern	Base	Gloss	F3 remote future
H	CVC	-fúk-	'pour on'	twááyè fúkè
H	CVVNC	-gúúng-	'cheat'	twááyè gúúngè
H	CVCVVC	-báraat-	'build wattle frame'	twááyè báráàtè
H	CVCVVNCVC	-gógombek-	'barge in'	twááyè gógóómbékè
L	CVC	-bèg-	'cut hair'	twááyè bégè
L	CVVNC	-fyèèng-	'shut off breath'	twááyè fyééngè
L	CVNCVVC	-shàmbaal-	'rejoice'	twááyè shámbáàlè
L	CVCVVNCVC	-bèraangir-	'call from afar'	twááyè béráángírè
L	CVCVCVVNC	-gòloloomb-	'flow'	gááyè gólólóòmbè
Ø	CVVC	-diih-	'beat'	twááyè dííhè
Ø	CVVCVC	-laalik-	'invite'	twááyè láálíkè

The data in (3.48) show that a prefix which is affixed directly to the main "lexical" verb of the remote future form affects the tone pattern of that verb in the way which is characteristic of subjunctive forms, causing it to exhibit the V_2 pattern. Compare the forms in the first column, where the verb stem has no prefixes, and exhibits the complex HH replacive H tones, to the forms in the following columns, where the tones following any lexical tone are the L tones of the V_2 pattern. The examples are given using both a H tone and a L tone object marker, in this case cl.1 'him/her' and cl.2 'them', in order to show that the basic effect on the verb stem is the same whether the prefix has H or L tone. The only difference is that following a H tone, a HL contour in a bimoraic syllable is realized on the surface, whereas it is realized simply as a H when it follows a L tone. The following data includes the usual verbs, with the addition of **-níg-** 'choke (someone)', **-kéngeer-** 'remember', and **-hàmagal-** 'call'. Underlined syllables show where the difference in stem-tone pattern between the first column and the remaining columns can be heard.

3.5 Tone on verbs

(3.48) Remote future, without and with prefixes on the main verb stem

UT	(F3) (no prefixes)	w/H tone obj.	w/L tone obj.	w/consecutive ná-
H	twááyè nígè	twááyè múnígè	twááyè bànígè	twááyè nánígè
H	twááyè g̱úúngè	twááyè múg̱úùngè	twááyè bàg̱úúngè	twááyè nág̱úùngè
H	twááyè kéng̱éèrè	twááyè múkéng̱èèrè	twááyè bàkéng̱èèrè	twááyè nákéng̱èèrè
L	twááyè ḇégè	twááyè múḇègè	twááyè bàḇègè	twááyè náḇègè
L	twááyè f̱ééngè	twááyè múf̱yèèngè	twááyè bàf̱yèèngè	twááyè náf̱yèèngè
L	twááyè ẖámágálè	twááyè múẖàmàgàlè	twááyè bàẖàmàgàlè	twááyè náẖàmàgàlè
Ø	twááyè ḏííhè	twááyè múḏììhè	twááyè bàḏììhè	twááyè náḏììhè
Ø	twááyè ḻáálíkè	twááyè múḻààlìkè	twááyè bàḻààlìkè	twááyè náḻààlìkè

The data in (3.49) show the addition of the same prefix, in turn, to each word of the remote future forms. In these forms, some speakers give two options as to the placement of the **ná-**.[92] As seen in the second column of (3.49), if the **ná-** is prefixed to the main verb stem (i.e. the second word of the form) the stem no longer displays the complex HH pattern. As seen in column three below, if the consecutive marker is placed instead in the *first* word of the form, the *second* word retains the normal subjunctive complex HH pattern. The last column in (3.49) also shows the placement of the negative markers in the remote future forms. The negative marker is always placed only in the first word of the verb stem (the prefix section) as shown below, and does not affect the realization of the complex HH pattern on the main verb stem.

---

[92]Other speakers allow the placement of **ná-** only directly before the main verb stem. There is some difference in the shade of meaning of the two: placement of the **ná-** in the first section of the form yields a consecutive or sequential meaning, which seems to focus more on the fact that the action will be done subsequent to an earlier, just mentioned, action in the remote future, while the placement of **ná-** in the second half of the verb gives a meaning of 'additionally, also' to the action expressed in the main verb, focusing on the fact that this action will also, additionally be done in the remote future, not necessarily subsequent to or consecutive with another action already mentioned.

(3.49) Remote future with **ná**- and negative marker

UT	F3	F3 (**ná**- on verb stem)	F3 (**ná**- on AUX)	F3 with NEG
H	twááyè fúkè	twááyè náfúkè	twànááyè fúkè	tùtááyè fúkè
H	twááyè gúúngè	twááyè nágúu̠ngè	twànááyè gúúngè	tùtááyè gúúngè
H	twááyè kéngéèrè	twááyè nákéngèe̠rè	twànááyè kéngéèrè	tùtááyè kéngéèrè
L	twááyè bégè	twááyè nábègè	twànááyè bégè	tùtááyè bégè
L	twááyè fyééngè	twááyè náfyèèngè	twànááyè fyééngè	tùtááyè fyééngè
L	twááyè hámágálè	twááyè náhàmàgàlè	twànááyè hámágálè	tùtááyè hámágálè
Ø	twááyè dííhè	twááyè nádìihè	twànááyè dííhè	tùtááyè dííhè
Ø	twááyè láálíkè	twááyè nálàalìkè	twànááyè láálíkè	tùtááyè láálíkè

3.5.4 Tone assignment in verbs with adverbial auxiliaries

In multiword verb forms with the verbal auxiliaries which we term "adverbial",[93] the form includes more than one phonological word, but only one subject prefix. In such forms the TAM-related stem-tone pattern is realized on the first auxiliary to the right of the prefixes, e.g. the **lúúngúlì** 'prematurely' of **twàngàlúúngùlì géénd**ì **lólà** 'we could prematurely go look' (from -**lól**- 'look') or the **kizi** of **ágákìzì géénd**à 'he will repeatedly go' (from -**géénd**- 'go'). A single verb form may have more than one adverbial auxiliary. However, it seems that only the first bears the stem-tone pattern dictated

---

[93] The adverbial auxiliaries are often adverbial in semantic content (adding information about time, manner etc.) but are verbal forms, and as seen from the tonal patterns here, are tonally treated as verbal in form. Most of the adverbial auxiliaries which precede such prefixless infinitives end in -**i**. This final -**i** is most likely a reinterpreted and repositioned form of the cl. 5 infinitive prefix found in some related Bantu J languages. A possible historical derivation of a sample form might be: ***twà-zíndùk-à í-hììng-à** (a hypothetical reconstruction of a possible original form with a cl. 5 infinitive prefix on -**hììng**- 'farm' giving the meaning 'we went early to farm' > **twàzíndùkì hííngà** (the actual form) 'we farmed early in the morning'.

3.5 Tone on verbs

by the TAM indicated by the prefixes. Any further auxiliaries,[94] as well as the semantically main (syntactically final) verb stem bear the simple stem-tone pattern of the infinitive (though they do not bear the infinitive prefix). The simple pattern is seen on **géèndì** 'going', and on **lólà** 'look' in **twàngàlúúngùlì géèndì lólà** (where the first auxiliary is **lúúngùlì**).

In the future form **túgágéèndì lágáánà** 'we will go and agree together', the suffixal L tone of the V₂ stem-tone pattern of the future tense appears on the second mora of the bimoraic first syllable of the adverbial auxiliary, -**géèndì** 'going', while the main verb, **lágáánà** 'agree together', exhibits the infinitive's simple stem-tone pattern for a H verb.

Following in (3.50) are a few examples of tone in multiword verb forms in which an adverbial auxiliary occurs after the prefixes and before the main verb stem. Note that the stem-tone pattern dictated by the prefixes appears on the adverbial auxiliary, while the main verb displays the H tone of the simple stem-tone pattern in the first free TBU position. This H tone then spreads to all non-final TBUs.

The TBU(s) which exhibit(s) the suffixal tone(s) of the stem-tone pattern of each verb form is/are underlined in each example of (3.50). Note that the tones on -**lágáánà** are always the same in the forms with the auxiliary, displaying the H tone of the simple stem-tone pattern.

(3.50) TAM	UT	Stem T pattern	w/o AUX	Gloss	w/AUX	Gloss
F2	H	V₂ (L)	túgálágàànà	'we'll agree'	túgágéèndì lágáánà	'we will go & agree'
P1	H	complex HL	twàlágààna	'we agreed'	twàgééndì lágáánà	'we went & agreed'
P2	H	simple (H)	túkálágáánà	'we agreed'	túkágéèndì lágáánà	'we went & agreed'
SBV	H	complex HH	tùlágáànè	'let's agree'	tùkízì lágáánà	'let's REP agree'
F2	L	V₂ (L)	túgáshàmbààlà	'we'll rejoice'	túgágéèndì shàmbáálà	'we will go & rejoice'
P1	L	complex HL	twàshàmbáálà	'we rejoiced'	twàgéèndì shàmbáálà	'we went & rejoiced'

---

[94]In the second auxiliary, which bears the simple stem-tone pattern, it is not clear why postlexical H-spread does not cause the H of the simple pattern to be realized also on its final syllable, since it is not final in its phrase, e.g **twàngàlúúngùlì géèndì lólà** 'we could go look too soon'.

TAM	UT	Stem T pattern	w/o AUX	Gloss	w/AUX	Gloss
P2	L	simple (H)	túkáshàmbá_á_là	'we rejoiced'	túkágé_é_ndì shàmbáálà	'we went & rejoiced'
S1	L	complex HH	tùsh_á_mbá_à_lè	'let's rejoice'	tùkízì shàmbáálà	'let's REP rejoice'
F2	Ø	V₂ (L)	túgál_à_àlìkà	'we'll invite'	túgágé_é_ndì láálíkà	'we will go & invite'
P1	Ø	complex HL	tw_à_l_á_álíkà	'we invited'	twàgéé_ndì láálíkà	'we went & invited'
P2	Ø	simple (H)	túkál_á_álíkà	'we invited'	túkágé_é_ndì láálíkà	'we went & invited'
SBV	Ø	complex HH	tùl_á_álíkè	'let's invite'	tùkízì láálíkà	'let's REP invite'

3.5.5 Tone assignment in monosyllabic verb stems

Monosyllabic verb stems are always in the *toneless* class. They present some quite interesting data because of the limited TBUs they have available for tonal association.

In verb forms where the monosyllabic verb stem is not extended in any way, i.e. is only -C(G)-FV, the grammatical tones of the stem-tone pattern link to a TBU which is technically part of the verbal prefixes. Recall that in non-monosyllabic verb stems, stem-tone patterns never interact with the tones on prefixes. In H or L verbs, of course, the radical has a lexical tone which associates to the first TBU of the verb stem, so that any "suffixal" tone of the stem-tone pattern, in order to associate to a mora in the prefixes, would have to violate the constraint against association lines crossing. But even in the case of a [CVVC or longer] toneless verb, where there is no lexical tone on the radical, there is a domain boundary between prefixes and stem which is never crossed in tonal association. The exception to this is the case of monosyllabic stems.

In Kifuliiru, only a monomoraic syllable is permitted in word-final position. Thus a monosyllabic verb stem, though consisting underlyingly of CV, does not become bimoraic when the FV is added. The result of the addition of the FV is -CGV, and not -CGVV. Thus the stem is not only a single syllable, but a single mora. No thorough study has been made regarding this topic in Kifuliiru,[95] but apparently because the monosyllabic verb stem alone

---

[95] For some studies on minimality issues, see McCarthy and Prince (1990) and Hyman (1995).

3.5 Tone on verbs

does not meet the requirements for a minimal verb stem, the usual domain boundary between the prefixes and the stem is ignored in these forms. The final TBU of the prefixes is reinterpreted as part of the stem for tone assignment purposes.

Thus we find forms such as the subjunctive (SBV) **tú-mwè** 'let's shave', where the H tones of the complex HH form link to the toneless subject prefix, while the FV bears default tone.[96] Similarly the future (F2) example, **tú-gáà-mwà** 'we will shave', displays the L tone of the V_2 stem-tone pattern on the second mora of the bimoraic tense prefix.[97] In the future form, the fact that initial linking of the stem-tone pattern's single L tone is to the prefix, rather than to the FV, indicates that the FV is not available for initial linking in such a form.

In the complex HL recent past (P1) forms of monosyllabic roots, e.g. **twààmwà** 'we shaved', **ààgwà** 'he fell', **bààfwà** 'they died', **mwààlyà** 'you (PL) ate', etc., there is further evidence that initial tone association will not link a tone to the FV. In a form such as **twààmwà** 'we shaved', we see that no H tone appears in the surface form, despite the fact that this stem-tone pattern has a H tone which links to the first free TBU. As shown below in (3.51), this lack of H tone stems from the triple-linking constraint, which disallows the linking of the H tone. The H tone is then deleted by T-drop (3.8.4). Linking the HL of the stem-tone pattern in any way other than that shown below in (3.51) would produce forms with a surface H tone. If the L tone of the TAM marker and the H of the stem-tone pattern were both linked to the prefix vowel, and the final-L linked to the FV, this would result in an initial LH contour. An initial LH contour followed by an L tone is subject to application of LH raising, LH > H/# _ L, and would result in the incorrect surface output *****twáámwà**.

So we see that in the case of a monosyllabic verb stem with prefixes, the FV must still be extratonal, since the only TBUs available for initial tone assignment of the stem-tone pattern tones are in the penultimate syllable. By virtue of its penultimate position in the word, it is able to take two association lines. The linking situation seen in these verbs is the very same as that seen in the corresponding complex HL forms of L-tone CV(VN)C verbs, where the H grammatical tone also drops out.

In the monosyllabic verbs, the other tone linked to the penultimate syllable in addition to the grammatical tone of the stem-tone pattern is the L tone of the P1 prefix **à-**, as can be seen in the derivation in (3.51).

---

[96] See following paragraphs for explanation of why we do not posit that the right-linking H links to the FV, later being lowered by MR (even though this would also produce the correct surface tones in this case.)

[97] The first mora of the -**gaa**- tense prefix bears the lexical H tone of the tense prefix.

(3.51) **tw-àà-mo-à** (1PL-P1-shave-Fa) 'we shaved' (Ø)

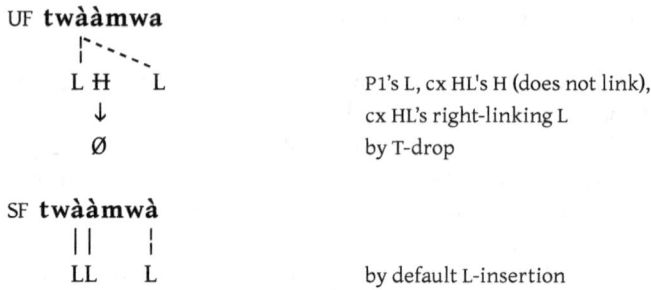

UF	**twàà̀mwa**		
	L H L		P1's L, cx HL's H (does not link),
	↓		cx HL's right-linking L
	Ø		by T-drop
SF	**twààmwà**		
	‖ ǀ		
	LL L		by default L-insertion

In (3.51) we see that the initial linking of the tones of the stem-tone pattern in **twààmwà** is to the second mora of the long prefix vowel, just as we saw earlier in the future form, **tú-gáà-mwà** 'we will shave', where the L tone in **gáà-** is the L tone of the V₂ pattern.

The chart in (3.52) gives a full paradigm of monosyllabic forms. The basic forms are found in the first column of verb forms, with passive and causative forms in the remaining two columns.

(3.52) Monosyllabic verb root in various conjugated forms†

TAM form	CV **mo**- 'shave'	+ PS	+ CS
INF	kúmwâ	kúmwéébwâ	kúmwéésâ
P2	túkámwâ/ túkámwà	túkámwéébwâ	túkámwéésâ
PROG	tùlì múù=mwâ	tùlì mú=mwéébwâ	tùlì mú=mwéésâ
P1	twààmwà	twàmwéébwà	twàmwéésà
SQ	twàànámwà	twànámwéèbwà	twànámwéèsà
TL	tùmwà	tùmwéébwà	tùmwéésà
CND/POT	twàngààmwà	twàngàmwéébwà	twàngàmwéésà
CND Pres.	twàngàmwíírì	twàngàmwíírwì	twàngàmwésîìzì
w/O1‡	twàngàmúmwîìrì	twàngànámwîìrwì	
RS	tùmwíírì	tùmwíírwì	tùmwésîìzì
RS.FRUS	tútámwīīrì	tútámwììrwî	tútámwèsììzî
F1	twà=múù=mwâ	twà=mú=mwéébwâ	twà=mú=mwéésâ

3.5 Tone on verbs

TAM form	CV **mo-** 'shave'	+ PS	+ CS
P3	twáàlí mwīìrì	twáàlí mwììrwî	twáàlí mwèsììzî
CND.C.F.PST	twángámwììrì	twángámwīīrwì	twángámwèsììzî
SBV	túmwè	tùmwéébwê	tùmwéésê
F3	twáyéé=mwè	twááyè mwéébwê	twááyè mwéésê
F3 w/O1	twááyè múmwè	twááyè námwèèbwê	twááyè námwèèsê
CON	tùnámwè	tùnámwèèbwê	tùnámwèèsê
CND.PERS	túkìmwè	túkìmwèèbwê	túkìmwèèsê
F2	túgáàmwà	tuágámwèèbwâ	túgámwèèsâ
F2 w/O2	túgáábàmwà		túgábàmwèèsâ
IMP.S	mwâ	mwèèbwâ	mwèèsâ
IMP.P	mwî	mwèèbwî	mwèèsî

†For more details on the formation and semantic usage of the various verb forms, see chapter 9 "Verb words and phrases" in Volume 2 of this set.

‡I include an object prefix (either H: cl. 1 **mú-** or L: cl. 2 **bà-**) in forms where it clarifies the presence of underlying contours either in the form with the object, or the preceding row's form without the object. In forms where the presence of an object does not clarify contours, or is not semantically compatible, I omit the forms with objects in order to make the length and complexity of the paradigm more manageable.

In the P2 (unmarked past) non-extended form above, **túkámwà** 'we shaved', there were two variations elicited. One has a final H tone, and the other does not. Since there is a variation here, we assume that either there is optional H-spread onto a FV in a monosyllabic verb, or that the final H is an intonational tone. The fact that two variations were elicited perhaps means that the form is in flux. It may be given a final H tone because it is similar in surface form to a passive (having Glide-FV ending) and the passive forms all have a H tone on the FV in the simple stem-tone patterns.

The infinitive in (3.52), which is also a simple stem-tone pattern form, was elicited consistently with a final H tone. This is either an indication that the FV can be assigned a tone in cases where there are only two syllables in the word or perhaps, or, as hypothesized above, that forms are being regularized so as to have a final H tone on any verb which has a simple stem-tone pattern and ends with G-FV.

In the case of a multiword verb form, a monosyllabic stem is encliticized to the preceding auxiliary before initial tone assignment. When this cliticization takes place, the final vowel of the auxiliary is lengthened. For example, compare the following forms with adverbial auxiliaries, the first with a monosyllabic stem and the second with a two-syllable stem: **ágágéèndíì=nywâ** 'he will go and drink'[98] with **ágágéèndí tēgà** 'he will go and trap'.[99]

Extended forms of the CV verb roots, i.e. any forms which include the resultative, causative, or passive morphemes, are derived in just the same way as any toneless non-monosyllabic forms.

3.5.6 Tone in reduplicated verbs

In a reduplicated verb, any underlying lexical tone of the radical is not reduplicated.[100] There is at most one lexical tone, which, as is usual in verbal forms, appears on the first (leftmost) syllable of the stem. The suffixal stem tone directly follows any lexical tone, and is realized over the extent of the reduplicated verb stem.

For example, in looking at the infinitive form **kúgàná-gánà** 'to squeeze repeatedly, knead' can be seen that the lexical L tone of the verb stem, seen on the syllable directly following the infinitive prefix, **kú-**, is not repeated in the right section of the form. All syllables which follow the lexical tone of the radical are tonally "free" and therefore susceptible to spreading of the H suffixal tone of the infinitive form. The fact that the lexical tone appears only on the leftmost TBU indicates that the whole reduplicated verb stem is being treated as a single unit. A few examples follow in (3.53). Forms are normal and straightforward for each stem-tone pattern.

---

[98]The source of the falling contour on the final vowel of the aspect is not immediately apparent, but is not assumed to be verbal in origin. The same contour is found on the lengthened final vowel of the host word in phrases with a nominal, verbal, or adjectival enclitic, e.g. **ínyúùmbáà=mbî** 'the bad house'.

[99]The H tone at the end of the auxiliary here is due to leftward H-shift (see 3.12.2).

[100]The picture is more complex in reduplicated nouns, some of which seem to exhibit a single pattern spread across the two parts of the word, while in others, the basic pattern seems to be reduplicated, recurring on the second section.

(3.53) Reduplicated verbs in various stem-tone patterns

TAM	Stem-tone pattern	H verb 'divide out' RDP	L verb 'squeeze' RDP	Ø verb 'writhe' RDP
Inf	simple (H)	kúgábá-gábà	kúgàná-gánà	kúgáyá-gááyà
P1	complex HL	twàgábà-gàbà	twàgàná-gánà	twàgáyá-gááyà
F2	V₂ (L)	túgágábà-gàbà	túgágànà-gànà	túgágàyà-gààyà
P2	simple (H)	túkágábá-gábà	túkágàná-gánà	túkágáyá-gááyà

3.5.7 Overview of verb forms by stem-tone pattern

The data in table 3.3 give an overview of thirty-nine distinct verb forms, grouped by stem-tone pattern. Negatives are generally included only where the negative form has a different stem-tone pattern from the positive form.

We have chosen verbs which have three syllables (CVCVC-FV) within the verb stem (stem includes radical, extensions, and FV). When working with tone, short forms often mean complex tone interaction. It is much easier to see basic tone patterns in a word with enough syllables to display each tone on a separate syllable. Given that most verbs have a lexical tone, and all verb forms are assigned a stem-tone pattern consisting of at least one, perhaps two, tone(s) there will necessarily be some sort of process(es) going on in a CVC-FV verb stem, e.g. -**fúk-a** 'pour liquid on' or -**bèg-a** 'cut hair, take ugali', in order to accommodate the two or more tones on the single available TBU.

In a non-toneless CVCVC-FV verb, on the other hand, the lexical tone of the verb always appears alone on the first syllable of the stem, while the tone(s) of the stem-tone pattern appear (in non-passive, non-causative forms) on the penultimate syllable. In a toneless verb with three stem syllables, the two tones of any complex stem-tone pattern appear on the first two syllables of the stem. The longer verbs, then, give the opportunity to observe (fairly) clearly what the tone(s) of each stem-tone pattern is/are.

Except for the imperative and infinitive forms, all the forms in table 3.3 use the first-person plural subject prefix (**tu-**, **tw-**). The verb stems are separated from any prefixes on the stem by a hyphen. A clitic is separated from the verb stem by a cliticization mark (=). Prefixes are not separated from each other by hyphens.

The asterisk (*) on the names of some tense/aspect forms in table 3.3 indicates two (or more)-word verbs in which only the first word exhibits the tonal qualities of the stem-tone pattern under which the form is listed. Some of the forms have such short and immutable forms in the first word that it is impossible to determine conclusively what the tonal pattern is, so we have just placed them where it seems they might fit. The second part of the verb exhibits a separate stem-tone pattern. Where the second part has no prefix (P1.FRUS) or is preceded by a progressive marker (i.e. F1, F1.NEWLY, P3, and all the progressives (PROG) except for PROG.INTL) the stem-tone pattern on the second part is simple, since these are morphologically prefixless infinitives. In the PROG.INTL and F2.NEWLY forms, the second verb is morphologically and tonally identical to the F2 future, and thus is characterized by the V₂ stem-tone pattern. In P1.FRUS, the second word is prefixless, but takes the V₂ stem-tone pattern.

Table 3.3. Verb forms[a] listed by stem-tone pattern

Stem-tone pattern	TAM	H -góluk[b] 'we...return'	L -fùkam- 'we...kneel'	Ø -laalik- 'we...invite'
Simple (H)	Infinitive	kú-gálúkà	kú-fùkámà	kú-láálíkà
	Future, imminent (F1)	twà=mú=gálúkà	twà=mú=fùkámà	twà=mú=láálíkà
	Past, unmarked (P2)	túká-gálúkà	túká-fùkámà	tú-ká-láálíkà
	Contrary-to-fact (C.F.P2)	ngá=(...) túká-gálúkà	ngá=(...) túká-fùkámà	ngá=(...) túká-láálíkà
V₂ (L)	Future, unmarked (F2)	túgá-gálùkà	túgá-fùkàmà	túgá-làòlìkà
	Subjunctive (SBV) (w/neg or other prefix)	tùtá-gálùkè	tùtá-fùkàmè	tùtá-làòlìkè
	Continuative (CON)	túná-gálùkè	tùná-fùkàmè	tùná-làòlìkè
	Intervening time (INTV)	tùká-gálùkè	tùká-fùkàmè	tùká-làòlìkè
	Future, remote (F3) (w/prefix on main verb)	twááyè nágálùkè	twááyè náfùkàmè	twááyè nálààlìkè
	Conditional contrary-to-fact persistive	túkì-gálùkè	túkì-fùkàmè	túkì-làòlìkè
	Conditional timeless (CND.TL)	tú-gálùkà	tú-fùkàmà	tú-làòlìkà

3.5 Tone on verbs

Stem-tone pattern	TAM	H -gáluk[b] 'we...return'	L -fùkam- 'we...kneel'	Ø -laalik- 'we...invite'
	Conditional not-yet (CND.NOT.YET)	tútàzì gálùkà	tútàzí fùkàmà	tútàzí lààlìkà
	Not-yet (NEG of RS/P1)	tùtàzì gálùkà	tùtàzí fùkàmà	tùtàzí lààlìkà
	(NEG) P3-YET	tùtáàlì záàzì gálùkà	tùtáàlì záàzí fùkàmà	tùtáàlì záàzí lààlìkà
Complex HL	Recent past (P1)	twà-gálùkà	twà-fùkámà	twà-láálíkà
	Sequential (SQ)	twàná-gálùkà	twàná-fùkámà	twàná-láálíkà
	Contrary-to-fact Pot./con. (CND.C.F)	ngá=(...)twà-gálùkà	ngá=(...)twà-fùkámà	ngá=(...)twà-láálíkà
	Potential (POT)/ Conditional (CND)	twàngà-gálùkà	twàngà-fùkámà	twàngà-láálíkà
	POT/CND contrary-to-fact	twàngà-gálwìrì	twàngà-fùkámírì	twàngà-láálísírì
	Resultative (RS)	tù-gálwìrì	tù-fùkámírì	tù-láálísírì
	Timeless (TL) w/máángò 'when'	(máángò) tù-gálùkà	(máángò) tù-fùkámà	(máángò) tù-láálíkà
	*Progressive (PROG)	tùlì mú=gálúkà	tùlì mú=fùkámà	tùlì mú=láálíkà
	*Progressive, persistive PROG.PERS	tùkìrì mú=gálúkà	tùkìrì mú=fùkámà	tùkìrì mú=láálíkà
	*Progressive, newly PROG.NEWLY	tùkòlà mú=gálúkà	tùkòlà mú=fùkámà	tùkòlà mú=láálíkà
	*Progressive, intentional PROG	tùgwètì túgá-gálùkà	tùgwètì túgá-fùkàmà	tùgwètì túgá-lààlìkà
	*Previous PROG	tùshùbà mú=gálúkà	tùshùbà mú=fùkámà	tùshùbà mú=láálíkà

Stem-tone pattern	TAM	H -gáluk[b]	L -fùkam-	Ø -laalik-
		'we...return'	'we...kneel'	'we...invite'
	*Previous contrary-to-fact PREV.C.F	tùshùbà túgá-gálùkà	tùshùbà túgá-fùkàmà	tùshùbà túgá-làalìkà
	*Immediate future newly (F1.NEWLY)	tùkòlà bù=gálúkà	tùkòlà bù=fùkámà	tùkòlà bù=láálíkà
	*Future newly (F2.NEWLY)	tùkòlà túgá-gálùkà	tùkòlà túgá-fùkàmà	tùkòlà túgá-làalìkà
	*Frustrated recent past (P1.FRUS)	tútámálì gálúkà	tútámálí fùkámà	tútámálì láálíkà
Complex LL	Conditional contrary-to-fact (CND.C.F.PST)	twángá-gálwìrì	twángá-fùkàmìrì	twángá-làalìsìrì
Complex LH	RS.FRUS	tútá-gálwìrì	tútá-fùkàmírì	tútá-làalìsírì
	Past resultative (P3)	twáàlì gálwīrì	twáàlí fùkàmírì	twáàlí làalìsírì
	*P3 (w/aspect)	twáàlí kìzí gálúkà	twáàlí kìzí fùkámà	twáàlí kìzí láálíkà
	Conditional resultative (CND.RS)	tú-gálwīrì	tú-fùkàmírì	tú-làalìsírì
	Direct imperative (imperative singular) IMP.SG	gálūkà/ gálùkà	fùkámà	làalíkà
Complex HH	Subjunctive (SBV)	tù-gálúkè	tù-fúkámè	tù-láálíkè
	Future remote (F3)	twááyè gálúkè	twááyè fúkámè	twááyè láálíkè
Complex LH-I	Direct imperative (IMP.PL)	gálùkî	fùkàmî	làalìkî

[a]For more details on the verb forms, see Volume 2.

[b]The non-resultative forms are from the verb **kúgálúkà** 'to return (INTRANS)' but due to a slight oversight, the resultative forms instead reflect the transitive form of the same verb: **kúgálúlà** 'to return something'. Tones are identical in the transitive and intransitive forms.

3.6 Extratonality of the final syllable in nouns and verbs

In table 3.3 observe that for the H-tone verbs and the L-tone verbs, the lexical tone of the verb is realized on the first syllable of the verb stem, so that the tone of the first syllable of the stem remains constant (except in the subjunctive complex HH forms, where there is replacive H tone in the V_1 position of every verb) while the following syllables of the stem vary according to the stem-tone pattern. In the toneless verbs, the first tone of the stem-tone pattern always appears on the first syllable of the stem, causing the first syllable of the stem to have H tone in a stem-tone pattern with a H tone, and L tone in a stem-tone pattern with a L tone.

3.6 Extratonality of the final syllable in nouns and verbs

The final syllable of every regular non-monomoraic noun[101] is "extratonal". This is to say that the final syllable is "invisible" to, or at least ignored by, the initial tone assignment rules.[102] This fact is observed in the numbers of possible tonal patterns found on multimoraic nouns. When there are two total TBUs in the noun stem, the number of possible patterns is not four, H(H) L(L) HL and LH, as expected, but only two, H and L. In isolation, the final syllable bears a default L tone. This indicates that the final syllable is not available for lexical tone assignment. The number of tone patterns reaches the maximum number, four, H(H) L(L) HL, LH only when there are three or more total TBUs in the noun stem. Only the non-final TBUs of regular nouns can be assigned lexical tones on the underlying level, while the final one remains extratonal.[103]

The final vowel of verb forms is also extratonal. It could possibly be argued that rather than being extratonal, the final vowel (FV) of verbs is not assigned an initial tone because it is not yet present in the form at the time of initial tone assignment.[104] However, because regular nouns are not generally analyzed as having a separate FV morpheme, and yet nouns have an extratonal final syllable as well, the analysis of a FV which is present but extratonal seems justified in verbs. This FV is not assigned a tone until the point of "visibility" which comes near the end of the lexical cycle.

---

[101] A "regular" noun here is any noun that does not bear a specific H tone suffix. There are a good number of such H-final nouns in Kifuliiru. In such nouns, the H suffix tone is appended to one of the four regular tone patterns.

[102] For more information on extraprosodicity/extratonality in Bantu languages, see Hyman (1995) and Bickmore and Doyle (1995).

[103] There does seem to be a non-segmental H tone suffix used on certain nouns, e.g. a noun which is a shortened form of a longer word, e.g. **máhòòyé** 'famous person', from the verb **kúhóóyéká** 'to be widely acclaimed', or **Tímó** 'nickname for **Tímótéò** (Timothy)'.

[104] This would fit in with the analysis that a tone is initially assigned to the vocalic passive extension and to the final vowel of the causative, later undergoing delinking and relinking.

The following are some arguments for the extratonality of the FV of verbs in Kifuliiru:

As already noted, tone patterns in nouns make it clear that in non-exceptional cases a lexical tone will not link to the final syllable of a word. A noun having two total syllables in its stem, i.e. the stem is (C)VCV,[105] can exhibit only one lexical tone, not two.[106] Since the majority of nouns are derived from verbs,[107] it is not surprising that verbs, as well, have extratonal final morae.

Tone patterns in verbs, as well, point clearly to the extratonality of the final vowel. Though each verb root has only one lexical tone in its uninflected form, all surface verb forms have grammatical tones as well. Still, the only cases in which the final vowel of a verb form may bear a lexical or grammatical tone is in the case where there is a causative or passive suffix. A likely reason for the non-extratonality of the FV in these forms could be the underlying (if not synchronically underlying, at least underlying at some point in history) assignment of tone to the vocalic extension itself. Since this TBU formed part of the final syllable of the verb, this yielded a non-extratonal final syllable, though not a non-extratonal FV. At the point when the FV became interactive with the word, the vowel of the extension underwent glide formation and lost moricity. Thus the lexical or grammatical tone associated to it was then delinked and subsequently relinked to the FV. Over time, this was reinterpreted as initial association to the FV, with the process of glide formation taking place before initial tone association.

It is clear from the mid (LH) tone on the lexically L-toned root vowel in cases like **túkábēgà** 'we cut hair/broke ugali (P2)' that even though the lexical root tone L is already associated to the vowel of the stem, the H of the far past tense also links to that same syllable. Though this is a single-mora syllable, both tones link to that single non-final syllable of the verb stem. The FV is not an option which the suffixal tones have for linking in the initial association of tones in non-passive, non-causative forms.

In verb stems with only a single non-final syllable (CV(VN)C-FV) and a complex (two toned) stem-tone pattern, e.g. **twàmúbègà** 'we cut his hair', the lexical tone (in this case, L) plus the two grammatical tones (in this case, H and L) all attempt to link to the single available syllable (underlined) because the FV is not available for linking. Because of constraints against linking more

---

[105]In a noun, the "root" is the part which follows the prefixes. In non-derived nouns, the root is monomorphemic.

[106]As mentioned in the discussion of the identity of the TBU in (3.2), further research is needed to determine whether a single-mora penultimate syllable of a noun, as that of a verb, can bear two tones.

[107]A rough count of 400 randomly chosen nouns shows that approximately sixty percent are immediately recognized by speakers of the language as being derived from known verbs. This percentage might be higher if thought and discussion were given to the subject.

than two tones to any one syllable, one of the three tones, in the case of the complex HL forms, the H, ends up being deleted (3.7.3). If the FV were available as a TBU at that point, two tones would link to the non-final syllable, and one to the FV, and no tones would be deleted. For example, in toneless verbs with a complex stem-tone pattern, where there is no lexical tone, there are only two grammatical tones (H and L) vying for position on the penultimate, so that both tones are able to link, and appear together on the penultimate syllable, e.g. **twàmúdíìhà** 'we beat him'.

As seen in 3.5.5, even in the case of monosyllabic (CG-FV) verb stems, such as -**fwa** 'die', -**lya** 'eat', etc., it appears that the FV is not normally assigned tones by initial tone association.

3.7 General characteristics of tone association in Kifuliiru

The following are the general characteristics of tone association in Kifuliiru:
- Tone is assigned to the syllable according to the edge-in association convention.
- A penultimate syllable, whether monomoraic or bimoraic, bears two tones. (Likely true only of verbs.)
- Any penultimate syllable which is singly linked following initial tone association is always assigned a second tone by lexical level tone spread rules.
- No single syllable in any position may have more than two association lines.

The first of these is a known linking strategy across languages. The next two reflect the general tendency in Bantu to give special treatment to the penultimate position of a word. The last is probably a common phenomenon in all languages. This section deals with all of these general linking characteristics.

3.7.1 Edge-in linking and double-linking of the penultimate

We posit that in Kifuliiru initial tone association is to the syllable, and that tone is associated according to a modified version of the edge-in association convention. The original version of the convention was proposed by Yip (1988) and reformulated by Hewitt and Prince (1989). It is shown in (3.54), with the adapted Kifuliiru version of it shown in (3.55). We also posit that the penultimate syllable has two underlying tonal nodes and is always doubly linked underlyingly.[108]

---

[108] In some cases this means the spreading of a tone from the first node of the penultimate onto the second node.

It is often noted in Bantu languages that the penultimate syllable position in the word has a special status in both phonology and tone assignment. In some Bantu languages, this is the position where stress is placed at the word level. Kifuliiru does not have a penultimate stress pattern,[109] but there is, nonetheless, special treatment of the penultimate syllable. It is the only syllable which is given two association lines.

Goldsmith (1976) in his original formulation of autosegmental phonology, proposed automatic contouring as a possible universal linking constraint. By this he meant the assignment of two tones to a final mora in the case that there were more tones than there were TBUs. In Kifuliiru, since the FV is extratonal (3.6) it makes sense that any "automatic contouring" which happens would apply to the penultimate rather than the ultimate position. This in fact is the case. However, in Kifuliiru, this double linking of the penultimate does not apply only in cases where there are more tones than TBUs. Instead, a penultimate is always double linked. H and L spread rules associate an extra tone to any singly-linked syllable in the penultimate position.[110] In the derivation of a verb with a stem-tone pattern which has only a single tone (i.e. simple or V_2) we do not show the extra association line to the second node of a monomoraic penult. But in theory, such a line always exists.

This double linking of the penultimate is, in many forms, aided by association of tonal melodies according to the edge-in linking convention. This linking convention is as shown in (3.54) as proposed by Hewitt and Prince (1989):

(3.54) Edge-in association convention:
For a tonal melody /**a**...**z**/: link **a** to the initial melody anchor;
  a. link **z** to the final melody anchor;
  b. link any remaining melodemes left to right.
We propose a fairly heavily modified version of this for Kifuliiru, as shown in (3.55).

---

[109]We have not researched stress in Kifuliiru. Tone- and pitch-related phenomena are much more significant. Any observations regarding stress would be made in terms of tone, pitch, and vowel length, which are the determining factors in placing stress. Stress is not the factor that determines the placement of tones or length. In terms of vocal volume, the volume is higher near the beginning of an utterance and drops over the course of the utterance. Utterance-final syllables often have unvoiced vowels.

[110]Such a contour may later be simplified by rules, and the resultant tone may be the same as the original tone of that syllable, or it may instead be the same as the tone received by spreading, depending on the surrounding tonal environment.

(3.55) Modified edge-in association convention (adapted for Kifuliiru):
  a. For a combined tonal melody /a...z/: link **a** to the leftmost available TBU in the domain;
  b. link **z** next. If **z** was the left-hand tone in its melody of origin, link it immediately to the left of **a**; if not, link it to the rightmost available TBU in the domain;
  c. link any intervening tones, starting with the leftmost one, to the next most peripheral TBUs on the left or right, according to their left or right placement in their melody of origin.[111]

Recall that the tonal melody on any given verb stem is a combination of two melodies (see example (3.18)), each of which may have up to two tones. The two melodies are the lexical melody, consisting of the lexical root tone (if any) plus the extension tone (if any), and the grammatical melody, consisting either of a left-linking tone only, or of a left-linking and a right-linking tone. The grammatical melody is overlaid on the lexical melody, resulting in what we have termed the combined tonal melody. This combined tonal melody consists of one to four tones. A toneless verb in non-passive, non-causative form has no lexical melody at all. Every verb, however, has at least a left-linking grammatical tone.

Clauses (3.55b, c) both refer to the placement of a tone in its original melody, either the lexical melody or the grammatical melody. A tone which was originally the left-hand tone in its melody will link only toward the left edge of the domain, while a tone which was originally the right-hand tone in its melody will link only toward the right edge of the domain.

In the association of any melody, the first slot to be filled is the leftmost in the domain: the first syllable of the stem. It is obligatory that this position be filled by initial linking. The lexical tone of the root, if present, links here. If there is no lexical tone in the root, the left tone of the grammatical melody fills this leftmost position. The rightmost slot, on the other hand, is only optionally filled at initial linking. If neither the lexical nor the grammatical melody has a right-hand tone, the rightmost slot may remain empty until filled by spread or default rules.

In any combined melody consisting of four tones, two will be left-linking and two right-linking. In a verb with a four-tone combined melody, when

---

[111]Because of the variation in the possible combinations of tones underlyingly present in any given verb form (e.g. two lexical with one (left) grammatical; one lexical (either left or right) with two grammatical; no lexical with either a right or left grammatical, or both (see 3.5.2)), it is impossible to predict the linking positions either in terms of a straight left to right or right to left progression, or in terms of an alternating application to left end/right end (or vice versa). The only way to predict where a tone will be placed is to refer (a) to its placement in the combined melody and (b) its placement in its original melody.

the verb stem has four available TBUs it at first seems possible to posit that the association of the "intervening tones" (or even of all the tones) is done in a straight left to right manner. In a verb with more than four available TBUs, it seems that one needs to posit that all four tones are associated to the peripheral (edge) TBUs in an alternating fashion, left edge first, then right, then left, and followed by right again. However, such linking strategies only work because any melody consisting of four tones has two left-linking tones followed by two right-linking tones. As soon as any one of the four tones is missing, it becomes evident that the left or right placement of a tone in its original melody is the determining factor in whether it will link towards the right end or the left end. Left or right placement of a tone on the verb stem is not determined merely by a linking convention. Each tone of the melody is intrinsically either a left-linking tone or a right-linking tone. A lexical root tone, for example will only link to the leftmost position in the verb stem, while an extension tone will *only* link to the rightmost available position.

For example, in a non-toneless verb in which the lexical and the grammatical melodies each consist of only one tone, both tones link towards the left, with the lexical root tone first, followed by the grammatical tone. The future form **túgá-gógòmbèkà** 'we will intrude' is such a form. The single lexical H tone is evident on the first syllable of the stem, which is the leftmost syllable in the domain, while the single L grammatical tone, links directly to its right. If, on the other hand, the verb is an underlyingly toneless, passive form, in that same future tense the lexical melody would consist only of a right-hand extension tone, while the grammatical melody would consist only of a left-linking tone. In this case the grammatical tone links to the leftmost syllable, while the H tone of passive links to the rightmost syllable: **túgá-làálìkwâ** 'we will be invited'.

Notice that even though (3.55) is heavily modified from the original edge-in linking convention in (3.54), we still posit that the leftmost tone is associated first to the left edge, followed by the association of the rightmost tone (if any) to its proper place, rather than assuming that linking of all left-hand tones precedes the linking of the right-hand tones. The reason for positing edge-in linking is found in the selection of tones that is permitted to link in the situations that involve T-drop (3.8.4). In such situations, there is only one syllable, but two tonal root nodes (3.7.2) available for tone association, and three tones needing to link. It is clear in these situations that the order of linking is leftmost tone first, rightmost tone second. The tone which would link third is the one which is deleted for lack of space. In the complex stem-tone patterns, where the combined tonal melody consists of lexical root tone, grammatical stem tone (left), grammatical stem tone (right), the tone which is dropped is the left-hand tone of the stem-tone pattern. If the linking had proceeded in a straight left to right manner, the left-hand tone of the lexical pattern and the left-hand tone of the grammatical pattern would be the ones which were allowed to associate. Instead it is the right, not the left, of the two grammatical tones which associates, indicating that its linking must precede that of the left-hand tone of the grammatical pattern.

As regards multiple association lines to a single surface syllable, we noted initially that in a noun whose stem has a surface bimoraic penultimate, each of the two morae in the penultimate syllable bears a tone, so that the PB reflexes of LH or HL both show up on the bimoraic syllable, while the final TBU receives a default L tone. For example, PB *-pàndé 'piece' (LH) becomes FLR lú-háàndè (11-side) (HL) and PB *-kúndò 'knot' (HL) has the reflex FLR kí-fūūndò (7-knot) (LH). These patterns indicate that each mora in a bimoraic penultimate may bear a separate lexical tone, and thus that a single bimoraic syllable may bear two different lexical tones. It does not necessarily follow from this that a monomoraic syllable in the penultimate position can also bear two tones. However, evidence indicates that in verbs, at least, it is clearly the case that a monomoraic penult can bear two tones[112] at the underlying level.

A good proof for double-linking of the tones on a surface penultimate mora in verbs can be found in the passive form of any L-tone verb stem with CVC shape and a complex HL stem-tone pattern. For example, take the passive of -bèg- 'cut hair' in the P1 tense: twààbégwà 'we got our hair cut', and compare this with the same form except with the addition of the conjunctive prefix, ná-: twànábēgwà 'and (then) we got our hair cut'. In each of these passive forms, the L lexical tone of the verb and the H tone of the passive extension both link to the e of -bèg-. In the first form, twààbégwà, the tautosyllabic LH is simplified to H by the rule of LH raising because it occurs between two L tones (LH > H/L _ L). In the second form, twànábēgwà, the preceding H tone allows the LH to be realized as a surface mid tone.

The very presence in twààbégwà of a surface H tone on the first syllable of the lexically L verb stem bèg- would be evidence enough that there has been double linking of this syllable, since the L lexical tone of the verb always links to the V_1 position of the stem, and only in combination with an underlying H tone could it ever be realized as a surface H tone. By adding the conjunctive morpheme to the verb form, giving twànábēgwà, we see further proof that L and H are actually both linked to the e of -bèg-. With no changes to the verb

---

[112]Some speakers pronounce a LH associated to a single mora with the same tone as they would pronounce a LH associated to a bimoraic syllable. A HL contour on a monomoraic syllable is always simplified to H by rule, and is never phonetically discernable, so it is impossible to demonstrate other than theoretically that there may be double-linking of HL on a single mora.

form except for the simple addition of the H-toned 'sequential' **ná**- prefix, producing **twànábēgwà**, the LH linked to the V_1 position of the stem actually surfaces as LH (a level, phonetically mid tone). The LH is realized as LH in **twànábēgwà** because the preceding H tone of the prefix prevents the rule of LH raising from taking place in this form, by replacing the preceding L tone in **twààbégwà** with the H tone of the consecutive prefix.

Those speakers whose dialect does not allow LH to be realized on a single mora pronounce the tone on the V_1 position of the stem of **twànábēgwà** not with a H tone as it was in **twààbégwà**, but with a L, **twànábègwà**. This is because these speakers have the rule: monomoraic LH > L/H_ L. This provides further evidence that there is double linking (both L and H) on this syllable. All of these contour simplification rules apply here only because there is an underlying LH on this syllable in the UF to begin with, thus showing that the single mora in the penultimate of the verb stem is indeed double-linked.

In all passives of recent past (P1) forms in CVC roots, the H tone of the complex HL is able to link to the first vowel of the stem together with the lexical tone of the verb, only because double linking is allowed in the penultimate position. Because the final-linking L tone of the complex HL links to the FV in a passive or causative P1 form, the H tone of complex HL and the lexical tone of the verb both link to the V_1 position of the stem. The H tone of the passive is then deleted by T-drop (3.8.4). A derivation of **twààbégwà** 'we had our hair cut' is given in (3.56) to elucidate this explanation.

(3.56) **tu-à-bèg-ú-a** (1PL-P1-cut.hair-PS-Fa) 'we had our hair cut' (L)

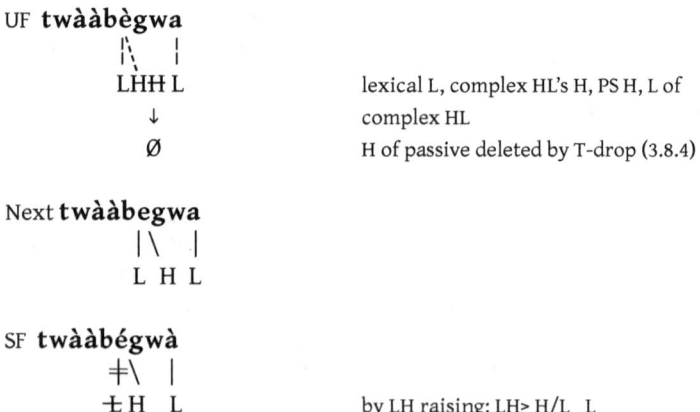

                            lexical L, complex HL's H, PS H, L of
                            complex HL
                            H of passive deleted by T-drop (3.8.4)

                            by LH raising: LH> H/L _L

The major point of the derivation in (3.56) is that double linking is sanctioned on the penultimate syllable. This derivation also shows that such double linking is not restricted to a bimoraic syllable, but that even a single mora can have two association lines.

3.7.2 Syllable, with modifications, as TBU

Next let us present the argument for the syllable as the underlying TBU, earlier summarized in (3.2).

First, in many Bantu languages we read of rules which place a H tone on a certain mora of a verb stem, or which spread a tone one or two morae to the right, etc. In Kifuliiru, there are no such tone association rules which target the mora.[113] Tone assignment here can be explained without necessarily making any reference to the mora.

Secondly, because there is never contour in an antepenultimate bimoraic syllable, but there are bimoraic syllables in that position, positing tone assignment to the mora necessitates a rule of antepenultimate contour simplification. This rule would delink a tone from the antepenultimate syllable, following rightward spread of that tone onto the following syllable. It seems to make more sense to link the tone initially to the syllable to the right of the bimoraic antepenult, since it ends up there anyway.

Lastly, the argument for the syllable as TBU is inextricably linked to the double-linking qualities of the penultimate syllable. We are faced with the fact that a bimoraic penultimate syllable bears two tones, as does a monomoraic penultimate syllable. But even though a monomoraic penultimate syllable bears two tones, the *penultimate mora* of a bimoraic syllable bears only *one* tone. This means that it is the penultimate syllable, not the penultimate mora, which is singled out for special linking.

It is also true, however, that we need to assume some sub-unit within the syllable in order to account for tone spread phenomena on a penultimate syllable, whether monomoraic or bimoraic. Because initial tone association in Kifuliiru follows edge-in linking, there are tones which associate to a leftmost free TBU and those which associate to a rightmost free TBU. When the left-hand TBU of a penultimate syllable is linked, the tone of the preceding syllable will *not* spread onto the penultimate (whether or not the second TBU of the penultimate is linked). When only the right-hand TBU of a penultimate syllable is linked, tone *will* spread onto that syllable. Thus we have evidence of two distinct positions, a left node and a right node, within a single penultimate syllable. In a bimoraic syllable, "mora" makes a handy name for this

---

[113]There is one phonetic rule which does mention the mora, that of single mora HL simplification, which phonetically interprets a HL contour on a single mora as H. The mora is also a significant unit in the determination of vowel shortening parameters.

subsyllabic TBU. However, to talk of the two morae of a *mono*moraic syllable is a contradiction in terms.

If we were to assume that the linking of two tones to a monomoraic penultimate syllable is merely due to "automatic contouring" of some sort, theoretically the penultimate would accept two tones, no matter what their origin. There would not be any problem in linking a second tone by rightward tone spread onto a monomoraic penult as long as that penult was not already doubly linked. The rule would not know or care whether a single already-linked tone on the penultimate had been linked from the left or from the right. But if there are underlyingly two nodes in every penultimate: a left and a right node, then to link another tone by tone spread onto a penultimate syllable which already has a linked left node would result in crossing of association lines, which is disallowed by the "well-formedness condition" (Pulleyblank 1986:11). This constraint against the crossing of lines is exactly what is evidenced by the characteristics of tone-spread onto a penultimate syllable in Kifuliiru.

With Hubbard (1995:144) we "assume in accordance with Zec (1994) that mora and syllable tiers are part of universal grammar and languages cannot opt out of either one...". Since the syllable tier is present, there seems to be no reason to avoid using the syllable as the TBU if it seems to fit the data better. Thus we have chosen to posit linking to the syllable via the tonal root node (TRN) with the stipulation that a penultimate syllable has two TRNs, while a non-penultimate syllable, whether monomoraic or bimoraic, has only one TRN (3.2).

We will assume that these TRNs are aligned with the syllable, as shown below in (3.57). This allows a penultimate syllable, whether monomoraic or bimoraic, to be linked to two tones and explains why a singly-linked penultimate syllable may be targeted by rightward tone spread if its single tone was applied by edge-in linking from the right and may not be so targeted if its single tone was applied by edge-in linking from the left.

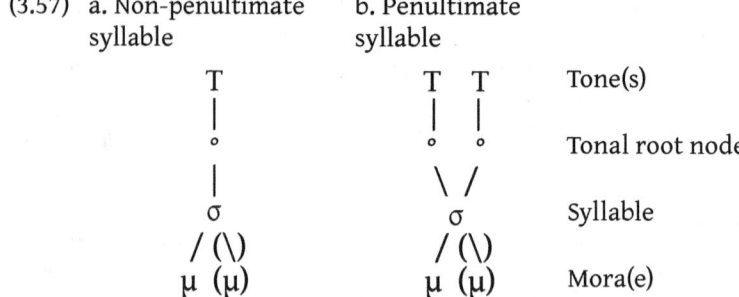

3.7 General characteristics of tone association in Kifuliiru

Though a bimoraic penultimate syllable and a monomoraic penultimate syllable behave identically with respect to underlying tonal linking, on the surface, tonal contours are much more easily observed on bimoraic syllables.[114] So we will look first at a verb with a bimoraic penult as we show how the linking of a left-hand node prevents tone spread from targeting a penultimate syllable, while the linking only of a right-hand node does not. Keep in mind that Kifuliiru has both H-spread and L-spread.

In a verb with a bimoraic penultimate in which only the right-hand mora/node is linked to a tone, spread rules *do* target the penultimate syllable. This is shown by a form like the complex HL recent past form **gàgòlólóòmbà** 'it flowed'. In a verb with the complex HL stem-tone pattern, there are two grammatical tones. In **gàgòlólóòmbà** the lexical L of the radical is associated to the initial TBU of the stem, while the initial tone H of the complex HL grammatical melody links to the leftmost free TBU, the first **ló**, immediately following the lexical L. The final grammatical L of the complex HL links to the *right-hand* node/mora of the bimoraic penult, because this is the rightmost free TBU since the FV is extratonal. That takes care of initial tone association. Next, the grammatical H tone on **ló** spreads onto the following syllable, linking to the left-hand mora of the bimoraic penultimate whose right-hand mora is linked to the final grammatical L. The resulting HL contour is seen in the surface form of the penultimate.

By contrast, there is no tone spread onto a bimoraic syllable whose left node is linked. Let us look at another, shorter, complex HL recent past form, **twàtábààlà** 'we helped (someone)'. First, edge-in linking will associate the lexical H tone of the radical to the first syllable of the verb stem. Because the FV is extratonal, the two morae of the penultimate then represent the leftmost and rightmost free TBUs of this stem. Thus edge-in linking will associate the two tones of the stem-tone pattern to the two morae of the penultimate syllable, H to the left mora and L to the right. The grammatical H is then lowered by the application of Meeussen's rule, resulting in a LL linking to the penultimate syllable. Because the left-hand mora of the penultimate is linked, tone spread will not target this syllable. There is thus no contour on this penultimate.

One might assume that tone spread is not permitted to target the penultimate syllable of **twàtábààlà** simply because the penultimate has two tones already (the H and L of the complex HL stem-tone pattern)[115] and three tones

---

[114]LH contours are heard more clearly on bimoraic syllables than on monomoraic ones, and HL contours are phonetically simplified to H on a single mora, so that they do not surface at all on a monomoraic penult.

[115]The H of the stem-tone pattern does not appear on the penultimate as H because it is lowered by MR, due to its juxtaposition to the lexical H tone of the verb stem.

may not be linked to a single syllable. Indeed, this is a factor in the example just mentioned. So let us look at another example, one in which there is only one tone linked to the penultimate, but this tone is the only tone in its stem-tone pattern and so is linked to the left-hand mora of the penultimate. (Recall that both the lexical tone of the verb and the initial tone of the grammatical stem-tone pattern link at the left end of the verb stem.)

Such an example in which the linking of the left-hand mora of the penultimate blocks tone spread is found in the V_2, prefixed-subjunctive form **tùmútábààlè** 'let's help *him*'. In this form, the H lexical tone of the radical links to the leftmost mora of the stem. Next, the L of the V_2 form, being the initial (as well as the only) tone of its melody,[116] is linked by edge-in linking to the leftmost available TBU, which at this point is the left-hand mora of the bimoraic penult. Then, because this left-hand mora/node is linked, H-spread from the lexical tone of the radical will not target the penult. L-spread will subsequently spread the L tone of the left-hand mora of the penult to the right-hand mora as well. Thus H-spread is not permitted to create a HL contour on this syllable even though it has only one tone at the time H-spread applies.[117]

Now let us look at verb with a monomoraic penult. We see exactly the same tone spread parameters. Tone spread, which progresses from left to right, *does* target a monomoraic penult which is already linked only on its right node, but does *not* target a penultimate which already has a tone linked to its left node. We will look first at a three-syllable verb in which we do see tone spread, **twàhàmágálà** 'we called (someone)'. This verb is similar in all respects except for the lack of bimoraic penult to **gàgòlólóòmbà** 'it flowed', where we saw H-spread target (the initial mora of) the penultimate syllable. In the same (complex HL) recent past form of the three-syllable verb **twàhàmágálà**, the linking is carried out just as we saw in **gàgòlólóòmbà**. The L-lexical tone of the radical is linked first to the initial syllable of the verb stem. The H of the complex HL pattern links to the leftmost free TBU, which is the syllable directly following the initial syllable of the stem. The L of the complex HL links to rightmost available TBU, which is the right-hand node of the penultimate (because the FV is extratonal). Yet though in **twàhàmágálà** this final L of the stem-tone pattern links to the penultimate, we see that the penultimate syllable displays a surface H tone, not a L tone. This is because

---

[116]The fact that the grammatical L is linked to the left-hand mora of the penult rather than the right-hand mora also means that the lexical tone of the verb and the L of this pattern are each still counted (by edge-in linking) as the initial, and thus left-linking, tone of its own distinct melody and not as the left and right edge members of some general "verbal melody".

[117]One could instead explain this in an ad hoc manner by ordering L-spread to take place before H-spread, but assuming that spread rules apply from left to right as the environment is found, H-spread would apply before L-spread had linked the second mora of the penultimate.

3.7 General characteristics of tone association in Kifuliiru

H-spread from the grammatical H tone has targeted the *left-hand node* of the monomoraic penultimate, just exactly as it targeted the left-hand mora of the penultimate in **gàgòlólóòmbà**. The difference is that in **twàhàmágálà**, the resulting HL contour is on a monomoraic penult. An underlying HL contour occurring on a single mora is simplified in phonetic utterance to a H tone, by the phonetic rule of single-mora HL simplification. Thus we get a surface H tone on the penultimate syllable of **twàhàmágálà**.

Next we will show that tone spread does *not* target a monomoraic penult in which only the left node is linked by initial tone association. In order to find such a form, we need a verb with a stem-tone pattern which has only a single tone in its melody, such as the simple or V_2 stem-tone patterns. Let us take, for example, the F2 future form **túgágálùkà** 'we will return' which has a V_2 stem-tone pattern. The H lexical tone, being the initial (and only) tone of the lexical melody, links to the leftmost TBU of the radical, while the L grammatical tone, likewise the first and only tone in its melody, links to the left-hand node of the penultimate syllable. Then, because the left-hand node is linked, there is no H tone spread onto the penultimate, even though it is still only singly linked. Subsequently, the L tone linked to the left-hand node spreads also to the right-hand node, resulting in a L tone on the penultimate: **túgágálùkà**. If tone spread had targeted the penultimate in this form, we would see instead the surface form *__túgágálūkà__.

Some might express doubt as to whether there is *really* a contour underlyingly on a penultimate such as that of **twàhàmágálà** where we posited an underlying HL which is phonetically simplified to H. They think that perhaps the final L tone of the stem-tone pattern remains floating until after the visibility of the FV where it can then link. To one not familiar with the principles of tone-linking in Kifuliiru, this floating hypothesis at first seems like it might be a viable possibility, at least in a stem-tone pattern in which the final-linking tone of the grammatical melody is L.[118] However, when working with a pattern in which the final tone is H, such as complex LH or complex HH, it is clear that such a final tone always links to the penultimate, and never to the FV, in a non-passive, non-causative form. Only in a passive or causative verb does it link to the FV.

Moreover, it is clear from the linking patterns of Kifuliiru, the tone-spread phenomena, and from the surface tones of verbal forms, that the penultimate is double linked in all these forms. For example, in a non-passive complex LH form, such as **tútáfyèèzírì** 'we had just pinched something, but...' both

---

[118]But, it would leave unexplained the fact that complex HL verbs such as the L verb **gàgòlólóòmbà** 'it flowed', the Ø verb **twàmúdíîhà** 'we beat him', and the H verb **twànágúùngà** 'and we cheated' all have a HL contour in the penultimate, while P2 (unmarked past, simple stem-tone pattern) verbs have no such contours: **túkágòlólóómbà**, **túkámúdííhà**, **túkágúúngà**.

the L and the H of the stem-tone pattern are linked by initial tone association to the monomoraic penultimate. How do we know this? We look at the stem-tone pattern (as determined by study of verbs of all three tonal types and of many different CVC patterns) and simply follow the edge-in linking procedures. The L tone of the radical links to the first syllable of the stem. The initial grammatical L links to the left-hand node of the penultimate syllable, while the final grammatical H links to the rightmost available TBU, which, because the FV is extratonal, is the right-hand node of the penult. This results in a LH contour there, which is phonetically interpreted as H, by the rule of LH raising. The linking follows the same principles in every case. In light of the contour simplification rules of the language, the H surface tone found on this syllable is completely consistent with an underlying LH contour there.

Let us add another H tone extension to the mix and see the results. The passive form of **tútáfyèèzírì** 'we had just pinched something, but...' is **tútáf-yèèzìrwí** 'we had just been pinched, but...'. Here the linking follows the same principles, but the FV is not extratonal, because it is a passive form. Thus the L tone of the radical is linked to the first syllable of the stem. Next, the L grammatical tone of complex LH links to the left-hand node of the following syllable, which is the monomoraic penultimate. At the right end of the verb, edge-in linking associates the final H tone of the complex LH pattern to the FV, and the H tone of the passive to the right-hand node of the penult. Once again we have a resultant LH contour on the penult. Here, however, it surfaces as a L tone because the following grammatical H tone on the FV creates the environment for the phonetic rule of LH lowering.

Thus we can summarize the three possibilities for the linking of any penultimate syllable as follows:
- In the first option, the penultimate bears two tones, each of which is a lexical or grammatical tone assigned by initial tone association. (In this case it already has two association lines and may not be further linked to any tone by any process.)
- In the second option, the penultimate is initially assigned a single lexical or grammatical tone. If this tone is right-linking tone, i.e. the second tone of its melody, it links to the right-hand node. The syllable is then assigned another tone by tone spread from the syllable to its left. On the other hand, if the initially linked tone is the first tone in its melody, it links to the left-hand node and is then spread onto the following node by tone-spread rules.
- In the third option, the penultimate was not assigned any tone by initial tone association, and consequently its tone

3.7.3 Constraint against triple-linking to a single syllable

In (3.7.2), we noted that a non-penultimate syllable in Kifuliiru has only one TRN (tonal root node) to which tones can be associated. A penultimate syllable has two TRNs and must have two tonal association lines. At the same time, two nodes is the maximum for any single syllable. There is a constraint in Kifuliiru against creating three association lines to a single syllable in any position, whether that syllable is monomoraic or bimoraic. This constraint is reflected in the rule of T-drop which is observed in various contexts (3.8.4).

As might be expected, the contexts in which T-drop is operative are found in CV(VN)C-FV verb forms, where there is a single non-extratonal syllable in the stem. In addition, the situation where three tones are competing for position on a single syllable is found only in verbs with a complex stem-tone pattern. In such a pattern there are two suffixal tones, one of which ideally links to the first free TBU of the stem, and the other of which is a final-linking tone. Any verb which is not toneless also has a lexical tone, which brings to three the tones vying for position on the stem. Thus in a non-toneless CV(VN)C verb with a complex stem-tone pattern, two suffixal tones plus a lexical tone compete for association lines to the same single syllable of the verb root.

Let us look, for example, at a lexically L CV(VN)C verb with the complex HL stem-tone pattern, e.g. **twààbègà** 'we cut hair' (from CVC -**bèg**-) or **twàfyèèngà** 'we pinched something together' (from CVVNC -**fyèeng**-).[119] (For an overview of complex HL forms, see 3.5.3.3.3) In such a verb, the H tone of the complex HL pattern, which ideally links in the V_2 (second vowel) position of the verb stem, does not link. Note that there are no surface H tones at all in L verbs of this form. In both of the verbs above, if there were an underlying LH contour in the verb stem, it would be realized in this environment as a H tone, because it is preceded by a L-tone prefix and followed by a L FV. This is the environment where the phonetic realization rule of LH raising (LH > H/L _ L) would take effect.

Contrast those forms with a verb with a bisyllabic base, for example, **twàbètúlà** 'we carried something on our heads' (from CVCVC -**bètul**-) where the H tone of complex HL links to the left-hand node of the penultimate, and does show up on the surface. Similarly, in the applicative forms of the CV(VN)C verbs, such as **twàbègérà** 'we cut hair APL' or **twàfyèèngérà** 'we

---

[119]Though **fyèeng**- does have two non-final *morae*, it has only one non-final *syllable*. It is triple-linking to a single syllable which is disallowed by the constraint. This, of course, disallows any triple-linking to a single mora, as well.

shut someone's breath off APL', the H tone of the complex HL pattern shows up in each case on the underlined applicative extension.[120]

Also contrasting with the complex HL forms are the simple and V_2 stem-tone patterns. In these patterns with a single grammatical tone (H in simple and L in V_2) the grammatical tone of the stem-tone pattern *is* permitted to link to the only non-final syllable of the stem of a CV(VN)C verb stem. The far past (P2) tense gives an example of linking in a simple stem-tone pattern. In this tense, L-tone verbs of CVC and CVV(N)C surface with a mid tone on the stem vowel, e.g. **túkáb̄ēgà** 'we cut hair', (cf. **túkábàb̲égà** 'we cut their hair' where the preceding L tone allows the LH to surface as a H tone, due to LH raising) and **túkáf̲y̲ēēngà** 'we shut off someone's breath' (similarly, cf. **túkábàf̲y̲ééngà** 'we shut off their breath', where LH raising also applies.) The underlying LH tone in the initial syllable (underlined) of the verb stem in all these simple stem-tone pattern forms is a combination of the radical's L tone and the H grammatical tone of the P2's simple stem-tone pattern.

In another example, the future (F2) form (which exhibits the V_2 stem-tone pattern) e.g. **túgágéèndà** 'we will go' (from -**géend**- 'go') we see that the L suffixal tone of the future tense's V_2 stem-tone pattern has linked to the second mora of the bimoraic first syllable of the stem (underlined) directly following the verb's lexical H tone, and creating a HL contour.

Thus in the complex stem-tone patterns the V_2-linking tone is forced to drop out, and in the simple and V_2 stem-tone patterns, the V_2-linking tone is permitted to link. The crucial difference between the complex stem-tone patterns and non-complex simple and V_2 stem-tone patterns is that in the non-complex patterns there is only one grammatical tone, whereas the complex patterns have two. Thus, in the non-complex patterns, there is no situation in which three tones vie for position on the single available syllable. In the complex patterns, on the other hand, there are three tones competing for association to that same spot. Double-linking (to the penultimate syllable) is allowed. Triple-linking is never allowed to any syllable. Thus the reason that the H tone of the complex HL fails to link in verbs such as **twààbègà** 'we cut hair' (from CVC -**bèg**-) and in **twàfyèèngà** 'we pinched something together' (from CVVNC -**fyèeng**-) is not some ad hoc constraint against linking a H grammatical tone to the first syllable of the verb stem. It is not a "marked" quality of the complex HL pattern. It is due instead to a simple and well-motivated constraint against triple-linking.

That the constraint which disallows the linking of the grammatical H tone is a constraint against triple-linking, rather than being a constraint specific

---

[120]The final L of the complex HL pattern links to the right-hand node of the same syllable, but does not find phonetic realization because the resulting HL contour is linked to a single mora and undergoes single mora HL simplification.

3.8 General rules affecting tone at the word level

to the complex HL pattern against linking of a H tone to CV(VN)C verbs, is further demonstrated by the fact that both the H and the L grammatical tones of any complex pattern *will* link to a toneless verb, where they are the only two tones needing to link. In a toneless verb form exhibiting a complex HL pattern, such as **twànádîîhà** 'and we beat (someone)' the H tone of the complex HL pattern links to the (underlined) first syllable of the stem along with the pattern's right-linking L tone. The linking of both these tones to the same syllable is what produces the HL contour on that underlined syllable.

3.8 General rules affecting tone at the word level

3.8.1 Tone-spread rule

There is one simple lexical-level tone spread rule in Kifuliiru which includes H-spread and L-spread. For clarity, they are listed in derivations as H-spread or L-spread, according to the tone being spread, but both H and L spread operate identically and can be formulated as a single rule as shown in (3.58).[121] Both of these rules are iterative and spread a linked tone rightward onto any free non-final TBUs within the domain of a word stem. Both will target the free left node of a penultimate syllable regardless of whether the right-hand node is linked. Neither will target any linked TBU. A linked tone blocks the rightward progression of tone spread. As shown in the rule below, T-spread will not target a word-final TBU. This is evident from all the examples.[122]

The lexical-level tone (T) spread rule can be formalized as in (3.58).

(3.58) σ σ...σ σ]$_w$
         |̣͎͎͎͎͎͎͎͎͎͎͎
         T

---

[121]It could also be considered that all L tones which are not lexical or grammatical in origin are provided by default insertion, but it seems more intuitive that the process be considered a spread rule, since its effects are identical to H-spread, except that they involve L tones. A final L tone not provided by initial tone association can be considered to be provided by a postlexical T-spread rule, if it occurs within a phrase. If such a L tone occurs phrase finally, it can be considered a L boundary tone, which is never applied within a phrase, but only at phrase boundaries. Such a L is a default boundary tone, since a H boundary tone is "marked", and only occurs in certain environments, where it is conditioned by semantic and discourse criteria.

[122]We posit that there is another rule of postlexical T-spread which is permitted to spread a tone onto word-final syllable within the phonological phrase, as long as the word-final syllable is not also phrase final. Such a H tone provided by postlexical spread is different from a H boundary tone which indicates non-finality, since a word whose penultimate is not linked to a H tone does not undergo postlexical H-spread. A H boundary tone can occur after either a H or a L penultimate, and is not placed within a phrase, but at a point which might otherwise be considered final.

The configuration in (3.59) shows the constraint that T-spread will *not* target a linked TBU. This constraint is discussed below in (3.61) and (3.63).

(3.59) *σ   σ
       |---|
       T   T

Various examples of H-spread within verbs can be seen in (3.60). The lexical tone of each radical is given in the column at left. Besides their original lexical tone listed in the UT "Lex. T" column, verb forms in the infinitive all exhibit the grammatical "simple" stem-tone pattern, a H tone (listed under "Gram. T") which links to the first free syllable of the verb stem. In the verbal examples below, it is this infinitive H tone which then spreads onto the following syllables.

In the nouns in (3.60), we are assuming that since these are nouns derived from verbs, the two underlying tones each link to the leftmost free TBU, beginning with the underlying tone of the verb radical. Thus we are assuming that the nominal tone in these lexical items is the tone which links to the second TBU from the left, and that it is this tone that spreads onto the following syllable (See 3.10.2 for further discussion of linking patterns in deverbal nouns).

For clarity of presentation in (3.60), we separate the examples into H-spread and L-spread. All underlined syllables have received their tones by the T-spread rule. Note that no word-final syllables are targeted by lexical level T-spread.

(3.60) Tone spread within the word

H-spread within the word

Lex.T	Gram.T	Form	Gloss
H	H	**kú-gábá-gábà**	15-divide.out-RDP
L	H	**kú-gàná-gánà**	15-knead.with.hands-RDP
Ø	H	**kú-gáyá-gááyà**	15-writhe.in.pain-RDP
H	H	**kú-fúkúmúlà**	15-pour.out
L	H	**kú-bèráángírà**	15-call.from.a.distance
HH	---	**í=kí-shókóólóló**	AU=7-thick.clump.of.bushes
HH	---	**ú=bú-sángáánírà**	AU=14-old,.worn.out.clothing
HH	---	**ú=mú-lángáálíro**	AU=3-hope,.expectation
LH	---	**ú=mú-jwàngáráró**	AU=3-uneasiness
H	L	**tú-gá-gábà-gàbà**	1PL-F2-divide.out-RDP

3.8 General rules affecting tone at the word level   221

L-spread within the word

Lex.T	Gram.T	Form	Gloss
L	L	tú-gá-gànà-g<u>à</u>nà	1PL-F2-knead.with.hands-RDP
Ø	L	tú-gá-gàyà-g<u>à</u>àyà	1PL-F2-writhe.in.pain-RDP
H	L	tú-gá-fúkù<u>m</u>ùlà	1PL-F2-pour.out
L	L	tú-gá-bèràà<u>n</u>gìrà	1PL-F2-call.from.afar
LL	---	ká-shùngù-sh<u>ùù</u>ngù	1a-very.tall.thing
LL	---	ú=lú-hàhà<u>l</u>ìzì	AU=11-concern/care
LL	---	ú=lú-jàndàgìzì	AU=11-laziness
LL	---	í=ky-ùngù<u>l</u>ìrà	AU=7-edible.leaves.of.squash.plant

Besides the constraints against spreading to a word-final syllable and against targeting a linked syllable, T-spread also seems to be limited by domain boundaries within the word. The tone of a prefix does not spread, even if there is a toneless morpheme directly to its right. Not only does a prefix tone not spread onto a stem, a prefix tone does not spread onto another prefix, either. For example, the negative marker, **ta**-, is toneless (3.9). However, even though it is a toneless morpheme, a H tone on a preceding prefix is never spread onto it by H-spread, as shown by forms such as **kú-t<u>à</u>-géénd-à** (15-NEG-go-Fa) 'to *not* go'.

The lexical tone of a stem never spreads. This fact is simply attributable to the presence of the suffixal tone of a stem-tone pattern, which is always linked directly to the right of the lexical tone in any verb form. If the lexical tone were thus able to spread onto a following linked TBU, it would produce surface forms other than the ones actually observed. Verbs such as the V_2 future form **túgágúúngìrà** 'we will cheat for/at' would instead be *****túgágúúngírà** if the lexical H tone of the stem were allowed to spread onto the penultimate, the left node of which is instead linked to the L tone of the V_2 pattern.

In contrast, depending on the number of syllables in a given verb stem, a grammatical tone may be followed by unlinked TBUs. A grammatical tone on a verb stem will spread to the right within the verb stem up to but not onto any TBU which is already linked to a tone. This is seen in (3.61), where the verb is toneless and the grammatical tone links to the leftmost TBU of the stem, and in (3.63). Such a grammatical H tone may spread onto a penultimate syllable whose left node is free, as happens in the complex HL recent past form **gàgò<u>lóló</u>òmbà** 'it flowed', or the resultative form **tùbèr<u>á</u>ngíìrì** 'we have called from afar', where the grammatical H of the complex HL links to the leftmost free TBU and spreads onto the left-hand node (both underlined) of the bimoraic penultimate whose right-hand node is linked to the final grammatical L.

It is not only bimoraic penultimate syllables which are given a second association line by tone spread rules. The following derivation of the toneless verb -**biik**- 'put', in the recent past (P1) passive of causative form **twàbíkíísíbwà** 'we were caused to put (something)', which has the complex HL stem-tone pattern, shows that a monomoraic penult is also assigned an extra tone by spreading. Contour simplification rules subsequently phonetically simplify all contours thus produced on monomoraic syllables. Though such contours are sometimes neutralized by simplification, in other cases, the effect of tone spread is still perceptible in that the resultant tone is that of the spread tone rather than the tone which was originally linked to the syllable in question. In the derivation in (3.61) we see that in a position where one would expect to find the H of passive, lowered by MR to L, there is instead a surface H tone. The derivation in (3.61) shows H-spread onto the following bimoraic syllable as well as onto the left node of the singly-linked penultimate syllable. Recall that the superscript **r** shown on the H and L in first stage of the derivation below indicates that the tone is linked (only) to the right-hand node of the penultimate syllable. Thus the left-hand node is still available for linking by H-spread and such spread does not violate the constraint in (3.59).

(3.61) **tw-à-bík-íísí-bw-à** (1PL-P1-place-CS-PS-Fa) 'we were caused to put something' (Ø)

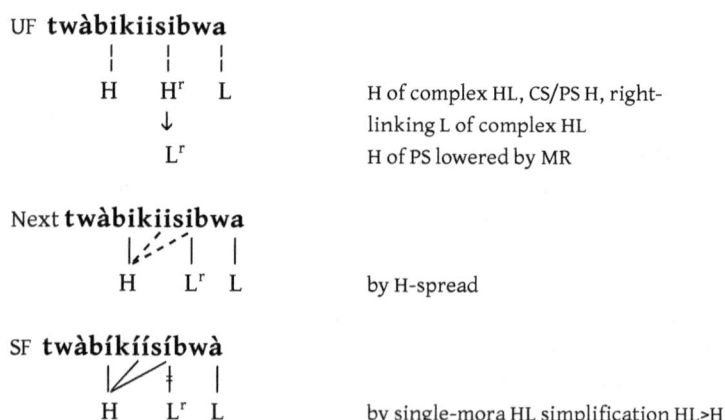

Note that in (3.61), if H-spread had not placed a H tone on the penult, there would be a L tone there from the lowered H of the passive, rather than the H tone seen in the surface form. Thus, not allowing H-spread onto the already linked penultimate would result in an incorrect surface output.

3.8 General rules affecting tone at the word level

For a comparable form, except illustrating L-spread instead of H-spread, we can look at a verb identical to that in (3.61) but with H lexical root tone. In the derivation in (3.62), the effects of L spread onto the penultimate are neutralized by the phonetic rule of LH raising, which interprets a LH as H when it occurs between two L tones. This allows the H tone of the passive to surface as a H tone.

(3.62) **tw-à-fúk-ììsí-bu-à** (1PL-P1-pour.on-CS-PS-Fa) 'we were caused to pour on something' (H)

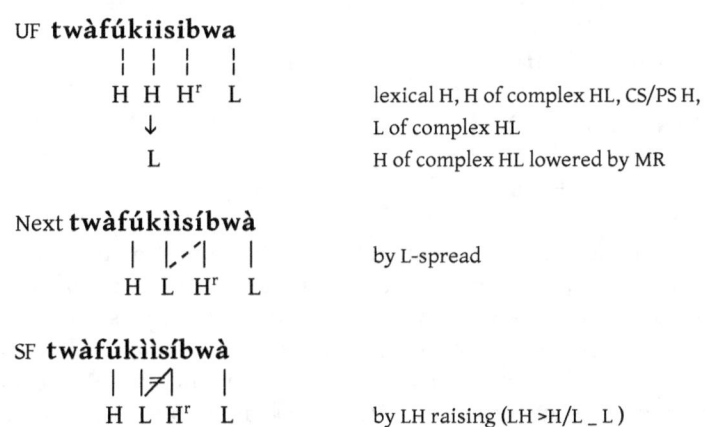

Because of contour simplification, T-spread is easiest to see in a verb with a bimoraic penult. An example similar to that in (3.61), but with a bimoraic penult, is seen in (3.63) in the conditional contrary-to-fact form **twàngà-bègésíìbwì** 'we recently could have been caused to cut hair (but were not)', which also exhibits the complex HL pattern. As seen in this example, though H-spread is permitted to link the H to the left node of the singly linked penultimate syllable, it is not permitted to target the right node, because a L tone (the H of passive, lowered by MR) was already linked there. H-spread onto the second node of the penult here would yield the incorrect output *__twàngàbègésííbwì__.

(3.63) **tw-àngà-bèg-ésíì-bw-ì** (1PL-CND-cut.hair-CS+RS-PS-Fi) 'we could have been caused to cut hair' (L)

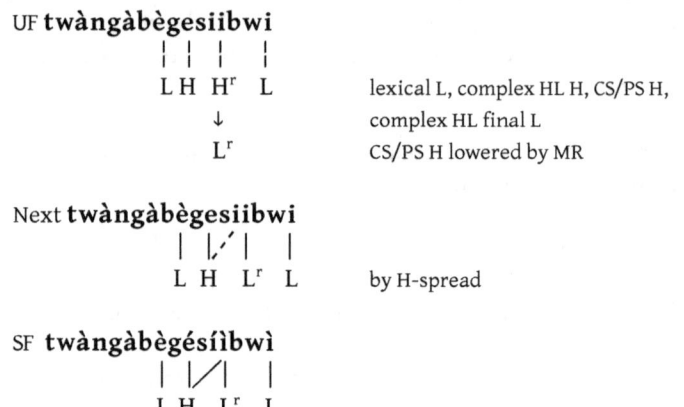

UF **twàngàbègesiibwi**
   | | | |
   L H Hʳ L   lexical L, complex HL H, CS/PS H,
       ↓   complex HL final L
       Lʳ   CS/PS H lowered by MR

Next **twàngàbègesiibwi**
   | |⸍| |
   L H Lʳ L   by H-spread

SF **twàngàbègésíìbwì**
   | |⸍| |
   L H Lʳ L

The same phenomenon of H-spread onto the penultimate can also be observed in any other non-causative, non-passive form of a verb with the complex HL stem-tone pattern. As seen above in (3.61), it is not only *bimoraic* penultimate syllables which are given a second association line by tone spread rules. The following derivation (3.64), of a complex HL recent past form without passive or causative, shows once again that a *monomoraic* penult is assigned an extra tone by spreading.

In the derivation in (3.64) we see that in the penultimate position, where one would expect to find the final-linking L tone of the complex HL stem-tone pattern, there is instead a surface H tone. The final-linking tone of stem-tone pattern always links to the penultimate in non-passive, non-causative forms. However, the final-linking L which is linked to the right node of that syllable by initial tone association is then joined by a H tone, linked by H-spread to the left node. This produces a HL contour. A HL contour on a single mora always surfaces as H tone because of the rule of single-mora HL simplification. Thus the H tone on the penultimate syllable of **twàbèráángírà** 'we called from afar' is the result of the double-linking of the penultimate by the rule of H-spread. Without H-spread onto the left node of the penult, we would get the incorrect surface outcome ***twàbèráángìrà**.

(3.64) **tw-à-bèráángír-à** (1PL-P1-call.from.afar-Fa) 'we called from afar' (L)

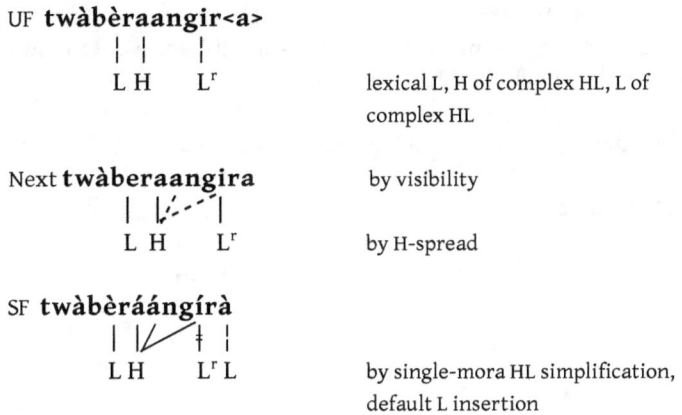

UF **twàbèraangir\<a\>**

    L H   L^r lexical L, H of complex HL, L of complex HL

Next **twàberaangira**

                         by visibility

    L H   L^r by H-spread

SF **twàbèráángírà**

    L H   L^r L   by single-mora HL simplification, default L insertion

In (3.65) we see a derivation in which L-spread targets two following free TBUs, the left and right nodes of the penultimate, which were both free since the stem-tone pattern has no right-linking tone. The spread is shown as a single line, but is assumed to link to both TBUs.

(3.65) **tú-gá-gúng-ìisi-bw-a** (1PL-F2-cheat-CS-PS-Fa) 'we will be cheated' (H)

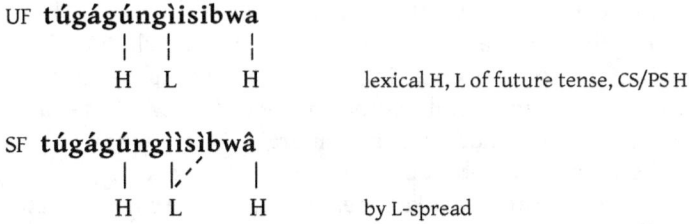

UF **túgágúngìisibwa**

    H   L   H   lexical H, L of future tense, CS/PS H

SF **túgágúngìisìbwâ**

    H   L   H   by L-spread

The passive of causative forms in the imperative singular, e.g. **dìhìisìbwâ** 'be caused to beat someone!' present another case where a L tone is seen to spread, this time only onto the left-hand node of the penult, since the right-hand node is linked. In this form, the stem-tone pattern is the complex LH. The derivation in (3.66) shows the passivized causative of the imperative singular of the toneless verb -**diih**- 'beat', **dìhìisìbwâ** 'be caused to beat someone!'

Here we see that the rule of T-spread spreads the L tone onto the surface penultimate syllable, the right-hand node of which was already linked to the H tone of PS. This sets the stage for the rule of LH lowering to interpret the LH as L, since there is a following H. A lack of L spread here would result in a H surface tone on the **si** syllable, ***dìhìisíbwâ**.

(3.66) **dìh-ììsì-bw-â** (beat-CS-PS-Fa) 'be caused to be beaten!' (Ø)

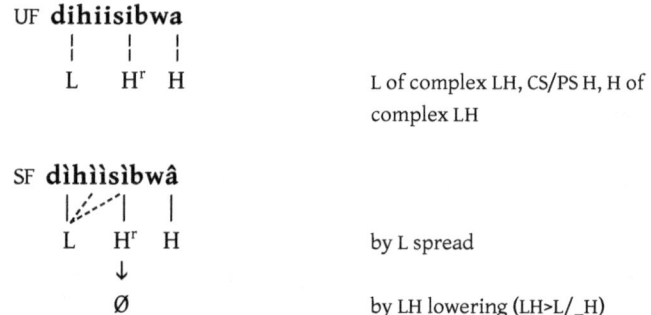

3.8.2 Contour simplification rules

Any penultimate syllable will eventually receive two association lines, if not by initial tone association, then by H-spread or L-spread. As seen in 3.7.2, double-linking is the rule on even a monomoraic penultimate syllable. Yet for the most part, tonal contours may not be realized on a single mora. Thus there is an obvious need for some contour simplification rules, including those which will simplify a tonal contour on a single mora. Note that the following rules apply only to tautosyllabic combinations of tones (i.e. two tones linked to a single syllable, whether bimoraic or monomoraic). These are all considered to be rules of phonetic interpretation.

In a case where there are two like tones associated to a single syllable, there is theoretically no question of the phonetic interpretation. Thus we posit no rule to "neaten up" situations such as that found in a case like the unmarked past (P2) in (3.67), where a H-toned CVC radical like **-fúk-** 'pour out' ends up with two H tones in the derivation of **túkáfúkà** 'we poured out something'.[123]

---

[123]Theoretically some sort of merger rule could be assumed to merge like tones.

3.8 General rules affecting tone at the word level   227

(3.67) **tú-ká-fúk-à** (1PL-P2-pour.out-Fa) 'we poured out something' (H)

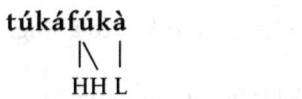

HH L   lexical H and suffixal H of P2, default L

There are rules which affect tautosyllabic LH contours and those which affect tautosyllabic HL contours. A summary of the realizations of contours is given in (3.68). Contours listed all occur in penultimate position. The symbol # signifies a word boundary. Dashes, signifying that such a situation does not occur, are shown for all combinations which would assume a contour in a final syllable. All listings for HL contours below further assume that the HL contour occurs on a bimoraic syllable, since a HL contour is simplified to H on a syllable having only a single mora. Recall also that LH does not signify a rising contour but a "mid" tone phonetically equivalent to a downstepped H.

(3.68) Summary of contour simplification in Kifuliiru

Realizations of LH			Realizations of HL		
# LH L	→	H-L	# HL L	→	HL-L
# LH H	→	L-H	# HL H	→	HL-H
# LH #	→	---	# HL #	→	---
L LH L	→	L-H-L	L HL L	→	L-H-L
L LH H	→	L-L-H	L HL H	→	L-H-H
L LH #	→	----	L HL #	→	----
H LH L	→	H-M-L	H HL L	→	H-HL-L
H LH H	→	H-L-H	H HL H	→	H-HL-H
H LH #	→	----	H HL #	→	----

3.8.2.1 *LH contour simplification*

The rules which determine the phonetic realizations of LH are summarized in (3.69).

(3.69) a. LH raising   LH > H/L _ L or /# _ L
       b. LH lowering   LH > L/_ H
       c. Single mora LH simplification   LH > L/when linked to a single mora
           (some dialects)
       d. LH realization as LH (mid)   LH > LH (level mid tone)/H _ L

There are thus four rules which act to interpret LH sequences within words. Three of them simplify the contour to a simple H or L tone. The last spells out the environment in which the LH is realized as a level mid tone. The first, (3.69a) is a raising rule, by which LH surfaces as H, while (3.69b, c) are lowering rules, causing LH to be realized as L.

The effects of these rules cause three different phonetic realizations of the underlying LH contour, depending on the tonal context. The three realizations can be observed in the context of a noun with an underlying LH tone pattern, as exemplified by the cl. 3 noun **ú=mwéēndà** 'debt' as shown in (3.70).[124]

(3.70) a. **ú=mwéēndà**   'a debt'
       b. **mwééndà**   'debt'
       c. **mwèèndá yùgwó**   'It's a debt, that.'

In (3.70a) **ú=mwéēndà**, the LH surfaces as a level mid tone, since the tautosyllabic contour is in a penultimate syllable, and is both preceded by the augment's H tone and followed by the L tone of the ultimate syllable. In (3.70b) **mwééndà**, the LH contour surfaces as H due to the action of the LH raising rule (3.71), since here the contour is in phrase-initial position and is followed by the L tone of the ultima. In (3.71c) **mwèèndá yùgwó**, LH surfaces as a L tone due to the effect of LH lowering for which conditions are met by the H tone on the ultima. The H on the ultima in this position is the result of the spreading of the H tone of LH, which can take place because the final syllable of **mwèèndá** in **mwèèndá yùgwó** is in non-phrase-final position.

In a phrase such as **ú=kúkùùndá Múzíbò** 'to love Muzibo', we see evidence that the rules of contour simplification are active at the postlexical level. In isolation, the infinitive **ú=kúkūūndà** has a LH contour realized as a mid tone on the penultimate syllable. In the context of a phrase, the process of postlexical H-spread spreads the H tone from the right-hand node of the penultimate mora to the final mora of the infinitive because it is in non-phrase

---

[124]Note that in order to create an environment in which the LH is followed by a H, it is necessary to put the word in the context of a noun phrase. However, here we are still looking only at the realization of contours which are found word internally.

3.8 General rules affecting tone at the word level

final position.[125] This means that a H tone follows the LH contour on the verb stem, causing the rule of LH lowering to take effect. This produces a L rather than mid tone on the penultimate: **ú=kúkùùndá Múzíbò**, since there is now a H tone following the LH contour, meeting the conditions for LH lowering.

This shows that this simplification rule acts at the postlexical level, refiguring the surface tone according to the postlexical tone changes around it. (For discussion of phrase level tone rules such as postlexical H-spread, see 3.12.) The phonetic rules acting on LH sequences now follow.

3.8.2.1.1 LH raising

A tautosyllabic LH is phonetically simplified to H when preceded and followed by L, or when it is in phrase-initial position and followed by L.

LH raising: LH → H/L _ L or # _ L

Figure (3.71) provides possible configurations.

(3.71) a. σ σ σ   σ σ σ   b. $_w$[σ σ $_w$[σ σ
       |/\ | > | /\ | /\ | > /\ |
       L L H L   L H H L   L H L   H H L

     c. σ σ σ]$_w$ σ σ σ]$_w$
        |/|\ > |/\ |
        L H^r L   L H H L

This rule as stated in (3.71a) is easily exemplified in L stem verb forms like **ákábàfyééngà** 'he shut off their breath', where the L-toned cl. 2 object marker **bà-** preceding the stem causes the following LH (lexical L plus suffixal H of simple stem-tone pattern) to surface as a level H tone on the bimoraic stem syllable. Compare this to the same form, but without an object marker, **ákáfyēēngà** 'he shut off (someone's breath)', or the same form with a H-toned cl. 1 object marker **mú-**: **ákámúfyēēngà** 'he shut off his breath', where in either case, the H-toned prefix preceding the stem allows the following underlying tautosyllabic LH to surface as a mid tone.

As formalized in (3.71b) the rule states that the same raising of LH to H takes place when the underlying contour occurs word initially. Assuming

---

[125]By comparing this phrase with another in which there is no LH contour on the verb, we can see that the cause of the final H on the verb in the phrase **úkúkùùndá Múzíbò** is from H-spread and is not a H boundary tone. An example is the future form, where there is no LH contour in the verb stem, and its final syllable is L: **ágákùùndà Múzíbò** 'he will love Muzibo'.

that in the imperative singular of a lexically L verb the initial tone is LH, comparing the sound of imperatives of lexically H verbs such as **fúkà** 'pour!' and **gúùngà** 'cheat!' with those of lexically L verbs such as **bégà** 'cut hair!' (with underlying initial LH) and **fyēēngà** 'pinch shut!' shows that the pitch of the initial tone of the L verbs and that of the H verbs is quite comparable.

As shown in (3.71c), even when the L which forms the tautosyllabic LH contour is the same L (being only spread onto the penultimate, and not comprising a separate underlying tone) there is still phonetic simplification of the contour. This is another indication that this rule is phonetic and not a lexical level rule, since a lexical level rule would theoretically require that there be an L preceding the L of the LH contour for the rule to apply. By the phonetic rule of LH raising, the L which was spread onto the left node of the penultimate by T-spread is functionally delinked from the penultimate, allowing the H tone to surface as a phonetic H. We posit however, that these rules do not actually delete tones or association lines, but simply interpret the underlying sequence.

An example of the situation shown in (3.71c) is seen in **twàngàgúngìsíízì** 'we could have caused someone to cheat', where there is an underlying LH contour on the bimoraic penultimate syllable, formed by L-spread from the preceding syllable followed by the H of the causative morpheme. It is realized at the same pitch as a simple H tone would be pronounced in that position. Because of downdrift, the pitch of this H is lower than that of a H tone which preceded any L tones within the word. Basically all the rule in (3.71c) says is that there is no discernable difference between the pitch of a H tone affected by downdrift and that of a LH contour which follows and precedes a L tone.

An example of the same rule affecting LH in the phrase-initial environment can be seen in the adjective **mw-ēērù** (3-white), which seems to have an initial H tone in isolation. However, it can be shown that the tone on the initial syllable is actually LH. When this same adjective is preceded within the phrase by a noun, the noun, which would normally have a final L tone, instead has a final H tone. This final H tone is the result of leftward H-Shift conditioned by the L initial tone of the following adjective (3.12.2) e.g. **úmúlòòndó mwēērù** 'the white garment', the LH tone is phonetically discernable, since it is between a H and a L tone. Contrast this with a phrase in which the following adjective has an initial H tone, such as **úmúlòòndò múlà** 'the long garment'. Though the initial H tone of the adjective is lowered in pitch due to downdrift, the lack of a final H tone on the noun shows that this adjective has an underlying initial H instead of LH as was seen in **mwēērù**. Thus the apparent initial H tone in **mwēērù** when pronounced in isolation is due to the phonetic interpretation rule of LH raising.

3.8 General rules affecting tone at the word level   231

The examples in (3.72a–g) provide a comparison of the phonetic realizations of words which have initial LH tone realized as H due to LH raising, and those which have initial LL, HL, or HH tone. Examples (3.72b, d) demonstrate the effects of LH raising.

(3.72)   Tone of
           Initial syll.   Surface   Gloss
    a.   LL   bw-òòfì   14-shortness
    b.   LH   mw-áákà   3-year
    c.   LL   bì-ìngì   2-many
    d.   LH   bí-írù   2-black
    e.   LL   bà-àndì   2-other (demonstrative)
    f.   HL   bí-ìjâ   2-good
    g.   HH   ky-óóbà   7-fear

In **mwáákà**, (3.72b) as well as **bíírù**, (3.72d) there is still underlying initial LH tone, though the initial phonetic tone is H.[126]

3.8.2.1.2 LH lowering

The phonetic interpretation rule of LH lowering applies only to tautosyllabic LH contours and requires only that the following environment be specified as a word-final H tone. The rule results in the realization of LH simply as L. The rule can be formalized as in (3.73).

(3.73) LH lowering

$$\begin{matrix} \sigma \\ \wedge \\ LH \end{matrix} \rightarrow \begin{matrix} \sigma \\ \wedge \\ LL \end{matrix} / \_\_\begin{matrix} \sigma]_w \\ | \\ H \end{matrix}$$

LH lowering is best exemplified in L-stem verbs with a penultimate bimoraic syllable in V_1V_2 position.[127] In unmarked past (P2) forms, which display the simple stem-tone pattern, we find examples like (3.74) **ákáfyèèngwá** 'he had his breath shut off'.

---

[126]Because the prefixes of both of these forms have underlying H tone which is not able to link to the prefix itself, there is a floating H tone to the left. In isolation, these forms are phonetically **bíírù** 'black' and **mwáákà** 'year', since LH is realized as H initially in the phrase. Within the phrase, these forms still trigger leftward H-shift, because the initial L is still there underlyingly (see 3.12.2 for details on LHS).

[127]The same phenomenon is present in a verb with a monomoraic penult, but the contrast is easier to hear in a longer segment.

In (3.74) the lexical H tone of the passive, realized on the FV, provides the environment for the rule of LH lowering to interpret the LH contour on the first syllable of the radical as L.

(3.74) **á-ká-fyèèng-w-á** (1-P2-cut.off.breath-PS-Fa) 'he had his breath shut off' (L)

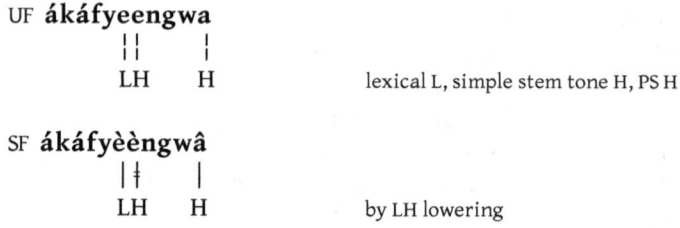

Compare the surface form in (3.74) to the non-passive form **ákáfyēēngà** 'he pinched off (someone's) breath', where there is no H tone following the LH contour on the stem. Since there is instead a L tone following in this case, the LH contour is phonetically realized as a level mid tone.

Examples such as **kútàfyèèngwâ** 'to not have one's breath shut off' demonstrate that LH lowering is not sensitive to whether a H or a L tone precedes the LH contour. In **ákáfyèèngwá**, (3.74), the tone preceding the underlying LH on **fyee** is the H of the P2 tense marker, and in **kútàfyèèngwâ**, also a form with simple stem-tone pattern, it is the negative marker, with surface L tone, which precedes. The rule operates in both cases.

3.8.2.1.3 Single-mora LH simplification

A third rule concerning LH is needed for some speakers.[128] A tautosyllabic LH contour on a bimoraic syllable is pronounced as a level mid tone by all speakers when it follows a H and precedes a L. However, for some speakers, this is *only* permissible when the LH is linked to a bimoraic ((C)VV) syllable, but not when it is linked to a single mora. For speakers who never pronounce LH as a mid tone on a single mora, another rule is necessary:

(For some speakers) a LH linked to a single mora is simplified to L when preceded by a H and followed by a L.

---

[128]This is probably an areal feature, though it may instead be generational. The speakers I noticed it in are those born after 1970 or so. However, we have never attempted to determine the exact parameters, and since we are no longer resident in the area, casual observation is impossible.

(3.75) Single-mora LH simplification

$$\begin{matrix} \mu & & \mu \\ \wedge & > & | & /\mathrm{H}\_\mathrm{L} \\ \mathrm{L\,H} & & \mathrm{L} \end{matrix}$$

This can be exemplified in a L-toned CVC verb stem such as -**bùt**- 'give birth, produce offspring'. In the far past, speakers who pronounce a LH on a single mora would pronounce this as **ákáḇūtà** 's/he gave birth', while those who do not pronounce LH as a mid tone on a single mora would pronounce this with a L tone on the stem, **ákáḇùtà**.

3.8.2.2 HL contour simplification

There are two basic phonetic rules for interpreting the surface realization of an underlying HL contour. These are single-mora HL simplification, and post-L HL simplification.

3.8.2.2.1 Single-mora HL simplification

Any HL contour which is linked to a single mora is phonetically simplified to H. This rule can be stated as:

(3.76) Single-mora HL simplification

$$\begin{matrix} \sigma & & \sigma \\ | & & | \\ \mu & & \mu \\ \wedge & > & /\!\!\not\!\!\wedge \\ \mathrm{H\,L} & & \mathrm{H\,L} \end{matrix}$$

This can be seen to operate in cases like the future (F2) forms of H stem CVC verbs. In (3.77) we see the H verb -**fúk**- 'pour out something'.

(3.77) **tu-gáa-fúk-a** (1PL-F2-pour.out-Fa) 'we will pour out something' (H)

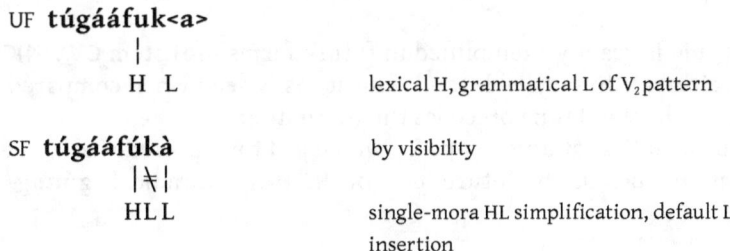

UF **túgááfuk<a>**
  |
  H L   lexical H, grammatical L of V₂ pattern

SF **túgááfúkà**   by visibility
  |≠|
  HL L   single-mora HL simplification, default L
                                 insertion

It might be tempting to claim that the L in a case like that in (3.77) is never associated to the penultimate syllable in the first place, but rather that it remains floating if there is only a single mora in the penultimate, and then associates to the FV when that becomes visible. However, there are two reasons that we assume instead that the grammatical L is associated to the penult, to the right of the lexical tone of the verb.

The first reason for assuming linking of the L tone in such cases is that when the contour involved is LH rather than HL, the LH combination in the speech of many speakers is not simplified, and can actually be phonetically discerned, for example in the P2 form **tú-ká-bēg-à** (1PL-P2-cut.hair-Fa) 'we cut hair'. In this case, the underlying and surface LH tone on the lexically L verb stem -**bèg**- is due to the double-linking of the penultimate syllable by the lexical L tone and the grammatical H tone of the simple stem-tone pattern. Thus in a parallel case, such as that shown in (3.80), where the only difference is that the lexical tone of the verb is H and the grammatical tone is L, instead of vice versa, we assume that the grammatical L is similarly permitted to link, and is then simplified by the rule of single-mora HL simplification.

The second reason for assuming that there are two linked tones in a position like this is that the H tone of a HL contour in the penultimate syllable of verbs is often the result of an application of the H-spread rule which links a H tone to a syllable which is already linked to the right-linking L tone of a verbal stem-tone pattern (see, for example, the derivation in (3.61)). This shows that there are both a left and a right node in the penultimate that must have tones associated with them.

3.8.2.2.2 Post-L HL simplification

A tautosyllabic HL contour is simplified to H if it is preceded by a L tone within the word. This can be formalized as follows:

(3.78) Post-L HL simplification

```
 σ σ       σ σ
 | /\   >  | /≠
 L H L     L H L
```

This rule is readily exemplified in future forms of H stem CVV(N)C verbs with a bimoraic first syllable, and is most easily seen when compared to the situation where a H tone precedes the HL contour.

Let us look first at an example in which a H tone precedes an underlying HL contour, such as the future form of the H-toned radical -**gúung**- 'cheat

3.8 General rules affecting tone at the word level

(by overcharging)'. The form **tú-gá-gúùng-à** (1PL-F2-cheat-Fa) 'we will cheat someone' is such a form, as is the same form with a H-toned cl. 1 object prefix, **tú-gá-mú-gúùng-à** (1PL-F2-O1-cheat-Fa) 'we will cheat *him*'. In both these cases there is a H-toned prefix preceding the radical, so that the underlying HL is allowed to surface phonetically on the radical as seen in the derivation of **túgámúgúùngà** in (3.79).

(3.79) **tú-gá-mú-gúùng-à** (1PL-F2-1.O-cheat-Fa) 'we will cheat him' (H)

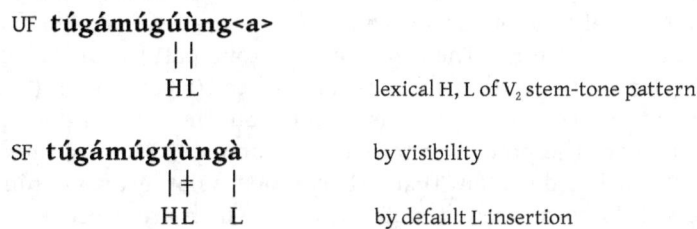

lexical H, L of V_2 stem-tone pattern	
by visibility	
by default L insertion	

The HL on the bimoraic first syllable of the radical (-**gúùng**-) is the result of linking both the lexical H tone of the radical and the suffixal L tone of V_2 stem-tone pattern to this same penultimate syllable.

Compare the form in (3.79), where the syllable linked to the HL is preceded by a H-toned prefix, to (3.80), an example in which the same underlying contour is preceded by a L-toned prefix. By substituting the cl. 2 object prefix **bà**- for the cl. 1 object prefix **mú**- seen in (3.79), we get **tú-gá-bà-gúúng-à** 'we will cheat them', in which the a L tone precedes the H-toned radical.

(3.80) **tú-gá-bà-gúúng-à** (1PL-F2-O2-cheat-Fa) 'we will cheat them' (H)

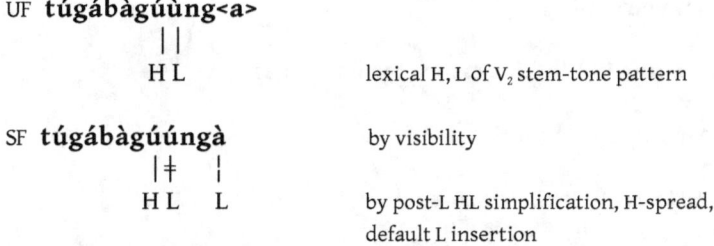

lexical H, L of V_2 stem-tone pattern	
by visibility	
by post-L HL simplification, H-spread, default L insertion	

In such a form the L-tone prefix preceding the verb stem triggers post-L HL simplification, and causes the HL contour on the bimoraic stem syllable to surface as a simple H tone (-**gúúng**-).

Any L-tone prefix which immediately precedes the radical has exactly the same effect on the underlying HL tone on the bimoraic penultimate first syllable of a verb radical. Compare, for example, **tú-gá-kì-géénd-à** (1PL-F2-PERS-go-Fa) 'we will still go' with **tú-gá-géènd-à** (1PL-F2-go-Fa) 'we will go', in which -**géend**- 'go' has a HL contour.

Further examples showing that a HL contour will surface following a H tone, but not following a L tone, are given in (3.81). The verb used is -**gáaj**- 'count', a verb with lexical H tone shown in (3.81a–d) in the recent past (P1) form. Each of the forms in (3.81a–d) has an underlying HL contour, of which the H is the lexical tone of the verb and the L is the final tone of the complex HL stem-tone pattern. (The H of the stem-tone pattern in each case is dropped by T-drop.) Note that there is no surface HL contour in (3.81a) or (3.81b) where the preceding prefix has a L tone, but the contour does appear in (3.81c, d) where the preceding tone is H. Example (3.81e) is a unmarked past form (P2) included to show that a HL contour is not just something that happens on all bimoraic penultimate syllables which are preceded by a H tone and followed by a L tone. HL does not occur in form (3.81e) because there is no lexical L tone present in the tonal configuration of the P2 tense, and thus no underlying contour on the penultimate syllable.

(3.81) | Verb | Gloss | Tense |
|---|---|---|
| a. **tw-à-gááj-à** | 'we counted' | P1 |
| b. **tw-à-bì-gááj-à** | 'we counted them' (cl. 8 **bì**) | P1 |
| c. **tw-à-mú-gáàj-à** | 'we counted him' (cl. 1 **mú**) | P1 |
| d. **tw-à-ná-gáàj-à** | 'and we counted' | P1 |
| e. **tú-ká-gááj-à** | 'we counted' | P2 |

3.8.3 Meeussen's rule

Meeussen's rule in Kifuliiru can be formalized as:

(3.82) Meeussen's rule (MR)

HH > HL (within specified domains only)

Meeussen's rule is active in Kifuliiru only in verb stems of two stem-tone patterns: complex HL and complex HH. This rule is named after the Belgian linguist who first pointed it out, and is the label often given to any rule which eliminates one or more of the lexical or grammatical H tones present in a given target domain. Ntihirageza (1998:282), in her survey of Meeussen's rule

3.8 General rules affecting tone at the word level

(MR) across Bantu languages, points out that MR is not really one single rule, since it is applied differently in different languages, and thus needs to be formalized in many different ways.

The main differences in the application of Meeussen's rule as observed across languages are that the domains in which the rule is applied are different, and the triggers and targets, while all H tones, frequently need to be further specified as to what domain they are a part of. Another difference is that in some languages the rule is iterative,[129] affecting a string of H tones, while in others, only a single H tone is targeted. In Kifuliiru, the targeted H, rather than simply being deleted, is lowered, producing a L tone which blocks further application of the rule unless there is another H to act as a second trigger within the domain of operation of the rule.

Ntihirageza also points out that even within a single language, MR usually applies to some domains but not to others. She notes that in some languages, this domain may be the phrase, while in others, it is the phonological word or subportions of the phonological word. She emphasizes that the one "constant" in MR application over all the languages surveyed is that the rule only operates when there are two adjacent H tones. It is the adjacency of the triggering H (the one on the left) and the targeted H (the rightward one) that is necessary for the application of the rule. Moreover, both the trigger and the target must be specified in each language as to their domain(s). This means that both trigger and target must be within some certain domain, or across a certain domain boundary, e.g. within the same phrase, within the same word, or trigger within one specified domain and target within another specified domain, etc.

In Kifuliiru the only instances in which MR has been observed is in the stem of verbs with the complex HL or complex HH stem-tone patterns. That is, MR applies only when the trigger and target are both within a subportion of the word, and applies only in two specific stem-tone patterns. In other Kifuliiru stem-tone patterns, and in other word classes, MR has not been observed to apply at all. For example, in the noun **í=kí-mény-éés-ô** (AU=7-know-CS-o) 'a sign' there are underlyingly at least three H tones, and none is targeted by MR. The augment, the noun prefix, and the root all have lexical H tone, and none of them is lowered to produce a contour. In simple stem-tone passives such as **ákágálúlwâ** there are three lexical H tones and a grammatical H tone (the H of the past tense marker **ká-**), which links also to the mora to its left, the lexical H tone of the verb **-gálul-** 'return (TRANS)', the lexical H tone of the passive marker, **u-**, and the H grammatical tone of the simple stem-tone pattern. None of the tones in such forms is lowered by MR.

---

[129]That, is, even where there is a single H trigger, the rule targets every H tone found within the domain of the rule.

In Kifuliiru verbs, of the seven basic suffixal stem-tone patterns, MR operates only in the complex HL and complex HH stem-tone patterns. (For details of the complex HL pattern, and evidence of the activity of MR, see the section on complex HL under 3.5.3.3.3.)

The data in (3.83) illustrate very briefly the operation of MR in the complex HL pattern. The syllables to which the grammatical H tone of the complex HL pattern is associated are underlined. Note that this H tone is lowered by MR only in the verbs with a H lexical tone, (3.83a, b). MR does not lower this grammatical tone in the verbs where there is no preceding lexical H tone *within the domain of the stem* to serve as a trigger for the rule. In (3.83e, f) though the first syllable of the stem has a H tone, there is no lowering, since this is a toneless verb, and that single H tone is the grammatical H of the stem-tone pattern. Thus in (3.83e, f) there is a potential trigger, but no target, for MR. Note in the final column that although the H-toned sequential (SQ) **ná-** prefix directly precedes the lexical H tone of the H verbs (3.83a, b) and directly precedes the H grammatical tone in the Ø verbs, there is no application of MR, because the prefixes are outside the domain of the verb stem. For MR to apply, both the trigger and target must be in the domain of the verb stem.

(3.83)	UT	Gloss	Cl. 1 subject	with sequential **ná-**
a.	H	'agree together + APL'	à-<u>lágààn-ìr</u>-à	à-ná-<u>lágààn-ìr</u>-à
b.	H	'return +APL'	à-gá<u>lùk-ìr</u>-à	à-ná-gá<u>lùk-ìr</u>-à
c.	L	'carry on head + APL'	à-bè<u>túl-ír</u>-à	à-ná-bè<u>túl-ír</u>-à
d.	L	'call from distance'	à-bè<u>rángír</u>-à	à-ná-bè<u>rángír</u>-à
e.	T	'invite + APL'	à-<u>láálík-ír</u>-à	à-ná-<u>láálík-ír</u>-à
f.	T	'cook +APL'	à-<u>déék-ér</u>-à	à-ná-<u>déék-ér</u>-à

MR also does not apply between two H-tone prefixes. This is shown by examples such as **àná<u>múshúlì</u>kà** 'and he hit him', where the H tone of the cl. 1 object marker **mú-** interacts neither with the following H tone of the verb stem, nor with the preceding H tone of the sequential **ná-**. MR is active, however, as is seen from the lowering of the grammatical H tone of complex HL. The L tone on **lì** is the result of the application of MR triggered by the H tone of the verb stem **-shúlik-** 'hit'.

As mentioned above, in Kifuliiru the action of MR lowers a H to L rather than deleting it. Thus, there will be an underlying L wherever MR has applied. In Kifuliiru this L blocks further applications of MR within the domain unless there is a second trigger-target sequence.

3.8 General rules affecting tone at the word level

The following derivation demonstrates MR's application in the complex HL stem-tone pattern. MR is active in all verbs with the complex HL pattern. In (3.84) we show another recent past (P1) form.

(3.84) **tw-à-gógòòmbék-à** (1PL-P1-forced.something-Fa) 'we forced something where it didn't belong' (H)

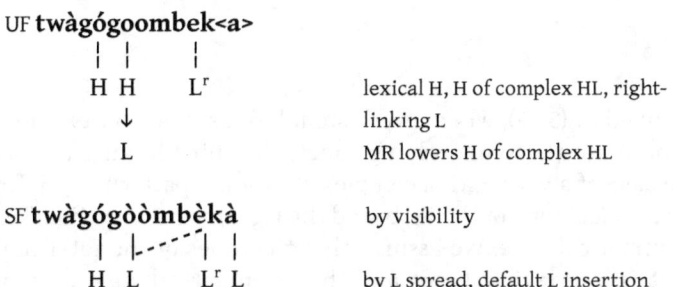

Note that in the H verb **twàgógòòmbèkà**, it is the H tone of the complex HL stem-tone pattern which is lowered by MR. In a toneless verb, by contrast, there is no lexical H tone, so that the only H tone is that of the complex HL. Thus, in toneless forms, there is no application of MR, and the surface tones remain H, as in **twàláálíkírà** 'we invited (someone) for someone or at someplace'.

The reason that we term this lowering "Meeussen's rule" rather than just saying that some tenses have a "polar" tone is that the H of causative or passive can also be targeted by this rule. For examples, see the second and third derivations in (3.34).

3.8.4 T-drop

The rule of T-drop is Kifuliiru's response to the problem presented by three tones competing for association to a single available syllable, as described in (3.7.3). We saw in that section that in the case of the complex HL pattern, it is the initial (left-linking) H tone of the grammatical melody that is dropped, while the final (right-linking) L tone is permitted to link. This rule of T-drop applies in the process of initial tone association. The tone, finding no available node, is deleted without ever linking. The formula in (3.85) thus shows that linking of three tones to one syllable is not permitted, and the third-linking tone of the three is the one which is dropped. This is undoubtedly related to the fact that initial linking is done from the edges inward (see (3.55)), so that the first tones to link are those at the periphery of the tonal melody. The tones (T) in (3.85) are numbered according to their order of association.[130]

(3.85) T-drop

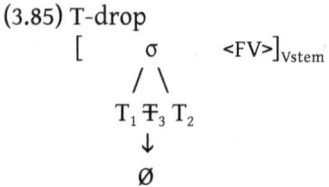

As symbolized in (3.85), when a verb stem has a single non-extratonal syllable and there are three underlying tones, the third-linking tone is deleted.[131] In the case of a verb with a complex stem-tone pattern, the leftmost T indicates the lexical tone of the verb, and the rightmost T the "final" or right-linking grammatical tone. We assume that the tones of the total combined melody, that is, the lexical tones and the grammatical stem-tone pattern tones are all present before the initial tone association takes place. The lexical tone of the verb links to the first free TBU of the stem, and the final tone of the combined melody must link next. This makes the left-linking tone of a complex stem-tone pattern the "middle tone" which links last. It is the tones which link first that are given linking priority when there are three tones vying for one position. The order of linking is determined by the convention stated in (3.55).

That the lexical tone of the verb and any right-linking tones are given preference over the grammatical stem tone of the complex HL is shown by a case like **twànáfyèèngà** (from -**fyèèng**- 'pinch shut'). Here it is the lexical L of the

---

[130]The third-linking tone here is shown as the middle tone, as would be the case in which there are only three tones in the combined tonal melody. In cases where the three tones are instead the three initial tones of a four-tone melody, and thus do not include the final tone, our formulation of edge-in linking posits that it is the rightmost of the three remaining tones which will link third. Thus T_3, the deleted tone, would be in the rightmost position in such a case.

[131]In the case of a passive verb, the lexical and the stem-tone melodies each have two tones. The question of which tone drops by T-drop in verbs with a monosyllabic base can only be theoretically determined in such forms. In the passive of a C(G)V(VN)C verb, the final tone of the grammatical melody links to the FV, which is not extratonal in these forms. The lexical tone of the radical links to the left-hand node of the initial syllable of the verb stem. It is, then, impossible to determine empirically whether it is the H of passive or the initial tone of the stem-tone pattern which is allowed to link to its right. This is because in a complex HL (or HH) form the initial grammatical tone and the H of passive are identical, and in complex LH forms, the effects of phonetic contour simplification rules make it impossible to discern which tone is dropped. Theoretically, however, if the linking of the two middle tones of a four-tone melody proceeds from left to right, the left-hand grammatical tone links before the H tone of the passive, and thus it will be the H of the passive which is deleted.

3.8 General rules affecting tone at the word level

verb and the final-linking L tone of the complex HL stem-tone pattern which associate to the two free morae of the verb, while the grammatical H tone of the complex HL pattern, which ideally links to first free TBU, is dropped (see derivation in (3.86)).

The example of **twànábēgwà** 'and we had our hair cut' illustrates that in a verb with one more free TBU, the H tone of complex HL can also fill the rightmost T slot in the formula given in (3.85). In this verb stem there are four tones and only three spots available for linking. The lexical L tone of the verb links to the first available TBU, the left-hand node of the penultimate syllable. The final-linking L associates to the FV, which is not extratonal in a passive form. The grammatical H tone and the passive H tone both vie for position on the right-hand node of the penultimate. Though practically it is impossible to tell whether it is the grammatical H tone or the H tone of the PS which is dropped, our linking convention in (3.55) predicts that it will be the H of passive which is the third-linking tone, and thus is deleted. The double-linking of the lexical L and the grammatical H creates a LH contour in the V_1 position, which is reflected in the mid tone on the surface form.

The linking of the H of the stem-tone pattern to the V_1 position in this verb form demonstrates that it is not some "constraint" against having a H tone link to this position which prevents the grammatical H tone of the stem-tone pattern from linking there in the non-passive form. Only the constraint against three association lines to a single syllable keeps that grammatical H from linking in forms like **twànáfyèèngà**.

A derivation is shown in (3.86) for **tw-à-fyèèng-à** 'we pinched something shut' a L-toned CVVNC verb stem in the complex HL pattern. The lexical L tone of the verb and the final-linking L are permitted to associate to the V_1 and V_2 positions (both in the first syllable of the stem) while the H of the complex HL is dropped out by T-drop because the leftmost and rightmost tones link first, leaving no free TBU for the third tone.

(3.86) **tw-à-fyèèng-à** (1PL-P1-pinch.shut-Fa) 'we pinched something shut' (L)

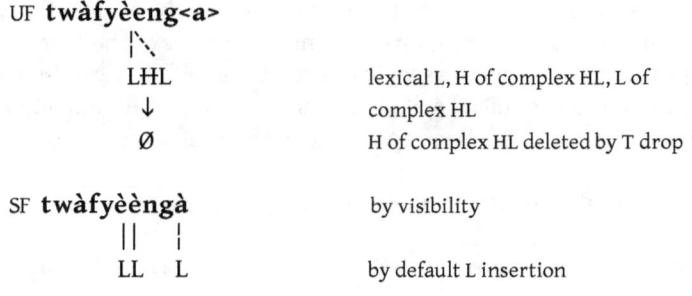

In (3.87) is a derivation of the passive form of the active verb shown in (3.86). Note that the H tone of passive is deleted by T-drop during initial tone association. The H tone of the stem-tone pattern remains H and finds surface realization in the H tone which is the phonetic interpretation of the LH contour on the initial syllable of the verb stem: **twàfyééngwà**.

(3.87) **tw-à-fyèèng-w-à** (1PL-P1-pinch.shut-PS-Fa) 'we were pinched shut' (L)

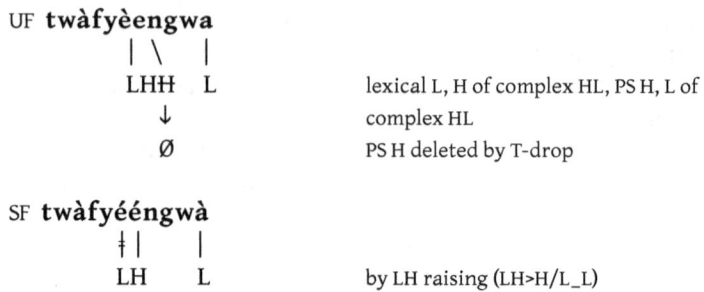

By contrast, in a passive verb of the same tense but with a lexically *toneless* verb stem, both the grammatical H tone and the H of the passive *are* able to link, since without any lexical tone, there are only two tones which need to link on the two available TBUs of the penultimate. Because both H tones link in a toneless verb, the environment for the application of MR is met, and (when there is a preceding H tone, such as provided by the **ná-** sequential marker) the HL contour derived by MR is audible. A good example is **twànádííhwà** 'and we were beaten'. For more verbal derivations involving T-drop, see (3.32), (3.51), and (3.56).

3.8.5 Lexical level H float

The underlying tone of certain prefixes (e.g. all the nominal and adjective prefixes, and pronominal prefixes of cl. 1, 4, and 9) is a H tone. When this H tone is for some reason unable to link to the word of which the segmental portion of its morpheme is a part, it remains floating to the left of the word in question. This process is referred to as lexical level H float. If the word in question has H tone linked to the initial syllable, or if an initial (H-toned) augment is cliticized to such a word, the floating H tone of the prefix is deleted.[132]

The rule of lexical H-float may be formulated as follows:

---

[132]Note that the augment is a morpheme which operates at phrase level (7.2, volume 2).

3.8 General rules affecting tone at the word level

(3.88) Lexical H float

a. [σ ... σ]_{N or Adj}
         |
    (H) L

b. [σ ... σ]_{N or Adj}
         |
    (H) H

c. [σ] = [σ ... σ]_{N or Adj}
     | |
     H (H)   L

(3.88a) shows that a floating H precedes a word-initial L tone. (3.88b) shows that a floating H is deleted when a H tone follows. (3.88c) illustrates that if an augment or other H-toned clitic is cliticized to the word, the floating H tone is deleted.

When, in word formation, a CV prefix is juxtaposed to a regular C-initial stem, the H tone of the prefix associates to the syllable comprised of the segmental portion of the prefix. However, there are four cases in which the H tone of the prefix is not able to link, or to remain linked, to the prefix itself. These cases are the following:

- the prefix consists of a nasal only, as in cl. 9, e.g. **m-bèhò** (9-cold).
- a CV prefix is juxtaposed to a V-initial stem, so that the vowel of the prefix coalesces or elides with that of the stem, e.g. **má-ìgìrìzó > mìgìrìzô** (6-teachings).
- the vowel of the CV prefix is realized as a glide (**w** or **y**) before a V-initial stem and thus is unable to bear a tone, e.g. **kí-ùbì > kyūūbì** (7-wing).
- (less commonly) a noun seems to have a prelinked lexical tone with a floating tone to the left. Such exceptional noun stems seem to have two tones, the rightmost of which is prelinked to the first TBU of the noun stem. Thus the first of the noun's lexical tones must link to the prefix. Such a case is seen in **mù-gózì** (3-rope), plural **mì-gózì** (4-ropes) where the noun seems to have underlying LH tone, of which the H links to the first TBU of the stem, leaving the L to link to the prefix.[133]

---

[133]One source of such a situation is seen when the noun is derived from a verb which originally had an initial (L-toned) reflexive prefix. The vowel of such a prefix may drop, but the L

The H tone of the prefix, if unable to associate to a TBU in the prefix, is always blocked, probably by the linked lexical tones of the stem, from moving rightward across the domain boundary between prefix and stem. Even in monosyllabic words, where the boundary between prefixes and stem seems to be ignored, stem tones always move left into the prefixes. Prefix tones are never seen to link rightward across the domain boundary that separates them from the stem. Thus the unlinked H tone remains floating to the left. In cases where it is followed by a L tone to its right, it is not deleted by rule. Such a L tone results whenever a H-toned prefix is affixed to a stem which begins with a L-toned vowel, e.g. **bá-ìngì** > **bììngì** (2-many), **má-ìgìrìzó** > **mìgìrìzô** (6-teachings), **ú-a-ìtù** (1-A.M-1PL) > **wììtù** 'our'.

The presence of this floating H is not noticeable until the word which it floats to the left of is used in a non-initial position in a phrase or clause. This is the point at which the postlexical rule of leftward H-shift (LHS) (3.12.2) allows such a floating H tone to associate to the final TBU of the word preceding it within the utterance.

In the third column of (3.89) we show a noun followed by an adjective whose prefix has an initial H tone, -**la** 'long/tall'. In these examples, because the adjective's prefix has H tone, there is no floating H tone to the left of the adjective, and therefore no LHS. This is seen by the fact that the final tone of the nouns is L. In the last column, by contrast, the prefixes of the adjective have initial L tone. In these cases, the floating H tone is present, and LHS does occur. This is evidenced by the H tone on the final syllable of the noun.

(3.89)	UF of noun	Gloss	+ H-initial adj -**la** 'long/tall' NO LHS	+ L-initial adj -**ofi** 'short' LHS applies
a.	**ú=mú-fùmù**	AU=1-doctor	úmúfùmù múlà	úmúfùmú mwòòfi
b.	**íí=m-bùtò**	AU=9-seed	íímbùtò nyírà	íímbùtó nyòfi
c.	**ú=lú-sìkù**	AU=11-day	úlúsìkù lúlà	úlúsìkú lwòòfi

In (3.90) we see that cl. 1a nouns, such as 'grandfather' and 'grandmother', which have no segmental prefix, still seem to have a tonal H prefix which does not link to the cl. 1a noun and remains floating to the left if the noun is L initial. In (3.90a) the noun has initial L tone, while in (3.90b) the noun has initial H tone. Both of these nouns are used in the verb-object construction

---

tone remains. This seems to be the case with **í=kìbùùngù** 'cloud', which has an alternate pronunciation: **í=kíyìbùùngù**. In the case of **ú=mùgózì**, this would suggest derivation from a verb **kúyìgózâ**, though I do not know if such a verb is attested, and have not asked speakers for an evaluation of this option.

bàsìgà 'they left...'. In (3.90a) where the noun is L initial, we see the floated H tone of the L-initial noun linked to the final TBU of the preceding verb, **bàsìgá** 'they left', while in (3.90b) where the noun is H initial, there is no LHS. This indicates that the floated H is deleted when the noun has initial H tone.

(3.90) a. **bàsìgá shòòkùlù**   'they left grandfather'   (LHS applies)
       b. **bàsìgà náákùlù**   'they left their grandmother'   (no LHS)

Further evidence that this floating H is a prefixal tone which has been unable to link is seen in the associative pronouns. LHS applies in the noun-plus-associative pronoun construction in (3.91a) where the tone of the cl. 1 pronominal prefix (**ú**-) is H, and it has not been able to associate to the pronoun itself because the **u** is realized as **w**. LHS is *not* seen in (3.91b) where the tone of the cl. 2 pronominal prefix (**bà**-) is L.

(3.91) a. **úmúfùmú wììtù**   'our doctor'   (LHS applies)
       b. **ábáfùmù bììnyù**   'your (PL) doctor'   (no LHS)

Example (3.92) shows that there is a floating H tone preceding the cl. 2 L-initial adjective **bììngì** 'many', which triggers LHS, but that preceding the associative (possessive) pronoun **bììnyù**, which also has an initial L tone, there is *no* floating H tone, and thus no LHS. This is seen by comparing the final syllable of **á=bákàzì** 'women' in (3.92a) with that in (3.92b). There is no floating H tone preceding the associative pronoun because the cl. 2 *pronominal* prefix does not have a H tone like the adjective prefix, but rather a L tone. This L tone links to the pronoun prefix, leaving no tones floating. LHS cannot take place if there is no floating H tone to shift leftward, so the final syllable of the preceding noun displays the default L tone.

(3.92) a. **á=bákàzí bììngì**   'many women'   (LHS applies)
       b. **á=bákàzì bììnyù**   'your (PL) women'   (no LHS)

3.9 Lexical tone of verbal affixes

3.9.1 Lexical tone of verbal prefixes

There are both derivational and inflectional verbal prefixes. The only derivational prefixes that appear on verbs are the infinitive prefix and the set of subject relative markers, both of which signify that the verbal stem is being used nominally.[134] All of these derivational prefixes have H tones.

---

[134]The subject relative markers, **ú**, **í**, **á** may be interpreted as clitics. The "object relative"

Inflectional prefixes include both subject and object markers, as well as the TAM prefixes, and the negative marker. Inflectional prefixes may be H, L, or toneless. Table 3.4 gives an overview of verbal prefixes and their underlying tones. In table 3.4p, q two separate-word inflectional auxiliaries are included, even though they are not prefixes per se, because their presence is what dictates the tone pattern on the following word of the verb. They are a defining part of the main verb, which retains its full verbal properties in these forms, rather than being expressed as an infinitive.

Table 3.4. Lexical tone of verbal prefixes

	Prefix	Gloss	Underlying tone of pfx.	Example	Gloss
a.	ú=kú	AU=infinitive (cl. 15)	H tones on each	ú=kúgééndà	'to go'
b.	n- | u- | a-	subject prefixes I, you, s/he, etc.	all Ø but can bear gram. T	wàgééndà/ úgéèndà	'you went' 'if you go'
c.	ta-	negative(NEG)	toneless	úkútàgééndà	'not to go'
d.	ká-	unmarked past (P2)	H spreads one TBU to the left	ákágééndà àtákágééndà	'he went' 'he did not go'
e.	gá(a)-	unmarked future (F2)	H spreads one TBU to the left	ágágéèndà àtágágéèndà	'he will go' 'he will not go'
f.	tá-	resultative, frustrated (RS.FRUS)	H spreads one TBU to the left	átágéézīrì àtátágéézīrì	'he had just gone' 'he had not just gone'
g.	à-	recent past (P1)	L	nàgééndà	'I went'
h.	àngà-	conditional/ potential (CND/POT)	LL	nàngàgéénda nàngàgéézìrì	'I would go' 'I would have gone'
i.	ángá-	conditional/ potential contrary-to-fact (CND.C.F.PST)	H H	nángágéézìrì	'I would have gone'
j.	ná-	additive/ sequential	H	nànágéèndà	'and I went'
k.	ká-	subsequent distal (INTV)	H	ùkágéèndè	'...(and then) you will go'

marker is also a clitic, rather than a prefix, e.g. **bó** in the following: **ábándú bó=twààbònà**, literally 'the people (the ones) whom=we saw'.

3.9 Lexical tone of verbal affixes

	Prefix	Gloss	Underlying tone of pfx.	Example	Gloss
l.	kì-	conditional contrary-to-fact subjunctive (CND.C.F.)	H on preceding TBU, L on ki-	úkìgééndè ùtákìgééndè	'if you had gone' 'if you hadn't gone'
m.	kì-	persistive (PERS)	L	ágákìgééndà àkìgéézìrì	'he will still go' 'he is still (having) gone'
n.	Ń- | kú- | mú-	(object PFX) 1SG, 2SG, cl. 1	H	àmúgééndèrà	'he went to/for him'
o.	yì- | tù- | mù- | bà- | gù- etc.	(object PFX) reflexive, 1PL, 2PL, cl. 2, cl. 3, etc.	all L	àbàgééndèrà	'he went to/for them'
p.	ááyè	remote future (F3)	H L (separate word)	wááyè gééndè	'you will go (someday)'
q.	áálí	continuing state past (P3)	HL H (separate word)	twáálí géézīrì	'we were in the state of having gone (P2)'

Note that in row (b) the subject prefixes are all underlyingly toneless. Unless they bear a grammatical H tone or are followed by one of the verbal prefixes discussed below which may spread its tone leftward onto the subject prefix, they have L surface tone, supplied by default L insertion.

The negative marker is also toneless. This is shown by the fact that in cases where it does not occur in a position which conditions a H tone, it is seen with a default L tone, e.g. à-tà-géénd-à 'he did not go' (P1) or kú-tà-géénd-à 'to not go'. Only when it occurs in positions which condition H tone does it have a H tone. Thus, for example, when it precedes a "marked" prefix which assigns a H tone to any morpheme to its left (see following paragraph) the negative marker bears a H tone, e.g. àtákágééndà 'he did not go (before yesterday)', àtágágèèndà 'he will not go', àtátágéézīrì 'he had not just gone (but...)'. If the negative marker had an underlying lexical L tone, the combination of tones on it when it occurs with a H tone (especially one coming from the left, as with the H due to the "marked" prefixes) would result in a LH tone, which preceding a H tone is always realized as L. Since the ta- has a surface H tone preceding these three H prefixes, we can be sure that it does not have underlying L tone, but is toneless.

There are three verbal tense prefixes which spread their tone one TBU to the left, as seen in rows (d–f). These are future (F2) **gá-**, unmarked past (P2) **ká-**, and frustrated resultative (RS.FRUS) **tá-**. In these cases, the tone of the tense prefix is realized on the tense prefix itself *as well as* on whatever syllable is directly to the left of the prefix: always either the subject marker or the negative marker, but not both the negative marker and the subject marker, since the tone spreads only one TBU leftward.[135] The **kì-** prefix of the conditional contrary-to-fact subjunctive (see table 3.4, row l) operates in a similar way, except that the prefix itself bears a L tone while the TBU to its left is assigned a H tone.

There is also prefix with a H tone which does not spread one TBU to the left. This is not technically a tense marker, but the intervening time marker **ká-**.

The data in (3.93 b, d) take the example of the future (F2) tense prefix, and by contrasting it with recent past (P1) forms (3.93 a, c), show how these left-spreading prefixes project a H tone onto whatever morpheme is directly to their left. Note that there is no H tone on the first-person plural subject prefix, **tu-** (**tw-** before a vowel) in (3.93a, c, or d) but that the subject prefix does have H tone in (3.93b) where it is directly to the left of the F2 prefix **gá-**. Note that the toneless negative marker **ta-**, which had L tone in the P1 form in (3.93c) bears the H tone in (3.93d) since it now comes directly to the left of the F2 prefix. In (3.93d) the subject marker **tu-** has its normal default L tone since it is no longer directly to the left of the F2 **gá-** prefix.

(3.93) a. Recent past (P1) **tw-à-fùkám-à** (1PL-P1-kneel-Fa) 'we knelt'
b. Future (F2) **tú-gá-fùkàm-à** (1PL-F2-kneel-Fa) 'we will kneel'
c. P1 with negative **tù-tà-fùkám-à** (1PL-NEG+P1-kneel-Fa) 'we didn't kneel'
d. F2 with negative **tù-tá-gá-fùkàm-à** (1PL-NEG-F2-kneel-Fa) 'we will not kneel'

There are other cases, however, where the subject prefix is assigned a H tone, which, when used with a timeless or resultative form, signals a subjunctive usage.[136] The H tone on the subject prefix always indicates conditionality

---

[135]Cheryl Black points out that this is similar to the H tone anticipation found in Kinande prefixes (another Bantu J language) as described in Mutaka (1990) and Black (1995). In Kifuliiru, there is one other H tone tense/mood prefix, which does not trigger H tone anticipation, so H-tone anticipation is perhaps not a general rule of the language in this case, but a property of these specific prefixes.

[136]It is interesting that the timeless, simple resultative, and subjunctive forms are the only forms which have a null tense marker following a subject prefix.

3.9 Lexical tone of verbal affixes

or some action or state not yet realized. In all the forms with this H-tone subject prefix, the stem-tone pattern is always the V₂ pattern. This is the same pattern used with all subjunctive forms which have any prefix other than a simple toneless subject marker. The use of this tone pattern in these forms with a H-tone subject marker indicates that these are subjunctive forms, by virtue of the H tone on the prefix, even though they do not use the subjunctive FV -**e**. The stem-tone pattern on the non-subjunctive forms, without the H subject prefix is in each case complex HL. Examples are found in (3.94), where the first of each pair shows the form with the unmarked L-tone prefix, and the second of the pair shows the use of the marked H-tone prefix:

(3.94) a. Timeless (no H tone on subject when used with **máángò** 'time when') **máángò tùláálíkà** 'when(ever) we invite'

w/H prefix (and without **máángò** 'time when') **túlààlìkà** 'if/when we invite'

b. Timeless (w/NEG) **àtààlì yéèhè** 'it is not he'
w/H prefix **átàlì yéèhê** 'if it is not he'

c. Timeless (w/NEG plus **ná** 'and') **tùtànáyìkàrábà** 'and we did not wash'

w/H prefix **tútànáyìkàràbà** 'if we have not also washed'

d. Timeless (w/**tazi** 'not yet') **tùtàzì híkà** 'we have not yet arrived'

w/H prefix **tútàzì híkà** 'if we have not yet arrived'

e. Resultative **tùbwátîìrì** 'we were sitting'
w/H prefix **túbwàtììrì** 'if we are sitting'

As noted in row (n) of table 3.4 the singular "personal" object markers (first-through third-person singular) all have H tone, while all the other object markers, represented in row (o) of table 3.4, including the reflexive **yì**-, have L tone. Because the first-person singular object marker consists only of a nasal, it cannot bear its own H tone, and this tone is realized on the prefix directly to its left. For example, observe the tone of the negative **ta**-. In (3.95a) the ta- has L tone, while in (3.95b) it bears the H tone of the following H-toned first-person singular object prefix, **n-**.

(3.95) a. à- tà- shúlìk -à 'he did not hit (anyone)'

b. à- tá- n- júlìk -à 'he did not hit <u>me</u>'

In (3.96), taken from the context of a traditional narrative, the L-toned conditional contrary-to-fact prefix **kì-** appears with surface H tone due to the following first-person singular object marker, in **úkímbwìrìrè** 'if you had told me'.

(3.96) **Ú-<u>kí-m</u>-bwìr-ìr-è**   **háá-hà-lyá** ‖ **ngá= n-dà-gù-sìg-à** |
2SG-C.F-O1.SG-tell-APL-Fe   E-16-there.R   then= 1SG-NEG-O3-leave-Fa

kú= kì-ryá kí-tì.
17= 7-that.R 7-tree

'If you had told me right there ‖ then I would not have left it (my heart) | at that tree.' (12.026)

3.9.2 Lexical tone of verbal suffixes

Derivational suffixes on verbs include all the typical Bantu "extensions" such as applicative, reciprocal/comitative, reversive, etc. These are all toneless except for the passive **-u** and causative **-i**, both of which are H toned (see 3.5.1.2 for discussion, as well as examples in the causative/ passive sections under each stem-tone pattern in 3.5.3). Inflectional suffixes include the resultative **-ir**, and the FV, both of which are toneless. In most non-subjunctive cases the FV is **-a**, in subjunctive it is usually **-e**, and in the resultative forms, which have the resultative **-ir**, the FV is **-i**.[137] The suffixes in table 3.5 are listed basically in order of occurrence from left to right, though the extensions within the first row are not presented in any special order, and the final vowels, including the final **-i** of the resultative, occur only in final position (in mutually exclusive distribution).

---

[137]Speakers from some areas are influenced by Mashi and pronounce the final vowel of the resultative form as **-e** rather than **-i**, but the standard Kifuliiru form is **-i**. However, **-e** is the more usual form of the resultative FV in most other present-day Bantu languages, as well as the proposed proto-form of this morpheme.

3.9 Lexical tone of verbal affixes

Table 3.5. Lexical tone of verbal suffixes

Suffix	Meaning/Gloss	UT
-ir/-er | -an | -am | -(u)ul/ -(o)ol |-(u)uk/-(o)ok | -ik/-ek | -at | -al | etc.	applicative, reciprocal, positional, reversive (TRANS), reversive (intr.), neuter/impositive, contactive, extensive, etc.	Ø
-ir-i	resultative[a]	Ø
-í/-iisí	causative (CS)-	H on (final) - i
-ú (following C) -bú (following V)	passive (PS)	H
-a	FV	Ø
-e	FV (SBV)	Ø

[a]This suffix is traditionally called the perfective ending in the original terminology of Bantu studies.

In the examples in (3.97) the toneless verbal extensions, exemplified by applicative -**ir**, (as well as by -**am**, which is lexicalized as a part of the root in the L verb) are assigned grammatical suffix tones either by initial tone association or by the rules of H or L spread, and thus reflect the stem-tone pattern of each verbal form. All underlined syllables in (3.97) bear either a grammatical stem tone or a tone spread from that tone. H-spread can be seen in the INF + APL + PS row where the H grammatical tone of the infinitive form's simple stem-tone pattern is seen on the extension(s). L-spread is noted in all the F2 rows, where the grammatical L tone of the future's (F2) V_2 stem tone pattern is reflected on the extension(s). A look at the FV in passive (PS) forms also illustrates the point that the passive extension, underlyingly -**ú** but on the surface -**w**, has a H tone which shows up on the FV in these forms.[138] The inflected forms in (3.97) all have cl. 1 subject marking, **a-**.

---

[138]The passive H tone is realized on the FV in stem-tone patterns which have only one tone, which links to the leftmost free TBU. In passive forms of tenses which have a "complex" stem-tone pattern, i.e., a pattern with a final-linking grammatical tone in addition to the left-linking grammatical tone, the H of passive ends up associated to the mora to the left of the FV, though its presence is sometimes neutralized by contour simplification rules.

(3.97)   H-tone verb   L-tone verb
Infinitive   **kúgá<u>lú</u>kà** **kúfù<u>ká</u>mà**
Gloss   'to return'   'to kneel'
INF + APL + PS   kú-gá<u>lúk</u>-ír-w-â   kú-fù<u>kám</u>-ír-w-â
F2   á-gáá-gá<u>lù</u>k-à   á-gá-fù<u>kà</u>m-à
F2 + APL   á-gá-gá<u>lùk</u>-ìr-à á-gá-fù<u>kàm</u>-ìr-à
F2 + APL + PS   á-gá-gá<u>lùk</u>-ìr-w-â   á-gá-fù<u>kàm</u>-ìr-w-â

3.10 Tone on nouns

3.10.1 Lexical tone in noun affixes

Nominal prefixes, and in some cases, suffixes,[139] have their own lexical tones. Both the augment and nominal concord prefix in all classes have a lexical H tone, e.g. **í=kí-rèmà** (AU=7-cripple) 'crippled person'.[140] The H tone of the nominal prefix(es) never spreads onto the noun stem/root, presumably because the lexical tone of the noun is linked to the leftmost free TBU in the stem.

In the case of V-initial noun roots (and V-initial adjective roots as well), however, there is interaction between the prefix tone and the root tone.[141] The vowel coalescence which results from the addition of a V-final prefix to a V-initial noun root may result in tone perturbation. Since the prefixes have H tone, the two tones interacting at such boundaries are always either HL or HH. The coalescence of a H prefix with any L-initial root results in an initial LH. The coalescence of a H prefix with a HL root results in HL.

---

[139]Underived nouns do not have suffixes, but many nouns derived from verbs do involve derivational suffixes. Most nominal suffixes seem to be toneless or perhaps L, while others bear H surface tone. Stative verbal adjectives (a type of deverbal adjectives) have a final H-toned -**e** suffix. Many such words have been lexicalized as nouns, and still exhibit the final H tone. More analysis could be done on H-final nouns.

[140]More research could be done on cl. 1a/2a. In cl. 1a there is no true segmental prefix, but there does seem to be a non-segmental H-tone prefix, as shown by the occurrence of leftward H-shift preceding cl. 1a nouns which have initial L surface tone. As for other classes, there are certain surface exceptions to the fact that a prefix bears H tone, most of which result from vowel coalescence between the vowel of the prefix and the first vowel of a L-toned V-initial stem, and the subsequent elision of the prefix tone in favor of a L-tone on the initial syllable of the noun (e.g. **ú=bú-ìtègèèrèzè** > **ú=bwìtègèèrèzè** (AU=14-wisdom), a deverbal noun which includes part of the L-tone reflexive marker as the initial syllable). There are also a limited number of exceptions which may be actual exceptions, such as **ú=mù-gózì** (AU=3-rope).

[141]Such interaction never occurs at morpheme boundaries in verbs because there are no V-initial verb roots. All verb roots which are V initial in PB are in Kifuliiru given an epenthetic initial **y**.

The perturbation H + L > LH in the root-initial syllable of a V-initial noun can be seen in such words as the cl. 11 **ú=lwīījì**, from **ú=lú-ìji** (AU=11-river) 'river', cl. 6 **ámīījì**, from **á=má-ìji** (AU=6-water) 'water', and cl. 1 **ú=mwāānà**, from **ú=mú-àna** (AU=1-child) 'child'. In accordance with the LH simplification rules (3.8.2.1), when LH is followed by a H tone, it is realized as L, as seen in **mwìtání**, from **mú-ìtáni** (1-murderer) 'murderer', derived from the reciprocal form of the L-tone verb **-yìt-an-** (-kill-RCP-) 'kill (each) other'.

The combination H + HL > HL can be seen in V-initial nouns such as the cl. 3 noun **ú=mwîìmbù** (from **ú=mú-îìmbu**) (AU=3=harvest) 'harvest', derived from the H-tone verb **-yíímbul-** 'harvest'.

3.10.2 Lexical tone in noun roots

There are four underlying tone patterns in underived nouns, as seen in (3.98). These are H(H), L(L), LH, and HL. The maximum number of basic tone patterns found in bisyllabic noun stems of three or fewer surface morae is four.[142] Nouns of different CV configurations are listed separately.[143] We assume edge-in linking and a two-tone nominal melody for underived nouns.

---

[142] In noun stems of three or more syllables, there are some exceptional patterns, including a number of compound nouns which demonstrate combinations of the tonal patterns plus prefixes e.g. (**mú-tó-kì-íkò** H-H LH L 'ashes', from **mú-tò** 'lesser one', and **kí-ìkò> kìíkò** (phonetically **kííkò**) 'fireplace').

[143] Nouns of more than two syllables tend to be compound or derived from verbs, so their tone patterns are more complex. They are included here for comparison.

(3.98) Tone patterns in C-initial noun stems

Stem morae	Stem syllables	H	HL	L	LH
1	1 CV	úú=bú- lá AU=14-intestine	----------	úú=bú- là AU=14-length	----------
2	2 CV-CV	í=kí-rígò AU=7-spring	----------	í=kí-rìmì AU=7-sore.throat	----------
3	2 CVV-(N)CV	í=kí-háángò AU=7-patch	í=kí-húùmbù AU=7-fox	í=kí-hììzà AU=7-round.house	í=kí-haāngò AU=7-covenant
3	3 CV-CV-CV	í=kí-mínìkà AU=7-epidemic	í=kí-kómèrè AU=7-wound	í=kí-nògòshò AU=7-hoof	í=kí-shàkúlò AU=-7-mortar
4	3 CV-(N)C VV-CV	í=kí-bólóógò AU=7-shouting	í=kí-tángààzà† AU=7-sthg. amazing	í=kí-bòndòòlà AU=7-field. fertile.again	í=kí-gàndáárò AU=7-funeral. wake
4	3 CVV-(N) CV-CV	í=kí-rííndímà AU=7-weasel-like.animal	í=n-góóránè AU=9-trouble	í=kí-kòòjòkà AU=7-broken-off.piece	í=kí-gùùngúlì AU=7-person.without.family
4/5	4 C(G)V-CV(V)-CV(V)-CV	í=kí-shókóólólò AU=7-thicket	í=kí-gúkùzìmù AU=7-ant	í=kí-bèrèkàànà AU=7-hot.fire	ú=mú-jwàngárárò AU=3-uneasiness

†This word is derived from a verb, and the tones here may reflect the verbal relative construction rather than a nominal tone pattern. Most nouns which have this CVCVVCV syllable pattern and a H tone on the first syllable of the stem seem to have a H HL L tone pattern on the stem, e.g. á=kà-vútáàlè (AU=12-chameleon) or í=kìhúhúùtà (AU=7-strong. stormy.wind) rather than a H LL L pattern as shown here. The L in the HL contour of these latter forms probably reflects edge-in linking of a lexical L tone to the right-hand node of the penultimate.

3.10 *Tone on nouns* 255

We posit that in nouns with monosyllabic stems, such as those in first row of (3.98), the final syllable is not extratonal at the time of initial tone association. For this reason, the final syllable of such a word may bear either a H or a L tone.

In cl. 5 nouns with monosyllabic stems and LL underlying tone pattern, e.g. **í=ì-gì** (AU=5-egg), (PL **mágì**), it is possible to see that the initial tone of a monosyllabic noun stem associates to the prefix syllable. Cl. 5 is unique in that its usual nominal prefix consists not of CV but only of V. Because the prefix is V only, the addition of the augment, which also consists only of a vowel, increases the mora count by one, but does not add another syllable to the noun. It does, however, result in a bimoraic penult, on which tonal contours may surface.

In the case of monosyllabic cl. 5 stems, the augment always seems to be included in citation forms in order to add a mora.[144] The initial syllable, consisting of the augment plus prefix, each of which consists of **i-**, is added to the stem before tone association, in order to provide the minimal two syllables necessary for a stem and the minimum of two non-extratonal TBUs necessary for tone assignment. The augment and prefix each has its own tone, while a noun stem has two tones. So even if one assumes that in a noun with a monosyllabic stem the final syllable is assigned a tone in initial tone association, there are still three tones competing for linking on the initial (and at the same time, penultimate) syllable. The initial tone of the noun stem is associated to the prefix syllable, along with the H tone of the prefix. We assume that the H of the augment is first shunted leftward by lexical H float and then deleted because of the following H tone (3.8.5). Examples of cl. 5 nouns in which a lexical L of the noun stem occurs on a prefix are **í=ì-rò** (AU=5-sleep), **í=ì-twè** (AU=5=head), **í=ì-ndà** (AU=9=louse), etc.,[145] as seen in derivation (3.99).

---

[144]In cases where the augment is precluded, such as following a locative marker or a copula, the monosyllabic stem is encliticized to the preceding word and receives a lengthened initial vowel by the rule of clitic-related vowel lengthening (2.3.1.2.5).

[145]It is only in monomoraic stems like this where there is a long vowel in the penultimate syllable that tones are definitely observed to link leftward across the boundary between the prefixes and the stem, though it may happen in other cases of monomoraic stems, such as **i=kí-mí ~ í=kí-mé** (AU=7-dew) or **í=ín-dá** (AU=9-abdomen). In such cases, the fact that the stem tone is H, just as the prefix tones are, makes it impossible to tell audially if the stem tone is linking across boundaries. The linking of stem tones on a prefix syllable can be observed in monomoraic verbs where there is a bimoraic penultimate prefix syllable, such as in **twàmúù=mwà** 'we are shaving (someone)'.

(3.99) í=ì-rò (AU=5-sleep) 'sleep' (LL)

    UF **iiro**
       |\ |
       | \ |
    HH LL   H of augment, H of noun prefix, lexical
     ↓   L L of noun
     Ø   by Lexical H-float (b)

    SF **îìrò**
      || |
    HL L

Straightforward nouns with bisyllabic stems were discussed under 3.3.2 and will not be revisited here. For nouns consisting of three or more syllables, especially the derived and compound nouns, it is difficult to determine the number of underlying tones and the manner in which tones are associated. Further research would be needed to make any comprehensive statement as to how the tone of these longer forms is assigned. Compounds such as **í=kígúkùzìmù**, the HL four-syllable noun given in (3.98), seem to have a combination of two nominal tonal patterns, or in the case of a noun derived from a verb plus a noun, of a verbal pattern plus a nominal pattern. Nouns of three or more syllables which are not compounds are generally derived from extended verbs, as are the remaining three- and four-syllable nouns in (3.98).

We assume edge-in linking for the nouns simply because this has been shown to be the case in verbs and we have no reason to believe that it is not the case for nouns as well. The tone patterns in at least some derived nouns, e.g. **bú-dérédéèndè** (14-few.remaining.things) give evidence for edge-in linking. Since the L tone of a HL contour on the penult of a noun is never produced by rules, but only results from an underlying HL contour, such a contour in the penult of a four-syllable noun must be produced by the initial linking of a L tone to the final active TBU. Edge-in linking of a HL pattern, followed by rightward tone spread would produce the tone configuration of a noun like **bú-dérédéèndè**.

Another question to consider is whether the monomoraic penult of a noun can bear two tones, as that of verbs can. Looking at a deverbal noun such as **kí-tóbérò** (7-food.fed.to.animals) (from the H verb **kútóbérà** 'to feed animals') it is most natural to assume that it has a HH pattern. However, if the penultimate syllable of a noun has two nodes for tone association, and if we assume that T-spread will spread the H tone of the antepenult onto the penult as we saw to be the case in verbs, the underlying pattern in such a noun could be either HH or HL. Assuming tone spread, if the melody of the noun were HH,

3.10 Tone on nouns

the underlying tone on the antepenult would be H and on the penult, HH. If, on the other hand, the melody of the noun were HL, the antepenult would have an underlying H, while the penult would have an underlying HL, with the right node linked to the L, and the left node linked by T-spread to the H tone. Since a HL is realized as H on a single mora, this would mean that the HH and HL patterns would merge in a noun with a monomoraic penult.

There are nouns such as **mú-jōkà** (3-snake) in which a stem-initial penultimate syllable has an underlying LH contour, which surfaces as a mid tone. This contour, however would be the result of an underlying LH pattern, both tones of which associate to the penultimate syllable. LH contours in a non-stem-initial position, produced by tone spread are not attested. Instead we find nouns such as **ká-gúlìrò** (12-market) in which spreading of the stem-initial H tone would result in a LH (mid) tone on the penultimate syllable. However, instead of LH tone, the tone on this syllable is L. This could mean that tone spread will not target the left node of a penultimate of which only the right node is linked. It could alternatively mean that there are more than two underlying tones in such a noun, and that both nodes of the penultimate are linked by initial tone association.

Looking at a noun with a bimoraic penult, in the cl. 14 noun **bú-gáshààne** (14-blessing) derived from the L verb -**gàshaan**- 'be blessed', we see a H tone on the antepenult and a L tone on the (bimoraic) penult. This indicates that T-spread does not target the left-hand node of the penultimate even in a case where the penult is bimoraic. The only reason for this, if such spreading follows the pattern found in verbs, would be that this left node has already been linked to a tone by initial tone association.

There are two possible reasons that the left node of the penultimate in such a noun would be already linked at the time of T-spread's application. One option would be to posit that linking in nouns is not edge-in, and that such a noun has only a two-tone nominal melody. If such were the case, the two tones of the nominal melody would link from left to right, the first being associated to the initial TBU of the stem, and the second linking directly following it, on the left node of the penultimate. The other option would be to posit that there are more than two tones underlyingly, at least in deverbal nouns. This assumption is compatible with edge-in linking. These three tones would theoretically include the tone of the original verb radical, and the remaining tones could be either a holdover stem-tone pattern from a verbal form or nominal overlay melody.

In deverbal nouns which have a bimoraic penult, we find penults having not only LL and HH but also HL.[146] The one solution that works for deverbal

---

[146]The fact that in my [not recently compiled] list there are no LH penults in nouns with three or more stem syllables may mean nothing more than that they were elicited from a speaker

nouns of all three of the tone patterns attested in the penults is that of assuming three underlying tones. Because there are not only nouns like **bú-gáshàànè** (14-blessing) and **kí-bólóógò** (7-wailing.of.many.people) with LL and HH penults, but also nouns like **kígógóòlwà** (7-fresh.bark.of.banana. plant) with a HL contour in the penultimate syllable, we could posit an underlying three-tone pattern. Thus there might be a HHL melody in a noun like **kí-gógóòlwà**, while **bú-gáshàànè** or **ká-gúnùùzà** (12-great.hardship) would require a three-tone melody of HLL.

Example (3.100) shows more nouns with three or more morae in the stem, with various syllable and mora patterns. These are nouns for which the usually-assumed two-tone nominal patterns, with edge-in linking, followed by T-spread of the leftmost tone would adequately explain the tone patterns. A three-tone pattern would also be explanatory in these nouns. Tones on the nominal prefixes, all cl. 7 in (3.100) unless otherwise labeled, are all H. The final tone in each case is a default L. The numbers 1, 2, 3 above the columns refer to syllable positions in the stem. LL, HH, LH, etc. listed together in a single column indicates a bimoraic syllable.

(3.100) Tone in multisyllabic nouns of various CV patterns

UT	(1)	(2)	(3)	Final Syll.	Noun	Gloss
HH	HH			L	kí-fúúlà	'fallow field'
HH	H	H		L	kí-míníkà	'epidemic'
HH	H	HH		L	kí-bólóógò	'cry (of many together)'
HH	HH	H	H	L	kí-rííndí-mà	'weasel-like animal'
HH	H	HH	H	L	kí-shókóólólò	'thicket'
LL	LL			L	kí-hììzà	'round house'
LL	L	L		L	kí-nògòshò	'hoof'
LL	L	LL		L	kí-bòndòòlà	'fallow field, fertile again'
LL	LL	L		L	kí-kòòjòkà	'small broken-off piece'
LL	L	L	LL	L	kí-bèrèkàànà	'big fire with hot coals'
HL	HL			L	kí-shóòlà	'small remote village'
HL	H	HL		L	kí-vúléèrwè	'lack of sunshine'
HL	H	HL		L	mú-jámbîìrà	'1-slimmed-down person'

whose pronunciation of LH was not especially easy to hear.

UT	(1)	(2)	(3)	Final Syll.	Noun	Gloss
LH	LH			L	**kí-hāāngò**	'covenant'
LH	L	H		L	**kí-shàkúlò**	'mortar for grinding'
LH	L	HH		L	**kí-gàndáárò**	'funeral wake'
LH	LL	H		L	**kí-gùùngúlì**	'person w/o family'

The nouns in (3.101) are some of those which, assuming edge-in linking, would argue for more than two underlying tones.

(3.101) Tone patterns not explainable by two underlying tones

UT	(1)	(2)	(3)	Final syll.	Noun	Gloss
HLL	H	L		L	**ká-gúlìrò**	'market'
HLL	H	HL		L	**kí-tángààzà**	'amazing thing'
HLL	H	HL		L	**kí-gúkùzìmù**	'ant (sp.)'
LHH	L	H	H	L	**mú-jwàngárárò**	'uneasiness'
LHLH	L	HL[†]		H	**n-gùngúùlâ**	'battle between armies'

[†]This example seems to violate the rule by which HL is realized as H following a L, and is probably a compound, of which the final segment is a monosyllabic clitic.

3.10.2.1 H final nouns

As noted in the basic overview of nominal tone characteristics given in (3.3.2), the usual case is for a noun to have a final L tone in isolation. However, there are nouns which have a final H tone, and some observations can be made about them.[147] Nearly without exception, nouns with a final H tone fall into one of five categories. The final H tone in the last two categories of these seems to come from a H-toned suffix. The five categories of H final nouns are these:

---

[147]Out of a random group of 1,500 nouns, 106, or about 7 percent, had H tone on the final syllable. Of these, twenty had monosyllabic roots (in which the final mora is not toneless), thirty-nine ended in a suffixal H-toned **-e**, thirty-one had an ending which contained a glide (**w** or **y**) or a causative-type morpheme. This leaves only sixteen (just over 1 percent) as "exceptional", with no obvious reason for their H-tone ending. Note that a final H tone is given a short falling contour when in utterance final position.

- Monomoraic roots which have H lexical tone, e.g. **á=má-tê** (AU=6-saliva). The final syllable of a monomoraic noun root is not extratonal, and bears a lexical tone, either H or L.
- Loan words from French, such as **àrìjâ** 'silver', from the French 'argent', which are accented in French on the final syllable.
- A type of nickname, shortened name, or "label" for a certain type of person. Many of these words are cl. 1a, e.g. **Sèngô** (shortened nickname form of the proper name **Sèngòróóngè**).
- Nouns which are substantively used stative verbal adjectives. These adjectives all have a tone pattern consisting of the tone of the verb radical, a L tone which follows this and spreads rightward, and a final H-toned -**é** suffix. Examples are **máhòòyê** 'person talked about a lot', **kítàbìkê** 'wide, expansive thing'.
- Some of the nouns derived from verbs which have a causative or passive extension also have a final H tone. Passive and causative morphemes in verbs are analyzed as having an underlying H tone. It is not clear just how this carries over into nouns, but especially from examples such as (3.102d), one might posit that there is still a H tone connected with the causative morpheme in this noun, since there is no H tone to the left which could spread onto the FV. However, no organized study has been done on the way verbal extension tone relates to tone on the nouns derived from them. It is clear from examples (3.102e, f) that the H tones of CS and PS are not always present in a nominal form. Examples of words in which the H extension tone seems to carry over into the noun are seen in (3.102a–d).

(3.102)

	H-final noun	Gloss	Related verb	Gloss
a.	**í=ígézô**	'trial'	**kú-gé-z-â**	15-try-CS-Fa
b.	**í=kífúúsô**	'means of escape'	**kú-fúú-s-â**	15-escape-CS-Fa
c.	**á=kátyábírízô**	'thunder'	**kú-tyábírí-z-â**	15-thunder-CS-Fa
d.	**í=kyèèrèsô**	'sign'	**kú-yèèré-s-â**	15-show-CS-Fa
e.	**ú=múbùtìrwà**	'native (of a place)'	**kú-bùt-ír-w-â**	15-give.birth-APL-PS-Fa
f.	**ú=múbùgùzà**	'tax.collector'	**kú-bùgú-z-â**	15-pay.fee-CS-Fa

3.11 Tone on other parts of speech

In general, it can be noted that only verbs seem limited to a single tone on their underlying radical. Other parts of speech may have more than one underlying tone. A few observations will be noted in this section regarding the tonal behavior of adjectives, demonstratives, associative markers, and numerals.

3.11.1 Tone on adjectives

The adjective prefixes, just as the nominal prefixes, are all posited to have an underlying H tone. In the case of adjectives whose stems begin with a consonant, the H tone of the adjective prefix associates to the prefix, e.g. **ú=lúsìkù lúgùmà** 'one day', **áá=kábwá kásírè** 'the mad dog', etc.

In cases where the adjective stem begins with a vowel, there is coalescence between the vowel of the prefix and the initial vowel of the stem, or the vowel of the prefix is changed to a glide, i.e. **y** or **w**. In these cases, if the stem has an underlying L (e.g. -**òfì** 'short', cf. **ú=múúndú mwòòfì** 'the short person') or LH tone (e.g. -**èérù** 'white', cf. **áá=kábwá kēērù** 'the white dog'), the H tone of the prefix is not realized on the prefix when the adjective is used in context, but rather is shifted leftward, linking to the final mora of any preceding word within the phrase **ú=múkàzì** 'woman' versus **ú=múkàzí mwòòfì** 'short woman' (3.12.3). If a vowel-initial adjective stem begins with an underlying H tone (e.g. -**íìjá** 'good', cf. **ú=lúsìkù lwíìjâ** 'the good day') the resulting adjective has an initial H tone and there is no leftward H-shift.

The adjective stems, like nouns, are posited to have an underlying one- or two-tone melody of H, HL, LH, or L (for a listing of the basic adjectives with surface tones see Vol.2, 4.1.1). A few examples of adjectives with C-initial and V-initial stems are provided in (3.103). Note in these examples that a V-initial adjective stem with an initial L tone, such as -**òfì** 'short', though pronounced with all L tones in context when following a noun, e.g. **ú=múúndú mwòòfì** 'the short person', in isolation form, it is somewhat difficult to judge the pitch of the initial syllable. In (3.103) it is transcribed as L.

(3.103) Samples of Kifuliiru adjectives with concord

Cl.	-bì 'bad'	-káyù 'fierce'	-íjá 'good'	-òfì 'short'
1	múbì	múkáyù	mwíìjâ	mwòòfì
2	bábì	bákáyù	bíìjâ	bòòfì
3	múbì	múkáyù	mwíìjâ	mwòòfì

The class of words which we call stative verbal adjectives are productively derived from verbs and have a more verbal tonal configuration. These forms are most often used following a copula, constituting what might be called a predicate adjective or participle. Though they take the adjective prefixes with typical H tone, the tone on the stem itself is a more typically verbal pattern. The underlying tone of the verb, if any, appears on the first syllable of the stem, followed by L tones which spread over the rest of the non-final syllables. In the case of a toneless verb, all non-final stem syllables have L tone. The final suffix is H toned -**é**. One example is **mú-hàmìk-ê** (3-closed.securely-Fe) from **-hàmik-** 'close securely'.

(3.104) Some stative verbal adjectives

UT	Verb base	Gloss	Derived adj. (cl. 7)	Gloss
Ø	-baaj-	'carve wood'	**kíbààjé**	'carved'
L	-bààngik-	'stick together'	**kíbààngìké**	'stuck together'
H	-láámbik-	'lay out'	**kíláámbìké**	'laid out'

3.11.2 Tone on demonstratives

Demonstratives include all the members of the word class which when used attributively, precedes the noun, and which uses the set of demonstrative[148] prefixes. This includes all the words which express the normal deictic meanings of demonstratives, e.g. this, that, etc. (7.7) as well as **-ndi** 'other' (different set) and the set of words formed like **ú=wààbò** 'fellow'.

The demonstrative prefixes of classes 1, 4, and 9 (the only classes for which the demonstrative prefix in most cases[149] consists only of a vowel) have an underlying H tone (see discussion preceding (3.106)), while those of other classes have a L tone. The H-tone prefix in classes 1, 4, and 9 can be seen in (3.105), where prefixes with H tones are underlined. Compare especially the prefix of cl. 1, where the prefix has H tone, with that of cl. 3, which, though segmentally the same, has L tone. Prefixes of classes 2, 3, and 7, shown in (3.105), are representative tonally of the prefixes of all the other classes.

---

[148]The demonstrative prefixes are also used for the enumeratives and for the pronominals.

[149]The only case in which the demonstrative prefix has a CV shape in cl. 1, 4, and 9, is when used with **-ndì** 'other', in which case a **g** is added, as shown in the first column of the examples in (3.105).

3.11 Tone on other parts of speech

(3.105) Cl. -**ndi** 'another'

		Copulative 'It's that one (distal)'	Attributive 'that...' (distal)	Gloss
1	ú=gúù-ndì	ú-līīrà	ú-lììrá múúndù	'that.D person'
4	í=gíì-ndì	í-rīīrà	í-rììrá míkóóndè	'those.D bananas'
9	í=gíì-ndì	í-rīīrà	í-rììrá nyúùmbà	'that.D house'
2	á=bààndì	bà-líírà	bà-líírá báándù	'those.D people'
3	ú=gùù-ndì	gù-líírà	gù-líírá múkóóndè	'that.D banana'
7	í=kìì-ndì	kì-ríírà	kì-ríírá kíjúúmbù	'that.D potato'

In the distal forms in (3.105), if one compares the attributive (pre-noun) forms, it might appear that MR is applying, since the H tone on the first mora of the stem of the demonstrative seems to be lowered following the H-tone prefix, e.g. **gùlíírá múkóóndè** 'that.D bananas', but **úlììrá múúndù** 'that.D person'. However, note the H tone on the final syllable of each attributive form. The rule of postlexical H-spread (3.12.1) has spread a H tone from the preceding syllable onto the final syllable of the demonstrative, e.g. **úlììrá múúndù**. This is yet another indication that rather than an instance of MR application, this is instead a case of an underlying LH tone on the demonstrative stem. The LH is subject to LH raising (LH > H/L_ L or #) and so appears as H following the L-tone prefixes, e.g. **gùlíírà**. It is only following the H-tone prefix where it surfaces as a LL (preceding a H tone, because of LH lowering, e.g. **úlììrá múúndù**) or as LH (between a H and a L, e.g. **úlīīrà**).[150]

That the final mora of forms such as cl. 1 **úlììrá** and cl. 4/9 **írììrá** has H tone when used attributively, i.e. preceding a noun, is most probably only an indication that the H of the underlying LH melody is allowed to spread onto the final mora (by postlexical H-spread) when the demonstrative is not final in its phrase.

A significant feature of demonstratives is the use of a syntactic tonal overlay. Two of the demonstrative forms, the proximal contrastive (**ùùnó/úúnò, bànó/bánò, gùnó/gúnò** 'this.P.C', etc.) forms, and proximal (**ùùyú/úúyù, yàbá/yábà, yùgú/yúgù** 'this.P', etc.) have two different replacive tonal overlays, chosen according to their two different syntactic usages, as shown in (3.106). This overlay is LH for attributive (e.g. 'this' man', 'this' dog', etc.) or

---

[150] LH > L/_ H, and LH > H/L_L, or L _# or #_ L. LH is pronounced as LH (a non-contoured mid tone) only in the environment /H_L.

substantive/pronominal use, e.g. 'this (one)', and HL for copulative use (i.e. when it means 'It is this/that one'). These forms do not exhibit any underlying lexical tone apart from that which is assigned according to this syntactic usage. The patterns override any other tones on prefixes or on the word as a whole. These patterns, seen in (3.106a, b) are the same for all classes.

(3.106)

Gloss	Attributive (pre-noun)			Copulative or isolation		
	Cl. 1	Cl. 2	Cl. 3	Cl. 1	Cl. 2	Cl. 3
a. this (contrast. proximal)	ùùnó	bànó	gùnó	úúnò	bánò	gúnò
b. this (proximal)	ùùyú	yàbá	yùgú	úúyù	yábà	yúgù
c. this (nearby)	ùùyó	yàbó	yùgwó	ùùyó	yàbó	yùgwó
d. that (remote)	ùùlyá	bàlyá	gùlyá	ùùlyá	bàlyá	gùlyá
e. that (distal)	úlìirá	bàlíírá	gùlíírá	úlīirà	bàlíírà	gùlíírà

The nearby demonstrative forms (**ùùyó, yàbó, yùgwó**, etc.) and the remote forms (**ùùlyá, bàlyá, gùlyá**, etc.) seen in (3.106c, d) do not exhibit the syntactic overlay. They use a standard LH tone in both attributive and copulative forms. There is no variation in tone between classes, either in the tone of the prefixes or of the stem/word.

The distal demonstrative forms for (**úlīirà, bàlíírà** 'that.D/those.D', etc.) seen in (3.106e) are also most simply analyzed as not having the syntactic overlay.[151] They have a single tonal configuration in both attributive and copulative forms. This is an underlying LH tone, the H of which spreads onto the final syllable in the attributive form, due to post lexical H-spread, because they are not phrase final but rather followed by a noun. However, in the distal forms, each class prefix also has its own underlying tone: H in classes 1, 4, and 9, and L in the other classes.

The demonstrative form 'other' (**gúùndì, bàándì**, etc. exemplified in (3.105)) also uses one standard tonal configuration for both attributive and copulative use, but the stem in this case has L tone, while the tone of the prefixes varies by class, with cl. 1, 4, and 9 prefixes having H tone, and the prefixes of the remaining classes having L tone.

---

[151] Assuming a basic LH stem with L or H prefixes, according to class, and then putting on a LH or HL suffixal overlay would also give the correct output, if one assumed no extratonal vowels, and the application of T-drop in initial tone assignment.

3.11.3 Tone on associative markers

The associative marker (A.M) and the conjunctive morpheme, **na** 'CNJ' which is basically a non-agreeing associative marker[152] seem to be underlyingly toneless at the lexical level, but at the postlexical level, both exhibit polar tone, so that they are H toned before a noun beginning with a L tone, and L before a noun beginning with a H tone, e.g. **á=bììrà bà=dáàtà** 'the friends of father', **ú=lúsìkù lwàà=kánà** 'the fourth day', versus **á=bììrà bá=shòòkùlù** 'the friends of grandfather', **ú=lúsìkù lwá=kàbìrì** 'the second day'.

Because of its usual coalescence with a following augment, the polarity of the A. can be observed only when the A.M precedes the prefixless cl. 1a/2a nouns and the ordinal numerals, as shown in (3.107). If the A.M had H tone only preceding a L-initial noun or adjective, we might attribute this to leftward H-shift (3.12.2) and in fact that most probably is a factor in these cases. However, the A.M also exhibits polar behavior preceding the ordinal numerals, exemplified in (3.107d, e) which, not having an underlyingly H-toned prefix, do not trigger leftward H-shift.[153] Note how the A.M has H tone preceding the L-initial noun in (3.107a) and the L-initial ordinal numerals in (3.107d, e) but L tone when it precedes the H-initial words in (3.107b, c, f, g).

(3.107) Polarity of the A.M exemplified   Gloss
  a. **á=bììrá⁺ bá=shòòkùlù**   'the friends of grandfather'
  b. **á=bììrá bà=náákùlù**   'the friends of his grandmother'
  c. **á=bììrá bà=dáàtà**   'the friends of his father'
  d. **ú=mwììrá wá=kàbìrì**   'the second friend'
  e. **ú=lúsìkù lwá=kàshàtù**   'the second day'
  f. **ú=mwììrá wàà=kánà**   'the fourth friend'
  g. **ú=lúsìkù lwàà=kánà**   'the fourth day'

⁺The H tone at the end of **mwííra/bííra** 'friend/friends' is due to postlexical H-spread of the H of the underlying LH contour on the stem.

In any other cases where the associative marker is used, the noun following it nearly always begins with the augment, and there is obligatory coalescence

---

[152]When used as a verbal prefix, **ná-** always has H tone.

[153]We are here assuming that the **ka-** prefix, when used with numeral roots to indicate ordinality, is L-toned, as are the other prefixes of the numerals. The ordinal numerals are always preceded either by an associative marker (e.g. **ú=múkàzì wá=kàshàtù** 'the third woman' or by the word **úbùgírà** 'repetition(s), time(s)' which undergoes postlexical H-spread in a phrase, e.g. **ú=bùgírá á=kána** 'four times', where the ordinal seems to have the augment, so it is difficult to test definitively whether or not the ordinals trigger leftward H-shift.

both of vowels (the vowel of the A.M and of the augment) and of tones when the monosyllabic A.M is procliticized to the following noun, as shown in (3.108). All the augments have H tone, while the A.M, being polar toned, has L tone when it precedes the augment. In tonal coalescence, the rightmost tone seems to have precedence over the left one in cases where there is also vowel coalescence.[154] Thus, when the L tone of the vowel of the A.M is merged with that of the following H-toned augment, the result is a H-toned vowel. The A.M takes on the H tone of the augment in every case where these two elements are juxtaposed.

(3.108) Coalescence of vowel of A.M   Gloss
         with the augment
  a. á=bììrà bó=mwààmì   'the friends of the king'
  b. á=bììrà bá=bányérè   'the friends of the girls'
  c. á=bàànà bé=nyúùmbà   'the children of the house'
  d. ú=múkìrà gwéé=ngáàvù   'the tail of the cow'

Besides the associative markers, several other clitics also seem to have no underlying tone, but to exhibit polar behavior. These include the conjunctions **si** 'but obviously', the comparative conjunction **nga** 'like/as', the pronominal locative and object enclitics which may be used with verbs, and possibly others. In (3.109), a short selection taken from a natural narrative, are two examples of **si** 'but obviously' which show its polar nature. In the first instance, it precedes a L-initial word and exhibits H tone, while in the second occurrence, where it precedes a word which begins with a HL contour, it exhibits L tone.

---

[154]This is exemplified when a H-tone nominal prefix is affixed to a vowel-initial noun stem with an initial L tone, such as **kí-ìbùùngù > kìbùùngù** 'cloud' (derived from the verb -**yìbùùng-** 'move one's self').

(3.109) W-áá-n-dàrè ‖ à-ná-bwîr-à | ùyó   mú-shààjà: ‖
       1-A.M-9-lion   1-SQ-tell-Fa   that.N+1 1-old.man

   «Sí w-à-láhìr-à   ‖ kwó= W-à-n-gáàvù | à-tà-lì
   OBV 2SG-P1-refuse-Fa CMP= 1-A.M-9-cow   1-NEG-is

   há-nò. ‖ Sì   y-óòyô | à-gwétí á-gáá-lír-à.
   16-here.P.C OBV E-that.N+1 1-PROG 1-INTL-cry-Fa

'Lion ‖ told | that old man: ‖ It's obvious you denied ‖ that Cow | is here. ‖ But it's obvious that that very same one (Cow) | is now crying.' 105 038

In (3.110) are examples of the polar behavior of two of the verbal object enclitics. Note that the clitic has L tone in (3.110a, c), where it follows a H tone, but H tone in (3.110b, d), where it follows a L tone.

(3.110)   Polar-toned verbal object clitics   Gloss
     a. **ngéndì kúshàhúlírá=yè**   'that I go belittle him for you'
     b. **ndágákúhà=yê**   'I will not give him to you'
     c. **ànákìzì lùfìná=kwò**   'and he repeatedly treads on it'
     d. **byó=ngákúbààgìrà=kwô**   'which I will slaughter you on'

3.11.4 Tone on numerals

Regarding tone on numerals and their prefixes, it should first be noted that only the numbers two through seven are morphologically numerals,[155] which take the numeral/pronoun prefixes. The number one is morphologically an adjective, and other number words, 'eight', 'nine', 'ten', 'hundred', 'thousand', etc. are nouns.

The numeral prefixes, which comprise all the plural classes only, since the number 'one' is an adjective rather than a numeral, are all L-toned (or perhaps toneless) except for cl. 4, í- which has a H tone. The cl. 4 prefix is also the only numeral prefix which consists only of a vowel.

The numeral words -**biri** 'two' and -**shatu** 'three' both seem to be toneless. This observation is based on the way that the H tone of the cl. 4 prefix í- spreads onto the first mora of the numeral root with these two numerals, while this spreading does not happen in other numerals. Notice in (3.111a) that the tone of the first syllable of the number two (underlined) has H tone

---

[155] The forms for 'six' and 'seven' are compounds, derived from a verb-plus-noun, but seem to pattern morphologically as numerals.

when preceded by the H-toned cl. 4 prefix, whereas in (3.111b), where it is preceded by the L-tone cl. 2 prefix, it has L tone. In (3.111c, d) the same observation can be made regarding the number three. In (3.111e, f), where the number is -**tāānu** 'five', rather than the toneless numbers -**biri** 'two', and -**shatu** 'three', there is no spreading of the tone of the prefix onto the numeral, because the numeral five is not toneless, but has underlying LH tone (-**tāānu** 'five'). In (3.111f) the underlying LH tone on **bàtááànù** is realized as H, because the preceding L-toned cl. 2 prefix **bà-** triggers the rule of LH raising (LH > H/L _).

(3.111) Tone on numerals

a.	-**biri** 'two'	**í=míkóóndé íbírì**	'two bananas'
b.		**á=bányéré bàbìrì**	'two girls'
c.	-**shatu** 'three'	**í=mítìmà íshátù**	'three hearts'
d.		**á=bányéré bàshàtù**	'three girls'
e.	-**taanu** 'five'	**í=míkóóndé ítāānù**	'five bananas'
f.		**á=bányéré bàtáánù**	'five girls'

The numeral -**ná** 'four', has a lexical H tone. The H of this is realized on the prefix rather than on the numeral root, because the root is monosyllabic, and the final (and only) mora of the root is extra-tonal.[156] In the case of the cl. 4 prefix, which is already H toned, there is no change in the tone of the prefix. It remains H. All the other prefixes, which normally have surface L tone are realized as H preceding this numeral, e.g. the cl. 4 **í=míkóóndé ínà** (phonetically **í=míkóóndíìnà** 'four bananas'),[157] cl. 10 **í=nyúùmbà zínà** 'four houses', cl. 6 **á=mábòkò gánà** 'four arms', cl. 2 **á=bányéré bánà** 'four girls'.

The numeral -**tāānù** 'five', has underlying LH tone, e.g. **í=míkóóndé ítāānù** 'five bananas' but **í=nyúùmbà zìtáánù** 'five houses' (LH > H/L_). 'Six' and 'seven' are deverbal numerals, descended from a copula clause using -**li** 'is' plus the nominal forms **ndatu** 'six' (possibly from a cl. 10 plural of -**shatu** 'three') and **nda** 'seven' (etymology uncertain). -**lííndàtù** 'six' has an underlying HL tone, e.g. **íí=mbébá zìrííndàtù** 'six rats', while -**lííndà** 'seven', has underlying H tone, **á=bányéré bàlííndà** 'seven girls'. A H tone never spreads onto the final syllable of a numeral in phrase final position.

---

[156]Or perhaps the morpheme -**na** 'four' lexically has both a H and a L tone, the L of which is realized on the stem and the H on the prefix.

[157]Postlexical vowel coalescence takes place between the final vowel of the noun and the vocalic prefix of the numeral. Then, because there is only one mora following, the vowel length is retained. The resyllabification at the postlexical level then finds a bimoraic penult, and the HL tone which would lexically have been realized on the prefix and stem of the numeral then shifts left, producing a HL contour on the long **i**.

3.12 General rules affecting the tones of words on the phrase and clause level

Tone on words in phrases and clauses differs from tone on the isolation form of the words only in the following five ways, all of which result in a change only in the tone of the word-final syllable in a non-phrase-final word. The five instances are listed here and exemplified in the sections below:
1. Postlexical H-spread: When there is another word following within the phonological phrase, a H tone in the penultimate syllable of a word spreads onto the word-final syllable, provided that it has no other underlying tone which would block that H-spread. If there is no penultimate H tone to spread, just as when the word is final in its phrase, the final tone of the word is L (3.12.1).
2. Postlexical leftward H-shift: When conditions for leftward H-shift are met within the phrase, the leftward shifting of a floating H tone causes the tone of the final mora of the preceding word within the phrase to be raised to H (3.12.2).
3. Postlexical tonal changes due to coalescence of vowels at word boundaries: When there is coalescence at a word boundary between the final vowel of one word, and the initial vowel of the following word, if the tones of the two vowels do not have the same tone quality, tone changes take place (3.12.3).
4. Intonational raising before a non-final pause: When there is a non-final pause within a sentence, the final syllable pronounced before the pause may be given a raised-pitch H tone in order to signal that the speaker is only pausing, and has not completed what he is saying (3.12.4).
5. Final H contouring: Just as in isolation forms, when there is no word following within the phrase, a word-final H tone is given a short falling contour (3.12.5).

In regard to intonational boundary tones, it can be noted that there is most often no difference between the intonation of a statement and that of a question. There may optionally be a special intonation given to yes-no questions. This intonation seems to consist of slightly raising the pitch of the final word, rather than letting it drop as is usual in utterance-final position, and giving it a falling contour on the final syllable. Questions are also grammatically marked either by the monosyllabic (cliticized) question marker, **ka**, or by the use of an interrogative word such as **nyáàndì** 'who?', **bíkì** 'what?', etc. so the special question intonation is not necessary to distinguish meaning.

A question is provided in (3.112) to illustrate the optional question intonation.[158]

(3.112) Ùyó   mú-shósì ‖ à-ná-shùbí   dēt-à: ‖ «Sí=   n-àà-túm-á |
       that.N+1   1-man   1-SQ-AGAIN say-Fa   OBV=   1SG-P1-send-Fa

       W-à=lú-kwàvù   há-nò!   ‖   Ká=   mù-tà-zì   mú-bààg-â?»
       1-A.M-11-rabbit   16-here.P.C   Q   2PL-NEG-YET   O1-slaughter-Fa

'That man ‖ again said: ‖ «But I sent | Rabbit here! ‖ Haven't you slaughtered him yet?»' (626.034-5)

3.12.1 Postlexical H-spread

A H tone on the penultimate mora of a word may spread onto the word-final syllable as long as that word-final syllable is not also utterance final, and as long as the word has no underlying tone on that final syllable.[159] This happens whether the initial tone of the following word in the utterance is H or L.

In (3.113a, b), we see the condition for H-spread met in the noun phrase ending in -îjá 'good', since the penultimate syllable of the first word in the phrase has a H tone. (The penultimate tones are shown by tone markings and also listed as H or L in the "Pen.T" column.) In the "Isolation" column, we see that all the nouns have L tone on the final syllable. However, in the "Phrase" column, there is H tone on the final syllable of the first two examples (underlined). H-spread has spread the H tone of the penultimate onto the final syllable of the word.

Examples (3.112c, d) are included for contrast. In these two examples, the conditions are not met for H-spread in the phrase column, since there is no H tone on the penultimate syllable of the first word in the phrase. Thus there is no H tone on the final syllable of the noun in the context of the phrase. The usual default L boundary tone occurs there.[160]

---

[158]This is taken from a story which was being read. It is my contention that the "optional" question intonation is triggered by what people are taught in school about how to read a question mark in the text, and not by any linguistic cues.

[159]A H intonational tone can replace an underlying tone on the final syllable of a word, but H-spread does not target a syllable with an underlying tone.

[160]The H boundary tone, discussed in (3.12.4) occurs only at the end of a non-final phrase or clause on the discourse level, to signal a non-final pause which might otherwise be interpreted as the end of the discourse, and/or to raise the pitch register. It does not serve as a 'default non-final tone' found in all non-utterance-final syllables. The default tone is still L in a word-final position not subject to postlexical H-spread.

3.12 General rules affecting the tones of words on the phrase and clause level

(3.113) Phrases with and without H-Spread

	Isolation	Gloss	Pen. T	Phrase	H-spread	Gloss
a.	ú=múshósì	'man'	H	ú=múshósí mwîijâ	yes	'a good man'
b.	í=nyámà	'meat'	H	íí=nyámá nyîijâ	yes	'good meat'
c.	í=bígóòjè	'maize'	L	í=bígóòjè bîijâ	no	'good maize'
d.	ú=múkàzì	'woman'	L	ú=múkàzì mwîijâ	no	'a good woman'

The L tone which appears on the final mora of the initial nouns in the phrases shown in (3.113c, d), as well as that on any noun in isolation or in phrase-final position, can be considered a default L tone. The default tone is assigned to the final vowel if there is no lexical tone assigned to the final mora and the conditions are not met for postlexical H-spread. This default L tone also serves as a boundary tone in utterance-final positions. Lexical level H-spread is not considered, however, to be blocked in isolation forms by the presence of a boundary tone, but rather to be subject to a non-finality constraint which keeps it from spreading the H tone onto a final mora.

Example (3.114) shows that utterance level H-spread is not limited to noun phrases. A H tone on the penultimate syllable of a verb within a clause will also spread onto the word-final syllable (3.114a–c), as will a H tone on the penultimate syllable of a verb followed by a complement clause, as in (3.114d).

(3.114)

	Isolation	Gloss	Phrase	Gloss
a.	ú=kúkūùndà	'to love'	ú=kúkùùndá Múzíbò	'to love Muzibo'
b.	ákáshúlíkà	'he hit'	ákáshúlíká Múzíbò	'he hit Muzibo'
c.	ú=múshósì	'man'	ú=múshósí àgééndà	'the man went'
d.	ákámbwíírà	'he told me'	ákámbwíírá kwó=ágágééndà	'he told me that he will go'

3.12.2 Postlexical leftward H-shift

Leftward H-shift is a process by which the H tone of a nominal/adjective prefix, if unable to link to a mora within the word with which it is lexically associated, links instead to the final mora of the preceding word within the phrase. We posit that the H tone is left floating at the lexical level by the rule of lexical level H-float (3.8.5).

The most commonly seen case of leftward H-shift is in a noun phrase in which a non-phrase-initial noun or adjective begins with a L tone, e.g.

ú=múkàzí mwòòfì 'the short woman'. Here the final mora of ú=múkàzí has the H tone of leftward H-shift because the H tone of the adjective prefix is unable to link to the adjective. Compare this with ú=múkàzì múlà 'the tall woman', in which there is no leftward H-shift because the H tone of the adjective prefix mú-, of mú-là (1-tall), is realized on its own prefix.

The reason that this shifting takes place before a noun or adjective beginning with a L tone is that nominal and adjective prefixes are underlyingly H toned. If the H tone cannot link to the prefix itself, either because of coalescence with a vowel initial L-toned stem, as in the case of the adjective ny-òòfì (9/10-short), or because of an exceptional L-toned prefix, as mù-gózì (3-rope), or the lack of a segmental nominal prefix, as in the cl. 1a noun shòòkùlù 'grandfather', the H tone which is part of the prefix remains floating at the lexical level and postlexically links leftward to the end of the previous word within the phrase (e.g. ú=múkàzí mwòòfì 'a short woman', ú=gúùndí mùgózì 'another rope', àsìgá shòòkùlù 'he left grandfather').

Observation of the selected environments where leftward H-shift occurs preceding associative (possessive) pronouns show that it is triggered not by the presence of some sort of general H "boundary tone" but rather by a H-tone left floating by the rule of lexical level H-shift. Preceding associative pronouns which have an (underlyingly) L-toned prefix, there is no leftward H-shift. But preceding those with an underlyingly H-toned prefix whose tone is not realized on the prefix, there *is* leftward H-shift. For most noun classes, the pronominal prefix used on associative pronouns has a L tone. However, in classes 1, 1a, 4, and 9 the class prefix consists only of a vowel and its lexical tone is not a L tone, but instead, a H tone. Because a vowel-only prefix is changed to a glide (w or y) before the vocalic stem of the associative pronoun, the H lexical tone of these prefixes is not able to link to the prefix of the associative marker, and is thus subject to lexical level H-float. This floating H tone of the associative pronouns (of these four classes only) is associated by leftward H-shift at the postlexical level to the final mora of the preceding word in the phrase. With associative pronouns of the other classes, in which the prefix has L tone, there is no leftward H-shift (LHS).

The examples in (3.115a–c) show the classes where LHS takes place with associative pronouns. Row (3.115d) gives an example of a class for which the prefix tone is L, and consequently, where LHS does not take place, even though the associative pronoun has initial L tone. Row (3.115e) gives an example in which the prefix of the associative pronoun bears the H tone of the following morpheme, and shows that in this case as well, there is no LHS, since not only is the prefix underlyingly L-toned, but any floating H would be deleted rather than shifted leftwards in this environment, as it precedes a H tone.

3.12 General rules affecting the tones of words on the phrase and clause level

(3.115) Leftward H-shift (LHS) preceding associative pronouns

	Cl.	Noun	Assoc. Pfx.	Surface	Gloss	LHS
a.	1	ú=múfùmù	ú-	ú=múfùmú wììtù	'our doctor'	yes
b.	4	í=mítìmà	í-	í=mítìmá yààgè	'his spirits/hearts'	yes
c.	9	í=mbùtò	í-	í=mbùtó yààwè	'your seed'	yes
d.	10	í=mbùtò	zì-	í=mbùtò zààwè	'your seeds'	no
e.	6	á=máhèèmbè	gà-	á=máhèèmbè gááyò	'its (cl. 9) horns'	no

The word whose final mora undergoes raising can be of any morphological category, e.g. a noun, as in (3.116) and (3.117); a demonstrative, as in (3.118); a verb, as in (3.119) and (3.120); or an associative marker, as in examples (3.121a–c) below. The final syllable of any word which precedes (within a phrase) a H prefix tone which has been left floating by lexical H-float, undergoes LHS. The syllable in question is underlined in the examples below.

In (3.116), we see that in the final column, where the adjective begins with a L tone, leftward H-shift takes place, so that the final mora of the noun has H, rather than L tone. It has L tone when not affected by LHS, as seen both in the noun in isolation and in the noun when followed by an adjective with H initial tone.

(3.116)

Noun	Gloss	w/H-initial adj -lá 'long/tall'	w/L-initial adj -òfi 'short'
ú=múfùmù	'doctor'	ú=múfùmù mú-là (no LHS)	ú=múfùmú mw-òòfi (LHS)
íí=mbùtò	'seed'	íí=mbùtò nyí-rà (no LHS)	íí=mbùtó ny-òfi (LHS)
ú=lúsìkù	'day'	ú=lúsìkù lú-là (no LHS)	ú=lúsìkú lw-òòfi (LHS)

In the case of an adjective which has the cl. 9 prefix, which consists only of a nasal, N- and is not tone bearing, we also see leftward H-shift taking place,[161] as in (3.117).

---

[161] There are also other processes happening in the examples in the first column. Resyllabification takes place postlexically, with the final vowel of the initial word functioning both as (short) final vowel of the first word and as a lengthened (by the following NC) initial syllable of the following adjective. Thus, phonetically, the "shared" vowel is lengthened, as well as having H tone.

(3.117)

Cl. 9/10 noun (N- prefix)	Gloss	Nouns of classes with CV prefix	Gloss
í=nyúùmbá n-gùmà (LHS)	'one house'	ú=múfùmù mú-guma (no LHS)	'one doctor'
í=ngáàvú n-gùmà (LHS)	'one cow'	ú=lúbùtò lú-gùmà (no LHS)	'one seed'
shààlí n-gùmà (LHS)	'some firewood'	ú=lúshààlì lú-gùmà (no LHS)	'one firewood'

In (3.118a) we see that the final syllable of the demonstrative -**ndi** 'other' is given a H tone by leftward H-shift when it is followed by a noun in which the H tone of the prefix was not able to link to that prefix and in (3.118b) that no LHS takes place when the prefix bears its own H tone.

(3.118)

	Noun	Surf. T of N Prefix	Gloss	'another x'	LHS?
a.	ú=mùgózì	L	'rope'	ú=gùùndí mùgózì	yes
b.	ú=múkóóndè	H	'banana'	ú=gùùndì múkóóndè	no

Leftward H-shift can affect the final tone of a verb whose object begins with L tone,[162] as seen in (3.119). In (3.119a) the object **shòokùlù** 'grandfather' begins with a L tone. A contrasting example is shown in (3.119b) in which LHS does not take place, because the object, **Múzíbò** 'lastborn' (proper name) begins with H tone. Both objects are cl. 1a nouns.

In (3.119c) leftward H-shift is seen to raise the final tone of the copular verb -**li** 'is' before a noun with L-tone prefix, while in (3.119d) there is no raising of the final tone of -**li** preceding a noun which begins with a H-tone prefix.

---

[162] Most objects following a verb begin with H tone, since the nominal prefixes all are H toned. There are however quite a few nouns of cl. 1a (the prefixless class) which start with a L tone, and a few exceptional nouns of other classes.

3.12 General rules affecting the tones of words on the phrase and clause level

(3.119) Leftward H-shift in verb + nominal complement (NC)

	Initial T of NC	LHS?	Phrase	Gloss
a.	L	yes	á-gáá-bèg-<u>á</u> shòokùlù	'he will cut grandfather's hair'
b.	H	no	á-gáá-bèg-<u>à</u> Múzíbò	'he will cut Muzibo's hair'
c.	L	yes	gù-<u>lí</u> mù-gózì	'it (cl. 3) is a rope'
d.	H	no	gù-<u>lì</u> mú-kóóndè	'it (cl. 3) is a banana'

Leftward H-shift is seen not only in verb-plus-object constructions, but also within a verbal construction involving an auxiliary followed by a prefixless infinitive with L initial tone. When an adverbial auxiliary is included in a compound verb, the semantically main predicate is reduced to an apparently prefixless infinitive which is a separate word from the prefixes and auxiliary, e.g. **à-gáá-shùbì géédà** 'he will go again' (from **-shùbi** 'again', and **-géend-** 'go'). In this example, **géédà** is the "prefixless" infinitive.

We consider such forms to be infinitives because they still exhibit the simple stem-tone pattern assigned to all infinitives in Kifuliiru. Historically we posit that these infinitives had the cl. 5 prefix, **í-** used synchronically in some related languages (such as Kinande) as the unmarked infinitive prefix. This class prefix is not used at all synchronically for infinitives in Kifuliiru, and the initial **í-** of these "prefixless" forms has been reinterpreted in Kifuliiru as the final vowel of the adverbial auxiliary. Thus the "infinitive" in these forms has lost its segmental prefix. However, it is clear from their triggering of leftward H-shift that these infinitives have not lost the tonal element of their prefix, which remains floating to the left. Since an infinitive is a nominal form in Kifuliiru, such a prefixless infinitive, if initially L-toned, triggers leftward H-shift. This means that whenever this "prefixless" infinitive is a lexically L-toned verb stem, its initial tone will be L, and the final mora of the preceding auxiliary will have a H tone, due to leftward H-shift, e.g. **àgááshùb<u>í</u> dētà** 'he will say again' (from **-dèt-** 'speak').

If, on the other hand, the prefixless infinitive is a lexically H or toneless verb stem, its initial tone will be H, and the final mora of the auxiliary will not receive a H tone from leftward H-shift.

Examples of verb forms with the adverbial auxiliary are given in (3.120a–e). These forms are in the future tense in the adverbial auxiliary forms, because this tense has a V_2 stem-tone pattern, which has a suffixal L tone and does not occasion any H suffixal tones on the auxiliary which might confuse the evidence. The examples in (3.120a–c) do not exhibit leftward H-shift, because the main verb (a prefixless infinitive) begins with a H tone. In (3.120d, e) the final infinitive has an initial L tone, and thus leftward H-shift does take place.

(3.120) Leftward H-shift in verb phrases

UT	Stem	Gloss	Verb phrase	Gloss	LHS?
a. H	-lól-	'look'	ágágéèndì lólà	'he will go look'	no
b. H	-géénd-	'go'	ágálúúngùlì gééndà	'he will go too soon'	no
c. Ø	-bwaatal-	'sit down'	ágáshùbì bwáátálà	'he will sit down again'	no
d. L	-fùkam-	'kneel'	ágááshùbí fùkámá	'he will kneel again'	yes
e. L	-hàmagal-	'call'	ágálúúngùlí hàmágálà	'he will call too soon'	yes

A H word-final tone due to the phenomenon of leftward H-shift has not been documented preceding a L-toned associative marker (A.M)[163] as in the phrase 'the doctor of x' shown in (3.121). The final tone of the word **ú=múfùmù** 'doctor' is not raised, even when the tone of the A.M following it is L, as seen in (3.121a, b).

Though the A.M, not being a noun or an adjective, does not trigger leftward H-shift onto the preceding noun, the A.M can itself be targeted by leftward H-shift. Examples (3.121c, d) show leftward H-shift causing the tone of the A.M to become H. This is seen in that when the noun following the A.M begins with a H tone, as it does in (3.121a, b) the A.M has L tone, but when there is a noun with initial L tone following the A.M, as in (3.121c, d), the A.M's tone is raised to H. The A.M is thus considered to have a polar tone.

---

[163]The A.M seems to be underlyingly toneless. It has a L surface tone preceding a H-initial noun with no augment, and H preceding a L-initial noun with no augment. When an augment follows the A.M, there is vowel coalescence, and the resultant vowel has the H tone of the augment.

3.12 General rules affecting the tones of words on the phrase and clause level

(3.121) Leftward H-shift and associative markers

	Init. T of noun	Noun (cl.1a)	Gloss	'doctor of x'	LHS onto A.M?
a.	H	náákùlù	'my grandmother'	ú=múfùmù wà=náákùlù	no
b.	H	Kálùkù	'proper name'	ú=múfùmù wà=Kálùkù	no
c.	L	Ngòjé	'proper name'	ú=múfùmù wá=Ngòjé	yes
d.	L	shòòkùlù	'grandfather'	ú=múfùmù wá=shòòkùlù	yes

3.12.3 Postlexical tonal changes due to coalescence of vowels

Another instance in which a difference of tone is seen between the isolation form of a word and the contextual form is when the final TBU of the preceding word bears the initial H tone of the following word due to coalescence of the vowels, and consequently coalescence of the tones, at a word boundary.

In Kifuliiru there are no closed syllables, so every word ends with a vowel. Word-initial V(V)- syllables are also quite common, in large part due to the frequent use of the nominal augment, which always has the shape of a H-toned V. Thus there is a high incidence of vowel juxtaposition at word junctures, especially when the second word is a noun, as in a sequence of verb plus object. In normal speech, when vowels are juxtaposed across word boundaries within the phrase, vowel coalescence takes place. Only in unusually slow speech do such vowels remain separate. The resulting vowel qualities in coalescence across word boundaries are discussed in 2.3.1.2.2. Here we look only at what happens with the tones when the vowels coalesce. The following are preliminary observations.

- When the two tones are alike, i.e. H + H or L + L, as in (3.122a, b, g) they merge into a single tone of the same quality.
- When a L tone is followed by a H, as in (3.122e, f) the resulting tone is H.
- When a H tone which is the result of H spread within the phrase is followed by a L tone which is the result of default L-insertion, as in (3.122c) the resulting tone is H.
- When there is a H tone which is not the result of H-spread, but rather is a lexical H tone, at the end of a word, followed

by a L tone at the beginning of the next, as in (3.122d) the result is a falling contour.

The tones in the "Tones" and "Word sequence" columns of (3.122) are not the tones of the words in isolation, but reflect the process of postlexical H-spread in cases where it applies.

(3.122)

	Tones	Word sequence	With coalescence	Gloss
a.	H+H>H	ákábòná í=mbènè	ákábònéémbènè	'he saw a goat'
b.	H+H>H	ákábwíírá ú=mwīīrà	ákábwíírómwīīrà	'he told the friend'
c.	H+L>H	ákákèngéérá àyííjí ndíbítà	ákákèngééráyííjí ndíbítà	'he discovered that he had come and run from me'
d.	H+L>HL	kwó àgééndà	kwáágééndà	'that he went'
e.	L+H>H	ààsìgà úmwīīrà	ààsìgómwīīrà	'he left the friend'
f.	L+H>H	ààsìgà ámbwîîrà	ààsìgámbwîîrà	'he left having told me'
g.	L+L>L	ààsìgà àtùbwíírà	ààsìgàtùbwíírà	'he left having told us'

3.12.4 Intonational raising indicating a non-final pause

At any non-final point within an utterance, when a pause is inserted, it may be signaled by a raising of the tone on the final mora of the word which immediately precedes the pause. If the pause is at a normal pausing place within the sentence, such as following the topic of the sentence, the raise may consist of no more than a lack of further drop in pitch. At a pause such as that a person makes when unsure of what to say next, or at a dramatic pause, the pitch is usually higher than a normal H tone. Whereas the second H tone of a HLH sequence is lower in pitch than the first, a pre-pause H in the same position would be as high as or higher than the initial one. Thus such an intonational H tone is not affected by the normal pitch lowering process of downdrift (3.13). A pre-pausal H is a deliberate raising of pitch and is not realized as a short falling contour, as an utterance-final lexical H tone is. Such characteristics are typical of a boundary tone as described by Hyman (1990).

The example in (3.123) shows two subsequent repetitions of a short clause of which the speaker knew he was to give two repetitions. Pre-pause raising is signified in (3.123) and (3.124) by an up-arrow *preceding* the raised syllable, e.g. **zèè né** 'today' indicating that the H tone which follows has a higher pitch than a non-pre-pausal H would have in that same position in the utterance.[164] That the final syllable of **zèè né** has an acute rather than a circumflex accent shows that the pre-pause H tone does not get a falling contour, whereas in the utterance-final version of the word, **zèènê**, the final lexical H tone does get a slight falling contour, as is normal for a H tone in utterance-final position:

(3.123) á-gá-lù-báámb-á zèè né   á-gá-lù-báámb-á zèènê
'he will peg it out today'   'he will peg it out today'

Example (3.124) shows not a list intonation, but a normal pause following the introduction of the topic of a sentence. The final syllable of **twóóshì** 'all' would normally have a L tone since it is at the end of its phrase, but instead the pitch of the final syllable is raised to indicate that there is more following within the sentence.

(3.124) **nó=**   **tw-áásó**   **tw-óó shí |** ...
         and+AU=   13-leaves   13-all

'...and all the leaves .....'

3.12.5 Final H contouring

When there is no word following within the utterance/breath group, any word-final lexical H tone, such as that in **bú-hyá** (14-pit) is pronounced as a short falling contour, **búhyâ**. This is due to the presence at the postlexical level of a L boundary tone. Final H contouring applies to any word with a final lexical H tone, but does not apply to the H boundary tone which signals a pause in non-final position (discussed in 3.124). Examples of final H contouring are given in (3.125).

In (3.125) each of the words found in the "Isolation form" column at left has an underlying H tone on its final syllable. In the phrases in each pair of examples in (3.125) the first example (3.125a, c, e), shows the H-final word used in non-utterance-final position in its phrase, where its final H tone does not undergo contouring, and remains H. In the second example of each pair,

---

[164]This arrow convention is not used in the marking of other examples throughout this book. In the context of sentences, there is frequent application of the pre-pause H. Wherever a H tone not marked as a circumflex is seen preceding a non-final punctuation mark such as a comma or semicolon, that H tone is a product of pre-pause raising. A final H tone not affected by raising will be given a short falling contour (see final H contouring above) and is marked by a circumflex accent.

(3.125b, d, f), the same word is used in utterance-final position, and final H contouring applies.

(3.125) Final H contouring

	Isolation Form	Gloss	Form in context	Gloss
a.	búhyâ	'hole'	àgwà múú=bú<u>hyá</u> búlà	'he fell in a deep pit'
b.	búhyâ	'hole'	àgwà múú=bú<u>hyâ</u>	'he fell in a pit'
c.	kwô	'complementizer'	àdètà <u>kwó</u>=bàgéén dà	'he said that they went'
d.	kwô	'cl. 17 pronoun'	bàháábwà=<u>kwô</u>	'they were given (some of) it'
e.	àgáábègwâ	'he will be shaved'	ágáábè<u>gwá</u> káhàlà	'he will be shaved bald'
f.	àgáábègwâ	'he will be shaved'	léérò àgáábè<u>gwâ</u>	'this time he will be shaved'

3.13 Downdrift

Downdrift, sometimes called automatic downstep, is a very evident phenomenon in the Kifuliiru language. Downdrift is the process by which the pitch of an utterance is progressively lowered following a low tone. Because of downdrift, a H tone following a L tone is not as high in pitch as a H tone which preceded that L tone.[165] This lowering affects all domains and is gradual but progressive. On a scale where 6 is the highest pitch and 1 is the lowest pitch, a sequence of HL, HL, HL might have pitches of 6-4, 5-3, 4-2, etc. This is just a rough approximation. More study could be done on the precise syntactic conditions governing downdrift and pre-pause raising within the clause, sentence, and paragraph.

No real study has been made in Kifuliiru on the topic of pitch and downdrift. However, just from casual observation, it is clear that the pitch, as well as the intensity of the speech, gradually drops over the course of an utterance. The loss of intensity often causes the final syllable of a word in isolation, or an utterance-final word to be voiceless.

Downdrift has noticeable effects on pitch even in a short sentence. The domain over which downdrift continues before a true return to initial pitch

---

[165] As noted above, a H tone due to pre-pause raising is not subject to downdrift and may be higher than the previous H tone, whether or not a L tone has intervened.

seems to be roughly equivalent to a short paragraph. The highest pitch and highest intensity appear at the beginning of the paragraph, and the lowest pitch and lowest intensity at the end.

Following in (3.126) is an illustrative sentence from the beginning of a natural narrative text. Because it is still the beginning of the text, the pitch and intensity do not drop as low as they would at the end of the text. However, even in this first sentence, the effect of downdrift can be seen in the phonetic measurements of both intensity (first graph) and pitch (second graph), shown in figure 3.1.

(3.126) **Lú-sìkù   lú-gùmà | W-à-n-gwáàrè ‖   á-ká-géénd-á   à-gwéétí**
       11-day   11-one   1-A.M-9-quail   1-P2-go-Fa   1-PROG

       á-gáá-kààz-á   mú=   kú-lóóz-á   by-ó   á-gáà-ly-à.
       1-INTL-scare.up-Fa IN.STATE 15-get.CS-Fa 8-O.R 1-F2-eat-Fa

'One day Quail went scaring up (insects, etc.) in order to look for something to eat.'

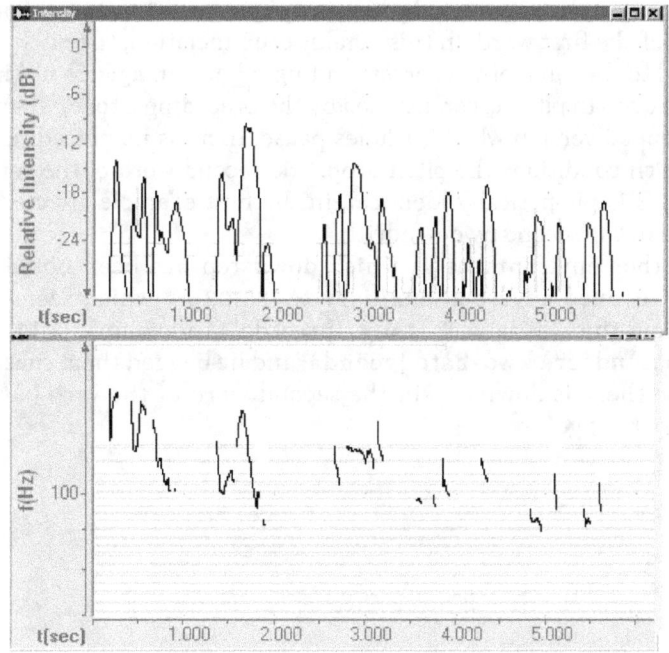

Figure 3.1. Intensity and pitch of a narrative-initial sentence.

3.14 Floating L tones and (non-automatic) downstep

Non-automatic downstep (or "downstep") is a drop in pitch exactly like that of downdrift, but one which is not conditioned by a L tone which appears on the surface. Instead it is occasioned by a L tone that is not associated to a TBU and therefore is not realized phonetically in the surface form. Such underlying tones without phonetic realization often result from the diachronic loss of a segmental morpheme, without the loss of the tone which was lexically associated with it. Downstep in Kifuliiru is not a common phenomenon, but has been noted following a H tone which replaces a L tone due to intonational raising at a pause (see 3.12.4).

When such a pre-pause H tone replaces what would have been a L tone in word-final position, downstep follows it. The L tone which was replaced, though not realized phonetically, still conditions the lowering of a following H tone. For example in **ágágéè ↑ndí ↓réétà** (the up arrow indicates that the tone of **ndí** is upstepped high, while the down arrow indicates downstep of the high tones which follow) 'he will go bring something', the H tone on **ndí** is a pre-pause tone which displaced a L tone, so the following word, **réétà** 'bring', has downstepped H tone on the underlined syllable. By contrast, the default pronunciation with no medial pause is **ágágéè ↑ndí ↓réétà**, with a L tone at the end of the first word. In this default pronunciation, the pitch of **réétà** is identical to the pitch of the corresponding syllable in **ágágéè ndí !réétà**, but here the drop in pitch is conditioned by the preceding L tone, whereas in the downstepped version which includes pause, there is no preceding surface L tone which conditions the pitch drop. The second word of the verb form in both cases is phonetically identical, in the first example affected by downstep and in the second by downdrift.

The other environment in which downstep has been noted is following the H-toned adverbial auxiliary **té** (PRIOR),[166] which seems toderived from the L-tone verb -**tàng**- 'precede'. An example (3.127) is found in **ànábàtèndéérà kwó=bàté ↓gēēndà** 'and he begged them that they first go'. Here there is downstep in the second word of the verb **bàté ↓gēndà** 'that they first go'.

---

[166] Pronounced by some people as **tí**.

(3.127) Ùyó   mw-ààmì | à-ná-bà-tèndéér-à | kwó= bà-té   ↓gēēnd-à ||
that.N+1 1-king   1-SQ-O2-beg-Fa   CMP= 2-PRIOR go-Fa

bà-ká-yîj-è   gù-ndì mú-lègè-règè.
2-INTV-come-Fe 3-other 3-day-RDP

'That king | begged them | that they first go || and then come back | another day.' 24 007

4
Derivational processes

Bantu languages are rich in derivational processes. In Kifuliiru, nouns can be derived from verbs and from adjectives. They can also be derived from other nouns by prefix changes, by the addition of a formative, or by compounding two words together.

Verbs can be derived from nouns, from ideophones, and from adjectives. Verbal auxiliaries as well as adjectives and adverbs can be derived from verbs. Semantic variations of a verb can be derived from a verb radical by the suffixation of verbal extensions. The verbal extensions are discussed separately (see chapter 5 Verb Stems).

4.1 Noun derivations

Noun derivation is a rich and common process in Kifuliiru. Nouns can be derived from verbs, adjectives, other nouns, a formative plus a noun root, a verb root plus a noun root, from ideophones, and by reduplication. In looking over a random list of 380 (non-infinitive) nouns with a 38-year-old Kifuliiru speaker, there were fewer than sixty nouns (~ 15 percent) for which he could not think of a related verb. It is our impression that older speakers with more extensive vocabulary could find related verbs for an even greater percentage of nouns.

We remind the reader that in this chapter, compensatory vowel lengthening is not indicated. Kifuliiru words are indicated orthographically except for the fact that tones are marked and clitics indicated by = rather than with an apostrophe. Vowels are phonetically lengthened following a glide (**y** or **w**) and preceding a NC (**mb, nd, ng**). Only vowel lengthening for which there is no obvious surface trigger is written.[1] Keep in mind, as well, that any long vowels are shortened when three or more morae follow within the word.

4.1.1 Nouns derived from verbs (deverbal nouns)

4.1.1.1 Infinitives

The Kifuliiru infinitive is structurally nominal and consists of an optional augment with the cl. 15 prefix (**ú**)=**kú**-, the final vowel -**a**, and H tone on all non-final morae following the first mora of the verbal stem. Infinitives often function nominally, and can be used in the same ways as any other noun. Except for a very few irregular verbs which might be said to have no infinitive form, every verb has an infinitive, making this nominal derivation from a verb stem a completely productive process.

In (4.1), the cl. 15 infinitive noun **kú-kùnd-án-à** (15-love-RCP-Fa) 'to love each other' functions as the head of a noun phrase, in which it is modified by the cl. 15 nearby demonstrative **yù-kwô** (that.N-15) 'that.N' and the associative pronoun **kw-à-bò** (15-A.M-2) 'their'. This NP, **yùkwó kúkùndánà kwàbò** 'that.N loving each other of theirs' is in turn, the complement of the locative phrase headed by the cl. 18 marker **mú**.

(4.1)   **Mú**=   **yùkwó**   **kú-kùnd-án-à**   **kw-à-bò**...
      18   that.N+15   15-love-RCP-Fa   15-A.M-2

'In their loving each other ... (lit., that loving each other of theirs...)'
(42 011)

The infinitive, though nominal in its usual syntactic function, still retains significant verbal qualities. In this sense, it is unique among deverbal nouns. For example, it may still include a negative marker as **kútàgéndérérà** 'to not progress', seen in (4.2).

---

[1] As in the derivation of **múbùúvì** 'potter' from **kúb-mbà** 'to work clay', a NC sequence (here **mb**) is sometimes simplified by rule to a simple C (here **v**). In such a case, the compensatory lengthening is retained, even though the triggering NC sequence is no longer observable.

4.1 Noun derivations

(4.2) À-ná-gì-gánùùl-ìr-à   ú=bú-kénì   bw-é=   kí-hùgó |
1-SQ-O.4-converse-APL-Fa   AU=14-poverty   14-A.M+AU=   7-land

nó=   kú-tà-géndérér-á   kw-à-kyò.
and.AU=   15-NEG-make.progress-Fa   15-A.M-7

'And he discussed with them the poverty of the land |and its lack of progress (lit., the to not make progress of it.)' (23 004)

An infinitive may also include an object prefix, as seen in (4.3) where there is a first-person singular object, **n-**: **kú-n-gúl-íís-â** 'to sell me'.

(4.3) **Hálìkò   yùkwó   kú-n-gúl-íís-â   kw-ì-nyù ||**
But   that.N+15   15-O1-buy-CS-Fa   15-A.M-2PL

kù-tá-Ø-mù-jéngèè-z-é | kù-tá-Ø-ná-mù-bììk-è
15-NEG-SBV-O2.PL-be.sad-CS-Fe   15-NEG-SBV-ADD.V-O2.PL-put-Fe

mw-ó=   lú-háhàlìzì.
18-AU=   11-worry

'But your selling me (lit., that to sell me of yours) || should not make you sad | nor should it worry you (lit., it should not put into you worry).' (Gen 45:5)

Example (4.3) also shows that the H-toned nominal prefix which marks an infinitive has a corresponding toneless cl. 15 verbal subject agreement prefix, as seen in the two verbs which follow it: **kùtámùjéngèèzê** 'it should not cause you to be sad' and **kùtánámùbììkè=mwô** 'it should not put in you'. These verbs both agree with the infinitival subject of the sentence: **yùkwó kú-n-gúl-íís-á kwìnyù** 'that.N selling me of yours'.

Infinitives may be formed from any verb, and thus often include extensions, such as passive, applicative, causative (as seen in (4.3) **kú-n-gúl-íís-â**), etc.

4.1.1.2 Deverbal nouns with agentive suffix

Non-infinitive nouns can be derived from verbs by the suffixation of the agentive suffix, **-i** (which is historically derived from the high close vowel i̧ in Proto-Bantu.) In (4.4) we see cl. 1/2 nouns which are usually termed "agentive nouns" because they indicate "the person doing x" where "x" is some action denoted by the verb from which the noun is derived.

(4.4) Deverbal nouns with agentive suffix

	Verb base	Gloss	Noun stem	Noun	Cl.	Gloss
a.	-bìb-	'scatter seed'	-bìbì	múbìbì	1/2	'seed scatterer'
b.	-bùmb-	'work clay'	-būūvì	múbūūvì	1/2	'potter'
c.	-biij-	'carve wood'	-bīījì	múbīījì	1/2	'woodcarver'
d.	-byal-	'plant'	-byázì	múbyázì	1/2	'sower'
e.	-dúb-	'fish'	-dúbì	múdúbì	1/2	'fisherman'
f.	-hìiv-	'hunt'	-hìivì	múhìivì	1/2	'hunter'
g.	-bùt-	'give birth'	-bùsì	múbùsì	1/2	'parent'
h.	-hìng-	'farm'	-hīīzì	múhīīzì	1/2	'farmer'
i.	-kòl-	'work'	-kòzì	múkòzì	1/2	'worker'
j.	-lèg-	'accuse'	-lèzì	múlèzì	1/2	'accuser'
k.	-lér-	'hold on lap'	-lézì	múlézì	1/2	'nanny'
l.	-tábaal-	'help'	-tábáázì	mútábáázì	1/2	'helper'
m.	-tu-	'cut'	-twì	mútwì	1/2	'cutter'

The cl. 1/2 agentive noun can then be used as the base for further derivation, by replacing the cl. 1/2 prefix with a different class prefix, such as the cl. 14 **bú-**, which often indicates an abstraction, e.g. the corresponding abstract of **mútábáázì** 'helper' in (4.4,1) is **bútábáázì** 'help'.

The fact that the agentive suffix is derived historically from the high close vowel **-i̧** is the reason that it triggers spirantization in certain consonants. This spirantization can be observed in (4.4b, d, g–l), e.g. **-byal-** 'plant' > **-byaz-** in **múbyázì** 'planter'. The **-i** suffix used in the derivation of agentive nouns is phonologically identical to the verbal "short" causative extension **-i**.

Observation of derived nouns with this suffix in Kifuliiru seems to indicate that besides having an agentive meaning, this suffix can also be used to indicate the result of the action of the verb, cf. examples in (4.5). Both this usage and the agentive usage perhaps imply an identity with the verbal causative extension, considering the fact that this suffix and the causative extension are phonologically identical in Kifuliiru.

Some examples of **-i** as a suffix on nouns which indicate the result of the action of a verb are found in (4.5). In the examples in (4.5), the use of this "agentive" suffix in a non-agentive noun cannot be said to be the result of the derivation of these nouns from an agentive noun by a change of class prefix, because a corresponding cl. 1 agentive noun is not attested (except in the case of (4.5d) where the noun **múbùsì** 'parent' does exist).

(4.5) Non-animate deverbal nouns with agentive extension

	Verb base	Gloss	Noun stem	Noun	Cl.	Gloss
a.	-huut-	'flow'	-húúsì	múhúúsì	3/4	'strong wind'
b.	-kòler-	'do for'	-kòlèzì	múkòlèzì	3/4	'act, deed'
c.	-gók-	'stoop'	-gósi	í=ígósì	5/6	'neck'
d.	-bùt-	'give birth'	-bùsi	kíbùsì	7/8	'generation'
e.	-shàl-	'vomit'	-shāzì	kíshāzì	7/8	'vomit'
f.	-huut-	'flow'	-húúsì	mbúúsì	9/10	'wind'
g.	-shòlogot-	'feel nauseated'	-shòlògòsì	shòlógósì	9/10	'nausea'
h.	-gòlomb-	'flow'	-gòlóóvì	mágòlóóvì	6	'water'
i.	-hàhalir-	'be concerned'	-hàhàlìzì	lúhàhàlìzì	11	'concern'
j.	-jàndagir-	'be lazy'	-jàndàgìzì	lújàndágízì	11	'indolence'
k.	-shóbol-	'be able'	-shóbózì	búshóbózì	14	'ability'
l.	-mény-	'to know'	-ményì	búményì	14	'knowledge'

4.1.1.3 Other deverbal nouns

Nouns can also be derived from verbs by the addition of other suffixal vowels. These derived nouns can end in (non-spirantizing) **i**, or in **e**, **a**, **o**, or **u**. They are discussed below according to which final vowel they use.

The derived forms in (4.6) all end in -**i**. Many belong to cl. 14, the abstract class, and several to cl. 5, but several classes are represented. Most seem to indicate a state or a product that is the result of the action of the verb, much as those in (4.5). However, there is no spirantization of the consonant which precedes the suffix in the examples in (4.6), even of the consonants such as **r**, as in (4.6d, i), or **k**, as in (4.6k), which did undergo spirantization in (4.4) and (4.5). It appears that these nouns which are derived from verbs which have an -**ik** or -**ir** extension have undergone the dropping of the final consonant of the verb base. Thus the final vowel in these cases may be the vowel of the original extension rather than a nominalizing suffix as such. It is possible that at least some such nouns are the source of the verbs rather than vice versa, but this is only conjecture.

In (4.6h–k), there is no obvious extension in the source verb, and yet the final consonant does not undergo spirantization. Thus, the final -**i** would appear to be a different suffix from the agentive/causative one seen in (4.4) and (4.5), even though the semantic meanings seem to be similar to those in (4.5). It is also possible that they are both the same suffix, but that this suffix conditioned spirantization only at certain times in the past, and the verbs not showing spirantization were lexicalized at a period in which the spirantization process did not apply.

(4.6) Deverbal nouns ending in -**i** (non-agentive)

	Verb base	Gloss	Noun stem	Noun	Cl.	Gloss
a.	-**búlik**-	'pay "hit man"'	-**búlì**	mbúlì	9/10	'payment for murder'
b.	-**laalik**-	'invite'	-**làalì**	múlàalì	3/4	'invitation'
c.	-**tàmbik**-	'go around edge'	-**tàmbì**	bútàmbì	14	'periphery'
d.	-**tìrik**-	'talk into refusing'	-**tìrì**	lútìrì	11	'reluctance, refusing'
e.	-**yírik**-	'give extra'	-**îrì**	bwîrì	14	'bonus, extra'
f.	-**dábagir**-	'be lazy, shiftless'	-**dábàgì**	ídábàgì	5	'intentional laziness'
g.	-**gàbíís**-	'resist'	-**áábì**	bwábì	14	'obstinacy'
h.	-**gámb**-	'go make plans'	-**gâmbì**	ígâmbì	5	'plot'
i.	-**raakar**-	'be angry'	-**ráákárì**	búráákárì	14	'anger'
j.	-**haat**-	'be stubborn'	-**háàtì**	káháàtì	12	'bossiness'
k.	-**daak**-	'curse'	-**dàakì**	ídàakì	5/6	'curse'

The derived forms in (4.7) all end in -**e**. As with the non-agentive -**i** final nouns above, many of the deverbal nouns with this ending are abstracts and fall in cl. 14.

(4.7) Deverbal nouns ending in -**e** (non-agentive)

Verb base	Gloss	Noun stem	Noun	Cl.	Gloss
-**gàl**-	'be rich'	-**gàlè**	múgàlè	1/2	'rich person'
-**sòrek**-	'mature (human)'	-**sòrè**	músòrè	3/4	'young person'
-**bòn**-	'see'	-**bòné**	ííbònê	5/6	'vision'
-**húb**-	'make error'	-**húbè**	búhúbè	14	'mistake, failure'

4.1 Noun derivations

Verb base	Gloss	Noun stem	Noun	Cl.	Gloss
-hùgw-	'feel unfamiliar'	-hùgwé	káhùgwê	12	'loneliness'
-káruuk-	'be courageous'	-kárùùké	búkárùùkè	14	'courage'
-rámb-	'live long'	-ráàmbè	búráàmbè	14	'life'
-lángashaan-	'shine'	-lángàshànè	búlángàshànè	14	'radiance'
-lóóz-	'want'	-lóòze	búlóòzè	14	'will, desire'
-lyanirw-	'be painful'	-lyànìrwè	búlyànìrwè	14	'pain'
-shàmbaal-	'rejoice'	-shàmbààlè	búshàmbààlè	14	'joy'
-shèreber-	'be spoiled'	-shèrèbèrè	búshèrèbèrè	14	'corruption'

The derived forms in (4.8) all end with an -o suffix, and are found in all classes except for the locative classes, cl. 15, and cl. 1/2. There seems to be no single meaning attached to this suffix, though several seem to denote an instrument or means or place for carrying out the action of the verb.

(4.8) Deverbal nouns ending in -o (non-agentive)

Verb base	Gloss	Noun stem	Noun	Cl.	Gloss
-yámbal-	'wear'	-ámbálò	mwámbálò	3/4	'garment'
-sheeg-	'sup'	-shéégò	múshéégò	3/4	'supper'
-tèg-	'trap'	-tégò	mútégò	3/4	'trap'
-hétam-	'be curved, bent'	-hétò	múhétò	3/4	'bow (for hunting)'
-shùvy-	'answer'	-shùvyò	íshùvyô	5/6	'answer'
-bùnd-	'lie in hiding'	-būndò	íbūndò	5/6	'lair of animal'
-buuz-	'ask'	-búúzó	kíbúúzô	7/8	'question'
-tòndeek-	'begin'	-tòndékò	ndòndékò	9/10	'beginning'
-baaj-	'carve away'	-máájò	máájò	9/10	'adze'
-bùt-	'give birth'	-bútò	lúbútò	11/10	'seed'
-yìmb-	'sing'	-īmbò	lwímbò	11/10	'song'
-shy-	'grind'	-shyó	lúshyô	11	'stone grinding trough'
-kùnd-	'love'	-kūndò	rúkúndò	11	'love'
-jábuk-	'cross over'	-jábò	kájábò	12	'other side (of river, etc.)'

The derived nouns in (4.9) all end in the final vowel **u**, which has no single predictable meaning. Some of the radicals contain the vowel **u**, so that perhaps the final **u** is a copy of this vowel. Other verbs in (4.9) include an extension which begins with **u**, e.g (4.9a, c, d, g, i, l). In these cases, it seems that either the final C of the extension is dropped when the derived noun is formed, or perhaps it is an indication that the noun was primary. These nouns also fall in a variety of classes, as can be seen in (4.9).

(4.9) Deverbal nouns ending in –**u** (non-agentive)

	Verb base	Gloss	Noun stem	Noun	Cl.	Gloss
a.	-láguz-	'divine'	-lágù	múlágù	1/2	'diviner'
b.	-fùm-	'doctor'	-fùmù	múfùmù	1/2	'doctor'
c.	-yímbul-	'harvest'	-îmbù	mwîmbù	3/4	'harvest'
d.	-sháhul-	'take a report'	-sháhù	músháhù	3/4	'report'
e.	-tùmit-	'spear'	-tùmù	ítùmù	5/6	'spear'
f.	-líbuuk-	'suffer'	-líbù	málíbù	6	'sufferings, trials'
g.	-hèmagir-	'pant, breathe hard'	-héèmù	kíhéèmù	7/8	'hard breathing'
h.	-gùg-	'gather'	-gùgù	kígùgù	7/8	'crowd'
i.	-shúmbul-	'take back sthg'	-shûmbù	shûmbu	9/10	'thing reclaimed'
j.	-sheeny-	'cut firewood'	-shèènyù	shéényù	9/10	'axe'
k.	-fu-	'die'	-fù	lúfù	11	'death'
l.	-sázuur-	'be angry and vocal'	-sáàzù	kásáàzù	12	'anger'

The nouns in (4.10) all end in an -**a** suffix, and represent many noun classes. There seems to be no one common semantic meaning.

(4.10) Deverbal nouns ending in -**a** (non-agentive)

	Verb base	Gloss	Noun stem	Noun	Cl.	Gloss
a.	-shaaj-	'get old'	-shààjà	múshààjà	1/2	'old man'
b.	-zìmb-	'steal'	-zìmbà	múzìmbà	1/2	'thief'
c.	-báy-	'smell'	-báyà	í=íbáyà	5/6	'smell'
d.	-bùt-	'give birth'	-bùtà	íbùtà	5/6	'descendant'
f.	-démb-	'indulge oneself'	-démbà	ídémbà	5/6	'self-indulgence'

4.1 Noun derivations

	Verb base	Gloss	Noun stem	Noun	Cl.	Gloss
g.	-baaj-	'chip off, carve'	-bàaja	kíbààjà	7/8	'plot leveled for house'
h.	-gány-	'be worried'	-gányà	í=ígányà	5/6	'complaining'
i.	-tàl-	'lay out to dry'	-tàlà	kítàlà	7/8	'drying platform'
j.	-shánul-	'comb'	-shánúlà	kíshánúlà	7/8	'comb'
k.	-zìng-	'wrap, tangle'	-zìngà	nzìngà	9/10	'tangled thing'
l.	-koojok-	'break off'	-kòòjòkà	híkòòjòkà	19	'small piece'

4.1.1.4 Nouns with n-da plus verb

The formative **n-da** 'I don't ...' (or perhaps 'one who doesn't'),[2] contains the verbal negative marker **ta-**. This formative (**nda**) can be used with or without a class prefix, and combines with various verbal bases to form compound nouns of cl. 1a.

Related forms include the negative pronominal copula which expresses lack of something, e.g. the cl. 8 **ndáá=byò** 'there are none'. All of these negative copulas begin with **ndáá:** (cl. 1 **ndáá=yè**, cl. 2 **ndáá=bò**, cl. 3 **ndáá=gwò**, etc.) The lengthening of the vowel in these cases (cf. the cl. 3 form with additional prefixes **ndà=ná-kí-gwò** (NEG-ADD.V-PERS-3) 'and there is no longer any cl. 3' where the vowel is short) argues for the fact that this formative may be (or have originally been) a clitic, rather than a prefix, and thus be affected by the phonological rule which lengthens the vowel of a proclitic when it is joined to a word of fewer than three morae.

There are at least two of these derived forms which are used adverbially, as well as nominally. These two are the cl. 11 **lúndàtwìkà** 'endlessly' from the verb **kútwíkà** 'to be cut', and the cl. 12 form **kándàhárùùrwâ** 'innumerable', from the verb **kúhárúúrà** 'to count'.

This affixation of noun prefix + **nda-** seems to be, or to have been, quite a productive process, and there are numerous examples of such words. Most of them are seen to be somewhat pejorative. Some examples of these **nda-** nouns are seen in (4.11).

---

[2] The morphological origin of the initial **n-** is uncertain. It is probably derived either from the first-person singular subject marker **n-**, or from a cl. 9/10 nominal prefix.

(4.11) Nouns formed with (GNP-) **nda-** plus root

Verb stem	Gloss	Noun	Cl.	Gloss
-bònek-	'be evident'	**ká<u>nd</u>àbònèkà**	1a/2	'person not seen'
-hùs-	'set off trap'	**ká<u>nd</u>àhùsà**	1a/2	'person alert to danger'
-shék-	'smile, laugh'	**<u>nd</u>àshékà**	1a/2	'person who doesn't laugh'
-twaz-	'pay attention'	**<u>nd</u>àtwàzâ**	1a/2	'person who won't listen'
-gálulw-	'be returned'	**<u>nd</u>àgálùlwâ**	1a/2	'person not sent back'
-siim-	'be pleased'	**<u>nd</u>àsììmà**	1a/2	'person who is never pleased'
-ményw-	'be known'	**mú<u>nd</u>àménywà**	3/4	'unknown person'
-gábik-	'be stubborn'	**mú<u>nd</u>àgábìkà**	3/4	'person not taking advice'
-yúvw-	'hear'	**mú<u>nd</u>ùùvwâ**	3/4	'person who won't listen'
-bòn-	'see'	**mú<u>nd</u>àbònà**	3/4	'person who can't see'
-hánuulw-	'be advised'	**mú<u>nd</u>àhánùùlwâ**	3/4	'person not taking advice'
-lúhuuk-	'rest'	**mú<u>nd</u>àlúhùùkà**	3/4	'person who doesn't rest'
-kùl-	'grow'	**mú<u>nd</u>àkùlà**	3/4	'person who doesn't grow much'
-gólolw-	'be straightened'	**mú<u>nd</u>àgólòlwâ**	3/4	'person who won't be corrected'
-hímb-	'be exhausted'	**mú<u>nd</u>àhímbà**	3/4	'person who doesn't get tired'
-bègw-	'have hair cut'	**mú<u>nd</u>àbègwà**	3/4	'person who won't get haircut'
-hánuus-	'ask advice'	**mú<u>nd</u>àhánùùsâ**	3/4	'person not seeking advice'
-bwirizibw-	'be corrected'	**mú<u>nd</u>àbwìrìzìbwâ**	3/4	'person who does not take advice'
-ly-	'eat'	**mú<u>nd</u>àlyà**	3/4	'person who doesn't eat'

Verb stem	Gloss	Noun	Cl.	Gloss
-bètulw-	'be carried'	múndàbètùlwâ	3/4	'person who will not be carried'
-haan-	'give to others'	múndàhààna	3/4	'person who doesn't share'

4.1.1.5 *'one having'* -ene

The root -ènè 'one having' is a noun root of cl. 1a, with its plural in cl. 2. It seems perhaps to be derived from an irregular resultative form of the verb phrase: **kúbá ná** 'have (lit., be with)'. As a noun, it means 'owner of', or 'one having something', e.g. **mwèné ndálò** 'the one who owns the field', **mwènè=yô** 'the one who owns it'. In the idiomatic phrases **mwèné wìtù** 'our relative', **mwènè wìnyù** 'your (PL) relative', **mwènè wàbò** 'their relative' (of which the plurals are all formed by changing **mwènê** to **bèènê**) it means 'relative'. It may also function as a comparative conjunction, meaning 'like' or 'of the same type', e.g. **íbíndú mwènè bínò** 'things like these (lit., things the relative of these)'.

The example **mwènè=yô** 'the one who owns it' shows one of the idiosyncrasies of **mwènê**: it is the only non-verbal lexical item to which a pronominalized object may be syntactically cliticized. This quality, along with its semantic and segmental resemblance of the verb phrase **kúbá nâ** 'to be with, have' (with the **na** changed to a -**an** extension, a bit of imbrication, and the final vowel changed to -**e**), suggests the word's verbal origins. This is a unique form, and not characteristic of a productive process. An example in context is given in (4.12).

(4.12) Kú=yù-kw-ò ‖ yù-lú   lú-hàzì | tw-à-lù-héérez-á |
      Therefore   this.P-11 11-rooster 2PL-P1-O11-give-Fa

   mw-ènè =lwô.
   1-owner =11

   'Therefore ‖ this rooster | we gave it to | its owner (lit., the one having it).' (634 031)

When used in the plural with no complement, as in (4.13), **bèènê** means 'owners', **íbyá bèènè** are 'the (things) which belong to someone else', i.e. they are not just free for the taking.

(4.13) W-é=   rì   mú=   génd-á   ú-gáà-ly-à |
      2SG-FOC= is   PROG= GOING-Fa 2SG-INTL-eat-Fa

   í=by-á=   bè-ènè.
   AU=8-A.M=   2-owners

'You are the one who goes around eating | the (food) of someone else.'
(634 031)

4.1.2 Nouns derived from adjectives

A noun of any class may be derived from any type of adjective of that class. Since it involves no affixation or alteration of form, this is not so much a case of derivation as it is an alternative function of an adjective form. The structure of such a noun is identical to that of the adjective. The only differences are that as a noun, the form is no longer used attributively, but instead is used substantively, e.g. in the NP **(ú=)múndú múbí** 'bad person', the noun **múndù** may be omitted, being understood, but no longer expressed, and **múbí** takes over the nominal function: **(ú=)múbí** 'the bad (person)'. The nominal form may take an augment, while the adjective used attributively may not.

The derivation of nouns from adjectives is a highly productive process. The base adjective may be underived, or it may itself be derived from a verb. It is common to productively derive a noun from an adjective, which in turn is derived from a verb using the adjective suffix **-é** (described in 4.3.2). See (4.14m) for an example, from the verb **-yándik-** 'write'.

In (4.14a–k) we see nouns of cl. 1/2 which have been derived from adjectives. Most examples of derived nouns below are shown in cl. 1 and cl. 8, as these are most common, but any class could have been used. Abstract nouns derived from adjectives are also commonly used, e.g. (4.14n) **búgùmâ** 'unity' from **-gùmâ** 'one'.

(4.14) Nouns derived from adjectives

	Adj. stem	Gloss	Derived noun	Gloss
a.	-bì	'bad'	(ú=)múbî	'bad (person)'
b.	-éru	'white, pure'	(ú=)mwērù	'pure (person)'
c.	-òfi	'short'	(ú=)mwòfì	'short (person)'
d.	-îjá	'good'	(ú=)mwîjâ	'good (person)'
e.	-gùma	'one/some'	(ú=)múgùmà	'one (person)'
f.	-hámu	'large'	(ú=)múhámù	'large (person)'

	Adj. stem	Gloss	Derived noun	Gloss
g.	-gùmaana	'alive, well'	(ú=)múgùmààna	'alive/well (person)'
h.	-là	'long, tall'	(ú=)múlà	'tall (person)'
i.	-síre	'possessed'	(ú=)músírè	'possessed (person)'
j.	-lébe	'a certain'	(ú=)múlébè	'a certain (person)'
k.	-īru	'black'	(ú=)mwīrù	'black (person)'
l.	-ìngi	'many'	(í=)bìngì	'many (things)'
m.	-yándiké	'written'	(í=)bíyándìkê	'written (things)'
n.	-gùmá	'one/some'	(ú=)búgùmâ	'unity'

4.1.3 Nouns derived from other nouns by prefix change

4.1.3.1 Diminutive/pejorative derivations

The cl. 19 singular prefix **hí-**, with its plural most often in cl. 13 **tú-** but sometimes in cl. 14 **bú-**, is used to derive diminutive nouns, or sometimes pejorative ones, from an unmarked nominal form. For example, the noun **mùgózì** 'rope' will yield **hìgózì** 'small rope' or **tùgózì** 'small ropes'. Especially with cl. 9/10 nouns, the diminutive prefix is sometimes added to the normal noun prefix rather than substituting for it, e.g. **hí-ny-ûmbà** (19-9-house) 'small house'.[3] Retention of the original prefix is possibly done to avoid losing the identity of the original noun, as well as perhaps having some phonological basis in the syllabification of the original noun.

The more commonly used diminutive plural is in cl. 13, but cl. 14 is also used: e.g. the plural of **hí-kólò** (19-monkey) 'monkey' is either **tú-kólò** or **bú-kólò**, and there are other nouns which also take either plural. The cl. 14 **bú-** is often used when there are a great many small things, e.g. a flock of birds, large group of monkeys, many little seeds, etc. Cl. 14 is also generally used for the diminutive plural of items in cl. 12, for which the normal non-diminutive plural is in cl. 13 **tú-**.

When counting non-specific things, such as when teaching a child how to count, the progression is **hí-gùmà, bù-bìrì, bù-shàtù**... (19-one, 14-two, 14-three...), and not **hí-gùmà,*tù-bìrì, *tù-shàtù**... etc.

In its non-diminutive, non-pejorative use, cl. 14 is not a plural class, but takes its plural in cl. 6, e.g. **bú-lámbò** (14-mountain), **má-lámbò** (6-mountains). However, when used in a diminutive sense, the cl. 14 **bú-** is always plural.

---

[3] One reason for assuming that the **ny-** is a prefix rather than part of the noun is that there is a related noun, **kyûmbà** '(inner) room', of which the diminutive is **hyûmbà**. However, the status of the **ny-** is debatable in this word, and the interpretation may differ from speaker to speaker.

Though this plural use of the cl. 14 form does not always indicate a pejorative connotation, it seems to be the class of choice if the speaker wishes to indicate a lack of respect toward the items being mentioned using the diminutive form, e.g. **bú-fwáráŋgà** (14-a.few.paltry.pieces.of.money) (cf. the normal cl. 9/10 **í=fwáráŋgà** 'money').

In (4.15) **bú-** is used as the plural prefix for the cl. 9/10 **nyámà** 'meat', to pejoratively indicate the gangrenous spots in the flesh of a mistreated child.

(4.15) **Bù-lyá   bú-ny-ámá | ú-bú-tá-málí   tòndéér-à**
      14-that.R 14-9-meat   S.R-14-FRUS.INTL-ALREADY begin-Fa

      ú=kú-ból-à ‖   bà-ná-bù-lyó-s-à.
      AU=15-rot-Fa   2-SQ-O14-leave-CS-Fa

'That flesh | which had already begun to rot ‖ they removed it.' (409 072)

Note that in (4.16i, k), the original noun is in cl. 12, which takes its usual plural in cl. 13, which is also the plural of the diminutive class, cl. 19. Cl. 12 in Kifuliiru is not overtly diminutive. The cl. 12 **kányúni** 'bird' may refer to a big bird or a small bird. Likewise, cl. 13, as a plural for cl. 12, may or may not be diminutive. In such a case, the use of the cl. 14 plural, as **búnyúni** 'small birds', in (4.16k) gives an option that leaves no room for doubt as to whether diminutivity is inferred. The same is true of other cl. 12/13 nouns such as **kábwâ** 'dog', **túbwâ** 'dogs'. The plural of cl. 19 **híbwâ** 'small dog' is always stated as **búbwâ** 'small dogs'.

(4.16) Diminutive derivation using **hi-/tu-/bu-**

	Cl.	Base noun	Gloss	Dim. sing	Dim. plural	Dim. gloss
a.	3/4	**mùgózì**	'rope'	**hìgózì**	**tùgózì**	'small rope(s)'
b.	3/4	**múgàzì**	'mountain'	**hígàzì**	**túgàzì**	'small mountain(s)'
c.	5/6	**íhèmbè**	'horn'	**híhèmbè**	**túhèmbè**	'small horn(s)'
d.	7/8	**kíndù**	'thing'	**híndù**	**túndù**	'small thing(s)'
e.	7/8	**kítáábò**	'book'	**hítáábò**	**tútáábò**	'small book(s)'
f.	9/10	**mbútò**	'seed'	**híbùtò**	**túbùtò**	'small seed(s)'
g.	11/10	**lùfwàbê**	'alphabet letter'	**hìfwàbê**	**tùfwàbê**	'small letter(s)'
h.	11/10	**lúhândè**	'side'	**híhândè**	**túhândè**	'small piece(s)'
i.	12/13	**kájùmbà**	'box'	**híjùmbà**	**tújùmbà**	'small box(es)'

4.1 Noun derivations

	Cl.	Base noun	Gloss	Dim. sing	Dim. plural	Dim. gloss
j.	12/13	kálìrà	'island'	hílìrà	túlìrà	'small island(s)'
k.	12/13/14	kányúnì	'bird'	hínyúnì	túnyúnì/búnyúnì	'small bird(s)'

In (4.17) we have an example of the use of the class 14 plural **búnyúni** 'small birds'.

(4.17) Bà-lì   mú=   shény-á ‖ ú=w-àbò   ná-yé |
      2-are PROG= get.firewood-Fa AU=1-SAME.SET ADD.P-1

      à-lì   mú=   yìt-à ‖ ú=**bú**-nyúnì.
      1-is   PROG= kill-Fa AU=14-birds

'They are getting firewood ‖ and their fellow also | he is killing ‖ birds.' (210 059)

Another example of the pejorative/diminutive used in context is found in a story where birds were singing in an attempt to bring forth water from a spring in a time of drought. In this example, the cl. 6 (a plural class but used for liquid masses) noun **á=mī-ījì ~ á=mā-ājì** (AU=6-water) is diminutivized using the pejorative/diminutive plural class, either 14 **ú=bwījì** or 13 **ú=twījì**. However **bí-dákà** (8-mud), also a noun which has no singular form, is diminutivized using the singular cl. 19 in (4.18).

The wagtail bird speaks, and the first small bit of moisture begins to appear, but no actual water is visible. At this point, the noun **ú=bw-ījì** (AU=14-water) is used to describe it. As noted above, the cl. 14 prefix often seems to have more of a pejorative connotation than its cl. 13 counterpart. Note also the cl. 19 diminutive **hídákà** 'little bit of mud'.

(4.18) Ú=**bw**-ìjí | **bú**-kòlà   mú=   nyény-á   ‖
      AU=14-water 14-is.NEWLY PROG= yield.to.persuasion-Fa

      n-é=   **hí**-dâká ‖ hì-kòlì   lób-ìr-ì.
      CNJ-AU= 19-mud 19-is.NEWLY be.wet-RS-Fi

'...(pej/dim) water | is beginning to yield to persuasion ‖ and the (dim) mud ‖ is beginning to be wet.' (204 043)

When the wagtail has managed to call forth still a bit more water, it is expressed using **ú=tw-īj̄ì** (AU=13-water) 'water' with the cl. 13 diminutive, rather than cl. 14 as before.

(4.19)

Ú=tw-ìjí |	tw-à-tòndéér-à	ú=kú-yîj-á |	tú-nììnî.
AU=13-water	13-P1-begin-Fa	AU=15-come-Fa	13-little

'(Dim) water |began to come | a little.' (204 045)

Finally, when there is a decent amount of water visible, the non-diminutive cl. 6 form **á=māājì** 'water' is used to describe it.

(4.20)

Mbw-à=	Ø-yùs-è	ú=kú-dèt-á	«ndóó» ||
As.soon.as-1=	SBV-finish-Fe	AU=15-say-Fa	ndoo

á=mà-àjí ||	gà-ná-yàmí	bòn-ék-à.
AU=6-water	6-SQ-IMMED	see-NEU-Fa

'When he finished saying «ndoo» || the water || suddenly appeared.' (204 048)

4.1.3.2 Augmentative/pejorative derivations

Though much less frequently used than the diminutive, Kifuliiru also employs the cl. 7 prefix **kí-** either as augmentative or as pejorative/augmentative. An example is found in the following, where the normal cl. 12 prefix of the noun **ká-nyúnì** (12-bird) has been replaced by the cl. 7 prefix, **kí-**, to emphasize the large size of the bird, which is reinforced by the adjective phrase **kíhámú** 'big':

(4.21)

Kú=	yìkyò	kí-hé |	mú=	kí-shúkà ||	mw-áàlì	rì-ìr-í |
17=	that.N+7	7-time	18=	7-bush	18-P3	is-RS-Fi

í=kí-nyúni |	kí-hámù.
AU=7-bird	7-big

'At that time | in the bush || there was |a bird | big.' (610 006)

The sometimes pejorative nature of the cl. 7 prefix is indicated mainly by its usage in many terms for persons whose mental or physical capacities are not in line with normal ranges, e.g. **kíshūūshù** 'mentally impaired person', **kítúzì-túúzì** 'person who has lost his mind', **kívírà** 'stupid or foolish person', **kíyíngí-yíngì** 'mentally impaired person', **kízéèzè** 'fool, simpleton', **kílèmà** 'crippled person', but these are not truly derivational uses of the prefix, since there are no related forms with alternative prefixes. However, the cl. 7 prefix has been observed in derivational use as a pejorative prefix for the word thief, which, in its unmarked form is **múzìmbà** 'thief'. Children in the village sometimes taunt an accused thief, chanting **Kízìmbá voleur! Kízìmbá voleur!** 'thief! thief!'. (**Voleur** is French for 'thief'.)

4.1.3.3 *Personifying prefix*

As an optional device in fictional narratives, usually those in which animals figure as at least some of the main characters, the characters, usually animals but sometimes even humans in the same story, are cited with what seems to be a "personifying" clitic, **w-a** (1-A.M) which then triggers cl. 1 agreements on other parts of speech. Since the only form in the language which in cl. 1 takes the form **w-a=** is the associative marker (A.M), it seems that this is basically an associative marker being used to indicate that a general noun is being used as a proper name for a character in the narrative. For example **wà=lúkwàvù** 'Rabbit', cf. **lú-kwàvù** (11-rabbit), **wá=ndàrè** 'Lion', cf. **n-dárè** (9/10-lion), **wá=kèrê** 'Frog', cf. **kèrê** (1a+frog), **wà=múndù** 'Person' cf. **mú-ndù** (1-person), etc. As is usual with an A.M, the **w-a=** precedes, rather than displaces, the normal class prefix of the noun, and in every case, the resulting noun takes cl. 1a agreements, rather than agreement with the original class of the noun. The tone of this clitic, as of all A.M s, is polar, that is, H preceding a L tone, and L preceding a H tone. As with all proclitics, the vowel of **wa=** is phonetically lengthened when followed by fewer than three morae.[4] The difference between the usual A.M and this usage is that usually there is an antecedent with which the A.M agrees. In this case, the A.M agrees with no cl. 1 antecedent, but serves to mark the inclusion of the following noun in class 1a.

---

[4] We are not indicating this predictable, non-phonemic vowel length in our examples.

(4.22) Personifying clitic for characters in certain narratives

Cl.	Prefix	Noun root	Gloss	Derivation	Gloss
1	mú-	-ndù	'person'	**wà**=múndù	'Mr. person'
1a	Ø	-kèrê	'frog'	**wá**=kèrê	'Mr. frog'
3	mú-	-shálàbìrà	'lizard'	**wà**=múshálàbìrà	'Mr. lizard'
7	kí-	-hómà	'puff adder'	**wà**=kíhómà	'Mr. puff adder'
9	n-	-dàrè	'lion'	**wá**=ndàrè	'Mr. lion'
9	n-	-gáàvù	'cow'	**wà**=ngáàvù	'Mr. cow'
9	m-	-beba	'rat'	**wà**=mbébà	'Mr. rat'
9	n-	-gwî	'leopard'	**wà**=ngwî	'Mr. leopard'
9	Ø	-shúúlì	'bull'	**wà**=shúúlì	'Mr. bull'
11	lú-	-kwàvù	'rabbit'	**wà**=lúkwàvù	'Mr. rabbit'
11	rù-	-mùngù	'hyena'	**wá**=rùmùngù	'Mr. hyena'
12	ká-	-mándà	'hawk'	**wà**=kámándà	'Mr. hawk'

Example (4.23) demonstrates the cl. 1 agreements with the form **w-à=shúúlì** (1-A.M=bull): the demonstrative, **ùyó** 'that.N-1' and the cl. 1 subject anaphoric pronoun **a-** on the verb **ákálángíízâ** 'he looked at' both agree with the new cl. 1a noun, **wà=shúúlì**.

(4.23) Ùyó   w-à=shúúlí | ìrì   á-ká-lángííz-á   w-á-ny-ànà
       that.N+1 1-A.M=bull when   1-P2-look.at-Fa 1-A.M=9-calf

       mú=   ká-bándà | à-ná-mánùk-à.
       18=   12-valley   1-SQ-went.down-Fa

'That bull | when he looked (from afar) at calf in the valley | he went down.' (631 007)

4.1.3.4 Abstract derivations

There are many abstract nouns, usually of the cl. 14 GNP **bú-**, but also (rarely) in cl. 11, with a **lú-** prefix. Most of these are related to nouns of cl. 1/2. Note that (4.24l) is an abstraction (derived from the verb -**génd-** 'go') using cl. 11 rather than cl. 14. Some of these cl. 14 nouns, such as in (4.24b), have a locational nuance, in addition to a true abstract meaning.

(4.24) Abstract nouns with corresponding noun of cl. 1/2

	Cl.	Cl. 1 noun	Gloss	Cl.	Abstract noun	Gloss
a.	1/2	**mújâ**	'slave'	14	**bújâ**	'slavery'
b.	1/2	**múngérè**	'herdsman'	14	**búngérè**	'place of herding'
c.	1/2	**múgùmààna**	'one who is well'	14	**búgùmààna**	'wellness'
d.	1/2	**mwírà**	'friend'	14	**bwírà**	'friendship'
e.	1/2	**mútùùdù**	'humble person'	14	**bútùùdù**	'humility'
f.	1/2	**múléévì**	'prophet'	14	**búléévì**	'prophecy'
g.	1/2	**múnyérè**	'young woman'	14	**búnyérè**	'girlhood'
h.	1/2	**mwéngè**	'clever person'	14	**bwéngè**	'cleverness'
i.	1/2	**mútàbánà**	'young person'	14	**bútàbánà**	'boyhood'
j.	1/2	**mwánùkè**	'very young baby'	14	**bwánùkè**	'infancy'
k.	1/2	**mwìtánì**	'murderer'	14	**bwìtánì**	'murder, killing'
l.	1/2	**múgéézì**	'traveler'	11	**lúgéézì**	'trip, journey'

4.1.3.5 Language names

As a rule, language names in Kifuliiru are marked by the cl. 7 prefix **kí-**, which is derived from the cl. 1/2 noun, denoting the person of the group which speaks the language. From the cl. 1/2 **múbèmbê** 'Bembe person' is derived **kíbèmbê**, 'the Bembe language'. The cl. 7 prefix is used in the Kifuliiru term, even though the languages may be called by other names by those who actually speak them. For example, Bembe people, southern neighbors of the Bafuliiru, themselves call their language **ébèmbê**, and the Tembo call their language **chítèmbò**. The exception to the consistent Kifuliiru use of the cl. 7 prefixes for language names is **máshì**, which in Kifuliiru takes the cl. 6 prefix **má-**. This term is the same one used by the neighboring Shi people for their own language.

(4.25) Language names marked by **ki-, ma-**

Cl. 1 noun	Gloss	Language name	Gloss
múbángú-bângù	'Mubangu-bangu person'	<u>**kí**</u>**bángú-bângù**	'Kibangu-bangu language'
múbèmbè	'Mubembe person'	<u>**kí**</u>**bèmbê**	'Kibembe language'
múfùlììrù	'MuFuliiru person'	<u>**kí**</u>**fùlììrû**	'Kifuliiru language'
múhàvù	'Muhavu person'	<u>**kí**</u>**hàvù**	'Chihavu language'
múnyárwándà	'Rwandan person'	<u>**kí**</u>**nyàrwàndâ**	'Kinyarwanda language'
múnyíndù	'Munyindu person'	<u>**kí**</u>**nyíndù**	'Kinyindu language'
múrégà	'Murega person'	<u>**kí**</u>**règâ**	'Kirega language'
múrûndì	'Burundian person'	<u>**kí**</u>**rûndì**	'Kirundi language'
múrúngwâ	'White person'	<u>**kí**</u>**rúngwâ**	'White person's language'
mútèmbò	'Mutembo person'	<u>**kí**</u>**tèmbò**	'Chitembo language'
múfáráànsà	'French person'	<u>**kí**</u>**fáráànsà**	'French language'
múshì	'Mushi person'	<u>**má**</u>**shì**	'Mashi language'

4.1.3.6 Place names

A place name may be derived from a noun or verb by the use of the cl. 14 **bu-** prefix. This process is not confined to Kifuliiru, as can be observed from a look at the map of Africa, where such town names as **Bù-líndwê** (a mountain village) derived from the passive verb **-líínd-w** 'be waited for', **Bú-nìà**, **Bú-tèmbò**, **Bú-kávù** (from **bú-kààfù** (a Mashi word) 'place of cows'), **Bú-rûndì**, home of the **Bá-rûndì**, with its capital **Bù-júmbúrà**. The Kifuliiru pronunciation of "Uvira", the major town of the Kifuliiru-speaking area, is **Bú-vīīrà** 'place of the Viira people'. This derivational process is productively used in naming places after the people who live there, as shown in (4.26).

(4.26) Place names marked by **bu-**

People name	Gloss	Place name	Gloss
Bábángúbângù	'Bangu-bangu people'	**búbángúbângù**	'land of Bangu-bangu people'
Bábèmbè	'Bembe people'	**búbèmbè**	'land of Bembe people'
Báfùlììrù	'Fuliiru people'	**búfùlììrù**	'land of Fuliiru people'
Báhàvù	'Havu people'	**búhàvù**	'land of Havu people'
Báviīrà	'Viira people'	**búviīrà**	'land of Viira people'
Bányíndù	'Nyindu people'	**búnyíndù**	'land of Nyindu people'
Bárûndì	'Burundian people'	**búrûndì**	'land of Rundi people'
Báshì	'Shi people'	**búshì**	'land of Shi people'
Bárégà	'Lega people'	**búrégà**	'land of the Lega people'
Báhàráàbù	'Arab people'	**búhàráàbù**	'land of the Arab people'

4.1.4 Nouns derived from another noun by the addition of a formative

There are several formatives which combine with noun roots or with various pronominal formatives to produce derived nouns. These derived nouns are of basically three types: (a) kinship terms: father, mother, husband, wife; (b) nouns denoting an animate being as either female (woman or girl) or a child; and (c) nouns formed using the conjunctive, which denote the owner or possessor of some thing or quality.

4.1.4.1 Formatives na 'mother of' and she 'father of'

A similar method of producing a derived noun is observed with **-na** 'mother of' or **-she/-sho** 'father of' to a noun root (see **nyínà** 'his mother' and **yîshè** 'his father' for these formatives used as roots or suffixes). Nouns having an initial **na-** or **she-** formative are always of cl. 1a, and therefore do not have a gender-class prefix preceding the formative. This derivational process is infinitely productive with proper names, since **na-/she-** can be prefixed to any name to indicate the mother or father of a child of that name. The fact that a vowel of the formative is lengthened when there are fewer than three morae following within the word, as in **náákùlù** 'his...grandmother' and **shòòkùlû** 'grandfather', (4.27d, l), indicates that these formatives are/were clitics.[5] In at least some cases however, the combinations seem to have been lexicalized

---
[5] There is a rule which lengthens the vowel of a proclitic when its host word consists of three or fewer morae.

with the long vowel. The tone of these formatives is polar, i.e. H preceding a L tone and L preceding a H tone.

(4.27) **na-** and **she-** with kinship terms and proper names (cl. 1a)

		Noun	Gloss
	a.	<u>nyí</u>-nà ~ <u>ní</u>-nà	'his/her/their mother'
	b.	<u>nyó</u>kò	'your mother'
	c.	<u>nyó</u>kó-kùlù	'your grandmother'
	d.	<u>náá</u>=kùlù	'his/her/their grandmother'
	e.	<u>ná</u>=vyàlà	'his/her/their mother-in-law'
	f.	<u>nyáá</u>mà vyàlà	'my mother in law'
	g.	<u>nà</u>=Mútētò	'mother of Muteto'
	h.	<u>ná</u>=Shàmbààlê	'mother of Shambaale'
	i.	<u>ní</u>=íhāshà	'mother of twins'
	j.	yî-<u>shè</u>†	'his/her/their father'
	k.	yî-<u>shò</u>	'your father'
	l.	<u>shòò</u>=kùlû	'his/her/their/my/your grandfather'
	m.	<u>shé</u>=vyàlà	'father-in-law'
cf.	n.	dáàtà vyàlà	'my/our father-in-law'
	o.	<u>shó</u>=vyàlà	'your father-in-law'
	p.	<u>shè</u>=Mútètò	'father of Muteto'
	q.	<u>shé</u>=Shàmbààlé	'father of Shambaale'
	r.	<u>shèè</u>=bújâ	'slave master or owner of animal (lit., father of slavery)'

†The morpheme **yî-** is also found in the cl. 1a kinship term **yîba** 'her husband', see (4.1.4.2).

It is interesting that in the terms for mother, comparing **nyínà** 'his/her/their mother' and **nyókò** 'your mother', the common element, assumedly representing 'mother' seems to be **ni** (~ **ny-** or **nyi-**) while the possessive elements would seem to be **-nà** in (4.27a) and **-ókò** in (4.27b). However, comparing these with (4.27d, e, g, h, i) it seems that the element which represents 'mother' is **na-**. In (4.27i) the vowel of the **na-** formative coalesces with the initial **i** of **íí-hāshà** (5-twin). The term **máàwê** 'my/our mother' has no obvious common element with any of these. The same is true for the grandmother terms, where **múgààkà**, the term used for reference or direct address to 'my/our grandmother' bears little resemblance to the grandmother terms found in (4.27c, d).

Note also in (4.27j, k) that the formative is **she** for third-person relationship, but **sho** for second-person relationship. However, in (4.27l) the formative in the word grandfather is not **she** but **sho**, even though not necessarily expressing a second-person relationship. It is not clear how this came to be.

The root **vyàlà** 'in-law' is interesting in that it is usually used with a proclitic such as **na** or **she**, or in conjunction with another kinship term, e.g. **dáàtà vyàlà**. However, with a slight tonal change, it is found as a noun stem with the cl. 1 prefix **mú-** as **múvyâlà** 'child of maternal uncle'. The fact that this seems to have a common root with in-law terms undoubtedly says something about the traditional kinship system and common traditional choice of marriage partners. The same root is also found without a prefix in the context of the possessive locative, e.g. **í=mwàbó vyàlà** 'at their in-laws' place' (cf. **í=mwàbò** 'at their place') or **í=mwítù vyàlà** 'at our in-laws' place'.

Besides **vyâlà**, the only other non-possessive term which forms a word with the **she** proclitic/initial formative is **shéébújâ** 'slave master, animal owner' seen in (4.27r).[6]

4.1.4.2 Formatives mùká 'wife' and yîbà 'husband'

As seen in (4.28), **mù-ká-** (1-wife), (plural **bà-ká-** (2-wives), neither form ever expressed without a possessor)[7] is used as a root in the various possessive forms of the word 'wife', and **yîbà** (PL **báyîbà**) 'her husband' (used with or without an expressed possessor) as a root in various possessive forms of the word 'husband' (cf. **yîshè** 'father'). All forms are of cl. 1a and take their plurals in cl. 2.

In one case, the two formatives (**mùká** and **yîbà**) are combined into a single word, see (4.28g). The forms which, for semantic reasons, are not commonly found in singular are listed as plurals in (4.28). The form in (4.28g), **mùká yîbà ~ mùkíîbà** 'the (other) wife of her husband',[8] can also be used with the

---

[6] The adverb **sésèèzì~shéshèézì** 'morning' may also historically contain this morpheme. The word **kúsèèzì~kúshèèzì** 'tomorrow' seems to have the same root. This would indicate that the morning was expressed as 'the father of tomorrow'.

[7] The words **mùká** 'wife (of)' (cf. **múkàzì** woman), and **yîbà** 'husband (of)' while having no obvious inherent possessive element, may be used together with a proper noun (and with no associative particle) to indicate possession: e.g. **mùká Bíháyò** 'the wife of Bihayo' or **yîbá Bídètwà** 'the husband of Bidetwa'. There is only one other noun which may be used similarly without an associative element: **múgálà** 'son (of)', e.g. **múgálá Bíháyò** 'son of Bihayo'. Though **mùká** and **yîbà** may not be followed by separate possessive element (either associative particle or full forms of 'my', 'his', 'your' etc.), this is not true of **múgálà**, which may be used with a full associative pronoun ('my', 'his', etc.), e.g. **múgálá wààgè wá=Kìízà** 'his son Kiza' (Kiza being the name of the son, not of the father). Such an utterance assumes that there are other sons from whom Kiza is being differentiated.

[8] This term is used not only to refer to a co-wife, but also, with a separate following possessive,

possessive elements seen in (4.28i, j), as **mùkííbànié** 'the wife of my husband' or **mùkííbàlò** 'the (other) wife of your husband'. **Mùká** or **yîbà** can also be used preceding a proper name to signify the spouse of that person, e.g. **mùká Bíháyò** 'the wife of Bihayo', **yîbà Kábègétwâ** 'the husband of Kabegetwa'.

(4.28) Formatives **-ka** and **yiba** with possessive elements

	UF	SF	Gloss
a.	mù-<u>ká</u>-à-ni-é	mùkáànié	'my wife'
b.	mù-<u>ká</u>-à-u-é	mùkáàwê	'your (SG) wife'
c.	mù-<u>ká</u>-à-g-é	mùkáàgê	'his wife'
d.	bà-<u>ká</u>-a-itú	bàkíìtû	'our wives'
e.	bà-<u>ká</u>-a-inyú	bàkíìnyû	'your (PL) wives'
f.	bà-<u>ká</u>-a-ba-ó	bàkáàbô	'their wives'
g.	mù-<u>ká</u>-yîbà	mùkíìbà	'the wife of her husband'
h.	mù-<u>ká</u>-yîshò	mùká-yîshô	'the wife of your father'
i.	mù-<u>ká</u>-dáàtà	mùká-dáàtà	'the wife of my father'
j.	mù-<u>ká</u>Bíháyò	mùká-Bíháyò	'the wife of Bihayo'
k.	<u>yîbà</u>-ni-é	yíbànié	'my husband'
l.	<u>yîbà</u>-lò	yíbàlò	'your (SG) husband'
m.	yîba	yîbà	'her husband'
n.	<u>yîbà</u>Kábègétwá	yîbà-Kábègétwâ	'the husband of Kabegetwa'

4.1.4.3 Formative -ānà 'child'

The root **-ānà** 'child' combines with the noun roots denoting various birds or animals to form compound words which denote the young of that animal, e.g. the cl. 7 **kyánà-hènè** 'baby goat', cf. **í=mbènè** 'goat'. As in the example just given, such compounds usually have a cl. 7 prefix, **kí-** with the plural in cl. 8 **bí-**, but can also have a diminutive cl. 19 prefix, **hí-**. The use of **-ānà** to form the name of a young animal is not a completely productive process, since this derivation is commonly done in reference to certain animals, but not to others. It is possible that this is being lost as a productive process, as older speakers tend to use it more widely than younger ones. For animals whose young is not indicated by the prefixation of the root **-ānà** 'child', an associative phrase is used, e.g. the cl. 19 **hyànà hyé=mbógò** 'baby water buffalo' or **úmwàná wé=ngwî** 'baby leopard', etc.

---

to refer to the wife of one's husband's brother. A man refers to his brother's wife as **mùkáànié wànì**.

The noun created using **kyánà-** (cl. 7 plus formative) can be the source of further derivation by the substitution of the cl. 19 **hí-** diminutive prefix, e.g. **kyánà-hènè** 'baby goat' > **hyánà-hènè** 'little baby goat'. The root **-ānà** 'child' is also used in the derivation of words for other progeny, as shown in (4.29).

(4.29) Formative -ana plus noun

	Cl.	Noun	Gloss	Cl.	Derived noun	Gloss
a.	1a/2	**nyínà**	'his/her mother'	7/8	**kyàná-nyínà**	'child of maternal aunt'
b.	7/8	**kíbùzì**	'sheep'	7/8	**kyáná-bùzì**	'lamb'
c.	7/8	**kígûndù**	'banana plant'	7/8	**kyáná-gàkà**	'shoot of a banana plant'
d.	9/10	**ngókò**	'chicken'	7/8	**kyáná-gókò**	'chick'
e.	9/10	**mbénè**	'goat'	7/8	**kyánà-hènè**	'kid (of goat)'
f.	9/10	**ngúlúbè**	'pig'	7/8	**kyánà-kúlúbè**	'piglet'
g.	12/13	**kányúnì**	'bird'	7/8	**kyányá-nyúnì**	'baby bird'
cf. h.	12/13	**kábwà**	'dog'	7/8	**kíbwānà**	'puppy'

4.1.4.4 Formative -kàzì 'woman'

The cl. 1 Kifuliiru noun root **-kàzì** (cf. **múkàzì** 'woman')[9] can be used derivationally as a formative to denote a specified type of woman. From the noun **mújá** 'slave' one can derive **mújàà-kàzì** 'slave woman'; from **mwámì** 'king' is derived **mwámì-kàzì** 'queen', etc. Examples are seen in (4.30). This is a productive process with ethnic names as in (4.30g-k), but not with most common nouns. The presence of a long vowel in the base noun in (4.30a) and of a HL contour on the final syllable of the base noun in (4.30b, c) indicates that **kàzì** is not a suffix.[10] It is either a clitic or a separate word, but does not become part of the same word as the base noun.

---

[9] The formative **lume/rume** is fairly common in Bantu, denoting a male (cf. Std. Kiswahili **mwanamume** 'man' (Congo Kiswahili **mwanaume** 'man' or **dume** 'male'). In Kifuliiru, however, this formative has been observed in only one instance: **í=mbwá-rúmè** '9/10-male dog'. It is said that this compound has its origins in Mashi, Kifuliiru's neighbor language to the north. The idea that this word may not be of true Kifuliiru origin is further reinforced by the fact that it uses the cl. 9/10 form **m-bwâ**, whereas the usual Kifuliiru term for 'dog' is the cl. 12 **ká-bwà**.

[10] Long vowels are shortened if three or more morae follow in the word. Underlying HL contours occur only in a penultimate syllable, and a H tone is realized with a phonetic HL contour only if it is word final.

(4.30) Compound noun stems formed by noun root plus formative -**kazi**

	Cl.	Derived noun	Gloss
a.	1/2	**múléévì**-**kàzì**	'prophetess'
b.	1/2	**mújáà**-**kàzì**	'slave woman'
c.	1/2	**múhyâ**-**kàzì**	'recently married woman'
d.	1/2	**mwálì**-**kàzì**	'daughter-in-law (lit., sister-woman)'
e.	1/2	**mwámì**-**kàzì**	'queen (king-woman)'
f.	9/10	**mbwâ**-**kàzì**	'female dog'
g.	1/2	**múfùlììrù**-**kàzì**	'Mufuliiru woman'
h.	1/2	**múmísìrì**-**kàzì**	'Egyptian woman'
i.	1/2	**múrûndì**-**kàzì**	'Murundi woman'
j.	1/2	**múnyárwándà**-**kàzì**	'Rwandan woman'
k.	1/2	**mùyàhúdì**-**kàzì**	'Jewish woman'

4.1.4.5 Formative -nyérè 'girl'

The formative -**nyérè** (cf. cl. 1 **mú**-**nyérè** 'girl') is suffixed to a complete noun to indicate that the person denoted is a girl. The use of this as a formative is exemplified in the word **múlùzì**-**nyérè** 'daughter of the king, princess' (cf. **múlùzì** 'prince, son of king'). Other examples are given in (4.31).

(4.31) Words formed by noun root plus formative -**nyere**

Cl.	Derived noun	Gloss
1/2	**múlùzì**-**nyérè**	'king's daughter
1/2	**múlámbò**-**nyèrè**	'girl of the **múlámbò** clan'
1/2	**múhámbà**-**nyèrè**	'girl of the **múhámbà** clan'
1/2	**múshímbì**-**nyèrè**	'girl of the **múshímbì** clan'
1/2	**mútùmbà**-**nyèrè**	'girl of the **mútùmbà** clan'
1/2	**múfùmù**-**nyèrè**	'healer's daughter'
1/2	**mwàndísì**-**nyèrè**	'writer's daughter'
1/2	**ngéézì**-**nyèrè**	'escaped daughter'
1/2	**ngáálé**-**nyèrè**	'rude daughter'
1/2	**mbéézí**-**nyèrè**	'lost daughter'
1/2	**múkòzì**-**nyèrè**	'girl who is a servant or worker'
1/2	**mbábúsì**-**nyèrè**	'far away daughter'

4.1.4.6 Conjunctive nouns derived with formative na

As in many Bantu languages, **na** is a syntactic element closely related to the associative markers. It is used with a conjunctive meaning between nouns, or as a sequential prefix within verbs, etc. All nouns with this as a formative are of cl. 1a, and take their plural in cl. 2, e.g. **nàhánò** 'lord (lit., the one having this place)', **bánàhánò** 'lords'; **nàhámwàbò** 'their master (lit., the one having their place)', **bánàhámwàbò** 'their masters', etc. The meaning of **na-** in this context is 'the one having'.

In these constructions, the formative **na-** is followed by a complete noun or pronoun with its own prefix. In (4.32a–e) and perhaps (4.32i), the formative is added to a noun which has been derived from a verb. In (4.32f–h) the formative is added to various types of pronominal/locative elements, and in (4.32j–l) the formative is added to a noun.

There are stems of many other words (all of cl. 1a) beginning with this formative which are not synchronically traceable to another lexical item, e.g. **nákásàrè** 'hawk', **nàfúúfúlù** 'owl', etc.

(4.32) Derived nouns with formative **na-**

	Cl.	UF	Surface	Gloss
a.	1a	na-bú-yì-súmà	nábwìsùmà	'a car/cart' (cf. -**sum**- 'buy food')
b.	1a	na-bú-yì-gíra	nábwìgìrà	'self-reliant person (one doing things by self)'
c.	1a	na-mu-fwiri	nàmúfwīrì	'widow (having one who has died)'
d.	1a	na-bà-góòkwà	nábàgóòkwâ	'disease causing crooked fingers'
e.	1a	na-kí-mínīkà	nàkímínīkà	'mass-murderer (one wiping out people)'
f.	1a	na-hánò	nàhánò	'lord (one having this place)'
g.	1a	na-mw-àní	nàmwànî	'spouse (one of in my place)'
h.	1a	na-há-mwàbò	nàhámwàbò	'their master (one having their place)'
i.	1a	na-ká-sàrè	nàkásàrè	'hawk' (perhaps from **kusára** 'to crave, long for')
j.	1a	na-kí-béngà	nàkíbéngà	'name of valley with a pond (having a pond)'
k.	1a	na-kú-zìmù	nàkúzìmù	'death personified (one having the underworld)'
l.	1a	na-kí-óyá	nàkyôyâ	'a person w/hairy body, or a hairy edible leaf'

Another class of words is distinguished from those in the preceding section by the fact that the formative **na** is preceded by a noun class prefix. The noun from which the derived noun is formed always retains its gender prefix as well, e.g. **múná-mwānà** 'the one with a child', cf. **mw-ānà** (1-child). Words of this type are in many classes, but never in cl. 1a, as all of the words above.

This method of forming compound noun stems is the only method which is still completely productive today. A compound noun of this configuration may be made from any noun just by adding a gender-class prefix plus **na-**.

(4.33) GNP plus formative **na-** plus full noun

Cl. of root	Derived noun	Gloss
1	**mú-<u>ná</u>-mwānà**	1-with-child
3	**mú-<u>ná</u>-múbêmbè**	1-with-leprosy
4	**mú-<u>ná</u>-mísí**	1-with-strength
6	**mú-<u>ná</u>-máhúkù**	1-with-wanting.everything
7	**mú-<u>ná</u>-kíshèkè**	1-with-sugarcane
8	**mú-<u>ná</u>-kíbèèshà**	1-with-lies
9/10	**mú-<u>ná</u>-mbâmbà**	1-with-arguing
11	**mú-<u>ná</u>-lúsháàgwà**	1-with-honor
12	**mú-<u>ná</u>-kádàlì**	1-with-not.listening
14	**mú-<u>ná</u>-búményì**	1-with-knowledge
6	**kí-<u>ná</u>-mīījì**	7-with-water 'wild edible tuber'
14	**kí-<u>ná</u>-bwēngè**	7-with-intelligence 'computer'

4.1.5 Compound nouns derived from two words

4.1.5.1 *Nouns derived from a verb root plus noun*

Compound noun stems may be formed from a nominal prefix plus verb root plus noun root. The noun root at the end can be interpreted as the object of the verb which precedes it. The verbal segment of the word always retains its final vowel, **-a**, though in pronunciation this **-a** undergoes elision in the case of a vowel initial prefix (cl. 5) on the following nominal element, as in (4.34a, e).

The noun root which follows the verb always retains its gender prefix, though the compound stem's initial gender prefix is the one which determines concord markings with other parts of the sentence.

4.1 Noun derivations

(4.34) Nouns composed of GNP + verb stem + complete noun

	PFX-verb + PFX-noun	Surface	Gloss
a.	<u>kí</u>-zìmyâ + <u>í</u>-zūūbà	kízìmízūūbà	(7-extinguishing-5-sun) 'very many'
b.	<u>ká</u>-mír-a + <u>bú</u>-ndù	kámírábúndù	(12-swallows-14-ugali) 'throat for swallowing food'
c.	<u>ká</u>-míra + <u>mì</u>-íji	kámírámīījì	(12-swallows-6-water) 'throat for swallowing water'
d.	<u>ká</u>-fwa + <u>bú</u>-shâ	káfwàbùshà	(1a-dies-14-worthless) 'good-for-nothing person'
e.	<u>na</u>múli + <u>í</u>-kòndo	námùlíkòndò	(1a+I.eat-5-navel) 'praying mantis'
f.	<u>ká</u>-hòla + <u>má</u>-sìga	káhòlàmàsìgà	(12-cools-6-cooking.stones) 'wee morning hour'
g.	<u>kí</u>-lónda + <u>mw</u>-ēzi	kílóndámwēzì	(7-born.after-3-moon) 'bright morning star'
h.	<u>n</u>-dètéra + <u>há</u>-bìri	ndètéráhábìrì	(1a-speaks-at-16-two) 'double-talker'
i.	<u>kí</u>-lya + <u>m</u>-bébà	kíryàmbèbà	(7-eats-9/10-rats) 'type of viper'
j.	<u>má</u>-hòna + <u>n</u>-vùlà	máhònànvùlà	(6-drops-9-rain) 'October'
k.	<u>n</u>-da-hùsá + <u>kí</u>-sìnga	ndàhùsákísìngà	(1a-doesn't.set.off.traps) 'inveterate womanizer'
l.	<u>n</u>-da-gíra + <u>mw</u>-ìra	ndàgírámwìrà	(1a-doesn't.make-1-friend) 'proper name'
m.	<u>ná</u>-mú-lòba + <u>Ø</u>-fwì	námúlòbâfwì	(1a-PROG-catch-Ø-fish) 'species of bird'

4.1.5.2 Nouns derived from noun plus noun

There are a few nouns derived by the compounding of two nouns, rather than a verb plus a noun. In these noun-noun compounds, each of the nouns retains its usual class prefix. The class of the compound noun, as always, is indicated by the initial noun's prefix.

(4.35) Nouns derived from complete noun plus complete noun

Noun + noun	Derived noun	Gloss
<u>mú</u>hánda + <u>nj</u>óvu	**múhándá-njóvù**	(3-toilet-9-elephant) 'thorn bush'
<u>ny</u>ûnda + <u>má</u>shììji	**nyûndà-máshììjì**	(9-eagle-6-river.plain) 'big bird (sp)'

4.1.6 Nouns derived from ideophones

A noun may be derived from an ideophone, as seen in (4.36).

(4.36) Nouns derived from ideophones

Ideophone	Gloss	Derived noun	Cl.	Gloss
nyáàwù	'meow'	**ny-áàbù**	9	'cat'
shwâ	'swishing sound'	**lú-shwâ-shwà**	11	'sound.of.passing. thru.plants'
nyààfù	'sound of hitting'	**mú-nyààfù**	3	'flexible.stick'
dígí	'sound of hard rain'	**mú-dígí-dígì**	3	'long.hard.rain'
shólyô	'sparrow's call'	**kí-shólyô**	7	'sparrow'
ngwà-ngwà	'pigeon's call'	**kí-ngwà-ngwà**	7	'pigeon'
syô	'sound of partridge chick'	**mú-syô**	3	'baby.partridge'
gùùgù	'male pigeon's call'	**ná-kí-hùgùùgù**	7	'large.dove'
gìtì-gìtì	'loud footsteps'	**ná-búgìtì**	1a	'one.who.walks. loudly'
syô-syô	'sound of chick'	**hy-áná-syôsyò**	19	'chick'
gútù	'sound of rapid drinking'	**námúgútúúlò**	1a	'one.who.drinks. quickly'
zíbù	'a sting'	**ká-zíbúlò**	12	'something.which. stings'
dítì	'sound of falling'	**mú-dítímbò**	3	'fall'

4.2 Verb derivations

4.2.1 Verbs derived from nouns

Though in most related noun-verb pairs the verb is considered to be primary, it is not clear that this is always the case. In some it is difficult to tell whether the noun or the verb is etymologically prior. There are also two related verbs in which the extension does not have the vowel that would be expected, given the vowel height harmony rule that affects the extensions. This might indicate that they are derived from a noun rather than vice versa.

Notice that in these two reversive/separative forms, the extension has the mid vowel **o** rather than the high vowel **u**, even though the extension would be expected to take the **u** form rather than the **o** form following a verb root containing the high vowel **i** (*-sínguuka, *-sínguula). This might indicate

4.2 Verb derivations

that the **o** has been retained from the noun from which these verbs might have originally been derived. The **búsíngò** noun indicates 'tools (sticks, string, etc.) needed to start a fire without matches'.

(4.37) Verbs possibly derived from nouns

Noun	Gloss	Derived verb	Gloss
bú-síngò	14-fire.starting.tools	kú-síngóókà	15-be.burned.up
bú-síngò	14-fire.starting.tools	kú-síngóólà	15-burn.up.something

4.2.2 Verbs derived from ideophones

The derivation of verbs from ideophones is quite common. Some such verbs are given in (4.38).

(4.38) Verbs derived from ideophones

Ideophone	Gloss	Derived verb base	Gloss
pwâ	'breaking of egg, jug, etc.'	-pwamuul-	'throw down and break open'
gúlù-gúlù	'fire crackling'	-gulumir-	'flames to crackle'
dígì-dígì	'sound of hard rain'	-digiirir-	'rain long and hard'
gó-gó	'sound of swigging'	-gongomer-	'swig quickly'
gótò-gótò	'sound of gulping'	-gòtomer-	'gulp down liquid'
dútù	'rope breaking'	-duuduk-	'rope to snap suddenly'
bù-bù	'dull sound'	-bùbul-	'have dull sound'
m!	'preglottalized mm'	-kuum-	'grunt in surprise, pain'
zíbù	'sting!'	-zìbul-	'sting, bite (of a snake or insect)'
píì	'when finished off'	-píís-	'many people to be killed (CS)'
dúgù-dúgù	'glug-glug'	-dúgumul-	'pour out liquid'
vwò	'sound of water'	-vwom-	'draw water'
pó	'bam!'	-poop-	'strike, chop something hard'
pû	'run off fast'	-puumuk-	'run away'

Ideophone	Gloss	Derived verb base	Gloss
kû	'thud'	-k<u>uu</u>nyuk-	'fall'
syê	'bang'	-s<u>ye</u>kan-	'bump each other'
kyô	'chirp'	-k<u>yoo</u>l-	'chirp'
tó	'sound of dripping'	-t<u>oo</u>ny-	'drip'
shàà	'water sound'	-sh<u>aa</u>m-	'begin boiling'
kótò	'sound of breaking'	-kò<u>to</u>l- /-gò<u>to</u>l-	'break'
júgù	'noise from container'	-jùg<u>u</u>mul-	'shake and hear sound'

4.2.3 Verbs derived from adjectives

Adjectives can also be a source of verbal derivation. Such derivation is accomplished by adding the inchoative morpheme -h- 'become' to the end of the adjective followed by the verbal final vowel. The final vowel of the adjective is thus the vowel which precedes the inchoative -h in the derived verb. In the case of a monosyllabic adjective, the final vowel of the base adjective is also lengthened. For example, the adjective -bí 'bad' becomes **kúbííhà** 'to become bad', while -là 'long' becomes **kúlááhà** 'to become long'. In the case of (4.39d) -**nììnî** 'small' where the monosyllabic adjective is reduplicated in its adjectival form, only the monosyllable is used in the verbal derivation.

Note that the adjective listed as the source of (4.39e), -**nóvù** 'soft', is itself probably derived from the verb **kúnògà** 'to be soft'. That the derivation has thus gone full circle indicates that the adjective -**nóvù** has been lexicalized. The same is probably the case for all adjectives.

(4.39) Verbs derived from adjectives

	Adjective	Gloss	Derived verb base	Gloss
a.	-bì	'bad'	-bi<u>ih</u>-	'become bad'
b.	-là	'long'	-la<u>ah</u>-	'get long'
c.	-lèma	'lame'	-lèma<u>h</u>-	'become lame'
d.	-nììnî	'small'	-ni<u>ih</u>-	'be scarce'
e.	-nóvu	'soft'	-nóvu<u>h</u>-	'become soft'
f.	-síre	'possessed'	-síre<u>h</u>-	'become possessed'
g.	-ángu	'light'	-yángu<u>h</u>-	'become light'

	Adjective	Gloss	Derived verb base	Gloss
h.	-òfi	'short'	**-yòfih-**	'become short'
i.	-ùgi	'sharp'	**-yùgih-**	'become sharp'
j.	-zíto	'heavy'	**-zídoh-**	'become heavy'

4.2.4 Verbs derived from related verbs by way of extensions

Extensions can be used to derive a verb from a related verb. For example, **kúgúlíísâ** 'cause to buy (i.e. sell)' is derived from **kúgúlà** 'to buy' by the suffixation of the causative extension -**íís**. The process of derivation by extension can be an extremely productive one. Because there are so many extensions used in derivation, and because they can co-occur and interact with each other, this subject is treated separately in ch. 5 "The Verb Stem".

4.2.5 Verbal auxiliaries derived from verbs

Most of the adverbial auxiliaries are derived from verbs still in synchronic usage. The adverbial auxiliaries, several of which can occur in a single verb form, are followed by a non-prefixed verb stem with the infinitive tone pattern.

The adverbial auxiliaries seem to have been formed not by an intentional process of derivational affixation, but by gradual grammaticization of the vowel coalescence between the final vowel -**a** of the first verb and the cl. 5 infinitive prefix, **i**- that was originally the first morpheme of the following verb. Synchronically they are lexicalized as -**i**-final grammatical morphemes.

Many of these auxiliaries still have the same basic meaning as the source verb. They are found in (4.40a–l). Other adverbial auxiliaries are obviously derived from a verb, but the meaning has been skewed. These are found in (4.40m–r). Finally, there is one, **kizi** 'repeatedly' for which no related verb has been even tentatively identified. It is possible that it is instead related to the non-agreeing adjective **ngíìsì** 'each, every'.

(4.40) Verbal auxiliaries derived from verbs

	Verb base	Gloss	Derived AUX	Gloss
a.	-génd-	'go'	-géndi	'going'
b.	-hík-ir-	'arrive-APL'	-híkiri	'arriving'
c.	-lèng-	'pass'	-lèngi	'to become fierce'
d.	-sìgal-	'remain behind'	-sìgali	'remaining'
e.	-yíj-	'come'	-yíji	'coming'
f.	-tám-	'come to end'	-támi	'after this' (usually w/ neg- 'any more')
g.	-tàng-	'come first'	-tàngi	'be first'
h.	-zínd-	'come to end'	-zíndi	'lastly'
i.	-zínduk-ir-	'go early in morning-APL'	-zíndukiri	'early in the morning'
j.	-lóóz-	'want, seek after'	-lóózi	'wanting'
k.	-mény-	'know'	-ményi	'knowing'
l.	-yìji-	'know (RS)'	-yìji	'knowing'
m.	-bùl-	'lack'	-bùli	'subsequently, afterwards'
n.	-kòl-	'work'	-kòli	'new state'
o.	-mál-	'be finished/ finish off'	-máli	'already'
p.	-línd-	'wait'	-líndi	'after great duress'
q.	-lúnguul-	'go without detours'	-lúnguli	'prematurely'
r.	-tàng-	'come first'	-té	'do before something else'
s.	---		-kìzi	'repeatedly, usually, always'

Example (4.41) illustrates the use of four of these auxiliaries, **té** 'first', **géndi** 'going', **bùli** 'afterwards', **yíji** 'coming':

(4.41) Ù-Ø-lék-é   n-**dé**   géndî   nywà á=mì-ìjí |
      2-SBV-leave-Fe   1SG-FIRST   GOING   drink AU=6-water

   tù-ká-**bùlì**   yíjí   gànúúl-à.
   1PL-INTV-SBSQ   COMING   converse-Fa

'Let me first go and drink water | (and) afterwards we'll come and chat.'
(54 018)

4.3 Adjectives derived from verbs

4.3.1 The closed set

Many adjectives are derived from verbs. The following adjectives are part of a finite set of adjectives which is encoded in the lexicon. The examples in (4.42) with the exception of (4.42m-o) employ the suffix -**u**, which is also attested in other Bantu languages as an adjectival derivational suffix.[11] In (4.42a, b) this suffix seems to condition spirantization (i.e. root-final **(m)b** and **g** become **v**), while in the others it does not.

(4.42) Adjectives derived from verbs

	Verb base	Gloss	Derived adjective	Gloss
a.	-**jámb**-	'get thin'	-**jáàvù**	'tasteless'
b.	-**nóg**-	'be smooth'	-**nóvù**	'smooth'
c.	-**dúkul**-	'be red'	-**dúkùlà**	'red'
d.	-**hám**-	'get big'	-**hámù**	'big'
e.	-**kay**-	'be fierce'	-**káyù**	'fierce'
f.	-**kùl**-	'grow'	-**kùlù**	'great, bigger, older'
g.	-**lémb**-	'be soft'	-**lêmbù**	'soft'
h.	-**nún**-	'be sweet'	-**núnù**	'sweet'
i.	-**lúl**-	'be bitter'	-**lúlù**	'bitter'
j.	-**yèruuk**-	'to get white/clean'	-**ērù**	'white'
k.	-**yír**-	'to get dark'	-**írù**	'black'
l.	-**tíb**-	'be dull'	-**íbù**	'dull'
m.	-**hy**-	'be ready, ripe'	-**hyàhyâ**	'new'

---

[11]*-ų is reconstructed by Meeussen (1967) as an adjective derivational suffix.

	Verb base	Gloss	Derived adjective	Gloss
n.	**-lyalyani-**	'deceive'	**-lyâlyà**	'deceptive'
o.	**-maat-**	'be empty'	**-māātà**	'empty'

4.3.2 Productive derivations of stative verbal adjectives

Adjectives can be productively derived from verbs by the suffixation of -**é** to the verb stem in place of any other final vowel, and the use of the nominal/adjectival prefixes, rather than any verbal prefixes. This is a productive process, as is the formation of the infinitive. However, unlike the infinitive, these adjectives may not include the negative marker nor have object prefixes, nor contain any productive (non-lexicalized) extensions. For example, in **úmúndú múshúlìkê** 'a person who has been hit' (from **-shúlik-** 'hit') we note that there is no passive morpheme in the adjective **múshúlìkê** to indicate that the "subject" of the verbal root is the undergoer of the action. The verbal nature of these adjectives is restricted to the fact that they share a common radical with a verb, and are used as participles, following a copula.

Another example of a stative verbal adjective is -**tùlé**, e.g. **í=nyûngú ndùlê** 'a pot with a hole', from the verb **tùl-** 'make a hole'. Although this derivational process is productive, and adjectives of this type can theoretically be formed from any action verb, they do not occur very frequently in our texts.

As is true of all adjectives, these forms can also be used as substantives, e.g. **ú=múshúlìkê** 'a person who has been hit'. Thus these adjectives are also a source of derived nouns.

(4.43) Some stative verbal adjectives

Verb base	Gloss	Derived adjective	Gloss
-baaj-	'carve wood'	**-bààjé**	'carved'
-bàngik-	'stick together'	**-bàngìké**	'stuck together'
-hàmik-	'close tightly'	**-hàmìké**	'closed'
-lámbik-	'lay out'	**-lámbìké**	'laid out'
-shùk-	'clean, wash'	**-shùké**	'washed, cleaned'
-shwek-	'tie up'	**-shwèké**	'tied'
-tèrek-	'place, store'	**-tèrèké**	'stored, placed'
-yándik-	'write'	**-yándìké**	'written'
-tùl-	'make hole'	**-tùlé**	'having a hole'

Verb base	Gloss	Derived adjective	Gloss
-laalik-	'invite'	**-lààlìké**	'invited'
-yóky-	'roast, burn'	**-yôkyé**	'roasted'
-yígul-	'open'	**-yígùlé**	'open'

4.4 Adverbs derived from verbs

There are various adverbs, many of them reduplicated, which are derived from verbs. Most commonly they have either a **ká-** (12) or **lú-** (11) prefix, as seen in (4.44).

(4.44) Adverbs derived from verbs

	Verb base	Gloss	Derived adverb	Gloss
a.	**-jòjober-**	'to walk slowly in shame'	**lú-jóbé-jóbè**	11-slowly.in.shame
b.	**-kúbiriz-**	'do something quickly'	**ká-ngúbí-ngúbì**	12-in.a.hurry
c.	**-yìtónd-**	'to be careful, cautious'	**lú-tóó-lútô**	11-furtively.behind
d.	**-gálam-**	'to lie on the back'	**ká-ngálí-ngálì**	12-on.the.back
e.	**-gálam-**	'to lie on the back'	**lú-gálì**	11-on.the.back
f.	**-gálam-**	'to lie on the back'	**bú-gálàmà**	14-on.the.back
g.	**-dwàng-**	'join together'	**dwàvwé-dwàvwê**	be.very.many
h.	**-tyógool-**	'renege'	**lú-tyôgò-tyôgò**	11-insincerely
i.	**-shuush-**	'to do quickly'	**ká-shúùshì**	12-quickly
j.	**-fúdéét-**	'to walk backwards'	**kí-fúdéètè**	7-backwards

In general, verbal extensions are dropped or shortened in the adverbial forms: -jòjob-er- > jóbé-jóbè, -kûb-iriz- > -ngúbí-ngúbì, -gál-am- > -gálì (-ngálì).

There is evidence in (4.44g) of stages of derivation. From the base verb -dwàng- 'join together' what seems to be the adjectival suffix -u was added. It would seem more intuitive with a verbal base to interpret the suffixal -u as a passive suffix but the passive has not been observed to cause spirantization a preceding stop. In this case we see spirantization of the velar stop to v, with subsequent effacement of the preceding nasal, resulting in the change of -dwang- > -dwav-.

5

Verb Stems

As is typical in Bantu languages, verbs are the most complex word category in Kifuliiru. This chapter begins with the structure and function of the verb stem itself. The Bantu verb is commonly regarded as consisting of a root with various affixes.[1] In Kifuliiru the components of a verb are: initial prefixes (including subject, tense, negation, aspect), object prefixes (including the reflexive object prefix), root,[2] extensions, and final vowel (FV). The root and extensions together make up what is called the verb base (also called the derivational stem), and the base together with the FV makes up the (inflectional) stem. If there is an incorporated object marker, or markers, these are included with the stem in what is referred to as the macrostem. For example, the verb **tú-ká-mú-shòn-óól-à** (1PL-P2-O1-climb-RV.T-Fa) 'we lowered him down' can be divided as in (5.1)

---

[1] Many thanks to Thilo Schadeberg for helpful comments on an earlier draft of this chapter.
[2] The "root" is also called the radical.

(5.1)

tu	ká	mú	shòn	ool		a
1PL	P2	O1	climb	RV.T		Fa
[initial prefixes† (relativizer, subject, negative, TAM, etc.]	[(object prefix(es)‡	[root]	(suffix(es)] (including extensions)		[FV]
			[--------------base-------------]		
		[----------------stem----------------]		
	[-----------------------macrostem-----------------]		

†For Bantu in general, what is often called the "initial" position in verbs is usually filled by a relative marker or certain negative prefixes. In Kifuliiru, only the relativizer occurs preceding the subject prefix. The "initial prefixes" include all prefixes which precede the object prefix.

‡Kifuliiru verbs can take a maximum of two object prefixes, of which one is either the reflexive yì- or first-person singular ń-. When there are two object prefixes in the same verb, the first-person singular or reflexive will always occur in the position immediately to the left of the radical.

As seen in (5.1), the verb stem can thus be formalized as [verb root (+ext)^n + final vowel]. The number of extensions in a stem is most often either none or only one. It is not rare, however, to have two. The number of extensions seldom reaches three unless one or more of the extensions can be considered "frozen" or lexicalized as a part of the verb root. Four seems to be the maximum number of recognizable extensions per verb. The extensions comprise a broad set of morphemes which add various components of meaning to a verb radical or stem, and may affect the stem's valence. Discussion of the extensions forms the majority of this chapter.

As also seen in (5.1), the object prefix(es), if present, always appear to the immediate left of the base, and are counted as a part of the macrostem. In a multiword verb form, e.g. a form with an auxiliary, the object is always included in the final part, along with the radical, e.g. the recent past **àgéndì múbwírà** 'he went and told him', or the present progressive **àlì mú=múbwírà** 'he is telling him', in both of which the object **mú**- 'him' is prefixed to the (lexical) root.

To the right of the verb base is the obligatory final vowel: a single -**a**, -**e**, -**i**, or the more complex -**ir**-**i**, depending on the form of the verb. The choice of the final element is determined by the tense/aspect/mood of the verb, and is thus, just as the prefixes are, a part of the inflectional affixation of the verb. The default final vowel is -**a**, with -**e** being used for subjunctive and certain irrealis forms, -**i** for the imperative plural, while -**ir**-**i** is used for resultative forms. The -**ir**-**i** is a unique suffix which, though not a single vowel, is, like the FVs of -V configuration, both final and inflectional. This suffix interacts phonologically with the verb base in complex ways that the single FVs do not. For this reason, the addition of the resultative ending is a major aspect of the formation of the verb stem. The formal aspects of the resultative are presented in (5.9).

5.1 Extensions: General considerations

Bantu verbs are famous for their wide variety of "extensions". Extension is the term commonly used for non-final, semantically definable derivational verbal suffixes in Bantu languages.[3] "Semantically definable" is to say that an extension adds a certain semantic component of meaning to the verb to which it is suffixed.

Extensions of the shape -VC- do not have any underlying tone, so that a syllable added by such an extension is subject to the association of a grammatical tone, or to the high or low spread of a grammatical tone. There is "some slight evidence" (Schadeberg, 2003a:72) that the tone of causative (*-i̧) and passive (*-u), the only two extensions of -V- shape, may have had a high tone in Proto-Bantu. Both of these extensions have an underlying H tone in Kifuliiru.

Eleven verbal extensions have been reconstructed for Proto-Bantu (PB): causative *-i̧-/-iC-i̧-; applicative (also called dative) *-ir-; impositive *-ik-; neuter *-ik-; positional (stative) *-am-; reciprocal (associative) *-an-; extensive *-al-; contactive (tentive) *-at-; reversive (separative) transitive *-ul-; reversive (separative) intransitive *-uk-; and passive *-u-/-ibu (Meeussen 1967). These reflexes are all found in Kifuliiru. In addition, Kifuliiru has lexicalized a combination of two of these extensions to form the intensive -e(e)rez/-i(i)riz, and also uses as an extension the emphatic, which is a reflex of the PB repetitive *-ag ~ -ang. This brings the total number of distinct extensions in Kifuliiru to thirteen. For listing of Kifuliiru reflexes, see under "Productive extensions" (5.5) and "Non-productive extensions" (5.6).

As can be observed in the preceding list, in general, extensions are of the shape -VC-. Only two, passive and causative, consist in basic form only of -V, and each has an allomorph of the shape -VCV-. In Kifuliiru the vowel of the -VC extensions is lengthened in some cases, resulting in an extension of the shape -VVC. In addition, -e(e)rez/-i(i)riz or -iirir/-eerer intensive has the

---

[3] Most scholars are of the opinion that original verb roots in Bantu were basically of CVC structure. Thus any verb stem with extra syllables is considered to have been added to at some point in history. Any "added" syllable for which no common semantic meaning is discernable is referred to as an expansion rather than an extension. These expansions are not productive synchronically and are considered a part of the lexical root of the verb. Thus they always precede any extensions.

shape -V(V)CVC-. Formally this is a reduplicated applicative -**ir**/-**er** with a lengthened vowel, usually followed by the short causative -**i**. Semantically it has a single meaning synchronically unrelated to those parts, and thus appears to have been lexicalized in Kifuliiru as an extension in its own right.

All the -VC- extensions which have vowels other than **a** are subject to vowel height harmony. This means that whether a high (**i** or **u**) or mid (**e** or **o**) vowel occurs in the extension depends on the height of the vowel in the preceding syllable of the verb, whether this vowel is in the radical itself, or is part of a previous extension. Throughout this section, one will see -**er**/-**ir**, -**ol**/-**ul**, etc. (See also 2.3.2.1).

Besides the basically -VC- extensions, there is also the inchoative, -**h**, which consists only of -C-,[4] and which, though a post-radical component of the verb stem, is not a true extension, but rather a derivational suffix of a different nature. Inchoative -**h** does not add semantic information to a verb stem but rather functions to change the word class of an adjective to a verb. All the other extensions are added only to words which are already verbs, and do not change these verbs into any other word class (part of speech). Since -**h** is a recognizable element of some verb stems, it is listed in the comprehensive table of extensions and expansions, and is discussed under non-productive extensions.

There is one other verbal suffix which in most Bantu languages functions differently from the extensions. This is the morpheme which across Bantu appears as -**ag**, -**ak** -**ang**, etc. and is usually associated with habitual, repeated, or imperfective action. This morpheme, which is seldom given a title in the literature, is most often referred to as the "pre-final" -**a(n)g**, and so called because of the position it has in the verb. It is treated separately from extensions by Meeussen (1967:110) and others, because in most languages it is an inflectional suffix, occurring only with certain tense/aspect forms of the verb, and often forming an obligatory part of the defining morphology those tenses or aspects. In Kifuliiru this pre-final suffix appears as -**ag**, and is not inflectional, but a derivational suffix which denotes special emphasis. This morpheme which we call emphatic, functions as an extension and is discussed below with the productive extensions, which are each treated individually in 5.5.

5.2 Degrees of productivity in extensions

In the literature on Bantu extensions, an evaluation of "productivity" is usually given for each extension. This evaluation is most often based on whether

---
[4]Though when it is added to a -CV adjective (e.g. -**bí** 'bad') the vowel of the adjective is lengthened in the verb e.g. **kúbííhà** 'to be(come) bad'.

5.2 Degrees of productivity in extensions

or not the extension commutes with other extensions, and/or with zero. To say that one extension "commutes with" another means that each of these two (or more) extensions can be used with the same verb root, with a predictable meaning change, e.g. the reversive transitive -**ul** commutes with the reversive intransitive -**uk** in -**gálul**- 'return' (reversive transitive) and -**gáluk**- 'return' (reversive intransitive), etc.

To say that an extension commutes with zero (an unextended verb root), simply means that the extension can be removed from the verb, leaving an unextended verb root which can also be used without an extension, and which differs predictably in meaning from the extended form. For example, in -**kól**- 'work' and -**kòl-er**- 'work for someone', the only difference is the presence or absence of the applicative extension -**er**, which here has the meaning of doing the action of the verb on behalf of someone else.

The most productive extensions always commute at least with zero. Nonproductive extensions, such as contactive and extensive, typically occur in a very limited set of verbs and in many cases commute neither with the same radical having a different extension, nor with a non-extended verb. However, the typical component of meaning they add is still discernable upon investigation.

A completely lexicalized or "frozen" extension is one for which the typical meaning of the extension is not discernable in the meaning of the verb as a whole.

In many cases there are pairs of extensions that are identical except for the fact that one has a double vowel and the other a single vowel, e.g. -**uk**/-**uuk** 'reversive intransitive'. These double vowels would appear to have been formed at least in some cases by the dropping of an **l/r** consonant from a succession of extensions (-**uluk**, > -**uuk**, -**ulul** > -**uul**, -**erez** > -**eez**, etc.). This hypothesis of the origin of the long vowel form (in at least some cases) is substantiated by the fact that some forms in which the extension is -CVCV- alternate, with no meaning change, with a form having a double vowel, e.g. -**hèmbulul**- ~ -**hèmbuul**- 'give a starving person food'.

It is worthwhile noting that, with the exception of the applicative extension, -**ir**/-**er**, in Kifuliiru the extensions with the long vowels (e.g. -**uuk**) seem to be the more synchronically productive ones, while the short vowel extensions (e.g. -**uk**) tend to be the lexicalized, unproductive ones. This is true, at least to some extent, of the reversive extensions, both transitive and intransitive, e.g. -**bìsh**- 'hide something', -**bìshuul**- 'bring something out of hiding'; -**shwek**- 'tie something', -**shwekuul**- 'untie something'; -**tèg**- 'set trap', -**tèguul**- 'get something out of trap'; -**shòn**- 'climb up', -**shònook**- 'climb down', -**shònool**- 'lower something down'; -**gób**- 'be tongue-tied',

-góbook- 'become un-tongue-tied', -góbool- 'loosen someone's tied-down tongue'; -lúh- 'be tired', -lúhuuk- 'rest', -lúhuul-, 'give someone a rest', etc.

It is always true for the causative that the extension with the long vowel is the more productive one. The productive "long causative" ending -iisi[5] generally surfaces as -iis, e.g. -siim- 'be pleased' -simiis- 'cause someone to be pleased'. The only source of a surface -is form, on the other hand is from a verb that ends in **ik** (whether part of the radical or an extension) plus the "short causative" -**i**, -hík- 'arrive' > -hís- 'cause something to arrive'.

There are many "frozen" or lexicalized extensions in which different vowel length is observed. There is no discernable reason in these cases for the difference in the length. Examples of lexicalized minimal pairs that differ only in the length of the vowel in the extension: -**kúnduul**- 'run very fast', -**kùndul**- 'water be red from suspended soil particles after rain', neither of these seem to have any relationship with -**kùnd**- 'love'; -**níngúl**- ~ -**nóngól**- 'lop off with a single blow' and -**nìnguul**- 'give birth to a single male offspring and no other children', cf. **kí-nínga** (7-only.child), -**láluk**- 'be drunk', -**láluuk**- 'sleep around in various places'.

5.2.1 Productive extensions

For an extension to be classified as productive, it must be added to a verb radical which can also occur without the extension, or with a different extension. Furthermore, a productive extension is one which adds a recognizable component of meaning to a verb. In addition, we can say that a highly productive extension is one which may be suffixed to a large number of verbs. Extensions which are most productive in Kifuliiru are the applicative, causative, reciprocal/mutual/comitative, intensive, emphatic, and to a lesser extent, reversive transitive and reversive intransitive.

The applicative extension -**ir**/-**er** is an example of one that is highly productive in Kifuliiru. It can be added to most verbs, adding the meaning of doing the action of the verb to or for someone, or at a particular place. With this applicative extension, an intransitive verb (which in its unextended form is able to have only a subject) becomes able to take an object as well as the subject, e.g. -**tíbit**- 'run' may be applicativized to -**tíbit-ir**- 'run to (a person or place)'. This added object can then be incorporated into the verb, if this is called for by discourse considerations, e.g. **àmútíbìtìrà** 'he ran to/from him'. Another example of a highly productive extension is the causative. It can be added to the great majority of verbs and gives a causative meaning,

---

[5] The final **i** of -**iisi** undergoes glide formation (> **y**) when it precedes a vowel, and is absorbed by the preceding **s**. See 5.5.5.1.

5.2 Degrees of productivity in extensions

e.g. the causative form of **kúlálúkà** 'become drunk', is **kúlálúsâ** 'to cause to get drunk'.

Thus a productive extension can be used synchronically in the derivation of various forms of a verb. For each of the productive extensions in table 5.1, the majority of its occurrences fit into this category.

Table 5.1. Productive extensions

Causative	-i/-iisi/-eesi
Passive	-(b)u/-ibu/-ebu
Applicative	-ir/-er
Reciprocal (including comitative and mutual)	-an
Reversive transitive	-ul/-ol
Reversive intransitive	-uk/-ok
Intensive	-(i)iriz/-(e)erez
Emphatic	-ag

5.2.2 Non-productive extensions

A non-productive extension is one which is used with a limited number of verb stems. Though it still adds a certain predictable shade of meaning to a verb, often it does not alternate (with a predictable meaning difference) with another verb having the same root but no suffix, or the same root but with a different suffix.

An example of an extension with very limited productivity in Kifuliiru is the contactive -**at**, which denotes physical contact and occurs with a small set of verbs including -**fùmbat**- 'grasp in the hand', and -**hàgát**- 'hang from the shoulder'. In these cases, it is clear that the -**at** still has something to do with contact. The verb -**fùmbat**- is related to the non-extended verb -**fùmb**- 'close together (hands, eyes, etc.)', but the extended form, along with the semantic notion of contact also includes the unpredictable restriction of reference to the hand only. As for -**hàgat**-, there seems to be no related unextended or alternatively extended verb in use currently.

Neuter, impositive, and positional all have quite limited productivity. They are not used with many verbs, but still usually commute either with at least one other extension or with an unextended verb. See table 5.2.

Table 5.2. Non-productive extensions

Contactive	-at
Extensive	-al
Neuter	-ik/-ek
Impositive	-ik/-ek
Positional	-am

5.2.3 Lexicalized extensions

Besides the classifications of productive and non-productive extensions, we find that there are many lexicalized or "frozen" extensions. A lexicalized extension is one which has become an essential part of a lexical verb root, and which often no longer retains a discernable semantic tie to the original meaning of the extension. Most of the extensions which fall into the productive category will also be found in "frozen" form in at least a few verbs. In the cases in which an extension has become "frozen", the shade of meaning has shifted at least slightly so that the original combination of radical plus extension has synchronically taken on a specific meaning which is either partially or completely different from the meaning one would expect to result when a given root is modified by a given extension.

A good example of a lexicalized extension is the verb -**hémber**- 'set a string trap'. Though this would appear to contain a root -**hémb**- followed by the applicative extension. The verb -**hémb**- means 'smear'. While this activity may well have once had to do with preparing some type of trap, the meaning of -**hémbér**- is no longer divisible into these semantic components. Thus the -**er** in -**hémbér**- is considered to be a "frozen" extension, which no longer has the predictable meaning of doing something for someone or at some place. Even though the applicative extension itself is a productive extension, in this instance this sequence of -**er** has become frozen in relation to a specific verb root.

In addition, many verb stems include extensions which are reduplicated or partially reduplicated, and the reduplicated form may be frozen with a special meaning. Examples of this are found in -**sháng-ul-ul**- 'hand out shares', cf. the related form -**shángiir**- 'share together', which contains what appears to be a partially reduplicated applicative extension, -**iir**, rather than -**ir**, and the related noun **lú-shángì** (11-collection). Note also the unrelated (at least semantically) -**sháng-ul**- 'wear something out', and its related form -**sháng-uk**- 'be worn out'.

5.3 Relative order of extensions

Several extensions may be added successively to a radical, though the number does not usually exceed two productive extensions. If there are three (or four) extensions, at least one is lexicalized.

Any extension which is added to an already extended verb alters the meaning of the extended verb, not that of the original radical. Thus the order of extensions is, at least to an extent, dependent on which extension is semantically prior. This would imply that such derivation is cyclic in nature, with the verb stem going through repeated "cycles" of affixation. Any frozen extensions, since they have become a lexical part of the verb radical, are found further to the left than an added "productive" extension would be. For this reason, then, the more productive extensions (causative, applicative, passive, etc.) are further from the radical than the less productive ones.

Hyman (2003d) presents the claim that there is a "default" templatic suffix order across Bantu, which he denotes as C-A-R-P: Causative, Applicative, Reciprocal, Passive. He states that there is a tension between this canonical template and potential conflicting orders which are driven by the semantic composition of a given verb stem. When such a conflict occurs, the outcome is determined by the language-specific ranking of this "CARP template" constraint as compared to other constraints which opt instead for the accurate reflection of semantic compositionality. If the CARP template is ranked as more important, it will govern the order of the suffixes even when semantically, a different order would be expected.

Kifuliiru does not present any clear evidence of diverging from the CARP template of suffix ordering, though there is a language specific constraint that causative must appear directly to the left of the final vowel, or of the passive morpheme, if there is one. In order to meet this constraint, as well as to maintain the CARP order, the short causative (CS) is repeated at the end of the verb, e.g. -**húb-iis-an-i-a** (-err-CS-RCP-CS-FV) 'cause each other to err'. In verbs where extensions have a different order, e.g. -**hún-iz-a** 'cause to appear to sleep' from -**hún-ir-i-a** (-sleep-APL-CS-FV), the extension which appears to be "out of order", in this case, the applicative which appears to the left of causative, has been lexicalized as a part of the root, and therefore not is subject to any morpheme ordering constraints at the derivational level.

Similarly, the reciprocal, if not lexicalized, follows the applicative, e.g. -**kòl-er-an-** 'work for others', -**tùm-ir-an-** 'send to each other'. There are, however, several verbs in which the reciprocal is lexicalized, and thus precedes the applicative, as in -**sánganir-** 'go meet someone who is coming', etc. The applicative in such cases may be productive or may itself be frozen.

The general order of the extensions in Kifuliiru is exemplified in table 5.3. The final vowel, though not an extension, is included to show its relative position in the verb stem.

Table 5.3. General order of extensions within the verb

Root	POS	CNT	EXT	RV	NEU/IMPS	CS$_1$	APL	RCP	EMP	CS$_2$	PS	FV	Gloss
-shénd	am			uk			ir					a	'lean back on'
-gúng	am		al									a	'slump in sadness'
-gwàng			al		ik							a	'push a weak one'
-háng			al		uk							a	'get very dry'
-gál	ab	ad			ik							a	'lay s/o down'
-gál	ab	ad			i	s^a						a	'CS s/o to be laid down'
-hùmb	at	al										a	'get thinner'
-fùmb		ad			ik							a	'hand sthg to s/o'
-kwáb		ad			uk							a	'do immed.'
-tùm							ir	an				a	'send to s/o'
-gáb				ul	ik			an				a	'be separate from s/o'
-shób				ok				-an				a	'be possible'
-shób				ol								a	'be able'
-hùl				uk			ir					a	'appear to/at'
-kàb				ul			ir					a	'throw away'
-gúl					iis					i	bw	a	'be sold'
-gúl					iis							a	'sell'
-sìnd-					ik		ir					a	'shove down'
-bw-		at	al					an			w	a	'sit together'
tòndee(r)					z				ag	y		a	'begin now!'
-shùk				uul	uk							a	'over-dilute'

Note the following co-occurrence restrictions: When reversive transitive and reversive intransitive co-occur, transitive always precedes intransitive. Neuter and impositive never co-occur. Reversive intransitive and neuter/impositive never co-occur.

^{a}The causative is not really -s, but -i. It is realized on the surface, however, by the spirantization of the k of the impositive -ik to s, and listed here as -s so that reading across the columns yields the surface form of a verb stem.

5.3 Relative order of extensions

The extensions which are semantically more basic to the meaning of the verb precede these which are more incidental. Thus, the reversive always precedes applicative e.g. **-hùl-uk-ir-** 'come out to', and never *-**hùl-ir-uk-**.

The positional always precedes both the reversive and the applicative, e.g. **-shénd-am-** ~ **-shénd-am-uk-** 'lean back while sitting'; **-shénd-am-uk-ír-** 'lean back against something'.

A productive reciprocal, such as the comitative **-an** in the following example, tends to be the rightmost of the -VC extensions, e.g. **kú-bà-shúmbík-án-à** 'to stay with them for a while' > **-shúmbik-** 'stay a while in a place not one's own', plus **-an** 'comitative', cf. **í=shûmbì** 'AU=encampment'; **-gáb-ul-ik-an-** 'be divided from each other' from **-gáb-** 'divide' < **-gábul-** 'divide out' < **-gábulik-** 'be divided out'.

Some extensions may group together to indicate a single meaning. Such "compound extensions" are included in table 5.4.

Table 5.4. Compound extensions

Compound EXT	Form	Examples	Compare with
APL + CS = INTS	**-iiriz/-eerez**	**-bèr-ééréz-** 'cut repeatedly/ intensively'	**-bèr-** 'cut'
RCP + PS = MUT	**-anw**	**-béér-ánw-** 'stay together with each other'	**-béér-** 'stay'
NEU + RCP	**-ikan/-ekan**	**-yùv-ííkán-** 'be heard'	**-yùvw-** 'hear'

There is also a special conventionalized form of the applicative which is used only with causative verbs. This could be considered to be a type of compound extension as well. Its surface form is **-k-iz-/-k-ez-** or **-g-iz-/-g-ez-**, e.g. **-yú-k-iz-** 'finish a task for someone or at some place', from **-yús-** 'complete a task' (see 5.6.1.2 "Special forms for applicatives of causative verbs").

That a conventionalized form of the applicative is used for causative verbs would imply that the causative extension is affixed prior to the applicative, and this does seem to be the usual case, as noted above. However, there are also numerous forms, such as **-tòndeez-** ~ **-tòndeer-** 'begin', in which the causative follows what seems to be a lexicalized applicative. Other examples of such forms are **-lèngez-** 'lift and move someone or something', from **-lèng-** 'pass by', and **-lèng-er-** 'pass by APL', or **-hónyolez-** 'to mock someone' from the ideophone **hóónyò!** (a mocking word).

Another consideration in the ordering of extensions is the fact that the causative and the passive extensions are always placed as far to the right as possible. This constraint is usually attributed to phonological considerations, reflecting the fact that these are the only two extensions which consist only of a vowel. If both passive and causative are used in a single verb, the passive is always found to the right of the causative, with the combination appearing as (-**iis**)-**i**-**bw**.

As noted above, in many cases the causative morpheme appears to the left of another extension. In such a case the causative -**i** always occurs (again) to the right of the added extension. This maintains the "right ordering" of the causative, and is exemplified by the conventionalized form of the applicative used with causative verbs, e.g. -**gúl-iikiz**- 'sell to someone' (from -**gúliis**- 'sell'), and with the emphatic extension, e.g. **bùùz-àg-y-â** 'ask, now!' (from -**buuz**- 'ask'). The exception to this is the passive, which *always* directly precedes the final vowel, e.g. with the passive verb -**buu-z-i-bw**- 'be asked', there is no repeated causative following the passive -**w**.

The emphatic extension -**ag**, though of VC form, also appears as far to the right as possible because semantically its meaning is applied to the whole verb. It directly precedes the passive in a passive (or pseudo-passive) verb e.g. **ànágwánágwà** 'and he was found (EMP)', from -**gwanw**- 'be found (in some state)'; **yùv-àg-w-â** 'listen, now!'[6] It directly precedes the rightmost realization of the causative in a causative verb, e.g. **bùùz-àg-y-â** 'ask now!'. Though the passive and causative sometimes occur together in the same verb, the emphatic has not been observed in such a verb.

5.4 Extensions and their relationship to valence

Altering the valence of a verb is not the main purpose of any extension. The extensions have basically semantic rather than syntactic functions, and their effect on valency is peripheral and often dependent on the meaning of the unextended verb. Nonetheless, they can be generally classified according to their effect on valence.

Ten out of fifteen[7] of the extensions alter the valence of the verb, i.e. they either increase or reduce the number of arguments (i.e. patient, goal, ben-

---

[6] Though this is usually not considered to be a true passive, but one of the very rare CVCw-underived verb bases. Thus it is a pseudo-passive form, with passive-type morphology, but no passive meaning. In the context of this verb, one hears, sometimes even from the same speaker, alternation between treating the **w** as a passive, with right placement, as done in **yùv-àg-w-â** 'listen now!' (the most common form) or treating it as a part of the stem, as in **yùvw-àg-â** 'listen now!', or resultative **yùvíítwî** (less common) ~ **yùvwíítì** (more common), or as both (!) as in **kúyùvwíírwâ** (not common, but attested) a variant of the well-attested form **kúyùvíír-wâ** 'to feel for/towards someone', as in **kúyùvíírwá índèngèèrwà** 'to feel pity for someone', or **kúyùvíírwá úlúùgì** 'to feel jealous of someone'.

[7] Earlier we mentioned thirteen distinct extensions. Of these, the reciprocal has three separate functions which differ in their effect on valence. Thus for this listing we separate out the

5.4 Extensions and their relationship to valence

eficiary, instrument, location, etc.) which may be used with the extended verb as compared with the unextended form of that verb. For example, the passive extension reduces valence by eliminating reference in the verb to the agent of the action, and turning the patient or goal (who/whatever is acted upon by the non-passive verb) into the grammatical subject. The applicative extension, on the other hand, increases valence by adding an object, thus creating a transitive verb from an intransitive radical, or a ditransitive verb from a simple transitive radical. The phenomenon of a valence-increasing extension resulting in ditransitivity when added to a transitive verb is seen with both the causative and the applicative extensions.

As seen in table 5.5, valence-increasing extensions in Kifuliiru are: causative, applicative, reciprocal (comitative use only), contactive, and impositive.

Valence-neutral extensions in Kifuliiru are: mutual (reciprocal plus passive combination), reversive transitive, intensive, emphatic, and extensive (which is almost exclusively used with intransitives).

Valence-reducing extensions in Kifuliiru are: reciprocal, passive, reversive intransitive, neuter, and positional.

---

three uses of the reciprocal: reciprocal, mutual, and comitative, bringing the total to fifteen.

Table 5.5. Extensions and their relationship to valence

Extension name	Form	Productive ?
Valence increasing		
Causative	-(iis)i	yes
Applicative	-ir/-er	yes
Reciprocal (comitative)	-an	yes
Contactive	-at	no
Impositive	-ik/-ek	no
Valence neutral		
Reciprocal (mutual)	-an-w	yes
Reversive transitive	-ul/-ol	yes
Intensive	-(i)iriz/-(e)erez	yes
Emphatic	-ag	yes
Extensive	-al	no
Valence decreasing		
Reciprocal	-an	yes
Passive	-(ib)u	yes
Reversive intransitive	-uk/-ok	yes
Neuter	-ik/-ek	no
Positional	-am	no

It will be noted that five of the fifteen extensions listed here are valence-neutral. That is, these extensions do not usually affect the final valence of the verb to which they are suffixed. However, this is not to say that their use is totally unrelated to valence. Instead, with the exception of intensive and emphatic, the valence of the stem is a factor in determining which verbs a valence-neutral extension may be used with.

The reversive transitive nearly always results in a transitive verb, but since it is suffixed mostly to verbs which are already transitive, or occurs with a root which is never used in unextended form and is found only with this extension, it can rarely be said to increase valence, cf. -bìsh- 'hide something', -bìshuul- 'reveal something'. The illusion that the reversive transitive extension increases valence comes only from comparing a verb that has the reversive transitive extension to a related verb that has reversive intransitive extension, which is a valence-reducing extension.

The extensive is nearly always added to a verb which is already intransitive, and does not change this valence.

Only the intensive and the emphatic can be freely added either to a transitive or intransitive verb and have no affect on valence.

That effect on valency is not the main function of extensions is evidenced by the reciprocal extension -**an**, which functions in all three categories. It is valence-increasing in its "comitative" use with an intransitive verb (cf. -**taah**- 'go home', **taah**-**an**- 'go home with'), valence-neutral when combined with passive and used as "mutual" (cf. -**tuul**- 'live', -**tuul**-**anw**- 'live together with'), and valence-decreasing when used as a true reciprocal with a transitive verb (-**seezer**- 'say good-bye to someone' (requires a complement), vs. **seezer**-**an**- 'say good-bye to each other' (takes no expressed complement).

While the basic reciprocal (as opposed to mutual and comitative) does not change the *semantic* valence, it does decrease *syntactic* valence. The basic reciprocal is always used with a transitive verb, which remains semantically transitive following the addition of the extension. However, the patient can no longer be syntactically indicated by the use of an expressed object. The patient is included, semantically and grammatically, by the plural subject marker which is necessitated by the addition of the reciprocal extension. For example, the phrase **á-n-júlìk-à** (1+P1-O1.SG-hit-Fa) 'he hit me' has both subject and object indicated (here the object is indicated by the incorporated **n**- following the subject prefix of the verb), but **twàshúlìkànà** 'we hit each other', may not have a syntactic object indicated in Kifuliiru, neither incorporated nor represented by a noun following the verb. Reference to the agent and patient has been merged in the subject marker. Thus the reciprocal is included in the valence-decreasing category.

The mutual function of the reciprocal is especially interesting valence-wise, in that it is used with intransitive verbs, and is a combination of the valence-increasing comitative and the valence-reducing passive. This results in a verb with unchanged valence.

5.5 Productive extensions

Table 5.6 gives a list of productive extensions, with Proto-Bantu reconstructions and Kifuliiru examples.

Table 5.6. Productive extensions in Kifuliiru, exemplified

Extension	PB	FLR reflex	FLR base	Gloss	FLR e.g. w/ extension	Gloss
Causative	*-i̧ (ic-i̧)	-í or -iis-í-[a]	-lím-	'farm'	-lím-iis-í- > límiis-	'cause s/o to farm'
Passive	*-u/-(i)bu	-ú or -(i)bú	-lím-	'farm'	-lím-ú- > -límw-	'be farmed'
Applicative	*-il/-el[b]	-ir/-er	-lím-	'farm'	-lím-ir-	'farm for s/o'
Reciprocal	*-an	-an	-bòn-		-bòn-aan-	'see each other'
Rev. INTRANS	*-uk/-ok	-(u)uk/-(o)ok	-shòn-	'climb'	-shòn-ook-	'climb down'
Rev. TRANS	*-ul/-ol	-uul/-ool	-shòn-	'climb'	-shòn-ool-	'let down'
Intensive	---	-iirir/-eerer/-iiriz/-eerez	-bùg-	'apply coating'	-bùg-iiriz-	'apply coating thoroughly'
Emphatic	*-ag/-ang	-ag(ag)	-génd-	'go'	-génd-ag-	'go, now!'

[a] The final -i of the causative -iis-i is separated off by a hyphen because in cases where the causative is followed by another extension (except passive, where the final i remains stable and precedes the passive -bu) a final i appears to the right of the additional extension, e.g. -hub-<u>iis</u>-an-<u>i</u>-a 'cause each other to do wrong'. It thus seems that perhaps the short causative -i and the final -i formative of the long causative are one and the same. This final formative of the causative is separated from the initial formative -iis in such cases, with the other extension interrupting the long causative morpheme.

[b] Many times these proto-forms which are subject to vowel harmony are represented with an upper case vowel, with the upper case signifying that the vowel is subject to harmony, e.g. *-Il applicative, *-Uk reversive intransitive, etc.

These extensions are all discussed at some length below in this section. For each one, a section on structural details is presented first, followed by a discussion of meaning and function, and including examples in natural context.

5.5.1 Causative

5.5.1.1 *Causative structural considerations*

The causative extension -**i**/-**iisi**- may surface segmentally as -**y**-, -**s**/-**z**, or as -**iis**/-**ees**, depending on the phonological and morphological properties of the verb involved, as seen in (5.2).

(5.2)	CS ext.	Surface	Non-CS	Gloss	CS ext.	Gloss
a.	-i	-y	-yùm-	'be dry and hard'	-yùm-y-	'cause to be dry and hard'
b.	-i	-s	-yút-	'be finished (task)'	-yús-	'finish (a task)'
c.	-i	-z	-nòg-	'be soft'	-nòz-	'make soft'
d.	-iisi	-iis	-síím-	'be pleased'	-sím-iis-	'please s/o'
e.	-eesi	-ees	-kòl-	'work'	-kòl-ees-	'cause to work, use'

The synchronic underlying forms are -**i**, known in Bantu literature as the short causative, and -**iisi**/-**eesi**, called the long causative. Depending on the phonological quality of the preceding consonant, the short causative -**i** may surface as **y**, as in (5.2a), or it may cause spirantization of the preceding consonant to **s** as in (5.2b), or to **z** as in (5.2c).

It should be noted that the causative, no matter how it surfaces segmentally, has an inherently H tone which links as far to the right as possible in the verb form.

Causative -**i**, causes spirantization of many preceding consonants (see 2.3.2.5). This means that it causes a voiceless consonant to become **s**, or a voiced consonant to become **z**. After causing spirantization, the causative -**i**, whether the short causative, or the final -**i** of the long causative, undergoes glide formation to -**y** if it precedes a vowel. It is most often the case that it directly precedes the final vowel of the verb. Then, because of the phonological rule of **y**-absorption following an **s** or **z**,[8] the **y** does not appear on the surface. This leaves the spirantization of the final consonant of the verb base as the only indication of the causative extension, e.g. -**kìr-a** 'be saved from sickness

---

[8]Hyman (2003c) speaks of this same sort of phonological occurrence in Luganda as absorption of the palatalization by the preceding palatal consonant. In Kifuliiru a **y** (causative) may occur following the palatal fricative **sh**, (cf. **kúbìshyâ** 'to grind them' versus **kúbìshà** 'to hide something') so though there is **y**-absorption following **s** and **z**, absorption is triggered only by **s** and **z**, and not by all palatal consonants, in this language. This same disappearance of **y** following **s** and **z** also occurs in other environments besides the causative in Kifuliiru.

or danger', when used with the causative undergoes **kìr -i-a > kìz-i-a > kìz-y-a > kìz-a** 'cause someone to recover or be rescued'.

In the case of the long causative, the same rule of **y**-absorption following an **s** or **z** prevents the final **i** of **-iisi/-eesi** from appearing on the surface in any cases except where the passive **-bu** follows the causative. In all other cases, the causative is followed by a vowel, which causes the final **i** of **-iisi/-eesi** to be changed to the glide **y** and undergo **y**-absorption.

The short causative, **-i**, e.g. **-yùm-i- > -yùmy-** 'cause to be dry and hard' (cf. **-yùm-** 'be dry and hard'), is found with verbs of all syllable patterns, except for unextended monosyllabic verb stems (i.e. those whose base consists only of CV). The short causative is often found with verb bases which include another extension, even a frozen one.

(5.3) Short causative examples: -i

	Non-CS form	Gloss	CS form	Gloss
a.	**-laah-**	'be long'	**-laah-y-**	'cause to be long'
b.	**-yùm-**	'be dry'	**-yùm-y-**	'cause to be dry'
c.	**-kàn-**	'be firm, mature'	**-kàn-í-**†	'cause to be firm'
d.	-----‡		**-buuzani-**	'ask each other'
e.	**-hèr-**	'life to come to an end'	**-hèz-**	'bring to an end'
f.	**-hék-**	'come to an end'	**-hés-**	'finish off'
g.	**-nòg-**	'be soft, pliable'	**-nòz-**	'make soft'
h.	**-hùluk-**	'come out'	**-hùlus-**	'take out'
i.	**-kòmeerek-**	'be wounded'	**-kòmeeres-**	'wound someone'
j.	**-góngomer-**	'gulp down'	**-góngomez-**	'make someone gulp'
k.	**-gwèjer-**	'lie down'	**-gwèjez-**	'lay someone down'
l.	**-bálal-**	'fly'	**-bálaz-**	'put aloft'
m.	**-lyogool-**	'joke, talk lightly'	**-lyogooz-**	'cause frivolity'

†Though the causative **-i** does undergo glide formation preceding the FV in such cases, it is still written as **i** following **n** in order to distinguish it from the palatal nasal, which is symbolized as **ny**, since we are not using IPA symbols here.

‡This form has no synchronically used form which is interpreted as non-causative. **kúbúúzâ** to ask, may possibly have its origins in the causative of a hypothetical verb root *-**bu-ul-a** 'speak (separative)' (attested only in

kúbúul-an-a 'take someone to court' and the intensive form kúbúlírízâ 'to ask intensively, interrogate' where the vowel is shortened by the mora-based vowel shortening rule). Cf. also kúbwírà 'to tell someone something'.

When it follows **h**, **m**, or **n**, as in (5.3a–d) the short causative is realized as the palatal glide -**y**. Note that in (5.3d) it is the "repeated" short causative which shows up following the **n** of the reciprocal extension. The segmental representation of the final **i** of the leftward causative morpheme has been deleted following the **z** (or displaced rightward to a position following the reciprocal -**an**), i.e. -**buuz**- (**i**)-**an**-**i**- > -**buuz**-**an**-**i**-.

In other cases, the short causative is realized on the surface only by spirantization of the final C of the -VC- extension, as in (5.3e–m). This is because it is the short form of the causative which is usually found following another extension, and most of the extensions end in **t**, **k**, **l**, or **r**, segments which are phonologically subject to spirantization by the spirantizing suffixes (causative, agentive, and resultative). As mentioned above, the causative -**i**, when followed by the final vowel, becomes -**y**, which is always deleted or absorbed following an **s** or **z**, leaving only the spirantization of the final consonant to indicate the causativity. Thus -**hùluk**- 'come out', with the addition of the causative becomes -**hùluk-i**- > -**hùlus-y**- > -**hùlus**- 'put out, take out', etc.

The short causative, or the final -**i** of the long causative, shows up on the surface as an -**i** when it precedes the passive -**bu**, as seen in (5.4).

(5.4) Passives of causatives

	Non-passive CS	Gloss	CS form	Gloss
a.	-**gwas**-	'cause to be caught'	-**gwasibw**-	'be caused to be caught'
b.	-**buuz**-	'ask'	-**buuzibw**-	'be asked'
c.	-**kàni**-	'cause to be firm'	-**kànibw**-	'be caused to be firm'
d.	-**simiis**-	'make s/o happy'	-**simiisibw**-	'be pleased, made happy'
e.	-**gúliis**-	'sell'	-**gúliisibw**-	'be sold'
f.	-**yégerez**-	'welcome'	-**yégerezibw**-	'be welcomed'

The long causative seems historically, and probably until recently, to have been used mostly following non-extended verb roots, i.e. -CV-, -CVC-, or -CVVC- roots, as seen in (5.5a–g). With a CV-only verb base the "long causative" is always used, e.g. the causative of kú-tw-à 'cut' is kú-tw-íís-â 'cause to be cut off'. Compare kúhísâ 'cause to arrive' (from kúhíkà) and kúhíísâ 'cause to get ripe/cooked', from kúhyâ.

(5.5) Long causative examples: **iis-i/-ees-i**

	Non-CS	Gloss	CS	Gloss
a.	**-siim-**	'be happy'	**-simiis-**	'cause to be happy'
b.	**-mény-**	'know'	**-ményees-**	'cause to know'
c.	**-dùk-**	'insult'	**-dùkiis-**	'cause someone to be insulted'
d.	**-líh-**	'pay'	**-líhiis-**	'cause someone to pay'
e.	**-nún-**	'taste good'	**-núniis-**	'cause something to be sweet'
f.	**-gír-**	'do/make'	**-gíriis-**	'have something made'
g.	**-nywaan-**[†]	'be in harmony'	**-nywaniis-**	'cause others to be in harmony, reconcile'
h.	**-yándík-**	'write'	**-yándikiis-**	'cause to be written, register'
i.	**-shóbol-**	'be able'	**-shóbolees-**	'cause to be able'
j.	**-mánul-**	'get something down'	**-mánuliis-**	'cause someone to get something down'
k.	**-sìmbah-**	'honor, obey'	**-sìmbahiis-**	'cause to honor'
l.	**-yìmul-**	'chase away'	**-yìmuliis-**	'cause to be chased away'

[†] **kú-nywáán-à** literally means 'to drink together', but has been lexicalized with this specialized meaning of 'being in harmony' or 'making a covenant together'. The form **kú-nywáán-ísâ** (even with the reciprocal extension **-an**) in non-causative form has only a CGVVC verb base.

Though the long causative is usually found with verb bases which do not include an extension, this is not to say that it never occurs with an extended radical, as is seen in (5.5g–l). Its current use with extended radicals is at least partially due to the fact that the long causative has become the more productive form of the causative extension.

In some of the cases in which the short causative does not follow another extension, it is a lexicalized (frozen) form. These frozen forms have taken on specialized meanings, not totally predictable from the combination of the root plus causative. There is often also a productively derived causative form of the same verb which uses the long causative, as seen in (5.6).

5.5 Productive extensions

(5.6) Lexicalized forms of the short causative

Base	Gloss	Long CS	Gloss	Short CS	Gloss
-gér-	'measure'	----		-géz-	'try, attempt'
-hík-	'arrive'	----		-hís-	'bring home a wife'
-yòng-	'suck milk'	-yòngees-	'assist to nurse'	-yòz-	'nurse a baby'
-gúl-	'buy'	-gúliis-	'sell sthg to s/o'	-gúz-	'put sthg up for sale'

5.5.1.1.1 *Placement of the causative*

The causative extension is always placed immediately to the left of the final vowel, unless the passive is also present, in which case it appears immediately to the left of the passive morpheme, which directly precedes the final vowel. In the case where a further extension is added to a causative verb, the short causative morpheme -i is repeated (or displaced rightward) to a position at the right of the added extension. For example, in -húb-iis-an-i- 'make others do wrong', the causative extension appearing directly after the radical is the long causative, appearing as -iis, while the short causative, -i, follows the mutual extension, -an. In -lám(u)s-an-i- 'to greet each other',[9] both the leftward causative and the repeated one which follows the reciprocal -an, are the short causative.

This occurrence of the causative morpheme following the added extension appears to be triggered by the constraint that the causative be as close as possible to the final vowel, among the "final" suffixes of the verb: causative, passive, and FV. The repetition allows the original causative base of the verb to retain its causative identity, either through the spirantization of the final consonant or by the presence of the surface -iis or -ees form of the causative, while the "active" causative morpheme, the spirantizing vocalic portion of the morpheme, still appears in rightmost possible position.

The "rightward re-appearance" of the causative morpheme is found not only with reciprocal forms, but is observed whenever a causative verb is put in the resultative form. Look for example at the resultative, àgúlìsíízì 'he has sold'. This is a resultative form of -gúl-iis- 'sell', (a causative form of -gúl- 'buy') and in it we see the resultative morpheme -ir becoming spirantized to -iz

---

[9] The verb -lamus- 'greet' could be considered a pseudo-causative, i.e. a verb which has no synchronic non-causative form. Such verbs are sometimes not considered to be true causative forms, but only to be interpreted as such by speakers because of their structural similarity to causative forms. In Kifuliiru, any verb with an s or z in the C_2 position is interpreted as a causative.

by the (repeated) causative extension which follows it. The underlying form **à-gúl-iisi-ír-i-ì** 'he has sold' becomes **à-gúl-ìsí-íz-ì** 'he has sold'.

In some languages this sort of phenomenon in the causative has been described as "cyclic spirantization", i.e. segments such as **t**, **l**, **k**, **g**, etc. at the end of subsequent extensions being spirantized to **s** or **z** in the context of a causative verb. It does seem that the process of extension itself is cyclic, i.e. the original causative form (CS), once derived, e.g. -**gúl-iisi-** 'sell' then goes through the derivational process again for the addition of the additional extension, or as in this case, the resultative (RS) ending, as seen in (5.7).

(5.7) -gúl-iisi-ir-i > -gúl- -iisi -ir -i -i > -gúlisiizi
 buy-CS-RS-Fi   buy   CS   RS CS Fi   'sell (RS)'

However, it is clear from observing what happens to an extended causative in a case where the verb base ends in a final consonant which is not phonologically subject to spirantization, that this subsequent spirantization is not simply a morphological "spirantization" process, but is being caused by the presence of the short causative morpheme itself preceding the final vowel. The repeated causative thus appears as -**i** when following **n**,[10] as in the ending -**an-i-a** on the reciprocal form **kú-yág-áz-án-i-â** 'make each other angry' from the causative verb -**yágaz-** 'make someone angry', (cf. -**yágal-** 'get angry') or as -**y** in the -**ag-y-a** at the end of verbs with the emphatic (EMP) morpheme -**ag**, like **bùùz-ág-y-à** 'ask EMP!'.

More examples are found in (5.8). Glosses for the column with mutual/reciprocal (MUT/RCP) would be '...each other', while the glosses for the verb with emphatic would remain unchanged if the emphasis is merely a discourse usage to draw attention to the event. Note that the original causative morpheme, shown in the CS base column, becomes a glide and is deleted by rule when followed by a vowel. Thus each of the forms in the final two columns (underlyingly) contains two instances of the causative morpheme.

---

[10]The causative -**i** is indicated as such following **n** in order to distinguish the **n** + CS from a palatal nasal, which is indicated as **ny**. The failure of a long vowel in the CS base to shorten in the reciprocal and emphatic forms is evidence that there are only two moraic segments (i.e. the vowel of the MUT/RCP or EMP extension, plus the FV) following it within the word, indicating that the vocalic causative morpheme does undergo glide formation preceding the FV. If it remained vocalic and moraic, any long vowel farther left in the verb would be shortened by phonological rule.

5.5 Productive extensions 345

(5.8) Repeated CS morphemes with MUT/RCP and Emp extensions

CS base	Gloss	CS base + MUT/ RCP + CS	CS base + EMP + CS
-shùv-i-	'answer'	-shùv-an-i-	-shùvy-ag-i-
-shágan-i-	'shake'	-shágan-an-i-	-shágan-ag-i-
-gíriis(i)-	'CS to be made'	-gíriis-an-i-	-gíír-iis-ag-i-
-heerez(i)-	'give'	-herez-an-i-	-herez-ag-i-
-tòndeez(i)-	'begin'	-tòndeez-an-i-	-tòndeez-ág-i-
-shùbiriz(i)-	'put back'	-shùbiriz-an-i-	-shùbiriz-ag-i-
-lóóz-	'want'	-lóóz-an-i-	-lóóz-ag-i-
-hís-	'get a wife'	-hís-an-i-	-hís-ag-i-

No matter where the final -i of the causative appears or does not appear on the surface, there is only one H tone associated with this extension. This H tone is always right-linking, i.e. it always associates as far toward the right end of the word as possible.

5.5.1.1.2 Special forms for applicatives of causative verbs

In many Bantu languages, there is a special form for the applicative of causative verbs (i.e., forms which have both the causative and applicative extensions, and which mean 'cause something to be done for/to someone, or at some place'). The applicative extension in Kifuliiru is **-ir/-er**. One might assume that following the usual pattern of finding the causative morpheme following any added extension on a causative verb, this **ir/-er** would be "spirantized" to **-iz/-ez**. For example if **-gúliis-** is 'sell', then 'sell for someone' should be **-gúliis(i)-ir-a** > *-**gúliisiz-**. However, as the asterisk here implies, this does not happen. Instead, the form we find is **-gúliikiz-**. As Hyman (2003c:73) observes, it appears that "almost all of the fricating [spirantizing] languages show a tendency to establish a convention for turning causatives into applicativized causatives." These conventionalized forms usually involve either an **l** or a velar consonant (**k** or **g**). In Kifuliiru, they include both **k** and **g**. Hyman analyzes such forms in terms of "defrication" or what we will call here "despirantization", that is, restoration of a non-spirantized consonant in place of a consonant which has been spirantized by the effect of the causative morpheme.

The following examples explain what is meant by "despirantization". In the process of causativization, the final consonant of a root often undergoes spirantization, as seen in examples discussed in the previous section. For example, the causative form of **-nòg-** 'become soft', is **-nòz-** 'make soft'.

Here **g** has been spirantized to **z**. In forming the applicative of the causative verb -**nòz**-, the **z** is "despirantized" back to **g**, as in -**nòg-ez**- 'make soft APL'.

In the case of -**nòz**- and its applicative -**nògez**-, the despirantization seems merely to restore the original consonant of the root, i.e. **g** becomes **z** and then goes back to **g**. However, looking at other cases, we see that the result of despirantization is always a velar consonant, regardless of the specifications of the root's original final consonant. Thus a verb such as -**yút**- '(task) be finished' is causativized to -**yús**- 'finish a task', and the applicative of this causative is -**yúkiz**- 'finish a task APL' and not *-**yútiz**-. The final consonant of the base is not despirantized to its original form, **t**, but instead, to **k**. Notice also that in -**yúkiz**-, the "restored" consonant is not **g** as it was in -**nògez**-, but **k**, because the original consonant was voiceless.

Thus, though the velar consonant which results from despirantization does not match the original consonant in place of articulation, the voicing of the consonant does reflect the voicing of the original consonant in each case. That is, a voiceless consonant, which is always spirantized to **s**, is despirantized to **k** while a voiced consonant, which is always spirantized to **z**, is despirantized to **g**. This same situation is found in Mashi (Shi), a closely related language (Polak-Bynon 1975).

This regularization of the results of despirantization to a standard velar consonant, rather than restoring the original consonant of the radical, is what Hyman means when he says that a convention is established for forming these applicativized causatives. Many of the verbs in which this conventionalized form is seen are applicatives of those causative verbs which no longer have non-causative form in synchronic use. Such verbs which have no non-causative form are sometimes referred to as pseudo-causatives. For all causative verbs, the use of the conventionalized applicativized causative seems to be synchronically productive and regularly used.

Examples of applicativized causatives are given in (5.9). If a non-causative form of the verb is in use, it is listed in the "Source" column. Note that in the applicativized causative forms, the applicative is indicated by a change of the final consonant of the stem to **k** or **g**, followed by -**ir**-**i**/-**er**-**i** > -**iz**/-**ez**.

5.5 Productive extensions

(5.9) Examples of causative forms

	Source	Gloss	CS	Gloss	APL of CS	Gloss
With **z > g** in applicative						
a.	-----		**-buuz-**	'ask'	**-buugiz-/ -bùguliz-**	'ask or summon for s/o'
b.	-----		**-gááz-**	'turn to dry'	**-gáágiz-**	'turn to dry for s/o'
c.	-----		**-húúz-**	'praise'	**-húúgiz-**	'praise at'
d.	**-lóng-**	'to get'	**-lóóz-**	'look for, want'	**-lóógez-**	'look for s/o'
e.	**-sháág-**	'to leave'	**-shááz-**	'remove'	**-shháágiz-**	'remove for s/o'
f.	-----		**-tííz-**	'borrow'	**-tíígiz-**	'borrow for s/o'
g.	-----		**-tíz-**	'court (a girl)'	**-tígiz-**	'court for s/o'
h.	**-tuul-**	'live'	**-túúz-**	'CS to calm down'	**-túúgiz-**	'calm sthg for s/o'
i.	-----		**-bííz-**	'sweep'	**-bíígiz-**	'sweep for s/o'
j.	-----		**-twéz-**	'dip food in sauce'	**-twégez-**	'dip food in sauce for/at'
k.	**-shèréér-**	'be ruined'	**-shèreez-**	'ruin something'	**-shèreegez-**	'ruin for s/o'
With **s > k** in applicative						
l.	**-yút-**	'come to end'	**-yús-**	'complete something'	**-yúkiz-**	'finish a task for s/o'
m.	----		**-gùs-**	'push coals in fire'	**-gùkiz-**	'tend fire for s/o'
n.	**-gwat-**	'catch'	**-gwas-**	'CS s/o to be caught'	**-gwakiz-**	'CS s/o to be caught for s/o'
o.	-----		**-lámus-**	'greet s/o'	**-lámúkiz-**	'greet on s/o's behalf'
p.	**-duut-**	'be hot'	**-duus-**	'make sthg warm'	**-duukiz-**	'heat something for s/o'
q.	**-lyok-**	'leave'	**-lyos-**	'take out from'	**-lyokez-**	'take out for s/o'
r.	**-hík-**	'arrive'	**-hís-**	'bring home a bride'	**-híkiz-**	'take sthg somewhere for s/o'

	Source	Gloss	CS	Gloss	APL of CS	Gloss
	With **s > k** in applicative					
s.	**-sook-**	'go behind'	**-soos-**	'CS sthg to go around'	**-sookez-**	'CS to go around behind sthg'
t.	**-ny-**	'rain'	**-ny-ees-**	'CS to rain'	**-nyeekez-**	'CS to rain on'
u.	**-gw-**	'fall'	**-gw-iis-**	'CS to fall'	**-gwiikiz-**	'CS sthg to fall for s/o'
v.	**-tw-**	'cut'	**-tw-iis-**	'CS to cut'	**-twiikiz-**	'CS to be cut for s/o'
w.	**-gúl-**	'buy'	**-gúl-iis-**	'sell'	**-gúliikiz-**	'to sell to/for s/o'

Notice that in the verbs in (5.9t–w) the despirantization is affecting not the final consonant of the verb radical, but rather the **s** of the long causative.

The use of the conventionalized applicativized causative forms with the velar **k** or **g** seems perhaps never to have been regularized in causative verbs which include more extensions than just the causative alone. This is indicated by the fact that there are often several options for expressing the applicative of causative verbs which include other extensions. -**líng-ik-an-i-** 'make something ready, prepare something' seems to be a frozen applicativised causative (having lost the distinctive applicative meaning) of the reciprocal-causative form -**líng-aan-i-** 'make something ready' (a frozen causative of -**líng-aan-** 'be of the same size or type, be alike'). Synchronically, both -**líng-ik-an-i-** and -**líng-aan-i-** have the same non-applicative meaning. In order to synchronically applicativize -**líng-ik-an-i-** 'make something ready, prepare', the normal applicative extension plus the short causative, -**ir** + -**i** > -**iz**, must be added, giving -**líng-ik-an-iz-** 'prepare something for someone'.

However, the more widely used applicative form of this verb does not include the -**ik** extension at all; it is -**língaaniz-** 'prepare something for someone', derived (by addition of applicative plus repeated causative) from the form without the -**ik**, -**líng-aan-i-**. This might appear to be the causativized applicative form of -**língaan-** rather than the applicativized form of the causative, but there is no non-causative form of this verb attested with the meaning 'prepare'. Thus, this verb must be derived from the causative form -**líng-aan-i-** 'make something ready'.

There is another applicative form of a reciprocal causative which involves an unusual -**ik**. This is found in -**gwas-ik-an-i-** (hold-IMPS-RCP-CS-) 'hold something for each other' (from -**gwas-** 'hold for someone', which is the causative form (though with applicative meaning) of -**gwat-** 'hold'). In -**gwas-ik-an-i-**, the frication of the final consonant of the root is retained: -**gwas-**, rather than -**gwat**- (with the original non-causative form) or -**gwak**- (with the conventionalized applicative of causative form, though this conventionalized form is used in non-reciprocal forms, e.g. -**gwakiz**- 'catch someone at a place or for some misdeed'). There is no form*-**gwasirani**-, but -**gwasani**- and the cyclically spirantized version of this, *-**gwasizani**- do exist as options to -**gwas-ik-an-i**-.

The extent of variety seen in the formation of these causative-plus-reciprocal forms seems to indicate that forms with other extensions in addition to the causative are not used often enough with the applicative to have been really standardized in the language. Other somewhat anomalous forms are found in (5.10).

(5.10)	Non-CS	Gloss	CS form	Gloss	Frozen APL CS	Gloss
a.	-**mér**-	'grow'	-**méz**-	'CS to sprout'	-**mér-egez**-	'grow well'
b.	-**gér**-	'measure'	-**géz**-	'test'	-**gér-egez**-	'try hard'
c.	-**yòng**-	'suck milk'	-**yòngees**-	'CS to suck milk'	-**yònger-ekez**-[†]	'help nurse animal'

[†]***kúyòngéréésâ**, which would seem perhaps to be the underlying causative here, has not been attested.

The form in (5.10a) seems to be a lexicalized form. It has the meaning of an intensive form, which would normally have the applicative-plus-causative ending, -**iiriz/-eerez**. However, *-**mére (e)rez**- is not attested. Perhaps *-**mére (e)rez**- was reinterpreted somewhere along the line as a causative instead of an intensive, and then underwent having the -**rez** replaced by -**gez** by analogy with applicatives of causatives. The form in (5.10b) is another form with intensive meaning, which also has the unexpected velar consonant.

Although applicativized forms of causative verbs have a conventionalized form, the reverse is not true. In causativized forms of applicative verbs, there is no insertion of an extra **k** or **g**, or other special treatment. Such forms, however, are not common. Hyman (2003c:80) states that "Causativized applicatives are... rare in Bantu languages, and where they occur, the applicative is typically lexicalized with a special meaning".

In Kifuliiru the truth of this statement is not generally challenged. Though there are many verbs which fit the pattern of a causativized applicative, i.e. an ending of -**iza/-eza**, in the majority of them, the applicative extension has been lexicalized, no longer having the meaning components such an extension combination would lead one to expect. Often these extensions do not commute with other extensions or with zero. In cases where there does seem to be commutation with other extensions, the meaning of the causativized applicative has often shifted and become lexicalized, e.g. -báyiz- 'smell (transitive), sniff for a scent' which has the corresponding forms -báyir- 'smell to someone', and -báy- 'have an odor'. In other cases, it is the non-causative "applicative" form which is lexicalized, and without true applicative meaning, e.g. -yìngiz- 'cause to go in', is the causative of -yìngir- 'enter some place', but there is no synchronic form *-yìng- of which -yìngir- is the applicative form.

Another lexicalized causativized applicative that is widely used is found in the verb -lèngez- 'pick up and move', originally from the verb -lèng- 'pass', but now lexicalized. The simple applicative of -lèng-, -lènger- is used exclusively with the reflexive, giving a meaning of not staying in a place: -yìlènger- 'just pass by', (as is also true for some other verbs of motion, e.g. -yìgénder- 'just go on one's way'). The causative of -lèng- is -lèèz- 'cause to pass' or 'surpass', but this seems not to have a widely used applicativized form. Another similar example is found in -shùb- 'formerly be', -shùb-ir- 'go back to where one formerly was', -shùb-ir-i > shùbiz- 'cause someone to go back to where he was'.

A partial exception to the statement that causativized applicatives are usually derived from lexicalized applicative forms is found with locational applicatives, a few of which do still have the applicative-plus-causative meaning, e.g. -hùlukiz- 'cause to come out to some place' could be interpreted as the causative of the applicative verb -hùluk-ir- 'come out to some place', e.g. kúhùlúkírá ímbùgà 'go outside', the applicative of -hùluk- 'come out'. However, in these cases, since most of the non-causative verbs in question, just as -hùlukiz- end in -ok or -uk, the applicative of a causative verb is totally indistinguishable segmentally from the causative of an applicative verb.

In other words, does -hùlukiz- really come from -hùluk-ir-i- (-come.out-APL-CS-), with the applicative followed by causative? Or is the derivation -hùlus-ir-i- > -hùlukiz-, involving the conventionalized applicative form of the causative verb -hùlus-? It is not possible to definitively determine the derivation, except in verbs for which the applicative form has a frozen meaning which is different from the meaning of the basic causative form, e.g. -lyoker-, the applicative form of -lyok- 'leave' has come to be used only in the infinitive, and to mean 'starting from some point of time', while the causative form -lyos- means 'take out'. Thus when we find the form -lyokez- 'take out from some place' we can assume that it is the applicative form of the causative verb -lyos- 'take out' (-lyós-er-i- > -lyok-ez-) rather than the causative form of -lyoker- (-lyok-er-i- > *-lyokez-), etc.

The following example shows a rare instance of a productive causative of a non-locative applicative form. The verb involved is -yìm- '(ruminant animal) conceive' (the direct causative form of which is -yìmy-). The non-causative applicative form would be -**yìmir**- 'conceive for someone (i.e. to the owner's eventual financial benefit)'. The causative of the applicative is -**yìm-íz**- 'cause (a female ruminant animal) to conceive for some owner'. The example is found in a traditional story text in which one person's normal-looking cows have much bigger, stronger calves than anyone else's cows do.

(5.11) Í=shúúlí   y-à=   nyândì ‖
       AU=9+bull   9-A.M=   who

       ì-rí   mú=   kú-yìm-íz-á   w-êhè?
       S.R+9-be   PROG=   O2.SG-conceive-APL+CS-Fa   2SG-CTR.P

'Whose bull ‖ is causing (your cow) to conceive for YOU?' (621 065)

In (5.11) the incorporation into the verb of the second-person singular object **kú**-, referring to the owner, is definitive evidence that this is an instance of a productive applicative.

5.5.1.2 *Causative functions*

The productive causative extension always increases the valence of an intransitive verb, which is to say, it adds a syntactic argument, the causer, while the argument which was the subject/agent of the non-causative verb becomes the patient. For example, **Túlízó àhúbà** 'Tulizo made a mistake', but **Kìràgé àhúbìisà Túlízô** 'Somebody caused Tulizo to make a mistake'.

Suffixing the causative extension to a transitive verb, on the other hand, adds an extra semantic or logical argument: the actual agent of the action indicated by the non-causative verb; but the number of *syntactic* arguments usually remains stable. For example, **Ú=mwàmì àhìngà índálò** 'The king farmed the field' versus **Ú=mwàmì àhìngíísà índálò** 'The king had the field farmed (for him by somebody else)'. The king **ú=mwàmì** is the syntactic subject in both examples, but in the non-causative example, he actually did the farming, while in the example with the causative verb, he is only the causer of the action. Someone else, who is not directly referred to, actually did the work. The use of the causative with a transitive verb thus transforms the role of the syntactic subject from agent of the action to causer of the action, but does not necessarily add a syntactic argument.

So whether the verb is transitive or intransitive, the meaning of the causative extension is that the subject of the verb is the one who is 'causing something to happen'. If the original verb is intransitive, the "causation" expressed by the causative extension is aimed at an actor, at causing some*one* to do something, either directly or by the agency of someone else. If the original verb is transitive, the causation is generally aimed at an event, causing some-*thing* to happen, by the action of some usually unnamed agent (but see (5.12) below, where the agent, who is also the speaker, is named).

5.5.1.2.1 *Causatives of transitive verbs*

In the case of a causative of a transitive verb, the grammatical subject is the causer of the action, while the actual agent of the action is not usually expressed. The original object of a transitive verb remains the object of the causative verb. For example, **ànáhìngíísà índálò** 'and he had his field' (**índálò**) 'farmed' < **-hìng-** 'farm' (transitive). The object can be incorporated, as in **ànágìhìngíísà** 'and he had it (cl. 9) farmed'. The action here is performed by some unnamed (but hopefully duly rewarded) agent. Likewise, in **ákágwátíísá íngòkò** 'he had a chicken caught', the subject of the verb is the causer and not the agent of the action (who is being caused to act), while the object/patient is still the chicken. This can be seen by incorporating the object in this last example. Note that the incorporated object in **ákágìgwátíísâ** 'he had it (cl. 9) caught' is the cl. 9 object marker **gì-**, referring to the chicken, and not the cl. 1 object marker, **mú-** which would be the case if the object were the person doing the catching.

The addition of the causative extension to a verb always increases the potential valence of the verb by logically implying an agent of the action who is different from the grammatical subject of the verb. Thus the addition of the causative to a transitive verb causes it to be able to take two objects rather than just one. In most cases, as the two in the previous paragraph, the new agent is not expressed. However, in the event that the extra argument is then specified, it is interpreted as indicating the person being caused to perform the action of the verb, and may be expressed as an extra object of the verb, together with the original object of the transitive verb.

The following example illustrates such a case. The situation being described involves some people who enter a shop and ask the shopkeeper to get down some blankets from the shelf behind him for them to look at. When they are put off by his price, and refuse to buy them, the shopkeeper complains to himself 'They come making *me* get down my goods, and they don't buy from me!' In this example, the italicized 'me' is the extra object allowed by the addition of the causative in the verb **-mánuliis-** 'have someone get something down'. The non-causative form of this verb, **-mánul-** 'get something down' is a transitive verb, so the addition of the causative makes it possible for **-mánuliis-** to have an extra object, as indicated by the fact that the first-person object marker is used with it: **m-mánuliisa**[11] 'cause me to get something down', while the original patient/object, **ú=bútùùzì** 'goods' is still mentioned following the verb.

(5.12) **Zí-gá-yîjì**   **m-mánúl-íís-á**   ú=bú-tùùzì   bw-à-nî ‖
10-F2-COMING   O1.SG-go.down-CS-Fa   AU=14-goods   14-A.M-1SG

zì-tá-gá-ná-n-gúl-ìr-à.
10-NEG-F2-ADD.V-O1.SG-buy-APL-Fa

'They come making me get down my goods ‖ and they don't buy from me!' (520 052)

There is at least one instance in which the causative is used to imply assistance rather than direct agentive causation. This is in the case of -**bùtiis**- 'assist in childbirth', from the transitive verb -**bùt**- 'give birth'. With this causative, the expectant mother is usually the only expressed object of the verb, as in (5.13).

(5.13) **Á=bì-ì-tù** | **á-bá-àlì**   **m-bùt-íís-â**   ‖
AU=2-SAME.SET-1PL   S.R-2-P3   O1.SG-give.birth-CS-Fa

bá-n-dwâl-à   **í=rw-ījì.**
2-O1.SG-take-Fa   23=11-river

'My fellow (women) | who assisted me in childbirth ‖ took me to the river.' (201 111)

5.5.1.2.2 Causatives of intransitive verbs

With a causative formed from an intransitive base verb, the grammatical subject is also the agent of the action as well as the causer, e.g. **bànáhùlúsà múkáàgè** 'and they took out his wife' (-**hùlus**- 'take out (CAUSATIVE, TRANS)' < -**hùluk**- 'go out (INTRANS)'). In such a case, the agent/subject causes the intransitive action of the verb to happen to someone or something that would have been expressed as the subject of the original verb. That is, if the woman had come out on her own, she would have been the agent/subject rather

---

[11]There are no geminate nasals (or geminate consonants) in Kifuliiru, so the first-person singular object, morphologically N- is expressed with an nasal initial verb only by its H tone object, shifted leftward to the preceding morpheme or word. We include the segmental representation of the N- here to clarify the presence of the extra object.

than the patient/object of the verb, e.g. **múkáàgè ànáhùlúkà** 'and his wife came out'.

Example (5.14) further illustrates that the causative used with an intransitive verb indicates that the subject/agent of the verb is acting directly upon the object/patient. The causative verb here is -**hís**- 'cause something to arrive', which is derived from -**hík**- 'arrive'.

(5.14)   **Mbw-<u>à</u>=**   **<u>Ø-hí-s-é</u>**   **kàndì**   **yì-zó**   **n-yámà**
as.soon.as-1   SBV-arrive-CS-Fe   again   those.N-10   10-meats

mú=   **mw-à-gè** || **mú-ká-à-gè**   **à-ná-ráákár-à**   **bwénèènè.**
18=   home-A.M-1   1-wife-A.M-1   1-SQ-be.angry-Fa   very.much

'When he again brought those meats into his house || his wife became very angry.' (35 014)

5.5.1.2.3 *Causatives expressing instrumentality*

As is true in many Bantu languages,[12] instrumentality may be expressed by the Kifuliiru causative extension. An example of this instrumental use of a causative with an intransitive verb is -**kòla** 'work', -**kòleesa** 'use something', e.g. **áàlí kìzí kòléésâ ú=búlémbò** 'he was repeatedly using sticky sap'. Note that the causative increases the valence of the verb, so that an intransitive verb such as 'arrive' or 'work' which formerly allowed a subject as its only argument, is now able to take an instrumental object as well.

In (5.15) the person must go look for equipment with which to -**kàndiis**- 'make juice or beer'.

---

[12] Wald (1997:231–232) mentions that languages of a large area (South and Interior East Bantu) use the causative to express an instrument as a topical object, while the remaining areas use the applicative extension to perform this same function, e.g. Kiswahili: **tunalimia majembe** 'we are farming with hoes'.

5.5 Productive extensions

(5.15) ...ù-ná-gêndì   lóóz-á   í=bí-rúgú   ‖   né=   bì-ndì
       2SG-CON-GOING   look.for-Fa   AU=8-container   CNJ=   8-other

bí-kòlànwà | by-ó=   kú-kànd-íís-â.
8-equipment   8-A.M+AU=   15-make.beverage-CS-Fa

'...and you go look for containers ‖ and other equipment | for making beverages with.' (411 020)

However, though speakers can produce on demand such sentences as **tùlì mú=límíísá í=fùkà** 'we are digging with hoes', **tùlì mú=hìngíísá í=fùkà** 'we are farming with hoes', it is not natural in Kifuliiru to use the causative in this way to indicate instrumentality. The only verb commonly used in which the causative indicates instrumentality is the verb **-kòlees-** 'use' (from -kòl- 'work/do'). However, in lexicalized nominal forms, there is evidence that instrumentality (doing something *with* an instrument) was expressed in the past by the use of the reciprocal plus causative. Evidence of this is still seen in nouns such as **bí-lw-án-íís-ô** (8-fight-RCP-CS-o) 'fighting gear (swords, shields, etc.)'. A similar noun combines reciprocal plus passive, in **bí-kòl-àn-w-à** (8-work-RCP-PS-a) 'equipment', found in example (5.15) above.[13]

Causative is used to indicate instrumentality only with verbs which do not already include instrument in their argument structure. Many ditransitive verbs, especially those which include the impositive extension, include an instrument as one of their objects (see 5.18.2.2 on the inclusion of instrument as an argument in many impositive verbs).

Some Bantu languages also use the causative to express imitative behavior. This has not been observed in Kifuliiru. However the verb **-gír-** 'do, make' is used with the causative plus reflexive object marker, i.e. **-yì-gír-iis-** to mean 'pretend (lit., make oneself)'. The conjunctive **ngá** 'like/as' is used following this verb, e.g. **ànáyìgírìisá ngà=múlwāzì** 'and he pretended to be sick (lit. made himself like a sick person)' or **ànáyìgírìisá ngá=ágááshàlà** 'and he pretended he was going to vomit (lit. made himself like he will vomit)'.

5.5.1.3 Causative alternate forms

There are some verbs for which there is both a short causative form, with **i**, **y**, and a long causative form, with **-iis/-ees**. The long causative is always the

---

[13] These comitative uses of the reciprocal -**an** to indicate instrumentality are interesting in light of Wald's (ibid.) footnote regarding a reflex of the "proto collective extension (-an)" in Duala, a Northwest Bantu language of Cameroon in the verb meaning "use" which he lists as **-bol-anɛ** (do-COM/INSTR).

one used for synchronic derivation of a causative form, while the short forms tend to be lexicalized.

A frozen causative form of -**gwat**- 'hold, catch' is -**gwas**- 'assist'.[14] As seen in (5.16) this form uses the short form of the causative rather than the long one, found in -**gwatiis**-. The form -**gwas**- is often idiomatically used like an applicative form of -**gwat**-.

(5.16) **Ùl-ì   mú=   láálík-á   á=bá-ndú   b-ó=   kú-kú-gwá-s-á**
    2SG-are   PROG   invite-Fa   AU=2-people   2-A.M+AU=   15-O2-help-CS-Fa

   mú=   mí-kòlwà.
   18=   4-work

'You are inviting people to assist you in the work...' (020 021)

However, -**gwas**- is not always used in this specialized way, but can also used with true causative meaning. In (5.17) it is stated that "the trapper uses sap in catching birds" (i.e. causing the birds to be caught). The use of the causative instead of the non-causative form of the verb -**gwat**- indicates that the trapper is not catching the birds with his own hands, but is using some other agent to accomplish the action of the verb. In this case this involves an inanimate means, but the action can also be done by another person.

(5.17) **Mú=   kú-lémbék-á   kw-à-gè | á-àlí   kìzì   kòl-éés-á**
    18=   15-catch.birds-Fa   15-A.M-1   1-P3   REP   work-CS-Fa

   ú=bú-lémbó | mú=   kú-gwá-s-á   ú=tú-nyúnì.
   AU=14-sticky.sap WHILE   15-catch-CS-Fa   AU=13-bird

'In his trapping (birds, with sticky substance) | he repeatedly used sticky sap | in catching birds.' (623 004)

Other examples include -**gúl**- 'buy'; -**gúz**- 'put something up for sale', -**gúli-is**- 'sell (something to someone)'; -**lím**- 'farm', -**límy**- 'go look for work to get something to live on', and -**límiis**- 'to have a field farmed', or 'farm a field with some implement' (both of the meanings of -**límiis**- are, however, actually more commonly expressed using the verb -**hìngiis**- 'farm' -**hìng**- 'farm'). As

---

[14] It seems that probably this is the original form of the causative of -**gwat**-, but because it is often used as a lexicalized form with a non-causative meaning, the longer form of the causative, -**gwatiis**-, was created as an innovation, and is now often used when a true causative meaning is intended.

can be noted in these examples, when both long and short causative options exist, the short causative usually indicates direct causation in which the subject of the verb is the agent of the action, while the long causative shows indirect causation, in which the subject of the verb is not the agent of the verb's action, but merely the agent of the causation. One very illustrative example of this is found with the verb -**yìm**- '(female ruminant animal) to conceive'. The short causative is -**yìmy**- 'cause conception in a ruminant animal', while the long causative form is -**yìmiis**- 'arrange for ruminant animal to be mated'.

5.5.2 Passive

5.5.2.1 Passive structural considerations

Two allomorphs have been reconstructed for the Proto-Bantu passive, *-ʋ, used following a C, and *-**ibʋ** used following a V (Schadeberg 2003a:78). In Kifuliiru, both of these are reflected. The passive extension surfaces as -w (from -u) following a consonant, or -**ib-w/-eb-w** (from -**ib-u/-eb-u**) following CV- radicals. This gives active/passive alternations like -**bùt**- 'give birth', -**bùtw**- 'be born', and -**ly**- 'eat', -**lííbw**- 'be eaten', etc. The passive, like the causative, is one of the two extensions which includes a H tone.

The passive morpheme is always placed directly to the left of the final vowel in the verb stem. This means that it is always the final extension. If the causative extension also appears in the same verb as the passive, the causative -**i** will directly precede the passive -**bu**.

As stated above, the shape of the passive following C is -**u**. There is also a strengthened form which is used following a monosyllabic -CV- radical. The initial vowel of this allomorph undergoes vowel height harmony (VHH) with the preceding vowel of the stem. This form is -**ib-u/-eb-u**, e.g. -**mo**- 'shave' > -**mwebw**- 'be shaved'; -**tu**- 'break off' > -**twibw**- 'be broken off'.[15] Another form in which -**ebu** is found is derived from the verb -**nyw**- 'drink', (UF **nyo**-) the causative form of which is -**nywees**- 'give a drink to someone who can't drink by himself'.[16] The related noun, seemingly formed from the passive form of -**nyw**- is **kínywèèbwà** 'drink, beverage'.

---

[15] However, there are two passive forms of the verb -**ha**- 'give': either -**heebw-a** (rarely used, mostly archaic, reflecting -**ibu**) or the much more common -**haabwa** (reflecting -**abu?**) 'be given'). The unextended form of -**ha**- 'give' is synchronically little used. Its usual form is instead structurally a causativized applicative, e.g. **kú-hééz-â/kú-héér-éz-â** 'to give (sthg) to someone'. The unextended form only occurs when it includes an incorporated object and is followed by a cliticized second object pronoun, e.g. **ngá-kú-hà=kyô** 'I will give it to you'.

[16] There is, however, also a seemingly related form with a high-vowel extension (rather than the mid-vowel extension with **e**) **kúnywíísâ** 'to water a plant or a field'. This is, however a lexicalized form with a different meaning synchronically.

In Kifuliiru there is also another post-vocalic allomorph, **-bu,** which lacks the initial **i/e.** This **-bu** allomorph is used following the causative morpheme. This becomes evident when one looks at the vowel length and vowel harmony phenomena in causative forms. Let's look first at the length considerations. The causative morpheme is vowel final in its underlying form: (-**iis**)-**i**/-(**ees**)-**i**. Thus if we assume the **-ibu** form of the passive is used following a vowel, the passive of a causative should evidence the ending (-**iis**-/-**ees**)-**i**-**ibu,** with a double **i** preceding the **bu.** This, however, is not the case. There is no doubling of the vowel preceding -**bu** in forms such as -**gúl-iis-i̱-bw-a** 'be sold'. Instead there is retention of the original length in **íís.** This long vowel would be shortened by the phonological rule of mora-based vowel shortening if there were a long vowel preceding -**bw-.** But there is no length there. In any non-resultative form of a causative verb, e.g. -**gwasi̱bwa** 'be caught' from -**gwat-** 'catch' + -**i** (CS) + (PS), or -**simiisi̱bwa** 'be made happy' from **siim** 'be happy' + CS + PS, there is only a single **i** in the suffix combination.

Perhaps one could assume that the final -**i** of the causative has been deleted here by the phonological rule which deletes a glide following **s** or **z.** This is indeed what becomes of the final **i** in the surface form of a non-passive causative verb, e.g. -**gúliisa** 'sell' (from -**gúl-iis-i-a** > -**gúliis-y-a** > -**gúl-iis-a.**) However, the final -**i** is deleted only after it has been changed to a glide, -**y** due to the environment of a following unlike vowel. There is no rule that deletes the **i** when it is still vocalic. If one assumes that the passive appears as -**ibu** in a passive-of-causative form, its initial vowel is not an unlike vowel which would cause the final -**i** of the causative to undergo glide formation. So we that the environment for glide formation is not met, and it cannot be the case that the final -**i** of the causative has been deleted for that reason. If on the other hand, one assumes that there is no final **i** there, and the causative morpheme is only -**iis/-ees** then there are two problems. First, why is the post-vocalic form of the passive used in causative forms at all if the causative morpheme is not vowel-final? Second, it is not possible to assume deletion of the causative -**i** in forms where only the short causative is used, such as -**yók-y-a** (-roast-CS-Fa) 'roast'/-**yók-i-bw-a** (-roast-CS-PS-Fa) 'be roasted'.

Vowel harmony phenomena also point to a -**bu** allomorph in causatives. The vowel which precedes the -**bu** passive in causative forms never harmonizes with a mid-vowel of a radical, as happens with (non-causative) -CV- radicals, e.g. **mo-** 'shave' > -**mwebw-a** 'be shaved'. Instead, in causative forms the vowel preceding -**bu** is always **i.** Thus the form of the passive is not -**ebu-** in causative verbs whose radical has a mid vowel, for example, we find -**lyosi̱bwa** 'be taken out', and not *-**lyosebwa,** from -**lyok-** 'come out', and -**shèreezi̱bwa** 'be destroyed', and not *-**shèreezebwa** from **shèreez-** 'destroy'. The passive extension does not display vowel height harmony with the vowel of the stem in these cases simply because it has no initial vowel. The passive -**bu** directly follows the final -**i** of the causative morpheme, and this causative -**i** is the vowel which precedes the passive -**bu** in these forms.

5.5.2.2 Passive function

The passive extension functions to reduce the valence of a verb by one, by allowing a semantic patient/object to be expressed as the syntactic subject of the verb. This means that the action of the verb is being done to the syntactic subject. In (5.18) the lion (subject) "will be eaten" by the rat.

(5.18) **Ná-yò ‖ í-gá-lìì-bw-á | né=   yò   m-bébà.**
       ADD.P-9   9-F2-eat-PS-Fa   CNJ=   that.N+9   9-rat

'And it (lion) ‖ also will be eaten | by that rat.' (49 011)

If a verb is ditransitive to begin with, the passive does not make it intransitive, but renders it a simple transitive. This can be shown with the verb -**zìmb**- 'steal', which is ditransitive.[17] The malefactive (one being stolen from) is one of the syntactic objects, as shown by its incorporation in (5.19).

(5.19) **Iri n-àngà-mény-à ‖   ú-w-á-n-zìmb-á | yì-zí**
       If   1SG-CND-know-Fa   S.R.-1-P1-O1.SG-steal-Fa   this.P-10

   fwárángá   z-àà-nî |...
   money   10-A.M-1SG

'If I would know ‖ who stole my money from me (lit. who stole (from) me | my money....' (22 006)

Being human, the malefactive object is the object higher on the hierarchy, so it is the one which most often becomes the subject of the passive form -**zìmb-w**-. The derived cl. 1a noun **nàkúzìmbwâ** 'person who has been stolen from' is derived from the passive form of this verb. A passive verb of which the subject is the one stolen from is shown in (5.20), where the grammatical

---

[17] There are many such verbs in Kifuliiru which semantically may include (and syntactically allow) the incorporation of a malefactive object (one adversely affected by the action of the verb) without an applicative extension being added to the verb. For example, **kúlyâ** 'to eat' may have an incorporated malefactive object as **ákándyâ** (lit. 'he ate me') in the following: **wá=ngòkò náyè ákándyá í=nyámá yànì** 'Chicken also ate (me) my meat', meaning that the chicken ate the speaker's meat without permission.

subject of the passive verb is the **mwàmì** 'king', who has been robbed of his **í=ngáàvù** 'cow' which is expressed as the remaining object of the clause.

(5.20) **Kú=**   **yìkyó**   **ky-ànyà** || **mw-àmí** |
     17=   that.N+7   7-time   1-king

     á-àlí   **màlí**   **zìmb-w-â** | **í=n-gáàvù.**
     1-P3   ALREADY   steal-PS-Fa   AU=9-cow

'At that time || the king | had already had stolen (from him) | a cow.' (22 006)

It is clear, however, that not only the one stolen from, but also the thing stolen is an object of the verb **-zìmb-**. Look at (5.21) where the subject of the relativized passive verb is the very 'cow that was stolen' spoken of in (5.20).

(5.21) **B-à-gwán-à** || **à-bètw-ír-ì** | **í-fúmbá**   **ly-é=**
     2-P1-encounter-Fa   1-carry-RS-Fi   AU+5-packet   5-A.M+AU

     bì-jógòmbé | **by-ê=**   **yó**   **n-gáàvú** | **y-é=**   **bw-àmì** |
     8-intestine   8-A.M=   that.N+9   9-cow   9-A.M+23   14-kingdom

     í-y-à-zímb-w-à.
     S.R-9-P1-steal-PS-Fa

'They found || him carrying | a packet of intestines | of that cow | of the king | that was stolen.' (23 025)

When the patient of the verb's action, in this case the cow, is expressed as the subject of a passive verb, the malefactive object (in this case the king, from whom the cow was stolen) may not be expressed as an object. As seen in (5.21), the king gets into the statement only peripherally, by the reference in the preceding associative phrase that the cow was "of at" (cl. 9 associative marker plus cl. 23 locative marker) the kingdom.

Many times, the passive is used idiomatically with the verb **-gwat-** 'grab, take hold of' to express emotion, with emotion expressed as the "agent" of the passive. In the following example, the emotion is **ú=lúùgì** 'jealousy', but other examples of this same construction use **ú=bútê** 'anger', **ú=mwìzíngéérwê** 'sadness', **í=kyōbà** 'fear', **í=shōnì** 'shame', **í=kífùfù** 'deep grief, sobbing', etc.

5.5 Productive extensions

(5.22) <u>Bà-ná-gwât-w-à</u>   n-ó=   lú-ùgì.
       2-SQ-grab-PS-Fa   CNJ-A.M+AU= 11-jealousy

'And they were seized by jealousy.' (107 005)

In the majority of cases, an animate agent of the passive is not expressed. In (5.23) we are not told (here) who killed the old men (though it is explained earlier in the narrative.)

(5.23) Á=bá-shààjà | á-b-áàlì gì-yí-j-ì | bà-tá-kírí =hò ‖
      AU=2-old.person S.R-2-P3 O9-know-RS-Fi 2-NEG-PERS =16

      kéèrà | <u>bà-ká-yīt-w-à</u>.
      already   2-P2-kill-PS-Fa

'The old men | who knew it (a house) | are no longer around. ‖ Already | they were killed.' (23 025)

However, (5.24) shows an expressed agent of the action of the passivized applicative verb **ákáfw-ír-wâ** 'he was died to'.[18] A person who is bereaved is often cast as the grammatical subject of this passivized applicative verb. In (5.24) **músósí múgùmà** 'a certain man' is specified as the subject of the verb, while his deceased wife is the "agent" introduced by the conjunction **ná**=.

(5.24) Mú-sósí mú-gùmà ‖ <u>á-ká-fw-ír-w-á</u>   ná=   mú-ká-à-gè.
      1-man   1-certain   1-P2-die-APL-PS-Fa CNJ= 1-wife-A.M-1

'A certain man ‖ lost his wife (was died to by his wife).' (43 002)

Cf. also -bèg-/-bèg-w- 'shave hair/be shaved', -bwir-/-bwir-w- 'tell/be told', -gwat-/-gwat-w- 'grab/be grabbed', -lyos-/-<u>lyos-ibw</u>- 'get rid of/be gotten rid of', -sìg-/-sìg-w- 'leave/be left', -yìt-/-yìt-w- 'kill/be killed'. (See also the mutual use of the reciprocal extension, 5.5.4.5 for a specialized use of the passive).

---

[18]That this is the passive of an applicative form is clear by analogy with the monosyllabic verb **kúlyâ** 'to eat', of which the passive is **kúlííbwâ** 'to be eaten', e.g. **ú=búndú bùtàlììbwâ búzírá shògò** 'ugali is never eaten without accompanying relish' and the applicative is **kúlíírà** 'to eat APL', and the passive of the applicative, **kúlíírwà** 'to be eaten APL'.

5.5.3 Applicative

5.5.3.1 *Applicative structural considerations*

The applicative extension is also called "dative" or "prepositional". It means "to do for, to, or at", and its form is -**er** or -**ir**, subject to vowel height harmony, e.g. -**kòl**- 'do'/-**kòler**- 'do to/for', -**gáluk**-/-**gálukir**- 'return/return to', etc. A verb in which the applicative has been lexicalized, such as -**láhir**- 'refuse, deny' may also take a productive applicative, e.g. -**láhir-ir**- 'refuse someone something, deny something to someone'. Recall that none of the -VC extensions includes a tone.

Reduplicating the applicative and lengthening the first vowel has been observed in a few verbs, and gives the idea of intensifying or magnifying the action, or doing something on purpose, with the same result as the intensive. Thus while the applicative of -**gír**- 'do', -**gír-ir**-, means 'do for someone', or 'do at some place', -**gír-iirir**- with both reduplication of the extension and vowel lengthening, is 'do something on purpose, or with intensity and intention'. In many lexicalized forms, the applicative has a long vowel for no apparent reason, e.g. -**hòleer**- 'be comforted', -**kèngeer**- 'remember', -**yèmeer**- 'agree', etc.

5.5.3.2 *Applicative function*

The applicative extension -**ir**/-**er** means 'do something to, or for, someone, or at some place'. The applicative, then, is a valence-increasing extension, which allows a formerly intransitive verb to take an object, or a verb which is already transitive in unextended form to take an extra object. The applied object may be someone benefiting or being adversely affected by the action of the verb. It may also express a location where the action is taking place. When an applicative verb also includes the reflexive object prefix, it expresses intentionality. These three functions are discussed below.

5.5.3.2.1 *Applicative of benefit/detriment*

The addition of a benefactive/goal object seems to be the most common use of the applicative. For example the verb -**twal**- 'carry away' is a transitive verb. Example (5.25) shows how the applicative allows the goal as the added object argument: 'take something *to someone*'.

(5.25) À-ná-bì-twál-ír-à   náákùlù.
    1-SQ-O8-take-APL-Fa   1a+his.grandmother

'And he took them to his grandmother.' (35 013)

The statement in (5.25) could also be expressed with both objects pronominalized, as **ànámútwálírà=byô** 'and he took them to her'. Kifuliiru allows two object prefixes preceding the verb stem only when at least one of them is either the first-person singular or the reflexive. Here, since neither is first singular or reflexive, one of them must be encliticized (attached to the end of the verb). The animate beneficiary/goal of the verb is higher on the incorporation hierarchy than the inanimate patient of the verb, so **mú-** 'her' is the one which is incorporated in the pre-stem position of the verb, while the patient, **byô** 'them' is encliticized.

In (5.26) the applicative form -**gír-ir-** 'do to/for' allows the beneficiary to be expressed. Here the agent/subject is 'doing something for the leopard', in this case, giving him the liver of the animal he has trapped. Note that in the second use of -**gír-ir-** 'do for' in this example, the cl. 9 object **gì-** is incorporated into the verb, referring once again to the leopard, who is the beneficiary, but not incorporated, of the first applicative verb.

(5.26) À-ná-gír-ìr-à   ìyó   n-gwí ‖ ngá= kwókùlyà |
    1-SQ-do-APL-Fa   that.N+9 9-leopard like= like.thus

   á-ká-té   gì-gír-ír-à.
   1-P2-PRIOR   O9-do-APL-Fa

'He did for that leopard ‖ just as | he first did for it.' (35 013)

In (5.27) context determines that this is the detrimental/malefactive use of the applicative; the added malefactive argument is expressed by the incorporated **bà-** '2 (them)'.

(5.27) ...á=má-húbé g-á=   bá-ndú | bà-lì   mú=   bà-gír-ír-à.
    AU=6-wrong 6-O.R.+AU= 2-people 2-are PROG O2-do-APL-Fa

'...wrongs which people | are doing to them.' (523 008)

5.5.3.2.2 Applicative of location

In (5.28) the applicative -**er** adds to the meaning of the transitive verb -**deek**- 'cook' the meaning of doing something in a certain location, which in this case is the container in which the cooking is done.

(5.28) **À-ná-gêndí   húmb-à   ú=mú-hólè || à-ná-gù-déék-<u>ér</u>-á |**
      1-SQ-GOING   dig-Fa   AU=3-bitter.leaf   1-SQ-O3-cook-APL-Fa

      mú=   ny-ûngú | yé=   kí-byâ.
      18=   9-pot   9+A.M+AU   7-small.clay.pot

  'And she went and picked bitter leaves || and she cooked it | in a small pot | of clay.' (26 005)

This locational sense is also used often with verbs of motion or location, e.g. -**gáluk-/-gálukir**- 'return/return to', -**bàlam-/-bàlam-ir**- 'travel/travel to'; -**hík-/-hík-ir**- 'arrive/arrive at'; -**yìmáng-/-yìmáng-ir**- 'stand, stand at'; -**rágir-/-rágir-ir**- 'graze animals/graze animals at', etc. In each case, the location is expressed by a locative phrase.

5.5.3.2.3 Applicative plus reflexive: intent

As already noted with intransitive verbs, the applicative suffix when used in conjunction with the reflexive prefix conveys the notion of intention, or purpose. This is most often, but not always, used in connection with verbs of motion, so that the meaning is one of getting oneself out of some place, and doing it intentionally. In such a case, there is no added semantic argument. Syntactically, the reflexive represents an object, but the object refers, of course, to the same semantic referent as the grammatical subject of the verb. In (5.29) the combination of the reflexive **yi**- prefix together with the applicative -**ir** on **kànáyìpúrùmùk<u>ìr</u>à** 'and it just dashed (itself) off' conveys that there is intention involved. The unextended verb -**púrumuk**- 'dash off', lacks the explicitly intentional notion.

(5.29) À-ná-làsh-à   yàkó   ká-nyúnì ‖ hálìkò ‖
1-SQ-threw.at-Fa   that.N+12   12-bird   but

kà-ná-yì-púrùmùk-ir-à.
12-SQ-RFX-dash.off-APL-Fa

'And he threw something at that bird ‖ but ‖ it dashed off.' (07 014)

5.5.4 Reciprocal

5.5.4.1 Reciprocal structural considerations

The reciprocal extension is -**an**, e.g. -**shòmb**-/-**shòmb-án**- 'hate/hate each other', -**tábaal**-/-**tábaal-an**- 'help/help each other', -**shúlik**-/-**shúlik-an**- 'hit someone/hit each other', etc. It also may have the meaning of comitative and mutual.

The reciprocal extension -**an** can be used with true reciprocal meaning in nearly any transitive verb, but is also often found lexicalized without specific reciprocal meaning in forms such as -**kàndagan**- 'step on', from -**kànd**- 'press'; -**jùgumban**- 'be about to fall', from -**jùgumby**- 'shake (TRANS)',[19] -**lángashan**- 'be shining'; -**tuuban**- 'sweat'; -**vwaganan**- 'container or measure to be not quite full'.

5.5.4.2 Reciprocal function

The basic meaning of the reciprocal extension -**an** is that two or more actors are performing the same transitive action and each is patient or goal of the action of the other. Thus while semantically, a verb with this extension has two agents and two patients, syntactically the number of arguments which may be expressed separately with the verb is reduced, in that the patient may no longer be represented by a complement phrase. Each agent is also a patient, and vice versa, and this is signified by a plural subject prefix plus the inclusion of the reciprocal in the verb stem. In (5.30) the action is -**shòmb**- 'hate', which in unextended form takes an expressed object, but the addition of the reciprocal makes the verb -**shòmb-an**- 'hate each other', which cannot take an object.

---

[19]Note the apparently related forms **kújúgúmà** 'to tremble', **kújúgúmyâ** 'to cause to tremble', **kujùgúúvyâ** 'to shake something', **kújùngúbánà** 'to quake, wobble', and **kújùgúlà** 'to rattle around'.

(5.30) **Kú-lyók-ér-á**   yùlwó   lú-sìkù ‖ W-à-rú-mûngù |
15-leave-APL-Fa   that.N+11   11-day   1-A.M-11-hyena

ná=   W-à-lú-kwàvù | bà-ná-shòmb-**án**-à.
CNJ=   1-A.M-11-rabbit   2-SQ-hate-RCP-Fa

'And ever since (lit. leaving from) that day ‖ Hyena | and Rabbit | hated each other.' (621 065)

There is never an object complement phrase following a verb in which the reciprocal extension designates true reciprocity of action, since the reciprocal objects are implied by the inclusion of the extension in the verb. There is also no coordinate phrase following the verb when the reciprocal is used with true reciprocal meaning. When the reciprocal extension is lexicalized (or used comitatively, 5.9.2.2) **na** 'CNJ' may follow the verb. The reciprocal extension in the verb -**gwan-an**- 'encounter' in (5.31) is lexicalized, so that the conjunction **na** is added after -**gwan-an**- to introduce the person being met with. Note that the verb in this case also has a singular subject.

(5.31) **N-à-gwán-án-à** ‖   **ná**=   mw-ìrá   w-à-nì.
1SG-P1-meet-COM-Fa   CNJ=   1-friend   1-A.M-1SG

'I met (with) ‖ my friend.' (12 011)

In (5.32) we see another verb in which the reciprocal is lexicalized, and which has a following **na** 'CNJ'. The verb -**kùlikir-an**- is used somewhat idiomatically with a following **na** to mean 'according to'.

(5.32) **N-àná-yábììr-à**   í=n-gónì ‖   ú=kú-kùlíkír-**án**-à | **nó**=   bú-màsì |
1SG-SQ-meet-Fa   AU=9-stick   AU=15-follow-COM-Fa   CNJ=   14-witness

bw-ó=   tú-ká-yì-bòn-ér-á | tw-ényènè.
14-OR=   1PL-P2-RFX-see-APL-Fa   1PL-self

'And I took a stick ‖ according to (lit. following with) | the testimony | which we saw for | ourselves.' (634 030)

For other examples of the reciprocal in context, see also -**gwan**-/-**gwan-an**- 'encounter/encounter each other', -**hím**-/-**hím-an**- 'defeat/be in contention', -**seezer**-/-**seezer-an**- 'say goodbye/say goodbye to each other' -**siim**-/-**sim-aan**- 'like/like each other'.

5.5.4.2.1 Reciprocal of abstraction

Sometimes the reciprocal -**an** is used in place of an object in a transitive verb that is normally expressed with an object, to signify that the action is being spoken of abstractly, rather than in relation to a specific incident. For example, -**yìt**- 'kill', is not normally used without an object, but can be expressed as -**yìt-an**- (-kill-RCP-) 'kill others'. This use of the abstract reciprocal is also found in the related nouns **bw-ìtánì** (14-murder), and **mw-ìt-án-ì** (1-kill-RCP-AG) 'murderer'. Another example of the reciprocal of general application is -**beesh-er-an**- (lie-APL-RCP) 'lie about others'. Any such verb could, in the right context, be interpreted as truly reciprocal, rather than as an abstraction. It is the context, and not the form or any quality of the verb, that determines whether the speaker is referring to a specific incident, for example of two (or more) specific people acting on each other, or just the abstract idea of doing something to other people.

In (5.33) the verb -**yèrek-an**- 'show to' gives the idea of showing something to someone, without specifying who is being shown (see also "Neuter plus reciprocal" 5.6.3.2.1).

(5.33) H-í=gúlú   ly-ó=   kú-yèrék-<u>án</u>-á | kw-é=   mí-sòrè ||
16-5=in.order   5-A.M+AU=   15-show-RCP-Fa   CMP-AU=   4-young.people

y-áàlí   kwìr-ìir-í | ú=kú-kōl-à...
4-P3   must-RS-Fi   AU=15-work-Fa

'In order to show (others) | that the young people || ought | to work...'
(23 047)

5.5.4.2.2 Comitative use of the reciprocal

In intransitive verbs the reciprocal -**an** has the meaning of accompaniment rather than reciprocity. In such a case -**an** is glossed as comitative (COM) rather than reciprocal. This is a productive extension for verbs such as -**taah-an**- (-go.home-COM-) 'go home with' > -**taah**- 'go home'; -**gáluk-an**- (-return-COM-) 'return with' > -**gáluk**- 'return'; -**génd-an**- (-go-COM-) 'go with' > -**génd**- 'go'; -**sìgal-an**- (-remain-COM-) 'remain with' > -**sìgal**- 'remain behind, be left', etc. Intransitive verbs used with this extension are either verbs of motion or verbs of staying somewhere. The fact that these verbs are making use of the reciprocal extension in the comitative manner, and that this is not just a cliticized use of associative **na** 'CNJ' is shown by the fact that the object of accompaniment may be incorporated into the verb, and often is, as in the following two examples.

The object of accompaniment is sometimes animate, but not actively accompanying, as **ùyú mwānà** 'the child' in (5.34).

(5.34) **Ù-yú   mw-ānà | n-dá-gáá-mú-ly-à. || n-àmú=**
     this.P-1   1-child   1SG-NEG-F2-O1-eat-Fa   1SG-F1=

     n-àmú=   mú-tááh-án-á   í=kà-áyà ||
     1SG-F1=   O1-go.home-COM-Fa   23=12-village

     n-Ø-géndì   mú-lér-à.
     1SG-SBV-GOING   O1-raise.child-Fa

'This child | I will not eat him. || I am about to take him home to (my) compound || that I go take care of him.' (617 026)

More often, as in (5.35) the comitative object is inanimate, as **mí-tègò** (4-traps), here seen as the incorporated object.

(5.35) **À-ná-hùm-à | kw-î=   yó mí-tègó y-à-gè ||**
     1-SQ-touch-Fa   17-those.N=   4   4-trap   4-A.M-1

     à-ná-gì-génd-àn-à.
     1-SQ-O4-go-COM-Fa

'And he took some of | those traps of his || and he went with them.' (35 002)

Other examples of the comitative use of the reciprocal follow.

In (5.36) the object, being new information in the sentence, is not incorporated into the verb, but is specified by the noun phrase **í=bíhìmbò byó=búshâ** 'meaningless bruises'. However, it is clear that this is the syntactic object, since it is the only referent to which the comitative could refer. If the meaning of -**taah-an**- (-go.home-COM-) 'go home together with each other', the verb would also include the passive (see mutual below) and the complement phrase would not be permitted.

(5.36) **Bà-ná-tááh-án-à | í=bí-hìmbò | by-ó=   búshâ.**
     2-SQ-return.home-COM-Fa   AU=8-bruises   8-A.M+AU=   emptiness

'And they returned home |with bruises |meaningless.' (06 026)

In (5.37) we find a similar example, where **yàkó kábwâ** 'that.N dog' is the comitative object.

(5.37) Ùyó   mú-ndù ‖ à-ná-tááh-<u>án</u>-à
     that.N+1 1-person 1-SQ-return.home-COM-Fa

     yàkó   **ká-bwá** | í=   mw-à-g-è.
     that.N+12 12-dog 23= home-A.M-1-PR

'That person ‖ went home with that dog | to his place.' (11 040)

The example in (5.38) also has a non-incorporated object; the subject of the verb here is **ngóónà** 'crocodile' and the unexpressed referent of the substantive adjective **bígùmà** 'some' and the demonstrative **í=bìndì** 'others' is **bítúmbwê** 'fruit'.

(5.38) Y-ànáà-ly-à bí-gùmà ‖ y-ànà-tááh-<u>án</u>-á | í=bì-ndì.
     9-SQ-eat-Fa 8-some   9-SQ-go.home-COM-Fa   AU=8-other

'It ate some ‖ and went home with the |others (fruits).' (12 008)

See also -**bùng**-/-**bùng-an**- 'move/move with', -**génd**-/-**génd-an**- 'go/go with', -**kùlikir**-/-**kùlikir-an**- 'follow/follow with'.

The conjunction **na** 'and/with' is never used following a verb with a productive comitative extension. Note its absence in (5.34)–(5.38) above.

5.5.4.2.3 Mutual (reciprocal plus passive)

As stated above, when used with an intransitive verb the reciprocal has the meaning of accompaniment, rather than reciprocity. However, if two animate beings are considered to be actively accompanying 'each other' in an intransitive action such as coming, going, living, sitting, staying, etc., the passive is added following the reciprocal. Thus each subject is considered (at least grammatically) to be *accompanied by* the other. This use of the reciprocal plus passive we call "mutual", since the term reciprocal usually implies a transitive verb.

In (5.39) the mutual extension -**anw** is exemplified in the verb **twàyíjānwà** 'we came together (with each other)'

(5.39) Y-é=   tw-à-yíj-ānw-à.
       1-FOC= 1PL-P1-come-MUT-Fa

'He is the one I came with (lit. He is the one we came together with each other).'

Other examples are -**génd-anw**- (-go-MUT-) 'go together' from -**génd**- 'go', cf. -**génd-an**- (-go-COM-) 'go with something' or 'take someone and go'; **tu-shùb-anw-a** (1PL-been-MUT-Fa) 'we have been together', from -**shùb**- 'come from being somewhere'; -**laal-anw**- (-sleep-MUT-) 'sleep together'; -**beer-anw**- (-stay-MUT-) 'stay together'; -**bwatal-anw**- (-sit-MUT-) 'sit together', etc.

This construction can even be used with the copula -**li**, in the resultative form, as -**líínwì** 'be together'. In (5.40) the verb **mùlíínwì** means 'you (PL) are together'.

(5.40) W-êhê ‖ ná=   yà-b-ò   mù-lí-ínw-ì   ‖ mù-Ø-gálúk-è.
       2SG-CTR.P CNJ= those.N-2   2PL-are-MUT+RS-Fi   2PL-SBV-return-Fe

'YOU ‖ and those you (PL) are together with ‖ should return.' (Jdg 9:32)

Another example of the mutual in context is given in (5.41) the verb -**tuul-anw**- (-live-MUT-) 'live together', from -**tuul**- 'be habitually'. In (5.41) the verb **kàgéndì túúlánwâ** means '(that) it go and live together'.

(5.41) Há= n-yúmà   ká-ná-bòn-à   kwó= kà-géndì   túúl-ánw-á
       16= 9-after   12-SQ-see-Fa CMP= 12-GOING   live-MUT-Fa

       kúgùmá   n-é   shúúlí   y-é=   n-gáàvù.
       together   CNJ-AU=   9+bull   9-A.M+AU= 9-cow

'Afterwards it (dog) saw that it should go live together with the bull of a cow.' (45 004)

In addition to its use with verbs of staying and going, the mutual can be used with intransitive action verbs such as -**hìng**- 'farm', as in (5.42).

(5.42) Yà-bó=   bá-shósì | bá-tá-àlì   kìzì   hìng-ánw-à.
       those.N-2   2-men   2-NEG-P3   REP   farm-MUT-Fa

'Those men | weren't habitually farming with each other.' (523 046)

5.5 Productive extensions

In general, the applicative is not used in conjunction with the mutual extension, but in (5.43) the verb -**génd-er-anw**- means 'going together (time after time)'. This seems to be an incidence in which the use of the applicative and reciprocal in an intransitive verb carries an extensive meaning (5.5.4.2.4). As such, the use of the applicative plus mutual in the following example reinforces the habitual meaning carried by the auxiliary **kìzì** 'repeatedly'.

(5.43) **Bá-àlì kìzì génd-<u>ér-ánw</u>-á || bà-ná-kìzì láál-á |**
      2-P3   REP   go-APL-MUT-Fa   2-SQ-REP   slept-Fa

      ny-ûmbá n-gùmà.
      9-house   9-one

'They habitually went about together || and they habitually slept (in) | one house.' (01 003)

The fact that the use of the applicative with the mutual in an intransitive verb carries the same semantic meaning as the use of the applicative with the basic reciprocal in such a verb is a strong indication that the mutual (reciprocal plus passive) is not seen as being semantically separate from the use of the reciprocal without the passive. The mutual is merely the grammatical form of the reciprocal which is used with intransitive actions performed purposely in a mutual fashion rather than merely comitatively.

The reciprocal and the passive also occur together in the verb -**bùt-anw**- (-bear-MUT-) 'be born of the same mother'. In this case, however, it seems that the passive is prior, since the verb is otherwise ditransitive (a woman bears a man a child, (5.44)), or transitive (a man or woman produces offspring). However, the passive form of the verb, i.e. being born, is of course intransitive. Thus it seems that this is a case in which the passive was semantically and derivationally prior to the comitativity.

5.5.4.2.4 Reciprocal: Other uses

Combined with the applicative, the reciprocal with an intransitive verb can mean extensive or successive action, -**lèng-er-an**- (-pass-APL-RCP-) 'pass one after the other'. In (5.44) the verb **zíkálèngéránà** 'they had (successively) passed each other' shows that the days were many.

(5.44) Ìrí   sìkù   zí-ká-lèng-ér-án-à ‖   à-ná-mú-bùt-à
      when 10+day 10-P2-pass-APL-RCP-Fa 1-SQ-O1-bear-Fa

   kwó= mw-àná | w-ó=   bú-nyérè.
   17=   1-child   1-A.M+AU= 14-girl

'When the days had passed (one after the other) ‖ she bore him from there a child | of girl.' (615 005)

In the verb -**kùlikir-an**- (-follow-RCP-) 'follow, one after the other', even though the applicative is frozen in this case, the reciprocal has a very similar meaning. This verb is also used idiomatically in the infinitive form **úkúkùlíkíráná ná...** to mean 'according to...'

There are also multiple verbs in our database which contain a lexicalized -**an** which no longer directly carries reciprocal or comitative meaning, e.g. -**tuuban**- 'sweat', -**hòngobedekan**- 'be thin', -**jùgumban**- 'be about to fall', etc.

5.5.5 Reversive (transitive)

5.5.5.1 Reversive (transitive) structural considerations

The reversive transitive (also called separative transitive) extension is -(**o**)**ol**/-(**u**)**ul**, depending on vowel height harmony. Verbs having this extension are usually transitive and have a reversive or separative meaning, e.g. -**shòn**- 'climb up'/**shòn-ool**- (-go.down-RV.T-) 'let something down'. Often the "separateness" of the reversive transitive has been lost in lexicalized items containing this extension, e.g. -**hímb**- 'be exhausted' / -**hímbul**- 'hit repeatedly with a stick'. Perhaps the original meaning of -**hímbul**- was to hit for the purpose of "separating" someone from the expression of a state of exhaustion, but synchronically, it just means repeated beating of someone with a stick.

This extension often commutes with a non-extended verb, as in the example just given, or with a verb having reversive intransitive, as well as with verbs having an extension other than reversive intransitive, especially the impositive, meaning 'put something in some position'. Thus we find pairs/sets[20] like those given in (5.45).

---

[20]The lack of a form in a given spot in the grid does not necessarily mean that such a verb does not exist, but only that it was not found in our wordlist or texts. We did not try to elicit forms for this purpose.

5.5 Productive extensions

(5.45) Commutations of the reversive transitive

Non-RV	Gloss	RV TRANS	Gloss	RV INTRANS	Gloss
-shíngir-	'set price'	**-shínguul-**	'bargain s/o down'	**-shínguuk-**	'agree to lower price'
-shíng-	'set in ground'	**-shínguul-**	'pull out of ground'	-----	
-gúl-	'buy'	**-gúluul-**	'buy back'	-----	
-hán-	'punish'	**-hánuul-**	'give advice'	-----	
-báy-	'give off odor'	**-báyuul-**	'get rid of odor'	-----	
-shòn-	'climb up'	**-shònool-**	'let down from above'	**-shònook-**	'climb down'
-shálík-	'be hungry'	**-sháluul-**	'give a bit of food'	**-sháluuk-**	'assuage hunger'
-túmbik-	'cover'	**-túmbuul-**	'remove cover'	-----	
-laalik-	'invite'	**-laluul-**	'remind s/o to come'	-----	
-yòmek-	'put knife in'	**-yòmol-**	'pull knife out'	-----	
-shógek-	'insert sthg'	**-shógol-**	'to pull sthg out'	-----	
		-gálul-	'to return sthg'	**-gáluk-**	'return (INTRANS)'

There are also many cases where the reversive transitive form appears to be the only form of a verb in synchronic use, so that there is no commutation with an unextended form or a form which makes use of an alternative extension. This extension is sometimes found in reduplicated form, signaling intensity of the action (see 5.5.5.3).

We note that the **l** of the reversive transitive may instead be found as **r** in words (presumably) of Kinyarwanda origin. These are often lexicalized, though the reversive/separative meaning is usually still present, e.g. -**hòkooror**- 'hollow out something', -**kórootor**- 'noisily clear throat of phlegm', -**yóbor**- 'separate certain animals from the herd', -**hábur**- 'mislead someone purposely by giving wrong directions' (from -**háb**- 'get scared off path and get lost', cf. the same root with the -**ul** extension, -**hábul**- 'chase away by startling or scaring').

5.5.5.2 Reversive (transitive) function

As noted by Schadeberg (2003:77) regarding its use in Bantu languages in general, the extension is generally called reversive. Schadeberg, though, has called it separative, a label which seems to better reflect the semantics of this extension. It has a meaning of separating something from something else or from some position. In the following example involving the pair -**hán**- 'punish' / -**hán-uul**- (-punish-RV.T-) 'counsel, advise', the reversive seems to carry the meaning of keeping (or getting) someone out of (separate from) trouble and punishment.

Example (5.46) shows the verb -**hán-uul**- 'counsel' (cf. its causative form -**hán-uuz**- 'ask for advice').

(5.46) **Mú=kúbá | ú-w-àngà-bùl-á | á-bá-gá-mú-hánùùl-à ||**
Because   S.R-1-POT-lack-Fa   S.R-2-F2-O1-counsel-Fa

y-é= gá-ná-bùl-á | á=bá-gá-mú-zììk-à.
1-FOC=   F2-ADD.V-lack-Fa   S.R-2-F2-O1-bury-Fa

'Because the one who would lack |those who will counsel him || is the same one who will also lack | those who will bury him.' (51 031)

Depending on the meaning of the basic verb, the reversive transitive extension -**(u)ul/-(o)ol** in Kifuliiru sometimes can be interpreted as indicating the *reversal* of the basic action. In (5.47) we see both the unextended verb -**yáj**- 'spread something out' and its reversive transitive form -**yájuul**- 'gather back together something spread out'. However, it could also be seen as removing (separating) the spread out item from its spread out position.

(5.47) **Ngíísì mú-gùmà || à-ná-kìzì géndì yàj-úúl-á |**
each   1-one   1-SQ-REP   GOING   spread-RV.T-Fa

h-â= yàj-à.
16-O.R+1=   spread-Fa

'And each one || went to unspread (the bedding) | where he had spread (it).' (515 021)

Verbs which include the reversive transitive extension are, as the name indicates, transitive. However, in looking at cases in which there is an unextended verb, or a verb containing the same radical with a different extension

5.5 Productive extensions

(often the impositive), these also are generally transitive (-**shwek**- 'tie something'/-**shwekuul**- 'untie something'; -**bìsh**- 'hide something'/-**bìshuul**- 'unhide something'; -**túmbik**- 'cover something'/-**túmbuul**- 'uncover something'; -**ziik**- 'bury'/-**zuul**- 'unbury, dig up' (cf. -**zuuk**- 'resurrect, return from the dead'); -**shíng**- 'set up a pole in the ground'/-**shínguul**- 'take the pole out of the ground'. The following pair shows a slight meaning shift of the reversive: -**laalik**- 'invite someone'/-**laluul**- 're-invite (remind someone of invitation when all is ready'). And in the following pair, the impositive -**yòmek**- 'insert (knife into something)', and the reversive transitive form -**yòmol**- 'pull (knife) out', the impositive form is ditransitive (see Ditransitive impositives, under 5.6.4.2.2), while the reversive transitive form is only singly transitive. So it certainly cannot be properly said that the reversive transitive always increases the valence of a verb, though in most cases it does not decrease it either. There is one clear case where the valence of an extended verb is increased by the addition of this extension, e.g. -**shòn**- 'climb up' > -**shònool**- 'let something down' (cf. -**shònook**- 'climb down'). Altering valence is obviously not the main purpose or function of this extension.

5.5.5.3 Reduplication of reversive transitive

The reduplication of this extension is used in some cases to signal intensity of the reversive action. Thus, -**gólól**- is 'straighten out', while -**góloolol**- is 'really straighten out'; -**shéb**- is 'sift', while -**shébuulul**- is 'sift out every little lump and impurity'; -**shùk**- is 'wash', while -**shùkuulul**- is 'over-dilute a beverage'. In the case where one of these intensified forms commutes with reversive intransitive, only the final occurrence of the extension is changed from **l** to **k**: -**shùkuuluk**- 'beverage to be over-diluted'.

5.5.6 Reversive (intransitive)

5.5.6.1 Reversive (intransitive) structural considerations

The reversive intransitive extension, also called separative intransitive, is -**(o)ok**/-**(u)uk**, subject to vowel height harmony. There are many commutations with zero (i.e. an unextended verb), such as -**shòn**-/-**shònook**- 'climb up/climb down', and, -**bùng**-/-**bùnguuk**- 'move house/return from where one moved to', -**dúb**-/-**dúbuuk**- 'go out on the lake fishing/return from fishing'. There are also many commutations with reversive transitive, e.g. -**shínguul**-/-**shínguuk**- 'bargain someone down/agree to sell at a lower price'; -**shònool**-/-**shònook**- 'let something down/climb down', etc.

5.5.6.2 Reversive (intransitive) function

The reversive (separative) intransitive extension, -(**u**)**uk**/-(**o**)**ok**, is called intransitive because it reduces the transitivity of a verb to which it is added. Like its transitive equivalent above, it signifies separation, which can sometimes be interpreted as the reversal of the action expressed by the same radical without the extension. The affixation of this extension reduces the valency of a verb, and seems to cause some verbs to have a meaning very reminiscent of the neuter (5.6.3). Just as with the neuter, the valence of a verb characterized by the reversive intransitive is only one, the agent/subject, while with the reversive transitive generally gives a valence of two: patient/object and agent/subject.

5.5.6.2.1 Reversive intransitive as reversive or separative action

Examples (5.48) and (5.49) show the results of suffixation of the reversive intransitive to a transitive verb base, e.g. -**dúb**-/-**dúbuuk**- 'fish/return from fishing'. (5.48) first illustrates the use of the basic verb, -**dúb**- 'fish'.

(5.48) Ìrí   á-ká-b-á   á-kòlà   mú=   <u>dúb</u>-à ||
when   1-P2-be-Fa   1-is.NEWLY   PROG=   fish-Fa

à-ná-**dúb**-à   í=mòtò.
1-SQ-fish-Fa   AU=9+small.scaleless.fish

'When he was now fishing || he caught (lit. fished) a small fish.' (624 004)

In (5.49) we see the use of -**dúb**-**uuk**- 'return from fishing'.

(5.49) **Mú-shìjá**   w-à-wè || mángò   à-<u>dúb-ùùk</u>-à |
1-brother.of.female   1-A.M-2SG   when   1-fish-RV.I-Fa

á-gá-yîjì   kú-shít-à.
1-F2-COMING   O2.SG-impale-Fa

'Your brother || when he comes back from fishing | he'll come and impale you.' (624 029)

The verb pair -**shòn**-/-**shònook**- 'climb up, climb down' is another example where the reversive intransitive indicates a reversal of the action of the verb. Both of these, of course, are also interpretable as a process of separating oneself from the position reached in the action of the basic verb.

5.5.6.3 Reversive intransitive as neuter

The reversive intransitive can be used in exactly the same way as the neuter, in reducing the valence of the verb to one, with that one being an unspecified subject, e.g. -**shób-ok-** 'be possible' (cf. its usual usage **bìtàngà<u>shóbòkà</u> kwó...** 'it (cl. 8, unspecified) would not be possible that...') from -**shób-ol-** 'be able'. When this "neuter" usage is combined with a verb which is transitive in the unextended form, the reversive intransitive seems to have almost a passive effect, as -**kànguka** 'be startled', seen in (5.51).

The next pair of examples illustrates the basic and reversive forms of the verb -**kàng-** 'startle'. In (5.50) we see the basic form.

(5.50) Ù-lyá   mú-gómà || ú-ká-tù-<u>káng</u>-à || n-à-mú-yìt-à.
     1-that.R 1-enemy S.R+1-P2-O1.PL-startle-Fa 1SG-P1-O1-kill-Fa

'That enemy || who startled us || I killed him.' (602 038)

In (5.51) the same radical, but used with the reversive intransitive, -**kàng-uk-** means 'be startled', which is like the passive of 'startle'.

(5.51) Yîbà || ìrí   á-ká-mú-bōn-à || à-ná-<u>kàng-úk</u>-à.
     her.husband when 1-P2-O1-see-Fa 1-SQ-startle-RV.I-Fa

'Her husband || when he saw her || he was startled.' (208 038)

See also -**síngool-**/-**síngook-** 'burn something up/be burned up' for another illustration of the passive/neuter-type reversive intransitive.

5.5.6.3.1 Reversive intransitive expressing outward expansion

The reversive intransitive extension, seemingly only with intransitive verbs describing a state, can also indicate that the action represented in the radical is being increased to an expanded state (being spread or 'separated' outward from a central starting point). For example, -**hám-** 'get big', -**hám-uuk-** 'get very big, fat', -**lúg-** 'be many', -**lúg-uuk-** 'be very many'.

Example (5.52) illustrates the unextended verb -**lúg-** 'be many'.

(5.52) Í-sìkù | írí   zí-ká-<u>lúg-à</u> || mw-ànà w-à=   n-gáàvù ||
      10-day   when 10-P2-be.many-Fa   1-child 1-A.M=   9-cow

à-ná-fw-á   n-í=   shálì.
1-SQ-die-Fa CNJ-5= hunger

'The days | when they had been many || the child of the cow || died of hunger.' (105 035)

Example (5.53) illustrates the use of the reversive intransitive with this same radical -**lúg-uuk**- 'be very many'. Perhaps the separative meaning of the extension indicates that this is somehow perceived as expanding outward, with a very large amount being produced out of a small amount.

(5.53) Á=b-à   mw-í=   kòndò ly-à-wè || bá-gá-<u>lúg-ùùk-à</u>
      AU=2-A.M 18-5=   navel 5-A.M-2SG 2-F2-be.many-RV.I-Fa

mú= kí-húgó | ngá= lú-vù.
18= 7-world   like 11-soil

'The ones in your lineage || will be very many in the world | like soil.' (Gen 28:14)

In some cases this ending seems to be almost more like an impositive with an implied source, though a semantically separative idea is expressed in the glosses by '...out, ...up, ... away', etc. For example, -**hímb**- 'be exhausted', -**hímbuk**- 'get very tired *out* from working hard'; -**síngook**- 'be burned *up*'; -**kóngook**- 'be burned *up*'; -**tónyook**- 'leak *out* slowly (or tiptoe *away*)' (from -**tóny**- 'drip, rain gently'); -**dódook**- 'return home slowly, tired or discouraged'.

5.5.7 Intensive

5.5.7.1 *Intensive structural considerations*

There is one extension which is used exclusively to indicate intensive action: -**eerez** or -**iiriz**, subject to vowel harmony. Examples of this are -**shéker-**/-**shékeerez**- 'laugh at/really make fun of'; -**tínd-**/-**tíndiriz**- 'be late/be very late'; -**háviiriz**- ~ -**hábiiriz**- 'chase someone or something far away' (from -**háv-y**- 'chase someone or something away', which is CS of -**háb**- 'be scared off path and get lost').

This extension formally consists of the reduplicated applicative extension, with a lengthened vowel, followed by the causative **-i**, which causes spirantization of the final **r** of the applicative to become **z**. Both from the phonological shape of this extension and from the fact that it includes a right-linking H tone it can be assumed that this extension historically includes a causative extension.

It also appears that this extension not only undergoes vowel height harmony, appearing as **-(i)iriz** following a high vowel or **a**, and generally as **-(e)erez** following a mid vowel, but in certain cases the vowel may also be subject to rounding harmony, either with the vowel of the root, e.g. **-kòmb-** 'wipe last bits of food from bowl' /**-kòmboroz-** 'clean out bowl very thoroughly'; or harmony with the final vowel of a noun from which the verb seems to be derived, e.g. **-nàng-** 'hit target'/**-nànguruz-** 'hit the target spot on' (cf. **nângù** 'target', a word also used adverbially to describe speech, in which case it means 'clearly, explicitly'). That these extensions with the rounded vowels are *not* morphologically causative forms of the reduplicated reversive **-olol/-ulul** is suggested by the fact that there is no attested extension *-**oloz**[21] or *-**uluz**, but only **-oroz/-uruz**. The only source for this combination would be the intensive with rounding/height-harmonized vowels. The fact that these back-vowel variants include an underived **r** suggests Kinyarwanda influence.

5.5.7.2 *Intensive function*

The intensive extension **-iiriz/-eerez** indicates intensification, either by frequency of repetition or by increased vigor, of whatever action or state is conveyed by a verb. It does not affect the valence of the original verb. In (5.54) the intensive form **-yùv-iiriz-** 'listen closely' derives from **-yùvw-** 'hear'.

(5.54) Mú= yùkwó kú-yùv-<u>ííríz</u>-â ‖ à-yùvw-á í-ì-zù |
18= that.N+15 15-hear-INTS-Fa 1+P1-hear-Fa AU=5-voice

ly-à= mú-lùmùlá w-à-gè.
5-A.M= 1-younger.sibling 1-A.M-1

'In that listening closely ‖ she heard the voice | of her younger sister.'
(203 025)

In (5.55) the intensive of **-lèg-** 'accuse' is used in the form **bágákúlègèèrèzâ** 'they are intentionally fiercely accusing you'.

---

[21]There is one noun **kà-njókólózâ** (12-great.grandchild), a word related to **shòkùlù** 'grandfather', and **(bá)shòkùlúzà** 'ancestor(s)', but there are no verbs with this ending.

(5.55) Sí= bà-gwétì bá-gá-kú-lèg-èèrèz-á | kú= yà-gà gó-óshì!
OBV= 2-PROG   2-INTL-O2.SG-accuse-INTS-Fa   17= this.P-6 6-all

'Don't you see that they are really accusing you | in all these matters!'
(Mrk 15:4)

In (5.56), the verb -**búl-iriz**- means 'question intensely'. This is formed from the same root as -**buuz**- 'ask'.

(5.56) Yìkyó ky-ànyà || bá-àlì kìzì mú-búl-íríz-á | bwénèènè.
that.N+7 7-time   2-P3   REP   O1-question-INTS-Fa   very.much

'(At) that time || they were repeatedly questioning him | very intensely.'
(603 051)

5.5.8 Emphatic

5.5.8.1 Emphatic structural considerations

Unlike the inflectional pre-final -**ak**-/-**ag**-/-**ang**- suffix found in many Bantu languages, the emphatic -**ag**- (EMP) in Kifuliiru is a true extension. It co-occurs with any verb forms. Its use is determined by discourse and semantics, and it is not a defining or obligatory morpheme with any tense. It is rarely found in verb forms which include the final suffix -**ir-i**, but this is probably a consequence of semantics, since this final suffix tends to be used with verb forms which present background information, which in general, is not emphatic material. (See, however, (5.65) in this chapter where it does co-occur with -**ir-i**.)

Though its function is not inflectional, the emphatic retains its original pre-final position in the verb, even occurring between the two formatives of the -**ir-i** final. The suffix -**ag** in Kifuliiru occurs as far to the right in the verb base as possible, e.g. **gúl-āg-à** 'buy EMP!', **gúl-ìr-ág-à** 'buy (for/from someone) EMP!' It is placed to the right of other extensions except that it must occur to the left of the causative and the passive, e.g. **gúl-ììs-àg-y-â** 'sell EMP!', **bùùz-àg-y-â** 'ask EMP!' Note that the short causative is repeated following the emphatic,[22] as the -**y** seen in **gúl-ììs-àg-y-â** 'sell EMP!' The emphatic is not generally found with true passive forms, but in **yùv-àg-w-â** 'listen EMP!' it is followed by a pseudo-passive -**w**.

---

[22] Or, as noted earlier perhaps the long causative morpheme -**iisi** is simply interrupted by the emphatic: -**iis-ag-i**.

5.5 Productive extensions

Though the emphatic is a true extension in Kifuliiru, it is exceptional among the extensions in two ways. Firstly, it alone among the suffixes must appear in reduplicated form when used with verbs whose stem consists of -CV- only, e.g. **àná-ly-ág-ág-à** 'and he ate EMP' (from **-ly-** 'eat'), cf. the lack of reduplication in a verb with a longer base, as in **àná-gálùk-àg-à** 'and he returned EMP'. Thus with the verb **-fw-** 'die', it becomes **ùyíjì fwágágà** '(that you) come and die EMP'. Similar examples are **ànábáágágà** 'and he became EMP', from **-ba-** 'be'; **nió=gályàgàgà** (from **nie=úgályàgàgà**) 'I'm the one whom you will eat EMP' from **-ly-** 'eat'.

Secondly, it is unique in that it can also be used, somewhat colloquially, with lexical items, some of which may be used alone as non-verbal copular clauses, but which are not standard verbs, e.g. **bí-k-àg-ì** 'what EMP? from **bí-kì**? 'What kind (of things) (are they)?' or **hálìk-àg-ò** 'but EMP' from **hálìkò** 'but'. (For further discussion and examples, see 5.5.8.2.)

In such non-verb words, the emphatic is "infixed" immediately preceding the final vowel of the word. Thus the last vowel of the word, though not a separate morpheme as is the verbal FV, is reinterpreted in these cases as a separable unit by analogy with verbal forms. See example (5.57), where the emphatic is infixed just before the last vowel of the demonstrative **kwókùnô** 'thus'.

(5.57) Nà   kwókùn-àgô   ‖ kéèrà   à-yíjí   yáng-w-â ‖
      and   like.this.P.C-EMP already   1-COMING   marry-PS-Fa

      nà=   yîshé | á-tà-mény-à.
      CNJ=   1a+her.father 1+when-NEG-know-Fa

'And thus ‖ she already came and got married ‖ and without her father | knowing.' (616 040)

Other forms that commonly include the **-ag** emphatic suffix include the question words **kútì** 'how' (**kútàgì**), **háyì** 'where' (**háyàgì**), **bíkì** 'what' (**bíkàgì**), **nyândì** 'who' (**nyándàgì**).

When it occurs like this with parts of speech other than verbs, sometimes the initial vowel of the extension is a copy of the final vowel of the word to which it is attached, rather than being **-a**.[23] The word in which this is most commonly done is **hálìkògò** (from **hálìkò** 'but'), but one also hears **kwókùnògò** 'thus EMP',[24] and **nyándìgì** from **nyândì** 'who EMP'?

---

[23]One could also interpret these endings as **-gV** suffixes in which the V is a copy of the final vowel of the base word.

[24]In these cases the emphatic may be reinterpreted as a final suffix with a vowel which

The emphatic is most often used in the imperative, e.g. **géndàgà** 'go EMP!' and the sequential **ànágálùkàgà** 'and he returned EMP', but it is also common with the P1 past, and found with the infinitive, unmarked past, default future, present progressive, timeless, past state (a past perfect form), and subjunctive. This list is limited only by what we find in our present text corpus, since theoretically any verb form may be found with this extension.

When used in a multiword verb with an adverbial auxiliary, **-ag** is always suffixed to the leftmost adverbial auxiliary, rather than to the final verb, which is semantically "main" but grammatically sidelined and uninflected. Example (5.58) illustrates such a case with a polite imperative.

(5.58) É mú-shósì ‖ ù-Ø-kíz-<u>ág</u>-ì   géndì   húún-á |
       O   1-man   2SG-SBV-REP-EMP-Fi   GOING   ask-Fa

       í=by-ókúlyá | í=   mw-ì-tù.
       AU=8-food   23=   place-A.M-1PL

'Hey man ‖ always go ask (EMP) for | food | at our place.' (111 006)

Other examples of the emphatic extension on adverbial auxiliaries are seen in (5.59).

(5.59) Pre-final emphatic extension on adverbial auxiliaries

AUX	Gloss	Form	Gloss
-shúbi	'again'	ù-shúb-<u>ág</u>-ì yíjì n-yáng-à	'(that) you again EMP come and marry me'
-shúbi	'again'	tw-àná-shúb-<u>àg</u>-í tèrám-à	'and we went up again EMP'
-kòli	'newly'	bàkòl-<u>àg</u>-í gwètì bá-gá-hík-à	'they are now EMP arriving (intent.)'
-kìzi	'repeatedly'	á=bàkìz-<u>ág</u>-ì yíj-à	'the ones who always EMP come'
-kìzi	'repeatedly'	á-gá-kìz-<u>àg</u>-í n-gómbék-à	'he will always EMP hand-feed me'

5.5.8.2 *Emphatic function*

The emphatic extension **-ag** calls special attention to the verb with which it is used. It is often used to express immediacy in an imperative or polite command. It also precedes important turning points in a narrative discourse. It

---

reflects the final vowel of the base word.

can be used with any type of verb, and does not affect the valence of the verb in any way.

The emphatic is typically used in the customary parting greetings, which are in polite-command form. The one staying behind says, **Ùgéndágè bwija** 'You go EMP well', while the other replies, **Ùsígálágè bwija** 'You stay behind EMP well'. (The order of the statements is reversed if the one leaving initiates the repartee, but the statements themselves remain the same.)

The emphatic extension is also used to express the fact that an imperative should be carried out immediately. Often the first time a command is given, it is given without the emphatic, e.g. **Lèètá í=fwárángà!** 'Bring some money!' but if it is necessary for the person giving the command to repeat himself, it is nearly always done with the emphatic -**ag**, e.g. **Lèètágà!** 'Bring (it) EMP!'

As already noted, this is the only extension which can be used with words which are not overtly verbal. These words (both in emphatic and non emphatic form) are used in "verbless clauses" and have a copular function, though they have no other verbal qualities. For example, they cannot be negated, cannot express tense or aspect, etc. Both the non-emphatic and emphatic forms of **kútì** 'how'/**kútàgì** 'how EMP' are often used as informal greetings, especially by younger speakers.

In (5.60) we see the use of the emphatic with **háyì** 'where?' The speaker is frustrated, and so asks, "Where is (it that) he (is)?" using the emphatic form **háyàgì** 'where EMP'.

(5.60) **Háy-àgì   à-lì?**
       where-EMP   1-is

   'Where (EMP) is he?' (406 020)

In (5.61) it is infixed just before the last vowel of **hálìkò** 'but'.

(5.61) **Hálìk-àgò ǁ í=bí-rûndà   by-é   bw-àmì | by-áàlì kìzì**
       But-EMP   AU=8-corpses   8-A.M+23   14-kingdom 8-P3   REP

   bíík-w-á | mú ny-ûmbà | í-y-áàlì kìzì dèt-w-á | «Yóhò».
   place-PS-Fa   18   9-house   S.R-9-P3 REP   speak-PS-Fa   Yoho

   'But (EMP) ǁ the corpses of the kingship | were always placed | in the house | which was called | «Yoho».' (23 016)

In (5.62) -**ag** is suffixed (or infixed) to a question word, **kuti** 'how (is it)?'[25]

---

[25]**Kuti** 'how?' and the complementizer **kwo** 'that' both contain the cl. 15 concord prefix

(5.62) À-ná-yì-búúz-à: ‖ «Kút-àgì kwó= n-àmú= gír-à?»
  1-SQ-RFX-ask-Fa how-EMP CMP= 1SG-F1= do-Fa

'And she asked herself: ‖ «What (EMP) will I do now?»' (35 028)

This extension also has several uses within narrative discourse. It is used within quotes when the speaker wants to emphatically state a command, as shown in (5.63), where the quail tells the snake **tùlùùkágà** 'get down now EMP'. (The non-extended form of this verb is -**tuluuk**- 'get down'.)

(5.63) Y-àná-bwîr-à yùgwó mú-jòkà: ‖ «Ø-Tùlùùk-ág-à.»
  9-SQ-tell-Fa that.N+3 3-snake IMP.S-get.down-EMP-Fa

'And it told that snake: ‖ «Get down now (EMP).»' (13 008)

In material which does not represent repartee, the emphatic is used to build emphasis before a major turning point in the story. In (5.64) a woman went home with some rats, whose presence in her house introduces a turning point of the story.

(5.64) À-ná-tááh-án-ág-à ‖ yì-zó m-bébà.
  1-SQ-go.home-COM-EMP-Fa those.N-10 10-rats

'And she went home (EMP) with ‖ those rats.' (35 039)

The emphatic seldom co-occurs with a resultative form of the verb, because normally the important elements of discourse are presented as events rather than as the background material generally found in resultatives. One of the few cases of resultative with emphatic found in our texts is the following, a statement of presentational focus which introduces the antagonist in a narrative text.

(5.65) **Kízìgà há= bútàmbì ly-à-bò ‖ há-àlì**
  Surprise 16= beside 5-A.M-2 16-P3

  nà-tùùz-ìr-ág-ì | ú=mú-gèngè.
  ADD.V-live-RS-EMP-Fi AU=3-thorn

'Surprise there beside ‖ them also lived (EMP) | Thorn.' (523 053)

---

ku-. Thus they refer to verbal concepts, though usually having no explicit antecedent or referent.

For more details on the use of the emphatic extension as a precursor of important changes in the text, see Volume 2, 12.3.3.

5.6 Non-productive extensions and expansions

In Kifuliiru there are five generally non-productive extensions. Inchoative, though not an extension per se, is included in the list below and briefly mentioned in the text.

Table 5.7. Non-productive extensions

	Extension	PB	FLR	FLR stem[a]	Gloss	FLR w/ext.	Gloss
a.	Contactive	-at	-at	-fùmb-	'close together'	-fùmb-at-	'grasp with hand'
b.	Extensive	-al	-al	-gìshi	'rust'	-gìshi-m-al-	'rust'
c.	Neuter	-ik/-ek	-ik/-ek	-bòn-	'see'	-bòn-ek-	'be seen'
d.	Impositive	-ik/-ek	-ik/-ek	-fùmbat-	'grasp in hand'	-fùmbad-ik-	'hand sthg to s/o'
e.	Positional	-am	-am	-bìsh-	'hide sthg.'	-bìsh-am-	'be hidden'
f.	Inchoative	-p	-h	-lèma	'crippled'	-lèma-h-	'become crippled'

[a]Some of these in unextended form are full verb bases, with the addition only of a final vowel and prefix, cf. **kú-fùmbà** 'to close together'. Others such as **-gìshi** are instead noun stems, cf. **ngìshì** 'rust', **-lèmà** 'handicapped person'.

In addition to those suffixes listed in table 5.7, there are some lexicalized groups of segments which in Bantu are sometimes called "expansions." Expansions generally cannot be given a specific semantic label, nor do they usually commute with a verb of the same root which lacks the expansion. Still, they are recognizable segmental "units" within verb bases in Bantu. Several are mentioned in the list of extensions and expansions found in (5.3). Other suffixes (expansions) are also found in (5.22) "Various extension combinations".

5.6.1 Contactive

5.6.1.1 *Contactive structural considerations*

The contactive (CNT) (also called tentive) extension, -**at** is "not known to be productive in any language" (Schadeberg 2003a:77). Briefly, it adds to a verb radical a component of meaning denoting contact of two things or contact of various parts of one thing. Examples of verbs with this extension include -**bàlagat**- '(plant) begin to wither', -**fùmbat**- 'take hold of, grasp in hand', -**hà- gat**- 'hang on shoulder', -**líbat**- 'step on repeatedly, strike brutally', -**shàmat**- 'gather up, scoop up', -**vúbat**- 'pack inside cheek'.

Other verbs in Kifuliiru give the impression that this extension was also subject to vowel harmony, since in (5.66) we find several verbs in which it seems to appear with vowels other than -**a**.

(5.66) CNT   Examples

-**et**   -**tènget-er**- 'hold in arms'; -**béget**- 'hold in arms'; -**kéget**- 'munch, chew sthg crunchy'

-**it**   -**tíbit**- 'run'; -**tùmit**- 'throw spear at, or (animal) strike with horns'

-**ut**   -**nyúnyugut**- 'kiss'; -**kùgút**- 'chew a hard food'; -**lúgut**- 'throw'

-**ot**   -**hòdot**- 'trample'; -**shòlogot**- 'be nauseated'

It is also interesting to note that historically -**at** was sometimes was combined with -**ik** 'impositive', in which case it was changed (presumably by Dahl's law)[26] into -**ad-ik**, e.g. -**fùmbadik**- 'hand something to someone' (cf. -**fùmbat**- 'grasp in the hand'); -**hàgadík**- 'dress someone in poorly fitting clothes, drape something over someone' (cf. -**hàgat**- 'hang something over the shoulder'), -**límbadik**- 'throw something down', -**gálabadik**- 'lay something down', cf. **búgálàmà** 'on the back (adverb)', etc.

5.6.1.2 *Contactive function*

The contactive extension -**at** is found only in a small set of verbs. However, the notion of physical contact is often still observable in verbs with this extension, e.g., -**bábaat**- 'feel around without being able to see', -**fùmbat**- 'take hold of something', -**gwat**- 'take hold of something', -**hàgat**- 'hang something

---

[26] Dahl's law is a phonological dissimilation rule found in various Bantu languages, by which a voiceless stop becomes voiced if the consonant in the following syllable is also voiceless (Hyman 2003b:56).

on shoulder', -**kàngaat**- 'grab many things', -**líbat**- 'trample', -**shàmat**- 'scoop something up', -**vúbat**- 'put something in cheeks', -**yìshùmat**- 'be in depressed posture'.

Verbs with the contactive extension are for the most part transitive, and the few verbs for which there is a commutation with zero indicate that the extension does have the effect of increasing the logical semantic valence, and thus the potential grammatical valence of a verb, e.g. -**gwat**- 'take hold of something' > -**gw**- 'fall (INTRANS)'; -**fùmbat**- 'take hold of something in hand' (semantically involving two arguments: subject's hand, and thing grasped) > -**fùmb**- 'shut two body parts together as hands, eyes (eyelids coming together), mouth (lips coming together)', etc. (transitive, i.e. involves only the subject and the pair of objects closed together).

In (5.67) the verb -**bábaat**- 'grope around (as in the dark)' includes the contactive extension.

(5.67) Ù-lyá   mú-shósí   à-ná-vyûk-à | à-ná-bábààt-a   h-á=
       that.R-1 1-man   1-SQ-get.up-Fa 1-SQ-grope.around-Fa 16.OR-1=

àli bìis-ír-i kì-ryá kí-nyáátì.
P3 put-RS-Fi 7-that.R 7-trap

'And that man got up and groped around where he had put that (rat) trap.' (632 083)

5.6.2 Extensive

5.6.2.1 *Extensive structural considerations*

The extensive extension -**al**- is attested in most Bantu languages and often indicates an action spread over time or space. Though this extension sometimes commutes with other extensions, it is not one which may be generally added to a verb in order to modify the meaning. It occurs only with a limited number of verbs.

The verbs of which the following are the Kifuliiru reflexes are reconstructed in Proto-Bantu with the extensive extension (Schadeberg 2003a:77): -**bw-at-al**- 'sit' (cf. **lú-vû** 'earth, soil'),[27] -**yámb-al**- 'get dressed' (cf. -**yámb-ik**- 'put

---

[27] The **bu** found in various words for "sit" across Bantu, as in the Kifuliiru -**bw-at-al-a**, is thought to have its origins in the word for soil, -**bú** in PB (in Kifuliiru -**vù**) with -**at** '-contactive' indicating contact with the soil, and -**al** 'extensive' indicating the spreading of the person over the earth, or being in contact with the earth over a period of time.

clothes on someone else'), -**lw-al**- 'be sick' (cf. -**lw** 'fight'), -**sìg-al**- 'remain' (cf. -**sìg**- 'leave something or someone').

This extension may be reduplicated to -**alal**, as in -**bàngalal**- 'stand firm without moving, or be stubborn'; -**hàngalal**- 'get dry and hard, or be exhausted', -**jíngalal**- 'be dazed, stunned, stupefied'.

It may also appear as -**aal** e.g. -**shàmbaal**- 'be joyful, rejoice', -**tábaal**- 'help', -**hímaal**- 'be hoarse', -**gónyaal**- 'be bent over'; -**gángaal**- 'be unrestrainable', etc.

5.6.2.2 *Extensive function*

Though this extension sometimes commutes with other extensions, it is found only in a relatively small set of verbs. In cases where the extensive commutes with another extension or with zero, we find that most of these verbs are intransitive before the addition of the extensive. When used with a verb which is already intransitive, the extensive does not alter the valence of the verb, e.g. -**shùmbah**- 'remain a bachelor' < -**shúmbah-al**- 'remain a bachelor for an unusually long time' (cf. **mú-shúmbà** '1-unwed person').

There are a few cases in which this extension does reduce valence, removing the possibility of an object, from a verb which without the extension was transitive, e.g. -**gónyaal**- '(thing or plant) be bent up, wrinkled, withered' (intransitive) derived from -**góny**- 'fold, bend, wad something up', (cf. -**gókonyal**- '(person or animal) be hunched up from cold)'; -**sìg-al**- 'remain', an intransitive verb, derived from the transitive verb -**sìg**- 'leave something/someone'.

Though in general these extensive verbs are intransitive, some can have an optional object. It is possible that this may reflect the lexicalized nature of this extension in these verbs. With -**yámb-al**- 'get dressed, wear', the object is often omitted, e.g. **ùgéndì yámbálà** 'go get dressed'. However, the garment being worn may also be indicated, either as an incorporated object or a separate noun, e.g. **bànákìzì gìyámbálà** 'they repeatedly wore them' (**gì-** cl. 4 object prefix, referring to **mí-ròndò** (4-clothes), or **bànákìzì yámbálá íbíráátò** 'they repeatedly wore shoes'.

With the verb **lw-al-a** 'be sick', the sickness can optionally be expressed as the object of the verb, e.g. **àlwázírí ú=lúhérè** 'he is sick (with) scabies' of the extensive extension. In many of these verbs, the extensive meaning still comes across very clearly, e.g. -**hùmbatal**- 'be getting progressively thinner' (cf. -**hùmbat**- 'be very thin'); -**dwakal**- 'be defiled'; -**fùtikal**- 'be broken'; -**gàngajal**- 'be very dry'.

5.6.3 Neuter

5.6.3.1 Neuter structural considerations

The neuter extension is -**ek** or -**ik**, subject to vowel height harmony. Schadeberg (2003a:75) notes that "the neuter is generally homophonous with the impositive extension" (see following section). The difference between the two in most languages is merely one of meaning.[28] The subject of an impositive verb is an agent who places something in some physical position. The neuter, by contrast, denotes the results of some action without directly implying an agent, and its subject is the patient of the verb.

5.6.3.2 Neuter function

The neuter extension -**ik**/-**ek** is used with the meaning of 'happening to something', with no agent specified or implied, or with an unspecified indirect agency implied. The object of the action is expressed as the subject of the verb. Thus this extension is one which reduces the valence of a transitive verb.

Schadeberg (2003a:75) states that a more precise label would be "neutropassive" and notes that "verbs with this extension indicate that the subject is potentially or factually affected by the action expressed by the verb." He notes that whether the affect is factual or potential may be linked to the aspectual quality of the given verb form or inferred from the context.

He also states that in general in Bantu languages "(this) extension is best represented with two semantic classes of verbs: a) verbs of destruction 'be breakable/be broken' (INTRANS) 'be broken' < 'break' (TRANS), 'be splittable/be split' (INTRANS) < 'split' (TRANS), and b) experiencer verbs ('be visible' < 'see', 'be audible' < 'hear')."

In Kifuliiru we observe numerous instances of the use of the neuter extension, mostly with verbs of destruction or loss, with a few exceptions, e.g. -**bèr-ek**- 'break/be split apart' < -**bèr**- 'split/break (TRANS)'; -**yòn-ek**- 'be spilled, poured out', < -**yòn**- 'spill, pour out something'; -**tùl-ik**- 'have a hole' < -**tùl**- 'make a small hole in something'; -**teer-ek**- 'be lost' < -**teer**- 'lose something'; -**bùl-ik**- 'be lacking' < -**bùl**- 'lack something'; -**kòl-ek**- 'be done' < -**kòl**- 'do'; -**shál-ik**- 'be hungry' (cf. **ísháli** 'hunger'); -**bòn-ek**- 'appear, seem' < -**bòn**- 'something', etc.

Since this extension is valence-reducing, a verb which in the unextended form takes both a subject and a direct object, when used with the neuter

---

[28]Though there are some few languages of the Southeast where there are associated morphological or tonal differences between the two (Schadeberg, 2003a:74).

extension, takes only a subject. This subject is not the agent (since the agent is neither stated nor implied), but rather the patient of the neuter verb.

Example (5.68) illustrates the use of the neuter extension, by which the experiencer of the action, the thing which is broken, **lìryá ígì** 'that.R egg' is expressed as the subject of the verb, rather than the object. The agent is unspecified, and irrelevant to the discussion.

(5.68) **Mú=** yùkw-ò kú-gw-â ‖ lì-ryá í-gì | ly-àná-**bèr**-ék-à.
   18= that.N+15 15-fall-Fa 5-that.R 5-egg 5-SQ-break-NEU-Fa

'And in that falling ‖ that egg | broke.' (204 012)

The example in (5.68) is in contrast to the transitive equivalent -**bèr**- 'break'. In (5.69) -**bèr**- 'break' takes both a subject, **nyáàlí yàgè** 'her sister-in-law', who breaks a gourd, and an object, **ú=rúsóòzò lúgùmà** 'a certain gourd', which is broken.

(5.69) Ùyó   mú-nyéré à-ná-dèt-à ‖ kwó= nyáàlí   y-à-gè ‖
   that.N+1 1-girl   1-SQ-say-Fa   CMP= sister.in.law 1-A.M-1

à-**bèr**-à   ú=rú-sóòzò lú-gùmà | mú= ny-ûmbà.
1+P1-break-Fa AU=11-gourd 11-one   18= 9-house

'That girl said ‖ that her sister-in-law ‖ broke a certain gourd | in the house.' (624 027)

The verb form **àtágákìbònèkà** 'he will no longer be seen/appear' (cf. -**bòn**-) in (5.70) gives an example of the neuter used with an experiencer verb.

(5.70) Ùyó   mú-shósì | ìrí   bw-áàli kìzí yīr-à   ‖
   that.N+1 1-man   when 14-P3   REP   get.dark-Fa

à-tá-gá-kì-**bòn**-èk-à   há= m-būgà.
1-NEG-F2-PERS-see-NEU-Fa 16= 9-outside

'That man | whenever it was getting dark ‖ he would no longer be seen (appear) outside.' (109 004)

5.6.3.2.1 Neuter plus reciprocal

Though the neuter alone is used with the verb -**bòn**-, in other experiencer verbs, the neuter is combined with the "reciprocal" -**an** to denote experiencing by unspecified agents. (This is done with various types of verbs in Kiswahili to indicate potentiality, e.g. Sw. -**patikan**- 'be available', from Sw. -**pat**- 'get', Sw. -**uzikan**- 'be sellable' from Sw. -**uz**- 'to sell', etc.) Some Kifuliiru examples are -**yùviik-an**- 'be heard', from -**yùvw**- 'hear'; -**mény-eekan**- 'be known', from -**mény**- 'know'.

Another example of this combination is found in the verb -**yèrek-an**- 'show something'.[29] The valency reducing effect of the extensions is reflected in the fact that the non-reciprocal form is ditransitive, and can take two surface objects, i.e. -**yèrek**- 'show something to someone', while in this form, the understood multiple persons to whom something is shown may no longer be overtly expressed.

This same combination of extensions can also have a "cumulative" connotation, e.g. -**kòngobedekan**- ~ -**hòngobedekan**- 'be skinny from hunger'.

5.6.4 Impositive

5.6.4.1 Impositive structural considerations

Schadeberg (2003a:74) concludes that in Bantu in general, the meaning of the impositive extension is 'to put something into some position', and notes that "The impositive extension *-ɩk-[30] does not appear to be very productive in any particular language. It typically commutes with positional *-am- and separative *-ʋl-/-ʋk-, but commutation with zero is less common. In most languages it is [structurally] indistinguishable from the homophonous neuter extension".

In Kifuliiru this extension is well represented, e.g. -**lámbik**- 'lay something down', cf. -**lámbam**- 'lie down flat'; -**fwomek**- 'put in mouth'; -**hèngek**- 'tilt, make crooked', cf. -**hèngam**- 'be crooked'; -**hólobek**- 'put down into a hole', cf. -**hólober**- 'sink under water'; -**kómbek**- 'put soft food in mouth of a baby or sick person with one's finger', cf. -**kòmb**- 'wipe bowl with finger'; -**yámbik**- 'dress someone' cf. -**yámbál**- 'get dressed'; -**fùmbadik**- 'hand to someone', cf. -**fùmbát**- 'hold in hand'; -**shéndamik**- 'lean something up

---

[29] However, this is rarely associated with the unextended form **kuyèra** 'to be white, clean'.

[30] The special vowel of these reconstructed extensions indicates that they are subject to vowel height harmony and may appear either as a high or a mid vowel, depending on the preceding environment. A capital letter is also sometimes used to indicate this quality.

against something else', cf. **-shéndam-** ~ **-shéndamuk-** 'lean back, relax, while sitting', and **-shéndamir-** 'lean back on something'.

As seen in the preceding paragraph, in Kifuliiru this extension commutes not only with zero, (e.g. **-bònek-/-bòn-**), positional **-am** (**-hèng-ek-/-hèng-am-**), (**-lámbik-/-lámbam-**), and reversive (separative) intransitive **-uk** (**-shéndamik-/-shéndamuk-**), but also with applicative **-er** (**-hólobek-/-hòlober-**), (**-shéndamik-/-shéndamir-**), and extensive **-al** (**-yámbik-/-yámbal-**). In other cases there may be no other extension currently in use with the same radical (**-fwomek-**).

5.6.4.2 Impositive function

Schadeberg (2003a:74) notes that "For more than a century, the impositive extension *-**ik**- has been understood as a kind of causative, expressing typically "direct causation" (i.e. adding 'cause to' to an intransitive verb), but some 'locative' element of meaning has also been observed in several older descriptions". He comes to the conclusion, however, that in Bantu in general, the meaning of the impositive extension **-ik/-ek** is not basically causation, but is 'to put something into some position'.

This conclusion implies that verbs stems which include the impositive extension will be transitive, rather than intransitive like the verbs with the (generally) homophonous neuter extension. Transitivity, then, is a good indicator of whether a verb has the impositive or the neuter extension.[31]

In Kifuliiru, verbs with the impositive ending fall into two categories: transitive and ditransitive.

---

[31]This is to say that a verb stem which *includes* the impositive is transitive due to the component of meaning added by the impositive, and not to say that the original verb *stem* to which this extension *is attached* must be transitive. On the contrary, the verb stem (rarely an unextended one) to which it is attached is usually intransitive, so that the impositive increases valency. The neuter, on the other hand, usually commutes with zero, and produces an intransitive verb from a transitive root, reducing valency. The impositive and the neuter are distinguished as two separate extensions because they differ in the component of meaning which they contribute to the verb. It is thus their meaning which distinguishes them synchronically. However, Rhonda Thwing (p.c.) points out that if the two are generally used with different classes of verbs, one with transitive verbs, producing an intransitive result, and the other with intransitives, producing a transitive result, they could be as considered a single extension having two functions, the difference in meaning depending on the class of verb to which they are suffixed. In Kifuliiru the two are apparently in just such complementary distribution. However, since both uses of the extension(s) are for the most part lexicalized at this point, the base meaning of the verb stem to which they were attached is perhaps a moot point.

5.6.4.2.1 Transitive impositives

First, there are those transitive verbs which allow one object/patient and involve putting that object into a certain position or state, e.g. -**shéndamik**- 'lean something up against something else', -**fwomek**- 'put something into mouth', -**deedek**- ~ -**diidik**- 'throw heavy thing down, thud!', -**dèndek**- 'tie something to somewhere', -**dúgumik**- 'pour out liquid carelessly', -**dùndulik**- 'stuff (a bundle, suitcase, basket, etc.) until bulging', etc.

(5.71) gives an example of an impositive verb with a single object -**shéndamik**- 'lean something up against something else', in which the object, cl. 6 **ga**-, referring back to **má-tàvì** (6-branches), has been incorporated into the verb.

(5.71) **Bà-ná-tèm-à   á=má-tàvì ‖ bà-ná-gà-shénd-àm-ı̱k-à |**
     2-SQ-cut-Fa   AU=6-branch   2-SQ-O6-lean-POS-IMPS-Fa

   kú= lw-íngò.
   17=   11-tower

'And they cut branches ‖ and they leaned them up | against the tower.' (Jdg 9:49)

5.6.4.2.2 Ditransitive impositives, with instrumental object

The second group of "impositive" verbs are those which semantically allow two objects: a patient and an instrumental object, one or both of which may be expressed in any given instance. These verbs usually involve hitting, stabbing, etc., e.g. -**shúlik**- 'hit', -**gújik**- 'stab', -**yòmek**- 'insert knife/stab', -**shàdik**- 'throw something at someone', -**vuudik**- 'pummel with both fists', -**rárik**- 'beat with thick strap', etc.[32] With such verbs, it is not necessary to add the causative extension as an indicator of instrumentality, nor to mark the instrument by the conjunctive **na** 'with', because the verb itself semantically includes two objects, one of the objects being the victim of the action and the other, the instrument with which the action is carried out.

Following are some examples of impositive verbs which can include an instrumental object. Example (5.72) uses the verb -**shúlik**- 'hit', followed first

---

[32] Eleven of twenty-six other verbs denoting hitting, beating, pounding, etc. contain the reversive transitive or its causative form. In English there is the term "beat someone *up*". Judging from the use of the transitive separative in such verbs, in Kifuliiru the idea is more beating someone 'off' or 'out'. At least some of these verbs allow instrumental objects as well, e.g. **kúmúkúbúlá íí=ngónì** 'to hit him (with) a stick'.

by the receiver of the action, **yìkyó kíshégèshè** 'that.N hedgehog', which is followed by the instrumental object **í=ngóní ígánà** 'a hundred [strokes of a] stick'. Both objects are expressed; neither is incorporated into the verb in this case.

(5.72) Ú=lú-kwàvù | lw-àná-bà-bwír-à ‖ kwó= bà-Ø-shúlík-é yìkyó
      AU=11-rabbit   11-SQ-O2-tell-Fa   CMP= 2-SBV-hit-Fe   that.N+7

    kí-shégèshè | í=n-góní | í-gánà.
    7-hedgehog   AU=10-stick 5-hundred

'And the rabbit | told them ‖ to hit that hedgehog | [strokes of] the stick | one hundred .' (09 021)

The verb **-yòmek-** 'insert knife, stab' is another example of a verb which allows both an instrumental object and an object which is the target of the action. Below are several examples with incorporated and non-incorporated objects, depending on the different communication situations.

In (5.73), none of the objects is incorporated into the verb. All of the arguments of the verb (agent, patient, instrumental object, plus the oblique phrase expressing the location of the stabbing) are expressed by words separate from the verb.

(5.73) Yóhààbù ‖ à-ná-yàmí yòm<u>ék</u>-á ‖ Ámáàsà ‖
      Joab   1-SQ-IMMED insert.knife-Fa Amasa

    í=n-gòòtì   mú= ndâ.
    AU=9-dagger 18=   9-abdomen

'And Joab ‖ quickly stabbed ‖ Amasa ‖ [with] a dagger in the abdomen.' (2Sa 20:10)

In (5.74) the cl. 1 object **mú-** 'him', the patient, is incorporated into the verb, while the instrumental object, followed by the oblique location of stabbing, is mentioned after the verb.

(5.74) À-ná-<u>mú</u>-yòm<u>ék</u>-à   í=n-gòòtì ‖ mú= lú-bávù.
      1-SQ-O1-insert.knife-Fa AU=9-dagger 18= 11-side

'And he stabbed him [with] a dagger ‖in the side.' (2Sa 2:16)

5.6 Non-productive extensions and expansions 395

The example in (5.75) illustrates the use of the reversive form of the same radical -yòm-, as a simple transitive, with the dagger as the only object.

(5.75) Ùyó   mú-shósì ‖   à-ná-yòm-ól-à   í=n-gòòtì ‖
       than.N.1 1-man   1-SQ-withdraw.knife-RV.T-Fa AU=9-dagger

à-ná-gì-gótòméz-à | W-à=n-gwî.
1-SQ-O9-gulp+CS-Fa   1-A.M=9-leopard

'And that man ‖ drew out a dagger ‖ and shoved it into | Mr. Leopard.'
(632 062)

5.6.5 Positional

5.6.5.1 Positional structural considerations

The positional (also sometimes called stative) extension is -**am**. This extension is used in verbs which speak of a position, usually of the human body, but sometimes of other things. In our data there are several verbs in this category that have a lexically corresponding verb without a suffix, e.g. -**bìsh**-/-**bìsham**- 'hide/be hidden', -**zìng**-/-**zìngam**- 'fold, twist, wrap/be twisted in upon self', -**hàng**-/-**hàngam**- 'stop from doing something/be stopped from falling'; -**hòt**-/-**hòtam**- '(flames) die down/be lower, have shrunk down low'.

Others verbs have an (at least possibly) corresponding non-extended form but the positional form has been lexicalized with a specialized meaning, e.g. -**fùmb**- 'fold hands', -**fúmbam**- 'be hunchbacked from TB of the spine'.

Many verbs with the positional extension commute with or can be followed by the impositive extension, or the reversive transitive, e.g. -**hánam**- 'be up high', -**hánik**- 'put something up high'; -**shéndam**- 'lean back on', -**shéndamik**- 'lean something up against something'; -**lámbam**- 'stretch out to take a rest', -**lámbik**- 'lay something out'; -**zìngam**- 'be twisted in upon self', -**zìngool**- 'untwist, unwrap'. Also, -**gálam**- 'lie flat on back' (cf. adverbs **lúgálì** and **búgálàmà** both meaning 'flat on back') has related forms -**gál-ab-ad-ik**- 'lie someone down flat' (note strengthening of 'positional' -**am** > -**ab**, voicing of 'contactive' -**at** > -**ad**, preceding voiceless impositive -**ik**), and -**gál-aaj-uk**- 'fall backwards while sitting'.

The positional extension in some roots commutes with several other extensions, e.g. -**hèngam**- 'be crooked', is related to the following verbs with various extensions: impositive -**hèngek**- 'place in a tilted position';

applicative of causative (or possibly) impositive plus causative of applicative -**hèngekez**- 'cause something to lean against something'; causative of applicative -**hèngeez**- 'shut door, etc. only partially'; reversive intransitive -**hènguk**- 'straighten out, stand something up straight'; reversive intransitive plus reciprocal -**hèngukan**- 'take someone aside'; reversive transitive -**hèngul**- 'open something just a crack'.

Some others of the forty-plus verbs in our database which contain this extension are -**fùkam**- 'to kneel', -**góndam**- 'be bent over'; -**shènam**- 'stick out chest in pride', -**dìndam**- 'strike an impressive pose', -**shútam**- 'squat', -**yùbam**- 'lie down flat'.

In a few verbs, the suffix itself seems to have shifted meaning and become 'frozen', e.g. -**bàl-am**- 'journey' (possibly originally from -**bàl**- 'fly'), -**làng-am**- 'be very harsh' (cf. adj. -**làngi** 'harsh'), -**lègam**- 'be late'.

Though there are many cases in which -**am** follows a stem which contains **i, e, u,** or **o** (as it does in examples above), it seems that the positional extension -**am**, in other (lexicalized) cases has undergone vowel harmony, appearing as -**im/-um**, (but not -**em**, and probably not -**om**, except in combination with **ol**, next paragraph). Examples include -**hírim**- 'fall and roll over', -**líndim**- 'go down into the soil', -**gúgum**- 'brace oneself mentally to endure, be stoic', -**shúkum**- '(plant) wilt in sun', -**túndum**- 'shake', -**júgum**- 'tremble, shake', etc.

This extension/expansion is also often combined as -**amul**, -**imul**, -**omol**,[33] -**umul**, e.g. -**hálamul**- 'pull something out from the place where it was', -**líndimul**- 'bring down something from above'; -**dótomol**- 'peck (like bird)', -**jójomol**- '(bird) peck holes in something', -**búgumul**- 'shake off something, shake out something', -**fúkumul**- 'pour out', -**húlumul**- 'remove husks from grain'.

The positional also appears in combination with reversive intransitive -**amuk/-umuk/-imuk**, e.g. **shálamuk**- '(fetus) be miscarried', -**lándamuk**- '(cloth) be ripped', -**líndimuk**- 'slide or roll down'.

Two other verbs also have an -**im-al** suffix; the -**al** is extensive, and perhaps the initial **i** originates from the final vowel of a related noun or adjective: -**imal**: -**gìshimal**- 'rust', cf. **n-gishi** (9-rust), -**tìndimal**- 'be small, unimportant'.

---

[33] Theoretically the -**om** instances here could also be explained as partial reduplication of a CVC stem ending with -**om**, and then followed by the transitive reversive, i.e. -**dótomola** from -**tom**- (the **t** then having been voiced in the reduplicated first syllable by the formerly active Dahl's law) and -**jójomola** from -**jom**-.

5.6.5.2 Positional function

The positional extension, -**am**- as seen above, is used in verbs which speak of the position of the body or some other item.

One example of a positional verb in context is given in (5.76).

(5.76) à-ná-shút-àm-à   kw=í bwé mú= lw-ījì ‖ à-ná-tèg-à
       1-SQ-squat.down-POS-Fa   17=5   stone   18=   11-river   1-SQ-trap-Fa

       á=má-bòkò ‖   gírá   à-Ø-yábîr-è | á=mì-íjì.
       AU=6-hands   so.that   1-SBV-take.in.hands-Fe   AU=6-water

'And he squatted down on a stone in the river ‖ and he cupped his hands ‖ so that he could take | water.' (07 027)

By the nature of its meaning, a verb with the positional extension generally is intransitive. In the few instances in which the -**am** commutes with an unextended verb, the unextended verb has a valence of two, while the verb with the positional extension has a valence of one. For example, -**bìsh**- 'hide something', infers agent and patient, as subject and object, which are both routinely expressed with the verb. Compare this with -**bìsham**- 'be hidden'. Normally -**bìsham**- has only an agent/subject, who is also interpreted as the one acted upon by his own action, e.g. **àbìshámà** 'he has hidden (himself)'. Thus the meaning, here at least, is reflexive. The reflexive nature of the extension is further implied by the fact that if the incorporated reflexive object **yì**- is expressed, the positional extension may no longer be used. One can thus say **àyìbìshà** 'he hid himself', but it is ungrammatical to say ***àyìbìshámà**.

Surprisingly, it is possible however to have an incorporated object with the verb -**bìsham**-. In this case, since the verb is intransitive, the object expresses the person(s) being hidden *from*. In (5.77) is an example from our texts.

(5.77) **Kéèrà**   à-tù-bìsh-ám-à ‖   hálìkò   à-tù-dés-à ‖
       ALREADY   1+P1-O1.PL-hide-POS-Fa   but   1+P1-O1.P-speak+CS-Fa

       à-bìsh-ám-à ‖   mw-ô-mwò | mú= ny-ûmbà
       1+P1-hide-POS-Fa   E-in.there.N   18=   9-house

'Already he has hidden from us ‖ but he has talked to us ‖ he has hidden ‖ right here |in the house.' (106 050)

More commonly, a person who is affected by the action of a verb which has the positional extension, if mentioned, is expressed as an applicative object, as seen in the example below with -**fùkam-ir**- 'kneel down before/to' from -**fùkam**- 'kneel'.

(5.78) **Ná**= **yà-bó** **bè-èné** **w-ì-nyù** ||
CNJ= those.N-2 2-brothers 1-A.M-2PL

bá-gá-kìzí **kú-fùkám-ír-à.**
2-F2-REP O2.SG-kneel-APL-Fa

'And those brothers of yours || they will kneel before you.' (Gen 49:8)

There are, of course, verbs in which this extension is frozen, and seems no longer to have the meaning of physical position, e.g. -**làngam**- 'be harsh', -**bàlam**- 'make a journey'.

5.6.5.2.1 Positional followed by other extensions

When the extensive is used following the positional, the resultant verb is still intransitive, and refers to a body position, e.g. -**gúng-am-al**- 'slump as in discouragement and grief', -**mìn-am-al**- 'stand straight upright', -**túnd-am-al**- 'curl into a ball from sadness'.

When the impositive is used following the positional, i.e. -**am-ik**, the resultant verb is transitive, and refers not to an animate being, but to some inanimate thing being placed in some position e.g. -**shénd-am-ik**- 'lean something up against something else', -**yèg-am-ik**- ~ -**yègek**- 'set something on top of something else'.

5.6.6 Inchoative

The inchoative suffix -**h**, though it forms a part of a verb base, is not truly a verbal extension, since it is affixed to adjectives, and not to verbs. It is thus a part of the verb radical, rather than an extension. To complete the formation of the verb, the inchoative -**h** is followed by a final vowel. Note that the final vowel of the adjective is retained as the vowel which precedes the inchoative -**h**. For example, -**sírè** 'demon-possessed' is the source of -**síreh**- 'become possessed'; -**òfì** 'short' becomes -**yòfi-h-a** 'be short',[34] -**lèmà** 'crippled' yields -**lèma-h-a** 'be crippled', while -**zítò** 'heavy' is the source of the verb

---

[34]Kifuliiru has no vowel-initial verb stems. In the derivation of a verb from a vowel-initial stem, an epenthetic **y**- is always prefixed.

-**zído-h-a** 'be heavy'.[35] The true extensions may be suffixed following the radical formed by the addition of the inchoative, e.g. **mú-shúmbà** (1-unmarried person) > -**shúmbahal**- 'remain a bachelor for an unusually long time'.

5.7 Other suffixes (expansions)

Expansions are defined as verbal suffixes which cannot be identified as a recognized extension, and for which no firm meaning has been established across Bantu. In Kifuliiru, these are easiest to recognize and put a meaning label on when they occur in combinations with various recognized extensions.

-**ag** is probably the most frequently spotted expansion in Kifuliiru. It often seems to occur in verbs which have a semantic component of repetition, and thus may be historically related to the pre-final -**ag** which in many languages denotes repeated or habitual behaviour. The expansion -**ag**, however, is easily distinguishable from the emphatic extension which is the synchronic reflex in Kifuliiru of this prefinal -**ag**. Besides the difference in meaning, the two occur in different positions. In Kifuliiru the emphatic extension -**ag** always occurs in the rightmost (except for short causative and passive) extension position, and is always productive, whereas the expansion -**ag** is never found in prefinal position and is always lexicalized. Not only is it lexicalized, but when found in combination with other lexicalized expansions/extensions, it is the leftmost of the extensions.

The expansion -**ag** does not occur alone; rather, it most often occurs in combination with other lexicalized extensions, as in (5.79).

(5.79) Expansion -**ag**	combined with:	Base	Gloss
-**ag-al**	Extensive (EXT)	-**hànyagal**-	'have many troubles'
-**ag-az**	EXT + causative (CS)	-**dábagaz**-	'cause to be careless'
-**ag-ir**	Applicative (APL)	-**jéjagir**-	'lack strength'
-**ag-iz**	APL + CS	-**jéjagiz**-	'slowly help'
-**ag-uz**	Reversive (RV) TRANS + CS	-**nywáguz**-	'to hit with a switch'
-**ag-uk**	RV INTRANS	-**dìbaguk**-	'walk like fat person'
-**ag-an**	Reciprocal (RCP)	-**kàndagan**-	'trample'
-**ag-at**	Contactive (CNT)	-**bàlagat**-	'begin to wither or sneak away'

---

[35]Presumably the verb **kú-zídó-h-à** is frozen as a synchronically underived lexical item, since Dahl's law, which would create the voicing of the obstruent **t** in **zítò** > **d** in -**zídóha** before the voiceless **h** is no longer active in Kifuliiru. This probably implies that all the verbs in the closed set of verbs which includes the inchoative are lexicalized.

Several of the more frequently found combinations with -**ag** are highlighted here: -**ag**-**ir**: Many of these verbs have the meaning of repeated or prolonged action, e.g. -**hém**-**ag**-**ir**- 'pant, breathe heavily and quickly' (cf. -**heem**- 'swell'), also -**fwom**-**ag**-**ir**- 'pant'; -**kànd**-**agir**- 'trample down', cf. -**kànd**- 'to press'; -**tòndagir**- 'walk slowly and carefully', from -**tònd**- 'accumulate small bits until you have a lot'.

-**ag**-**ul**: Though it seems from (5.80a) that at least in some cases, the verb with -**ul** was primary, and that the -**ag** was interfixed before this final extension, in many cases this combination synchronically exhibits little of the transitivizing or separative/reversive nature of -**ul**. The combination **ag**-**ul** often seems to mean 'extra extensive', and is semantically more like a strengthened -**al** with -**gu**- interfixed. It is not clear whether the morpheme breaks should be as in **ag**-**ul** or **a**-**gu**-**l**.

(5.80)
-**hímbul**-	'hit with a stick'	-**hímbagul**-	'hit intensively with a stick'
-**hímb**-	'be exhausted'		
---------		-**bàmbagul**-	'expound on something you know nothing about'
-**génd**-	'go'	-**géndagul**-	'wander aimlessly'
-**hónd**-	'pound'	-**hóndagul**-	'strike very intensively'
---------		-**límbagul**-	'beat up thoroughly'
-**dìbir**-	'get fat'	-**dìbagul**-	'make fat'

Another combination, -**abula**/-**abuka**, is found in about twelve verbs other than those with radicals consisting of a consonant followed by -**ab**. -**ab** is not a recognized extension in Bantu. It seems that in Kifuliiru the -**ab** functions as a variant of -**am** 'positional', perhaps used with transitive verbs.[36] Some examples are -**yáj**- 'spread', cf. -**yájabul**- 'spread out, make something more expansive'; -**yándabul**- 'make wider', cf. -**yánd**- 'make smaller (esp. piles of things being sold at market)', cf. -**jándábuk**- 'become stretched out and saggy'; -**jàgabul**- '(exertion or journey) tire someone out', cf. -**jàgabuk**- 'have become tired out by exertion'.

---

[36] The intransitive verb **kúgálámà** 'to lie flat on back' (cf. adverb **lúgáli** 'flat on back') has a related transitive (and lexicalized) form **kúgál**-**áb**-**àd**-**ík**-**à** 'to lie someone down flat', in which we note strengthening of positional -A.M > -**ab**, (as well as the diachronic voicing of contactive -**at** > -**ad**, by Dahl's law preceding voiceless impositive -**ik**).

5.8 Various extension combinations

Table 5.8 gives an extensive (but not exhaustive) list of extensions, combinations of extensions, and expansions plus extensions found in our Kifuliiru working wordlist.[37] It lists sixty-two different extensions and combinations. This count does not include the possible passive form of the many combinations. Examples and comments are given for each listing. The high and mid vowel forms are listed together, with the mid-vowel form given first.[38] The numbers reflect the mid vowel/high vowel realizations found in the list. For example, the first row shows that we found no occurrences of the combination -**er-ek-a** and one occurrence of -**ir-ik-a**.

However, one can get a general idea of the comparative numbers of each. For example, in general, there tend to be more of the extensions with the high vowels (**u** and **i**) than with mid vowels (**o** and **e**) because the high vowels follow stems with a greater variety of vowels (**u**, **i**, and **a**) than do the extensions with mid vowels, etc. If there are long/short pairs, such as -**ok**/-**uk** versus -**ook**/-**uuk**, each is listed separately. All extensions/expansions are listed with a following final vowel to indicate word position.

Table 5.8. Extensions/expansions and combinations thereof

Ext(s) SF	Extension(s) and/or expansion	Comments and examples
-**er-ek-a** (0) -**ir-ik-a** (1)	Applicative +impositive/neuter	-**yì-dàh-ir-ik**- 'enter without permission' (possibly related to -**daah**- '(animal) return home') (cf. -**taah**- '(person) return home')
-**ek-eer-a** (1) -**ik-iir-a** (0)	Impositive +applicative w/long V	-**tèr-ek-eer**- 'participate in traditional worship', (extensions frozen) This contrasts with -**tér-ek-er**- 'get lost +applicative' from -**teer**- 'lose'
-**ek-er-a** (4) -**ik-ir-a** (16)	Impositive/ neuter +applicative	-**hèr-er-ek-er**- 'be completely finished off' (from a reduplicated form of -**hèr** 'come to end'); -**bùnd-ik-ir**- ~ -**bìnd-ik-ír**- 'cover with soil'

---

[37] The wordlist on which this chart is based was never designed to include all the extended forms of verbs, and productively extended verbs were, in fact, for the most part avoided, so the fact that some combinations have few representatives in the chart is not necessarily to say that they are extremely rare in the language.

[38] This is not intended to be a reflection on which one is the underlying or historically original form.

Ext(s) SF	Extension(s) and/or expansion	Comments and examples
-eek-a (0) **-iik-a** (0)	Impositive/ neuter with long V	Neuter/impositive never has a long vowel
-ek-a (82) **-ik-a** (160)	Impositive/ neuter	Mostly impositive, e.g. -**yòm-ék**- 'insert knife'; -**duul-ik**- 'to push fire up together'. Many "striking" verbs, e.g. -**shúl-ik**- 'hit', etc. Some neuter, e.g. -**kòl-ek**- 'be done'; -**kómeer-ek**- 'be wounded'; -**vùn-ik**- 'be broken'
-es-a (4) **-is-a** (8)	Causative of impositive	Causative of -**eka** verbs (-**ek** + **i**), e.g. -**yìyòndobes**- 'make self thin'; causative of -**ika** verbs (-**ik** + **i**) -**twis**- 'break something apart'
-y-a (52)	Causative	"Short" causative, e.g. -**gòh-y**- 'to blink', cf. **í=n-gòhè** (AU=9-eyelid); -**hám-y**- 'make larger' (cf. -**hám**- 'get big'); -**lááv-y** 'stretch out, unfold' (cf. -**lámb-uul**- 'straighten out'), -**jùgumby** ~ **jùguvy** 'shake something to hear what is in it'
-ees-a (12) **-iis-a** (23)	Causative	Productive "long" causative (NOT from -**eek-a** verbs, since there are none above) -**mèny-ees**- 'make known'; Productive "long" causative (NOT from -**iik-a** verbs, since there are none above) -**bùk-iis**- 'cause someone to be doctored'

5.8 Various extension combinations

Ext(s) SF	Extension(s) and/or expansion	Comments and examples
-k-ez-a/ -g-ez-a (1) -k-iz-a/ -g-iz-a (6)	Applicative of causative verb	Special form for applicative of a causative verb. -k goes with verbs whose causative form ends with s, -g with those which end with z, e.g. -nyékez- 'cause rain to fall on someone or something' (cf. -nyés- 'cause rain to fall'); -lóógez- 'look for someone', (cf. -lóóz- 'look for, want'); -lámukiz- 'greet someone for someone else' (cf. -lámus- 'greet'); -búúgiz- 'ask on someone's behalf' (cf. -buuz- 'ask', also -bùguliz-)
-os-a (4) -us-a (15)	Reversive INTRANS or radical-final -uk/ ok-+causative	Causative of -ok (-ok + i), e.g. -lyos- 'send away' (cf. -lyok- 'leave'); -lál-ús- 'intoxicate' (cf. -lál-úk- 'get drunk')
-oos-a (3) -uus-a (12)	Reversive INTRANS +causative	Causative of -ook (-ook + i), e.g. -shónd-oos- 'pick up carefully' (cf. -shón-ond-ol- 'pick up a small bit of something', with its CS, -shónd-ooz- 'glean in a field'); causative of -uuk (-uuk + i), e.g. -hán-uus- 'ask for advice' (cf. -hán-uul- 'advise, counsel')
-oz-a (12) -uz-a (46)	Reversive TRANS +causative, or radical of Cog-, etc. +causative	Causative of -ol-a or of verbs with stem of consonant + o + any voiced consonant subject to spirantization, e.g. Cong-, Cog-, Col-, etc. (-oC + i), e.g. -tom-oz- 'give someone firstfruits' (cf. -tóm-ol- 'taste firstfruits'), -nòz- 'soften by pounding', (cf. -nòg- 'be soft'); causative of -ul-a (-ul + i), e.g. -dúk-úz- 'make red' (cf. adj. 'red' -dúkul-); -gùng-uz- 'cheat'

Ext(s) SF	Extension(s) and/or expansion	Comments and examples
-ooz-a (8) -uuz-a (22)	Reversive TRANS + causative	Causative of -ool-a (-ool + i), e.g. -hòl-óóz- 'cool off something hot' (cf. -hòl- 'be cool, or to pass out'); causative of -uula (-uul + i), e.g. -bésh-uuz- 'expose a lie' (cf. -beesh- 'tell a lie')
-w-a (n/a)	Passive	Highly productive (-u + -a), e.g. -shúlikw- 'be hit' (cf. -shúlik- 'hit'), but can also be frozen, -yùvw- 'hear'
-ok-a (58) -uk-a (196)	Reversive INTRANS or impositive	Frozen form, e.g. -hód-ok- 'be cooked to the point of mushiness, (person) be limp from sleepiness'; gál-úk- 'return' (cf. -gál-úl- 'return something'); -hém-úk- 'have sudden uncontrollable urge to have something'.
-ook-a (17) -uuk-a (95)	Reversive INTRANS	Productive form, e.g. -shòn-óók- 'climb down' (cf. -shòn-óól- 'let down', -shòn- 'climb (up)'); -dúb-úúk- 'come back to shore after fishing' (cf. -dúb- 'fish with nets') -hem-uuk- 'unswell' (cf. -héém- 'swell up')
-ol-a/(78) -ul-a (242)	Reversive TRANS	Frozen form. -gób-ol- 'wean calf' (cf. mú-góbà 'udder'); -gól-ol- 'straighten something'; -bèt-ul- 'carry on head or top of shoulder'; -gúuk-ul- 'knuckle s/o on the head', cf. í-gúùkù (5-knuckle).

5.8 Various extension combinations

Ext(s) SF	Extension(s) and/or expansion	Comments and examples
-ool-a (50) -uul-a (123)	Reversive TRANS	Productive form, e.g. -shòn-ool- 'lower something from above' (cf. -shòn- 'climb up'). Also many frozen forms, including those having to do with hitting, e.g. -nòg-ool- 'hit someone until they are totally limp' (cf. -nòg- 'be soft, limp'); -hub-uul- 'rectify a wrong' (cf. -hub- 'err'); gán-uul- 'converse', including many which have to do with force, anger, completeness, etc. Many striking and throwing verbs, e.g. -hàt-uul- 'slap on face', (cf. -hàt- 'hit'); -dìk-uul- 'strike brutally'; -báy-uul- 'get rid of smell'
-ol-ol-a (2) -ul-ul-a (10)	Redup. reversive TRANS	-móg-ol-ol- 'rip or peel off long strips with hands' (cf. unredup. -móg-ol- 'peel off with fingernails, like a scab'); -hèmb-ul-ul- 'give a starving person food' (cf. redup. with one l dropped, e.g. -hèmb-uul- meaning unchanged)
-ool-ol-a (2) -uul-ul-a (4)	Redup. reversive TRANS	-hòl-ool-ol- 'revive unconscious person' (cf. -hòl- 'faint, become unconscious'); -kàm-uul-ul- 'wring out completely' (cf. -kàm- 'wring or squeeze, milk a cow')
-er-a (107) -ir-a (203)	Applicative	Highly productive as well as many frozen forms. -beesh-er- 'lie about someone' (cf. -beesh- 'lie'); -húb-ir- 'do wrong to someone' (cf. -húb- 'do wrong, make a mistake')
-er-er-a (10) -ir-ir-a (18)	Redup. applicative	Signals intensification or repetitiveness, e.g. -génd-er-er- 'continue' (cf. -génd- 'go'); -fúk-er-er- 'be steady, firm'; -bwir-ir-ir- 'reprimand' (cf. -bwi-r- 'tell')

Ext(s) SF	Extension(s) and/or expansion	Comments and examples
-eer-er-a (6) (i)ir-ir-a (5)	Double-redup. applicative intensive	Intensification, purposefulness, duration, e.g. -fùnd-eer-er- 'be placed well, fitting'; -lék-eer-er- 'forsake'; -vúm-eer-er- 'hum in agreement'; -nún-iir-ir- 'scratch a bad itch' (cf. -nún- 'be sweet'); -gír-iir-ir- 'do purposely' (cf. -gír- 'do')
-eer-ez-a (16) -iir-iz-a (18)	Double-redup. applicative +causative	Meaning may be intensive, or it may be an actual causative of an intensified -eer-er-a verb. 9 with e stem verbs, e.g. -bèr-éér-éz- 'cut repeatedly, lengthwise'; 1 with o stem -kóm-éér-éz- 'warn sternly'; 6 with u or i stem with d, h, f, v, z, e.g. -dùg- 'get too close', -dùm- 'speak poorly', -fúnd- 'store away carefully', -húng- 'make peaceful'. The i- form occurs with u, i, a roots, except not with u roots with du, fu, hu, vu (these take eerez). -háv-iir-iz- 'chase something far away' (cf. -háv-y- 'chase away', which is causative of -háb- 'be scared off path and lose way'); -mál-iir-íiz- 'finish off last little bit' (cf. -mál- 'finish')
-eer-a (47) -iir-a (35)	Applicative with long V	Mostly frozen forms, e.g. -tònd-eer- 'to begin'; -kóm-eer- 'get used to'; -hòl-eer- 'be comforted'; -fúb-eer- 'go at a hurried pace'. Often frozen with specialized meanings, but can be productive.

5.8 Various extension combinations

Ext(s) SF	Extension(s) and/or expansion	Comments and examples
-ez-a (81) -iz-a (64)	Applicative +causative	Causative of er-a, some frozen (count does not include -eer-ez-a or -eez-a verbs, but does include -er-ez-a and -ek-ez-a verbs), e.g. -bèr-ek-ez- 'make a loud cracking sound like a plank breaking' (cf. -bèr- 'cut'); -gér-eg-ez- 'try hard' (cf. -gér- 'measure, test'); -hòg-ez- 'eat gluttonously' (cf. -hòg-er- 'cause to eat a large quantity'); -hèz- 'bring to an end' (cf. -hèr- 'end') Causative of -ir-a verbs (ir + i + a), e.g. -dúm-iz- 'mother to respond vocally when her baby is crying'; -báy-iz- 'sniff at some odor' (cf. -báyir- 'smell to someone', -báy- 'smell' INTRANS)
-eez-a (16) -iiz-a (12)	Redup. applicative +causative	Causative of –eer-a verbs, e.g. -tònd-ééz- 'begin something' (cf. -tònd-éér- 'begin'); -hòl-ééz- 'comfort someone' (cf. -hòl-éér- 'be comforted'); -hèng-ééz- 'shut partially, and/or to peek after partial shutting'. Causative of -iira (iir + i + a), e.g. -dàt-ííz- 'make black', -hàng-át-ííz-/-bàng-át-ííz- 'bind or shut very tightly'
-Vmb-uk-a (4)	Expansion +reversive INTRANS	-dúk-úmb-úk- 'be intensely red' (cf. -dúk-ul- 'be red'); -gàl-amb-uk- 'look strange and abnormal'
ab-uk-a (7)	Expansion +reversive INTRANS	-jàg-ab-uk- 'be unable to do'
ab-ul-a (4)	Expansion +reversive TRANS	-jàg-ab-ul- 'cause to be weak'
-ag-al-a (11)	Expansion +extensive	-hàny-ag-al- 'suffer much calamity'

Ext(s) SF	Extension(s) and/or expansion	Comments and examples
-ag-az-a (6)	Expansion +extensive +causative	Causative of ag-al (-ag + -al + -i), e.g. -tur-ág-áz- 'thunder and lightning'
-ag-ir-a (22)	Expansion +applicative?	Many meaning repeated or prolonged action. -hém-ag-ir- 'pant, breathe heavily and quickly'; -from-ag-ir- 'pant'; -kànd-ag-ir- 'trample down' (cf. -kànd- 'to press')
-ag-at-a (1)	Expansion +contactive	-bàl-ag-at- 'run off and hide'
-ag-iz-a (7)	Expansion +applicative? +causative	Causative of ag-ir-a (-ag + -ir + -i), e.g. -jéj-ag-íz- 'carry or support, going slowly, as with weak person'
-ag-ul-a (20)	Expansion +reversive TRANS	Most with meaning of violence, ignorance, or repetition, e.g. -hímb-ag-ul- 'beat repeatedly with a sturdy stick' (cf. -hímb-ul- 'hit with sturdy stick')
-ag-uk-a (6)	Expansion +reversive INTRANS	-vw-ag-uk- 'spill and be scattered' (also -mw-ag-uk- same meaning)
-ag-an-a (6)	Expansion +reciprocal	-shób-ag-an- 'be twisted together like strands of or rope' (cf. -shób- 'be mixed up, twisted')
-h-a (54)	Inchoative	Derives verb from adjective, e.g. -yòfi-h- 'be short' (cf. -òfì 'short'); -yíji-h- 'be good' (cf. -îìjà 'good'); -tíbu-h- 'be dull' (cf. -tíbù 'dull')
-am-a (51)	Positional	-dìnd-am- 'strike an impressive pose, poise self for action'; -hàg-am- 'be stuck'
-am-al-a (3)	Positional +extensive	-gúng-am-al- 'sit slumped in sadness'

5.8 Various extension combinations

Ext(s) SF	Extension(s) and/or expansion	Comments and examples
-**aan**-**a** (38)	Interactive	'Do/be in relation to someone or something else', all frozen forms, e.g. -**gáb**-**aan**- 'distribute'. Count includes 7 with causative (-**aan**-**i**-**a**), e.g. -**líng**-**aan**-**i**- 'set in order'; 4 with RV INTRANS (-aanuka): -**lál**-**aan**-**uk**- 'be torn'; 4 with RV TRANS, 2 with -**aan**-**ul**-**a**: -**lál**-**aan**-**ul**- 'rip in two'; 2 with -**aan**-**ur**-**a**: -**sób**-**aan**-**ur**- 'explain'; 1 with APL (-**aan**-**ir**-**a**): -**gásh**-**aan**-**ir**- 'bless'; 2 with APL + CS (-**aan**-**iz**-**a**) -**bàng**-**aan**-**iz**- 'twist the truth'
-**an**-**a** (67)	Reciprocal +comitative	Productive form. -**kaab**-**an**- 'borrow from/lend to' (cf. -**kaab**- 'lend, borrow')
-**an**-**an**-**a** (3)	Redup. reciprocal	-**sók**-**an**-**an**- 'be surrounded' (cf. -**sook**- 'pass behind something' or perhaps -**sók**- 'squeeze in amongst')
-**an**-**w**-**a** (5)	Mutual comitative +passive	Used to make a reciprocal of an INTRANS verb, e.g. -**génd**-**an**-**w**- 'go together with each other'; -**yíj**-**an**-**w**- 'come with each other'. Also used for the comitative of a passive, e.g. -**bùt**-**an**-**w**- 'be born of the same mother', etc.
-**ek**-**an**-**a** (3) -**ik**-**an**-**a** (2)	Neuter +comitative	Indicates something being done (neuter) by multiple non-subject actors. -**mény**-**eek**-**an**- 'be known' (cf. -**mény**- 'know'); -**gáb**-**ul**-**ik**-**an**- 'be divided up' (cf. -**gáb**- 'divide'); -**yùv**-**iik**-**an**- 'be heard' (cf. -**yùv**-**w**- 'hear')

Ext(s) SF	Extension(s) and/or expansion	Comments and examples
-ik-an-i-a (4)	Causative +applicative +reciprocal +causative	These are frozen forms, either the applicative of a reciprocal causative, e.g. -**gwás**-**ik**-**an**-**i**- 'assist one another', or possibly the causative of a verb with both impositive and reciprocal, etc., e.g. -**líng**-**ik**-**an**-**i**- 'prepare something'; -**báng**-**ik**-**an**-**i**- 'force together'
-ig-an-i-a (1)	Applicative +reciprocal +causative	-**tìrígani**- ~ -**tìriginy**- 'fall down, miss the mark'
-uk-an-a (4)	Reversive INTRANS +comitative	-**háb**-**uk**-**an**- 'run off with somebody's stuff'
-at-a (11)	Contactive	-**hàmb**-**at**- 'follow incessantly, like a male animal following a female in heat'; -**shàm**-**at**- 'gather up, scoop up'
-ad-ik-a (15)	Contactive +impositive	These all seem to have a causative meaning and often have to do with putting something inside, or throwing something down, e.g. -**yì**-**hàmb**-**ad**-**ik**- 'put self inside of something'
-at-al-a (1)	Contactive +extensive	-**hùmb**-**at**-**al**- 'get progressively skinnier'
-at-ul-a (4)	Contactive +reversive TRANS	-**kàm**-**at**-**ul**- 'wring out completely' (cf. -**kàm**- 'wring something out, milk a cow')
-ot-ol-a (1)	Contactive	Possibly result of vowel harmony on -**at**-**al** (contactive + extensive), or the mid vowel version of -**at**-**al**, e.g. -**yòng**-**ot**-**ol**- 'nurse too often' (cf. -**yòng**- 'baby to nurse')

5.8 Various extension combinations

Ext(s) SF	Extension(s) and/or expansion	Comments and examples
-al-a (34)	Extensive	-shúmb-a-h-al- '(man) to stay unwed a long time' (cf. -shúmb-a-h- '(man) to stay unwed' (these also probably contain -h inchoative) and múshúmbà ('bachelor')
-al-al-a (6)	Redup. extensive	-hàng-al-al- 'get dry and hard, like clay, or, of a person, be exhausted'
-az-a (32)	Extensive +causative	Causative of -al-a verbs (-al + i) -bál-az- 'make something fly' (cf. -bál-al- 'fly')
-aal-a (14)	Redup. extensive	-shàmb-aal- 'rejoice'
-aaz-a (10)	Redup. extensive +causative	Causative of -aal-a verbs (-aal + i) -húm-aaz- 'blind or blindfold someone' (cf. -húm- 'be blind')
-al-ik-a (10)	Extensive +impositive	Most seem to be connected with force or carelessness, e.g. -dànd-al-ik- 'do something carelessly', -yi-bwand-al-ik- 'flop oneself down backwards'.
-Vb-al-a (5)	Expansion +extensive	These are CVC -Vbala verbs, where the V2 is a copy of the stem vowel. It is not clear whether there is a morpheme break between the vowel and the b, e.g. -gùd-ub-al- '(clouds) to become dark and threatening' (cf. -yùlubal- 'get black'); -gòng-ob-ál- 'become very thin from hunger' (cf. -góng-ob-ók- 'have become very thin').
-ek-al-a (0) -ik-al-a (3)	Expansion +extensive	-hwìj-ík-ál- 'temporarily forget and be fooled' (cf. múhwìjà 'fool')

5.9 The resultative final: Structural considerations

The resultative -**ir-i** is a verbal suffix which, unlike most verbal suffixes, is not regarded as an extension or expansion, but as filling the slot of the final vowel in certain tenses/aspects. The resultative suffix is reconstructed as proto *-**i̧d-e**, (or *-**i̧de**).[39] It collocates only with certain TAMs, and itself comprises a vital part of their definition. Another quality which separates -**ir-i** from the extensions is that it may be used with a verb of any semantic class. This is not generally true of the extensions, each of which, in general, collocates with some verbs and not with others.

The extensions are defined by their position between the verb root and the final vowel. The resultative, by contrast, though of the configuration -VCV rather than -V, functions in the place of the final vowel. The fact that it can be interrupted by certain morphemes such as passive (where it becomes -**ir-w-i**) and causative (where it becomes -**iz-i**) is, in Schadeberg's words, "best understood as a mismatch between phonological and morphological structures. These two extensions [passive and causative] consisting of a single vowel both compete for the last position in the string of extensions; this is a phonological competition, and phonology misreads the non-canonical [i.e. not of the usual single -V shape] final suffix -**iri** and interprets it along canonical lines (i.e. as a -VC extension plus -V final vowel), hence -**ir-i**" (Schadeberg p.c.). So from a morphological point of view, the resultative is considered to consist of a single, verb-final morpheme which directly follows the verb base.

In Kifuliiru, however, there is evidence that even in the morphological realm -**ir-i** is treated as two formatives. Phonological considerations may cause the vowel-only extensions, i.e. causative -**i** and passive -**u**, to be placed directly to the left of the final vowel. One cannot claim, however, that strictly phonological reasons lead to the placement in Kifuliiru of the -VC emphatic extension, -**ag**, between the two formatives of -**ir-i**, e.g. **hâlí nátùùz-ìr-ág-ì** 'there also lived EMP...' (non-emphatic form: **hâlì nátùùzìrì**). The emphatic extension in Kifuliiru corresponds historically to the "prefinal" inflectional morpheme found in many Bantu languages with a meaning of repetition or habitualness, and its rightward placement in the verb (and its placement

---

[39]There are two schools of thought as regards the representation of this morpheme. Some (e.g. Schadeberg (p.c.), Nurse (p.c.)) represent it as a single formative, while others (notably Hyman 1995) represent it as consisting of two separate formatives, *-**id** and *-**e**. Those who hyphenate it do so because when the passive and causative morphemes co-occur with *-**id-e**, they are inserted between the two parts. Hyman (1995:3) says: "As is generally recognized by Bantu scholars, *i̧**d**- is a separate formative from the final vowel -**e** that co-occurs with it." All consider *-**id-e** to be a single morpheme, with a unified function/meaning, however. Because this suffix is interruptible, we will use the hyphenated form, in order to clarify where the passive or causative occurs in relation to it and to simplify morpheme-by-morpheme glossing (or in this case, formative-by-formative glossing).

5.9 The resultative final: Structural considerations

before the final vowel of the resultative) is more likely related to its morphological heritage rather than to any of its phonological characteristics.

Though the proto-form of the resultative is considered to be *-ɨd-e, and in most Bantu languages its final vowel is still found as -e, in Kifuliiru its final vowel is -i. In some peripheral parts of the Kifuliiru-speaking area, it is pronounced as -e, and at the time the orthography was finalized, a few speakers from these areas wanted to symbolize the resultative final vowel as -e. However, the final consensus of speakers from all parts of the Kifuliiru speaking area was that in "pure Kifuliiru" it is pronounced as i, and that the use of a final -e in some areas is due to influence from neighboring languages, especially Mashi or Kinyindu.[40]

The structural considerations of the formation of the resultative stem are discussed here, rather than with the various conjugated forms in which they are used. We have done this for two reasons. First, though the resultative stem is used in various TAM forms, the segmental form of resultative stem is the same in all of them. Second, there is a significant amount of phonological interaction involved in the formation of the resultative stem, which is better treated here than under the specific forms in which these stems are used.

The specific verb forms which include this suffix are discussed under the various TAM forms of the verb. Very briefly and generally speaking, it can be said that forms with the resultative suffix are not used to refer to an event, but to a state, and used to present background material in a discourse. This may be a background state resulting from a previous action, e.g. -mánuk- is 'go down', while àmánùs-ìrì means 'he is in the state of having gone down (and is still down there)', while àshúlìs-ìrì (from -shúlik- 'hit') means 'he has hit (someone)' and infers that the results of this hitting have not yet subsided (e.g. someone may be injured, someone might still take revenge, restitution needs to be made, etc.) The resultative form with other prefixes may indicate an unrealized or contrary-to-fact state, e.g. (úkìmúyìté) n-àngà-shàmbí-írì '(if you had killed him) I would have been happy'.

5.9.1 Interactions of the resultative with the verb stem

The resultative suffix historically had the first degree (high) vowel *ɨ, and though its reflex in Kifuliiru does not have the extra-high vowel, it still causes either spirantization (2.3.2.5) or effacement of the final consonant of a verb base (2.3.2.3.2). The phonological changes conditioned by the juxtaposition of the resultative and a base final consonant are laid out in (5.81).

---

[40] We posit that the optional rule of final vowel devoicing (2.3.1.2.3.1), frequently applied to resultative forms, might have played a role in the raising of this final vowel by de-emphasizing the quality of the vowel and making it more susceptible to harmony with the preceding vowel.

(5.81) Effect of resultative on final C of verb base

	Verb base	Gloss	RS stem

Base forms ending with **y, h, b, mb, m, n** : NO CHANGE

a.	**-káy-**	'be fierce, angry'	**-káy-ir-i**
b.	**-yùgih-**	'get sharp'	**-yùgih-ir-i**
c.	**-yòboh-**	'be afraid'	**-yòboh-ir-i**
d.	**-jàmb-**	'become thin'	**-jàmb-ir-i**
e.	**-hím-**	'surpass'	**-hím-ir-i**
f.	**-shòn-**	'climb'	**-shòn-ir-i**

Base forms ending with **k, t** : SPIRANTIZATION

g.	**-heek-**	'carry'	**-hees-ir-i**
h.	**-sook-**	'go around'	**-soos-ir-i**
i.	**-yùbak-**	'build'	**-yùbas-ir-i**
j.	**-zùnguluk-**	'go around and around'	**-zùngulus-ir-i**
k.	**-fùndik-**	'become engaged'	**-fùndis-ir-i**
l.	**-shálik-**	'be hungry'	**-shális-ir-i**
m.	**-yìgut-**	'be full, satisfied'	**-yìgus-ir-i**
n.	**-dèt-**	'speak'	**-dès-ir-i**
o.	**-hàgat-**	'carry on shoulder'	**-hàgas-ir-i**

Base forms ending with **r, l, nd, ng, g** : SPIRANTIZATION

p.	**-goor-**	'have need'	**-gooz-ir-i**
q.	**-lól-**	'look at'	**-lóz-ir-i**
r.	**-kùnd-**	'love'	**-kùùz-ir-i**
s.	**-yìmang-**	'stand still, stop'	**-yìmaaz-ir-i**
t.	**-tèg-**	'trap, set trap'	**-tèz-ir-i**

Base forms with passive **-ir-w-i** : SPIRANTIZATION of base-minus-passive

u.	**-kùnd-w-**	'be loved (passive)'	**-kùùz-ir-w-i**
v.	**-yùbak-w-**	'be built (passive)'	**-yùbas-ir-w-i**
w.	**-bwat-al-**	'sit down'	**-bwat-i-ir-i**
x.	**-bwat-al-ir-**	'sit down at/on'	**-bwat-al-i-ir-i**
y.	**-yèm-eer-**	'agree'	**-yèm-i-ir-i**
z.	**-yìj-ul-**	'be full to top'	**-yìj-w-ir-i**
aa.	**-gól-ol-**	'straighten out'	**-gól-w-ir-i**

5.9 The resultative final: Structural considerations

Base forms with reciprocal/mutual: IMBRICATION (see below)
bb.	**-hoob-er-an-**	'hug each other'	**-hob-er-i-in-i**
cc.	**-kw-an-an-**	'be deserving, fitting'	**-kw-an-i-in-i**
dd.	**-shób-ok-an-**	'be possible'	**-shób-ok-i-in-i**
ee.	**-bwat-al-an-w-**	'sit together'	**-bwat-al-i-in-w-i**

As shown in (5.81a–f), a verb base ending in **h, b, mb, m, n** does not undergo spirantization or deletion of the final consonant. Further examples of verbs with no change in the final C of the verb base include **h**: -sìmbah- 'obey, honor' > -sìmbah-iri; **y**: -báy- 'have odor' > -báy-iri; **b**: -lób- 'get wet' > -lób-iri; **mb**: -shòmb- 'hate' > -shòmb-iri; **m**: -yùm- 'get dry and hard' > -yùm-iri; **n**: -shòn- 'climb' > -shòn-iri.

As shown in (5.81g–o), the final **k** or **t** of a verb base undergoes spirantization to **s**. Further examples of verbs in which the final **k** or **t** of a verb base is spirantized to **s** include -hík- 'arrive' > -hís-iri; -gáluk- 'return' > -gálus-iri; -maat- 'eat relish without accompanying staple' > -maas-iri.

As seen in (5.81r–t), the voiced segments **g, ng,** and **nd** are spirantized to the voiced fricative **z**, and the latter two are further altered by nasal effacement in most dialects so that **nd** or **ng** becomes simply **z**. In the remaining dialect, the nasal does not undergo effacement, so that **nd** and **ng** become **nz**. Further examples showing spirantization of **g, ng,** and **nd** to **z/nz** include -lèng- 'pass' > -lèèz-iri (one dialect -lèènz-iri), -géend- 'go' > -géez-iri (one dialect -géenz-iri), while -sìg- 'leave' > -sìz-ir-i.

An **l** or **r** in C_2 position is spirantized to **z**, as shown in (5.81p, q) above, e.g. -teer- 'lose' > -teez-iri; -twal- 'take away, carry' > -twaz-iri; -tuul- 'live' > -tuuz-iri; -bùl- 'lack' > -bùz-iri.

However, as seen in (5.81aa), an **l** or **r** in C_3 position (or farther right) in the verb base, is treated differently from an **l** or **r** in C_2 position. While the C_2 **l** or **r** is spirantized, an **l** or **r** in a position farther to the right than C_2 position undergoes imbrication.[41] Imbrication refers to the process by which the reflex of the Proto-Bantu *-ɨde morpheme (resultative in Kifuliiru) interacts with various segments to which it is juxtaposed, so that the verb base and the resultative appear to have merged into a single distinctive resultative form which in some cases cannot be easily parsed into separate morphemes.

Sometimes imbrication involves only the effacement of a consonant and subsequent merging of the vowels which are then found in juxtaposition. For

---

[41] Imbrication is the term used by Bastin (1983) to refer to the process by which a formative such as -iri fuses with a verb base, causing internal modifications to the base, instead of simply being suffixed. This same process is variously referred to in the literature as "ablaut" (Kisseberth and Abasheikh 1974), "fusion" (de Blois 1975), or formation of a "modified base" (Ashton et al. 1954; Givón 1970; Mould 1973).

example, when -**ir-i** is suffixed to -**gálul**- 'return something', the resulting form is -**gálw-iri**. A verb with a reciprocal extension -**an**, on the other hand, undergoes a more complex imbrication process by which the final suffix appears not as **iri** but as **ini**, e.g. -**gáluk-an**- 'return with (someone or something)' with the addition of **iri** becomes -**gáluk-i-ini**. This process is attested in Kifuliiru not only with **l/r** but also with **n** and (in lexicalized forms) with **t**, as is common in Bantu languages.

Thus a C_3 **l** or **r**, whether a segment of the extensive -**al**, applicative -**ir/-er**, or reversive transitive -**ul/-ol**, seems to be right-displaced by the initial formative of -**ir-i**- suffix, effectively interrupting the extension by the infixation of the resultative, as well as dividing the two formatives of -**ir-i**. The **r** of the resultative is totally effaced preceding the **l/r** of the original extension. The vowel of the extension is also open to interact with the vowel of the resultative morpheme. Lexical level vowel coalescence rules dictate that a non-back vowel totally assimilates to the **i** of the extension, e.g. -**bwatal**- 'sit' + **iri** > -**bwata-ir-l-i** > -**bwata-i-l-i** > -**bwatiiri**,[42] while the applicative form of the same verb -**bwatalir-iri** sit at/on + **iri** > -**bwatali-ir-r-i** > -**bwataliiri**; -**yèmeer**- 'agree' + -**iri** > -**yèmee-ir-r-i** > -**yèmee-i-r-i** > -**yèmiiri**.

(5.82) a. 'sit'   -**bwatal**-   -**iri**   > -**bwata-ir-l-i**   > -**bwatiiri**

   b. 'sit at/on'   -**bwatal-ir**-   -**iri**   > -**bwatali-ir-r-i**   > -**bwataliiri**

   c. 'agree'   -**yèmeer**-   -**iri**   > -**yèmee-i-r-i**   > -**yemiiri**

   d. 'return (TRANS)' -**gálul**-   -**iri**   > -**gálu-ir-l-i**   > -**gálwiri**

Note that while a front or mid vowel **i**, **e**, or **a**, shown in (5.82a–c), coalesces with the vowel of the resultative to form a long **ii** in the surface form, a back vowel, **o** or **u** becomes a glide, **w**, as in (5.82d). Other examples are -**shóbol**- 'be able' > -**shóbwiri**; -**shwek-uul**- 'untie, open' > -**shwekwiri**.

5.9.2 Irregular resultatives

There are several irregular resultative forms in Kifuliiru. At least some of these same verbs are irregular in nearly the same ways in many Bantu languages, which implies that such forms were already in use in some stage of Proto-Bantu. The irregular resultative forms in Kifuliiru are found in (5.83).

---

[42] **l** is pronounced as **r** when it follows a high vowel.

5.9 The resultative final: Structural considerations

(5.83) Irregular resultatives

	Verb base	Gloss	RS
a.	-mény-	'know'	-yìji
b.	-bòn-	'see'	-bwini
c.	*-ha(at)-†	'give (contactive)'	-hiiti
d.	-gwat-	'have'	-gweti
e.	-fùmbat-	'hand to'	-fùmbiiti
f.	-yámbal-	'put on (clothes, etc.)'	-yámbiiti
g.	-yùvw-	'hear'	-yùvwiiti

†This form is only a possible reconstruction of the base form, and is not synchronically recognizable by speakers as the source of the resultative form -**hiiti**. They do see -**hiiti** as a form of the verb 'to give', but there is no *-**haat**- in current usage, so the base form is instead considered to be -**haabw**- 'be given'.

The form **yìjì** 'know' (5.83a) synchronically is only one of the resultative forms of -**mény**- 'know'. Besides -**yìjì**, -**mény**- also has a regular resultative form -**ményiri**, which has been observed mostly in the contrary-to-fact resultative verb form, e.g. **ngá=wàngàményìrì** 'if you knew (but you don't)'.

-**bwini** (5.83b) is irregular in two regards. Synchronically the -**in** form of the resultative is used only with verbs having the reciprocal/ mutual extension, which -**bòn**- does not have. Secondly, a CVC verb synchronically does not undergo imbrication, probably because of minimality constraints.[43]

While in (5.83c) *-**haat**- (the contactive form of 'give') is not a synchronically existent form, and unrecognized by speakers, it seems that -**hiiti** 'having' derives originally from -**ha-at-a** (give-contactive-FV). -**gweti** 'have', (5.83d) is historically from -**gwat**- 'hold', though synchronically, -**gwasiri** is the resultative of -**gwat**-. -**fùmb-iit-i** (5.83e) 'holding in the hand' is irregular only because it contains a non-productive imbricated form of the resultative, -**iiti**. It is derived from a synchronically used verb which contains the non-productive contactive extension -**at**, e.g. -**fùmb-at**- 'grasp in the hand'. **yámb-i-it-i**

[43]Hyman (1995) posits that in Cibemba, minimality plays a role in determining which verbs undergo imbrication, i.e. the verb must meet a certain minimum length criterion in order to undergo imbrication. It is interesting that in the irregular forms which have been passed down, (e.g. -**gweti** 'have' (from -**gwat**-), -**bwini** 'see' (from -**bòn**-), -**hiiti** 'have' (from *-**haat**-?), the imbrication seems to have taken place with no regard to minimality conditions, whereas in synchronic use, monosyllabic forms, whether mono- or bimoraic, do not undergo imbrication, but only spirantization, e.g. -**twal**- 'take, carry away' -**twal + ir** > -**twaz-ir**, and it is the longer forms that undergo imbrication, e.g. -**twal-ir + ir** > -**twal-i-ir**. Thus it seems that historically there was perhaps no constraint against imbrication in monosyllabic forms.

'wear', (5.83f), synchronically is the resultative of **-yámb-al-** 'put on clothing', but apparently was historically from **-yámb-at-** with the contactive **-at** rather than the current extensive extension, **-al**. **-yùvw-it-i**, the resultative of **-yùvw-** 'hear, feel', (5.83g) apparently also was associated at one time with a contactive extension.

-yùvw-it-i 'heard' is sometimes interpreted by speakers as a passive form. In such cases, instead of **-yùvwiiti** (non-passive) it is heard as **-yùviitwi**, with the **-w** shifted rightward into the passive position. The meaning is identical in both forms.

Note that the irregular lexicalized forms in (5.83) include two different irregular (imbricated) forms of the resultative, **-ini** (as in **-bwini**) and **-iti** (as in **-fùmbiiti, -yámbiiti, -hiiti, -gweti**). The **-ini** form of the resultative, besides being found in the irregular form **-bwini**, also appears in synchronically derived forms of verbs whose final extension is the reciprocal extension, **-an**, as in (5.84a, b). A **-CVn-** base, however, does not undergo imbrication synchronically, perhaps because of minimality constraints. The lack of imbrication in **-CVn-** verbs is shown by examples like (5.84c, d). In **-kàn-** 'be strong, mature', the resultative is **kàn-ir-i** (not *-kan-in-i or *-ki-ini); and the resultative of **-shòn-** 'climb', is **-shòn-iri**, (not *-shonini or *-shiini).

Various theories have been put forth as to the exact phonological or morphological mechanisms responsible for deriving the imbricated forms **-iin**, from **-an + ir**, (and **-iit**, from **-at + -ir**). Assuming that the process laid out above in (5.82) is valid for the examples given in that set, it would likely work the same for verbs with **-at** or **-an** endings. For other possible treatments of this process, see Hyman (1995) for a quite thorough evaluation of various explanations of similar phenomena in Cibemba.

(5.84) Resultatives of reciprocal forms

	Verb base	Gloss	RS stem
a.	**-kùlikir-an-**	'follow each other'	**-kùlikir-iin-ì**
b.	**-shóbok-an-**	'be possible'	**-shóbok-iin-i**

Compare to non-reciprocals ending in /n/

	Verb base	Gloss	RS stem
c.	**-kàn-**	'be strong, mature'	**-kàn-ir-i**
d.	**-shòn-**	'climb'	**-shòn-ir-i**

Though the imbricated **-in** form of the resultative is still widely found in verbs whose stem ends with the reciprocal/mutual extension **-an** (see two examples in (5.84a, b), there is evidence that regularization with the unmarked

5.9 The resultative final: Structural considerations

resultative form is underway in such cases. Perhaps this is especially true in cases where that extension has been lexicalized as a part of the verb base. That the forms are in flux is evident from the use of resultatives like -**kumaniri** (not *kumiini) from -**kuuman**- 'gather together', and -**zòbaaniri** (not *zòbiini) from -**zòbaan**- 'be snarled, twisted, or woven together'. Also, a speaker gave both -**tùngiini** and -**tùngaaniri** as possible resultative forms of -**tùngaan**- 'straighten, line up, make perfect'.

While it seems that most verbs which contain the synchronic reciprocal extension -**an** may still form their resultatives with the imbricated form -**iin**, the verbs ending in -**iit/et** listed in (5.83c–e) are the only forms observed which have this imbricated form with the **t**. Observation of the synchronic derivation of the resultative from a verb base ending in **t**, whether or not it obviously contains the non-productive contactive extension -**at**, reveals that the **t** is spirantized to **s**, e.g. -**hàgat**- 'carry over shoulder in a bag or sheath' > -**hàgas-ir-i**, -**gwat**- 'hold' > -**gwasiri**; also -**yìgút**- 'be satiated (with food)' > -**yìgús-iri**.

It should be noted that both standard forms of the copula 'be', -**ba**- (**kú-bâ** 'to be') and -**lì** 'is/are' have regularly formed resultatives: -**bi-ir-i** (e.g. **írí àngàbíírì** 'if he were') and -**ri-ir-i** (e.g. **áàlí ríírì** 'he was (in the state of being ...)'. On the other hand, the "marked" copula -**kòla** 'be now (as opposed to an earlier state)', has no distinct resultative form, but instead may be used "as is" in syntactic contexts which usually call for forms with final -**iri**, e.g. **áàlí kòlà né=ndâ** 'she was newly in the state of being pregnant', cf. the use of resultative form (**riiri**) of **li** 'be/is' with this verb form: **áàlí rììrí múlùzì-nyérè** 'she was a princess'.

5.9.3 Resultatives of causatives

The resultative of a causative verb always ends in -**siizi/-ziizi**. When a resultative suffix is added to a verb stem which includes the causative morpheme (and thus whose surface base ends in **s-i** or **z-i**),[44] the causative morpheme -**i** is repeated between the -**ir** of the resultative suffix,[45] and the resultative's final **i**, causing the **r** to be spirantized to **z**. Thus, for example, from -**simiis**- (UF -**siim-iisi-**)[46] 'make happy', (from -**siim**- 'be pleased, happy') we have the

---

[44] All non-passivized causative forms of a verb base end in -**s** or -**z** in their surface forms. This -**s** or -**z** results either from the spirantization of the consonant preceding the short causative morpheme, -**i**, or is the **s** of **iisi**, the long causative morpheme. Thus, all causative verbal bases underlyingly end in -**si** and -**zi**. The passive of a causative would end in -**sibwa** or -**zibwa**.

[45] The short causative morpheme is repeated after any following suffix except the passive or the final vowel. E.g. with the emphatic, -**ag**, a non-causative form ends in -**ag**-FV, e.g. **híkàgà!** 'arrive, EMP' but the causative form ends in -**ag-y**-FV, e.g. **hísàgyà!** 'cause to arrive, EMP'.

[46] Recall that the mora-based vowel shortening rule (2.3.1.2.6) causes any long vowel to be

following derivation: -**simiisi-ir-i-i** > -**simiisiizii** > -**simisiizi**. The additional causative -**i**, which follows the -**ir** of the resultative, precedes the final vowel of the resultative, also **i**. Since both vowels are identical, they would normally merge as a single long vowel, but since a long vowel is disallowed word-finally in Kifuliiru, the length on the final **i** is simply deleted.

Below in (5.85) are several examples of lexicalized causatives in which derivation of the resultative is shown. Note that whether the causative is lexicalized or productive, the short causative must be added preceding the final vowel (in the case of a resultative form, preceding the final -**i** of **ir-i**).

(5.85)
Base[†]	Underlying	Step 1	Surface
-**hís**-	-hik + i + ir + i + i	-his-i-iz-i-i	-hísiizi
-**yús**-	-yut + i + ir + i + i	-yus-i-iz-i-i	-yúsiizi
-**simiis**-	-sim-iisi + ir + i + i	-sim-isi-iz-i-i	-simisiizi
-**hèrekez**-	-her-eker-i + ir + i + i	-her-ekez-i-iz-i-i	-hèrekeziizi

[†]Note that glosses of each 'Base' above are as follows: -**hís**- 'bring home wife', -**yús**- 'finish', -**simiis**- 'please', and -**hèrekez**- 'escort in parting'.

The forms in (5.86) are comparable to those above in (5.85), but instead of showing the derivation, in (5.86) we show the resultative of the causatives in a conjugated verb, demonstrated by the simple resultative form.

(5.86)
Base	Gloss	Resultative[†]	Surface
-**gùs**-	'tend (fire)'	àgùsíízì	'he has tended the fire'
-**buuz**-	'ask'	àbúzîizì	'he has asked'
-**hís**-	'bring home a wife'	àhísīīzì	'he has married'
-**lóóz**-	'look for, want'	àlózīīzì	'he wants'

[†]Note the tones in these conjugated forms. The different tonal patterns seen on these verbs are due to the difference in the underlying tone or lack of tone of the verb root. The underlying root tones (L, H, or toneless) are shown by the markings in the column which lists the unconjugated root only. For a complete explanation of the grammatical tones seen in these forms, and their interactions with the underlying root tone, see section on the Complex HL pattern (3.5.3.3.2).

---

shortened when three or more morae follow within the word. Thus the addition of a suffix with a long vowel, or of suffixes totaling three or more morae, triggers the shortening of a long vowel to the left.

5.9.4 Resultatives of passives

The resultative of passive form is derived by suffixing the usual -**u** (> **w**) immediately preceding the final -**i** of -**ir-i**, giving -**irwi**. Examples are -**yùbasirwi** 'is built' from -**yùbak-** 'build', and -**sìgiirwi** 'is left behind' from -**sìgal-** 'remain behind'.

In the resultative form of the passive of causative verbs, the ending is always -**siibwi** or -**ziibwi**, e.g. **bìgúlìsííbwì** 'they (cl. 8) have been sold' (from -**gúliis-** 'sell'), or **àhèrékézíìbwì** 'he has been escorted' (from -**hèrekez-** 'escort guest partway home'). Note the long **ii** in these endings. We posit that the source of this long vowel is the resultative -**ir-**, minus its **r**, plus the repeated short causative -**i**, as shown below in (5.87).

Assuming that the form of the passive morpheme following a causative is -**bu**, and not -**ibu**, we must have an explanation for the fact that there is a double **i** preceding the -**bw** in -**siibwi/-ziibwi**. Noting, as stated in 5.9.3, that the ending of the resultative form of a causative verb is always -**siizi/-ziizi**, also with a double vowel, it seems likely that the derivation of the resultative-passive-causative ending -**siibwi/-ziibwi** is the following.

(5.87) -(ii)s)i/(s/z)i   -ir   -i   -bu   -i   >   -(ii)siibwi or -ziibwi

    long/short CS   RS   repeated   PS   RS FV   PS RS of CS
                               (short) CS

To explain this further, the origins of this ending seem to have involved some imbrication (fusing of morphemes). First, the addition of the causative morpheme causes a verb stem to end in -**si** or -**zi** as shown at left in (5.87). Sometimes, as in the case of -**shálik-** 'be hungry' > -**shálik-i-** > -**shálisi-** 'cause to be hungry', or -**yòng-** 'suck milk' > -**yòng-i-** > -**yòzi-** 'cause to suck milk', this -**si** or -**zi** is simply a spirantized form of the original final consonant of the verb base, followed by the short causative, -**i**. In other cases, the -**si** is the final part of the long causative morpheme (-**iisi/-eesi**) e.g. -**yándik-** 'write' > -**yándik-iisi-** 'cause to write'.

In forming the resultative of the causative, we saw that the -**ir** of the resultative suffix was followed by a repeated short causative morpheme, which caused the **r** to be spirantized to **z**. In this passive form, we see that the short causative which follows the resultative -**ir** causes not spirantization, but total effacement of the **r** of the resultative.[47] Thus the first -**i** of -**siibwi/-ziibwi**

---

[47]The **r** is taken off from the resultative morpheme preceding the causative -**i** for the same reason that the **r** or **l** of an extension such as applicative or reversive transitive is deleted preceding the resultative -**ir**, which also begins with a spirantizing -**i**, e.g. the resultative of **kú-gál-úl-à** 'to return sthg' is **a-gál-ul-ir-i** > **à-gálw-ìr-ì** 'he has returned sthg', while the

is the formative -**ir** with the **r** removed, and the second **i** is the repeated short causative. This imbricated form, rather than being synchronically derived, has likely become lexicalized as the passive form of the resultative of a causative, i.e. -**iibwi**, which is selected for use as the passive form of causative verbs.

---

resultative of **kú-gálúl-ír-à** 'to return sthg to someone or some place' is **a-gál-ul-ir-ir-i** > **àgálùl-ì-ìr-ì** 'he has returned sthg to someone or some place'.

Appendix:
Determining word boundaries, and related orthography issues

The issue of word boundaries is a topic not merely of theoretical importance, but also of practical importance because of its many orthographic implications for those who would want to develop their languages. In this appendix we show how we have applied phonological and tone rules to the question of the determination of orthographic word boundaries in Kifuliiru.

The issue of the "word" in Bantu has been the subject of much discussion over the years.[1] There is a history of controversy in the decision of whether Bantu languages should be written conjunctively, with many morphemes joined together in a single word, or disjunctively, dividing off each morpheme as a separate word. Some articles address issues of wordhood in relation to specific morphemes. For example Meyers (1990) in his study of Chishona word structure, challenged the standard analysis of Bantu class markers as a part of the morphological noun word, claiming rather that they are independent syntactic constituents. Bresnan and Mchombo (1995) in turn challenge

---

[1] In Guthrie (1948), for instance, an article on Bantu word division, the author concluded that the "wordhood" tests of his day could not give conclusive proof that a sequence of morphemes is a word. Instead, he advocated beginning with a sentence, and dividing it only where there is clear evidence for a break between "pieces" or "distinct pieces" (these are the terms he used instead of "words"). Rather than word breaks, he posited "open junctions and semi-open junctions" and instead of nouns and verbs (which he felt were "European terms") he opted for "nominal segments" and "verbal segments".

Meyers' analysis, showing that except for the locative class markers, noun class markers in various Bantu languages do not meet their syntactic tests for lexical integrity.

Here we have not approached the data with Bresnan and Mchombo's battery of syntactic tests. Instead we present primarily phonological evidence that distinguishes between lexical and postlexical levels. Is phonological evidence a valid test of such differentiation? Meyers (1990) claims that phonological evidence can only prove that the class marker is a part of the same phonological word as the stem, and not that it is a part of the same morphological word.

In Kifuliiru, however, there are three phonological processes that allow one to distinguish between lexical and postlexical levels. For this reason, phonological evidence cannot be so easily eliminated as a valid indicator of the syntactic status of a given morphemic unit. The relevant processes are vowel shortening, vowel lengthening, and vowel coalescence/elision. In addition, true tonal contours occur only word-penultimately, giving more phonological input in determining word boundaries. And for the determination of word breaks within verbal constructions, besides these phonological indicators, there are several morphological clues as well that reveal the presence of a word boundary.

We do not, however, suppose that the issue of word breaks is a simple one. Hyman and Katamba (2005) show that two phonological criteria which were previously assumed to be "litmus tests for wordhood" in Luganda, another Bantu J language, do have their exceptions. These two criteria are the shortening of long vowels at the end of a word, and the fact that a word may not contain more than one HL tonal sequence. The overall conclusion of the article is that any attempt to cut language into well-defined segments, whether sentences, syllables, even morphemes or phonemes, will continually meet with complexities and contradictory evidence, but that linguists should continue to attempt definition and to hypothesize why such contradictions exist.

With the complexity of these issues in mind, we do not attempt in this section to definitively "pin down" the word in Kifuliiru in linguistic terms. We do present some of the linguistic criteria we have found helpful in determining practical orthographic word boundaries that reflect the perceptions of speakers of the language, in hopes that these will be of help to those faced with practical orthographic decisions in related languages.[2]

In this appendix, orthographic representation of data will be labeled as such. In orthographic representation, long vowels which are the result of rule

---

[2] Any orthographic decisions, no matter how strong the linguistic indications for them might be, should still be thoroughly tested with as many speakers of the language as possible, to make sure that they fit the perceptions of the majority of speakers as closely as possible.

application are not indicated as lengthened, since this is done automatically by speakers of the language.³ Other vernacular examples in this section will be transcribed with all vowel length indicated, since vowel length plays a role in much of the discussion.

1 The relevant units: words, affixes, and clitics

The failure to distinguish between morphologically bound monosyllabic affixes, which are an integral part of a word, and monosyllabic units which are separate words⁴ phonologically cliticized to another whole word, is one major cause of the confusion regarding word boundaries in Bantu. Morphologically, there is massive affixation in Bantu languages, largely of monosyllabic morphemes. Polymorphemic words are the rule rather than the exception. This fact is widely recognized. What is not so often noted is that many, if not most Bantu languages seem to have some degree of phonological constraint against independent monosyllabic words. In the presence of such a constraint, such words are often phonologically joined (cliticized), by postlexical rule, to a preceding or following word. They are separate at the lexical (word) level and yet phonologically joined to a "host word" at the phrase level.

To add to the confusion, the term "clitic/enclitic" has been used at times as a grammatical word class, as if a "clitic" were a single grammatical class definable by syntactic and semantic usage, like a noun or a verb. Here we will present evidence, using not only semantic and grammatical criteria, but also phonological evidence from vowel coalescence and vowel lengthening/shortening rules, and from tonal contours, giving a set of linguistic criteria for differentiating affixes, clitics, and words in Kifuliiru.

1.1 Words

The "lexical integrity principle states that words are built out of different structural elements and by different principles of composition than syntactic phrases" (Bresnan and Mchombo 1995:181).

---

[3]The same can be said for the great majority of tone marking. Except for a few grammatical minimal pairs, marking tone in Kifuliiru is superfluous and is considered to be a device designed to ensure that correct spelling remain the domain of a few elite. As a diplomatic Mufuliiru told me regarding a trial orthography in which tones were marked on all verb stems and certain grammatical functors, "The tone marks are very nice. They help foreigners pronounce our language correctly." Of course there are some grammatical tone markings which actually assist readers.

[4]Such monosyllables qualify as words if, for our purposes, we define a "word" as any unit which is independent and unbound at the end of the lexical (word-building) cycle of the grammar.

Words are generally understood to be independent syntactic units. In turn they are the building blocks of larger units: phrases, clauses, sentences, etc. There are several semantic and grammatical characteristics usually considered indicative of independent words. A given word may or may not exhibit all of the following characteristics: REFERENTIAL INDEPENDENCE, the ability to clearly communicate meaning in isolation; CONCEPTUAL UNITY, the conveyance of a single unified semantic or grammatical concept; MOBILITY, an assessment of the degree to which a certain unit may function in different word order configurations or with different word classes; SEPARABILITY, the possibility of having various words intervene between the word in question and a following or preceding word; and SUBSTITUTABILITY, the ability of the unit in question to be replaced by a unit which is clearly an independent word (Van Dyken and Kutsch Lojenga 1993:7). To determine whether a given morphemic unit is a word, or merely a part of a word, it must be first evaluated on these "lowest common denominator" criteria which distinguish a complete word from a lower level unit such as an affix, clitic, radical, stem, etc.

SEPARABILITY, the ability of a unit to be separated from another unit by intervening morphemes or words is probably one of the most important in distinguishing between affixes and monosyllabic words. We will posit that if any *whole word* (which meets several of the above criteria) can stand between a given morpheme and the word on which it *seems* to be "dependent", then that morpheme is also a separate word at the syntactic level.

This is obviously oversimplified from a linguistic point of view, but for orthographic purposes, we may refer to a morpheme or group of morphemes which meet all of the tests above as a "lexical word". It has passed through the lexical component of the phonology and emerged as a syntactically independent unit. A noun, for example, is always a word. It names a single concept. It is separable as a constituent of a sentence, and can stand on its own as a meaningful unit. It may be moved around in the sentence, according to its syntactic function as object or subject.

In Kifuliiru a typical noun consists of a noun class prefix[5] plus a stem: e.g. **mú-shósì** (1-man). The stem may be compound, as in the cl. 1a noun **námúlòbáàfwì** '(a.1a) 'fish-eating hawk (lit. with catching fish)'. Though this compound could be considered a clause, it refers to a single concept and has been lexicalized as a unit which for which another noun, such as **kányúnì** 'bird' can be substituted. A word has mobility, and if a noun, for example, is moved, it moves as a unit, together with its prefix. A verb may be even more complex, but still forms a unit, and has mobility as a unit. A verb form usually begins with a subject prefix, may have a negative marker preceding the tense

---

[5] Which in some cases is a null prefix, such as in cl. 1a words, and in cases where the N- prefix of cl. 9 is deleted by phonological rule before a fricative, e.g. **fíízì** 'big bull'.

prefix, and may include an incorporated object marker, all of which precede the verb radical. The stem itself consists of a radical, often followed by one or more derivational "extensions", plus a mandatory final vowel, e.g. **à-tá-ká-tù-sóm-éés-â** (1-NEG-P2-O1Pl-read-CS-Fa) 'he did not send us to school'. Despite its polymorphemic nature, such a verb is a single word.

1.2 Affixes

Affixes are building blocks for word formation. They are both morphologically and phonologically bound to a stem or radical. They function as units only at the lexical (word-building) level, never functioning independently at the postlexical level. Typical of Bantu languages, Kifuliiru makes extensive use of (mostly monosyllabic) prefixes and, to a slightly lesser degree, suffixes, in word formation. For example, the noun **mú-shósì** (1-man) has a cl. 1 prefix, while the verb **à-géénd-à** (1-go-Fa) 'he went' has both a prefix and a suffix attached to the radical, -**géénd**- 'go'. The radical without any obligatory affix(es) is not an entire word, nor can any of the affixes function syntactically as independent words.

One of the main features which distinguishes an affix from a cliticized monosyllabic word is that of inseparability. A word functions as a complete unit on the syntactic level. An affix, on the other hand, while it may well have a discernable meaning, never functions syntactically without the stem to which it is attached. For example, the subject marker on a verb may be separated from the verb stem by another affix, such as a tense marker, or negative marker, but both affixes are still attached to the verb stem, and never function independently. An independent word may never stand between an affix and the root to which it is morphologically bound.

In Kifuliiru, a noun class prefix is always an affix. Locative markers, on the other hand, while sometimes presented in the literature as "noun prefixes", function syntactically, at least in Kifuliiru, as monosyllabic words rather than as prefixes.[6] If we compare, for example, the cl. 19 diminutive nominal prefix, with any locative marker, we see that there is an essential difference between the two in terms of separability. The diminutive prefix usually replaces the normal noun class prefix of a noun which is being diminutivized. In some cl. 9/10 nouns, however, the noun class prefix is null, so in such cases, it appears that the diminutive is added to a complete noun. Even when added to a complete word, however, it is still clearly an affix and not a clitic, because it is inseparable from the noun to which it is attached. Compare **shááhò** (9+bag) and

---

[6]There are morphemes of the locative class which do function as bound prefixes on verbs, pronouns, demonstratives, etc. but in the case of nouns, the locative markers are never affixed at the lexical level.

its diminutive, **hí-shááhò** (19-9+bag), with the phrase **ììyó gíindì shááhò** 'that other bag' and its diminutive counterpart **yììhyó híindì híshááhò** 'that.N other small bag'.[7] Note that the **hí-** prefix is never separated from the noun (or modifier) to which it is attached. Rather, it remains attached to the noun, and the modifying words within the phrase have matching concord prefixes.

A locative marker of any class also precedes a whole noun, e.g. **shááhò** (9+bag), **mú=shááhò** (18=9+bag) 'in the bag'. However, the locative marker, unlike the diminutive prefix, *is* separable from the word to which it is phonologically attached. Observe how the locative marker appears only at the left of the phrase as modifying words are added: **mú=gíindì shááhò** 'in another bag', **mú=ííyò gíindì shááhò** 'in that other bag'. Clearly the **mú** is independent from any other specific word class, and rather is joined phonologically to the word that happens to follow it within the phrase. Thus, the locative marker, in contrast to the noun class prefix, *can* be separated from the noun to which it seems to be attached. It simply remains the head of the phrase, attaching to an entire phrase; there is no concord within the noun phrase that agrees with the cl. 18 locative marker. The modifiers in the noun phrase still have the cl. 9 agreement, **mú=ííyò gí-ìndì shááhò** (18=9+that 9-other 9+bag) indicating that the class of **shááhò** 'bag' has not changed to cl. 18. Below in 2, we present phonological evidence which shows that the locative is indeed attached phonologically to the word following it, but as a cliticized monosyllabic word, and not as an affix.

Bresnan and Mchombo (1995) give the historical background for the fact that the locative markers are not prefixes as the other noun class markers are. They assume the class markers to be, as Greenberg (1977, 1978) proposed, historically descended from classifying determiners or articles. In the evolution of morphologically bound affixes, a syntactic word such as an article "first becomes phonologically reduced and bound to an adjacent constituent [i.e. cliticized], and then becomes morphologically bound as an affix" (Bresnan and Mchombo 1995:212). This process of historical change has been completed in the case of non-locative class markers, which have become morphologically bound as prefixes, but is incomplete in the case of the locative class markers, which have retained their status as separate syntactic elements of noun phrases.

A related point of confusion in the orthographies of many Bantu languages regards word breaks in complex verb forms. Such word breaks are often unrecognized because of inadequate reference to indicators found in phonological and tone rules. Without such linguistic clues, word division, especially in complex verb forms, is merely a matter of guesswork, and is often neglected

---

[7] It is also possible that the noun nyúùmbà is interpreted as having no segmental prefix. The cl. 9 prefix is realized as ny- prevocalically, and as Ø before a nasal-initial noun stem.

entirely, resulting in very long verbs that are daunting to the reader. The problem of word division in verbs is further complicated by the existence of "gray areas" that reflect an interim stage in the progressive grammaticization of morphemes from clitics to morphologically-bound affix status.

In looking at these issues in Kifuliiru, we have found multiple linguistic clues, both phonological and syntactic, which can help to determine whether a given unit is an independent word, a clitic or an affix. The same linguistic clues we bring to bear on the issue of prefix versus proclitic are also useful in looking at the question of suffixes, and the features which distinguish them from enclitics.

1.3 Clitics

We can define a clitic in Kifuliiru as a monosyllabic word which is phonologically bound to another word. In Kifuliiru, as in many Bantu languages, not only are words polymorphemic in general; there is also a constraint against independent monosyllabic words within an utterance.[8] The corrective strategy which is usually applied to a monosyllabic word within a phrase or clause is cliticization. The monosyllabic word is phonologically joined (cliticized) to a neighboring lexical word, creating what might be called a phonological word. A phrase like [áámágí gíbáátà] 'the eggs of the duck' (orthographically, **amagi gi'baata**) contains only two phonological words. This phrase is, however, formed syntactically from five distinct lexical units consisting of seven morphemes: **a=ma-gi ga=i=i-baata** (AU=6-egg 6+A.M=AU=5-duck). (Hyphens within the gloss indicate morpheme breaks, while an equal sign indicates cliticization.)

C. M. Doke, who studied many Bantu languages, but did most of his work on those in South Africa, referred to clitics in Bantu as "monosyllabic words which have lost their separable power and attached themselves to some other word, partaking of the phonetic entity of that word." (Doke 1943:58). Though he does not elaborate on how a word can lose "its separable power," the fact that his definition is perfectly applicable to a clitic in Kifuliiru is perhaps evidence that a constraint against monosyllabic words is a feature of many, if not most, Bantu languages.

In order to be a clitic, then, a unit must not only be monosyllabic, but it also must qualify as a word (i.e. a unit functioning at the syntactic rather than lexical level.) As seen above in the section on "Words", the identity of a monosyllable as a word, rather than an affix, is partly determined by its

---

[8] Monosyllabic interjections do exist in Kifuliiru, e.g. **E!** (with a glottal stop) which expresses surprise, displeasure, etc. Another such interjection is **Yoo!** an expression of sorrow, sympathy, etc. Ideophones used as interjections are also often monosyllabic. It is possible as well to use a monosyllabic noun as a complete utterance, or to use a monosyllabic imperative form of a verb.

syntactic property of separability. It will be shown below that in many cases clitics in Kifuliiru can also be distinguished from affixes by reference to several phonological processes which are diagnostic in determining their status.

The second part of our definition of a clitic says that the unit on which the clitic is dependent is also a whole word. Cliticization involves the dependence of a monosyllabic *word* upon another *word*,[9] whereas affixation involves an interdependence of *subword* units or a subword unit and a word. A definition of clitics as 'phonologically bound morphemes that attach to whole words' (Schadeberg 2003b:152) avoids stating that such phonologically bound morphemes are also syntactically words. However, it will be shown by phonological evidence that in Kifuliiru, clitics are, at some level, words. This is shown by the fact that clitics are affected by postlexical rules, which operate only on whole words, and do not affect combinations of morphemes below the word level.

Not all clitics are grammatical functors. The fact that a word is a clitic is not materially related to its syntactic function or word class, nor to its semantic meaning, or lack thereof. Often, monosyllabic words do have functions which are largely grammatical, such as the nominal augment or the associative marker in Bantu. The semantic elusiveness and syntactic functionality of such words may add to the illusion that they must be affixes rather than words. However, it is not grammatical functionality or lack of semantic concreteness, but rather the combination of phonological dependence on another word and identity as a functional unit above the word level, which defines a clitic as a clitic.[10]

A monosyllabic noun or verb is phonologically no more able to stand alone than a monosyllabic functor such as a question marker or nominal augment. For example, a monosyllabic noun such as **n-dá** (9-abdomen), is never found uncliticized in normal speech without either the augment or a locative prefix or some other strategy for adding syllables to the word (**íí-ndâ** 'the abdomen/ pregnancy' or **múú=ndâ** 'in the abdomen', **í-búùndà** (5-pregnancy). Though **ndâ** is a complete noun without any addition, because it is a monosyllabic word, it does not stand alone. Likewise, a verb stem, such as **-lyâ** 'eat' in **à-géendíì=lyâ** (1+P1-GOING=eat) 'he went to eat' is also a "clitic" when it has no prefixes,[11] (cf. **àgééndì bwáátálà** 'he went to sit') though **-lya** itself is clearly a verb stem.

---

[9] Sometimes the word to which a clitic is attached is another monosyllabic word, e.g. the underlined portion of the verb **àlì múù=lyâ** 'he is eating'. The phonological word formed by the two clitics thus consists of a proclitic and an enclitic, acting as "hosts" for each other.

[10] Klavans (1985) distinguishes between syntactic and phonological clitics. This seems to be a valid distinction even in Kifuliiru. We posit that in Kifuliiru, and perhaps in all Bantu languages, however, that all cliticization is basically phonologically motivated, whether or not it also involves grammatical aspects.

[11] See the discussion on single syllable verb stems as clitics in 4.1.2.

Since the rule of monosyllable cliticization makes the clitic a part of another word, some aspects of the phonetic realization of a clitic and its host, e.g. tone, vowel length, etc., are a reflection of the fact that they have become a single unit. Because of this phonological interdependence, it may be helpful for smooth reading that the orthography somehow indicates the relationship between a clitic and the word to which it is joined. In one version of the Kifuliiru orthography, all clitics[12] are marked by an apostrophe, to show that they are phonologically a part of the word to which they are attached, while still representing a separate syntactic word rather than an affix. After a thorough trial of this option, the language committee later decided that marking all clitics in this way entails the use of too many apostrophes. They made the decision that apostrophes should be used only in cases in which there has been vowel elision.

2 Phonological indicators of word boundaries

Though word boundaries are determined in large part on the basis of semantic and syntactic criteria, input from phonological rules is often helpful in cases where word boundaries are in question. In Kifuliiru, the phonological indicators of word boundaries are abundant. The determination of word boundaries may be informed by the assessment of whether or not the following rules apply to a given unit:

- Compensatory vowel lengthening
- Clitic-related vowel lengthening
- Mora-based vowel shortening
- Vowel coalescence: Lexical level or postlexical level?
- Restriction on tonal contours

Examples will be given to show how each rule is useful in the determination of word boundaries.

---

[12] All except the augment. Because at the time the orthography began to be used more widely we were not yet convinced that the augment was a clitic and not an affix, the apostrophe is not currently used with augments in the Kifuliiru orthography. However, since the augment is written as a part of the noun, rather than as a separate unit, e.g. orthographically **abandu** 'people', readers never make the mistake of trying to read the augment as a separate unit. Also, because the augment in Kifuliiru is used extremely frequently, marking it with an apostrophe would be cumbersome.

2.1 Compensatory vowel lengthening

There are two rules of compensatory vowel lengthening in Kifuliiru.[13] One specifies that a vowel is lengthened preceding a nasal plus consonant (NC) sequence, such as **nd**, **mb**, or **ng**. The other states that a vowel is lengthened following a non-word-final glide, i.e. **y** or **w**. These two rules are alike in that they both increase the vocalic morae in a word to compensate for the lack of moricity in a segment of that word that was moraic at some point. These vowel lengthening rules inform word boundary decisions in that their application indicates the presence or absence of a word break either following a glide or preceding a NC sequence.

Thus, if a vowel *is* lengthened following a glide, it is clear that that vowel is not in a word-final position. If it is not lengthened following a glide, it is either word-final or followed within the word by three or more morae. For example, in the phrase **ùùlyá múbì** 'that bad person', the fact that there is no lengthening of the final **a** of **ùùlyâ** indicates that there is a word break following it, and the demonstrative and noun form a phrase, but are not joined as a single word.

The pre-NC lengthening rule, on the other hand, is not so helpful in determining the presence of a word break preceding the NC. This rule operates not only within the word, but to a limited extent across word boundaries within a phrase. Thus, the presence of vowel lengthening preceding a NC cluster is not always a clear indication that there is no word break between the lengthened vowel and the NC. An example of a phrase is where slight vowel lengthening before the NC occurs despite the word break is found in the clause **mbù=yííjì ngírá búlìgò** 'with the intention that you come and do me harm'. In this clause, though the verb form, **ùyííjì ngírà** 'you come (and) do me', consists of two words, in pronunciation at normal speed,[14] there is slight phonetic lengthening of the final **i** of the auxiliary preceding the word-initial **ng** which follows within the phrase: [**ùyííjììngírà**]. We know, however, that this verb consists of two words by noting that the rule of mora-based vowel shortening (see 2.3) has not shortened the long vowel which follows the **y** in **yííjì**. Since the mora-based shortening rule does not allow two long vowels in a single word, we know there is a word break following the auxiliary. Thus we still have a linguistic indicator that this verb consists of two words, an auxiliary, **yiiji** 'coming', and a main verb, **gira** 'do'.

---

[13]Because these rules are part of the speaker's innate understanding of his language, the vowel lengthening produced by them need not be indicated orthographically. A reader who speaks the language will automatically apply the rules at the appropriate spots.

[14]The pronunciation can be slowed so that the two words are pronounced separately, and in this case, there is no lengthening of the final **i**.

2.2 Clitic-related vowel lengthening

Another process in Kifuliiru which is helpful in distinguishing between affixes and clitics is that of clitic-related vowel lengthening. This is a process by which the vowel of a monosyllabic proclitic is lengthened[15] when fewer than three morae follow it within the newly created phonological word of which it is a part, and by which the final vowel of a host word is lengthened when a verbal, nominal or adjectival enclitic is added. The vowel of an affix is not lengthened by this rule, because it is a postlexical rule, which does not apply to units that function beneath the syntactic level. The lengthening, whether of a proclitic or of the final vowel of the host, preceding the enclitic, is not contrastive and is not indicated orthographically.

The application of this lengthening rule in proclitics can be exemplified by the augment. The augment, which appears as **a**, **i**, or **u**, in harmony with the vowel of the following syllable, is lengthened when cliticized to a word of fewer than three morae. As can be seen in (1a), the augment **i** is lengthened when followed by the noun **kí-hê** (7-time), which contains only two morae. The augment retains its short vowel when followed by the three-morae noun **kí-nógò** (7-hole) (1b). Note that the cl. 7 prefix **kí-** is not lengthened in either case, because it is an affix, and not a monosyllabic word, and as such is not subject to clitic-related vowel lengthening. Similar examples with cl. 2 augments are given in (1c, d).

---

[15] One could also posit that the vowel in these morphemes is underlyingly long, regardless of the number of following morae, and that the rule of mora-based vowel shortening then shortens the vowel when three or more morae follow. We have not made that assumption. For the reasoning behind this decision, see the discussion of the clitic-related vowel lengthening in 2.3.1.2.5.

(1) a. /í=kí-hé/   íí=kíhê   AU=7-time
     b. /í=kí-nógò/   í=kínógò   AU=7-hole
     c. /á=bá-nà/   áá=bánà   AU=2-four
     d. /á=bá-àná/   á=bāānà   AU=2-child

Another example in which this lengthening process is helpful in differentiating clitics from affixes is in locative markers. These are often referred to in the literature as locative "prefixes",[16] but a look at the linguistic evidence shows that in use with nouns, locatives are clitics in Kifuliiru. These markers include the cl. 16 **há**, 17 **kú**, 18 **mú**, and 23 **í**.[17] In (2a) the vowel of the locative marker **há** is lengthened before the noun **kítì** 'tree', which contains only two morae. However that locative marker retains its short vowel when occurring before the noun **lwííjì** 'river', which contains three morae.

(2)   Underlying   Gloss   Surface   Gloss
     a.   /há=kí-tì/   16=7-tree   háá=kítì   'at the tree'
     b.   /há=lú-ìji/   16=11-river   há=lwīījì   'at the river'

2.3 Mora-based vowel shortening

One of the most helpful indications of word breaks in Kifuliiru is found in the mora-based vowel shortening rule. This rule states that any long vowel is shortened if there are three or more morae following within the word. Rules with similar effects exist in several Bantu languages,[18] operating over different domains, such as the word, the phrase, etc. in different languages.[19]

---

[16] Locative class concord prefixes do exist, and are found in demonstratives **múnò** 'in here', verbs **hálì** 'there are', **hákábá** 'there were', adjectives **hálà** 'far' (e.g. **á=háándú hálà** 'a far place'), **hágùmà** 'one place, certain place', etc. Vowel lengthening is not observed in the prefixes, no matter how few morae follow. The locative markers attached to full nominal forms are, on the other hand, clitics rather than prefixes. In these there is vowel length when fewer than three morae follow.

[17] This last locative, **i**, is referred to in the literature with various labels: as 23, (which is a renumbering of Meeussen's 24 (Katamba 2003); as 24 (Meeussen 1967, Schadeberg 2003), and as 25 (Guldemann 1999 and Bastin 2003). Gauton (1999) states that locative class 24 is reconstructed as **ka-** and that locative cl. 25 is reconstructed with the same form as cl. 9, **n(I)-**, and not as **i-**. We are using only the cl. 23 label for the **i** locative.

[18] Similar shortening (or lack of lengthening) is found in the context of reduplicated verbs in Luganda (Hyman 1992) and works at the level of a prosodic phrase in Chimwini (Hayes 1989).

[19] In the case where such a rule works over the domain of the phrase, it would probably not be of significant help in determining word boundaries, but only phrase boundaries.

The domain of this shortening rule in Kifuliiru is the phonological word.[20] The rule shortens any long vowel followed by three or more morae. Since there is also a constraint against (phonologically) word-final vowel length in any phrase position in Kifuliiru, the combined effect of these two rules is that long vowels may appear only in the antepenultimate or penultimate syllable of a word.

The rule's usefulness in determining word boundaries is clear. If there is no phonetic lengthening following a glide in a non-final syllable, or preceding a NC sequence within a word, it is clear that there are at least three morae following within the word. On the other hand, if the long vowel in a word is still long despite the presence of an enclitic which brings to three the number of morae following it, this shows that the clitic is not counted as a part of the phonological word. For example, in Kifuliiru, monosyllabic pronominal objects, may be joined to the end of a verb. Does such an object become a part of the verb, or is it peripheral to it? The easiest way to find out is to check for patterns of vowel length in the host to which the clitic is attached. If a long vowel in the antepenultimate position of the host word remains long, as it was without the clitic, the clitic has not become a part of the phonological word.

Take for example the applicative verb **kubiikira** 'put something away for/at', which has a long vowel in the antepenultimate position. When it is followed by a monosyllabic pronominal element, does this clitic become a part of the phonological word? Looking at the vowel length in **àmúbííkírà=kyô** 'he put it (cl. 7) away for him', we see that the vowel of the radical, -**biik**- is not shortened, i.e. -**biikira** > -**biikira=kyo**. (The vowel length in the radical is just the same as it is with only two morae following in the non-applicative form **àmúbíìkà=mwô** 'he put him in there', or in **àmúhéèzà=kyô** 'he gave it to him'.) Contrast this with a form in which suffixes, rather than clitics bring to three the number of morae following. Adding the intensive extension gives such an example where three morae within the suffixes causes the shortening of the underlyingly long vowel of the radical: -**bíík-iriz-a** becomes -**bikiriza**. The lack of shortening in **àmúbííkírà=kyô** indicates that the enclitic is not counted as a mora in the same lexical word as the verb stem, and thus that though the pronoun is encliticized, there is still a word break between the verb and the pronoun. This indicates that orthographically, it would be a mistake to write the clitic as a part of the verb stem in the same manner one would indicate a suffix.

---

[20]The phonological word seems to include a phrase with a phrase level proclitic, such as an associative phrase, e.g. **bya'baandu** 'of the people', but does not include an enclitic, nor a proclitic which functions at clause level, e.g. **kwo** 'that', **ka** 'question marker'.

2.4 Lexical and postlexical level vowel coalescence

Another feature of Kifuliiru which is helpful in determining the difference between clitics and affixes is the fact that there are two sets of rules of vowel coalescence, one set which works at the lexical (word-building) level, and another which works at the postlexical (syntactic) level. This makes it possible in many cases[21] to determine if a juncture is that of an affix plus a stem or a monosyllabic clitic plus another whole-word unit.

At the lexical (word-building) level, total assimilation of non-high vowels to any following vowel is the rule. There are no exceptions to this rule.

At the boundary of a prefix or suffix with a root or stem, the following rule of vowel coalescence always applies: A non-high, non-back vowel[22] (e[23] or **a**) assimilates totally to any following vowel at morpheme boundaries within the word. The result is a long vowel. Examples are shown in (3), where prefixes, all ending in **a**, assimilate totally to the following vowel.

(3)

Cl.	Prefix	Stem	Word	Gloss
2	bá-	-ìra	bììrà	'friends'
2	bá-	-eru	bēērù	'white'
6	má-	-enge	mēēngè	'mental abilities'
2	bá-	-ana	bāānà	'children'
6	gá-	-óòhê	góòhê	'they'
16	há-	-òfi	hòòfì	'near'
2	bá-	-ùbasi	bùùbásì	'builders'

Vowel coalescence at the postlexical (syntactic) level, on the other hand, that is, coalescence at the boundaries of syntactic words, results in what can be termed partial or reciprocal assimilation, following this rule: When a

---

[21] In some cases, such as the juxtaposition of two identical vowels, or the glide formation that takes place when the first of two juxtaposed vowels is a high vowel, the result of vowel coalescence is identical under both rules. In the remaining cases, however, the result of the coalescence is different at the two levels.

[22] A high vowel, whether front or back, always undergoes glide formation when followed by a vowel. A mid back vowel (found in such cases only due to vowel height harmony in verbal extensions where the underlying vowel might be underlyingly represented by a high back vowel), also undergoes desyllabification to **w**.

[23] Since prefixes in Kifuliiru never have mid vowels, and verbal extensions contain mid vowels only as a result of vowel height harmony, the only case in which an **e** has occasion to be followed by another vowel is in the case of an applicative extension (which could arguably be underlyingly represented as -ir) harmonizes to a mid vowel and is followed by the perfective (resultative) ending, which begins with an **i** which conditions the deletion of the **r**, thus leaving the **e** (or **i**) of the applicative juxtaposed to the following **i**. The result in this case is **ii**.

non-high vowel (**e**, **o**, or **a**) is juxtaposed to any other vowel at a word boundary, the result is a long vowel[24] which exhibits the height of the first vowel (i.e. non-high) and the "backness" (or lack of it) of the second vowel. (Note that we have classed **e** as a front vowel, **o** as a back vowel, and **a** as neither front nor back.) For example, the coalescence of **e** (a non-high front vowel) with **u** (a high back vowel) results in **o** (a non-high back vowel). Examples follow in (4).

(4)	Vowels	Underlying	Orthographic	Gloss
a.	e+u > oo	yé=ùùlyá	yolya	'he is that.R very one'
b.	e+u > oo	yé=ú-gá-yáng-à	yo'gayanga	'she whom you will marry'
c.	e+i > ee	yé=í-gá-vwèjàgìr-à	ye'gavwejagira	'he whom it (cl. 9) will devour'
d.	o+a > aa	bó=á-ká-bùng-án-à	ba'kabungana	'those he moved with'
e.	o+i > ee	mwó=í-sìkù zì-biri	mwe'siku zibiri	'in there two days'
f.	a+i > ee	ya=í-n-gòkò	ye'ngoko	'of the chicken'
g.	a+u > oo	ya=ú-mú-ndù	yo'mundu	'of the person'

As noted above, when two vowels coalesce, they form a long vowel. However, whether or not the surface result is a long vowel depends on prosodic factors: when there are three or more morae following within the word to which a proclitic is attached, the long vowel is shortened by the mora-based vowel shortening rule, discussed in 2.3.

Even though they seem to reflect postlexical vowel coalescence rules, the emphatic demonstratives, such as **yóòlyâ** 'that.R very (one)' (from **yé=ùlyá** lit. 'he is the one who is that.R one', orthographic representation **yolya**) in (4a), are written as a single word, because the combination has been lexicalized, as witnessed by the fact that the unit now functions syntactically as a modifier or pronoun, and that the emphatic copula **ye** 'he is the one', which was originally a part of the demonstrative may precede it, e.g. **yé=yóòlyâ** 'he is (the one who is) that.R very one'. The conflict between evidence of postlexical level coalescence in these words, which indicates that they are (or were) two words, and the syntactic evidence that that this combination has been lexicalized is one of the "gray areas" of word breaks. When the two types of evidence conflict, the syntactic evidence is given more weight in determining orthographic word breaks than the phonological evidence. Of course, the

---

[24]With the exception that word finally, a phonemic long vowel is not allowed.

reaction of speakers of the language to the various orthographic options is also a very important factor.

Associative phrases give further insight into the application of the postlexical level coalescence rules, as well as into how they interact with monosyllable cliticization and the mora-based shortening rule. The associative marker is a clitic added to a complete word at the postlexical level. When there is coalescence between the vowel of the associative marker and the augment, the quality of the vowel produced by the coalescence is characteristic of postlexical rather than lexical level coalescence. With lexical level coalescence, the vowel **a** always assimilates completely to a following vowel (e.g. **a** + **i** > **ii**). As seen in (5 a, c, and d), this is not the case, thus giving further evidence that the associative marker is a separate word, and not an affix.

(5) Underlying   Phonetic   Gloss
  a. /á má-gí <u>ga í</u> í-bááta/   áá=mágí gí=báátà   'the eggs of the duck (cl. 5)'
  b. /á má-gi <u>ga í</u> n-gòkò/   áá=mágí géé=ngòkò   'the eggs of the chicken (cl. 9)'
  c. /á má-hèèmbe <u>ga í</u> n-káàvu/ á=máhèèmbè gé=ngáàvù   'the horns of the cow (cl. 9)'
  d. /ú lú-háànde <u>lwa í</u> kí-hùgo/ ú=lúháàndè <u>lwé=kíhùgò</u> 'part of the country (cl. 7)'

Note in (5a) that preceding cl. 5 nouns, the associative marker (or any other proclitic) has a final -**i** vowel in the surface form, though it has a final -**e** preceding nouns of any other classes which have an **i** augment. Compare the cl. 5 associative phrase with the examples from cl. 9 (5 b-c) and cl. 7 (5 d), which also have an **i** augment.[25] We assume that coalescence in the case of cl. 5 is "marked" and does not follow the default coalescence rules, in order to preserve the shape of the cl. 5 prefix.[26]

The examples in (5) also show that the vowel of the cliticized A.M is shortened when three or more morae follow within the word. Example (5b), where there are only two morae following the A.M, is the only example in the set above in which the vowel of the A.M remains long, because all the others have three following morae.

---

[25] The coalescence of the A.M with augments of cl. 4, 7, 8 (all of which have **i** augment) is identical to that shown for cl. 9.

[26] This "markedness" may have developed due to the fact that the cl. 5 prefix **i** was preceded by an identical augment **i**.

Further examples illustrating the application of postlexical vowel coalescence and mora-based vowel shortening are given in (6).

(6) Associative marker and vowel coalescence

	A.M	AU=noun	Surface	Gloss
a.	lwa̱	í=kítí	lwé̱é=kítì	'of the tree (cl. 7)'
b.	lwa̱	á=bāānà	lwá̱=bāānà	'of the children (cl. 2)'
c.	lwa̱	ú=lúhù	lwó̱ó=lúhù	'of the skin (cl. 11)'
d.	lwa̱	ú=mwāānà	lwó̱=mwāānà	'of the child (cl. 1)'

2.5 Tonal contours

In Kifuliiru, a tonal contour may surface only on the penultimate syllable of a word. A contour, whether HL or LH, never occurs, either underlyingly or on the surface, in any non-penultimate syllable. Thus, whenever there is a surface realization of HL or LH (except where HL occurs utterance finally due to the phonetic Final H Contouring rule, see 3.12.5) it flags the penultimate syllable of a word.

Knowing that a contour at the word level occurs only penultimately is very helpful in determining word breaks in multiword verb phrases. Since verbs in Bantu languages are highly agglutinative, it is tempting for those making orthography decisions to write multiword verbs as single words, assuming that they are simply multimorphemic, when they may actually contain word-level auxiliaries. An example of a multiword verb form in which the HL contour signals a word break is the Kifuliiru past state verbs, e.g. áàlì gwèjíírì 'he was (in the state of) having lain down'. In such verbs, there is only one subject marker, so one might assume that there is only one word in the verb phrase. However, the HL contour on the first syllable is a linguistic indicator that that syllable is in the penultimate position in its word. Thus we know that a word break follows the syllable after the one which bears the HL contour.

This verb form which denotes an ongoing state in the past (P3) combines the past form of the copular auxiliary -li 'is' with a resultative form of the main verb. Tonally, the main verb stem in this form bears the grammatical tone characteristic of this tense. It does not take an infinitive tone as do main verbs in the majority of multiword verb forms (see 3.2). However, the presence of a HL contour in the auxiliary is a clear indication that there is a word break following the auxiliary, since a HL contour may occur only penultimately in a word.

(7) a. **á-àlí shúlìs-ír-ì**   'he was hitting'
　　　1-P3 hit-RS-Fi

　　b. **bá-àlí bòn-ès-ír-ì**   'they appeared/seemed'
　　　2-P3 see-CS-RS-Fi

In the case of these forms, the long vowel which bears the HL contour is word-initial when the subject is third-person singular, as shown in (7a). Speakers of the language did not like the idea of using a word-initial long vowel, as would have happened in third-person singular forms. In addition, in many other verb forms, an initial long vowel created by such concatenation of morphemes is often followed by three or more morae, and therefore not phonetically long. The orthographic indication of underlying length in cases where it is not phonetically realized can be helpful for readers, as it maintains a stable morpheme shape in all cases. However, it causes difficulties for writers, especially those who are linguistically naive,[27] when the written form does match the spoken form. To complicate matters, the most common site where phonetic word-initial vowel length *is* found is in nominal augments followed by a noun of only two morae. Here the length is neither underlying nor contrastive. Thus the decision was made not to use long word-initial vowels anywhere in the orthography.

Since the verbal auxiliary in this case always has only one mora, -li 'is', which follows the prefixes, the vowel length in the prefixes in this case is stable. Consistently using a long vowel to indicate the concatenation of the subject prefix and the tense prefix would present a problem, however, because orthographically, long vowels are not indicated following a glide, and a significant number of subject prefixes are vowel-final, yielding a glide when the prefix precedes a vowel-initial TAM prefix.[28] Therefore the orthographic convention of a circumflex accent over a short vowel was chosen instead to indicate this tense, e.g. **âli** 's/he was', **bâli** 'they were', **wâlì** 'you (SG) were', **atâli** 's/he was not'. The circumflex represents the semantic meaning of the

---

[27]Linguistically naive here means "not consciously aware of word categories such as nouns, verbs, etc., nor of the underlying morphological makeup of complex words." An orthography which is too complex in its rules will discourage learners and intimidate teachers, who will be afraid of making mistakes in front of their pupils.

[28]Having simple and, insofar as possible, exceptionless rules very significantly increases ease of writing. Once exceptions to rules are made, correct spelling becomes a much greater challenge. It is possible, however, to teach a few key exceptions that are based on semantic meaning, e.g. related to a specific tense or semantic item. If, on the other hand, exceptions are made on the basis of a grammatical class marking tones in all tense markers or only on the first syllable of verb stems, or marking vowel length only in verbs, or only in noun class prefixes etc., both the amount of instruction needed to teach the orthography and the level of education necessary to use it correctly increase very significantly.

past state, which readers interpret with the appropriate HL contour as well as the necessary vowel length. This diacritic is used orthographically only in the representation of this specific verb form.

It is the circumflex accent, then, which distinguishes this past resultative form of the copula, **áàlì** 's/he was' (orthographically **âli**) from the present form, e.g. **àlì** (orthographically **ali**) 's/he is', which can also be used as an auxiliary: e.g. **àlì mú=gééndà** 's/he is going'. Both the past and present forms of the copula can also be used as independent verbs, as shown in the following orthographic forms: **àlì hánò** 'he is here'; **âlì hánò** 'he was here'.

The use of the circumflex enables the past copula to maintain a stable orthographic representation whether used as an independent verb, e.g. (orthographic) **âlì mwámbází wó'lúgòlò** 'he was a wearer of a snake bone', or in a multiword verb form, e.g. (orthographic) **yé'wâlì kìzì sháágwà** 'he was the one who was respected'.

3 Grammatical indicators of word boundaries in verbs

There are several syntactic/grammatical indicators of word breaks within verbs. They are listed here, and exemplified and discussed in this section:

- Presence of multiple subject prefixes
- Presence of an infinitive form of the main verb following a conjugated auxiliary
- Absence of subjunctive FV on the main verb stem in subjunctive verbs
- Placement of the pre-final emphatic extension, **-ag**
- Realization of the grammatical tone of the verb on an auxiliary

3.1 Multiple subject prefixes

The presence of two subject markers in a given verb form is an unequivocal indicator that the verb form is made up of two words. Thus, forms like **à-gwéétí á-gágéèndà** 'he is intentionally going', **tù-kòlà tú-gágéènda** 'we are about to go', or **bà-nágéèndà bá-gálóòzâ** 'and they went looking for something', each of which have a subject prefix at the beginning of each word, are clearly two-word forms.

In such forms, the two verbs together are being used to express a single idea, but they are still two words. Further examples of verb forms with two subject markers are:

(8)

Form	Surface	Gloss
Progressive state with intention	bàgwéétí bágááshólà	'they are (intentionally) playing mankala'
New state with intention	tùkòlà túgááshólà	'we are about to play mankala'
Recent past frustrated with new state	útákòlà úgááshólà	'you (sg) were just about to play mankala, but....'
Previous state, contrary-to-fact	àshùbà ágááshólà	'he was going to play mankala (but didn't)'

3.2 Infinitive following auxiliary

When a conjugated auxiliary is followed by a typical infinitive form, there is a word break before the infinitive. Even when the infinitive occurs without the usual infinitive prefix, there is probably a word break preceding the infinitive. In Congo Swahili, such forms are common, e.g. **ame<u>kwi</u>sha ku<u>fi</u>ka ~ ame<u>kwi</u>sha <u>fi</u>ka ~ ame<u>i</u>sha ku<u>fi</u>ka ~ a<u>me</u>sha ku<u>fi</u>ka ~ a<u>me</u>sha <u>fi</u>ka** 'he has arrived'. As seen in these examples, the infinitive may or may not exhibit the usual infinitive prefix in such cases, but stress patterns (always penultimate in Swahili, and indicated above by underlining) still indicate the presence of two words. In Kifuliiru verbs, the usual form of the infinitive has a cl. 15 **kú-** prefix. Following an auxiliary, however, the infinitive is synchronically prefixless, e.g. **àgééndì lólà** 'he went to look'. Nonetheless, phonological factors still point to the presence of two separate words, and the tonal pattern found on the final word is that found in the infinitive (see also 3.5).

Verbs which include an auxiliary followed by a prefixless infinitive include forms that have a copular auxiliary (e.g. **-shùba** 'previously') as the first member of the verb phrase, while the second member is a prefixless infinitive preceded by the locative 18 **mú** 'in' marker. The cl. 18 locative has been grammaticized as a marker of progressive action, indicating that something is "in" the state of doing something. The use of the locative for such purposes is common; Bybee (1994:129) notes that "the majority of progressive forms in our database derive from expressions involving locative elements."

In its verbal use, the clitic **mu**, like the locative, is affected by the rule which lengthens the vowel of a clitic. In (9a) note the lengthening of the progressive aspect marker **mú**, when cliticized to the verb stem which contains only two morae.

(9) Surface Gloss
  a. àshùbà <u>múú</u>=gúlà 'he was buying something'
  b. àshùbà <u>mú</u>=byáálà 'he was planting something'

Because the progressive marker is still subject to the rule of clitic vowel lengthening, and in order to make it readily distinguishable orthographically from the two object prefixes of the same shape (**mú-** 'him/her', and **mù-** 'you PL', both of which are marked with orthographic tone) which may also occur in the pre-stem position in the verb, but which are not clitics, we have chosen to indicate progressive **mú** with the apostrophe which distinguishes clitics in Kifuliiru. The following orthographic forms illustrate the use of the three segmentally similar morphemes: **ashuba mu'gulira...** he was buying for (someone), vs. **agamúgulira** he will buy for him versus **agamùgulira** 'he will buy for you (PL)'.

The copulas which form the first word of these progressive verb phrases are self-standing verbs which may also be used as independent copulas, i.e. -**li** 'is', -**kòla** 'is now (not before)', -**shùba** 'was before (not now)'. Since these are all independent words, there is no reason to believe that the progressive phrase, e.g. **mú=byáálà** '(in) planting' or **múú=gúlà** '(in) buying', is "suffixed" to them in the case of a progressive verb form. Thus the orthographic representation for all these forms is with three words, of which the **mú** is indicated as a clitic, e.g. **ashuba mu'byala** 'he was planting (something)', **akola mu'byala** 'he is now planting (something)', and **ali mu'byala** 'he is planting (something)'.

Another very commonly occurring multiword verb form uses the prefixless infinitive preceded by one of the 'adverbial' auxiliaries: -**kìzi** 'repeatedly', -**gééndi** 'going', -**yííji** 'coming', -**zíínduki** 'early in the morning', -**shùbi** 'again', etc. These auxiliaries can be used with tenses and aspects which would otherwise be one word forms (e.g. **ágá<u>géèndì</u> byáálà** 'he will go plant', cf. **ágábyààlà** 'he will plant'), or they can be used with forms which have double subject markers (<u>àkòlà</u> <u>ágágéèndì</u> **byáálà** 'he is about to go plant', cf. **àkòlà ágábyààlà** 'he is about to plant') or in single-subject forms with a copular auxiliary as the first member, such as the progressive forms with **mú**, etc. (**àkòlà mú=<u>gééndì</u> byáálà** 'he is now going planting', **áàlì kìzì <u>géénd</u>ì <u>byáálà</u>** 'he always used to go plant', etc.).

Most of the adverbial auxiliaries, such as -**gééndi** 'going', from -**géénd-à** 'go' derive from a verb in current usage. Besides the fact that these auxiliaries are formed from verb stems, there are multiple linguistic arguments for a word break following each auxiliary. These include the morphological arguments found in 3.3 and 3.4, as well as the following two phonological arguments:

1) The phonetic realization of compensatory lengthening of vowels in adverbial auxiliaries demonstrates that there are fewer than three morae following within the word. This is phonological proof for a word break after the auxiliary, **géendi** in (10a), and **zíínduki** in (10b). The main verb following the auxiliary is not counted as a part of the same word. If it were, there would be more than three morae following in both these cases, and the long vowels in the auxiliaries would have been shortened.

(10) a. **tw-àná-géèndì síímb-à** 'and we went and jumped'
 1PL-SQ-GOING jump-Fa

 b. **à-tà-ná-zííndùkì hík-à** 'and he did not arrive early in the morning'
 1-NEG-SQ-EARLY.MORNING arrive-Fa

2) Given the appropriate grammatical tones, a falling contour is possible in adverbial auxiliaries with a long vowel. The presence of a falling contour demonstrates that the long vowel is in the penultimate position in its word. This is further phonological proof for a word break following the auxiliary, -**géèndì** in (11a), and -**yîìjì** in (11b). The main verb following the auxiliary is not counted as a part of the same word, or there would be more than one syllable following in both these cases. Because a falling contour only occurs on a long vowel, no falling contour is possible in a case where the auxiliary has a short vowel, as -**shùbi** in (11c). However, since such auxiliaries appear in the same syntactic "slot" as the ones which are obviously separate words, by analogy they also are assumed to be separate words.

(11) a. **tú-gá-géèndì síímb-à** 'we will go jump'
 1PL-F2-GOING jump-Fa

 b. **à-tá-gá-yîìjì tù-tábáál-à** 'he will not come (to) help us'
 1-NEG-F2-COMING O1.PL-help-Fa

 c. **à-tá-gá-shùbì tù-tábáál-à** 'he will not help us again'
 1-NEG-F2-AGAIN O1.PL-help-Fa

3.3 Subjunctive forms with no subjunctive FV

Single word subjunctive forms always end with the FV -**e**, e.g. **ùgéénde** '(may/that) you (SG) go', **tùbàtábààle** 'that we/let's help them', etc. However, in a subjunctive verb form to which an auxiliary has been added, making a multiword verb form, the subjunctive final vowel -**e** does not occur on either word,[29] e.g. **ùgééndí hìgúlíísâ** '(may/that) you (SG) go sell it (cl. 19)', **ùté gēēndà**[30] '(may/that) you (SG) first go'. It is only the tone and the lack of a tense marker on the first word of the form, and the context, which indicates that a two-word verb is subjunctive rather than indicative. The semantically main verb of most two-word verb forms is a prefixless infinitive, with the infinitive tone pattern. Because only the first word of the form has subjunctive tone, and the subjunctive final vowel and subjunctive tone do *not* appear on the semantically main verb, we can assume that there is a word break which intervenes.

Observe (12) below, showing that the subjunctive -**e** does not appear anywhere in subjunctive form with the auxiliary, due to the word break occasioned by the adverbial auxiliary, which has a stable final vowel.

(12) Subjunctive   Subjunctive with aux
    tù-síímb-è̱ 'let's jump'   cf. **tù-gééndì síímb-a̱** 'let's go jump'
    1PL-jump-Fe   1PL-GOING jump-Fa

    à-hík-è̱ 'may he   cf. **à-zííndúkí hík-a̱** 'may he arrive
    1-arrive-Fe   arrive'   1-EARLY.AM arrive-Fa   early in morning'

In subjunctive forms with adverbial auxiliaries the main verb does not exhibit the subjunctive FV, e.g. **ùté gēēndà** '(may you) first go', presumably because of the word break. Basic imperatives likewise never have the subjunctive FV -**e**, but rather the default FV -**a**, as in **géèndâ** 'go!'. Imperative forms with adverbial auxiliaries, such as **té=gēēndè̱**[31] 'first go', **té=shùbì yíímbè̱** 'first sing again', and **géèndì múbwììrè̱** 'go tell him' are interesting, however, because they *do* have a subjunctive final vowel (FV) on the main verb. Such hybrids between imperatives and subjunctives are somewhat uncommon forms. Most often, when a request or order is made using a verb with an adverbial auxiliary, the true imperative (a form with no subject prefix) is

---

[29] The remote future tense (F3) is an exception to this, e.g. **twááyè géèndè** 'we will go REM', since the FV -**e** does appear on the second part of these two word forms. The realization of the subjunctive tone pattern on the second word of the verb in this case indicates that the first word is a separate auxiliary, because any prefixes attached to the main verb cancel out the subjunctive pattern. For more details see the discussion in (3.5.3.3.7).

[30] The adverbial auxiliary **té** ~ **tí** 'first' is apparently a grammaticized and abbreviated form of **táángì** 'first' and has a floating L tone which causes downstep of the H tone of the following word. The final vowel of an adverbial auxiliary is invariable, so the **é** of **té** is *not* a subjunctive final vowel.

[31] As noted earlier **té** (~ **tí**) is also an auxiliary, though it does not have the characteristic shape and final -**i**. It is likely a shortened form of **táángì**. The elision of the vowel on which the final L tone was realized leaves a floating L tone, which is why this auxiliary conditions downstep in a following H tone.

not used. A subjunctive form is most often used to convey the order, e.g. **ùté gēēndà** '(may you) first go'. In this latter case, where the auxiliary has a subject prefix, it is a separate word, and the main verb, which occurs after the word break, has no subjunctive final vowel. It is only in the imperative-type form that we find the use of the subjunctive FV on the main verb of a form that includes an adverbial auxiliary. It is not clear why the main verb *does* have the subjunctive FV in imperatives which include adverbial auxiliaries. Imperative forms which do *not* involve adverbial auxiliaries never have the subjunctive FV, so to find it in these multiword imperatives is unexpected.

It is clear, however, from the fact that it is possible to have long vowels in the auxiliary in imperative forms such as e.g. **géèndì múbwììrè** 'go tell him', that though they exhibit the subjunctive final vowel (and the subjunctive tone pattern) on the main verb, these forms still contain separate words.

3.4 Placement of pre-final emphatic -*ag* extension

In the case of a multi word form which has only a single subject prefix, the placement of a pre-final extension can give a clue to word breaks. In verb forms with auxiliaries, we see that the emphatic extension, if it is used, is placed on the first verbal auxiliary[32] to the right of the prefixes. Because the emphatic extension -**ag** always occurs just before a final vowel (with the exception a passive or causative extension may intervene between empahtic and the FV), its placement indicates that a word break follows within the multiword verb. An example of the emphatic in a one-word verb form is shown in (13) followed only by a locative phrase, while its placement in two-word verb forms is exemplified in (14–16).

(13)   …gw-àná-sìgál-ág-á ‖   mú=   yìì-z-ó   nyámà.
         3-SQ-remain-EMP-Fa   18=   those.N-10-P.R   10+meat

   '…and it remained ‖ among that meat.'

(14)   **ù-tá-géénd-àg-ì**   **yì-bwátál-ír-à**
         2SG-NEG-GOING-EMP-Fi   RFX-sit-APL-Fa

   'Don't just go sit.'

---

[32] Often two or three auxiliaries are used within a single verb form, with a word break following each auxiliary.

(15) Háyí | h-à=   mú=   géénd-ág-í   kōl-à?
      where 16-O.FOC+1=   F1=   GOING-EMP-Fi work-Fa

'Where | is it that he is about to go work?'

(16) ...à-ná-kìz-ág-í   gù-bwíír-à.
      1-SQ-REP-EMP-Fi   O3.-tell-Fa

'and he repeatedly told it.'

Other examples of the placement of the emphatic extension in a multiword verb form are shown in (17).

(17) Surface   Gloss
      ù-shúb-ág-ì yííjì n-yááng-à   '(that) you again come and marry me EMP'
      2SG-AGAIN-EMP-Fi COMING
      O1.SG-marry-Fa

      bà-kòl-àg-í gwèètì bá-gáá-hík-à   'they are now arriving EMP'
      2-NEWLY-EMP-Fi PROG 2-F2-arrive-Fa

      bà-ná-géénd-àg-í zíík-à   'and they went and buried (s/o) EMP'
      2-SQ-GOING-EMP-Fi bury-Fa

      á-gá-kíz-àg-ì n-góómbék-à   'he will repeatedly hand-feed me EMP'
      1-F2-REP-EMP-Fi O1.SG-hand.feed-Fa

      ù-kíz-ág-ì géénd̀ì húún-à   '(may) you repeatedly go and beg EMP'
      2SG-REP-EMP-Fi GOING request-Fa

3.5 Grammatical tone of the verb stem

In most multiword verb forms, the grammatical tone of the verb form is realized on the auxiliary to which the prefixes are attached. This is not surprising, since in a single-word verb the grammatical tone is realized on the first free mora of the radical, which also occurs directly to the right of the prefixes. The semantically "main" (syntactically final) verb of a multiword form with an adverbial auxiliary is always given an infinitive tone pattern.

If the auxiliary and the main verb were combined as a single word, tone spread rules would apply to the grammatical tone, and there would be no infinitive tone realized on the main verb. Examples are given in (18), where

(18a–c) show single word verbs, while (18d–e) show verbs of the same two tenses, future (F2) and past (P2), with an auxiliary.

(18) Verb form Gloss and (comments)

    a. **ú=kú-shúlík-à** 'to hit' (Note infinitive H tone on underlined mora.)
       AU-15-hit-Fa

    b. **bá-gá-shúlìk-à** 'They will hit' (Note F2 L tone on underlined mora.)
       2-F2-hit-Fa

    c. **bá-ká-shúlík-à** 'They hit' (Note P2 H tone on underlined mora.)
       2-P2-hit-Fa

cf. d. **bá-gá-géèndì shúlík-à** 'They will go and hit' (F2 L occurs now on second mora of auxiliary, and not on the main verb)
       2-F2-GOING hit-Fa

    e. **bá-ká-gééndì shúlík-à** 'They went and hit' (Note that the auxiliary in this case has the H grammatical tone of the P2.)
       2-P2-GOING hit-Fa

The HL contour on the auxiliary in (18d) is further indication that there is a word break following it, since HL contour is only realized on penultimate syllables.

4 Other word break issues

4.1 Clause-level clitics

Besides phrase-level clitics such as the augment and associative marker, Kifuliiru also has several proclitics which introduce clauses: **mbu** 'that (unrealized)', **kwo** 'that', etc., **lyo** 'that's when', **bwo** 'since', **si** 'it's obvious', **ka** 'question marker', and **ti** <quote>. Examples of these, taken from texts, are presented in (19). As can be seen in the examples below, clause-level proclitics behave differently from proclitics which function at the phrase level, in that they are not subject to the rule of clitic-related vowel lengthening. Instead, they are lengthened only when there is coalescence between the final vowel of the clitic and the initial vowel of the following word, such as is seen in (19e), where the underlying form is **lyó ùbùtà**. The length thus produced is not subject to shortening by the mora-based shortening rule. The vowel of a clause-level clitic also seems to be subject to lengthening due to a following NC cluster, as in (19g and i), though there may be additional issues such as clitic-related lengthening involved as well. More research could be done on clause-level clitics. The highlighted clitics in (19) are aligned below.

(19) Proclitics before clauses

	Surface			Gloss
a.	àtànákìlííndìrà	mb<u>ú</u>=	nyínà àgálúkè	'and he did not still wait (for) his mother (to) return'
b.	bànágírá	mb<u>ú</u>=	bàgìtùmìtè	'and they tried that they spear it'
c.	ànábwîìrà bákáàgè	kw<u>ó</u>=	bàlì bàshàtù	'and he told his wives, (that) they are three'
d.	ká=kùtàlì	kw<u>ó</u>=	mwààmì àtùbwíírà	'Is it not how the king told us?'
e.	bìrì kwóòkwó	ly<u>óò</u>=	bùtà dúbà	'It's that way (because) that's when you give birth quickly.'
f.	kúú=yùlwó lúsìkù	ly<u>ò</u>=	múgáshíbùùkà	'On that day is when you will finish the funeral.'
g.	ámbáágírà úlúhàzì	bw<u>óò</u>=	ndí múgénì	'She slaughtered for me a rooster, since I am a guest.'
h.	tùtááhágé	bw<u>ó</u>=	wàláhìrà	'Let's go home since you refuse'
i.		s<u>ìì</u>=	ndí lúkúùngù	'But it's obvious I am dust'
j.		s<u>í</u>=	lùtàhùùmbá ngáá=nvùlà	'But it's obvious it is not finished like rain'
k.		k<u>á</u>=	bìrì úúkùlì	'Is it the truth?'
l.		k<u>á</u>=	mùtàzí múbààgâ	'Haven't you (PL) butchered him yet?'
m.		t<u>ì</u>=	léká kààndì	'(quote) leave (it) again'
n.	Mwààmí	t<u>í</u>=	náàngà	'The king (quote) no'

Other clause-level clitics are the words which function both as emphatic copulas and object relative markers: **níè** 1SG, **wê** 2SG, **yê** cl. 1, **twê** 1PL, **mwê**

2PL, **bô** cl. 2, **gwô** cl. 3, **yô** cl. 4, **lyô** cl. 5, **gô** cl. 6, **kyô** cl. 7, **byô** cl. 8, **yô** cl. 9, **zô** cl. 10, **lwô** cl. 11, **kô** cl. 12, **twô** cl. 13, **bwô** cl. 14, **kwô** cl. 15, **hô** cl. 16, **kwô** cl. 17, **mwô** cl. 18, **hyô** cl. 19, and **yô** cl. 23. Those that represent a noun class (i.e. all but the first and second persons) can also function as enclitic pronominal objects. None of these are affected by the clitic-related lengthening rule when joined as a proclitic to a word of fewer than three morae. Like the clitics shown in (19), they display a long vowel only when there is coalescence with the initial vowel of the host word, as in (20a), where the vowel of the clitic in **yéé=rì** 'it is the one' (underlyingly **yó=ìrì** (9-FOC 9-is)) is lengthened, whereas in (20b) the vowel of the clitic remains short, as it is followed by **ø-gáà-bà** '(he) will be', which has no overt subject marker, and thus no initial V. There is thus no coalescence of vowels in (20b). Note that the vowel coalescence which takes place in (20a) is postlexical (**o** + **i** > **e**) and not lexical.

(20) Emphatic copula as proclitic

a.	**ndáré**	**y<u>éé</u>=**	**rì**	**néé=mísì**	'The lion is the one who has strength.'
b.	**yóòyò**	**y<u>é</u>=**	**gáàbà**	**yîìbà**	'That.N same one is the one who will be her husband.'
c.	**kíshókómà**	**ky<u>ó</u>=**	**kìrì**	**néé=mísì**	'The cheetah is the one who has strength.'
d.		**ky<u>ó</u>=**	**kíkátùmá**	**ngáyîìjí bìshámà**	'That's why I came hiding.'

In (21) we see the same rules applying to the object relative markers, which are formally identical to the copulas above.

(21) Object relative markers as proclitics

	bìkí	**by<u>óò</u>=**	**lì múú=gírà**	'What is it that are you doing?'
bìnó	**byóókúlyá**	**by<u>ó</u>=**	**wàtùléétérà**	'this food which you brought us'
yùgú	**múhìní**	**gw<u>óò</u>=**	**gwéétì**	'this handle which you have'
	íkíhùgó	**ky<u>ó</u>=**	**kèré áàlí tùùzìrí=mwô**	'the country which the frog lived in'

4.1.1 Clitics attached to the ends of verbs

A monosyllabic pronominal element may be joined to the end of a verb in lieu of full incorporation as an object prefix. These enclitics are formed from the pronominal "o of reference", and include both locative and non-locative object pronouns, with the exception of the first- and second-person personal pronouns. They follow only verbs, and not other parts of speech. The presence of the enclitic enables a H tone on the penultimate syllable of the verb to spread onto the final vowel, if that final vowel has no other tone. This is just as would be the case with a non-cliticized following object, since H spread will take place whenever the verb is not final in its phrase.

Such an enclitic is not, however, a part of the same phonological word as its host, like a suffix is. The distinctness of a clitic is shown by the fact that the encliticized pronominal element does not count toward the number of morae needed to shorten a vowel within the verb stem. The vowel following the glide in -**gwaatir**- is not shortened, because the enclitic is not counted in the number of morae following it within the word: **bàmúgwáátírà=byô** 'they held them for him' (cf. **bàmúgwáátírà** 'they held (something) for him').

The positioning of HL contours within a verb having a pronominal enclitic also indicates that the enclitic is not counted as a part of the lexical word. This can be seen by the HL contour in the penultimate syllable of the host word in (22d) below, **ànágéèndà=yô**. If the clitic were considered by the tone rules as a part of the word, the long vowel would not fall in the penultimate syllable, and would therefore not have a surface contour, but a simple H tone, as happens when an extension (suffix) is added to the stem, as in **ànágééndèrà**.

(22) Forms cliticized at the end of verbs

Object pronoun	a)	**n-gá-kú-hèèrèz-á** 1SG-F2-O2.SG-give-Fa	**byò** O8		'I will give them to you'
	b)	**bà-ná-mú-fùmbádík-à** 2-SQ-O1-put.in.hand-Fa	**lwô** O11		'and they put it in his hand'
Locative pronoun	c)	**à-ná-mú-kùlíkír-à** 1-SQ-O1-follow-Fa	**mwô** O18		'and he followed him in'
	d)	**à-ná-géènd-à** 1-SQ-go-Fa	**yô** O23		'and he went there'

Just as these pronominal enclitics do not form a part of the same phonological word as their host, they do not seem tightly bound to the verb from the syntactic point of view either. If there is a following word within the clause, the pronominal element joins instead, as a proclitic, to that following word. Below are examples of a clause final clitic, (23), and one which is not clause final, (24). In the first example, **mwô** 'in there' refers to 'in the hole'. Because **mwô** is not followed by another word within the clause, it is cliticized onto the end of the verb -**tìbul-ir-** 'drop down'.

(23)   Á-ká-m-búúmb-ír-á | ú=mw-óóbó   mú-hámù ||
       1-P2-O1.SG-dig-APL-Fa   AU=3-hole   3-big

       à-ná-n-dìbúl-ír-à   =mwô | à-ná-túmbìk-ìr-à.
       1-SQ-O1.SG-drop.down-APL-Fa   =O18   1-SQ-put.cover-APL-Fa

'She dug me a | big hole || and dropped me down in there || and she put a cover (over it).' (35 033)

In (24) by contrast, there is a word following within the clause. In this case the **mwô** is not attached to the verb, but instead is cliticized to the object noun phrase **á=mīījì** 'water'. The fact that it is cliticized rightward in this case is shown by the (obligatory) vowel coalescence which takes place between the clitic (**mwô**) and the augment (**á**) of the cl. 6 noun, changing **mwô** (with final intonation) to **mwá** (with non-final intonation).

(24)   Tù-géèndì   húún-á   mw-á=   mīījì.
       1PL-GOING   request-Fa   18-AU=   6-water

'Let's go ask for water (in) there.' (35 033)

4.1.2 Single syllable verbs as enclitics

Cliticization is not restricted to grammatical "functor" words. A single syllable noun or verb is also cliticized. For example, when the main verb stem in a verb with an adverbial auxiliary consists of a single syllable, it may not stand alone, and is cliticized to the preceding auxiliary. Thus in a verb such as **ágágèèndíì=lyâ** 'he will go eat', the monosyllabic verb stem -**ly**- 'eat' is cliticized to the auxiliary **géèndi** 'going'. Once again we see that the encliticization does not cause enclitic to be counted as part of the same phonological word with its host. This can be seen by the fact that -**géèndì** still has a HL contour on the first syllable, which means that it is still considered to be in penultimate position. This would imply that a word break still immediately follows the final vowel of the auxiliary.

At the same time, the final -**i** of the auxiliary in such forms is lengthened before the cliticized monosyllabic verb stem, in this case -**ly**-. Moreover, the long **ii** which results from the pre-clitic lengthening also bears a falling tone, showing that it also is counted as penultimate, with the cliticized verb stem as the last syllable of the word. It is as though the first mora of the lengthened **i** functions both as a final vowel for the auxiliary and as the initial mora of a bimoraic initial vowel for the verb stem.

The motivation for this situation may lie in the diachronic origins of the form. Historically, the prefixless infinitives used following auxiliaries were cl. 5 infinitives, with an **i**- prefix. The original form of the auxiliary verbs most likely ended with the unmarked FV, -**a**, e.g. **àgéèndà ílyâ* 'he went to eat', or if the augment was used with the cl. 5 infinitive, **àgéèndà îìlyâ*. When the combination was pronounced together, the final -**a** of the initial verb was elided. Then, as the auxiliaries were grammaticized, the prefix of the following infinitive was re-lexicalized as the FV of the auxiliary, so that synchronically, the [non-monosyllabic] infinitives which follow the adverbial auxiliaries have no prefix, e.g. **àgéèndì lólà** 'he went to see'. Perhaps in the case of monosyllabic verbs, the prefix never was removed from the infinitive, since its removal would mean that the infinitive would no longer have met the minimum number of syllables necessary for a verb stem.[33] The retained prefix in these cases, and possibly even an identical augment, could thus be the cause of the extra length in the vowel. Such a scenario would also partially answer the question of why the **ii** seems to function on both sides of the word break, as a final vowel for the auxiliary and an initial one for the infinitive. The underlying makeup of the word synchronically might include a FV -**i** on the auxiliary as well as an **ii**- prefix on the infinitive which follows: e.g. **àgéèndì îìlyà*.

However, the cl. 5 infinitive is no longer in use in Kifuliiru. Speakers do not recognize **îìlyâ** as an infinitive form. Also, since in orthography, predictability and pattern are virtues, and since in all other cases the adverbial auxiliaries are followed by a word break and a prefixless infinitive, the decision stands to write such verbs simply as an auxiliary with a following prefixless infinitive: e.g. (orthographically) **agendi'lya** 'he went and ate'.

---

[33] Retention of the cl. 15 **ku**- prefix with monosyllabic verb stems is observed in Kiswahili, e.g. **ku-l-a** 'to eat' has the perfect form **a-me-ku-l-a** 'he has eaten', imperative **ku-l-a!** 'Eat!', **ku-f-a** 'to die' > **a-me-ku-f-a** 'he has died', but non-monosyllabic verbs do not retain the cl. 15 prefix, e.g. **ku-fik-a** 'to arrive' has the perfect form: **a-me-fik-a** 'he has arrived' (not *a-me-ku-fik-a).

4.2 Vowel coalescence, word breaks, and orthography

As in many orthographies, an apostrophe in Kifuliiru is used to indicate an elided vowel. After a thorough trial of using apostrophes to indicate *all* cliticization, whether involving elision or not, the decision was taken to reduce the number of apostrophes by using them only in cases in which there is mandatory vowel coalescence. Naturally, the decision to indicate all vowel elision by the use of an apostrophe sometimes obscures the identity of the original vowels. The only time this is less than ideal from a literacy point of view is when it obscures the original identity of a verbal subject prefix, e.g. **kwa'gagenda from kwo agagenda** 'that he will go'. The apostrophe indicates not only vowel elision, but cliticization, the melding of two words into one, a process that influences not only vowel quality, but also vowel length and tone realizations, as shown in the discussions above. The processes that take place at the boundary of a proclitic and a host are obligatory at all speech rates. The apostrophe alerts the reader to the fact that the words joined by it, though two lexical words, must be read together as one word. Seeing the apostrophe, the reader is able automatically to make all the adjustments necessary for correct pronunciation.

It should be noted that vowel coalescence commonly occurs in contexts other than just between a clitic and its host. At a normal rate of speech flow there is massive coalescence and elision at word boundaries within phrases and clauses, since all words end with vowels, and many begin with a vowel, such as the nominal augment clitic, or a vowel-initial subject prefix on a verb. However, in these non-clitic contexts, the coalescence is always optional rather than obligatory. In contrast to the obligatory coalescence that takes place in cliticization, the optional coalescence can be "undone", and the words pronounced separately, when speech is slowed down.

A spot where such optional coalescence is usually observed is between a verb and its object or complement. In (25) the final vowel **-a** of the verb coalesces with the nominal augment **u**, cliticized to the complement, and by the rule of postlexical coalescence, the resultant vowel is **o**. Thus the normal spoken form is **ngákúshúlikó músèègérè**. However, in careful speech, this can be pronounced as separate words: **ngákúshúlìkà̲ ú̲=músèègérè**.

(25) N-gá-kú-shúlìk-à̲   ú̲=mú-sèègérè.
     1SG-F2-O2.SG-hit-Fa   AU=3-kick

'I will kick you (lit. I will hit you a blow of the foot).' (407 023)

Likewise in (26) the verb **kyànábwíìrà** 'and it told' and the demonstrative **ùùlyá** 'that.R' coalesce at a normal speech rate to produce **kyànábwíìrò̠lyá múnyérè**. However, this form can be slowed down to **kyànábwíìrà̠ ùùlyá múnyérè** when the words are spoken at a slow rate.

(26) ...ky-àná-bwîîr-à̠   ù̠-lyá   mú-nyérè ‖   tì: «Yíímb-à»
      7-SQ-tell-Fa   1-that.R 1-girl   <quote>   sing-Fa

'...and it told that girl: ‖ <quote>: «Sing!»' (405 016)

The phonetic joining of non-cliticized words within a clause or phrase, since it is "undoable" at slow speeds, must be treated differently in the orthography from the process of cliticization. Sequences in which there is cliticization involving vowel elision cannot be divided into separate words, except by linguistically sophisticated speakers, even when the words are spoken at the very slowest rate. For example, **ú=kúgúlú kwéé̠=mbènè** 'the leg of the goat' will not be pronounced as **ú=kúgúlú kwá̠=íí=mbènè**, no matter how slowly and carefully it is enunciated. This is because the monosyllabic proclitics are obligatorily cliticized, resulting in two phonological words. The accompanying vowel coalescence is also obligatory. This sequence is therefore written as **úkúgúlú kwé'mbènè**.

Orthographic representation of cliticization can aid fluent reading. In orthography design, it is theoretically preferable to keep the shape of any given word as consistent as possible, since fluent readers read by word shape, rather than segment by segment or syllable by syllable. However, if practically speaking there will be a minimal amount of training available for readers and writers, it is helpful if the forms that people are expected to read and write are at least pronounceable and reflect the linguistic intuition of the speakers.

References

Ashton, E. O. et al. 1954. *A Luganda grammar.* London: Longmans.
Ashton, E. O. 1959. *Swahili grammar (including intonation).* London: Longmans.
Bastin, Yvonne. 1983. La finale-IDE et l'imbrication en bantou. (Annales, Série IN-8, Sciences Humaines, no 114.) Tervuren: Musée Royale de l'Afrique Centrale.
Bastin, Yvonne. 2003. The Lacustrine zone (Zone J). In Derek Nurse and Gérard Philippson (eds.), *The Bantu languages,* 501–528. London and New York: Routledge.
Bastin, Yvonne, A. Coupez, and M. Mann. 1999. Continuity and divergence in the Bantu languages; Perspectives from a lexicostatistic study. Tervuren: Musée Royale de l'Afrique Centrale.
Beavon, Keith H. 1990. The locative verb in Kóózime: Its semantic, phonological, morphological, and syntactic attributes. Unpublished manuscript.
Beavon, Keith H. 1991. Kóózime verbal system. In Stephen C. Anderson and Bernard Comrie (eds.), *Tense and aspect in eight languages of Cameroon,* 47–103. Summer Institute of Linguistics and the University of Texas at Arlington Publications in Linguistics, 99. Dallas: Summer Institute of Linguistics and the University of Texas at Arlington.
Beavon, Keith H. 2005. A phonology of Njyem. Unpublished manuscript.
Bickmore, Lee S., and Michael T. Doyle. 1995. Lexical extraprosodicity in Chilungu. *Studies in African Linguistics* 24(2):85–121.
Black, Cheryl. 1995. Boundary tones on word-internal domains in Kinande. *Phonology* 12:1–38.

Blanchon, J. A. 1990. The great *HL split in Bantu group B40. *Pholia* 5:17–29. CRLS. Université Lumière-Lyon 2.

Blanchon, J. A. 1998. Semantic/pragmatic conditions on the tonology of the Kongo noun phrase: A diachronic hypothesis. In Larry M. Hyman and Charles W. Kisseberth (eds.), *Theoretical aspects of Bantu tone*. Stanford: CSLI Publications.

Bresnan, Joan, and Sam Mchombo. 1995. The lexical integrity principle. *Natural Language and Linguistic Theory* 13:181–254.

Bybee, Joan, Revere Perkins, and William Pagliuca. 1994. *The evolution of grammar*. Chicago: The University of Chicago Press.

de Blois, K. F. 1975. Bukusu generative phonology and aspects of Bantu structure. Annales, 85. Tervuren: Musée Royale de l'Afrique Centrale.

Doke, Clement M. 1943. *Outline grammar of Bantu*. Grahamstown: Rhodes University.

Ehret, Christopher. 1999. Subclassifying Bantu: Stem-morpheme innovations. In Jean-Marie Hombert and Larry M. Hyman (eds.), *Bantu historical linguistics*. Stanford: CSLI Publications.

Gauton, Rachélle. 1999. Locative prefix stacking as a earlier viable locativising strategy in Bantu. In Paul F. A. Kotey (ed.), *Trends in African linguistics 3: New dimensions in African linguistics and languages*, 217–232. Trenton, N.J.: Africa World Press.

Givón, Talmy. 1970. On ordered rules and the modified base of ChiBemba verbs. *African Studies* 29:47–54.

Goldsmith, John A. 197A. Autosegmental phonology. PhD dissertation, MIT. Bloomington: Indiana University Linguistics Club. [Published by Garland Press, 1979.]

Goldsmith, John A. 1987. Stem tone patterns of the Lacustrine Bantu languages. In David Odden (ed.), *Current approaches to African linguistics 4*, 167–177. Dordrecht: Foris Publications.

Greenberg, Joseph H. 1977. Niger-Congo noun class markers: Prefixes, suffixes, both or neither. *Studies in African Linguistics*, Supplement 7, December 1977, 94–104.

Greenberg, Joseph H. 1978. How does a language acquire gender markers? In Joseph Greenberg (ed.), *Universals of human language*, vol. 3:47–82. Stanford: Stanford University Press.

Guldemann, Tom. 1999. Head initial meets head final: Nominal suffixes in Eastern and Southern Bantu from a historical perspective. *Studies in African Linguistics* 28:49–91.

Guthrie, Malcolm. 1948. *The classification of the Bantu languages*. London: Oxford University Press for the International African Institute.

Guthrie, Malcolm. 1970. *Collected papers on Bantu linguistics*. Gregg International Publishers. England. (From the article originally published as Bantu word division, *International African Institute Memorandum XXII*, 1948.)
Guthrie, Malcolm. 1971. *Comparative Bantu*, vol. 2. Farnborough, Hants, England: Gregg International Publishers.
Hayes, Bruce. 1989. The prosodic hierarchy in meter. In P. Kiparsky and G. Youmans (eds.), *Phonetics and phonology, 1: Rhythm and meter*, 201-260. San Diego: Academic Press.
Hewitt, Mark, and Alan Prince. 1989. OCP, locality and linking: The N. Karanga verb. *WCCFL* 8:176-191.
Hubbard, K. 1995. Morification and syllablification in Bantu languages. *Journal of African Languages and Linguistics* 16:137-155.
Hyman, Larry M. 1990. Boundary tonology and the prosodic hierarchy. *The phonology-syntax connection*, 109-125. Chicago: University of Chicago Press.
Hyman, Larry M. 1992. Moraic mismatches in Bantu. *Phonology* 9(2):255-265.
Hyman, Larry M. 1995. Minimality and the prosodic morphology of Cibemba imbrication. *Journal of African Languages and Linguistics* 16:3-39.
Hyman, Larry M. 1999. The historical interpretation of Bantu vowel harmony. In Jean-Marie Hombert and Larry M. Hyman (eds.), *Bantu historical linguistics: Theoretical and empirical perspectives*, 235-295. Stanford: CSLI.
Hyman, Larry M. 2003a. Basaá (A43). In Derek Nurse and Gérard Philippson (eds.), *The Bantu languages*, 257. London and New York: Routledge.
Hyman, Larry M. 2003b. Segmental phonology. In Derek Nurse and Gérard Philippson (ed.), *The Bantu languages*, 42-58. London and New York: Routledge.
Hyman, Larry M. 2003c. Sound change, misanalysis, and analogy in the Bantu causative. *Journal of African Languages and Linguistics*: 24:55-90.
Hyman, Larry M. 2003d. Suffix ordering in Bantu: A morphocentric view. In Geert Booij and Jaap van Marle (eds.), *Morphology Yearbook* 2002, 245-281. Dordrecht: Kluwer.
Hyman, Larry M., and Francis X. Katamba. 1990. Spurious high-tone extensions in Luganda. *Southern African Journal of African Languages* 10:142-158.
Hyman, Larry M., and Francis X. Katamba. 1999. The syllable in Luganda phonology and morphology. In Harry van der Hulst and Nancy A. Ritter (eds.), *The syllable: Views and facts*, 349-416. Berlin: Mouton de Gruyter.
Hyman, Larry M., and Francis X. Katamba. 2005. The word in Luganda. In F. K. Erhard Voeltz (ed.), *Studies in African linguistic typology*, 171-193. Amsterdam: John Benjamins.

Hyman, Larry M., and Armindo Ngunga. 1994. On the non-universality of tonal association 'conventions': Evidence from Ciyao. *Phonology* 11:25–68.

Jouannet, F. 1984. *Phonologie du Kifuliru (langue bantoue du groupe J)*. Paris: SELAF

Kaji, Shigeki. 1996. Tone reversal in Tembo (Bantu J.57). *Journal of African Languages and Linguistics* 17:1–26.

Katamba, Francis X. 2003. Bantu nominal morphology. In Derek Nurse and Gérard Philippson (eds.), *The Bantu languages*, 103–120. London and New York: Routledge.

Kisseberth, C. W. and M. I. Abasheikh. 1974. Vowel length in Chi Mwi:ni - a case study of the role of grammar in phonology. In A. Bruck, A. Fox and M. W. La Galy (eds.), *Papers from the Parasession on Natural Phonology*, 193-209. Chicago: Chicago Linguistic Society.

Kisseberth, Charles W., and David Odden. 2003. Tone. In Derek Nurse and Gérard Philippson (eds.), *The Bantu languages*, 59–70. New York: Routledge.

Klavans, Judith L. 1985. The independence of syntax and phonology in cliticization. *Language* 61:95–120.

McCarthy, John J., and Alan S. Prince. 1990. Foot and word in prosodic morphology: The Arabic broken plural. *Natural Language and Linguistic Theory* 8:209–283.

Meeussen, A. E. 1967. Bantu grammatical reconstructions. Musée Royale de l'Afrique Centrale, Série 8, Sciences Humaines, 61:81–121. Tervuren.

Meinhof, Carl. 1904. Das Dahlsche Gesetz. Zeitschrift der Deutschen Morgenländischen Gesellschaft 57:299–304.

Meinhof, Carl. 1932. *Introduction to the phonology of the Bantu languages*. Translated and revised(from Meinhof 1910) by N. J. Warmlo. Berlin: D. Reimer/E.Vohsen.

Meyers, Scott. 1990. Tone and the structure of words in Shona (Outstanding Dissertations in Linguistics). Garland Press: New York.

Mould, Martin. 1973. On reconstructing the modified base of Bantu verbs. *Studies in African Linguistics* 3:107–125.

Mutaka, Ngessimo Mathe. 1990. The lexical tonology of Kinande. PhD dissertation, University of Southern California.

Ntihirageza, Jeanine. 1998. Meeussen's rule: Complexity in a simple tonal rule. *CLS 34: The Main Session* 281–298. The Chicago Linguistic Society.

Nurse, Derek. 2003. Aspect and Tense in Bantu languages. In Derek Nurse and Gérard Philippson (eds.) *The Bantu languages*, 90-102. London: Routledge.

Polak-Bynon, Louise. 1975. A Shi grammar: Surface structures and generative phonology of a Bantu language. *Annales Sciences Humaines 8A.* Tervuren: MRAC.

Prince, A., and P. Smolensky. 1993. Optimality Theory: Constraint interaction in generative grammar. Technical Report 2. Rutgers Center for Cognitive Sciences.

Pulleyblank, Douglas. 1986. *Tone in lexical phonology.* Dordrecht: D. Reidel.

Schadeberg, Thilo C. 1999. Katupha's law in Makhunda. In Jean-Marie Hombart and Larry M. Hyman (eds.), *Bantu historical linguistics,* 379–394. Stanford, Cal.: Center for the Study of Language and Information.

Schadeberg, Thilo C. 2003a. Derivation. In Derek Nurse and Gérard Philippson (eds.), *The Bantu languages,* 71–89. London and New York: Routledge.

Schadeberg, Thilo C. 2003b. Historical linguistics. In Derek Nurse and Gérard Philippson (eds.), *The Bantu languages,* 143–163. London and New York: Routledge.

Snider, Keith. 1999. *The geometry and features of tone.* Dallas: Summer Institute of Linguistics.

Van Dyken, Julia R., and Constance Kutsch Lojenga. 1993. Word boundaries: Key factors in orthography development. In Rhonda L. Hartell (ed.), *Alphabets of Africa,* 3–20. Dakar: UNESCO and Summer Institute of Linguistics.

Wald, Benji. 1997. Instrumental objects in the history of topicality and transitivity in Bantu. In Rose-Marie Déchaine, Victor Manfredi, et al. (eds.), *Object positions in Benue-Kwa: Papers from a workshop at Leiden University, June 1994,* 221–253. The Hague: Holland Academic Graphics.

Yip, Moira. 1988. Template morphology and the direction of association. *Natural Language* and *Linguistic Theory* A.551–577.

Zec, Draga. 1994. *Sonority constraints on prosodic structure.* New York: Garland.

Person index

Abasheikh, M. I. 417
Banyimwire wa'Rusati, Mushonio 2
Bastin, Yvonne 1, 43, 79, 80, 146, 417, 436
Beavon, Keith H. 126
Bickmore, Lee S. 141, 204
Black, Cheryl . . . . .xiv, 249
Blanchon, J. A. 126
Bresnan, Joan 426, 428, 430
Brown, Bonnie xiv
Bukuru, Nakalali 2
Busongoye, Kamaro . . . . .xiv, 2
Bybee, Joan 4, 444
Cahill, Mike xiii
Coupez, A. 79
de Blois, K. F. 417
Doke, Clement M. 431
Doyle, Michael T. 141, 204
Ehret, Christopher 124
Gauton, Rachélle 436
Gilley, Leoma xiv
Givón, Talmy 417
Goldsmith, John A. 110, 111, 125, 143, 144, 146, 152, 158, 160, 207
González, Margaret xiv
Gourley, Lois xiv

Guldemann, Tom 436
Greenberg, Joseph 430
Guthrie, Malcolm . . . . .xviii, xix, 1, 123, 124, 125, 425
Hampshire, Jon. xiii
Heath, Teresa 126
Hewitt, Mark. 111, 206, 207
Hubbard, K. 114, 213
Huttar, George xiv
Hyman, Larry M.. xiv, xix, 65, 67, 79, 81, 83, 110, 115, 121, 139, 176, 196, 204, 280, 333, 341, 347, 348, 351, 388, 414, 419, 420, 426, 436
Jones, Rhonda Hartell xiv
Kaji, Shigeki. 126
Kashindi, Asile . . . . xii, 2
Katamba, Francis X. 139, 426, 436
Katyera, Sengoronge . . . . xii, 2
Kinyamagoha, Juma. . . . . .xiii, 2
Kisseberth, Charles W. 115, 121, 417
Koehler, Loren xiv
Kutsch Lojenga, Constance 429
Kwangiba, Kifuvyo 2
Kyula, Kazera 2
Lauber, Ed xiii
Martens, Lana xiv
McCarthy, John J. 196
Mchombo, Sam 423, 424, 425, 428
Meeussen, A. E. . . . . viii, 1, 111, 113, 123, 125, 139, 143, 144, 145, 146, 152, 160, 163, 166, 169, 183, 184, 185, 186, 214, 237, 240, 239, 321, 327, 328, 436, 462
Meinhof, Carl 8, 32, 34, 43
Mould, Martin. 417
Musobwa, Bahabwa 2
Mutaka, Ngessimo Mathe 249
Mwemera, Bugulube 2
Ngalonga, Mulubi. 2
Ngunga, Armindo. 110
Ntihirageza, Jeanine. 238
Nurse, Derek . . . . xiv, xvii, 4, 414
Odden, David. . . . . .xiv, 115, 121
Pagliuca, William 4
Payne, Doris xiv
Perkins, Revere. 4

Polak-Bynon, Louise 109, 348
Prince, Alan S.................................. 110, 111, 196, 206, 207
Pulleyblank, Douglas ....xiv, 213
Rasmussen, Kent..xiv
Schadeberg, Thilo C. ...xiv, 7, 184, 325, 327, 359, 376, 388, 389, 391, 393, 394, 414, 432, 436
Smolensky, Paul.. 110
Snider, Keith ....xiv, 110, 116
Wise, Mary Ruth...xiv
Ye, Mwana Adrian xiii
Yip, Moira 111, 206
Yunga, Mulogoto 2
Zec, Draga 213
Zihindula, Kibambazi...xiii, xvi, 2

Language index

Bembe 120, 305
Bukusu 114
Chichewa 114
Chilungu 141
Chishona 425
Chitembo 1, 126
Cibemba 79, 419, 420
CiTonga 114
Ciyao, CiYao 110, 114
Duala 357
Eastern Bantu 66
French . . . . xi, xxi, xv, 18, 24, 262, 303
Kihunde 1, 146, 158
Kikerewe 114
KiLega 114
Kinande 1, 146, 249, 277
KiNdendeule 114
Kinyarwanda 1, 2, 9, 24, 25, 43, 375, 381
Kinyindu 1, 2, 53, 415
Kirundi 1, 24, 25, 43
Kiswahili . . . . xv, 10, 24, 72, 75, 77, 104, 311, 356, 393, 455
Kóózime 126
Luganda 114, 139, 341, 426, 436
Makaa 126

Mashi 1, 2, 53, 109, 252, 306, 311, 348, 415
Njyem. 126
Proto-Bantu. 4, 7, 13, 14, 15, 32, 43, 67, 68, 70, 79, 89, 109, 123, 124, 126, 139, 143, 289, 327, 339, 359, 389, 417, 418
Runyambo 114
Yoombi. 126

Overall index

A
abbreviations xxiii-xxv
ablaut 417. *See also* imbrication
adjectives 14, 25, 31, 35, 49, 55, 57-60, **75-79**, 90, 98-100, 123, 137, 231, 244-246, 254, **262-264**, 269, 273-276, 287, **298-299, 318-319, 321-323**, 398, 400-401, 435-436
    prefixes 25, 49, 244-246, 246, 263-264, 273-276
        derived from verbs 321-323
        monosyllabic 57-58, 75-77, 98-100, 318
        stative verbal adjectives 254, 262, 264, **322-323**
        stems 25, 98, 263
        tone on 263
adverbs 287, 397
    derived from verbs 323
agentive 7, 19, 77, 83, 85-86, 90, **94-95, 289-291**, 343
applicative extension 33, 51, 61, 64, 67-69, 79, 141, 172, 190, 218-219, 252-253, 289, 327, 329-333, 335-338, 340, **347-353**, 356, 358-359, 361, 363, **364-367**, 373-374, 381, 394, 397-398, 400-401 403, 405, 407-410, 412, 418, 423, 437-438
    causative of 398, 409
    of benefit/detriment 364-365
    of causative 347-353, 397-398, 405
    of location 366
    plus reflexive 366-367
    relative order 333-336
    valence 336-339, 354, 356, 361, 364, 377-379, 391, 399
argument (of verb) 337, 353-354, 356-357, 364-367, 389, 396
aspect. *See* verb(s)
associative marker 3, 49, 56, 99, **100-102**, 267-269, 275, 278-279, 303, 313, 362, 430, 440-441, 450
    tone on 267-269, 278-279
    vowel coalescence in 100-102, 440-441
    vowel length in 100-102, 267-269
augmentative/pejorative 302-303
automatic contouring 111, 207, 213
automatic downstep (downdrift) 109, 117, 121-123, 231, 280, 282-284

autosegmental 109, 110-113, 207

B
back vowel glide formation 9, 46-47
back vowel height harmony 64-65, 66-67
Bantu xi, xvii-xxi, 4, 17, 27, 53, 55, 66, 79, 80, 83, 95, 104, 109-110, 114-115, 121, 125-127, 130-131, 139, 143-144, 161, 193, 204, 206-207, 212, 238, 252-253, 287, 311, 313, 321, 325-328, 333, 341, 347, 351, 356, 357, 376, 382, 387-389, 391, 393-394, 401, 402, 414, 415, 418, 425-427, 429, 431-432, 436, 441
    Bantu A 126
    Bantu J 143-144, 193, 426, 249
        south and interior East Bantu 356
benefactive 364-365
bimoraic syllable **114-117, 119-122,** 123-124, 126, 129, 132-133, 136-139, 148-149, 154-155, 164-166, 168-169, 172, 177, 179, 185-186, 191, 194, 206, 210, 212-215, 219, 223-225, 228, 231-233, 236-237, 257, 259-260
boundary. *See* domain boundary; word boundary
boundary tone 118, 120, 123, 127, 150, 176-177, 220, 230 271-274, 280-281

C
Cameroon xxvii, 126, 357
C-A-R-P (causative-applicative-reciprocal-passive) order 333
causative extension 13, 19, 28, 30-31, 44-45, 62-65, 67-69, 77, 83, 86-87, 90-93, 109, 111, 123, 131-132, 138-146, 150-152, 156-160, 166-175, 178-180, 182-187, 197, 199, 204, 205, 211, 216, 223, 225-226, 231, 240, 252-253, 261-262, 289-290, 292, 319, 327, 330-331, 333-338, **340, 341-361,** 376, 381-382, 394-395, 397-398, 401, 404-406, 408-414, 421-424, 448
    alternate forms 341, 357-359
    expressing instrumentality 356-357
    functions 353-359
    long causative 64, 67, 87, 168, 330, 340-345, 350, 357, 359, 382, 404, 421, 423
    of intransitive verbs 355-356
    of transitive verbs 354-355
    resultatives of 421-422
    short causative 67, 86-87, 92, 290, 327, 330, 333, 340, 341-346, 350, 357-360, 382, 401, 404, 421-424
    structural considerations 341-353
    tone in 139-141, 146, 150-152, 156-158, 159-160, 166-171, 173-175, 178-179, 180-181, 182-184, 186-187
c-deletion 46, 49-50, 79-83
circumflex 3, 112, 120, 150, 156, 179, 281, 442-443
cl. 5 infinitive prefix 77, 137, 146, 193, 319, 455
class prefixes 22, 25, 32, 45, 47-49, 76, 254-255, 264-266, 296, 299-303, 314-316
clitic(s) 3-4, 35, 47, 50, 52, 55-59, 60, 64, 71-72, 75-76, 97-105, 120, 186, 199, 244, 247, 257, 267-269, 271, 295, 297, 303-304, 307, 309, 311, 359, 365, 369, 427, **430-433, 435-440, 450-455**
    clause-level 57-59, **450-455**
    enclitic 54-55, 57-60, 102-104, 186, 256, 268, 295, 365, 433-434, 453-455

Overall index 471

evidence from tone, vowel length 98-100
evidence from vowel coalescence 100-102
locative markers as 56, 436
orthographic treatment 456-458
phrase level 101, 450
proclitics 23, 55-56, 101-104, 267-268, 295, 303-304, 309, 432, 435-437, 439-440, 450-452
single syllable verbs as 454-455
clitic-related vowel lengthening 55-59, 435-436, 445, 450
colloquial variants 20
combined melody 140, **142**, **208-209**, 241
comitative 331, 335, 337-339, 357, 367, **369-371**
compensatory nasal syllabification 43, 53
compensatory vowel lengthening 8, 26, 35, 45, 46, 48, **53-59**, 60, 99, 103-104, 114, 137, 287, 433-435, 446
complex stem-tone patterns 158-160
compound nouns 314-316
conceptual unity 428
conditional /potential xxiii, 13, 72, 129, 144-145, 160, 188, 201-203, 224 248-250
conjunctive(s) 357, 395
conjunctive verbal prefix 88, 163, 192-193, 210
conjunctive nouns with **na** 307, 313-314
consonant(s) 7-9, **11-35**, 46, 49, 52, 53, 68, 77, 79, 86, 90, 92-93, 161, 290, 291, 341, 355
Dahl's law 8, 12, 17, **32-33**, 388, 398, 401, 402
distribution 11-32

fortition (strengthening) 14, 17, 24, **38-39**, 77, 397, 402
initial 22, 28
labialized 9, **27-32**, 54, 96, 106
l/r rule 38
Meinhof's law 8, **34**, 43
nasal assimilation 40
nasal deletion 40-43
nasal syllabification 43
palatalized 9, 23, **27-32**, 54, 96, 106, 341-343
phonemes 8-9, 12
(pre)palatal 13, 44, 83, 341-343
rules affecting 38-45
voicing 38-40
y-absorption 44-45
y-deletion 77-79
y-epenthesis 70-71, 78, 137
contactive extension 12, 33, 69, 80, 82, 253, 327, 329, 331-332, 337-338, **387-389**
contour tones 3, 54, 100, 111, 112, 115-117, **120-123**, 133, 138, 148-151, 153, 155-156, 162-170, 173, 175, 177-181, 183, 185-186, 191, 196, 198-199, 207, 210, 212, 214-220, 223, 225
contour simplification 115, 120-121, 139, 151, 153-155, 159, 163-166, 167-170, 175, 179, 183, 185-186, 207, 210-212, 214, 216-217, 219, 223-226, **227-237**, 241, 253
HL contour simplification 153-155, 164, 168, 185-186, 212, 216, 219, 223- 225, **234-237**
LH contour simplification 228-234, 255
contrary to fact xxiii, 72, 74, 129, 144-145, 152, 160, 181, 188, 201-203, 224, 248, 249, 251, 415, 419, 444
conventions, general 3-6
copy rule, demonstrative 95-96

D

Dahl's law 8, 12, 17, **32-33**, 388, 398, 401, 402
dative. *See* applicative extension
default tone 120, 125, **127, 131**, 135-136, 143, 148, 152, 153, 154, 155,157, 176, 177, 196, 197, 204, 208, 210, 220, 226, 228, 234, 236, 240, 243, 247, 249-250, 260, 272-273, 279
defrication. *See* despirantization
deletion (rules) 22, 34, 40, 43, 44, 46, 49-50, 53, 64, 75, **77-88**, 90, 164, 360, 417, 438
Democratic Republic of Congo xv, xvi, xxvii, 1, 114
demonstratives
    copy rule 71, 95-96
    tone on 264-266
derivational processes (word formation) 15, 20, 25, 28, 31, 35, 38, 41, 51, 59, 64, 67, 77-78, 85, 94, 247, 252-259, 262, **287-323**
    adjectives derived from verbs 321-322
    adverbs derived from verbs 323
    derivational prefixes 247
    derivational suffixes 35, 252, 321, 328
    nouns, compound 314-316
    nouns, conjunctive, with **na** 313
    nouns, derived from adjectives 298-299
    nouns, derived from ideophones 316
    nouns, derived from nouns 299-314
        abstract 304
        augmentative/pejorative 302-303
        diminutive/pejorative 299-302
        by addition of formative 307-314
        kinship terms 307-310
        language names 305-306
        place names 306-307
        with personifying prefix 303-304
    nouns, deverbal 288-298
        agentive 289-291
        infinitives 288-289
        non-agentive 291- 298
    verb derivations 316-324
despirantization 347-350
desyllabification 27, 29, 31, 32, 46, 50, 438
diminutive/pejorative 299-302
ditransitive 337, 357, 361, 395-397
ditransitive impositives 357, **395-397**
domain 38, 59, 60, 102, 111, 115, 119, 131-132, 134, 163, 189, 208-209, 220, 237-240, 282, 436-437
    boundary 131, 195-196, 222, 245
double linking of penult 111, 115-116, 120, 131, 148, 153, 155, 206-207, 210-212, 219, 225, 227, 235, 242
downdrift 109, 117, 121-123, 231, 280, **282-284**
downstep 109, 121, 228, **284-285**, 447

E

edge-in linking 111, 115, 131, 140, 142, **206-209**, 212-217, 241, 256, 258-261
effacement 415, 417-418, 423. *See also* nasal effacement
emphatic extension 327, 328, 330, 331, 336-340, 346, **382-387**, 401, 414, 421, 443, 448-449
enclitic 54-55, 57-60, 102-104, 186, 256, 268, 295, 365, 433-434, 453-455

epenthesis rules 18, 25, 64, **70-77**, 98, 137, 253, 400
expansions 34, 69, 80, 327-328, 387, 398, **401-402**, 403
extensions 326-401. *See also* applicative; causative; contactive; emphatic; extensive; impositive; intensive; neuter; passive; positional; reciprocal; reversive transitive; reversive intransitive
   C-A-R-P (causative-applicative-reciprocal-passive) order 333
   combinations of 387, 401-413
   lexicalized (frozen) 24, 31-34, 65, 67-69, 78, 81-83, 85-86, 253, 326-327, **329-330**, 332-332, 345, 351-352
   productivity 328-332 (*see also* non-productive extensions; productive extensions)
   reduplicated 327, 332, 364, 375, 377, 381, 383, 390, 407-409, 411, 413
   relative order of 333-336
   tone in 139-141, 150-152, 156-158, 166-171, 173-175, 178-179, 180-181, 182-184, 186-187, 197, **252-254**
   and valence 326, 336-339
extraprosodicity 204
extratonal(ity)) 111, 113, 117-119, 123, 125, 127, 130, 134, 140-142, 150, 151, 153, 156, 157, 159, 164, 167, 173, 177, 179, 196, **204-207**, 214, 215, 217, 218, 241, 242, 257, 262, 266

F

falling (HL) contour 3, 54, 100, 111, 112, 115-117, **120-123**, 133, 138, 148-151, 153, 155-156, 162-171, 172, 175, 177-181, 183, 185-186, 191, 198-199, 210, 212, 214-220, 223, 225, 271, 280-281, 446, 455
   restrictions on 120-122
final vowel devoicing 52-53
first degree vowels 7, 18, 68, 89, 90, 415
floating L tones. *See* downstep
fortition (strengthening) 14, 17, 24, **38-39**, 77, 397, 402
frication. *See* spirantization
"frozen" (lexicalized) extensions 24, 31-34, 65, 67-69, 78, 81-83, 85-86, 223, 325-326, **329-330**, 332-333, 345, 351-352
frustrated resultative 129, 171-175, 197, 201, 203, 248-249, 300, 444
functional load. *See* tone
fusion. *See* imbrication
future xxiv, 64, 122, 129, 133-134, 138, 144, 152, 154-157, 184-198, 201, 203, 209, 216, 219, 222, 226, 230, 234-236, 247-250, 253, 277, 384, 447, 450

G

glide(s)/ glide formation 4, 8, 9, 13, 18, 25, 26, 28, 31, 44, **45-46**, 54, 59, 63, 70, 79, 91, 96, 103, 114, 137, 139, 141, 198, 205, 329, 341, 342, 346, 360, 418, 434, 437-438, 442
   back vowel 46
   high vowel 8, **44-45**, 70, 341, 342, 346, 418, 438-439
GNP(gender/number prefix) 25, 32, 47-49, 76, 254-255, 257-258, 260, 263-264, 296, 314-315
grammatical melody 133, **140-142**, **208-209**, 214, 216, 240-241
grammatical tone contrasts 128-129

H

harmony, vowel 35, 46, **64-70**, 316, 327, 340, 359-360, 364, 377, 380, 381, 388, 391, 393, 398, 412
    back vowel height harmony 66-67
    front vowel height harmony 67-69
    height harmony, asymmetrical/canonical 65
height harmony. *See* harmony, vowel
H-final nouns 261-262
high vowel glide formation 8, **44-45**, 70, 341, 342, 346, 438
HL simplification 153-155, 164, 168, 185-186, 212, 216, 219, 223-225, **234-237**
H-spread (T-spread) 127, 135-136, 146, 148, 151-152, 155, 157, **168**, 171, 185, 194, 198, 214-216, **220-227**, 229-231, 235-236, 253, 254, 258-260, 262, 264-267, 269-273, 279-280

I

ideophones 4, 15, 28, 30, 31, 287
    nouns derived from 316
    verbs derived from 317
i-epenthesis 70
    in monosyllabic words 75-77
    in NC-initial verbs 72-74
    to avoid n plus nasal 74-75
imbrication 49, 80-82, **417-420**, 423
imperative plural 144, 145, 158, 177, **179-181**, 203, 326, 385
imperative singular 5, 74, 104-105, 144, 145, 171, **175-179**, 203, 226, 231, 384, 385, 431, 447, 448
impositive extension 90, 253, 327, 331, 332, 334, 338, 357, 374, 377, 380, 387, 391, **393-397**
    ditransitive 357, 377, 395-397
    transitive 395

inchoative 78, 318, 328, 387, **400-401**, 410, 413
infinitive(s) 14, 33, 36-37, 44, 62, 66, 67, 69, 70, 83, 85, 86, 91-95, 105, 144, **146-150**, 177, **288-289**, 384, **441**, 443, 444-446
    prefixless, following auxiliary 188, 193, 194, 277-278, 319, 444-449, 455
    tone on 125, 126, 133-135, 137-138, 193-195, 198-201, 221, 247, 254, 277-278
intensive extension 60, 64, 67-69, 327, 330-331, 335, 337-340, 343, 351, 364, **380-382**, 408, 437
intervening time 152, 201, 249
intonational tones 36, 54, 118, 123, 153, 170, 176, 183, 198, 271, 272, 280, 284

K

Kenya 1, 114
kinship terms 307-310

L

labialized/labialization 9, **27-32**, 54, 96, 106
language index 467
left-linking tones **141-142, 208-210**, 215, 241
lexical (word-building) level 8, 38-40, 44-50, 54, 55, 59-60
lexicalized extension. *See* "frozen" extension
lexical melody **141-142, 208-209**, 216
lexical root tone 127, 136, 142, 205, 208, 209, 224
lexical tone contrasts 128
lexical unlike vowel assimilation 48-50
LH simplification 228-234, 255

Overall index 475

long causative 64, 67, 87, 168, 329, 340-345, 350, 357, 359, 382, 404, 421, 423
long vowel 3, 4, 7, 8, **10-11**, **34-37**, 43, 47-48, 50, 53, 55, 59-64, 96-97, 99-100, 102, 104, 106, 113-116, 119-121, 136-137, 143, 151, 157, 172, 186, 197, 288, 403, 418, 422-423, 426, 434-442, 446, 448, 452, 453-455. *See also* clitic related vowel lengthening; compensatory lengthening

M
macron, for mid tone 3, 112, 116
macrostem 131-132, 325-326
maps xxvii-xxviii
Meeussen's rule 144, 152, 160, 163, 166, 169, 184-186, 214, **237-240**
Meinhof's law 8, **34**, 43
melody 111, 115-117, 133, **139-143**, **207-209**, 215-217, 240-242, 255, 258-260, 263, 265
mid tone 3, 97, 112, 117, 119-121, 123, 125, 138, 148-149, 167, 172, 183, 205, 210-211, 219, 228-230, 233-234, 242, 259, 265
minimality 57, 81, 95, 100, 117, 187, 196, 257, **419-420**
minimal pairs/triplets (tone) 119, 127-130, 427
mobility 428
modified base 172, 417-420, 460, 462. *See also* imbrication
monomoraic 112, 114, 116-118, 120-122, 135, 153, 162, 165, 168, 179, 185-186, 195, 204, 206-207, 210-218, 223, 225, 227, 232, 257-259, 262
monomoraic roots 262
monosyllabic words 3, 4, 31, 35, 52, 55, 57-58, 60, 64, 70, 71, 75-77, **96-105**, 114, 118-120, 126, 130, 134, 186, 195-**199**, 206, 241, 245, 257-258, 261, 268, 270, 271, 318, 342, 359, 363, 419, 427-433, 435, 437-438, 440, 453-455, 457
 cliticization of 97-104
 elimination by morpheme addition 104-105
 tone in 195-199
mora 8, 53, 54, 59, **113-117**
mora-based vowel shortening rule 8, 36, 48, 50, **59-64**, 97, 100, 114-115, 157, 186, 212, 360, 421, 433-435, 436-441
morphologically governed rules 64-96
morphophonemic 11
Mozambique 114
multiple subject prefixes 443-444
mutual extension- reciprocal plus passive 330, 331, 337-339, 345, 346, 363, 367, 370, **371-373**, 411, 417, 419-420

N
nasal 8, 9, 14-20, 23, 28, 38, 53, 72-77. *See also* prenasalized consonants
 assimilation 10, 40, 76
 commutation rule 88-89
 deletion preceding another nasal 40-43
 effacement 10, **83-88**, 90, 93, 323, 417
 epenthesis to avoid N + N 74-75
 Meinhof's law 34
 moricity 114, 131
 N+C compensatory vowel lengthening 3, 55
 N+fricative 9-10, **83-88**
 syllabification 43
 strengthening following nasal 38-39
 voicing following nasal 8, 39

neuter extension 391-392
neuter plus reciprocal 393
neutro-passive. *See* neuter
non-productive extensions 331-332, 387-400
noun(s) 14, 18, 25, 27, 31, 33, 40-42, 49, 55-57, 77, 84-85, 88, 94, 105-106, **287-316**
    tone on 111, **116-120**, 199, 204-206, 221, 244-247, **254-263**
        H-final 261-262
noun class. *See* GNP
noun derivations 288-316
numerals, tone on 267, 269-270

O

"o" of reference 102, 453
optimality theory 110
optional **u** deletion 43, 53, 114
orthography 127, 129, 415, 425-428, 431, 433-435, 437, 439, 441-443, 456-458

P

p-lenition 15
palatalized 9, 23, **27-32**, 54, 96, 106, 341-343
passive 28, 30, 31, 35, 65, 68, **357-361**
    and tone 109, 111, 123, 130, 132, 139-141-146, 150-152, 156-158, 159-160, 166-170, 175, 178-183, 186-187, 197, 199
past(s) xxiii, xxiv, 4, 8, 45, 63, 122, 127, 129, 144-146, 158, 160, 162, 165-167, 171, 181, 188, 196, 198, 201-203, 205, 211, 214-216, 219, 222-223, 225, 227, 232, 234, 237, 238, 240, 247-250, 292, 326, 384, 441, 443-444, 450
penultimate 28, 36, 60, 71, 97, 100, 109, 111, 113, 115-116, 118-124, 129, 131-132, 135, 140-141, 144, 148, 151, 153-157, 159-160, 162, 164-166, 168-170, 172-173, 175, 177, 179-183, 185-186, 196, 200, 205, 206-220, 222-232, 235-237, 242-243, 256-260, 270-273, 311, 426, 437, 441, 444, 446, 450, 453-455. *See also* double linking of penult
perfective. *See* resultative
phoneme inventory 8-11
    realization and distribution 11-38
phonologically governed rules and processes 38-70
polar tone **112**, 125, 143-144, 158, 160-161, 165, **240**, 267-269, 278, 303, 308
positional extension 253, 327, 331, 332, 335, 337, 338, 387, 393-394, **397-400**
    followed by other extensions 400
post-glide vowel lengthening 54, 61
postlexical vowel coalescence 50-52
potential. *See* conditional
prenasalized consonants 9, 90, 93
pre-pause raising 183, 271, **280-282**, 284
prepositional. *See* applicative
proclitics 23, 55-56, 101-104, 267-268, 295, 303-304, 309, 432, 435-437, 439-440, 450-452
productive extensions 68, 87, 328-331, 333, 335, 338-386
prosodic length 59, 114, 117
Proto-Bantu 4, 7, 13-15, 32, 43, 67, 68, 79, 89, 123-125, 126, 139, 143, 327, 339-340, 359, 389, 417, 418
    first degree vowel 67, 68, 89, 289
    tone reversal from 109, **123-125**, 143

R

reciprocal extension 65, 68, 82, 234, 252-253, 255, 327, 330-331, 333, 338-340, 343-346, 350-351, 357, **367-374**, 393, 398, 401, 410-412, 418-421
    comitative 335, 337, 339, 357, 367, **369-371**
    mutual 330, 331, 337-339, 345, 363, 367, **371- 373**
    of abstraction 369
    reciprocal: other uses 373-374
reduplication 4, 10, 12, 17, 28, 37, 58, 69, 80, 95, 119, 287, 318, 323, 327, 332, 364, 375, 377, 381, 383, 398. *See also* verbs: reduplication
register tier theory 116
resultative 4, 8, 13, 19, 26, 30, 35, 46, 52-53, 61, 67, **79-83**, 85-90 **90-92**, 129, 138, 144-145, 152, 160-176, 181-184, 202-203, 222, 248-253, 326, 336, 343, 345-346, 372, 386, **414-424**
    deletion of final consonants in 46, 49, 77, 79-83
    irregular 418-421
    of causatives 345-346, 421-422
    of passives 423-424
    tone 160-175, 181-184, 202-203
resyllabification 270, 275
reversive intransitive extension 374, 377-380
reversive transitive extension 374-377
reduplication of 377
right-linking tone(s) 111, 126, **140-142**, 144, 150, 158-160, 169-171, 173, 175, 181, 185, 187, 196-197, **208-209**, 217, 220, 226, 235, 240-241, 347, 381

S

separability 428, 429, 432
separative. *See* reversive
short causative 67, 86-87, 92, 290, 327, 330, 333, 340, 341-346, 350, 357-359, 382, 401, 404, 421-424
shortening rule, mora-based 8, 36, 48, 50, **59-64**, 97, 100, 114-115, 157, 212, 360, 421, 433-435, **436-437**
simple stem-tone pattern. *See* stem-tone patterns
slow speech 3, 47, 52, 279, 434, 456
spirantization 7, 13, 18-19, 44, 68, 79-80, 82-83, **85-95**, 139, 161, 172, 290-292, 321, 323, 334, 341-347, 381, 405, 415-417, 419, 421. *See also* despirantization
stative 33, 65, 67, 90, 397. *See also* impositive
stative verbal adjectives 254, 262, 264, **322-323**
stem-tone patterns (verbal) 143-204
    complex HH subjunctives 127, 145, 152, 159, **184-192**, 194-196, 203-204, 216, 227, 238-239
    complex HL 144, 158, **160-170**, 194-197, 200, 202, 206, 210-211, 214-216, 218-220, 222-226, 237-243, 250, 422
    complex LH 145, 153, 158, **170-181**, 203, 216-217, 226-227, 241
    complex LL 145, 158, **181-184**, 203
    imperative plural (complex LH-IP) 145, **179-181**, 203
    imperative singular: another complex LH form 175-179
    simple pattern 125, 134-136, 142-144, **146-152**, 153, 160, 166, 194-195, 198, 200, 201, 207, 216, 219, 221, 230, 232, 233, 235, 238, 253, 277

V2 pattern 127, 136, 142-144, **152-158**, 160, 166, 186-193, 194-197, 200-201, 207, 216, 219, 222, 232, 234, 236, 253, 277

V2 subjunctives 127, 184, 186-193, 215, 250

verb forms listed by stem-tone pattern 201

subjunctive 5, 24, 41, 73, 75, 105, 127, 132, **144-145**, 152, 159, 177, **184-193**, 196, 201, 203, 204, 215, 248-250, 252, 326, 384, 443, 446-448. *See also* stem tone patterns: complex HH subjunctives, and V2

subjunctives with no subjunctive FV 188, 250, 443, 446-448

substitutability 428

suffixal stem tone 125, 133-134, 199, 239. *See also* stem-tone patterns

syllable structure 96-97, 105-107

syllable prominence 97

syllable "weight" 114

syllable, bimoraic **114-117, 119-122**, 123-124, 126, 129, 132-133, 136-139, 148-149, 154-155, 164-166, 168-169, 172, 177, 179, 185-186, 191, 194, 206, 210, 212-215, 219, 223-225, 228, 231-233, 236-237, 257, 259-260

syllable, monomoraic 112, 114, 116-118, 120-122, 135, 153, 162, 165, 168, 179, 185-186, 195, 204, 206-207, 210-218, 223, 225, 227, 232, 257-259, 262

syllable, with modifications, as TBU 212-218

syntactic tonal overlay 189, 265-266

T

Tanzania 1, 114

TBU. *See* tone-bearing unit

T-drop (tone drop) 153, 162, 167, 177-178, 196-197, 209, 211, 218, 237, **240-243**, 266

tense. *See* verb tense

tentive. *See* contactive

tonal contours. *See* tone, contour

tonal root node (TRN) 112, 116, 135, 209, 213, 218

tone association **109-117**, 123, 125, 131-136, 140-141, 148, 151, 153, 157, 158-159, 162, 164-165, 169, 175, 178, 195-196, **205-227**, 231, 240-243, 253, 257-259, 327

initial association 206-220 (*see also* tone: edge-in linking)

"automatic contouring" 111, 207, 213

tone-bearing unit (TBU) 72, 109-110, **113-116**, 118-119, 121, 125, 127, 130, 132, 133, 134,-136, 139-146, 148, 152-153, 155, 157-162, 164, 167, 168, 171-173, 175-177, 179-180, 189-185, 187, 189, 194-196, 199-200, 204-210, 212-218, 220-223, 226, 241-243, 245-249, 253, 254, 257-259, 279, 284

tone, boundary 118, 120, 123, 127, 150, 176-177, 220, 230, 271-274, 280-281

tone(s), contour 3, 54, 100, 111, 112, 115-117, **120-123**, 133, 138, 148-151, 153, 155-156, 162-170, 172, 175, 177-181, 183, 185-186, 191, 195, 198-199, 207, 210, 212, 214-220, 223, 225

restrictions on 120-122

tone contour simplification rules 115, 120- 121, 139, 151, 153-155, 159, 163-166, 170, 175, 179, 183, 185-186, 207, 210-212, 214, 216-217, 219, 223-226, **227-237**, 241, 253

Overall index

HL contour simplification 153-155, 164, 170, 185, 212, 216, 219, 223-225, **234-237**
LH contour simplification 228-234, 255
tone(s), contrastive surface 117-120
tone, default 120, 125, **127**, **131**, 135-136, 143, 148, 152, 153, 154, 155, 157, 176, 177, 196, 197, 205, 208, 210, 220, 226, 228, 234, 236, 240, 243, 247, 249-250, 260, 272-273, 279
tone, double linking of penult 111, 115-116, 120, 131, 148, 153, 155, 206-207, 210-212, 219, 225, 227, 235, 242
tone, downdrift 109, 117, 121-123, 231, 280, **282-284**
tone, downstep 109, 121, 228, **284-285**, 447
tone, edge-in linking 111, 115, 131, 140, 142, **206-209**, 212-217, 241, 256, 258-261
tone, final H contouring 271, 281, 441
tone, functional load 127-130
  grammatical minimal contrasts 128-130
  lexical minimal contrasts 128
tone, H- float rule (lexical) **244-247**, 257-258, 273-275
tone, H-spread rule. *See* Tone-spread
tone, initial association. *See* tone: association
tone, inventory 117-122
tone, L-spread rule. *See* tone: tone-spread
tone, leftward H-shift 199, 231-232, 245, 254, 263, 267, 271, **273-279**
tone, lexical root 136, 142, 306, 208, 209
tone marking conventions 3

tone, Meeussen's rule (MR) 144, 152, 159-160, 163-164, 166, 168-171, 181, 184-186, 214, **237-240**
tone melody 111, 115-117, 133, **139-143**, **207-209**, 214-217, 240-241, 255, 258-260, 263, 265
tone, mid 3, 97, 112, 117, 119-121, 123, 125, 138, 148-149, 167, **171**, 181, 205, 210-211, 219, 228-230, 233-234, 242, 259, 265
tone, phonetic realizations 122-123, 228
  postlexical tonal changes 271-285
  pre-pause raising 183, 271, **280-282**, 284
  reversal, historical (*see* Proto Bantu)
tone rules and conventions 206-244
  phrase/clause level rules 271-285
  word level tone rules 220-270
tone-spread 127, 135-136, 146, 148, 151-152, 155, 157-159, 162, 165-166, 168, 170-171, 173, 175, 179, 180, 183-185, 187-189, 194, 198-199, 206-208, 214-216, **220-227**, 229-231, 235-236, 253, 258-260, 264-267, 269-273, 279-280, 327
tone, triple-linking constraints 162, 164, 196, 206, **218-220**, 242
tone, well-formedness condition 110, 194, 213
tone, in verb stems **141-142**, **208-209**, 216. *See also* stem-tone patterns
toneless affixes 4, 127, 139, 141, 222, 247, **249-252**, **253-254**
toneless verbs. *See* verbs, toneless

U
Uganda 1, 114

V

V2 pattern. *See* stem-tone patterns
valence, extensions and 326, 336-339
verb(s) affixes 247-254
verbs, aspect 4, 56, 72, 79, 89, 126, 131, 133, 145-146, 201-203. *See also* (verb,) conditional, contrary to fact; (verb,) frustrated resultative; (verb,) imperative; (verb,) intervening time; (verb,) subjunctive
verb, base **131**, 134, 141, 147, 290-295, 298, 300, 301, 311, 317-323, **325-326**, 336, 340, 342-348, 378, 382-383, 387, 400-401, 414-417, 419
verb, conditional/potential xxiii, 13, 72, 129, 144-145, 160, 188, 201-203, 224, 248-250
verb, contrary to fact xxiii, 72, 74, 129, 144-145, 152, 160, 181, 188, 201-203, 224, 248, 249, 251, 415, 419, 443
verb derivations 316-324
verb, extensions. *See* extensions
verb, frustrated resultative 129, 171-175, 197, 201, 203, 248-249, 300, 444
verb, future(s). *See* verb, tense
verb, imperative plural 144, 145, 158, 177, **179-181**, 203, 326, 385
verb, imperative singular 5, 74, 104-105, 144, 145, 171, **175-179**, 203, 226, 231, 384, 385, 431, 447, 448
verb, infinitive. *See* infinitive
verb, inflectional prefixes 131, 247-252
verb, initial prefixes 62-63, 325-326
verb, intervening time 152, 201, 249
verb, past(s). *See* verb, tense
verb, potential. *See* conditional/potential

verb prefixes 127, 187-189, 222, **247-252**
verb, reduplicated 199-200, 436
verb, resultative. *See* resultative
verb stem 3, 10, 13, 19, 28, 122, 125, **131-132**, 321, **325-424**, 427, 429, 433, 437, 441, 444-445, 449-450, 453-455
verb, stem-tone patterns, list 201. *See also* stem-tone patterns
verbs, subjunctive 5, 24, 41, 73, 75, 105, 127, 132, **144-145**, 152, 159, 177, **184-193**, 196, 201, 203, 204, 215, 248-250, 252, 326, 384, 443, 446-448
verb suffixes (non-extension) 139, **252-254**, 326, 328, 382. *See also* resultative
verb, syllable structure inventory 106-107
verb tense
   future xxiv, 64, 122, 129, 133-134, 138, 144, 152, 154-157, 184-199, 201, 203, 209, 216, 219, 222, 226, 230, 234-235, 247-250, 253, 277, 384, 447
   frustrated resultative 129, 171-175, 197, 201, 203, 248-249, 300, 444
   past(s) xxiii, xxiv, 4, 8, 45, 63, 122, 127, 129, 144-146, 158, 160, 162, 165-167, 171, 181, 188, 196, 198, 201-203, 205, 211, 214-216, 219, 222-223, 225, 227, 232, 234, 237, 238, 240, 247-250, 292, 326, 384, 441, 443-444, 450 (*see also* stem-tone patterns)
verb tone 109-254
   combined melody 140, **142**, **208-209**, 241
   edge-in linking 111, 115, 131, 140, 142, **206-209**, 212-217, 241, 256

grammatical melody 133, **140-142**, **208-209**, 214, 216, 240-241
grammatical tone (*see* stem-tone pattern)
left-linking tones **142-143, 208-210**, 215, 241
lexical melody **141-142, 208-209**, 216
right-linking tones 111, 126, **140-142**, 144, 150, **158-160**, 169, 170-171, 173, 175, 181, 185, 187, 196-197, **208-209**, 217, 220, 226, 235, 240-241, 347, 381
stem-tone patterns (*see* stem-tone pattern)
verb(s), toneless 4, 28, 42, 84, 109-110, 112, 126, 128, **132-138**, 140, 142, 146-147, 152, 162-163, 165, 169, 177-178, 184, 187, 195-199, 201-204, 206, 208-209, 220, 222-223, 227, 239, 240, 243, 264, 277, 422
voicing rule, consonants 38-40
vowel(s) 7, 8, **10-11, 34-37**, 38, 45-77
    assimilation
        identical vowel assimilation 47-48
        lexical unlike vowel assimilation 48-50
        reciprocal assimilation 50-52
    coalescence 47-52
        postlexical coalescence 50-52
    compensatory lengthening 8, 26, 35, 45, 46, 48, **53-59**, 60, 99, 103-104, 114, 137, 287, 434-435, 446
    distribution 34-37
    final vowel devoicing rule 52-53
    first degree 7, 18, 68, 89, 90, 417
    glide formation 45-47 (*see also* glide(s)/glide formation)
    harmony (*see* vowel harmony)
    long vowels 3, 4, 7, 8, **10-11, 34-37**, 43, 47-48, 50, 53, 55, 59-64, 96-97, 99-100, 102, 104, 106, 113-116, 119-121, 136-137, 143, 151, 157, 172, 186, 197, 288, 426, 434-443, 446-448, 452-455 (*see also* clitic related vowel lengthening; compensatory lengthening)
    not allowed word-finally 60, 96-97
    optional **u** deletion 43, **53**, 114
    rules affecting vowels 3, 45-77
    shortening rule, mora-based 8, 36, 48, 50, **59-64**, 97, 100, 114-115, 157, 186, 212, 360, 421, 433-435, 436-441
    weakening 52-53
vowel harmony 35, 46, **64-70**, 316, 327, 340, 359-360, 364, 377, 380, 381, 388, 391, 393, 398, 412
    back vowel height harmony 66-67
    front vowel height harmony 67-69
    height harmony, asymmetrical/canonical 65

W

weakening, vowels 52-53
well-formedness condition 110, 195, 213
word boundar(ies) 37-38, 48, 50, 60, 101, 112, 228, 271, 279, 425-457
    grammatical indicators of 443-450
    phonological indicators of 433-443

Y

y-absorption 44-45
y-deletion 77-79
y-epenthesis 70-71, 78, 137

SIL International Publications

Additional Releases in the **Publications in Linguistics** Series

145. **Language death in Mesmes,** by Michael B. Ahland, 2010, 155 pp., ISBN 978-1-55671-227-2
144. **The phonology of two central Chadic languages,** by Tony Smith and Richard Gravina, 2010, 267 pp., ISBN 978-155671-231-9
143. **A grammar of Akoose: A northwest Bantu language,** by Robert Hedinger, 2008, 318 pp., ISBN 978-1-55671-222-7
142. **Word order in Toposa: An aspect of multiple feature-checking,** by Helga Schröder, 2008, 213 pp., ISBN 978-1-55671-181-7
141. **Aspects of the morphology and phonology of Kɔnni,** by Michael C. Cahill, 2007, 537 pp., ISBN 978-1-55671-184-8
140. **The phonology of Mono,** by Kenneth Olson, 2005, 311 pp., ISBN 978-1-55671-160-2
139. **Language and life: Essays in memory of Kenneth L. Pike,** edited by Wise, Headland, and Brend, 2003, 674 pp., ISBN 978-1-55671-140-4
138. **Case and agreement in Abaza,** by Brian O'Herin, 2002, 304 pp., ISBN 978-1-55671-135-0
137. **Pragmatics of persuasive discourse in Spanish television advertising,** by Karol J. Hardin, 2001, 247 pp., ISBN 978-1-55671-150-3
136. **Quiegolani Zapotec syntax: A principles and parameters account,** by Cheryl A. Black, 2000, 365 pp., ISBN 978-1-55671-099-5

SIL International Publications
7500 W. Camp Wisdom Road
Dallas, TX 75236-5629

Voice: 972-708-7404
Fax: 972-708-7363
publications_intl@sil.org
www.ethnologue.com/bookstore.asp

www.ingramcontent.com/pod-product-compliance
Lightning Source LLC
Chambersburg PA
CBHW071231300426
44116CB00008B/997